Britain and Europe
1500–1780

Britain and Europe
1500–1780

Ralph Houlbrooke

BLOOMSBURY ACADEMIC

First published in 2011 by:

Bloomsbury Academic

An imprint of Bloomsbury Publishing Plc
36 Soho Square, London W1D 3QY, UK
and
175 Fifth Avenue, New York, NY 10010, USA

CIP records for this book are available from the British Library and the
Library of Congress.

ISBN (paperback) 978-0-34058-119-3
ISBN (ebook) 978-1-84966-463-9

This book is produced using paper that is made from wood grown in managed,
sustainable forests. It is natural, renewable and recyclable. The logging and
manufacturing processes conform to the environmental regulations of the
country of origin.

Printed and bound in Great Britain by the MPG Books Group, Bodmin, Cornwall.

www.bloomsburyacademic.com

For Sam and Benjamin

GENERAL EDITOR'S PREFACE

Years, decades, centuries, millennia come and go but Britain's relationship with its European neighbours remains consistently complicated and, on occasion, acutely divisive. It forms the stuff of contemporary political arguments both in 'Britain' and in 'Europe', debate which is sometimes strident and ill-informed.

The heat may perhaps be excused on the grounds that there are issues of personal, national and continental identity at stake about which people have strong feelings. The ignorance, however, is not excusable. Whatever views may be taken about contemporary issues and options, here is a relationship which can only properly be understood if it is examined in the *longue durée*. That is what this series aims to do.

It becomes evident, however, that in regard to both 'Britain' and 'Europe' we are not dealing with fixed entities standing over against each other through two millennia. What may be held do constitute 'Britain' and what 'Europe' changes through time. The present is no exception. In a context of political devolution how Britain and Britishness is defined becomes increasingly problematic as new patterns of relationship across 'the Isles' emerge. And what are perceived to be new patterns turn out on examination to be reassertions and redefinitions of old identities or structures. So is it also with 'Europe'. The issue of 'enlargement' of the current European Union brings up old problems in a new form. Where does 'Europe' begin and end? At long last, to take but one example, the Turkish Republic has been accepted as a candidate for membership but in earlier centuries, for some, Europe stopped where the Ottoman Empire began, an outlook which can still linger, with violent consequences, in the Balkans. In effect, therefore, the series probes and charts the shifting of boundaries – and boundaries in the mind as boundaries on a map. Where Britain 'belongs', in any era, depends upon a multiplicity of factors, themselves varying in importance from century to century: upon ethnicity, language, law, government, religion, trade, warfare, to name only some. Whether, in particular periods, the islanders were, indeed, 'isolated' depends in turn not only on what they themselves thought or wanted to believe but upon the patterns prevailing in 'Europe' and what might be thought to constitute the 'mainstream' of its development. The historians in this series are well aware that they are not dealing with a simple one-to-one relationship. They are not committed to a common didactic agenda or rigid formula. Different periods require different assessments of the appropriate balance to be struck in tackling the ingredients of insularity on the one hand and continental commonality on the other. Propinquity has itself necessarily brought the communities of Britain into closer contact, in peace and war, with some continental countries than with others and to have established (fluctuating) affinities and enmities, but the connection is not confined to immediate neighbours. Beneath the inter-state level, different sections of society have had different sorts of relationship across the continent. There is, therefore, in reality no single 'British' relationship with something called 'Europe' but rather multilateral relationships, sometimes in conflict and sometimes in co-operation, across Europe both at the state and non-state levels which have varied in content and intensity over time. And what has been happening in the wider world has in turn affected and some-times determined how both 'Britain' and the countries of 'Europe' have per-ceived and conducted themselves.

The study of a relationship (just like the living of one) is one of the most difficult but also the most rewarding of tasks. There is, however, no single title for this series which really does justice to what is being attempted. To speak of 'Britain and Europe' does indeed risk carrying the imputation that Britain is not 'part of' Europe. To speak of 'Europe in British perspective' would mislead as to the extent of the concentration upon Britain which remains. To speak of 'Britain in Europe' or even of 'Europe in Britain' both have their difficulties and advantages. In short, in the event, there is something for everybody!

The difficulty, though perhaps also the urgency of the task, is compounded for historians by the circumstances of history teaching and learning in schools and universities in the United Kingdom where, very largely, 'British history' and European history' have been studied and written about by different people who have disclaimed significant knowledge of the other or have only studied a particular period of the one which has been different from the period of the other. The extent to which 'British history' is really a singular history and the extent to which it is a particular manifestation of 'European history' are rarely tackled head-on at any level. This series attempts to provide just that bridge over troubled waters which present European circumstances require. It is, however, for readers to decide for themselves what bridge into the future the past does indeed provide.

Keith Robbins

ACKNOWLEDGEMENTS

I was delighted to be asked to contribute a volume to this series under the distinguished editorship of Keith Robbins. I am grateful to him for his encouragement and unfailing confidence. He read the whole text in early drafts and made several helpful suggestions. I have been fortunate in being able to discuss various topics addressed in this book with friends and colleagues at Reading, including Alan Cromartie, Joël Félix, Rachel Foxley, Richard Hoyle, Esther Mijers, Helen Parish, Frank Tallett, Stephen Taylor and David Trim. However, the customary authorial acknowledgement of responsibility for all errors needs to be made with particular emphasis in this case. My heartfelt thanks go to Margaret Houlbrooke for her understanding, enthusiasm and staunch support during a period of work on this book that turned out to be longer than either of us imagined at the outset, and especially for reading the whole of a nearly final version of the text.

In the closing stages of preparing this book for publication I have been fortunate in working with Fiona Cairns as editor and Emily Gibson as production project manager. I should like to take this opportunity of thanking them for being unfailingly responsive, helpful and patient.

Ralph Houlbrooke,
Reading,
September 2010

CONTENTS

Contents

INTRODUCTORY NOTE

In this volume, as in *Britain in the First Millennium* (2001), the first in this series, 'Britain' means 'the mainland of Britain, with the Isle of Man and all the islands except Ireland and those islands lying immediately off the Irish coast'.[1] The United Kingdom of Great Britain came into existence in 1707. Before that, there were two kingdoms in Britain, England and Scotland, though James VI of Scotland became king of England in 1603, inaugurating a dynastic union of the two crowns, and was proclaimed King of Great Britain in 1604. Edward I, king of England, had completed the conquest of Wales in the late thirteenth century. The English parliament established an enduring boundary between England and Wales in 1536. In this book, 'Wales' means the entity defined by that act (including Monmouthshire) unless otherwise indicated.[2]

It is impossible for a historian of Britain to ignore Ireland. All English monarchs during the period 1500–1780 were also lords (until 1541), kings or queens of Ireland. This survey, while necessarily taking account of relationships between Ireland on the one hand, and the nations of Britain on the other, follows the precedent set by Edward James in the first volume in this series in treating Ireland 'as part of Europe', not 'as some kind of appendage to Britain'.[3]

Attempts to write 'British' history have been criticized on various grounds. One telling charge is that they have diverted attention from wider European developments and European comparative perspectives. Another is that 'British history is ... a covert form of Anglocentrism' because it is 'dominated by perspectives, periodisation, problem-framing and so on largely derived from English history'.[4]

It is precisely the purpose of this series to set the history of the whole island of Britain in its European context. One of the advantages of doing so is the possibility of exploring the distinctive and multifarious character of Scotland's independent connections with areas outside Britain, especially France, Scandinavia and the Baltic. However, this book certainly gives far more space to England than to Wales or Scotland. If found guilty of 'Anglocentrism', one can only plead in mitigation that England was overwhelmingly the wealthiest and most populous of those countries throughout the period covered here, as well as occupying by far the largest territory. On the whole, with some outstanding exceptions, English developments influenced events in Scotland more strongly than Scottish developments influenced events in England.

The 'Europe' of this book is the Europe of modern geographical convention. The notion that the north-western peninsula of the Eurasian landmass with its circumjacent islands constitutes a separate continent (one of three, before the discovery of America) goes back to antiquity. Separate maps of Europe appeared in the sixteenth century. They covered an area roughly corresponding with that of modern Europe, although it was not until well after this period that the Ural Mountains were recognized as its conventional eastern boundary. The concept of 'Christendom', of a community of nations sharing the Christian faith, long remained more significant for western Europeans than a sense of a shared European identity.[5] 'In the fifteenth century', however, 'Christendom was giving way to Europe; it became possible to be "European"'.[6] The transition was a gradual one, not complete for another century or two. Links between Britain and almost every part of Europe will be touched on in this volume. But in general it is the relationships between the British nations and the countries of western Europe and the comparisons that can be drawn between Britain and its more immediate neighbours that will concern us here.[7]

This book has four main strands between its introductory and concluding chapters. Five narrative chapters recount the main developments in Britain's political history during this period, with particular emphasis on the relations between different realms. Nine thematic chapters examine political, religious, economic and social developments, with some elements of comparison between Britain and her European neighbours. Three chapters form a third strand that explores contacts and connections between Britain and Europe. The three chapters of the fourth and final strand are concerned with the making of Great Britain, a new nation state. The volume is also divided into three main chronological sections. The first is devoted to the years between 1500 and the accession of James VI to the English throne in 1603, the second to the period between the accomplishment of the regal union and the parliamentary union of 1707 and the third to the decades between the parliamentary union and 1780 when Britain, about to lose much of her American empire, faced a hostile Europe, widespread discontent in Ireland, and accelerating economic and demographic change.

The name of the royal house whose members reigned in Scotland before James VI's accession to the English throne and over all Britain between 1603 and 1714 appears as 'Stewart' in the first period out of deference to Scottish usage, but as 'Stuart' after 1603.

A strict limit was placed on the number of endnotes allowed in this volume. I have drawn very heavily on the *Oxford Dictionary of National Biography*, but inclusion of references to all the biographies I have consulted would have resulted in a huge number of extra notes. I should, however, like to acknowledge my heavy debt to the *Dictionary*.

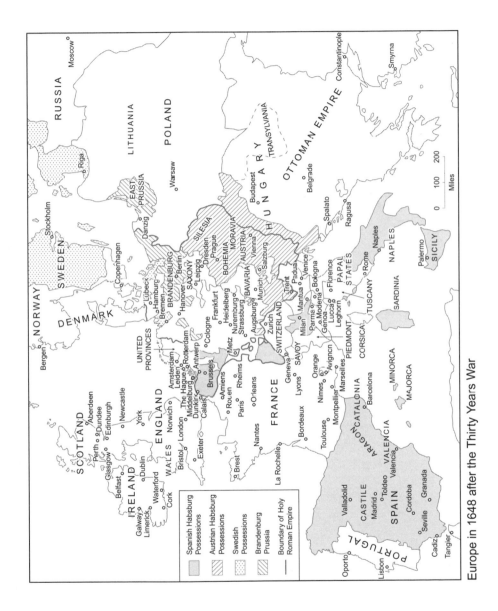

Europe in 1648 after the Thirty Years War

PART I

1500–1603

1

BRITAIN AND EUROPE IN 1500

Britain

Margaret Tudor, thirteen-year-old daughter of Henry VII, king of England, entered Edinburgh on 7 August 1503 in a great procession to be greeted with music, allegorical pageants and great popular rejoicing. The next day she was married to James IV, king of Scots, in Holyrood Abbey before clergy and nobles of both nations.[1] Margaret's father had gained England's crown by battle in August 1485. His claim to the throne was weak. However, he had in 1486 married Elizabeth Plantagenet, arguably the strongest claimant of the house of York. In 1489 it was agreed that their eldest son Arthur should marry Catherine, daughter of King Ferdinand of Aragon and Queen Isabella of Castile. This recognition was especially welcome to the recent usurper. The marriage eventually took place in November 1501. Arthur's death in April 1502 and his mother's in February 1503 cruelly dashed any satisfaction Henry may have felt in the newly established security of his dynasty, leaving him with only one son, the twelve-year-old Prince Henry.

James IV, sixth of the Stewart line that had ruled Scotland since 1371, had been crowned in 1488. Sixteen years younger than Henry VII, he had aspired to be a warrior king. His attempts to make trouble for Henry had achieved little, and they had finally made treaties of peace and marriage. The great-grandson of James and Margaret, James VI, was to become king of England a hundred years later. However, Henry's chief motive in arranging Margaret's marriage had been present security, not future dynastic union.

The two kingdoms that occupied most of the island of Britain were very unequal in territory and resources. England was some two-thirds larger in extent than Scotland. Both countries were overwhelmingly rural in character, but England's capital, London, with some 40,000–50,000 people, was several times larger than Edinburgh, and England had many more fair sized towns than Scotland. Mixed farming for the production of grain and livestock predominated in the south and east of England, where some 75 per cent of the population lived, pastoral farming in the uplands of the north and west.

England's principal manufacturing industry was the making of woollen cloth, by now her most valuable export, though half of the cloth exported was finished overseas. Cloth and wool together probably accounted for three-quarters of the value of English exports.[2] South-western England was the most important European supplier of tin, but that came a relatively poor third in terms of value.

Compared with many other kingdoms England possessed a relatively uniform framework of local government, above all the counties, whose sheriffs and justices of the peace were appointed by the crown. There were several areas where jurisdiction of various sorts had been delegated by medieval kings, but the greatest of these were under royal control in 1500. The king's courts stood supreme.[3] All land was ultimately held of the king, though by a wide variety of different tenures. Parliaments convened by the crown had a pre-eminent role in legislation and the granting of taxation. English politics had been exceptionally turbulent between 1450 and 1500, above all because of royal weakness or misjudgements, together with suspicion and hatred between royal kinsmen, rather than because of institutional or customary obstacles to the exercise of kingly authority.

English was spoken throughout the realm, except in parts of Cornwall and the Welsh borderlands. This provided the basis for a strong sense of national identity, despite the existence of distinctive local dialects. English was the dominant medium for private correspondence and a richly varied literature. A mongrel form of Norman French survived as the professional language of the common law. Latin remained the international language of learning and liturgy. It was also used in the majority of administrative and judicial records.

Various other territories belonged to the English crown. Wales, mostly upland or mountainous country, traversed by winding valleys, was comparatively poor and thinly settled. The lordships of the Welsh March enjoyed considerable internal independence, though several of them had come into the crown's hands by 1500. The last parts of Wales to be conquered had mostly been kept under the crown's direct control as the Principality of Wales and divided into shires in 1284. The council of the king's eldest son, the Prince of Wales, sat not in Wales but at Ludlow in Shropshire and its supervisory authority covered both the whole of Wales and the English border counties. The Welsh language of the overwhelming majority of the population was the one element to sustain a sense of shared identity in a geographically and administratively divided country. Some Welshmen, notably Henry Tudor's grandfather, had made successful careers in royal service. The Welsh were nevertheless widely regarded as a subject people, restricted by discriminatory legislation.[4]

The king of England was sovereign lord of various territories outside England. The Isle of Man had its own distinctive law, administration and language. The Channel Islands were the last remnants of the duchy of Normandy, formerly held by the English crown. On the French mainland the crown held Calais, together with its immediate hinterland. A colony English in population, language and law, fortified and strongly garrisoned, Calais was governed by a lord deputy. It was also the seat of the merchants of the Staple, who enjoyed the monopoly of English raw wool exports in return for helping to support the garrison.[5]

The lordship of Ireland was the greatest of the king's overseas territories. Anglo-Norman lords, with papal permission and under King Henry II's overall authority, had conquered much of the island in the twelfth century. Immigrants had subsequently created many towns and extensive rural settlements, but had never settled the remoter and less fertile areas. The colony's population had fallen sharply during the fourteenth century. The political authority of Gaelic-speaking chiefs had revived, and with it Gaelic culture. Some descendants of Anglo-Norman magnates had become almost indistinguishable from Irish chiefs. Lords who retained more of an English identity dominated much of the southern third of Ireland, but even they had adopted some Irish characteristics. Some of their tenants spoke English, but the towns, mostly on the coast, were the main strongholds of English language and culture.[6]

The lordship's government, including parliaments and shires, was modelled on England's. A recently built earthen rampart protected the 'Pale', an area around Dublin, seat of royal administration. The English lordships outside the Pale were largely independent in practice. Gerald Fitzgerald, eighth earl of Kildare, head of the dominant Anglo-Irish family, was chief governor or deputy for most of the time between 1478 and his death in 1513. When Kildare supported one pretender to Henry VII's throne and failed to act against another, the king eventually dismissed him. Sir Edward Poynings, sent from England as deputy with fresh troops in 1494, had the Irish parliament pass the statute later known as 'Poynings's Law'. It required the king's authorization for all meetings of that parliament, and his prior approval of all proposed legislation. After this assertion of royal power, Kildare was restored in 1496.[7]

Gaelic Ireland was thinly populated and predominantly pastoral. Its many lordships frequently engaged in warfare with each other or their 'English' neighbours. Land belonged collectively to a 'clan' or 'sept' whose members claimed descent from a common male ancestor. The leading men of the clan were supposed to select the chief's successor from a core descent group. Sometimes they accepted his choice. Alternatively, a bloody struggle might be necessary to decide the succession. A subject class worked the land. Successful clans expanded and absorbed or displaced smaller and weaker ones; various large clans broke into different branches. Gaelic chiefs sometimes allied and intermarried with 'English' magnate families. Gaelic Ireland shared its language and learning and a tradition of bardic celebration of heroic deeds with the Highlands and Islands of Scotland. Irish chiefs also employed troops of professional soldiers from western Scotland, the 'galloglass', some of whose leaders established clans in Ireland.[8]

Scotland was named after the Gaelic-speaking Scots, originally from Ireland, who had colonized the Islands and Highlands from the fifth century onwards. Their language had spread to most of Scotland by 1100. Yet 'Scots', the language dominant in the kingdom's south-eastern heartland by 1500, and one of the languages of official record from the fifteenth century, was descended from a dialect of old English spoken by Angles settling south of the Forth in the seventh century.[9] Edward I of England (1272–1307) had tried and failed to subjugate Scotland. In 1295–6 Scots opposed to his claims had made the first of a long series of Scottish alliances with France.

Scotland's land surface mainly consists of upland and mountain. Most of the soil is naturally harsh. The best land is concentrated in the southern Lowlands, along the east coast, and round the Moray Firth. The Highland massif was a formidable barrier to effective communication and control. Two-thirds of Scotland's population was probably concentrated in the Lowlands. Nearly all her towns lay there. Most of them were small places. Edinburgh had the lion's share of her export trade, in which wool was the most important commodity.[10]

Even in the more populous and settled areas, the king's authority was more limited than in England. Scotland south and east of the Great Glen was divided into sheriffdoms, but these were hereditary. The nobility possessed regalities, jurisdictions over their own lands, many of which entitled the holder to try every type of case except treason. Royal justiciars travelled on regular ayres for the enforcement of justice, but large areas of the country lay outside their circuits. Parliaments met frequently until James IV's reign, but granted very little taxation.[11]

The Gaidhealtachd or Gaelic-speaking region embraced in 1500 the Highlands and the Western Isles and the far south-west. The clan was the basis of lordship over much of this region. Throughout the Gaidhealtachd the institutional means of exercising royal overlordship were limited: kings' best hopes of enhancing their authority lay in the judicious settlement of noble disputes, the winning of co-operation against especially violent and disruptive magnates and reliance on carefully chosen local supporters. MacDonald lords had created the great semi-independent lordship of the Isles in western Scotland. Forfeiture of the lordship in 1493 failed to ensure effective royal control. In the far north, the Norse language of the Vikings who had once ruled all the northern and western islands survived in Caithness, Orkney and Shetland. Christian I of Denmark ceded the last two to James III as a pledge for payment of dowry in 1468–9.[12]

Britain was united in its loyalty to one institution, the Roman Catholic Church. Its largest and most beautiful buildings were cathedrals and abbeys. Its four ecclesiastical provinces (Canterbury and York in England, the recently established St Andrews and Glasgow in Scotland) contained between them twenty-one English and Welsh dioceses, and twelve Scottish ones. All the Welsh dioceses lay within the province of Canterbury. England contained some 9,000 parishes, Scotland about 1,000. There were also hundreds of monasteries and friaries, hospitals, almshouses and collegiate churches. The great majority of the students who took degrees in the universities (Oxford, Cambridge, St Andrews, Glasgow and Aberdeen, the last three all founded during the fifteenth century) went on to careers in the Church. Despite the existence of numerous local variations, the Latin mass would have been instantly familiar throughout Britain. The Church possessed vast landholdings.

Monastic foundation had almost ceased, but laity and clergy still made generous gifts and bequests towards the re-building and adornment of parish churches and the endowment of prayers for the dead. The cults of a host of saints, devotion to their images and relics, and pilgrimages to their shrines, provided foci for local loyalties.

Britain's European neighbours

France, England's nearest continental neighbour, almost twice as large as Britain in land area, was probably nearly five times as populous in 1500. France was a great kingdom, but also a much less close-knit one than England. The forms of the French language spoken in the north and south differed markedly. Roman law was dominant in the south, customary laws in the north. Several provinces on the edges of the kingdom had their own sovereign courts or *parlements*, distinct from the *parlement* of Paris, the most important in France. Kings seldom convened the estates-general, the national representative assembly. Many of the provinces had estates of their own.[13]

Since 1066 all kings of England had held land in France. Edward III's claim to its crown, made in 1340, was to remain part of his successors' royal style until 1801. As a result of Henry V's victories in 1415 to 1422, his son Henry VI had been crowned in Paris in 1431. However, the rival claimant Charles VII, scion of the French royal family of the Valois, aided by numerous Scotsmen in his hour of need, had subsequently defeated the English. After 1453 only Calais remained of the English crown's former French mainland territories. France remained a very important source of English imports of wine, dyestuffs, salt, linen and canvas. Guienne supplied wine to Scotland as well as England. Scotsmen served in the French kings' Scots guard, formed in 1455. Intellectual links with France were especially valuable for Scotland: many Scots studied at French universities, above all Paris.

England's early-fifteenth-century military success in France had owed much to the support of Philip 'the Good', duke of Burgundy. The duchy had been established for his grandfather, a younger son of the king of France. By judicious marriages successive dukes enlarged their territories, largely outside France, building up a powerful state. After King Louis XI of France seized the French duchy in 1477, the provinces of the southern Netherlands formed the heart of this 'Burgundian' state. The Duchess Mary, last of the Valois line, had married Maximilian of Habsburg. Their son Philip was duke in 1500. His Netherlands possessions, their area about half of England's, supported a population of similar size. These lands were fertile and intensively exploited. The southern Netherlands were also the most heavily urbanized region in Europe. Great rivers, the Rhine, the Meuse and the Scheldt, served as commercial highways. Both England and Scotland exported woollen cloth to the Netherlands, and imported a huge range of raw materials and manufactured goods that had been made there or passed through. These important commercial links made friendly relations between the British kingdoms and the rulers of those wealthy provinces highly desirable for both sides.

The Netherlands lay within the Holy Roman Empire, which extended from Holstein in the north to Siena in the south, from Lorraine in the west to Bohemia in the east. Within this enormous area, hundreds of secular and ecclesiastical states theoretically subject to the emperor enjoyed considerable autonomy in practice. By 1500, his authority was barely acknowledged south of the Alps. The emperor (Maximilian of Habsburg from 1493 to 1519) was first in rank among the rulers of Europe. Seven of the greater vassals, including the king of Bohemia, elected the emperor, who was always a member of the house of Habsburg from 1440 until 1740. The states of the empire were represented in the imperial diet or Reichstag.

Germany was the core of the Empire. The most important north German towns, including Lübeck, Bremen, Danzig and Cologne, had formed the powerful Hanseatic League to protect their commercial interests. With bases in London and other east coast ports, the League handled most of England's trade with Germany, the Baltic and Scandinavia. Germany supplied Britain with linen, canvas, fustians, metal goods (including fine armour) and a range of processed metals, including iron, steel, copper, brass and silver. Central Europe (especially the Harz, Bohemia, Slovakia, Hungary and the Tyrol) was Europe's main domestic source of gold and silver. This area experienced around 1500 a mining boom that helped to stimulate purchases of English cloth exported through Antwerp.[14] Many British scholars, Scotsmen in particular, attended German universities. Travellers from Britain to Italy frequently followed the Rhine. The Swiss Confederation, virtually independent of the Empire from 1499, controlled the western Alpine passes between Germany and Italy. Skilled and hardy Swiss soldiers were the most formidable mercenaries in Europe.

To the north of Germany, Norway, Sweden and Denmark had been under one ruler since 1397, though in practice kings based in Denmark had exercised only intermittent control over Sweden. Vast though these lands were, their total population was probably less than England's. The king of Denmark, however, controlled both shores of the mouth of the Baltic, and the Sound Tolls were an increasingly valuable jewel in the Danish crown. Scotland exported wool, cloth, skins and fish directly to Denmark and the Baltic lands, and imported flax, hemp and grain from there, and timber from Norway. In 1502 James IV, son of Margaret of Denmark, sent ineffective help to his uncle King Hans against the Hanse and Swedish and Norwegian rebels.[15]

In the south-eastern Baltic, Scottish merchants had founded their own suburb of Danzig over a century before.[16] A largely German city under Polish overlordship in 1500, it stood near the mouth of the great river Vistula, leading to the broad grain-growing plains of Poland. A royal marriage had in 1386 brought together Poland and Lithuania under one ruler. Poland/Lithuania, an enormous, relatively thinly populated territory with a powerful rural nobility, faced its first serious challenge from Russia, united under Moscow's leadership by the Grand Duke Ivan the Great, who seized slices of Lithuania. Ivan married in 1472 the niece of the last Byzantine emperor, whose capital,

Constantinople, had fallen to the Ottoman Turks in 1453. The Greek Orthodox Church of the former Byzantine Empire, in schism with the Roman Catholic Church since the eleventh century, was the mother Church of the eastern Slav nations and Romania. The fall of Constantinople left Muscovy as the only major independent polity professing the Orthodox faith, though not until 1589 was the patriarchate of Moscow established.

Meanwhile, the Ottoman sultans soon made themselves the foremost military power in Europe. As the capital of the Ottoman Empire, Constantinople became the continent's biggest city. Several features of the Ottoman polity made it exotic and alien in western European eyes. Fiercely devoted to Islam and its propagation by conquest, the sultans nevertheless, in accordance with Islamic precept, tolerated Judaism and Christianity, with resulting economic benefits. Their army was partly based on military fiefs, but at its heart was an elite of celibate slave warriors recruited by means of a compulsory levy of Christian children. Converted slaves also largely staffed the sultan's household and administration. Succession to the Ottoman throne, generally from father to son, was often decided by murder or bloody fratricidal struggle.

Hungary and Venice were the Ottomans' most important European neighbours, and had fought against them for much of the later fifteenth century. The great maritime republic of Venice had suffered some serious defeats, but still possessed several eastern Mediterranean islands, and some enclaves in mainland Greece such as Malvasia, from which the sweet 'Malmsey' wine popular in England took its name. Around 1500 a few English merchants still reached the Aegean. Intrepid pilgrims travelled to Jerusalem. The archbishop of Glasgow died on his way there in 1508, and James IV planned to make the journey.[17]

Italy was the heart of western Christendom. Rome was the seat of the pope, St Peter's successor and head of the Catholic Church, centre of the Church's governing bureaucracy and judicial institutions, and a major pilgrimage destination. A constant stream of business went to and from Rome, suits and petitions in one direction, sentences, dispensations, appointments in the other. Its possessions straddling central Italy made the papacy a considerable territorial power. The south of Italy belonged to the kingdom of Naples. In the north were numerous smaller states, mostly centred on great cities. Foremost were the republics of Florence, Genoa and Venice, and the duchy of Milan. The Apennine Mountains, Italy's formidably rugged spine, together with the interference of foreign powers and the territorial ambitions of the papacy, had prevented Italy's dominance by any one domestic ruler and encouraged local autonomy. The great Lombard plain was, together with the Netherlands, one of the two most intensively cultivated and heavily urbanized areas in Europe. Venetian and Genoese merchants handled much of England's trade with the Mediterranean, which included substantial imports of Italian luxuries, especially silk and satin fabrics and glassware. Italian merchants also brought Eastern and Levantine spices, silks and dried fruit. Three of the most famous universities in Europe, those of Padua (in Venetian territory), Bologna and Ferrara, attracted a steady stream of students from Britain.

Sicily and Sardinia belonged to the kingdom of Aragon, which embraced the fertile Ebro valley and eastern coastlands of the Iberian Peninsula. To its west lay the much larger kingdom of Castile, extending from the northern shore of the peninsula to its southern tip, much of its interior consisting of high plains intersected by river valleys and mountain ranges. The most intensively culti-vated lands lay in the south. Most of the largest cities of the peninsula were also in the south, including Granada, capital of the last Muslim kingdom of Spain, captured only in 1492. England imported Spanish wine, fruits, oil and iron. Bristol merchants played an important part in this flourishing trade. However, pilgrimage to the celebrated shrine of St James at Santiago de Compostella in Galicia possibly attracted more visitors to Spain from Britain than any other activity.

The marriage in 1469 of Ferdinand of Aragon and Isabella of Castile, fol-lowed first by Isabella's accession to the throne of Castile in 1474, and then by Ferdinand's to that of Aragon in 1479, had joined their kingdoms in what turned out to be an enduring union, though each kingdom kept its own distinctive institutions. It was to Catherine, daughter of these 'Catholic kings', that Henry VII married his son Arthur. The Spanish monarchs valued Henry above all as a potential collaborator against France either in diplomacy or in war. To this end they did their best to bring about peace between England and Scotland.

Relations between Castile and its western neighbour, Portugal, had been intermittently stormy. Their rivalry extended to overseas exploration. Christopher Columbus persuaded Queen Isabella to support his attempt to sail west to Asia. His 1492 landfall in the Bahamas preceded by only six years the arrival of the Portuguese captain Vasco da Gama in India. News of Columbus's discoveries soon reached England and quickened an existing interest in west-ern ventures. Bristol sailors had already been sailing far into the Atlantic, and the city supported the Genoese merchant John Cabot in a voyage of 1497 that resulted in the discovery of Newfoundland. Henry VII contributed a ship to his abortive second voyage. Bristol fisheries may have benefited, but royal interest in America was soon to wane.

Britain was not only geographically peripheral but also far less wealthy or densely populated than some other areas of Europe. Only London belonged even in the second rank of European cities. An oft-quoted Italian traveller through south-eastern England in Henry VII's reign thought it underpopu-lated in relation to its fertility and riches.[18] Britain's main exports were raw materials and unfinished goods. The two island kingdoms of England and Scotland were old enemies. Yet Britain's marginality and insignificance should not be exaggerated. England had shown a striking capacity for united action when ruled by able kings who had made good use of her exceptionally effec-tive parliament. English victories in France had not been forgotten. Among the numerous kingdoms of medieval Europe, England counted as one of the more important and powerful. In the sixteenth century, however, it was to be overshadowed by France and Spain. The French crown had extended its hold over previously semi-independent territories. A newly united Spain acquired a great empire in Europe and overseas. England's relations with Europe during the sixteenth century were to be strongly influenced by the rivalry between these two great powers.

2

DYNASTIC WARS AND RELIGIOUS CHANGES, 1500-58

Henry VIII's early wars with France and Scotland

The last years of Henry VII's reign were rife with uncertainty and fear. His wife and eldest son were dead. His own health deteriorated. Henry planned to marry again, but European royal deaths and bewildering diplomatic re-alignments complicated his matrimonial diplomacy.[1] Isabella of Castile died in 1504, the widowed Ferdinand of Aragon married a French princess and Ferdinand's son-in-law Philip of Burgundy died in 1506. Philip's sister Margaret refused to marry Henry, and Philip's widow Juana, whom he also considered, was mentally unstable. Dynastic insecurity and illness helped to make Henry harsh and suspicious. In April 1509 he died, aged fifty-two. In the event, his seventeen-year-old son Henry VIII enjoyed the first undisputed succession to the throne since 1422.

Henry VII had been fortunate that French kings had shown little interest in Britain because of their dynastic territorial claims in Italy. When Henry landed in France in 1492 in belated response to Charles VIII's successful invasion of Brittany, Charles had bought him off. Charles had then in 1494 embarked on what became an epic contest for control of Italy. Charles invaded Naples in 1495 to enforce his claim to the Neapolitan crown. At first successful, he was soon forced to withdraw by a coalition that included Ferdinand of Aragon, the Emperor Maximilian, the pope, Venice and Milan. His cousin and successor Louis XII (1498–1515) successfully asserted a claim to Milan inherited from his grandmother, and then invaded Naples, this time in co-operation with Ferdinand. The partners soon fell out, however, and Spanish forces conquered the whole of Naples. In 1512 a new coalition drove the French out of Milan. Francis I (1515–47), Louis's successor, recaptured it in 1515, and kept it when he made peace in 1516.

When Ferdinand of Aragon died in 1516, Charles of Habsburg, son of his 'mad' daughter Juana and Philip of Burgundy, became king of both Castile and Aragon, as Charles I, in principle as co-ruler with his mother Juana. The contest between the long-jawed Charles, dutiful, stubborn and purposeful, and the handsome, flamboyant and slippery Francis I, heads respectively of the royal houses of Habsburg and Valois, remained the mainspring of western European politics for over thirty years. In 1519 Charles won the imperial election to succeed his recently deceased paternal grandfather, Maximilian, and thus became Emperor Charles V. Growing tension between Charles and Francis culminated in war in 1521. In 1525 Charles's army captured Francis near Pavia in the most spectacular victory of the Italian wars. Once freed, Francis joined Pope Clement VII, Florence and Venice to try to prevent Habsburg domination of Italy. In the most notorious episode of the wars Charles's troops seized and sacked Rome in 1527. Francis was again defeated, and renounced all his Italian claims in 1529. The duchy of Milan, already a Habsburg satellite, came under Spanish rule in 1535.

Meanwhile, Henry VIII's accession in 1509 had transformed the atmosphere of the English court. Within two months he married his brother's widow Catherine of Aragon, belatedly implementing a marriage treaty made as early as 1503 but delayed by subsequent uncertainties. Young, and secure in his possession of the throne, Henry could now seek the other princely objectives of wealth and renown. Monarchs, like their greater subjects, sought to acquire land as a means of providing for children, gaining rule over men and rewarding followers for good service. Marriage was one route to territorial accumulation that had been followed with spectacular success by the houses of Burgundy and Habsburg. War was more doubtful, but if successful gained greater renown. The assertion of an inherited claim was a common pretext for 'just' wars, such as the Italian conflicts. Another was the fulfilment of an obligation to an ally faced with attack. The prince who fought for a kingdom might have to settle for less – a province or a stronghold – though this would not necessarily prevent the later re-activation of his claim. Sometimes the rewards of war were no more than financial – ransoms, or a pension or indemnity paid as part of the peace treaty, such as Henry VII had gained in 1492. Henry VIII commanded far smaller resources than either Francis I or Charles V. Only in alliance with one of the great powers did he have a realistic prospect of success in war, and even then hostilities were too expensive for England to sustain for very long. Some of Henry VIII's councillors favoured his standing aside from continental wars. His minister Thomas Wolsey allegedly retorted that if England sat in peace 'while the fools fought', they would ultimately make peace and join in attacking her. Sir Thomas More, relating this story, remained unconvinced: Wolsey's wisdom had helped 'the king and the realm to spend many a fair penny'.[2]

Henry VIII looked forward eagerly to war with France. The new anti-French league formed in 1511–12 gave him his opportunity as the ally of his father-in-law Ferdinand of Aragon and the pope (an important bonus for the conventionally pious king). A plan for an English attack on south-western France from Spain failed completely in 1512. Next year, however, Henry defeated the

French in Artois, and took Tournai, an island of French territory in Flanders. Henry made peace in August 1514 on honourable terms: an enhanced French pension, the marriage of his sister Mary to Louis XII and the high-maintenance acquisition of Tournai, cashed in for a further pension enhancement in 1518. These gains were small when set against the colossal cost of nearly one million pounds, met by using Henry VII's reserves and very substantial grants of parliamentary taxation.

The slippery slopes of Flodden in Northumberland witnessed in 1513 England's most important victory in the war. James IV, king of Scots, and Henry's brother-in-law, had set about constructing a formidable navy with French help. James tried to reconcile Louis XII and the pope in 1510–11. Offers of further help from Louis XII, and English highhandedness, including the assertion of Henry's suzerainty over Scotland, persuaded James to declare war on Henry in 1513. After he had seized some English castles, the earl of Surrey cut off his retreat. Forced into an untimely attack, the Scots suffered massive casualties, including the death of James himself.[3]

Thomas Wolsey's administrative contribution to success in war made him Henry's most trusted minister. Henry nominated Wolsey to the archbishopric of York, and in 1515 made him lord chancellor; the pope made him a cardinal. In foreign policy, Wolsey did everything he could to advance his master's honour and profit.[4] English resources had been exhausted. War was out of the question for the time being. In 1518, however, king and minister successfully exploited Pope Leo X's wish to promote a crusade and competing manoeuvres for English support by Francis I and Charles of Habsburg. By delaying the papal legate's entry to England until Wolsey had been granted a legateship *a latere*, and by then taking the lead in making the peace of London, signed by all the major powers, Wolsey and his king made the most of England's weak hand, achieving, briefly, an international prestige in peace-making that they could not have won in war. The afterglow lasted into 1520, when separate meetings took place with Charles and with Francis (in the fabulous setting of the Field of Cloth of Gold near Calais).

In 1521, after attempted mediation by Wolsey, Henry entered into alliance with Charles V. Francis I, the aggressor, was already losing ground, and Henry also had the pope's support: the international situation seemed favourable. At home, however, the most strenuous efforts had to be made to raise resources. In 1522–3, after an unprecedentedly thorough survey of different sources of wealth and of military resources, Wolsey raised big forced loans. Two expeditions to France in 1522 and 1523 achieved nothing. In 1523 Wolsey had to reduce a demand for parliamentary taxation. In 1525 news from Pavia re-ignited hopes of a successful invasion of France. Whether or not Henry really intended such action, he attempted to raise the non-parliamentary 'Amicable Grant' to finance it. Widespread resistance from taxpayers defeated the attempt.[5] The constraints imposed by his limited resources underlined Henry's second rank standing in Europe. This was a turning point in his reign. Henry felt let down by Charles V's unwillingness to help Henry make his own gains at France's expense. Henry made peace with France and Wolsey encouraged the formation of a new league against Charles V.

Scotland had posed no serious threat during Henry's second French war. His sister Margaret, guardian to her infant son James V after Flodden, had faced widespread mistrust, strengthened by the truce she soon concluded with England. When she married the young Archibald Douglas, sixth earl of Angus, other noblemen resented Angus's advancement. The king's council appointed James IV's paternal cousin, John Stewart, duke of Albany, governor of the kingdom and guardian of the young king. Previously an exile in France, courtier and trusted servant of Francis I, Albany tried but failed to mount a successful invasion of England during Francis's war with Henry, and finally left Scotland a disappointed man.

Meanwhile Angus had proved an unfaithful husband, thoroughly alienating Queen Margaret. Henry VIII, who saw their partnership as the best way of continuing English influence in Scotland, tried in vain to reconcile them. The determined Angus nevertheless gained a place among King James's regents, and took control of the king's person in 1525. Ruling in James's name, he had the fourteen-year-old king declared of age in 1527, and became chancellor.

Henry VIII's break with Rome

By 1527, Catherine of Aragon had borne only one surviving child, the Princess Mary, in 1516, and had not been pregnant for several years. Henry was concerned about the succession. His desire for Anne Boleyn, daughter of the treasurer of his household, was reinforcing growing doubts about his first marriage. Because Catherine was his brother Arthur's widow, a papal dispensation had been necessary to allow her marriage to Henry. Henry now became convinced that this marriage had flouted a scriptural warning (Leviticus 20: 21) against marrying a brother's wife. No matter that Deuteronomy 25: 5 strongly enjoined marriage to a brother's childless *widow*. Henry claimed that his marriage had been against God's Word. He also insisted, in face of Catherine's consistent denials, that her union with Arthur had been consummated. In May 1527 he had his marriage investigated by Wolsey and the archbishop of Canterbury, William Warham. But the annulment of the marriage could only be accomplished with papal authority. Henry's suit placed Pope Clement VII in an almost impossible position, because Charles V, Catherine's nephew, was dominant in Italy. Henry's invocation of Scripture challenged previous papal interpretation.[6] Eventually, in 1528, after temporary French successes, Clement empowered Cardinals Wolsey and Campeggio to hear the case in England, but proceedings did not open until May 1529 and were revoked to Rome after Francis I's crushing reverses in Italy.

Henry's quarrel with the papacy developed against a background of increasingly serious problems for Christendom. The Ottoman Empire had entered on a new era of dramatically rapid expansion with the conquest of Syria and Egypt and the assumption of control over the Holy Places in Arabia in 1516–17.

Suleiman I, 'the Magnificent', most celebrated of all Ottoman sultans, came to the throne in 1520. There followed in quick succession the fall of Belgrade (1521), the capture of Rhodes (1522) and the shattering defeat of King Lajos of Hungary at the Battle of Mohács (1526), leading to the conquest of much of the country that had been the eastern bastion of Christendom. In September 1529 the Turks launched their first attack on Vienna. Meanwhile, Charles's brother Ferdinand, his deputy in the Empire, faced a new problem there: the rapidly spreading influence of Martin Luther's evangelical message. Luther published his famous ninety-five theses against indulgences in 1517. He defended his doctrines at the Diet of Worms in 1521, only to see them condemned. The Elector Frederick of Saxony nevertheless sheltered him. A growing number of German princes and cities undertook evangelical reforms. They became known as 'Protestants' after protesting against the decision of the 1529 Diet of Speier to enforce the anti-Lutheran decree of the Diet of Worms. The Protestant Schmalkaldic League was inaugurated early in 1531.

In October 1529 Wolsey was indicted of praemunire, the offence of encroachment on royal jurisdiction, especially by ecclesiastical judges, and dismissed from his office of lord chancellor. In this way Henry was punishing Wolsey above all for failing to get his marriage annulled. Henry's faithful servant first and foremost, Wolsey as legate was nevertheless the supreme representative of papal authority. The charge against him was a warning to Rome. A new parliament, meeting in November, legislated against various ecclesiastical abuses. Efforts to change the pope's mind intensified in 1530. They included a petition from the nobility as well as a campaign to persuade the continental universities of Henry's case for annulment.

Meanwhile, however, a unilateral solution was taking shape. Its key elements would be a decision of Henry's case by the English Church and the recognition of royal supremacy over that Church. By September 1530 scholars working for Henry had gathered a substantial body of evidence, much of it rather dubious, in support of these radical ideas. The first move to enforce their acceptance came in December 1530, when all the English clergy were indicted on a charge of praemunire. The two convocations (assemblies of the clergy) of Canterbury and York agreed to pay £118,000 for their pardon. Then, when in January 1531 Henry suddenly required the Canterbury convocation to acknowledge him to be supreme head of the English Church, it attached the important qualification 'as far as the law of Christ allows'. Further intimidation followed in March 1532 when the Commons presented a supplication complaining about the clergy and church courts. Seizing on the first complaint, concerning the legislative power of convocations, Henry insisted that they should henceforth meet and legislate only with his consent, and that existing canon law be examined in order to ascertain its compatibility with English law. The Canterbury convocation submitted. After the death of the archbishop of Canterbury in August, Henry nominated to the pope as his replacement Thomas Cranmer, on whose co-operation he could rely. Clement VII appointed Cranmer in accordance with established procedures. Cranmer was soon to become a covert Lutheran.

Henry's unilateral solution could now be accomplished. Cranmer secretly married the king and Anne Boleyn in January 1533. In March, parliament passed an act declaring that England was an empire, i.e. independent of any external power; that both clergy and laity owed the king complete obedience, and that the English clergy were competent to deal with all matters of divine law. It prohibited appeals to Rome in all the most important types of church court case. Thomas Cranmer then declared Henry's first marriage invalid and upheld his second. In September Anne Boleyn bore a child, the Princess Elizabeth. Early in 1534 parliament declared the children of Henry and Anne successors to the crown. In April Henry appointed Thomas Cromwell, an able former servant of Wolsey's, his principal secretary.

By upholding the marriage to Catherine days before the Succession Act passed, Clement VII showed his firm refusal to accept Henry's solution. Many of the English clergy could not accept the king's policy or had serious doubts about it. Some noblemen sympathized with Catherine and deplored Henry's drastic actions. A defensive alliance with Francis I, made in June 1532, offered Henry some protection abroad, though Francis remained friendly towards the pope and strongly disapproved of Henry's solution. Henry also put out diplomatic feelers towards the German Protestant princes and concluded an alliance with the Hanseatic town of Lübeck in 1534. More important was Charles V's preoccupation with the growing Turkish threat. Khair-ad-Din 'Barbarossa', appointed admiral of the Ottoman Empire in 1533, took Tunis in 1534. Charles mounted a great expedition to Tunis in 1535 to re-instate the previous ruler.

Henry's sources of concern closer to home included Scotland. In June 1528, soon after his mother's marriage to the earl of Angus had been annulled, the young James V threw off his stepfather's irksome tutelage. Angus initially resisted and appealed for English help. Not until March 1529 did he agree to surrender his strongholds and withdraw into England. James then made reassertion of royal control over the borders his top priority. Raids by both sides culminated in December 1532 in James's summons of the Scottish host to resist English aggression. In July 1533, James sheltered a Welsh exile, James Gruffydd ap Powell, uncle to Sir Rhys ap Gruffydd, executed in 1531 on a flimsy charge of conspiring with the king of Scots to invade England. James had successfully curbed the Douglas interest despite its English backing. In the process he attracted the attention of Charles V, who made him a knight of the prestigious Burgundian order of the Golden Fleece in April 1532. Francis I, fearing imperial influence in Scotland, worked for an Anglo-Scottish peace, which was at last concluded in May 1534.[7]

By then a new threat to Henry VIII's rule was materializing in Ireland. In 1520, he had asserted royal authority by appointing an English lord lieutenant there. Henry refused to accept that the earl of Kildare was indispensable, but none of the alternative chief governors he chose between 1520 and 1530 lasted long. His spasmodic interference caused reciprocal irritation and suspicion, which were exacerbated by Thomas Cromwell's efforts to gain control of Irish patronage. Kildare was detained in England in May 1534. In June his son

Thomas denounced Henry's policies before the Irish council and then openly rebelled. He denounced Henry as a heretic, angled for conservative support in England and 'demanded an oath of allegiance to himself, the pope and the emperor'. Charles V despatched emissaries and some arms. Irish magnates had sought foreign aid before this, but calling the king a heretic was a new and ominous step. In October Henry sent to Ireland the biggest force despatched there since the fourteenth century. Only in August 1535 did Thomas, now himself earl of Kildare, surrender. An Irish parliament enacted the royal supremacy in 1536. In February 1537, in the wake of rebellions in northern England, Kildare and five of his uncles were executed as traitors at Tyburn – unprecedentedly severe treatment of the leading Anglo-Irish family.[8]

Confronted with papal obduracy, discontent at home and serious rebellion in Ireland, Henry acted to strengthen his authority, increase his resources and tighten his control over his dominions. Late in 1534 parliament passed the Act of Supremacy recognizing the king's supreme headship of the Church in England and his right to correct all heresies and abuses within it. A separate act made it treason to impugn the supremacy or speak maliciously of the king or queen. This act's victims included Thomas More and John Fisher, executed in 1535. More, Wolsey's successor as lord chancellor, deeply disapproving of Henry's moves to assert his control of the Church, had resigned in 1532. Pope Paul III had just made Fisher, bishop of Rochester and Catherine's tireless champion, a cardinal: his execution shocked Catholic Europe.

In its final session, early in 1536, the parliament summoned in 1529 authorized the dissolution of monasteries with incomes of under £200 a year, presented as a reform, but largely inspired by Henry's financial needs. External threats or fears of internal disorder helped inspire further measures to assimilate outlying territories to England and extend royal control. The most important of these reformed the government of Wales. Separate acts gave Calais parliamentary representation and returned to the crown judicial powers previously delegated to various local jurisdictions.

Catherine of Aragon died in January 1536. Her successor Anne Boleyn had failed to give Henry the son he wanted. She was suddenly arrested in May, tried on charges of incest and adultery, and executed. Henry seems to have believed the charges, made superficially plausible by Anne's own foolish behaviour. Her marriage to Henry was annulled. Anne's downfall raised the hopes of all friends of Catherine's daughter Mary. They were soon dashed. In June a swiftly summoned new parliament put any sons Henry might have by his new, third wife Jane Seymour at the front of the line of succession, while excluding both Mary and Elizabeth on the ground of their illegitimacy.

Another statute of 1536 stripped the pope of any remaining authority in England. The king exercised his ecclesiastical supremacy through the layman Thomas Cromwell, appointed vicegerent in spirituals in 1535. In 1536 Cromwell presided over a convocation that adopted the Church of England's first doctrinal statement to deviate from orthodox Catholic teaching. He subsequently issued directives to the clergy. Henry's measures of 1536 confirmed his determination to keep the royal supremacy and use it to impose his own priorities on the Church. They provoked a powerful popular response. In October a series of risings took place, first in Lincolnshire, and then in most of northern England beyond the Humber, the latter collectively known as 'the Pilgrimage of Grace'. The participants' grievances included the dissolution of the smaller monasteries, the king's employment of heretical advisers, the abolition of papal supremacy and Mary's exclusion from the succession. The pilgrims dispersed after receiving a promise of pardon that was broken after fresh small risings early in 1537. The risings received widespread support from people and clergy. A few noblemen were later severely punished for encouraging them, but the most important conservative magnates cautiously supported the king. The heads of some of the greater northern monasteries were also involved. The consequent forfeiture of these monasteries' property inaugurated the second phase of monastic dissolutions. When at last Queen Jane bore him a son, Edward, in October 1537, Henry's foremost goal was achieved, though Jane died soon afterwards.

In 1536 Charles V had been in no position to exploit the risings in England. Francis I had made a commercial treaty with Suleiman I and invaded Italy. In June 1538, however, Charles and Francis made a ten-year truce, followed by a personal meeting. The following January both undertook to make no separate agreement with Henry. Soon afterwards Pope Paul III despatched Cardinal Reginald Pole to Spain and France to win support for an attack on him. Henry was never convinced that Charles and Francis, two inveterate rivals, would really combine in action against him. His fourfold response was nevertheless decisive and energetic. A massive programme of shipbuilding and coastal fortifications was undertaken, largely financed by the accelerated dissolution of the greater monasteries, completed in 1540. Reginald Pole's brother and his kinsman the marquess of Exeter, one of England's foremost noblemen, were executed in 1538–9. To calm religious anxieties Henry set about showing other rulers and his own people that he was a truly Catholic king. In spring 1539, parliament passed the Act of Six Articles upholding some central Catholic doctrines and practices. Finally, Henry continued his quest for allies abroad. The German Protestant princes might be encouraged to restrain Charles V, but the Six Articles signalled Henry's determination not to be drawn into a Protestant confessional alliance. More promising was Duke Wilhelm of Cleves, very similar to Henry VIII in his religious stance, but allied to the Schmalkaldic League, France and Denmark. Wilhelm's succession to the duchy of Gelderland in 1539 posed an obstacle to Charles V's unification of the Netherlands under Habsburg rule. Henry married the duke's sister Anne, but when she came to England in January 1540, he could not consummate the marriage, and his third annulment closed this embarrassing matrimonial venture in July. It was swiftly followed by the execution of Thomas Cromwell. How far Henry's vindictive anger against this efficient servant was due to Cromwell's promotion of the Cleves marriage remains uncertain. The fact that he was charged with promoting heresy underlined Henry's resolve to move no further towards evangelical reform.

In 1541 Charles and Francis both sought Henry's friendship as they once more moved towards war. Catherine's death and Anne's execution had removed obstacles to co-operation with Charles. Jane had given Henry a son. He had successfully crushed rebellion at home, and vastly increased the wealth of the crown by plundering the Church. Francis's friendship now seemed much less valuable. He had annoyed Henry both by discontinuing his pension and by developing closer links with Scotland.

James V strongly favoured the French alliance. He chose two French brides. His nine months' absence on a visit to France in 1536–7 demonstrated his confidence in the stability of his realm. He brought back Francis I's daughter Madeleine, who died soon after her arrival in Scotland. In 1538, James married Mary of Guise, member of a powerful French noble family. Angus's continuing presence in England was irksome to James. In 1537 Janet Douglas, Angus's sister, was burnt at the stake for conspiring to poison the king and for treasonable contacts with her brothers. James also declined to follow Henry's advice to renounce the pope and seize church lands. He was perfectly satisfied with his existing relationship with the Church, which had become a source of revenue second only to his French dowries. In 1540 James led a naval expedition to assert his authority over the western Isles, his flagship a present from Francis I.[9]

Rough wooing, Reformation and the shadow of France

James seemed to slight Henry by not acting on his invitation to meet him at York in September 1541. In 1542, Henry resolved to bring his nephew to heel before going to war with France. An initial English attack accomplished little. James decided to counter-attack. Part of his army, sent towards Carlisle in a preliminary feint, was trapped and forced to surrender on Solway Moss in November. The English capture of several noblemen was unfortunate, but it was James's death three weeks later, leaving only a baby daughter, Mary, to succeed him, that seemed to give Henry a magnificent new opportunity. He hoped to marry Mary to his own son Edward. He counted on the support of 'assured Scots' among the Solway Moss captives and the co-operation of the governor of Scotland, James Hamilton, earl of Arran, heir presumptive to the Scottish crown and supporter of Protestant reform. In July 1543, commissioners concluded the Treaty of Greenwich, betrothing Mary to Edward. But Mary of Guise, who still held her daughter, as well as Cardinal Beaton, who soon became chancellor, and several noblemen, opposed Arran. Arran himself soon changed sides. In December Scotland's parliament renounced the treaty.[10]

In 1542 Henry had agreed with Charles V that they should undertake a joint invasion of France. Charles's desire for Henry's support, together with Henry's own vastly increased resources, offered the best prospect since 1513 of gains at French expense. After Anne of Cleves, Henry had married two more wives: Catherine Howard in 1540 (executed for adultery early in 1542) and Catherine Parr in 1543. Neither of them bore him a child. A statute of 1544 restored Henry's daughters Mary and Elizabeth to the line of succession to the throne, though without explicitly annulling their illegitimacy. After this precaution in case of his death in war, Henry crossed the Channel in June 1544 with a huge army of 40,000 men.

Instead of joining Charles V in marching on Paris he besieged the well-fortified coastal town of Boulogne. Charles repaid him by making peace in September on the day Henry entered Boulogne. England, now alone, faced a war on two fronts because Henry still hoped to force the Scots to accept the marriage agreed in 1543. Savage incursions into Scotland occurred in both 1544 and 1545. In a dramatic volte-face, Angus, Arran's long-standing foe, reacted to indiscriminate English wasting of his own lands by taking command as lieutenant of Scotland south of Forth, and defeating the English at Ancrum Moor in February 1545. French reinforcements arrived in June. A French fleet reached the Solent in July and landed forces on the Isle of Wight, though the English fleet soon regained control of the Channel. In June 1546 the Treaty of Camp ended the ruinously expensive war. English retention of Boulogne for eight years saved face. The military preparations and campaigns of Henry's last eight years had cost over two million pounds.

In Ireland, the lord deputy, Lord Leonard Grey, had attacked several troublesome Gaelic families with unprecedented vigour, provoking an exceptional alliance of the O'Donnell and O'Neill magnates of Ulster aimed at resisting the royal supremacy. They hoped for help from Pole, Charles V, Francis I or, especially, James V, but in vain. Grey defeated the league in August 1539. His successor Sir Anthony St Leger, appointed in 1540, inaugurated a more conciliatory policy. He sought to persuade the Gaelic chiefs to surrender their lands to the crown and receive them back as the king's tenants on terms that included descent by English rules of inheritance. They were to renounce their Gaelic titles for English ones, attend parliament and accept the extension of the machinery of government to Gaelic Ireland. The enforcement of the policy would necessarily be gradual. A number of chiefs co-operated at first. An unprecedented number of magnates attended parliament. In 1541 the Dublin parliament passed an act altering Henry's style to 'king' of Ireland. A local initiative, this was intended to remove any lingering belief in the pope's ultimate sovereignty that might be encouraged by the title 'lord'. One aim was to encourage the Irish chiefs to recognize Henry as their liege.[11]

Henry died on 28 January 1547, aged fifty-five. He had achieved his paramount goal of prolonging Tudor rule and enormously increased the authority, power and wealth of the crown. His settlement of the succession was nevertheless unsatisfactory. He had largely squandered the resources gained from the Church on a futile war. His religious policy had introduced new divisions. Protestants whom he himself had promoted would soon abandon his doctrinally conservative settlement. In his wrath one of the most terrifying kings in British history, he had broken or sent to the scaffold his best servants and several of the men and women he had most loved or honoured.

Henry's will named a council of sixteen to govern England until his son reached the age of eighteen. Henry's exclusion of his ablest conservative servants at a late stage crucially affected its balance. Two evangelicals, Archbishop Thomas Cranmer, and Edward Seymour, soon to be duke of Somerset, the new king's maternal uncle, were left in a dominant position. On 31 January, the council elected Seymour Protector of the realm and governor of the king's person. In March he received, nominally from Edward, authority to choose members of the privy council. This overrode Henry's will.

Francis I followed Henry to the grave in March 1547. His son Henry II (1547–59), a deadly foe of Charles V, favoured the Guise family, and resolved to stand by the young queen of Scots, daughter of Mary of Guise. In July, a small but formidable force sent by Henry swiftly captured St Andrews castle, held by Protestants who had in May 1546 murdered Mary's ally Cardinal Beaton. Somerset, who had already planned military action to enforce the treaty of marriage between Edward and Mary Stewart, responded by invading Scotland. In September, the Scots army, with Angus fighting bravely in the vanguard, was broken at Pinkie, outside Edinburgh. Somerset then garrisoned towns and strongholds from the Firth of Tay to the borders so as to underpin the pro-English 'assured Scots'. His propaganda appealed to the two nations' allegedly common ancestry and language and looked forward to a re-united Britain. The arrival of a substantial French army in June 1548 wrecked his strategy. The Scottish parliament agreed that Mary Stewart should be betrothed to Henry II's son Francis and removed to France. (Arran's support was secured by the grant of the French duchy of Châtelherault.) Somerset doggedly refused to accept his failure.

The Protector and Cranmer were meanwhile fast leading England towards a Protestant settlement with a series of measures including an act confiscating endowments for prayers for the dead (December 1547), and, early in 1549, an act introducing a new English Prayer Book. In the spring and summer of 1549 a unique sequence of popular risings shook England. Some of these were primarily concerned with religious grievances, others with economic ones. The biggest developed in the West and East Anglia. In Devon and Cornwall the new prayer book was the catalyst. The Norfolk rebels gathered in support of Somerset's policy of preventing the conversion of arable land to pasture, but their demand for the reversal of rent increases went far beyond anything he had offered. Both rebellions were put down only after Somerset, intent on continuing his war in Scotland, had tried in vain to avoid the use of force.

In August, Henry II laid siege to Boulogne. William Paget, Somerset's principal confidant, declared that England had been worn to the bone by her eight years' wars, while for France, which had been fighting for almost twenty-five years, four years' wars with England had been 'but as playings with us'. Henry II had said he would rather lose his own realm than abandon the Scots. England could not sustain the two-front war that was the inevitable consequence of any attempt to subjugate Scotland.[12]

Somerset's arrogant and abrasive manner, combined with his policies' disastrous consequences, had alienated his fellow privy councillors. John Dudley, earl of Warwick, led the coup that overthrew him in October 1549, and took power in February 1550 as lord president of the privy council. In March he made peace with France, giving up Boulogne. Peace with Scotland soon followed. Warwick avoided Somerset's mistake of neglecting the king, which had laid the Protector open to intrigues by his discontented younger brother, Thomas Seymour. Warwick's prospects of retaining Edward's confidence as his majority rapidly approached depended upon careful attention to his wishes. Edward's own commitment to Protestantism helped to ensure that the English Reformation would continue. The king's sister Mary, his heiress apparent, daughter of Catherine of Aragon, nevertheless gave hope to religious conservatives by refusing to end the celebration of mass in her houses. Edward himself told Mary that her disobedience was intolerable. Mary's cousin Charles V, watching the situation closely, sent in March 1551 what seemed like a threat of war if she were not allowed her mass.

England at this juncture was perilously weak and isolated. Peace had not made Henry II an ally. There had been incidents on the Calais border and reports of Franco-Scottish intrigues in Ireland. After disturbances in the Irish Midlands in 1546–7 rebel lands were declared forfeit and costly forts were built in the area to the west of the Pale to act as a protective screen. It seemed wise to conciliate Charles V at this point. But Edward could barely be persuaded to temporize, let alone give Mary explicit permission to hear mass. The council concluded in July 1551 a treaty with Henry II that provided for Edward's future marriage to Henry's daughter Elizabeth. The treaty gave a breathing space. Warwick (duke of Northumberland from October 1551) now dealt with Somerset, who had engaged in foolish plotting despite Warwick's attempts to conciliate him. He was condemned and then, in January 1552, executed. Soon afterwards, parliament accepted a more thoroughly reformed Prayer Book which came into use the following November.

In the autumn of 1551, having first made alliances with the Turks and German Protestant princes as well as removing any danger from England, Henry II declared war on Charles V. The emperor had overcome the Schmalkaldic League in 1547, achieving a short-lived supremacy in Germany. This was now shattered. In 1552, Henry seized the imperial cities of Metz, Toul and Verdun. Charles narrowly escaped capture by his German opponents. The English government had facilitated Henry II's triumph.

A Catholic Britain of Valois and Habsburg satellites?

Edward became mortally ill early in 1553. He resolved to exclude Mary and Elizabeth from the succession because of their illegitimacy. (Northumberland probably prompted this decision, fearing that Mary would blame him for recent religious measures.) Instead Edward chose Lady Jane Grey, granddaughter of Henry VIII's younger sister Mary,[13] who married Northumberland's son Guilford in May. When Edward died early in July, however, Mary, forewarned, fled to Norfolk and had herself proclaimed queen. Nobles, gentry and ordinary people went over to her in large numbers, followed by most of Jane's councillors. The plot against Mary had failed. Northumberland was executed. To religious conservatives the unexpected train of events looked like the result of a near-miraculous divine intervention.

Mary's first aim was to restore England to the Roman Catholic fold. Her second, formed soon after her accession, was to marry Charles V's son Philip. In her first parliament (October–December 1553), the Edwardian religious legislation was repealed. In November she refused the request of a House of Commons deputation that she marry an Englishman. A marriage treaty was concluded in January 1554. Philip would have the title of king, but his powers in England were carefully restricted. It was envisaged that a child of the marriage would rule over England and the Netherlands. Risings were planned in four counties to prevent the marriage, but only Sir Thomas Wyatt in Kent attracted many followers. Mary vigorously rallied support against him. He was defeated and executed, as were Lady Jane Grey and her father. Mary married Philip at Winchester in July. In November, Reginald Pole arrived as papal legate to reconcile the realm to Rome. Mary's third parliament (November 1554–January 1555) restored papal supremacy and repealed many other acts passed since 1529. Lay ownership of church lands was, however, confirmed, largely due to Philip's personal efforts.

Philip left England in August 1555. His English marriage had failed to produce the Habsburg heir that had been one of its main aims. The exhausted Charles V abdicated as ruler of the Netherlands in October 1555. Philip succeeded him there and (in 1556) as king of Spain. Charles's brother Ferdinand succeeded him as emperor in 1558. Philip faced new hostilities with France after a brief truce. Pope Paul IV, a Neapolitan who resented his native country's subjection to Spain, provoked a Spanish invasion of the papal states. In January 1557 one French army entered Italy to help Paul. Another attacked Flanders. Philip briefly returned to England to demand aid by virtue of a treaty of mutual defence between Charles V and Henry VIII. An April attack on Scarborough by a party of exiles from France persuaded Mary's reluctant councillors. An English force went to help Philip, arriving in time to assist in the capture of St Quentin in August. For Mary, her husband's war with the pope and Paul's revocation of Pole's legatine authority, followed by his summons to Rome to answer charges of heresy, were deeply distressing. A savage blow to English pride came in January 1558 when the duke of Guise took Calais in a brilliant surprise attack. In Ireland, the spectre of French and Scottish subversion revived with the war. The young earl of Sussex, appointed Deputy in 1556, had ambitious objectives: the 'plantation' of English colonists round the new garrisons west of the Pale, renamed Philipstown and Maryborough, attacks on several recalcitrant Gaelic chiefs and the expulsion of the MacDonalds from Ulster. In 1558 he launched an unprecedented attack on MacDonald territory in south-western Scotland, assisted by royal ships. Scotland, where Mary of Guise had become regent for her absent daughter Mary in 1554, had entered the war on Henry II's side. But although the regent summoned the host, the lords refused to cross into England.

When Mary Tudor died on 17 November 1558, her regime seemed, despite the loss of Calais, to be functioning effectively. Parliament had made a generous grant of taxation. The strengthened fleet had been used to reasonably good effect. At home, Catholic renewal continued, combined with repression of religious dissidents. Henry VIII's immense enhancement of the crown's authority had, paradoxically, facilitated the reversal of some of his other main achievements. England's first queen regnant had restored Roman Catholicism and entered a widely unpopular foreign marriage without encountering much resistance. England had faced the prospect of becoming a Habsburg kingdom. For Scotland, her queen now married to the heir to the French throne, future Valois rule seemed even more likely. But Mary Tudor's achievement died with her. She had failed to bear children or arrange her sister Elizabeth's marriage to a reliable Catholic prince.[14] Britain stood on the brink of dramatic, far-reaching and enduring changes.

3

ELIZABETH I, MARY STEWART AND JAMES VI, 1558-1603

Religious wars, revolts and new international alignments

Dynastic rivalries had dominated western European politics before 1558. In successive wars France, the strongest kingdom, had been pitted against the combination of Habsburg territories that the aggressive ambitions of French kings had helped to create. After 1558, however, a series of rebellions and civil wars within states brought a new instability to international relations. Religious militancy created new tensions both within and between states. A more activist brand of Protestantism had developed, widely distinguished as 'Reformed' or 'Pretended Reformed' by contemporaries, but retrospectively dubbed 'Calvinist', after its most influential theologian and organizer, John Calvin. Its adherents had a strong sense of an international Protestant cause. This in turn helped to create a shared militancy among defenders of the Counter-Reformation Catholic Church. Scotland experienced civil war and revolution in 1559–60 and 1567–73, France intermittently throughout the period 1562–1598 and the Netherlands from 1566 onwards.

When Elizabeth I succeeded to the English throne on 17 November 1558, France appeared dominant in Scotland, where Mary of Guise was regent for her daughter Mary Stewart. Mary Stewart was in France, where she had married Francis, eldest son of King Henry II, in April 1558. In Henry's eyes, Mary's claim to the English throne was better than that of Elizabeth Tudor, still tainted by illegitimacy. Henry looked forward to mastery of the British Isles. In this perilous situation, friendship with Habsburg Spain remained essential for England. Elizabeth nevertheless determined not to marry Philip II. Her most trusted adviser was the Protestant William Cecil, whom she made principal secretary of state, a post he had already held under Edward VI. Acts of Supremacy and Uniformity passed in April 1559 reversed Mary's religious settlement, restoring royal control of the Church of England and, with some modifications, the Prayer Book of 1552.

The peace of Cateau-Cambrésis (April 1559) ended Henry II's war with Philip II and England. It was soon followed by dramatic changes in Scotland. Mary of Guise had hoped to conciliate the Scots Protestant minority with limited concessions. Elizabeth Tudor's accession made her task more difficult by encouraging Protestants and alarming Catholics. In May 1559, the reformer John Knox, back in Scotland from Calvin's Geneva, his chief refuge since his flight from England in 1553, preached a powerful sermon in Perth, provoking disturbances that eventually developed into a wider rebellion by the Protestant 'Congregation', headed by a minority of powerful lords. Mary of Guise, assisted by French troops, fought back successfully. The resolute William Cecil overcame Elizabeth's reluctance to give the rebels help: first financial (from October 1559), later naval and military (from early 1560). Mary of Guise died in June 1560. The Treaty of Edinburgh, concluded in July, provided for the withdrawal of both French and English troops from Scotland. In August the Scots parliament abolished the mass and papal supremacy and adopted a Protestant confession of faith.

An effective French response at this critical juncture had been prevented by a combination of misfortunes. The formidable Henry II was fatally injured during a tournament in July 1559. Two separate fleets prepared for despatch to Scotland by the Guise-dominated regime of his son Francis II were severely damaged by storms. In March 1560 some Protestant nobles tried to overthrow the Guises. They failed, but the crisis diverted attention from Scotland. French Protestantism, powerfully reinforced by books and trained ministers from Geneva, had grown stronger during the 1550s, despite Henry II's hostility. His widow Catherine de' Medici, chosen regent when Francis II suddenly died in December 1560, tried in vain to contain the rising tensions that eventually resulted in the outbreak of civil war in 1562. In response to an appeal for help from French Protestants (or 'Huguenots'), Elizabeth intervened, her confidence greatly strengthened by success in Scotland, in hope of recovering Calais. This was an ill-advised step. For nine months in 1562–3 English troops held Le Havre till, weakened by plague, they were compelled to surrender by French forces re-united in their determination to drive out the old enemy.

Elizabeth's suspicion of foreign military ventures was reinforced by fruitless expenditure and a humiliating peace. Philip II and his advisers had watched with deepening disapproval England's Protestant settlement and Elizabeth's interventions in Scotland and France. Might the proximity of an officially Protestant England encourage religious dissent in the Netherlands? Once the centre of Charles V's empire, they had become an outlying dependency of the Spanish crown after the division of the Habsburg territories in 1556–8. Philip was permanently absent in Spain after 1559. Margaret of Parma, Philip's regent in the Netherlands, prohibited English cloth imports in the autumn of 1563. The pretext was a severe outbreak of plague in London, but the reasons also included English pirates' attacks on Catholic shipping and English support for Protestants in Scotland and France. The ensuing trade embargo ended only in December 1564.

Soon after the start of England's disastrous intervention in France, in autumn 1562, Elizabeth's life was threatened by an attack of smallpox. Settlement of the succession to the crown now seemed urgent. Elizabeth had been expected to marry, but, unlike her sister, had shown no inclination to do so. During Elizabeth's second parliament, meeting in 1563, the privy council helped to concert petitions from both houses of parliament asking Elizabeth to settle the succession.[1]

Mary Stewart, Queen of Scots, descended from Margaret Tudor, Henry VIII's elder sister, seemed to some an obvious successor. Henry, however, authorized by statute to name his successors after his own children and their descendants, had ignored the Stewart line. The widowed Mary Stewart had returned to Scotland in August 1561 without sacrificing her own claim to the English throne. French in upbringing, Catholic in religion, Mary was viewed with the deepest suspicion by many English Protestants, even though she did nothing to upset Scotland's Protestant settlement of 1560. In this she acted in accordance with the advice of her elder half-brother Lord James Stewart, one of James V's illegitimate sons, whom she made earl of Moray in 1562. Mary hoped that Elizabeth would recognize her as her successor in return for Mary's renunciation of her own claim to the English throne. Mary's able adviser William Maitland of Lethington encouraged this hope. Elizabeth, to her own displeasure, could not prevent this potentially explosive issue being debated in England, but she avoided any concession to the Queen of Scots.

In July 1565, Mary Stewart, her hopes of recognition so far frustrated, married her cousin Henry Stewart, Lord Darnley, son of Matthew, earl of Lennox. Through his mother, daughter of Margaret Tudor by her second marriage, Darnley could claim a place in the English line of succession. Rivals of Darnley's family and many Protestants disliked Mary's choice. Three of the most powerful Scottish nobles (Moray, the former regent James Hamilton who was earl of Arran and duke of Châtelherault, and the leading Protestant Archibald Campbell, earl of Argyll) joined in rebellion but were swiftly defeated. Mary bore a son, James, in June 1566. When the English parliament met the following autumn, William Cecil helped to co-ordinate pressure on Elizabeth to marry and settle the succession, unavailingly, but much to Elizabeth's chagrin.

The possibility of Elizabeth's marriage to the Archduke Charles of Austria, Philip II's cousin and third son of the Emperor Ferdinand, was actively explored during the mid-1560s in order both to meet the domestic demand for the queen's marriage and to strengthen Anglo-Habsburg relations. Charles's brother Maximilian, who became emperor in 1564, favoured toleration of Lutherans in his own territories and criticized Philip II's intolerant policy in the Netherlands. During the discussions, Elizabeth tried to emphasize the moderate nature of the English religious settlement and its surviving traditional elements. She instigated a campaign to make the English clergy wear officially required vestments. The Austrian negotiations nevertheless failed in 1567 because Elizabeth refused to grant Charles the right to hear mass.[2]

Meanwhile, Mary Stewart's brief success in Scotland had ended. Her son James's baptism in December 1566 with full Catholic rites, and celebrations signalling religious reconciliation, seemed to mark the height of Mary's triumph. The weakest element in her position was her feckless, jealous and loutish husband. Darnley had helped to murder Mary's Italian secretary David Rizzio in her presence in March 1566. When his own mysterious assassination in February 1567 was followed by Mary's indecently swift marriage to the earl of Bothwell in May, Mary's disunited regime was practically submerged by a tidal wave of scandal. Her re-marriage had greatly strengthened suspicions of her involvement in Darnley's murder. Her forces were swiftly defeated, and in July she was persuaded to abdicate in favour of her one-year-old son, and agree to Moray's becoming regent. When she escaped from confinement in May 1568, Moray routed her ill-assorted forces. Mary then fled to England. Elizabeth at first wanted to restore her, but was checked by a Scottish delegation's presentation of alleged evidence of Mary's complicity in Darnley's murder. Cecil hoped that investigation of the evidence would enable him to end Mary's political career for good, but Elizabeth would not allow the tribunal established for this purpose to complete its work. Moray's ultimate refusal to restore his half-sister presented Elizabeth with an unpalatable choice: accept the *fait accompli* or risk further destabilizing England's newly friendly neighbour.[3]

In 1566 Philip's regent in the Netherlands, Margaret of Parma, responding to a petition presented by some 200 noblemen, suspended the anti-heresy laws. There ensued in quick succession widespread Calvinist preaching, attacks on images, the establishment of many Calvinist congregations and an abortive armed rebellion. In August 1567 the duke of Alba arrived with a large Spanish army to begin a brutal repression. Refugees flooded into England. Alba's force caused considerable anxiety in both England and France about Philip II's possible aggressive intentions. In truth he already had too many commitments to undertake fresh hostilities. Spain had recently been engaged in intermittent warfare in the western Mediterranean with the Turks, who had mounted a long but ultimately unsuccessful siege of Malta in 1565. Spain's harsh treatment of her Morisco (converted Muslim) minority caused a long rebellion in Andalusia between 1568 and 1570.

Civil war broke out again in France in 1567, lasting, with a brief truce in 1568, until August 1570. During these years an informal international maritime coalition of militant Protestants from France, England and the Netherlands took shape, preying on Catholic shipping. Elizabeth sent munitions to the Huguenots. In November 1568 Spanish ships carrying money to pay troops in the Netherlands took refuge in England from storms and predatory Protestant captains. The money was taken ashore for safety. Militant Protestants saw an ideal opportunity to put pressure on Alba. The Spanish ambassador panicked, and urged Alba to seize English ships and merchants in the Netherlands, precipitating reciprocal English seizures and the first serious Anglo-Spanish quarrel.

The intermittent violence that plagued Ireland throughout the 1560s came to a head in 1569. The most important of the queen's representatives during this period, the earl of Sussex (till 1564), and Sir Henry Sidney (1565–71) were allied with rivals at Elizabeth's court, the duke of Norfolk and the earl of Leicester respectively, and court enmities helped to undermine their efforts. Both men hoped to deal with Ireland's problems by a mixture of military action against troublemakers, the 'plantation' of confiscated lands with English colonists, and the establishment in the provinces of English presidents with soldiers under their control.

Two struggles stood out from a complex of local rivalries. Both had roots running back well before Elizabeth's accession. One, between the queen's governors and Shane O'Neill, the most powerful chief of Ulster, originated in his claim to the headship of the O'Neills against the principle of primogeniture inherent in the English policy of surrender and re-grant. It was complicated by Shane's local conflicts with the O'Donnells and MacDonalds or MacDonnells, the latter Scots settlers whom the English government wished to have removed from Ulster. In 1566 Shane sought French assistance and negotiated with the earl of Argyll, who had been angered by Elizabeth's failure to support his opposition to the Darnley marriage. After years of intermittent campaigns against O'Neill by successive royal governors, it was the MacDonnells of Antrim who finally killed him in 1567 and sent his pickled head to Dublin.

Among the magnates of the south, there was a bitter rivalry between Thomas Butler, earl of Ormond, the queen's kinsman and Gerald Fitzgerald, earl of Desmond. James Fitzmaurice, captain of the Desmond Fitzgeralds while the earl was imprisoned in London, rose in rebellion in 1569, attacked English settlers, proclaimed Roman Catholicism and appealed to Philip II for help. Ormond gave crucial assistance in defeating the rebellion, which was savagely suppressed.

Mary Stewart meanwhile remained in England, both guest and prisoner. Elizabeth would not meet her, allow her to leave the country or send her back to Moray's keeping, seeing dangers in each course. Some English Catholics hoped that Mary's ultimate succession might lead to a restoration of their religion. The duke of Norfolk, the highest-ranking nobleman in England, took up the idea of marrying her himself, thus tying her firmly to an English subject who was a Protestant, albeit one with Catholic friends. Elizabeth forbade this match in September 1569, seeing it as a threat to herself. Then, suspecting that it was part of a bigger conspiracy, she summoned the Catholic earls of Northumberland and Westmorland to court. Instead, the fearful earls rose in rebellion, proclaiming their determination to restore Catholicism. Their poorly supported rising was quickly and brutally put down.

In February 1570, too late to help the rebels, Pope Pius V issued a bull excommunicating Elizabeth and absolving her subjects from their allegiance. Its full import was only gradually appreciated in Britain, but in retrospect it came to be seen as a political, religious and psychological turning point. Parliament, meeting in April 1571, responded with statutes making it high treason to bring papal bulls into England, to deny the royal supremacy or to call the queen a heretic. By this time, a plot was being laid for a Catholic rising to put Mary Stewart on the throne with Spanish help. A Florentine banker, Ridolfi, concocted it, but he gained the agreement of Mary, Norfolk and the Spanish ambassador. Philip II had disapproved of Elizabeth's excommunication. By 1571, he was nevertheless ready to support a Catholic coup in England, though Alba was determined not to give help until it had already achieved preliminary success. Spanish involvement in a plot on behalf of Mary Stewart, with her strong French connections, was an alarming demonstration of the extent to which fears and suspicions rooted in religious differences had undermined Anglo-Spanish friendship. The plot was discovered in August. Norfolk was convicted of treason in January 1572. After parliament met in May Elizabeth forbade consideration of a bill condemning Mary as a traitor, and withheld her consent from another bill excluding Mary from succession to the crown. By now, however, Mary was effectively a prisoner, her reputation severely damaged.

It was nevertheless possible that Charles IX of France or her Guise kinsmen might do something to help Mary Stewart, especially after the return of peace in France in 1570. Partly in order to prevent such help, Elizabeth entered into negotiations for her marriage to Henry, King Charles's younger brother. The negotiations broke down, like those with the Austrians, over the question of the queen's prospective husband's freedom to attend mass. However, when Spain and her allies inflicted a spectacular defeat on the Turkish fleet in the Battle of Lepanto (October 1571), shared concern about Philip's enhanced power helped bring England and France together in April 1572 in a defensive alliance, a better outcome for Elizabeth than a French marriage.

Two dramatic events of 1572 confronted both Spain and France with new and serious problems, giving England more freedom of manoeuvre. First, the 'Sea Beggars', free Netherlands Protestant captains preying on Catholic shipping, expelled from English harbours by Elizabeth in March, captured Brill in Holland, beginning a new revolt against Spanish rule. Alba, fearing an attack from France, held most of his forces further south, allowing the rebellion to spread rapidly through Holland. Many English and Scots volunteers soon arrived to help the rebels. This did not prevent an Anglo-Spanish treaty in 1574 settling the claims arising out of the two countries' reciprocal seizures of ships.

The most notorious episode of France's religious wars took place on 24 August 1572, St Bartholomew's Day. The volatile Charles IX, fearing reprisals for a botched attempt to kill the Huguenot leader Coligny, ordered on the advice of his mother and councillors an assassination of Protestant leaders that developed into a massacre of over 2,000 Protestants in Paris, and many more elsewhere.[4] Protestants throughout Europe were horrified. This infamous bloodletting precipitated a fourth civil war, and dogged resistance by the Huguenots in La Rochelle and the south of France.

After Mary Stewart's flight, Scotland suffered its own long, complicated and murderous civil war between her opponents and supporters (who included, for some time, a majority among the higher nobility). Two successive regents, the earls of Moray and Lennox, Darnley's father, were assassinated in 1570 and 1571. James Douglas, earl of Morton, became regent in November 1572, looking to England for support. By spring 1573, only Edinburgh castle still held out for Mary. Elizabeth, emboldened by the unlikelihood of French or Spanish intervention, sent siege guns to end its resistance.

Morton ultimately fell because he made that most fatal of all mistakes in a regent – failing to build a personal relationship with the king. He was greedy, and though certainly Protestant, not sufficiently zealous to satisfy the more militant Scottish reformers. In 1579, Darnley's cousin Esmé Stuart came to Scotland. Born and educated in France, some fourteen years older than James, with a charming and debonair personality, Esmé captivated the king and encouraged him to free himself from his childhood tutelage. James made him earl and later duke of Lennox. In December 1580 Esmé instigated Morton's arrest for his part in Darnley's murder, which was followed by his execution in June 1581. Lennox was wrongly suspected to be an agent of the Guises, and many people thought his conversion to Protestantism insincere. In August 1582 the earls of Gowrie and Angus, erstwhile supporters of Morton, seized James. He escaped in June 1583, and reclaimed power with the help of James Stewart, earl of Arran, previously an ally of Esmé's. Passed under Arran's auspices, the so-called 'Black Acts' of 1584 underlined royal power over the Church or Kirk of Scotland, seen as a source of unwelcome criticism of the crown. The unpopular Arran in his turn was overthrown in November 1585. This time, however, James, advised by the discreet and adroit John Maitland of Thirlestane, was able to achieve a more effective and enduring independence.

Despite the troubled transition from James VI's minority, Scotland escaped civil war after 1574. Henry III, who succeeded to the French crown when his brother Charles IX died that year, faced three more civil wars in the next six years. Meanwhile the Dutch rebels against Spanish rule held out in Holland and Zeeland, led by William, prince of Orange. In 1575 Elizabeth, anxious to avoid either her own direct intervention or French involvement in the Netherlands, tried to encourage reconciliation. The Netherlands would enjoy their 'ancient liberties' under Philip's sovereignty. Then, in 1576, royal authority suddenly collapsed when unpaid Spanish troops mutinied and later sacked Antwerp. The states-general, representing most of the Netherlands provinces, suspended the laws against heresy. Encouraged by this unexpected turn of events, Elizabeth gave them financial and diplomatic support. Religious tensions soon undermined the Netherlands' precarious unity, however, and in January 1578 the Spanish governor Don John inflicted a serious defeat on the states' forces.

The states-general needed a foreign patron who, unlike Elizabeth, was ready to intervene directly, and might also reassure Catholic Netherlanders. They turned to Francis, duke of Anjou, younger brother of Henry III of France. Elizabeth hesitantly moved from trying to prevent Anjou's intervention, fearing French dominance of the Netherlands, towards seeking to influence him in English interests. Anjou visited England to court Elizabeth in August 1579. The temptation to seize her last chance of marriage complicated her diplomacy. Such a match had obvious dangers. If Anjou succeeded his child-less brother Henry as king, England might become joined in regal union with her old enemy. Anjou as consort might threaten England's religious and politi-cal stability. English Protestant opinion was deeply hostile. By October 1579 the majority of Elizabeth's privy councillors were clearly against the marriage. Yet in 1580–1 Elizabeth still 'hovered uncertainly over the available options: the marriage, an alliance without marriage, and the role of Anjou's unofficial paymaster'. Only when she saw that the first two were completely impractica-ble did she fully accept the third.[5]

Meanwhile, the duke of Parma, governor-general of the Netherlands from October 1578, gradually mastered the rebellious provinces. In June 1580 Spanish troops successfully invaded Portugal in support of Philip II's claim to the throne, bringing under his control Europe's only other great overseas empire together with its ocean-going fleet. Philip had a lengthening list of grievances against Elizabeth. In the Netherlands, she had given his rebel-lious subjects financial help and allowed thousands of volunteers to aid their struggle. She had connived at predatory voyages to America by Francis Drake and others in 1571 and 1572–3, and in Drake's circumnaviga-tion of the globe in 1577–80, during which he had attacked Spanish colo-nies and ships. The potential for causing Elizabeth trouble in her own backyard was shown when James Fitzmaurice returned to Ireland in 1579 with papal support and Spanish connivance. He was soon killed, but the wavering earl of Desmond, prematurely declared a traitor, held out against sizeable English and loyalist forces until his eventual defeat by his old rival Ormond and his death in November 1583. In 1580 Philip approved the sending of Spanish and Italian reinforcements to the rebels in retaliation for Drake's activities. They were brutally massacred. Countless Irish people were slaughtered and the Munster countryside ravaged during the sup-pression of the rebellion.

By 1581 Elizabeth was ready to co-operate with France to check the Spanish reconquest of the Netherlands. But Henry III was unwilling to confront Spain. Such an alliance would outrage Catholic opinion in France. Militant French Catholics were increasingly critical of what they regarded as the king's inef-fectiveness in dealing with the Protestant minority. Henry, third duke of Guise, cousin of Mary Stewart, plotted during 1582–3 to invade England and place Mary on the throne. The Spanish ambassador in England was expelled because of his involvement, and Francis Throckmorton, his link with Mary, was executed. Anjou, Elizabeth's erstwhile suitor, died in June 1584, leaving a Protestant, Henry of Navarre, as heir presumptive to the French crown. Guise and other leaders formed a new league for the defence of the Catholic faith and Navarre's exclusion from the throne, and in December entered an alliance with Philip II.

Elizabeth I's undeclared war with Spain

Parma captured Brussels in February 1585. A stark choice now faced Elizabeth and her advisers: appease Philip II and accept his military dominance of the Netherlands, or greatly increase English aid so as to prevent this outcome. Spurred on by the sudden seizure of English shipping in Spanish ports, she allowed Francis Drake to attack the Spanish Caribbean colonies with a fleet that included some royal warships. In August Elizabeth took into her protection the surviving Netherlands provinces and agreed to send troops to help them.

With little military experience, Robert Dudley, earl of Leicester, the queen's favourite, commander of the English forces in the Netherlands, led an army of very mixed quality rife with personal rivalries. In a war of sieges, English soldiers achieved some minor successes, but Parma, one of the ablest commanders of the day, kept the upper hand. Elizabeth, horrified by the cost of operations, still hoped for peace, and insisted that Leicester maintain a defensive stance. Leicester infuriated Elizabeth by accepting the title of governor-general in January 1586, despite her resolute determination not to assume the sovereignty of the Netherlands. His inept interventions in Dutch politics served only to undermine the rebels' unity.

England's confrontation with Spain heightened fears of subversion at home. It was now clear that Roman Catholicism had not withered away in England itself as Elizabeth's government had originally hoped. Catholic priests trained overseas were reaching England in growing numbers, and parliament passed increasingly savage anti-Catholic legislation in 1581 and 1585. Mary Stewart's presence in England had already inspired a series of plots. The assassination of the Dutch leader William of Orange in 1584 prompted William Cecil (Lord Burghley since 1571) and the secretary of state Francis Walsingham to devise a Bond of Association whose numerous signatories swore to kill anybody who made an attempt on Elizabeth's life, and any person on whose behalf they acted. A statute of 1585 provided that any such prospective beneficiary who might be privy to such action against Elizabeth would be executed. Burghley had regarded Mary Stewart's very existence as a serious threat to Elizabeth and England since the 1560s. His colleague Walsingham at last secured the evidence he needed to destroy her when in 1586 she approved a plan by Anthony Babington, a young Catholic gentleman, to free her and assassinate Elizabeth. A special commission found her guilty. In 1586 the new parliament pressed for her execution, and Elizabeth reluctantly signed her death warrant in February 1587. Mary was executed a week later.

Shortly before the commencement of proceedings against Mary, in July 1586, after two years' preliminary negotiations, Elizabeth had entered into an alliance with James VI so as to counter the threat from the alliance between Spain and the French Catholic League. She also promised James an annual subsidy. James interceded for his mother energetically and repeatedly. The English government was careful to make clear his mother's condemnation did not affect his own rights, but Mary's death was a serious blow to his honour. Many

Scottish noblemen expected retaliation. Elizabeth showed rage at the execution, protesting that it had been implemented without her knowledge. William Davison, the secretary of state who had carried the signed warrant to the council, was fined and imprisoned. All this failed to appease James. Yet what could he do? If he turned to Catholic allies for his revenge, he was likely to be excluded from the English succession, and in any case such allies could not be relied on to help him. At first there were fears for the future of the alliance, but James eventually assured Elizabeth of his friendship when at last Philip II launched his attack on England.[6]

This attack, planned from 1585 onwards, was postponed when Francis Drake succeeded in destroying or capturing shipping and supplies in an expedition to Spain in 1587. Then at last in July 1588 the great 'Spanish Armada' sailed. According to the final plan it would proceed to the Netherlands, whence it would escort a large force of Parma's soldiers in troop transports to England. The expedition's most important aims were to end English assistance to the Dutch and gain religious freedom for English Catholics. Philip's plan was denied the good fortune essential for its success. The Armada was harried on its way up the Channel, forced by fireships out of its refuge in Calais harbour, savaged by the more effective firepower of the English fleet and finally blown northwards, eventually round Scotland, while Dutch and English ships kept Parma's transports bottled up in Flanders. Many of the Spanish ships were then wrecked on the rocky western coasts of the British Isles on the way home.[7] In 1589 an expedition under the command of Sir Francis Drake and Sir John Norris, veteran of the Netherlands wars, sailed to Spain in order to follow up the victory. The extensive involvement of private investors helped to divert effort from the destruction of the remaining Armada ships on the Biscay coast to a fruitless attempt to liberate Portugal, to be followed (it was hoped) by the admission of English merchants to the Portuguese East Indies. The expedition returned without achieving any of its goals. Philip now embarked on a massive naval building programme.

The spectacular failure of the Armada encouraged Henry III to try to free himself from the near-tutelage to which the Catholic League had reduced him. The king had Guise and his brother the cardinal of Lorraine assassinated in December 1588. This backfired badly. Furiously denounced by League supporters, he was himself murdered in August 1589. Before he died he recognized the Protestant Henry of Navarre as his successor. The Catholic League was determined to prevent Navarre (or Henry IV) making good his claim. Elizabeth sent money and soldiers to assist Henry in northern France. Leicester's stepson Robert Devereux, earl of Essex, led fresh forces to Normandy in 1591 to help Henry take Rouen. The campaign failed. Meanwhile Spanish forces had landed in Brittany. If Philip could consolidate his hold over Brittany and use the superb anchorage of Brest as a base, he could pose a formidable threat to England. Brittany thus became the main focus of English activity in France. Not until 1594 did the allies concentrate sufficient forces there to defeat the Spanish. Henry IV eventually took the upper hand in the civil war, above all because of his conversion to Catholicism in 1593. Henry gained Paris in March 1594 and in January 1595 declared war on Philip II. But he had his work cut out to fight Spain while subduing the remaining League forces and was glad to make peace for his exhausted kingdom in May 1598.

Parma had been forced to divert effort and resources first into the Armada campaign, and then to intervention in France. His inability to concentrate his forces against the Dutch did much to ensure the rebel provinces' survival. Between 1590 and 1594 the states' forces under Maurice of Nassau, son of William of Orange, steadily gained one important town or fortress after another. English forces and subsidies contributed to these successes. Leicester had finally left the Netherlands in December 1587 and died in 1588. The commander of the English field forces was now subordinate to Maurice of Nassau. In 1598, the year of Philip II's death, Elizabeth had the opportunity of joining Henry IV of France in making peace with Spain. Finally, however, she felt she could not abandon the Dutch, who offered her a new and financially favourable treaty to continue the war.

At sea, the main objectives were to cut off the flow of silver to Spain from her American mines and reduce her naval strength. Nearly all England's major naval campaigns, conducted by a combination of royal and private ships, were hampered by disagreements among the participants or downright indiscipline, and attempts to pursue divergent or incompatible goals. The fleet led by Lord Thomas Howard to intercept the treasure fleet in 1591 was too small for its task. Another expedition sent to the Caribbean in 1595 failed either to capture a treasure ship stranded in Puerto Rico or to seize the Isthmus of Panama. Both Francis Drake and John Hawkins, the expedition's two commanders, died during the voyage. The best-organized and most successful expedition set out for Cadiz in 1596, jointly commanded by the earl of Essex and the lord admiral, Lord Howard of Effingham. It destroyed several Spanish ships, but while the English forces took Cadiz, a richly laden merchant fleet in the harbour was fired to prevent its falling into their hands. In 1597, leading another expedition, Essex was frustrated by bad weather in the original aim of attacking the Spanish fleet in Ferrol, and then narrowly missed the returning treasure fleet off the Azores.

A struggle for Ireland dominated the last phase of the war. Ulster was the epicentre of resistance, led by Hugh O'Neill, grandson of the first earl of Tyrone. Himself recognized by the government as earl in 1585, Hugh was finally accepted as chief by the O'Neills in 1595. His position in Ulster was strengthened by the support of Hugh Roe O'Donnell, chief of a clan often hostile to the O'Neills. Tyrone's readiness to co-operate with the crown depended on acceptance of his supremacy in Ulster. This was incompatible with the aim of reducing the power of Irish overlords over their vassals and introducing English local administrative structures. In 1595 Tyrone defeated an English force, was proclaimed traitor and, together with O'Donnell, offered the kingship of Ireland to Archduke Albert of Austria, nephew to Philip II and newly appointed governor of the Spanish Netherlands. Tyrone made attacks on local forts or intruding government forces, but also repeatedly agreed truces or sought pardon. He was all the more dangerous because he had built up a formidable army, professionally trained. In 1598 he destroyed a government force at the Battle of the Yellow Ford, the biggest English defeat in Ireland in the whole course of the Elizabethan wars.

The earl of Essex was sent to Ireland in 1599 to crush Tyrone together with the largest army entrusted to any chief governor of that kingdom during Elizabeth's reign. Instead, he dissipated much of his army's strength in campaigns in Leinster and Munster before meeting Tyrone to agree yet another truce. He then returned to England suddenly, without permission. It was left to Essex's friend Charles Blount, Lord Mountjoy, appointed deputy in January 1600, to press home against Tyrone a strategy of three-pronged attack on Ulster that Essex had failed to maintain. In September 1601, long desired Spanish aid arrived in Ireland, but the force was small, and landed at Kinsale in the far south. It was rapidly invested by sea and land. Tyrone and O'Donnell had to march south to try to link up with it. Poor co-ordination between the Spanish and their allies allowed Mountjoy to rout the chiefs decisively on 24 December. The Spanish force surrendered to Mountjoy in January and was allowed to leave Ireland. Mountjoy had won the most decisive English land victory of the war. In the spring he resumed the campaign in Ulster. Tyrone finally submitted on 30 March 1603. A devastated Ireland had been more completely conquered than ever before. This military achievement was due to an unprecedented drive to raise, equip and supply English levies, ruthless destruction of rebel crops and stock, and the co-ordinated use of naval squadrons and land forces.[8]

The effective subjugation of Irish rebels was in Elizabeth's eyes a goal of highest importance, but neither she nor Burghley wished for complete victory over Spain, an unrealistic and hugely expensive goal. Essex, however, conceived a global strategy that included a blockade of Spain and English mastery of the East and West Indies. He believed that a crushing defeat of Spain was both desirable and feasible, seized every opportunity of command, spent his own money liberally in raising and equipping forces, and argued his views eloquently. He felt frustrated by what he saw as Elizabeth's and Burghley's timidity and the queen's indecisiveness.[9] Early enjoyment of the queen's favour, based on strong personal attraction as well as appreciation of his knightly qualities, made him too bold. Essex became a privy councillor in 1593, and tried to place his *protégés* in key positions. In what came to seem like a contest for place and patronage between Essex and the Cecils, William and his son Robert, Essex suffered repeated disappointments because of Elizabeth's deepening mistrust of his judgement and aims. Burghley died in 1598. Essex increasingly regarded Robert Cecil, secretary of state since 1596, with almost paranoid suspicion. He returned from Ireland to forestall any attempt by his rivals to exploit his failure against Tyrone. Instead he infuriated the queen. Disgraced, censured and deprived of a grant of sweet wine customs crucial to his finances, Essex decided to seize power from his perceived enemies by means of an armed coup. Forced into acting prematurely in February 1601, and mistakenly believing that London would support him, he was swiftly defeated, condemned and executed.

Elizabeth was now sixty-seven. Who would succeed her? Henry VIII's will had provided that descendants of his younger sister Mary should do so, but Elizabeth showed no sign that she favoured any of them. James VI of Scotland was the legitimate great-grandson of Henry VIII's elder sister Margaret. The claim of the Stewart line, ignored by Henry VIII, had been canvassed since the 1560s. James's mother had been condemned in England as a traitor, but all James's rights (though unspecified) had been expressly preserved. Since James was Protestant, opposition to his succession might be expected from Catholics. In 1594 a book pseudonymously published by the Jesuit Robert Persons aired the claim of the Infanta Isabella of Spain, daughter of Philip II, descended from Edward III of England through his son John of Gaunt. Essex, wrongly convinced that Robert Cecil secretly supported the Infanta, accused him of doing so in a letter he wrote to James VI in 1600. This was just the sort of mischief Persons had hoped to cause. Essex's determination to prevent Cecil from putting the Infanta on the throne was a powerful motive for his attempted coup. His death enabled Cecil to emerge as James's principal confidant in England and to prepare for his succession.

A considerable point in James's favour was the fact that he had two sons alive in 1603, thus holding out the prospect of an assured succession after his death. James had in 1589 married Anne of Denmark, thus creating a new tie with an old ally and trading partner. In Scotland James had tried to increase his authority gradually without alienating powerful interests. He needed the support of the Kirk. In 1592 the 'Golden Act' partly reversed the 'Black Acts' of 1584. However, James also tried to win the support of powerful Scottish Catholics and gain their outward religious conformity by showing them his trust and favour. In 1588 James made the earl of Huntly, the foremost Catholic magnate in Scotland, captain of his guard. In 1589, 1593 and 1594, however, James led forces against Huntly in person in response to Huntly's disobedience or treasonable dealings with Spain. On the last occasion Huntly was exiled. But when James failed to punish Huntly on his unauthorized return in 1596, churchmen demanded that he take action. One minister of the Kirk preached a bitter attack on the king. Subsequent riotous disturbances in Edinburgh, possibly the result of an abortive conspiracy by militant Protestants who hoped to force a change of policy, played into the king's hands. Moderate men's disapproval of the militants' intemperate behaviour helped James's subsequent measures to bring Edinburgh to heel and to strengthen his authority over the Kirk.

The succession of a Scottish claimant to the English throne, almost unthinkable in 1558, had become by 1603 the most likely, though by no means certain, outcome. Why and how? Unlike James V, subsequent Scottish rulers made attainment of the English crown a principal policy objective. However, without the acceptance of the Protestant Reformation by the rulers of both kingdoms, such an outcome would have remained much more improbable. Shared Protestantism loosened or severed previously strong ties between each of the British kingdoms and one of the foremost continental powers: between England and Spain, Scotland and France. Additionally, the relative weakness of the French monarchy between 1559 and 1598 removed what might otherwise have been an insuperable obstacle to the union of the British crowns. Henry II or a successor of comparable vigour and determination might well have fought hard to prevent the triumph of the Reformation in Scotland, let alone Scotland's slipping into England's orbit. France's internal religious divisions interacted with the personal shortcomings of her last Valois kings in a profoundly damaging way.

England's erstwhile king, Philip II of Spain, witnessed the successes of Protestantism in Britain with the deepest disapproval. His numerous commitments, and especially the need to face the persistent Turkish threat in the Mediterranean, nevertheless made him reluctant to intervene. From 1566, the revolt of the Netherlands absorbed a growing proportion of the Spanish monarchy's already overstretched resources. The foremost Catholic monarchies might have been weakened, but Elizabeth's key advisers remained only too acutely aware of England's own vulnerability in an unpredictable and volatile international situation. They persuaded her to take various steps that they perceived as defensive, culminating in intervention in the Netherlands. Philip II viewed these measures as increasingly blatant and impudent aggression.[10] Elizabeth could be seen as the leader of a Protestant coalition confronting Europe's foremost Catholic monarch and his allies. The perception that Elizabeth had fulfilled this role would continue to resonate in the Protestant imagination long after the exceptional circumstances of her war with Spain had passed.

England, like Spain, though for very different reasons, escaped civil war but faced serious rebellion in a dependent country – in her case Ireland. The failures of Tudor policy in Ireland forced the crown to complete, at immense cost, the conquest of that kingdom, a military triumph but a political tragedy.[11]

4

RULERS AND SUBJECTS

Rulers

Monarchs ruled most of Europe during the sixteenth century. Various other forms of government existed. There were aristocratic urban republics in northern Italy, and largely autonomous free cities in Germany. The Swiss Confederation consisted of a cluster of self-governing rural mountain cantons and cities. The United Provinces repudiated Philip II's sovereignty in 1581 as another free confederation. Most western European kings claimed 'imperial' authority in their realms, signifying that they had no earthly superior. Coronation ceremonies gave kings a special, sacred character.

The monarch's prerogatives varied from one kingdom to another. Those of the English crown included the making of war and peace, minting of coin, appointment of councillors and judges, summoning and dismissal of parliaments, confirmation of legislation, dispensing from certain laws, pardoning malefactors and granting honours and privileges to individuals and corporations. Scottish royal prerogatives were less extensive or less clearly established in some areas, such as foreign affairs.[1]

Most writers on royal power during the decades around 1500 conceived of it as limited. The eminent judge Sir John Fortescue, for example, distinguished during the 1460s between *dominium regale*, or royal dominion, and republican *dominium politicum*. The English monarchy was a hybrid. Its 'politic' element lay in the necessity of parliamentary consent to taxation, legislation and alienation of the royal demesne, and the king's need for good counsel. Fortescue regarded France as a 'regal' polity very different from England. The humanist Claude de Seyssel, in *La Grande Monarchie de France* (1519), nevertheless visualized it as a kingdom where royal power was 'bridled' by religion, justice and 'policy'. Irremovable judges should independently administer justice. 'Policy' included the king's obligation to take counsel, and good old laws that protected (for example) the order of succession to the crown and the royal patrimony. The term 'fundamental laws' entered common usage in sixteenth-century France. (It is first found in Scotland in 1597.) In Castile, religion and laws

concerning the succession and the inalienability of the royal domain were similarly viewed as limiting royal power. The Scottish philosopher John Mair
(1469–1550) thought that though the ruler could make laws, representatives of
the community might bind him in certain matters, and, in the last resort,
depose him for abuse of power. Some traditional coronation or inauguration
oaths included the maintenance of laws and liberties as well as justice.[2]

James V asserted that he was both loved and dreaded in Scotland. Whether
or not he was right, his claim neatly encapsulated the secret of successful
kingship.[3] Both Henry VII and Henry VIII erred on the side of tyranny. Henry
VIII's legacy was seriously flawed. Yet his masterful personality inspired both
fear and devotion. Government by a queen regnant from 1553 was a new experience for England. Both Mary and Elizabeth were courageous and determined.
They also tried to turn conventional expectations of their sex to their advantage, emphasizing their solicitude for their people. Elizabeth repeatedly
expressed her confidence that her people loved her. Indecisive in the face of
some complex situations, Elizabeth was consistent in her long-term outlook
and aims, but exercised her ultimate control over government in a cautious
and profoundly conservative manner. Her forty-year reliance on one principal
adviser, William Cecil, was unique in English history.

The sharpest contrast between England's and Scotland's experience of monarchical rule lay in the length of Scottish royal minorities. James IV and V were
strong and respected kings at home, brave, shrewd and sometimes ruthless, but
they engaged in disastrous wars with England and suffered untimely deaths.
Mary I, courageous and debonair, was undone by catastrophic marriages. James VI
was probably the least feared of sixteenth-century Scottish kings, but he was
eloquent, affable, approachable and generous. Extravagance was his foremost
weakness.

Before the 1550s, the leading continental rulers (Charles V, Francis I, Henry II)
were vigorous kings who inspired both respect and loyalty, though their
ruinously expensive foreign policies left heavy burdens of debt. The French
monarchy's problems of the years 1560–98 were largely due to royal minorities,
the mistrust inspired by Catherine de' Medici and Henry III, Henry's child-
lessness and the succession crisis that accompanied the end of the Valois
dynasty. Philip II of Spain was a conscientious and intelligent king, but
increasingly reclusive, inflexible and in thrall to his paperwork.

Courts and councils

The court, the ruler's entourage and its physical setting, was the heart of
kingly government, the foremost reservoir of patronage, the principal stage for
displays of royal magnificence and the arena for princely entertainments.
Intimate royal companions (the gentlemen of the privy chamber under Henry
VIII) performed special services in diplomacy and war. Noblemen or their sons
were given honorific court offices. The French court, particularly under
Francis I, the most splendid in Europe, was considerably larger than its English

counterpart. Stewart kings could only afford a relatively modest court, but their houses of Holyrood, Stirling and Falkland, although smaller in scale, nevertheless bear comparison with such Tudor palaces as Whitehall, Hampton Court and Nonsuch, or the great royal *châteaux* of the Louvre, Fontainebleau, Blois, Amboise and Chambord.[4]

In England the king's council was the principal advisory and executive organ of government. Its more active members included a few noblemen, but more men of outstanding ability from the gentry who had risen through the Church, the law or military service. Henry VIII's most brilliant advisers, Wolsey and Cromwell, were of still humbler origins. Several councillors held offices in the royal household. The core group of most active councillors became the 'privy council' in 1536 to meet the need for 'radical decisions and confidentiality'. Among the highest-ranking councillors were the lord chancellor and the lord treasurer. As lord chancellor (1515–29), Thomas Wolsey was Henry VIII's principal minister. The king's secretary, then from 1540 one of the two principal secretaries of state, became the monarch's chief link with the council. The secretaries sifted incoming information and correspondence about foreign and domestic affairs and received instructions for council agenda. As secretaries Thomas Cromwell (1534–40) and William Cecil (1558–72) acted as the foremost royal confidential advisers. William Cecil kept that role while lord treasurer (1572–98), to be succeeded by his son Robert (secretary from 1596).

The Scottish council was more informal and less well-documented than its English counterpart. During Mary I's difficult minority, in 1543, the privy council emerged, 'to take formal collective responsibility for decisions'. The chancellor was the senior minister, responsible for presiding over council meetings and sessions of parliament. Mary I's and James VI's ablest advisers were their secretaries, the brothers William Maitland of Lethington (1558–71) and John Maitland of Thirlestane (1584–91), also chancellor (1587–95). James VI gradually gained greater control over his privy council's membership, relying increasingly on able 'lairds' (lesser noblemen).[5]

Sound advice was considered essential for wise and effective government. But monarchs could seek advice from the councillors they trusted most, and indeed from outside the council. Policy was shaped by the monarch's personal priorities. The informal discussions that took place between the monarch and his intimate companions outside the council chamber largely went unrecorded. Councillors' most important advisory function was usually to help decide how best to achieve the monarch's chosen goals, though discontented subjects sometimes blamed bad advice for unpopular policies in order to avoid direct criticism of the ruler.

Wise advice was thought particularly necessary for queens. Mary Tudor pursued her main aims in face of the misgivings of different groups of councillors about one or other of those aims. Elizabeth never accepted that she was bound to act upon the advice of her privy councillors. Strong majority opinion nevertheless sometimes persuaded her to take steps she would rather have avoided, such as going to war with Spain in 1585, and signing Mary Stewart's death warrant in 1587, or dissuaded her from actions such as marrying the duke of Anjou in 1579. However, the councillors failed to persuade the queen to address the most urgent question of all, the succession. To avert a potentially disastrous crisis, Cecil twice put forward proposals for interregnum government by the privy council (1563) or a 'great council' (1585) pending a settlement by parliament, but these came to nothing.[6]

Councils played a part in the government of all the main European states. Secretaries became more important as keepers of agenda, memoranda and minutes. Some monarchs, like the kings of France and Spain, had various distinct councils with particular tasks. French kings used a small select group of intimate advisers that was more informal than the English privy council. Spain's exceptional number of specialist councils was largely due to the complex nature of its empire. In Scandinavia and Poland, unlike in western Europe, traditionally powerful noble councils existed. Swedish kings largely sidelined them, relying on humbler-born advisers.

Representative assemblies

Parliament was England's highest court and legislative and tax-granting assembly. The monarch summoned and dissolved it and decided its main agenda. Its House of Lords included judges, law officers, lay peers, bishops, and (initially) some abbots and priors. The number of seats in the House of Commons grew from 296 to 462 during the sixteenth century. By 1603, just under a fifth of the seats were occupied by knights of the shires, which had the largest electorates, many of which ran into the thousands. The rest were seats for the burgesses representing cities and boroughs, whose electorates varied in size. Many of them were small places, and the franchise was often limited to a few inhabitants. The great majority of the new constituencies created during the century were boroughs, often so as to provide seats for the servants of the crown or of favoured magnates. Contested elections were rare. A large majority of MPs were gentry. Members could show considerable independence, and their acquiescence could not be taken for granted. The Commons initiated grants of taxation. Legislation might be introduced in either house, but had to pass both and receive the crown's assent.

The frequent parliamentary sessions of 1529–59 enabled monarchs to obtain an exceptional amount of important legislation concerning the Church, succession to the crown, the scope of treason, new government agencies and local government changes. Other statutes introduced economic and social regulations and reforms. Parliament allowed individuals, corporations and interest groups to seek reform and redress. However, the crown was the driver of the most important legislation and the biggest intended beneficiary. Its measures met remarkably little parliamentary opposition. Fear, self-interest, loyalty, an outwardly united council, careful management, skilful propaganda, lack of unity among potential opponents, together with well-timed and forceful royal interventions, all played some part. There were initial anxieties about the crown's anti-papal measures in 1532–3. Opposition delayed the acceptance of Mary's religious programme. In 1559 the bishops made an almost united but vain stand against Elizabeth's ecclesiastical measures. Taxation demands (1523, 1532) and the hated Statute of Uses (1536) caused discontent in the Commons. During the 1540s, however, Henry VIII raised colossal amounts of taxation without opposition. Subsequent regimes, lacking his immense personal authority, made smaller demands. In 1555 the Commons successfully resisted a bill for the confiscation of exiles' property.[7]

Female rule inspired strong assertions of parliament's powers. England, John Aylmer insisted (1559), seeking to reassure his readers, was not a 'mere monarchy' but a mixture of monarchy, oligarchy and democracy. Aylmer claimed that the monarch could ordain nothing without parliaments if they used their privileges. He praised the members who had in 1539 resisted a bill to allow royal proclamations the force of statute. 'The most high and absolute power of the realm of England consisteth in the Parliament', wrote Sir Thomas Smith in 1565. During the first half of Elizabeth's reign, councillors' concerns about the queen's marriage, the succession and Mary Stewart were widely shared in both houses. Elizabeth's defensive attempts to prevent parliamentary discussion of church order and worship led to some clashes over freedom of speech. But they never came close to isolating the queen in face of majority opinion in council and parliament, unlike marriage and the succession.[8]

Elizabeth summoned parliament less often than her immediate predecessors, introduced less legislation and made smaller and less frequent requests for financial assistance. During her eighteen-year war with Spain, her military spending was only 20 per cent more in real terms than her father's between 1542 and 1547. The government made the case for taxation with care. Even so, the Commons reacted angrily in 1593 to a procedurally inept government attempt to bounce them into voting three subsidies. Hostility towards royal grants of monopolies burst out in a heated debate in 1601. Elizabeth revoked the most hated of these, promised that others would be subjected to judicial review and personally assured members of parliament that she valued her subjects' love above all and that their well being was her paramount concern.[9]

Scotland's unicameral parliament included representatives of the royal burghs as well as titled nobility, lesser nobility or lairds, and greater clergy. Early-sixteenth-century sessions were infrequent and poorly attended. Weaker regimes after 1542 depended more heavily on parliamentary help. Lesser nobles attended in greater numbers. The 1560 parliament introduced the Reformation. James VI's poverty forced him to summon frequent conventions of estates, like parliaments, but mainly used for tax-raising. They often resisted his demands. James and his advisers also introduced important parliamentary legislation, concerning among other things relations between crown and Kirk, the Kirk's representation by bishops in parliament, the parliamentary representation of shires, feuding and local government.[10]

Continental representative assemblies varied hugely in their effectiveness. France's estates-general seldom met, could not legislate and proved unwilling to approve grants of additional taxes. Several provinces possessed estates, but their inability to present a common front and social divisions within provinces made all but the strongest of them vulnerable in the long term. The states-general of the Netherlands consisted of delegates of the different provincial estates. The Habsburgs convened them often, usually as a preliminary step to the presentation of 'particular propositions' concerning tax to individual provincial assemblies. The consent of the Castilian *Cortes* remained necessary for the raising of over half the crown's income in 1601. But they had no legislative power, and after 1538 no longer included representatives of the nobility or clergy. They seldom opposed the government, but their ability to complain made them a useful safety valve. The *Cortes* of Aragon, Catalonia and Valencia survived, but gave the crown very limited financial help and played a correspondingly small part in government. The *Reichstag* of the Holy Roman Empire eventually became increasingly ineffective and hopelessly divided between Catholics and Protestants. Within the principalities of the Empire, estates varied hugely in vigour and effectiveness. The most powerful and frequently convened of all assemblies in the European kingdoms was the Polish *Sejm*, which from 1573 onwards elected the king. From 1505 no change might be made in the kingdom's common law without its consent. It was the supreme court of appeal and competent to hear serious charges against the chief officers of state. Fractious, determined to defend noble interests and limit royal power, it was not a constructive partner in government.[11]

Law and government

In the leading continental monarchies, unlike in England, rulers had the prerogative of making new legislation, but this was usually exercised in a cautious manner, after appropriate consultation, and often in response to requests or complaints made in representative assemblies. One of the most ambitious legislative measures was Francis I's great *ordonnance* of Villers-Cotterêts (1539). This reformed legal process, generally in line with Roman law principles, limited ecclesiastical jurisdiction, ordered all legal documents to be written in French, sanctioned the torture of suspected criminals to obtain confessions and forbade workers' combinations, among other things. However, French royal legislation was supposed to be registered by sovereign courts called *parlements*. The jurisdiction of the Paris *parlement*, the most important, covered almost half the country; seven peripheral provinces had their own. The judges of the *parlement* of Paris delayed for eighteen months the registration of Francis I's 1516 concordat with the pope, protested about the creation of new offices, opposed the establishment of new courts in 1552, refused to register Henry II's edicts establishing an inquisition, opposed religious toleration and delayed or refused the registration of several of Henry III's financial edicts. Various provincial *parlements* modified or failed to register some royal *ordonnances* or edicts.[12]

In England, where parliamentary statute was the supreme form of law, the other royal law courts had a different role from that of the *parlements*. In practice, however, judges' decisions in cases where existing law was ambiguous or insufficient effectively made law, creating precedents. The ancient royal courts, principally King's Bench and Common Pleas, administered the common and statute law and had long-established authority to remove cases from lower jurisdictions. From the later-fourteenth-century Chancery, which issued the writs necessary to commence actions in the royal courts, also offered justice, especially when no common law remedy was available. The king's council was supposed to ensure that justice was upheld. Its judicial work generated two new courts hived off under Henry VIII: Requests, offering justice to the poor and vulnerable, and Star Chamber, particularly concerned with riotous behaviour, intimidation by powerful men, perversion of justice and corruption or extortion on the part of royal officers.

England's forty ancient counties, together with the larger cities and towns, were the most important units of local government. The crown appointed in each county sheriffs and unsalaried justices of the peace from among the nobility and upper gentry, supervised by the justices of assize in their twice-yearly circuits. Tudor legislation gave the justices many new responsibilities, and their numbers grew considerably. Countless manorial and borough courts dealt with lesser disputes and offences. A dense network of church courts came under crown control in 1533. They enforced changes in religious observance, regulated sexual behaviour and granted probate of wills, among other things. Under Elizabeth I 'high' commissions with special powers reinforced the authority of these overworked courts.

All quasi-independent jurisdictions were brought under royal control by an act of 1536 that reserved to the king the appointment of all judges and the authority to pardon serious crimes. Another act of 1536 decreed the introduction of English law throughout Wales, the division of the Welsh Marcher lordships into shires and parliamentary representation of the Welsh counties and boroughs. A further act (1543) confirmed the Council in the Marches, established Welsh Great Sessions courts and provided for the appointment of sheriffs and justices of the peace. These statutes of 1536 and 1543 integrated Wales into the Tudor state. The Council in the North was reorganized in 1537 after the Pilgrimage of Grace. The two councils supervising the North and Wales and its marches gained wide civil and criminal jurisdiction and an important role in maintaining law and order in two outlying regions of the realm.

On both sides of the Anglo-Scottish border the marches stood half-ready for war even in peacetime. Clan-like groups preyed on neighbours across the border and their enemies in their own country. It was difficult to avoid using members of long-established local noble families as march wardens. More peaceful relations with Scotland brought a gradual decline in the endemic violence of border society.

In Scotland the Islands and western Highlands differed from the Lowlands in language, culture and social structure. Mountains and sea presented formidable barriers to sustained intervention, though both James IV and James V visited the Isles. The crown largely delegated local supervision to powerful magnates such as the earls of Argyll and Huntly. A statute of 1587 made all Highlands and border lords answerable for criminals on their lands. In 1588 Lowlanders complaining against Highland criminals were enjoined to come to Edinburgh courts.

Justice was outside direct royal control to a far greater extent in Scotland than in England. Much of the country was divided into some thirty sheriffdoms. The sheriff was an officer of the crown, but his office was hereditary. Within the sheriffdoms there were lesser courts, such as the private baron courts. Independent of the sheriffs were the regalities, private jurisdictions exercising delegated powers of royal justice even in cases of serious crime. Regalities (including some belonging to the crown) covered about half the country. Burghs possessed their own jurisdictions.

Royal justice ayres were held every few years, ostensibly to deal locally with serious crimes, but frequently as a means of making money or quelling political dissent. Sheriffdoms were gradually brought under closer royal control during James VI's reign. The Court of Session in Edinburgh, separated from the council in 1532, heard increasing numbers of cases concerning title to land. The act anent feuding of 1598 ordered that private feuds be submitted to royal justice. Kirk sessions, set up during the Reformation, promoted civility and order, trying to resolve family and neighbourhood disputes, and condemning violence and immorality. Crown and Kirk combined made a powerful alliance.[13]

Each major European realm had distinctive administrative and judicial structures. France's provinces each had a governor personally appointed by the king. Below the provincial level were ninety-three *bailliages* and *sénéchaussées*. The *baillis'* courts heard lawsuits, including appeals from inferior courts, punished crimes, published royal ordinances and supervised trade. From their courts appeal lay to one of the *parlements,* from them to the *grand conseil,* separated from the king's council in 1497–8. In the Netherlands the main elements of the judicial hierarchy were the district and urban magistrates, provincial *stadholders*, provincial high courts and the Great Council, the supreme court established at Mechelen in 1504. In both France and the Netherlands soon afterwards rulers ordered the recording and, to some extent, the systematization, of a huge variety of local laws. Appointment of Roman lawyers to the high courts was a key element in the consolidation of Habsburg control over the Netherlands. These courts drew business from lower ones by evocation and appeal. Their work in the Netherlands was the outstanding example of several broadly similar processes of princely state building within the Holy Roman Empire. In Poland, by contrast, the nobility limited the appellate jurisdiction of the royal courts: from 1518 onwards those courts could not hear appeals by peasants against their lords. The numerous middling and lesser nobility strongly supported during the sixteenth century the 'execution of laws', to prevent their infringement by the great magnates or the crown and protect the social dominance of the nobility as a whole.[14]

In Spain Aragon, Catalonia and Valencia retained their own administrations and law courts. In Castile, the crown appointed from 1480 *corregidores*, outsiders who held office for a limited term, to supervise government in all the major cities. Over large areas, however, magnates possessed delegated jurisdiction that included the administration of justice, collection of taxes, nomination of officials and raising of men for the crown. In order to meet its own pressing financial needs, the crown sold extensive lands and jurisdictions during this century. It also sold municipal offices. Appeals from lower courts lay to one of the *audiencias* of Castile or Aragon. Ultimate appeal lay to the councils of the different kingdoms. Only one institution under royal control had jurisdiction throughout Spain: the much-feared Holy Office or Inquisition, designed to root out non-Christian belief and heresy.

It was the duty of monarchs to uphold the laws and administer impartial justice. In practice many kings bent laws to their own wills. Henry VII, who exploited his feudal prerogatives for profit and used the threat of swingeing fines to instil fear, was exceptional in his deathbed acknowledgement that he had treated individuals unjustly. Henry VIII ruthlessly used weak charges of treason to destroy individuals whom he suspected of disloyalty, including some of the foremost English noblemen. From 1534 onwards several victims suffered by parliamentary act of attainder without normal legal process. The judges allegedly confirmed the legality of this procedure reluctantly and somewhat equivocally under pressure. Judges supported the Amicable Grant in 1525, even though such 'benevolences' had been forbidden by a 1484 act made 'by the consent of the body of the whole realm, which is the parliament'. After 1547, English governments, with some exceptions, were generally more cautious in bending the law for their profit and security.[15]

In Scotland James IV and James V vigorously exploited their rights as feudal suzerains. 'If there was a legal loophole James [V] would find it.' He ruthlessly punished individuals he thought to be his enemies. Both kings profited from remissions for serious crimes. Francis I struck down some of his most diligent servants, including a superintendent of finances and a chancellor, punishing their undoubted corruption with disproportionate severity for the sake of profit. His oppressive treatment of Charles de Bourbon, Constable of France, drove the Constable into Charles V's service. Philip II was usually scrupulously respectful of existing law, but believed that rebellion and heresy justified exceptional action. Alba's measures in the Netherlands, including disregard for even the highest nobles' privileges, badly damaged Philip's reputation. When in 1590 his disgraced servant Antonio Pérez fled to his native Aragon, whose justiciar claimed jurisdiction over him, Philip, against advice, pressed the Inquisition to prosecute him on an unconvincing charge of heresy. This resulted in riots, an unprecedented invasion of Aragon and the summary execution of resistance leaders, including the justiciar. Pérez himself escaped to France, and thence to England.[16]

Armed forces

Artillery and handguns contributed to far-reaching military changes. Massive, complex fortifications were developed to resist siege artillery, particularly in northern Italy and the Netherlands. Ships were designed to accommodate more guns below deck. Infantry with firearms could ravage charging cavalry, but had to be combined with pikemen. Armies grew larger, arming and supplying them more complex.[17]

England's defence depended above all on guarding the seas. Henry VIII's government built more ships, gave the navy administrative structure, 'institutional memory' and expert supervision in the shape of the navy board (1546), created new docks and began large-scale ordnance production overseen by the ordnance board. England alone secured a plentiful supply of small and medium-sized iron guns, though the biggest and best were still bronze. Elizabeth's government, though financially straitened, built several comparatively small, highly manoeuvrable and well-armed warships. Their nimbleness and an artillery re-loading rate far faster than the Spanish were crucial in 1588. In wartime, the crown pressed mariners and merchant ships into service. The strongest navy in northern Europe was vitally important for the defence of an otherwise second-rank power.[18]

England's small permanent land forces consisted of royal guards and a few garrisons. Arms practice was, however, compulsory for all able-bodied men, liable to be levied on a county basis for local or national defence. The training, equipment and funding of county forces were gradually improved. Lords lieutenant were first appointed for all counties in Edward's reign, and normally from 1585, assisted by gentlemen deputy-lieutenants. Two 1558 statutes provided for the taking of musters and the keeping of horses, armour and weapons. The Elizabethan council badgered gentry and towns to provide more modern weapons, and persuaded the counties to train selected men regularly from 1573 onwards. County forces were not legally liable to serve overseas. Henry VIII, strong and ruthless, used them during the 1540s nonetheless. During war with Spain, the privy council relied on county authorities to press for overseas service poor men from outside the trained bands. English armies also included forces raised by courtiers and other landowners (the main element in Tudor armies before the 1540s), foreign mercenaries and volunteers. The use of mercenaries was heaviest in the 1540s. Volunteers, especially veterans of continental wars, were particularly important in Elizabeth's reign. Henry VIII squeezed his realm to raise the century's biggest English army. Elizabeth's government maintained much longer-sustained and more widespread but smaller operations, placing on the counties much of the burden of raising men and supplies.[19]

Scottish hosts, bound to serve for forty days, were mostly raised by nobles from among their tenants. There was, intermittently, a royal guard. James VI tried to develop the traditional system of local musters or 'wapinshawings'. James IV built some formidable ships and used heavy guns against castles in the Western Isles. Subsequent Scottish governments could not maintain his navy.[20]

France had a permanent cavalry force, first raised in the fifteenth century, and financed by permanent taxation. Spain also created such a body, and was much more successful than France in establishing standing infantry forces. Commissioned captains were able to recruit many hardy volunteers from the austere Castilian uplands. Much of Spain's army was stationed in Italy, which bore a large share of its cost. Continuity fostered professionalism and development. New, better-armed Spanish infantry formations developed during the 1530s into the famous *tercios* of about 3,000 men combining pikes with firearms. Both Valois and Habsburgs also relied heavily on mercenaries. France and Aragon maintained Mediterranean galley fleets. Genoa switched alliances from France to Spain in 1528, reinforcing Spain's Mediterranean ascendancy. France also kept royal ships on her northern and western coasts. Castile inaugurated an Atlantic squadron in 1570, gained Portugal's ocean-going ships (1580) and undertook a galleon building campaign after 1588, but proved less successful than England in maintaining its sailing navy. Both the French and Spanish crowns hired and drafted merchant ships in time of war.[21]

Urban militias were the traditional backbone of the Netherlands armies, supplemented by noble retinues. Between c.1470 and 1559 rulers added a usually small standing mounted force, established several garrisons and hired large numbers of mercenaries. Once independent the United Provinces became a formidable new military power. Regular pay enabled them to raise a steady flow of recruits from Scotland, England and Germany as well as their own inhabitants. Innovative Dutch generals, especially Maurice of Nassau, developed earth fortifications, shallower formations, smaller tactical units, successive ranks of musketeers to maintain more continuous fire, and more systematic and intensive drill. The Dutch navy expanded rapidly.[22]

Revenues

Royal magnificence and armed forces depended on money. The English monarchy's two main income sources were lands and trade. The crown was the realm's greatest landowner. Henry VIII hugely expanded the royal estates, mainly at the expense of the Church, but had sold or granted the lion's share of the monastic lands by 1547. Substantial land sales, especially in order to help meet war costs, also occurred under Edward and Elizabeth. From 1484 to1604 the first parliament of every reign granted taxes on trade, 'tonnage and poundage', for the monarch's life. In 1558, Mary I's cash-strapped government increased outdated valuations, raised rates, and imposed new duties.

The crown also exploited various unpopular prerogatives to raise revenue. Henry VIII's land grants greatly increased the numbers of tenants-in-chief liable to feudal 'incidents', and thus the crown's feudal income. Between 1544 and 1551, governments minted massive quantities of debased coin.

Especially during the war with Spain, the crown granted or sold profitable monopoly rights of production or trade in given commodities to individuals. Purveyance, the levy of supplies for the royal household at a fixed price, amounted to a tax.

The crown also requested parliamentary grants of direct taxes, usually on the pretext of war or dangers to the realm's security. In Henry VIII's reign 'subsidies', taxes on individuals, were introduced, initially based on relatively accurate assessments. They remained the most important form of direct taxation, though yields fell after 1546 as assessment grew laxer. The crown sometimes invoked subjects' duty to give emergency help in order to raise forced loans or even gifts. Henry VIII failed to obtain the 'Amicable Grant' in 1525, but during the 1540s, at his most powerful, levied substantial extra-parliamentary taxes. Mary and Elizabeth raised some further forced loans. In 1534 the clergy were subjected to swingeing new permanent statutory taxes. Due to lax or conservative administration all the main crown revenues (rents, trade taxes, feudal dues, subsidies, clerical taxes) failed to keep pace with inflation during Elizabeth's reign.[23]

Scottish monarchs received comparatively tiny revenues. They included feudal dues, revocations of grants made during royal minorities (useful to this century's orphan monarchs), forfeitures for treason (especially in James V's reign) and payments for remission of penalties. The sale of charters by which tenants paid the crown a fixed feu duty instead of rent achieved immediate gains at the cost of a long-term reduction in income. Foreign dowries (or dower in Mary's case) were important for all the Scottish monarchs. Elizabeth I's subsidy to James VI was useful, though intermittently paid. James IV and James V exploited ecclesiastical patronage. James V, with papal consent, taxed the Church heavily. The crown shared with the Protestant clergy a third of the income of benefices of the old Church reserved by statute in 1562. Parliamentary direct taxation became more frequent from the 1580s. James VI increased taxes on trade. His governments also debased the coinage from the 1570s onwards. James's extravagance nevertheless kept his finances precarious.[24]

French and Castilian kings relied more heavily on taxation than did their British counterparts. They had made their main sources of revenue independent of their subjects' consent. These were the *taille*, a direct tax, in France, and the *alcabala*, a sales tax, in Castile. However, it was not until the second half of the century that there were major increases in the *real* yield of either of these taxes, and then much of the *taille* never reached Henry III's coffers. Meanwhile, governments in both countries had had to maximize other sources of revenue. The Church was one source that the Spanish crown exploited more effectively than the French, thanks to papal concessions. French indirect taxes were increased, especially the hated salt tax. The French crown began the large-scale creation of offices for sale in 1522. The long-term cost was considerable: officials were salaried, as well as exempt from personal *taille*. The Spanish crown's share of American bullion yielded a growing income between 1545 and 1600, and made it easier to raise loans, but even at its peak provided much less than a quarter of the crown's revenues. In Castile the *Cortes*, representing the cities, granted increasing amounts of direct tax. In 1590, with some difficulty, Philip II persuaded them to make a massive new grant, which the cities raised by taxing foodstuffs. In both countries, nobles were exempt from direct taxes. Small rural landholders and poor consumers shouldered a disproportionate share of the fiscal burden.[25]

In the Netherlands, the government persuaded the states to grant steadily increasing direct taxes, which provided most of its income by 1535–8. In the 1540s, after long negotiations, Charles V imposed taxes on exports and on profits from trade and land for a limited period. The different provinces also levied excises. Tax demands reached new heights in the 1550s. Alba's new sales tax helped precipitate revolt in 1572. In the north, after the revolt, most taxation was levied and administered by the provinces. Each was free to rely on a different mixture: Holland (the biggest contributor), drew nearly two-thirds of its revenue from indirect imposts. Rural inland provinces relied more on direct taxes.[26]

Most governments needed to borrow. Spending always outpaced revenue growth. English governments generally relied on forced loans or privileged lenders such as the City of London. Henry VIII, exceptionally, ran up a substantial debt at Antwerp. In Scotland, James VI borrowed from his own officials. The foremost continental rulers turned to financiers operating in such centres as Antwerp, Augsburg, Genoa, Lyons and Medina del Campo, and sold bonds and annuities as a means of tapping the wealth of a larger pool of investors, though only the big banker or financial syndicate could raise substantial sums quickly. It often proved impossible to maintain the high interest payments on such loans, let alone repay them. The only solution was to re-schedule them, as the Spanish monarchy frequently did from 1557 onwards. It also mortgaged an increasing proportion of its assets. By contrast, the cities and later the provinces of the Netherlands, which enjoyed the confidence of a unique concentration of investors, successfully raised money by issuing annuities and other forms of security funded by a variety of local taxes, on which they paid relatively low rates of interest.

Rebellions

The most important causes of resistance to governments in sixteenth-century Europe were religion, taxation and threats to local liberties and privileges. (Agrarian risings were largely directed against local ruling groups.) In England religious innovations helped provoke rebellions in 1536, 1549 and 1569, and gained support for Mary Tudor in 1553. Only in 1554 was Protestantism an important element in an English rising. Opposition to changes in worship was intertwined with concerns about church property. Taxation inspired widespread popular resistance in 1525. The Statute of Uses, an attempt to curb evasion of feudal dues, was a grievance in 1536. Local resentment of the innovating interference of a distant government was a strong element in 1536, 1549 and 1569. The succession to the throne was an important concern in several rebellions. Peers seldom led provincial rebellions, though they sometimes encouraged them. Most of the organizers were gentlemen, clergy or yeomen. Rivalries in court and council precipitated coups or plots at the centre of power, especially during Edward VI's reign. The single comparable episode in an adult monarch's reign was the earl of Essex's desperate, abortive attempt to remove his rivals by seizing the court in 1601.

The most momentously successful British rebellion of the century was the seizure of power by the Scottish Lords of the Congregation in 1559–60, a turning point in the island's history. The rebel leaders were a minority of the nobility and a group of militant clergy. A second revolution, in 1567, followed by civil war, consolidated the result of the first. Aristocratic attempts to seize the person of the monarch or remove rivals from the court by force were more frequent in Scotland than in England. Several assassinations occurred. Local aristocratic rebellions, such as those of the earls of Huntly, were largely intended to ward off royal interference. Donald Dubh MacDonald, last Lord of the Isles, was exceptional in pledging his loyalty to the English crown in an attempt to secure the autonomy of his lordship in 1545. There were no major popular rebellions like those of 1549 in England.

Religion was the most important and distinctive element in the great sixteenth-century continental rebellions. The French civil wars were complicated by royal minorities, magnate contests for control of the court, rivalry within the royal family, local peasant revolts, temporary *de facto* provincial secessions, a disputed succession, revolutionary Catholic seizure of Paris and foreign intervention. Numerous assassinations and horrifying massacres occurred.

Britain escaped France's fate, Scotland perhaps more narrowly than England. No effective leader of the scattered Catholic nobility appeared in either kingdom, and the focus of Catholic hopes, Mary Stewart, was all but a prisoner from 1568. A striking contrast between England and France was the relative weakness and lack of militancy of both Reformed Protestantism and the Catholic cause during the critical early Elizabethan years. A crucial difference between Britain and France was the use of parliaments as a means of establishing a legally binding national consensus.

Fiscal demands provoked resistance in several countries. A salt tax increase set off disturbances in south-western France between 1542 and 1548 that culminated in full-scale revolt. The rebels accused the king of breaking a promise made at his accession. After savagely suppressing the rebellion, the crown granted an amnesty, and in 1553 allowed the whole province of Guyenne to buy its freedom from the tax – an immunity that lasted until 1789.[27]

Some of the most protracted rebellions of the sixteenth century took place in dependent realms suffering unwelcome interference by outside overlords. Ireland presents an outstanding example. After the dangerous rebellion of 'Silken Thomas' Fitzgerald in 1534, the crown thenceforth appointed chief governors from outside Ireland. It aimed to make the quarrelsome and independent nobility, both Old English and Old Irish, more dependent on itself, while at the same time lessening the nobility's hold upon its own dependants by means of changes in land tenure and the extension of English law enforcement machinery. Many magnates saw these designs as intrusive and threatening. Half-baked Protestant Reformation was a further widely disliked element of interference. Confiscation, and (from the 1550s onwards) plantation, met resistance, suppressed with brutality and treachery soon amply repaid by those who suffered them. Determination to make Ireland pay for its own pacification resulted in the commutation of alleged military obligations into burdensome non-parliamentary taxes. Widely regarded as unlawful, they alienated the Old English. Major rebellions in every province punctuated Elizabeth's reign, culminating in Hugh O'Neill's 'nine years war' (1595–1603).

Existing Irish channels of advice and communication were neglected. After 1547 'Old English' members of the Irish privy council who criticized severer policies found themselves increasingly marginalized and mistrusted by English governors. Ireland's early-sixteenth-century parliaments gave a voice to the lordship's Old English inhabitants as well as serving crown interests. No parliament met under Edward VI, and only three under Elizabeth. The last of them (1585–6) threw out the chief government bills.[28]

Several continental rebellions were directed against foreign rulers. Sweden broke its union with Denmark in 1520–3. Charles of Habsburg alienated his new Castilian subjects through reliance on Flemish advisers and high-handed treatment of the *Cortes*. The resulting rebellion of the *Comuneros*, based principally in Castilian cities (1520–1), failed when the nobility turned against what seemed an increasingly radical and dangerous movement. Charles's timely stay in Castile from 1522 to 1529 enabled him to gain the kingdom's loyalty. When Charles's Netherlands became in turn a peripheral part of his son Philip's empire, no such response was forthcoming. Neglect of the nobility, infringement of provincial liberties, a repressive religious policy and hated taxes all helped to provoke rebellion. Eventually, the states-general of the truncated United Provinces abjured their allegiance in 1581 and succeeded in maintaining their independence.

There were many differences between the rebellions in Ireland and the Netherlands. Ireland was in many ways a backward kingdom, the Netherlands amongst the richest and most developed regions in Europe. Ireland's remoteness hindered foreign efforts to assist its rebellions. Yet in both cases aristocratic leaders sought to protect their position against a monarchy based outside their own country, demanded liberty of conscience and finally developed a patriotic ideology designed to unite diverse elements against a common enemy.[29]

Theories of resistance and royal power

Religious divisions induced an unprecedented number of authors to justify resistance to rulers. Cardinals Reginald Pole and William Allen invoked the need to preserve the unity of the Catholic Church and papal authority in tracts against Henry VIII and Elizabeth I. The Jesuit Robert Persons, questioning James VI's right to the English throne in 1594, argued that kings were partners with their people in a contract confirmed in their coronation oath, and subject to laws. The authority of a ruler bent on destroying the commonwealth (in which religion's preservation was the highest priority) might be revoked.[30]

English Protestant exiles developed resistance theories during the 1550s in response to Mary I's rule. John Ponet, Christopher Goodman and John Knox demanded the removal of rulers whose commands were contrary to God's Word. Knox's tract violently attacked female rule as against nature and God's ordinance. George Buchanan later justified Mary Stewart's overthrow and blackened her reputation. He also wrote a dialogue about the law of the kingdom among the Scots, eventually dedicated to his pupil James VI (1579). The true king, Buchanan insisted, gained power by popular consent and was subject to the law. He ruled for his subjects' benefit. Biblical injunctions to obey rulers did not apply to tyrants, who might be overthrown or assassinated.[31]

The French monarchy's involvement in treacherous violence against both Huguenots and Catholics encouraged the formulation of radical political ideas. During the 1570s, Theodore Beza, Calvin's successor at Geneva, and the anonymous author of the *Vindiciae contra Tyrannos*, both argued that 'inferior magistrates' or public officials might resist rulers who broke God's law. The foremost Catholic revolutionary ideologue Jean Boucher persuaded his Sorbonne colleagues to declare Henry III deposed. League writers saw true Catholic orthodoxy as essential in a successor to the throne, and justified Henry's assassination.[32]

The most influential political thinker of the religious wars was, however, the lawyer Jean Bodin. He deplored the effects of religious disunity. In *The Six Books of the Commonwealth* (1576) Bodin emphasized the king's moral duty to respect his subjects' rights of liberty and property and his need to observe the fundamental laws concerning the royal succession and domain. He should consult the estates and respect objections from the *parlement*. Bodin's work nevertheless owed its enduring influence to his insistence on the monarchy's possession of undivided sovereignty, and his consistent refusal to allow any other human authority to limit the sovereign.[33]

In Britain it was James VI of Scotland who expressed ideas of untrammelled sovereignty most eloquently and succinctly. In two tracts, *The Trew Law of Free Monarchies* (1598) and an advice book for his son Henry entitled *Basilikon Doron* (1599), James insisted that kings were accountable to God alone. No earthly laws could bind them. A good king would rule justly and observe the laws. His duty was to rule for his people's benefit. God had, however, enjoined obedience to kings and utterly forbidden resistance. James rejected Buchanan's claims.[34]

Conclusion

Several sixteenth-century European rulers found ways of enhancing their power, authority and resources. Their courts projected royal majesty through

lavishly splendid entertainments and ceremonial, and grand palaces magnificently adorned. Re-modelled or newly created councils and tribunals
assisted the making and execution of policy and made royal justice more
readily available and effective. Rulers reinforced the supremacy of royal
tribunals over other jurisdictions. They appointed a growing army of local
judicial, fiscal and administrative officials. Conflicts between dynastic states
demanded larger and better-equipped armies, and helped drive some of the
other changes already outlined. All these developments necessitated greater
financial resources, and stimulated fiscal ingenuity and innovation.

In no two kingdoms, however, was the course of development identical.
In England, Henry VIII and his ministers asserted and enforced the royal
supremacy, enlarged the royal household, created the privy council and new
prerogative courts, abrogated local jurisdictions, incorporated Wales, transformed the navy and enormously enhanced royal revenues by confiscations,
the spoliation of the Church, fiscal innovation and thrusting exploitation of
royal prerogatives. After c.1550, English governments were on the whole more
cautious, less innovative and more reluctant to resort to prerogative powers.
In comparison with most continental states, England had in parliament an
exceptionally active and effective national representative assembly. She maintained a relatively strong navy, but small permanent land forces. English rulers
did not create offices for sale, and relied for local law enforcement on growing
numbers of unsalaried justices of the peace.

Scotland remained a poor, peripheral kingdom. Its institutional development was interrupted by untimely royal deaths, military defeats and internal
conflicts. James V's Court of Session and the privy council that emerged during Mary I's minority proved lasting innovations, but James IV's relatively
powerful navy was impossible to maintain. Geography, the local power of the
Gaelic nobility and the existence of extensive regalities, all limited royal control over the localities. James VI's grasp on the reins of power was somewhat
uncertain at first, but he gradually achieved a more sustained consolidation of
royal authority.

All England's neighbours suffered serious rebellions or civil wars, relatively
short in Scotland, prolonged in France, the Netherlands and Ireland. England's
relative immunity from such upheavals was largely due to good fortune: the
failure of rebellions to spread beyond a particular region in 1536, 1549 and
1569, and the swift victories of Mary Tudor in 1553 and 1554. The Tudor
monarchy's biggest failure was in Ireland: eventual victory in 1603 carried a
terrible cost.

5

REFORMATIONS

The Catholic Church and the Protestant reformers

The sixteenth-century religious reformations split Europe and divided countries. They promoted a new ideological politics, precipitated rebellions and produced new international alignments. Protestant Reformations brought England and Scotland closer together (despite the tensions generated by differences between their reformations) but set Britain and Ireland on divergent religious paths.

Around 1500, the Roman Catholic Church commanded the spiritual allegiance of most of the inhabitants of western and central Europe. Popes elected by a college of cardinals ruled the Church with ceremonial pomp as monarchs with legislative, judicial and fiscal powers, and extensive patronage. The ecclesiastical hierarchy of wealthy and privileged prelates matched the upper echelons of lay society. A very large body of clergy, distinguished from the laity by their dress, tonsure and celibacy, conducted church services in Latin. They were supposed to give basic religious instruction, but most Christians had little direct acquaintance with the Bible, the foundation of their faith. The clergy's most important function was the celebration of Mass, the Roman form of the rite during which Christians commemorate in the Eucharist or Holy Communion Christ's Last Supper with his disciples. The bread and wine consecrated during Mass were, the Church taught, 'transubstantiated' into the substance of the body and blood of Christ. The laity might share only the bread, not the wine. Masses were sung not only for the living but also in huge numbers for the dead to secure their early release from purgatory, a place of punishment for the majority of Christians who, though saved, had died with sins to expiate. Among the clergy, several orders of monks and friars, based in monasteries and convents, were devoted to special tasks including worship, study, contemplation, and (more particularly in the case of the friars) education and preaching.

The Church recognized as saints thousands of men and women of exemplary life, pre-eminent among them Mary, Christ's virgin mother. Saints' cults were woven into every aspect of Catholic life. They were believed to assist and protect their devotees as well as interceding for them with God. Their relics and many of their images were believed to work miracles and attracted pilgrims.

The Church's perceived shortcomings attracted numerous critics during the centuries before 1500. One of the more radical was the Oxford theologian John Wycliffe (d. 1384). He had denounced the clergy's excessive wealth, challenged papal authority and attacked pilgrimages, the worship of saints and the doctrine of transubstantiation, all of which he considered idolatrous. He had demanded a translation of the Bible into English, a project undertaken by some of his followers, though soon forbidden. Repressed early in the fifteenth century, the Wycliffite 'Lollards' had survived as an underground movement. Renewed persecution under the early Tudors revealed the survival of Lollard ideas in London and elsewhere in southern England. However, the hundreds of parish churches rebuilt or embellished, and thousands of bequests showing devotion to saints and the desire for intercessory prayers and masses, testify to the continuing vigour of popular Catholicism.

More intensive study of ancient texts by humanist scholars led to new criticism of the Church. As early as the 1440s the Italian Lorenzo Valla had exposed as a forgery a key text used to justify papal temporal power and published a critical comparison of the Greek text of the New Testament with the Church's Latin version, the Vulgate. The Dutch humanist Desiderius Erasmus was, however, the first to publish the Greek New Testament with a new Latin translation (1516), revealing the shortcomings of the Vulgate. Erasmus looked forward to the day when even poor Christians would be familiar with the Gospels and the Epistles of St Paul. He mordantly satirized superstitious trust in relics, mechanically recited prayers, and ignorant and greedy monks and friars.

The European Reformation is conventionally taken to have begun in 1517, when Martin Luther, Augustinian friar and professor of Scripture at Wittenberg University, drew up his ninety-five theses against indulgences. In 1520 he published a series of tracts in which he attacked (amongst other things) papal supremacy, the distinction between priests and laity, the compulsory celibacy of the clergy, pilgrimages, masses for the dead and transubstantiation. He later rejected purgatory altogether, but, despite his denial of transubstantiation, never ceased to believe in the presence of Christ's body in the Eucharist. In Luther's eyes, all the institutions and practices that he condemned lacked scriptural authority. The Church seemed to Luther to encourage Christians to seek salvation through superstitious or idolatrous devotional practices. According to the doctrine of 'justification by faith' that Luther found in St Paul's letters, especially his Epistle to the Romans, faith in the crucified Christ is a gift from God to those whom He chooses. This God-given faith bears fruit in good works. Human beings are sinners, utterly incapable of achieving righteousness by their own efforts.

Another reformer, Huldrych Zwingli of Zurich, reached his own independent and radical critique of Roman Catholic traditions through his study of the Greek New Testament. Religious reforms in Zurich under Zwingli's influence included the removal of images from churches in 1524, a step beyond Lutheran teaching. Zwingli utterly rejected any belief in Christ's bodily presence in the Eucharist. When he met Luther at Marburg in 1529 this was the irreconcilable difference between them.

The third of the great sixteenth-century reformers was John Calvin, preacher and pastor at Geneva during the years 1536–8 and 1541–64. In Calvin's view the bread and wine were not only symbolic of Christ's body and blood as Zwingli had taught, but also, for those who partook of them with faith, the means by which they were lifted in spirit to his presence. This doctrine formed the basis of consensus among the Swiss churches in 1549, but did not satisfy the Lutherans. Calvin's lasting influence was due to his position as the leading reformer of the French-speaking world, the clarity and precision of his language, his exposition of an all-powerful God's predestination of some human beings to salvation, others to damnation, and his re-organization of the Genevan Church. Calvin became more explicitly rigorous about predestination as a result of controversy. His successors at Geneva further developed his thought on the subject. His *Ecclesiastical Ordinances* (1541) set out a structure based on that of the Church of the Apostles. Ministry was to be exercised by pastors, doctors (teachers), elders (with special responsibility for discipline) and deacons (concerned with charitable giving). The pastors and elders met weekly as a consistory. Here was the basic unit of a Presbyterian Church. The Huguenots in France were the first to create a national Presbyterian organization with a hierarchy of courts and assemblies.

The Reformation was first and foremost an evangelical movement that aimed to communicate the New Testament's message of salvation more effectively to Christian people. Teaching and preaching were the essential means to this end. Luther proclaimed the 'priesthood of all believers' but unguided individual interpretation of the Bible was a recipe for anarchy. Authority in the Church needed to be clearly located and securely underpinned. At the same time, all members of congregations were to play an enhanced part in the worship of God, and this meant that services must be conducted in the language of the people.

Martin Luther came to assign the chief responsibility for Reformation to the secular ruler because he denied the Church any coercive power, and depended personally on a godly prince, Frederick, elector of Saxony. Protestant rulers or civic authorities soon took control of the Church in several territories in the Empire and the kingdoms of Denmark and Sweden. This control was exercised through clergy, usually salaried 'superintendents' approved by the ruler.

The reformers had rejected papal authority. They were doubly sensitive to the possibility that their own authority might be discredited by the popular enthusiasm they had unleashed. When Luther's ideas of Christian freedom helped to inspire widespread peasant revolts in Germany in 1524–5, he disowned and savagely attacked the rebels. Some Zurich ministers questioned the validity of the baptism of infants, and the first adult baptisms took place there in 1525. The implications of 'Anabaptism' for the inclusiveness and unity of the Church were thought particularly dangerous. An enormous variety of Anabaptist groups later developed, differing amongst themselves in both belief and practice. In a particularly notorious revolutionary episode Anabaptists seized the city of Münster (1534) and introduced polygamy and community of property. Catholics and Protestants collaborated in suppressing them. Thereafter, most Anabaptists adopted a more pacific stance. The largest groups survived in Moravia, north Germany and the northern Netherlands.

The mainstream or 'magisterial' Reformation was established under the aegis of secular authorities. Within the Empire, however, the Emperor exercised supreme secular rule, and Charles V opposed the Lutheran Reformation from the beginning. Protestants soon developed arguments to justify defence of their reformation measures against unjust force, but did not go out of their way to flout imperial authority, which was valued by the free cities and other smaller states of the Empire. In the 1540s Charles belatedly focused his attention on Germany, but proved unable to enforce a Catholic provisional settlement with minor concessions to Protestants, and in 1552 suffered humiliating defeat. In 1555 the Religious Peace of Augsburg allowed sovereign princes and free cities of the Empire to choose between Catholicism and Lutheranism as the religion of their territories, with the proviso that the cities must allow Catholic worship. Recognition of religious diversity in an empire that owed allegiance to one ruler set a notable precedent.

There were various reasons for the Reformation's early successes. The eloquence and conviction of the preachers' messages, backed by an unprecedented exploitation of print and pictorial media, found the Church's defenders unprepared. The reformers' claims to be purging religion of unscriptural, superstitious, oppressive and ridiculous practices, and their attacks on the authority of a hierarchy all too vulnerable to charges of corruption, were powerfully persuasive. Their demand that a religion of pilgrimages, penance, purgatory and prayer for the dead be replaced by a Scripture-based faith that would inspire good works of practical charity clearly appealed to many. Initial hopes of social as well as religious enfranchisement may have gained popular support, but it soon became clear that change in the existing social order was not on the mainstream reformers' agenda. Rulers and urban oligarchies gained most, especially in greater control over their churches. Kings and princes seized large amounts of church property. Urban reformers were more successful in having such property used for socially beneficial purposes.

The chief elements of reformation were vernacular worship, a remodelled church order and a new confession of faith. Among 'mainstream' churches the 'Reformed' or 'Calvinist' congregations made the most radical changes in worship and church order. Protestants prepared several different confessions of faith, none of which commanded universal assent. The two most important were the Augsburg Confession of 1530, a deliberately moderate statement for presentation to Charles V on behalf of the Lutheran Churches, and the second Helvetic Confession of 1566. This was the confession most widely accepted by the Reformed Churches, including both Geneva and

Zurich. The split between them and the Lutherans over eucharistic doctrine proved permanent.[1]

The British reformations c.1520–63

Lutheran ideas reached England during the 1520s. England's foremost evangelical, William Tyndale, drew on Luther's as well as Erasmus's work in his translation of the New Testament, printed in Worms in 1526. To some extent Lollard survival prepared the ground for Lutheran ideas, despite the important differences between Lutheran and Lollard beliefs. However, a lively Catholicism still commanded the loyalty of most English people.[2] Henry VIII was no Protestant, but his break with Rome and attacks on the English Church made an English Protestant Reformation possible.

The Act of Supremacy (1534) recognized that Henry was supreme head of the English Church, possessing all 'honours ... profits and commodities' belong ing to that headship, together with all the correctional power and authority of spiritual jurisdiction. As in Scandinavia, exploitation of the Church's material resources swiftly followed the break with Rome. Parliament consented to heavy new taxes on the clergy (1534) and the dissolution of the monasteries (1536, 1539). Henry's church policy has variously been seen as governed by expediency and a 'ragbag of emotional preferences', or as a consistent programme of conservative reform. His assertion of the seven sacraments against Luther in 1521 had earned him the title of 'defender of the faith' from Pope Leo X. But Thomas Cranmer, his archbishop of Canterbury, became in key respects a secret Lutheran, while his vicegerent in spirituals Thomas Cromwell had evangelical sympathies. The Ten Articles of 1536, the first, incomplete statement of belief agreed by convocation after 1534, possibly influenced by a desire to maintain relations with the Protestant princes of Germany, mentioned only three of the seven Catholic sacraments, were carefully vague about the Eucharist and purgatory, and borrowed some Lutheran phrases about justification. Royal injunctions of 1536 and 1538 discouraged various aspects of saints' cults, and required that a Bible in English should be set up in every parish church. The version authorized for this purpose drew very heavily on William Tyndale's translation. The Act of Six Articles (1539), however, provided draconian penalties for denial of the doctrine of transubstantiation and breaches of vows of chastity, and upheld masses for the dead. The fuller treatment of doctrine in the King's Book of 1543 underlined the conservative aspects of Henry's religious settlement. He prevented England's acceptance of Lutheranism at what would otherwise have been a favourable moment.[3]

Following Edward VI's accession in 1547, homilies were published explaining justification by faith. Acts were passed providing for Communion in both kinds, and authorizing the confiscation of remaining endowments of prayers for the dead. Orders for the destruction of surviving images and the abolition of several religious ceremonies, together with the publication of a new *Order of Communion* in English, followed in 1548. Further acts ordering the use of an

English Prayer Book and permitting the marriage of the clergy were passed in 1549. The changes accomplished in worship during the years 1548–9 were more dramatic and profound than all those accomplished under Henry VIII.

After 1547, partly under the influence of continental exiles in England, Cranmer, given a unique opportunity of shaping religious policy under the boy king, moved beyond Luther. Communion, it was made clear in 1548, involved the *spiritual* eating and drinking of Christ's body and blood. This was underlined in a second Prayer Book, published in 1552. From 1550 wooden communion tables replaced the ancient stone altars, with their connotations of sacrifice. Scriptural texts were painted on white-washed church walls. A catechism and forty-two articles of faith issued by royal authority in June 1553 confirmed the Church of England's new doctrinal alignment.[4]

After Mary's accession in July 1553 England became the first officially Protestant state to experience a thoroughgoing Counter-Reformation. The Edwardian religious measures were nearly all repealed in October 1553. Re-union with Rome was completed in Mary's third parliament (November 1554–January 1555). The purchasers of monastic lands were, however, allowed to keep them, and the few re-foundations of religious houses were Mary's own work. The same parliament re-instated medieval laws for the punishment of heretics. Some 800 individuals, most, but not all, of them religious exiles, left England for Europe during Mary's reign. The Church's main efforts, co-ordinated by the Catholic reformer Cardinal Reginald Pole, archbishop of Canterbury, went into restoring Catholic worship, improving religious education, turning the universities into Catholic strongholds and winning over Protestants. If measured by the outward conformity of the overwhelming majority of the population, the Marian restoration was a considerable success. Mary and her advisers nevertheless underestimated the numbers of Protestants. Nearly 300 people were burnt to death for refusing to abjure their beliefs. Leading Protestant clergy such as Thomas Cranmer were prime targets, but most victims were quite obscure men and women, many of them poor. Some savage bursts of persecution occurred in the Netherlands, but the scale of this episode was unique in English experience. It provided invaluable material for Protestant propaganda.[5]

Elizabeth's first parliament, meeting in 1559, restored the royal supremacy. The queen was, however, recognized as 'supreme governor' rather than 'supreme head' of the Church in an attempt to make a woman's supremacy more palatable. The Act of Uniformity restored the Prayer Book of 1552, with some changes. In 1563 the Canterbury provincial convocation ratified a revised version of the 1553 articles of faith. After further fine tuning, they received statutory confirmation in the form of Thirty-nine Articles in 1571. The 'Elizabethan Settlement' was more conservative than that of 1552–3. Many Protestants regarded reformation, especially of worship, as a continuing process far from complete in 1553. The Queen soon made clear her unshakeable resolve not to move further. Elizabeth was probably at heart a more conservative sort of Protestant than her closest advisers. Initial resistance to the government's measures in the House of Lords was stronger than expected. Changes in the Prayer Book and the thirty-nine articles were possibly intended to appease conservative opinion at home and to avoid unnecessary provocation of Lutheran and even Catholic governments abroad.[6]

The Elizabethan Settlement left England's Church a curious hybrid, doctrinally aligned in key respects with the vanguard of 'Reformed' Churches, but liturgically much more conservative, and largely unreformed in government. It retained a land-holding episcopal hierarchy, cathedrals and church courts. Patronage, the right to nominate a clergyman to a 'benefice', mostly belonged not to congregations but to wealthy individuals and corporations. The crown's alienation of monastic property substantially increased the share of patronage belonging to the nobility and gentry.

Scotland's Reformation differed from England's above all in taking place without royal authority. Scotland had had few Lollards. Patrick Hamilton, burnt at St Andrews in 1528, became Britain's first evangelical martyr. During the 1530s and 1540s a small, widely scattered minority of nobles and lairds in the south-eastern Lowlands and Ayrshire became Protestants. Some heretics were burnt; many more fled abroad. The earl of Arran as governor of Scotland briefly favoured moderate reformation in 1543. Parliament permitted the reading of the Bible. George Wishart, strongly influenced by Swiss theology during his continental travels, preached widely in the Lowlands in 1544–6 before being tried and burnt in 1546. Protestantism received English support during Edward VI's reign. Bibles and prayer books were certainly useful, but assistance from Scotland's would-be conqueror was a mixed blessing. John Knox, who became a link between England, Scotland and Geneva, succeeded Wishart as Scotland's leading evangelist. Five lords 'professing Jesus Christ' drew up the First Band in December 1557, committing them to seeking moderate Protestant reforms. Joined by other nobles, they later headed as 'Lords of the Congregation', the more broadly based movement that developed after John Knox's return from Geneva in 1559.[7]

A well-attended parliament met in August 1560. It abolished the mass and papal jurisdiction and ratified a confession of faith quickly compiled by a small group of ministers led by Knox. This group was also responsible for the 'First Book of Discipline' partly approved by a thinly attended convention of greater nobles and lairds in January 1561. In December 1560 representatives of local congregations began to meet in what was later called the general assembly. In 1562 they endorsed the 'Book of Common Order', previously adapted from Calvin's liturgy by Knox for the use of British exiles in Geneva. By 1562 Knox and his colleagues had set out the framework of a kirk reformed in doctrine, worship and government. The most distinctive element of the Kirk's structure was the consistory or 'kirk session' that brought together ministers and elected elders drawn from the upper ranks of local society in the administration of discipline, education, alms and church maintenance. Kirk sessions, established in some places even before the Reformation parliament, spread rapidly thereafter. Reform was most successful at the grassroots. Where

Scottish kirk sessions worked effectively, underpinning religious instruction, regulating access to Communion, settling quarrels and imposing stiff penances on open sinners, they probably achieved a standard of Christian discipline unsurpassed in Europe. Regional synods began to meet in the 1560s. Ten or twelve superintendents were envisaged, but the full complement was never appointed. Scotland's was the first successful national reformation shaped by the example of the Genevan Church, and the only one initiated without the ruler's participation. The process was, however, an untidy one. The husk of the old Church remained. Many of the clergy, including some bishops, chose to co-operate with the new Kirk, but others did not. Only after Mary I's downfall in 1567 were vacant benefices reserved for ministers of the Reformed Church. The new Kirk was allocated only a small share of the income of the old Church in 1562, and it suffered continuing financial problems.[8]

Reformation and conflict in France and the Netherlands

In France, despite the early penetration of evangelical ideas, neither Francis I nor Henry II wavered in their Roman Catholic faith. Both kings viewed the papacy as a potential ally in their struggle with Charles V and had no grievance against it comparable with Henry VIII's. The crown was closely linked with the Church, 'eldest daughter' of the Roman Church, but proud of its own distinctive 'Gallican' traditions and liberties, a powerful bond of unity in a realm where local loyalties were strong. John Calvin and many other French Protestants found a refuge in Geneva, French-speaking but just outside French territory. From there a stream of newly trained pastors, books and letters of encouragement and advice contributed to the conversion of possibly 10 per cent of the French population by 1562. Support came above all from the nobility and from townsfolk, especially in the south of France. Some 1,200 local congregations were established. Their representatives met in local and national synods. The earliest national synod, convened in Paris in 1559, adopted a confession of faith drafted by Calvin, and a scheme of ecclesiastical discipline. These achievements, in face of a strong Catholic monarchy and intermittently severe persecution, showed a militancy and organizational capacity far more formidable than those displayed by the Protestant minority in England. Protestant support reached its high water mark in the early 1560s amid heady expectations that France might follow Scotland.

Catherine de' Medici, as regent for her son Charles IX, sought religious agreement, and in face of both sides' intransigence granted the Reformed Protestants ('Huguenots') limited freedom of worship. They now overplayed their hand, seizing churches and destroying images. The Guise family were to lead those many nobles who remained staunchly Catholic. The duke of Guise's killing of several Protestants gathered at Vassy in Champagne in 1562 provoked the first of a series of religious wars. Always a minority, the Huguenots were increasingly forced onto the defensive, especially after the Massacre of St Bartholomew in 1572, and had to accept that limited toleration or 'co-existence' was the most they could hope for. The crown's attempts at a settlement along these lines succeeded only when Henry IV, after accepting conversion to Catholicism as the price he had to pay for the crown, imposed the Edict of Nantes on an exhausted nation in 1598. Huguenots were allowed to worship freely in many carefully specified places without incurring civil disabilities and were granted numerous fortified towns and strongholds. Among the hereditary western European monarchies, France alone granted formal toleration to a religious minority, and then only after a long and terrible struggle.[9]

Several forms of religious dissent, including Anabaptism, had spread to the Netherlands, Britain's closest continental neighbour, before Reformed or Calvinist ideas arrived. The latter came both from the French-speaking southern provinces and from German towns, especially Emden, just across the border, where the Polish nobleman Jan Łaski established a Reformed church order in the 1540s with the ruler's support. Calvinist successes in Britain and France encouraged the formation of clandestine congregations in the early 1560s, especially in the southern Netherlands. They adopted in 1563 a confession of faith closely modelled on the French one of 1559. The suspension of the anti-heresy laws in 1566 was followed by an upsurge of open air preaching and a massive outbreak of iconoclasm powered by long-suppressed popular religious radicalism. Alba's subsequent brutal repression forced Protestants into outward conformity or exile. The first synod of the Netherlands Reformed Church met in 1571 at Emden.

The outbreak of the second phase of the Netherlands revolt in 1572, the liberation of the North, and later reconquest of the South, led to the establishment of the Reformed Church in the United Provinces and the crushing of Protestant dissent in the Spanish Netherlands. In the northern Netherlands the Reformed Church was the only one officially protected and promoted, but less than a tenth of the population even in the province of Holland belonged to it in 1587. It relied heavily on exclusion from Communion as a means of discipline. Although there was no official commitment to toleration after the revolt's early years, no very vigorous efforts were made to suppress Roman Catholic, Anabaptist or Lutheran congregations. The majority of the population of the Provinces were alleged to be Catholic in 1600.[10]

In eastern Europe Reformed Protestantism became the largest minority confession in Habsburg Hungary and Poland, and one of four recognized confessions in Transylvania. It spread even in the Empire itself, where the Palatinate became its foremost centre. This was contrary to the terms of the 1555 Peace of Augsburg and a source of tension and resentment.

Further reformation: England

Meanwhile, more militant Protestants sought further reformation in both England and Scotland. In England they shared the bishops' desire for a better qualified, preaching clergy, but also wanted to get rid of 'popish' elements such as the sign of the cross in baptism, kneeling at Communion and the surplice compulsory for clergy during church services. Vestments caused a first confrontation. Several London clergy who refused to wear the 'popish rag' were suspended in 1566. Elizabeth insisted on conformity. Some of her bishops disliked the surplice and other relics of Catholic worship, but most decided they were 'matters indifferent' that did not impair godly worship. They were shocked by what they thought needlessly bitter attacks by their uncompromising brethren who came to be called 'precisians' or 'puritans'. Some disillusioned English puritans became convinced that church government had to be changed both to make it conform more closely to the pattern of the apostolic Church and to achieve a more thorough reformation of worship. Thomas Cartwright set out the model of the Apostles' Church in lectures at Cambridge in 1570. John Field and Thomas Wilcox published *An Admonition to the Parliament* (of 1572) declaring that scriptural example required the introduction of a Presbyterian church order.

In 1576 Elizabeth, hypersensitive to any possibility that controversial issues might be aired in meetings of the clergy, ordered Edmund Grindal, archbishop of Canterbury, to suppress the 'exercises of prophesying'. These discussions of passages of Scripture by groups of clergy were intended to improve their scriptural knowledge and make them better preachers. Elizabeth had Grindal suspended from office when he objected. Grindal's successor John Whitgift, a more authoritarian figure, undertook a drive against puritan nonconformity in 1583. Organized in local conferences, puritan activists lobbied the parliaments of 1584–5 and 1586–7. There was sympathy with persecuted puritans, enhanced by the perceived danger from the 'papists', but little support for Presbyterian reforms. In 1587 the government confiscated a bill for a Presbyterian church order and Genevan worship that had been brought into the Commons. Biting satirical attacks on bishops in the clandestinely printed 'Marprelate Tracts' (1588–9) only discredited Presbyterians among more moderate Protestants. Thomas Cartwright and others were tried in 1591 for conspiring to impose Presbyterianism, but eventually released after acknowledging the royal supremacy.[11]

Much puritan energy, especially after the setbacks of 1587–91, went into less confrontational activities. With the connivance of sympathetic congregations, many ministers continued to use the Prayer Book selectively. Puritans also promoted strict observance of the Sabbath as a day set aside for religious duties. Puritan theology flowered during the 1580s and 1590s. The influential English Calvinists Dudley Fenner and William Perkins eloquently and ingeniously reconciled human effort and divine predestination. Despite the puritans' differences with Whitgift about church government and ceremonies, he defended the Calvinist beliefs that they shared. In response to an acrimonious controversy about predestination in Cambridge in 1595, Whitgift approved the 'Lambeth articles' that stated the doctrine of predestination in a much stricter and less ambiguous form than the thirty-nine articles. From eternity God had predestined a fixed number to salvation of his own will, not because he foresaw faith or good works on their part, and condemned the rest. However,

Elizabeth refused her consent to the articles. Many of the Church's most respected theologians shared these doctrines, but they were never officially adopted.[12]

An uncompromising minority of radicals separated from the Church. Their congregations were split by internal dissensions and some of their leaders were executed for sedition during the 1590s. Distinct from these groups was the Family of Love, founded by the Dutchman Hendrick Niklaes, who called on believers to strive for a perfection that would bring inward peace and joy. He wished the Family to operate *within* existing churches. Introduced into England during the 1550s, and difficult to detect, Familism became strongest in Cambridgeshire and the Isle of Ely.[13]

Further reformation: Scotland

From the 1560s onwards, many English churchmen admired the Scottish achievement of a more fully reformed Church. Sessions and synods offered English Presbyterians models for emulation. English puritans and Scottish reformers were natural allies. On the other hand, English church government offered a tempting pattern to those Scots politicians who wanted to use episcopal appointments to maintain crown control over the Church.[14] The episcopal office had never formally been abolished. In 1571 the regent Morton annoyed the Kirk by appointing an archbishop of St Andrews without consultation. An agreement was reached in 1572 about future episcopal appointments, but the results were unsatisfactory.

In 1574, Andrew Melville, the most prominent figure of the second phase of the Scottish Reformation, returned from Geneva to become principal of Glasgow University. He helped to draw up the *Second Book of Discipline*, largely a response to dissatisfaction with the existing framework of church government, which was formally adopted by the general assembly in 1581. This declared that ecclesiastical power flowed directly from God: the Kirk could not be subject to a temporal head. All ministers were of equal status. The assembly soon decided that no new bishops should be appointed. It drew up a scheme for fifty presbyteries (courts of ministers and elders from ten or twenty parishes), and the first thirteen were established. During the earl of Arran's brief seizure of power, parliament passed the 1584 'Black Acts', which approved bishops' disciplinary powers, forbade church assemblies without royal permission, and confirmed the royal supremacy and the competence of king and council to judge in spiritual matters. However, after Arran's downfall in 1585 the network of presbyteries was extended, and they received explicit recognition in the Golden Act passed by the parliament of 1592, though it also (crucially) kept for the king the right to decide the time and meeting place of general assemblies.

From 1586 James VI followed a conciliatory policy that reached its high point when in 1590, to rapturous applause from the general assembly, he praised Scotland's Church as the sincerest Kirk in the world and compared the

English communion service with the Catholic mass. He interceded with Elizabeth on behalf of English puritans in 1591. However, his leniency towards Catholics provoked increasingly harsh censure from kirkmen during the 1590s. In 1596, Andrew Melville, angered by James's response to a demand for action against the Catholic earls, famously told the king that there were two kingdoms in Scotland. James was only God's simple vassal, a member of the kingdom of Christ and the Kirk, not its head. But the intemperance of the criticism of James that reached its peak in 1596 assisted his subsequent assertion of his authority. Many kirkmen felt that confrontation had gone dangerously far. Thereafter, James cultivated the support of co-operative members of the assembly, and from 1600 once more began to appoint bishops after an interval of fifteen years.[15]

The impact of the British reformations

The British churches were exceptional in Protestant Europe in the extent to which their character was contested in internal struggles. In both England and Scotland reforming clergy had to work with Protestant rulers whose long-term aims differed from theirs in crucial respects. Elizabeth was concerned above all with obedience and outward conformity. Most of her bishops, let alone the puritans, were committed to active evangelization. The religion that took root in England was one in which visible symbols and ceremonies offered a reassuring element of continuity, and festivals and rites of passage provided occasions for conviviality. The creation of an academically qualified Protestant parish ministry took several decades. Increasing numbers of clergy were catechizing and preaching from the 1570s onwards, but many felt that their message fell on deaf ears.[16]

The impact of the Reformation was geographically uneven. London was one of the best-endowed preaching centres in Europe. Its exceptionally literate population provided a large readership for a varied and copious supply of religious literature. In England Protestantism put down its strongest roots in the south-east, in Scotland it flourished in the Lowlands. It was less successful in the English uplands and Scottish Highlands. Everywhere the support of local noblemen and gentlemen was important for the progress of reformation. Some provincial towns in both countries came to be known as Protestant strongholds, and in England some areas of rural industry containing clusters of literate craftsmen also provided fertile soil for Protestantism.

In Celtic language areas, Protestant churches achieved sharply contrasting degrees of success. Several religious books were published in Welsh from 1547 onwards, including the Book of Common Prayer and the New Testament by 1567, the whole Bible by 1588. Welsh bishops William Salesbury, Richard Davies and William Morgan were active participants in the project of scriptural translation. The Reformation helped to combine the preservation of Welsh cultural identity with integration into the Tudor State. The famous early separatist John Penry was Welsh, but Protestant dissent remained a negligible problem.[17]

Archibald Campbell, earl of Argyll, one of the foremost Scottish noblemen, a leader of the revolution of 1559–60, promoted the Reformation in the Highlands. His *protégé* John Carswell, bishop of Argyll, published the Book of Common Order in Gaelic together with a catechism in 1567. Yet the Bible was not published in Scottish Gaelic till 1801. Instead, clergy translated passages for oral transmission.[18] Most Highland parishes lacked qualified ministers long after the beginning of the Reformation, however. Few kirk sessions were established there before 1600.

Nowhere in Europe were official religious policies more conspicuously unsuccessful than in Ireland. Failure was not inevitable. Elizabeth's reign was a time of missed opportunities. Most of the livings in the Irish Church were miserably poor, and the great majority of the clergy were ill educated and quite unequal to the task of Protestant evangelization. Few effective bishops were appointed. Trinity College Dublin, the first Irish university college, was not founded till 1592, and then primarily served English Ireland. A Gaelic catechism was published in 1571, but although Elizabeth granted money for a Gaelic Bible in 1563, the New Testament was not published until 1603. By the 1580s Protestantism was coming to be associated with oppressive government policies and 'new English' intrusion into Irish affairs.[19]

In continental Europe, as in Britain, the Reformation faced serious difficulties in the countryside where most people lived, including an initial shortage of clergy and unavoidable reliance on time-serving former Catholic priests. The exacting work of inculcating Protestant belief was much less exhilarating than the initial attacks on the shortcomings of the Catholic Church. In the early days, ballads, plays and broadsheet caricatures had been used to attack 'popish' abuses, but once the Protestant churches were established, they tended to eschew these popular media. All too often Protestant sermons passed over the heads of their audiences. Theological disputes among Lutherans absorbed valuable energy. Reports on the effectiveness of basic religious instruction reveal marked contrasts between different areas.[20]

Catholicism and the counter-Reformation

Meanwhile, after its initial defeats, the Roman Catholic Church consolidated its position and began to recover lost ground. The Council of Trent (1545–8, 1551–2, 1562–4) introduced some important reforms, emphasized the pastoral role of bishops and decreed that every diocese should have a seminary for the training of clergy. New missionary orders set to work. The Jesuits, authorized by papal bull in 1540, were by far the most important of these, distinguished by their innovative educational programme, implemented in a rapidly expanding network of uniquely successful schools and colleges. The Catholic pastoral campaign included various familiar forms of devotion, used a wide variety of media, including print, ceremonies and visual arts, and emphasized the importance of simple, straightforward preaching.[21]

Close co-operation between the spiritual and secular arms made possible a rigorous repression of religious dissent and heresy. The chief weapons were the Inquisition and an index of prohibited books (first published in Spain in 1551, in Rome in 1559). The Spanish Inquisition, founded in 1478 in order to deal with backsliding Muslim and Jewish converts, was a council acting with papal authority but under royal control. An Inquisition was established at Rome in 1542 in order to counter Protestantism, which had infiltrated most parts of Italy without being adopted by any government. Efforts to strengthen Catholicism in the Empire, especially Bavaria and the Habsburg lands, began in the 1550s. The Jesuits played a leading part. Many of the Austrian nobility, allowed freedom of worship by the Emperor Maximilian II (1564–76) and his brother Charles, were Lutheran by 1580. But lack of effective organization and disagreements among the Lutheran clergy weakened their resistance to more determined efforts to restore Catholic dominance from the 1590s. Protestantism had made rapid advances in Poland, but was weakened by its own divisions. From the 1560s the Jesuits first helped to consolidate Catholicism among the majority of the nobility who had never abandoned it, and later achieved growing numbers of reconversions.[22]

Catholicism survived in most parts of England after 1559, and many priests, some of whom had managed to hold on to their livings in the established Church, continued to say mass. Partial or occasional conformity was a common strategy for both clergy and laity. The government did not at first press conservatives too hard, hoping to assimilate them in time. Several clergy had gone into exile, and some of these defended their Church in print. Englishmen who had gone abroad to be trained as seminary priests started to return as missionaries from 1574 onwards. The government responded to a series of internal and external threats with increasingly severe measures. An act of 1581 greatly increased fines for refusing to come to church services or attending mass and made it treason to convert or be converted to Roman Catholicism. A further act of 1585 declared all Roman Catholic priests ordained since 24 June 1559 to be traitors. Between 1581 and 1603, 191 Catholics were executed, of whom 131 were priests. Many more laity suffered fines or imprisonment of different degrees of harshness than suffered the ultimate penalty. This was a campaign of intermittent and occasionally brutal harassment rather than systematic extermination. The missionary clergy concentrated their efforts on the gentry and nobility. Catholicism tended to die out in areas of the country where it had initially been strong among the middling and lower ranks of society but lacked upper class leadership. Some Catholics invited persecution through their refusal to compromise; others behaved discreetly and continued to give the crown useful service. Many tried to distinguish between their religious duties and their allegiance. Only a small minority engaged in plots, while many more looked forward to a change of regime.[23]

The survival of popular Catholic observances was especially widespread in Wales. Missionary priests failed to exploit this potential reservoir of support because of the remoteness or poverty of so much of the interior. Welsh Catholics were heavily concentrated in the border counties, especially in Monmouthshire, where the conservative earls of Worcester offered some protection, and Flintshire, both close to areas where English Catholicism was strong.[24]

The local power of some Scottish magnates enabled them to maintain pockets of Catholicism so long as they did not defy the government openly. Visitors to Mary I's household could attend the mass celebrated there. The Jesuits sent to Scotland in the 1580s and the 1590s operated under the protection of Catholic nobles whose activities James VI partly tolerated for political reasons. Before 1603, however, the Highlands and Western Isles were neglected.[25]

In the Old English parts of Ireland attendance at mass remained widespread after 1559. Old English Catholics began to reject Elizabeth's ecclesiastical supremacy while protesting their loyalty to her as monarch. Merchants started sending their sons to continental Catholic universities and seminaries. Waterford parish clergy were already helping to support students at Louvain in 1564. In Gaelic Ireland Catholic bishops continued to function: three attended the Council of Trent. Many monasteries survived, especially in Ulster, where Jesuits were active from the 1560s.[26]

Around 1600 zealous British Protestants had reason to be pleased with the progress made in the restoration of 'true religion' since the 1530s. Yet the international situation was full of menace. Protestant advance had been checked. Protestant ranks were in disarray. British Protestants, disunited though they were in matters of worship and church order, were united in their hostility to the papacy and papistry. The Catholic revival sharpened this hostility and added an edge of fear. Critics of the papacy had long identified the pope with Antichrist, a usurper who would exploit Christ's authority to deceive his people. A 1536 statute extinguishing papal authority accused the pope of distorting Scripture's meaning so as to establish dominion over Christian people, usurping the king's rightful supremacy, robbing England of treasure and seducing its inhabitants into superstitious and mistaken opinions.[27] Persecution of the true Church was an old charge given new prominence by Mary's proceedings, exhaustively documented in John Foxe's *Acts and Monuments* (1563). The 1572 Massacre of St Bartholomew seemed to confirm papists' propensity for bloodthirsty cruelty. Protestants saw Pius V's 1570 bull excommunicating Elizabeth I as a particularly dangerous exercise of usurped authority. Catholic involvement was perceived in all the most threatening plots and rebellions against the Elizabethan regime. Did not the deaths of William of Orange and Henry III and the Babington plot in the 1580s underline papists' readiness to resort to assassination? Catholicism stood accused of appealing to the senses rather than the mind, of cultivating and exploiting groundless fears for profit and domination and of pandering to a deep-seated, idolatrous human desire to cherish, trust and worship the visible and tangible. British reformers saw all around them, among populations only recently deprived of Catholic worship, evidence of deep-rooted attachment to the 'dregs of popery'.

6

POPULATION GROWTH AND NEW HORIZONS

Populations

Europe's population rose by more than a quarter between 1500 and 1600 after a long period of demographic decline and stagnation following savage attacks of the plague in the fourteenth century. According to recent estimates, population rose faster in England than elsewhere in Europe, by some 80 per cent, from approximately 2,300,000 in 1500 to some 4,162,000 by 1601. By then it was fast approaching its probable 1315 peak of 4.25–4.5 million. Wales possibly had more than 200,000 people in 1500, but the scale of its demographic growth in this period is very uncertain. Scotland's population, approximately 700,000 in 1500, almost certainly grew, but it is impossible to say by how much. Ireland's probably increased from approximately 750,000 to approximately 1,000,000 in 1600. On the European mainland, the area of the modern Netherlands and Belgium may have contained about 2,350,000 people in 1500. According to the most widely cited estimates, France, with 16,400,000 people, Germany, with 12,000,000, and Italy, with 10,500,000, were the most populous countries in western Europe, while Spain and Portugal combined had 7,800,000. The northern Netherlands experienced the highest growth – possibly 58 per cent. Germany's population possibly grew by a third, Italy's by around a quarter, Spain's by a fifth, but France's may have increased by only 13–16 per cent, less than that of any other major western European country. The greater part of England's population growth occurred after 1550, but the French population, after savage civil strife, was hardly any larger in 1600 than in 1550.[1]

England experienced fewer checks to demographic growth than did most continental countries. First, her own territory was almost entirely free of the wars that devastated so many areas of the continent, including northern Italy during the first third of the century, and France and the Netherlands from the 1560s onwards. Secondly, although climatic deterioration affected much of western Europe, including Britain, in the 1590s, it hit the large semi-arid areas of Italy and Spain especially hard, resulting in widespread famine. Finally, while no part of Europe escaped epidemic disease, including the dreaded plague, it was marching armies and large grain shipments imported to alleviate famine that often brought disease in their wake. In northern Castile, which had completely escaped the ravages of warfare, plague and typhus following hard on the heels of dearth in the 1590s had terrible effects.[2]

Prices rose substantially in the sixteenth century. The pressure of a growing population that outstripped economic growth is now thought to be the main explanation. In England the average prices of grains increased nearly sixfold between the 1490s and the 1590s, and those of industrial goods two-and-a-half times, while agricultural wages little more than doubled. Prices of essential foods increased fastest, while the abundance of labour depressed real wages. Though population growth was the main driver of price inflation, increases in the money supply probably contributed to it. New supplies of precious metals came first from central Europe during the later fifteenth and early sixteenth centuries, and subsequently from Spanish America. In 1544–51 English rulers raised revenue and increased money supply by greatly reducing the coinage's precious metal content. However, it has proved difficult to estimate changes in the money supply with precision, let alone calculate their effects.[3]

England's population growth differed from that of other countries not merely in scale, but also in distribution. Around 1520, the estimated English urban population, i.e. people living in towns with 5,000 inhabitants, was 5–7 per cent of the total, compared with nearly 30 per cent in the Netherlands, nearly 25 per cent in Italy, just under 20 per cent in Spain and about 9 per cent in France. During the sixteenth century, the urban population grew by between 139 and 168 per cent in England, far faster than in any other country in Europe (though it remained relatively small). The growth of England's urban sector was distinctive not only in its speed but also in the fact that it was concentrated to an extraordinary degree in one prime centre: London.[4]

Cities, towns and industry

London and Westminster shared the functions of England's capital city. The population of the conurbation, including its suburbs, may have grown from 40,000–50,000 in 1500 to about 200,000 in 1600, with most of the increase occurring after 1550. Deaths outnumbered births in London as in all great cities. It depended on immigration to maintain its population, let alone increase it. A uniquely wide range of employment and relatively high wages attracted thousands of predominantly young immigrants every year.[5]

London was a centre of government, commerce and industry. The Exchequer and the law courts were in Westminster, the Mint, Customs House and Armouries in or near the Tower of London. Henry VIII greatly extended Whitehall as his main palace. He established naval dockyards at Rotherhithe. A surge in lawsuits in the Westminster courts, thirty years of exceptional parliamentary activity (1529–59), the expansion of the royal household and the scramble for crown patronage all brought business and great numbers of new seasonal or temporary residents to the capital. London had no university, but a legal training at the Inns of Court could be combined with a broader gentlemanly education. The capital became an increasingly important focus for the social life of the nobility and gentry. Sources of entertainment and instruction included court ceremony and spectacle, over a hundred pulpits, especially at Paul's Cross, and England's first commercial theatres. London also contained the country's largest concentration of luxury shops and artists' workshops.[6]

Antwerp's dominance of the north European trading network had increased London's share of English trade. The Merchants Adventurers who handled London's Antwerp trade included most of her richest men, all members of one of her twelve great livery companies. The concentration of mercantile wealth in London facilitated the formation of several new commercial companies between 1555 and 1601. London was also England's chief manufacturing centre. Cloth-making, leather-working, silk-weaving, brewing, ship-building and ship-repairs, printing, soap-making, sugar-refining, glass manufacture and brass gun founding all expanded rapidly or were first introduced there during this century. The suburbs, where industries could develop outside the city's jurisdiction, achieved the lion's share of London's growth between 1560 and 1600. Many immigrant craftsmen settled, often bringing valuable techniques and experience. Coal, imported from the north-east in rapidly increasing quantities, began to be adopted in a growing range of industrial processes.[7]

The relationship between crown and city was close and important to both partners. Customs collected in London provided 16 per cent of Elizabeth I's revenue. London merchants lent money to the crown and helped it repay its foreign debts. Ministers from Wolsey onwards took steps to ensure the capital's food supplies, monitor and contain plague outbreaks and curb London vagrancy. Governments – more especially those of Henry VII and Henry VIII – could be insensitive and heavy-handed in their dealings with the London oligarchy, especially in fiscal matters. But after 1550, governments consulted merchants about commercial policy more frequently and rewarded their co-operation with privileges and concessions. Elizabeth I underlined the importance of the relationship when she visited the City's new Exchange in 1570, and had it proclaimed 'The Royal Exchange'.[8]

Merchants were at the summit of society in London and other cities. Below them were retailers, independent craftsmen, employed journeymen, apprentices, domestic servants and, at the bottom, unskilled and casual workers. Admission to an occupational guild, craft or company (usually including both makers and sellers, employers and employed) entitled the member to work in the city. Charters granted by the crown or other lords generally concentrated effective power in the hands of a mayor and a bench of aldermen or similar officials. But urban ruling dynasties rarely endured, and the ranks of the business community were constantly renewed by the recruitment of outsiders.

Seven provincial towns, headed by Norwich, Bristol and York, had populations over 5,000 c.1520; about a dozen in 1600. They included the foremost ports and centres of cloth manufacture. All the largest towns of 1520, facing problems of adaptation and re-orientation, either grew more slowly than the national population or actually shrank. About 100 towns probably had between about 1,500 and 5,000 inhabitants around 1500. These middling towns possessed a relatively large range of crafts and services. Many also had a leading industry. They included most of the county towns and cathedral cities and a number of ports, as well as both university cities. Most contained schools, and an increasing number of almshouses and town halls. Almost all were meeting places for royal, ecclesiastical or municipal courts.[9]

Edinburgh, the biggest city in Scotland, probably grew faster than the country as a whole, but with a population of 18,000 at most in 1560 it may have been less than three times as large as Scotland's next largest city. Frequent sessions of parliament, the convention of royal burghs and the general assembly underlined Edinburgh's status as capital city during the later sixteenth century. The peripatetic royal court spent increasing periods at Holyrood. The establishment of the Court of Session by James V and the foundation of a new university in 1583 contributed to the prominence of lay professional people in the city's affairs. Luxury trades serving the court and aristocracy became more important. Edinburgh had the largest share of Scotland's overseas trade, paying 60 per cent of the customs in 1500, 72 per cent in the 1590s. She was, however, more directly subject to royal power than London. The crown repeatedly intervened in Edinburgh's affairs, and from 1553 to 1578 nominated the burgh's provost.[10]

Scotland's three major provincial towns, Dundee, Perth and Aberdeen, may have been the only ones with more than 2,000 inhabitants in 1560. There were forty-six 'royal burghs' in 1560, fifty-eight in 1640. The convention of royal burghs met regularly to safeguard their interests and decide how their tax burden should be shared. Lords also founded burghs in substantial numbers from the fifteenth century onwards. Their merchants, unlike those of the royal burghs, could trade only within the burgh. Some of them later gained royal burgh status, but most of them were small places. Provosts presided over the town council and 'head courts' in Scottish burghs. In several towns powerful merchant guilds regulated trade and industrial activities.[11]

In Ireland, Dublin, the seat of vice-regal government, containing some 5,000–10,000 people, was the foremost of the five Irish towns, all of them ports, which had populations of over 2,000 in 1500. Its commercial primacy was not as marked as that of London or Edinburgh. The foundation of Trinity College (1592) enhanced its importance as an educational centre.[12]

On the European mainland, Constantinople, capital of the Ottoman superpower, and a great commercial and industrial centre, had a far larger population than any other city. But in western Europe, London, which had been less populous than at least eight other cities in 1500, had by 1600 outgrown all others except Paris and Naples. Few other European capital cities matched London's combination of several different functions or its dominant role in national life. The population of Paris grew more slowly than London's, possibly from 100,000 to 220,000 between 1500 and 1600. The seat of government, administration, sovereign law courts and France's leading university, Paris contained royal palaces and numerous fine noble residences and was also a major centre of luxury goods production. However, it was not, like London, a seaport whose situation facilitated government interest in overseas trade. The city suffered badly during the civil wars, especially under siege in 1589–90. Naples, the biggest city in western Europe, whose population possibly increased from 150,000 to 281,000, was like London, its kingdom's foremost port and seat of government, as well as a major industrial centre. However, Naples was a subject kingdom. The city's external trade was largely in the hands of outsiders. Noble landowners dominated municipal government and social life, spending in the city much of the income from their rural estates.[13]

Madrid, Philip II's choice as Spain's capital, was a poorly situated, parasitic city of bureaucrats, patronage-seeking nobility and large numbers of mendicant poor. Lisbon anticipated London's later position as the booming port capital of a global commercial empire. But Portugal was a smaller country than England. Her empire was more vulnerable to foreign predators, and much more heavily dependent on foreign merchants and entrepreneurs for investment and distribution of its exports.[14]

The great city-states of Italy faced major challenges with varying degrees of success. Venice was Europe's principal supplier of eastern goods including silks, perfumes, pearls, ceramics, dyestuffs, cotton, various fine metal wares and, above all, spices. Her Arsenal was a unique combination of dockyards, factories and storehouses. The variety of her industries was unrivalled. During the later sixteenth century, however, she faced a growing range of predatory competitors and costly wars with Turkey. Venetian aristocrats increasingly withdrew from trade. The city may have had nearly 196,000 inhabitants in 1574. A catastrophic plague in 1575–7 sharply reduced her population, which never recovered its previous level. Genoa, much smaller than Venice, but once her chief rival in the Levant, had become closely involved with Spain and Portugal instead of the increasingly dangerous eastern Mediterranean. Her merchants traded with Seville, invested in Atlantic enterprises and controlled much of Sicilian commerce. Her financiers became the Spanish crown's principal bankers.[15]

The exceptional pattern of British urbanization stands out in comparison with Europe. In all the more populous European countries there existed, apart from any 'capital' city, several centres that were larger than any British provincial town. Many of the biggest were ports. Seville enjoyed a dominant position in Spain's American trade, which in turn stimulated industries in the city and the development of agriculture in its hinterland. By 1600, after rapid growth, it had surpassed the other Spanish ports of Barcelona and Valencia, both larger than Seville in 1500. In the north, Rouen, France's third most populous city and foremost port, was both the hub of a rural industrial hinterland and a financial centre, but it suffered severely during the civil wars. Early in the century, Antwerp became northern Europe's foremost port and then her chief money market. Italian firms in Antwerp taught northerners advanced business practices. The city suffered lasting damage during the Dutch revolt. Amsterdam later replaced Antwerp as the leading city of the Netherlands, and its population more than quadrupled during the century. Hamburg, some way short of 50,000 inhabitants in 1600, became Germany's most populous and important port. Danzig was the greatest of all Baltic cities, with a population of about 50,000 in 1600, largely German, but subject to the Polish crown.[16]

The biggest clusters of inland commercial and industrial cities were in northern Italy and the Netherlands. Northern Italian cities were the chief producers of silks, ceramics, fine leather goods, glass, gold and silver work, weapons, armour and a wide variety of other metal goods. The Netherlands cities made woollen cloth, linen and tapestry, and developed such newer industries as sugar-refining and soap-making. Liège produced all sorts of metalwork, including armaments. Local estates, *parlements* and fiscal courts helped to give several French cities an importance unmatched by any provincial capital in the more centralized English state with the possible exception of York. The fairs of Lyons attracted Italian bankers who arranged loans for the crown, though royal difficulties and the civil wars eventually destroyed their confidence. More enduring was the city's importance in printing and silk manufacture. Augsburg and Nuremberg produced clocks, firearms, gold and silver work, and bronze cannon. Spain's industries included cloth manufacture in Segovia and Valladolid, silks in Valencia and Granada, metal goods in Bilbao, Barcelona and Toledo, ceramics in Valencia and Seville and leather work in Cordoba.

Several continental cities were ruled by oligarchies with a strong hereditary element and aristocratic or quasi-aristocratic status. By contrast, the London corporation was predominantly recruited from outside the city altogether, bringing in new blood. Wealthy 'regent' or 'patrician' families that achieved some dynastic continuity governed the greater Netherlands and German cities. Occupational guilds regulated industries and ensured employers' control while also tending to protect small-scale workshop production. But patricians and external rulers limited their role in urban government or excluded them from it altogether. Venice was the outstanding example of a city governed by an urban nobility. The proportion of the nobility living in cities was higher than average in Spain as well as Italy and the Netherlands.[17]

Rural industrial activity was widespread in Europe. Mineral extraction mostly took place in the countryside. Motives for manufacturing there included freedom from urban guild restrictions, the availability of cheap labour and the proximity of raw materials, fuel or running water to drive machinery. Many country dwellers turned to manufacturing during slacker periods of agricultural activity or to supplement the earnings from holdings subdivided during a period of rising population. Rural industries were often closely linked with towns that they supplied with materials or with goods for finishing. Much rural industry depended on entrepreneurs who bought what workers produced or paid them for the work 'put out' to them. The rural manufacture of woollen cloth was especially widespread in Britain, and also common on the continent. The most important rural industries in Britain besides cloth-making were the mining of coal, tin, lead and iron, quarrying, construction and the making of goods of wood, metals and leather. Widespread continental rural industries included the mining of coal in the southern Netherlands and north-west Germany, of copper and silver in central Europe and of iron in several countries; metalworking, glass-making and the manufacture of linen, canvas, lace and silk yarn.[18]

The sixteenth century witnessed a considerable diversification of English industry, including the manufacture of various new fabrics, gunpowder, glass and paper. This was partly the result of a government policy designed to reduce England's dependence on imports and increase employment at home. Immigrants from Europe brought skills new to England. Iron was smelted in the Weald (where England's first blast furnace was built in 1496) and in South Wales. Wealden manufacturers, with royal encouragement, progressed from making cannon balls to cannon themselves in 1543–4. England soon became the foremost European producer and exporter of cast-iron cannon. To make superior bronze cannon, however, she needed copper. This was mined and smelted in Cumberland and Cornwall during Elizabeth's reign, but the industry's relative success was short-lived. On the other hand lead extraction in the Mendips and Derbyshire expanded substantially. The use of coal as a domestic and industrial fuel, aided by closeness to the sea, was more widespread in Britain than anywhere else in Europe. Coal shipments from north-eastern ports grew fivefold between 1508–11 and 1595–1600; coal imports into London grew ninefold between 1549–50 and 1605–6.[19]

Trade

The bulk of England's exports consisted of cloth. Sales of high-quality, soft-textured broadcloths and somewhat coarser kerseys rose sharply to their peak in the 1550s, remaining on an undulating plateau thereafter. During Elizabeth's reign England began to find markets for the lighter 'new draperies' whose manufacture was growing rapidly. Relatively small quantities of tin, lead, skins and fish made up the bulk of her remaining exports. England's imports were far more diverse than her exports. A London list of 1559–60 includes linens, canvas, wines, dyestuffs, oils, fruits, silk fabrics, iron, sugar, spices, metal goods, hops and flax.[20]

Antwerp was the major channel for England's early-sixteenth-century foreign trade. Then, in 1550–1, signs of glut in that market coincided with the growing hostility of the Emperor Charles V. Unpleasant awareness of the disadvantages of excessive dependence on Antwerp prompted the first serious efforts to diversify England's trade pattern. There followed voyages to Morocco (1551) and Guinea (1553), and an attempt to discover a north-eastern passage to the Far East (1553–4), which instead resulted in a new trade with Russia. Edward's and Mary's governments reduced the privileges of foreign merchants who had hitherto carried a substantial share of English exports. England's trade with the Baltic increased, and from 1573 her merchants began to return to the Mediterranean after a period of withdrawal. Disruptions of trade with the Netherlands from 1563 onwards also resulted in the establishment of alternative outlets for England's main trade with northern Europe.[21]

During the very period when a secure and highly profitable short-haul connection with Antwerp discouraged English exploration, the Iberian powers had with astonishing speed established transoceanic commercial and colonial empires. In the 1490s Portuguese captains had begun to bring Asian spices round the Cape. Portugal soon possessed a string of outposts reaching as far as the Moluccas and a substantial plantation in Brazil. After an initial shock, the Mediterranean spice trade recovered. Venice retained her leading position in it until around 1600. Spices brought to Portugal instead found their chief markets away from the Mediterranean, above all in Antwerp. Within little more than forty years after Columbus's arrival in the Caribbean, the Spanish had conquered much of central and south America, including Mexico (1519–21) and Peru (1531–6). The new empire soon yielded many commodities, including precious metals, dyestuffs and sugar. The manpower and supplies needed for the first stages of conquest came mainly from Spain, but Genoese and German businessmen and adventurers assisted in America's exploitation.

The effects of American precious metals on the Spanish economy are somewhat obscure. Spanish prices had already started to rise beforehand, and continued to do so after the collapse of precious metal imports. However, the opening of fabulously rich silver mines at Potosì in 1545 was followed by a rise in the exchange rates between Spanish and foreign currencies that probably gave imports a competitive edge. Spain notoriously sucked in goods from other countries, to the detriment of her own industries.[22]

France had challenged Iberian dominance in America, especially from the 1530s onwards. Intrepid Breton and Norman captains attacked Caribbean trade, explored Canada and attempted to establish colonies in Florida and Brazil. Huguenots were prominent in these ventures. The civil wars in France eventually stifled them. Only then did England become a major interloper in America. John Hawkins made three voyages to sell slaves to Spanish colonists in 1562, 1564 and 1567. Francis Drake sailed to plunder the Spanish Caribbean three times in 1570–2 and, together with Huguenots and escaped slaves, successfully ambushed a treasure train on the Isthmus of Panama in 1573. In 1577–80 he achieved the second circumnavigation of the globe. In 1585 and 1587 the first abortive attempts were made to establish English colonies in what is now North Carolina. Several English attacks on the trade and settlements of the Caribbean and Spanish Main took place from 1585 onwards.[23]

The diversification of England's trade, the increasing share of it in English merchants' hands, the growing importance of long distance routes and the need to build strong, well-armed ships for dangerous waters such as the Caribbean and the Mediterranean powerfully stimulated England's shipbuilding industry. Its shipping tonnage possibly rose from 50,000 to 67,000 tons between 1572 and 1582. The numbers of new ships, mostly built for

Londoners, the majority over 200 tons, grew rapidly during the war with Spain. London merchant syndicates, often working in alliance with 'predatory gentry', especially from the south-west, provided the necessary capital for the corsairs who plundered Iberian trade. Captures of valuable cargoes of pepper, sugar and dyestuffs made enormous profits for investors, yet cheapened these commodities, enhancing England's appetite for them.[24]

The eclipse of France and the troubles of the Netherlands gave England the incentives and the opportunity to challenge the maritime dominance of Spain and Portugal. However, the Dutch had hardly won their independence before they became formidable rivals in every area where English merchants had expanded or initiated trade during their years of opportunity: Russia, the Baltic, the Mediterranean and America. They already took the lion's share of North Sea herring stocks and carried large quantities of Baltic grain and timber. Immigrant merchants, especially southern Netherlanders and Portuguese Jews, supplied an expertise in 'rich trades' that the Dutch had hitherto lacked. The imposition of a Spanish embargo in 1598 stimulated Dutch efforts to open up a direct trade with the Far East before the belated foundation of the English East India Company in 1600.[25]

Scotland, meanwhile, had not enjoyed great commercial success. Cloth exports doubled between the 1470s and the 1530s, but rarely amounted to more than 4 per cent of the English total. They plummeted during the Rough Wooing, and never recovered their 1540 level before 1600. Total exports rose by a third between 1558–62 and 1593–7, artificially assisted by debasements of the currency, but barely reached the level of 1540, though they now included increasing quantities of salt and coal, the former greatly boosted by disruption of the Dutch salt trade with Spain. Scotland imported from Norway and the Baltic essential timber, iron, flax, hemp, tar and emergency grain supplies, from France salt, cloth, weapons and prodigious quantities of wine, and from the Netherlands diverse manufactures, cloth, dyestuffs and victuals. England became an increasingly important trading partner, providing Scotland with manufactured goods and receiving salt, fish, coal and other commodities in return.[26]

Agriculture

Only substantial increases in agricultural production could maintain the standards of living Europe had enjoyed in 1500. However, according to a recent comparative essay, agricultural output actually fell over much of Europe between 1500 and 1600. England and the northern Netherlands were both exceptions to this trend. According to these calculations, however, England's achievement was not particularly impressive, because an agricultural workforce that possibly grew by nearly two-thirds – more in proportional terms than that of any other country – achieved an output increase of less than a quarter.[27]

The foremost requirement of a growing population was an increased output of bread grains. For most of the century, price trends encouraged farmers to grow more corn. Between 1489 and 1563 several English statutes forbade the conversion of tilled land to pasture. Further acts passed from 1555 gave an added incentive to grow corn by permitting exports in times of abundance. Certainly the acreage under the plough was extended. However, big changes in existing patterns of land use could only be accomplished gradually. Crop rotations that incorporated a fallow period, typically every third year, and the addition of animal dung, were the basic means of maintaining fertility. In the mixed farming areas that covered much of England, arable and animal husbandry were complementary. 'Convertible' husbandry, the alternating use of land for arable and pasture, was one means of enriching the soil that spread after c.1560. Another was the addition of marl, lime, chalk, sand, ashes or seaweed. London's growing demand began to influence nearby counties, promoting agricultural specialization, the consolidation of market-oriented farms and intensive market gardening in her immediate vicinity.[28]

Although England's agricultural output growth failed to keep pace with her population, outright starvation was rare except after the poor harvests of 1596–8, and even then was limited to remoter pastoral areas, especially in the northwest. Imports from the Baltic helped meet the needs of London's poor. Famines were more frequent and widespread in Scotland. Cultivation was extended and in some places intensified as population grew, and some efforts were made to improve soil fertility, but its less developed economy and weaker market integration left its poor more vulnerable to the effects of harvest failure.[29]

The southern Netherlands practised the most efficient agriculture in Europe. According to one estimate output per agricultural worker there was nearly 50 per cent higher than in England in 1500. A dense cluster of cities created a high demand for agricultural produce and, together with cattle, copious supplies of manure to enrich the land. In the northern Netherlands, huge areas were drained and protected from flooding by dikes and canals. Reclamation accelerated markedly after the revolt. Meanwhile, Poland and its Baltic neighbours became Europe's chief granary. The amount of grain exported from the Vistula increased twenty-one-fold between 1491–2 and 1618. Reliable and plentiful supplies of Baltic grain encouraged a shift in the Netherlands into more profitable dairy products (in which a major export trade developed), as well as meat, fodder crops, flax, hemp and hops. The north Italian plain was another highly fertile, heavily urbanized area. Irrigation and assiduous manuring allowed a great variety of crops to be cultivated. Food supply was increased by the introduction of maize, a high-yield crop. Consortia of landowners undertook reclamation of marsh and waste. Agriculture also flourished in some fertile coastal areas of Spain and southern Italy.[30]

Over much of Spain and Italy, however, relatively low rainfall and intermittent droughts set limits to output growth. Methods used to provision the big cities included price controls, pre-emptive purchases and prohibitions on export, which discouraged producers and could result in hoarding. When famine struck, cities like Naples had to import grain from overseas. Hordes of country dwellers, impoverished by exorbitant rents and taxes, swarmed into the cities to seek relief. France and Spain were harder hit by famines than England. In both countries, but especially in Spain, there were greater natural obstacles to the internal movement of corn. The wars of religion had devastating effects on French agriculture during the last quarter of the century.[31]

Farmers

Most English and Welsh householders were tenant farmers. In England and much of Wales the manor was the basic unit of territorial lordship. It consisted of the lord's demesne, the tenants' holdings in the arable fields (subject to the same crop rotation), meadow, woodland and common pasture. Sixteenth-century population growth gradually altered the balance between tenant and landlord in the latter's favour. Landlords were able to raise rents on land under their own direct control, and entry fines on customary holdings. Tenants with growing numbers of children to provide for might try to do so by burdening their farms with bequests to non-inheriting children, by dividing them or by sub-letting parts of them. The numbers of small farmers increased, facing growing pressures, and eventually many, burdened with debts, had to relinquish their holdings and become cottagers or landless labourers. These developments were especially characteristic of some mixed farming areas, especially in the south-east. The 'yeomen', occupants of larger farms, especially if they were freehold or held on a long lease, were the best able to benefit from a growing population's demand for food, and to buy land from their less fortunate neighbours. It was prosperous yeomen, along with gentry, who were able to afford imported fruits and fabrics, home produced commodities such as glass, and grammar schooling for their children. In pastoral regions small farmers benefited to varying degrees from weaker manorial control, more extensive commons and greater possibilities of combining some other employment with agriculture.

Some Scottish tenant farmers enjoyed comparatively secure leases, but the majority were probably tenants-at-will, holding from year to year. Rents were largely payable in kind, often as a fixed share of the crop, and might be supplemented by various labour services. In Highland Scotland most clansmen were tenants-at-will of the chief or more important clan members. The precarious situation of many Scottish tenants was offset by 'kindness', the landlord's readiness to allow the tenant's heir to succeed to the holding. During the sixteenth century, the Church and the crown granted large amounts of land in hereditary 'feu ferme', a very favourable form of tenure. The more substantial tenants benefited most.[32]

Over much of Europe, the terms of leases became less favourable for the tenant farmer as the population increased. Tenant indebtedness was a widespread and growing problem, worsened by church tithes, royal taxes and, in Castile, by the crown's sale of much land previously regarded as common, which many peasants purchased only with the help of loans. Larger landholders and city dwellers snapped up land surrendered by farmers in both Castile and France during the ruinous 1590s.[33]

In much of eastern Europe, especially in Poland, nobles restricted their tenants' freedom of movement. Landowners exacted heavier labour services that enabled them to profit from western demand for grain, and took more land under direct management, but by 1600 these measures were not leading to a commensurate increase in yield. In the north-western Netherlands, in contrast, seigneurial control was weak. A high proportion of farms were relatively small but intensively cultivated to meet the growing demands of prosperous cities. An enormous variety of alternative employments lessened the problem of providing for non-inheriting children.[34]

Rural economic change sometimes provoked serious disorders. Lords' exactions resulted in several risings. The most formidable and widespread, the so-called Peasants' War, erupted in Germany in 1524–5. Grievances included excessive rents and dues, restriction on peasant rights and the privatization of land. Participants were savagely punished. In England, Kett's rebels (1549) shared several of these grievances. In France, a great wave of peasant risings occurred during the later civil wars in protest against ecclesiastical, royal and noble exactions.[35]

Nobles and gentry

All European societies included groups collectively described as 'nobility' whose titles and privileges manifested their high status. Their economic power rested primarily on the ownership of land. The English peerage and gentry increased their share of landownership at the expense of crown and Church during this century. The English distinction between the peerage, often termed 'the nobility', and the gentry was exceptionally sharp. Peers' titles, originally conferred by the crown, were hereditary. The gentry resembled in various respects the lesser nobility of other countries. Their highest rank, knighthood, was a personal distinction conferred by the monarch or an authorized representative. In principle, the adoption of the titles of 'esquire' and 'gentleman' denoting the second and third ranks of gentry was governed by fairly clear rules and conventions. However, it was not too difficult for men whose wealth enabled them to live like gentlemen to step onto the bottom rung of the gentry ladder. The numbers of gentry almost certainly grew far faster than the population at large. Existing gentry families established junior branches and economically successful yeomen and townsmen rose in status. (London's unique wealth and importance allowed a few oligarchs to rise to knighthood with exceptional rapidity.)

The nobility and the gentry shared concepts of honour, pride in lineage and attachment to an appropriate lifestyle whose key elements included generous hospitality and the employment of several servants, along with suitable pastimes, especially hunting. Prolonged internal peace and the strengthening of royal authority slowly changed the role and outlook of the upper classes.

Rents became more important; retinues that might be mobilized as armed followings less so. Castles were largely transformed into, or replaced by, country houses. Increasing numbers of young gentlemen received a classical education and gained some knowledge of the law in order to prepare themselves for service in parliament or local government as well as the preservation and enhancement of their own estates.[36]

The Welsh gentry were notoriously numerous, litigious and intensely proud of their ancestry. Many of them were poor. They patronized the bards, declaimers of elaborate traditional poetry. Office-holding, monastic land purchases and the abolition of partible inheritance in 1543 helped to consolidate the dominance of more substantial Welsh families. The Scottish nobility comprised both the peerage and the much more numerous barons or lairds. The boundaries of the nobility were blurred, but the most indisputable mark of a nobleman was tenure of lands and jurisdiction directly from the crown. The number of peers was similar to that in England, in a country with about a quarter of England's population. Lordship differed in various ways between Lowlands and Highlands. In both, however, lords enjoyed greater autonomy, military strength and sway over their tenants than in England. Kinship was more important, feuds were common and lords entered protective 'bonds of manrent' with their clients. The Highland clans were 'territorial associations, composed of a dominant kin-nexus and satellite family groups, that were held together by the paternalism and patronage of their chiefs and leading gentry who maintained an ethos of protection within the localities settled by their clansmen'. In the Highlands and Islands of Scotland, as in Gaelic Ireland, there was a 'traditional culture of raiding, feuding and feasting'. Bards celebrated chieftains' heroic deeds.[37]

In some countries, such as Old Castile and Poland, where all descendants of noblemen were allowed to retain noble status, nobles made up a large proportion of the population. Such nobilities inevitably included many poor members. In the Dutch Republic the revolt ended the creation of new nobility, and the numbers of existing noble families gradually dwindled, though noblemen were still preferred for naval and military commands.[38]

A widespread noble privilege that the English nobility did not share was exemption from certain taxes, especially direct ones. In various countries many offices were open only to nobles, or conversely conferred nobility. Offices of the latter sort were sold in large numbers by the French crown, but not in England. However, justices of the peace, sheriffs and heralds were given the title of esquire by virtue of their appointment if not already of that rank. Jurisdiction was an important element of noble power. The primacy of the king's courts in England was clear, and further strengthened in 1536. In Poland, by contrast, royal courts were excluded from interfering in disputes between lords and their tenants. In Castile, as in Scotland, nobles possessed extensive delegated royal jurisdictions. Several nobles in France still had courts with the power to inflict the death penalty, though subject to the oversight of royal judges. Disruptive feuds between nobles were endemic in

Poland, intermittent in Scotland and proliferated in France during the civil wars.[39]

Poverty and poor relief

During the sixteenth century real wages fell sharply. Dearth and economic slump could reduce many wage earners from precarious subsistence to abject poverty. Poor relief largely depended throughout this period on individual donors who contributed by means ranging from doles to almshouse endowments. Religious orders, too, were important before the Reformation (and afterwards in Catholic countries).

Various authorities, including the German Diet (1497) and Francis I (1536), declared each community responsible for its own poor. Several cities in Germany and the Netherlands introduced common poor relief funds and collections during the 1520s. Leisnig (Saxony) levied the first poor relief tax in 1523. Lyons started weekly distributions of food and money to listed poor, partly financed by a rate, in 1534, established two new orphanages and aimed to provide work for the able-bodied. A few Castilian towns adopted during the 1540s reforms like those already implemented in the Netherlands. New centralized institutions, specialized or multi-purpose, were founded in a number of continental towns. In Protestant Europe the buildings or endowments of dissolved religious foundations were sometimes used for relief.[40]

The London corporation founded or took over between 1544 and 1557 five institutions to cater for the sick and disabled poor, the insane, orphans and the wilfully idle. Some other towns introduced their own poor relief schemes. England's distinctive contribution was, however, a functioning *national* poor relief system. English legislation progressed from voluntary to compulsory alms, and transferred supervision from ecclesiastical to secular authority. The main innovations were regular voluntary collections (1536), obligatory almsgiving (1552 and 1563), appointment of overseers of the poor and assessment by the justices of the peace (1572), and provision of stocks of material for the involuntarily unemployed (1576). The great poor law of 1598, slightly amended in 1601, consolidated previous legislation and authorized justices to tax some parishes to help others that could not support their own poor. The English process of experiment and improvement, facilitated by parliamentary debate, was exceptional. These laws did not provide a secure entitlement to adequate relief. Their gradual implementation was a notable achievement nonetheless. The Scottish poor remained mainly dependent on voluntary alms despite legislation of 1575. Kirk sessions collected and disbursed contributions.[41]

After the early-sixteenth-century spread of municipal schemes, the Counter-Reformation re-asserted the importance of the voluntary principle and the Church's prerogative of supervising charitable institutions. New religious orders, societies and confraternities, hospitals of different sorts and charitable loan funds were all favoured forms of Catholic relief. Parish funds remained under clerical supervision.[42]

Education

The principal purposes of education were the inculcation of Christian duties, including obedience to earthly superiors, and training appropriate to one's social rank and intended profession. Learning to read, useful for the first of these purposes, was the most important function of 'primary' education. Writing came later. In England the level of literacy seems to have improved during the sixteenth century, though very unevenly. London was more literate than the rest of the country. The clergy, gentry, merchants and skilled professionals were the most literate groups. Craftsmen and tradesmen became markedly more literate. Improvement was evident among yeomen, but very slow among small farmers. Labourers and the majority of women were the least literate groups. The hierarchy of literacy revealed by this sort of evidence was very similar in Spain and Languedoc, suggesting that the structure of literacy was shaped above all by economic and social incentives and opportunities.[43]

After whatever elementary schooling their parents could afford, the great majority of the working population were trained by means of service or apprenticeship. England's 1563 Statute of Artificers made apprenticeship compulsory for a wide range of occupations. Attendance at a grammar school where Latin was taught was considered appropriate for boys destined for a career in the professions or commerce. A classical education might be continued at the university as a preparation for careers in the Church, law or medicine. In Britain, as elsewhere, the numbers of grammar schools were already growing fast before the Reformation. Religious change brought initial disruption, but in England monarchs, individual patrons and groups of townsfolk re-endowed old schools and established new ones. In Scotland, despite the reformers' ambitious aims, relatively few parish schools were founded before 1600. On the continent both Protestant and Catholic reformers assigned schools a crucial role in the inculcation of right belief. German Protestant principalities such as Württemberg and Brandenburg achieved impressive increases in school numbers. The Jesuit order was exceptionally successful in founding good schools, colleges and academies all over Catholic Europe, several of them in key areas vulnerable to Protestant advance.[44]

New universities were founded in Spain, Italy, Germany, the Netherlands and Scotland (at Edinburgh and Aberdeen), and new colleges at Oxford and Cambridge. By the early seventeenth century, some 2.4 per cent of young men in the appropriate age group attended universities in England, 2.8 per cent in the United Provinces and nearly 3 per cent in Castile, compared with an estimated European average of about 1 per cent a century earlier.[45] English common lawyers underwent their own unique training at the Inns of Court.

Growing quantities of printed material, issuing from scores of European presses, increased individual exposure to the written word. Nearly 90 per cent of all books published in Europe before 1601 were produced in a 'core' zone that comprised the countries where presses had first been established (Germany, Switzerland, Italy, France and the Netherlands). A third of all European books were printed in Germany, and 38 per cent of all books in Latin, the international learned language. Most of the countries in the 'core' zone had many vigorous urban centres. The existence of flourishing presses in several Netherlands cities complicated government efforts at censorship. In France, the breakdown of royal authority and the proliferation of bitter polemic during the civil wars boosted the output of print. England, achieving little more than 3 per cent of total publishing output, belonged with Spain and Scandinavia among the 'peripheral regions'. The crown was able to limit most English printing to London, though England also imported large numbers of books from abroad. The crown's early efforts to prevent the printing of heretical or seditious books culminated in Mary's reign. She also granted the Stationers' Company incorporation in 1557 and gave it a near-monopoly of printing. In 1559 a theoretically stringent system of licensing was established, but in practice Elizabethan censorship was never consistent or comprehensive.[46]

Conclusion

England's population probably increased faster than that of any other European country during the sixteenth century. The proportion of that population living in towns remained smaller than in much of Europe, especially Italy, Iberia and the Low Countries, but London's dramatic demographic growth made it western Europe's third largest city by 1600. London was not only the seat of government, but also England's foremost commercial and industrial centre. Cloth exports from the capital rose steeply until the 1550s. Their hitherto clear upward trend then ceased, but English merchants gained a larger share of England's trade, extended its range, established direct links with the sources of various imports and found new markets for English exports. Industries new to England were established, partly with help from continental immigrants, including many refugees from religious persecution. England probably achieved a larger proportional increase in agricultural output than most other countries, even though it was far from enough to maintain the standards of living of the majority. She was fortunate above all in avoiding wars on her own territory. In this respect her experience was very different from that of the neighbouring Netherlands. Rebellion and reconquest badly damaged Antwerp and other cities of the south and caused a great migration of people and capital to the northern provinces. There, the newly independent Dutch Republic embarked on a path of rapid economic growth, especially in overseas commerce.

Scotland fared less well than England during the sixteenth century. Her population, reined in by wars, dearths and epidemics, grew more slowly than England's. Some expansion of the cultivated area took place. From a low base, coal and salt production rose sharply during the second half of the century, and contributed to an overall growth of exports after a deep slump in the 1540s. Export growth over the century as a whole was relatively modest, however, and there was no major expansion of the geographical range of Scotland's trade.

7

CONTACTS AND CONNECTIONS: RENAISSANCE AND REFORMATION

England and Scotland were linked with the rest of Europe by commercial, diplomatic, religious, intellectual and artistic networks. The most sustained international contacts took place in the peripatetic entourages of rulers and in ports, university cities, seats of government, at international fairs and financial centres. Britain was uniquely dependent on maritime connections, but most European countries relied on them to some extent. The great overland road or river routes also made foreign merchants, diplomats, scholars and exiles a relatively familiar sight in parts of rural Europe.

Commerce

Privileged merchant companies controlled the most lucrative branches of English overseas trade, maintaining premises and agents in staple towns overseas. The English cloth trade with the Netherlands was the preserve of the Merchants Adventurers, based in Antwerp. Much of the cloth exported to the Netherlands was finished there. A lot of it passed on to inland markets. England obtained in Antwerp local products such as fine textiles, arms and armour, German copper, metal wares and fustians, Portuguese spices and sugar, and Italian luxury goods, including silks and glassware. The Scottish staple in the Netherlands, controlled by the Convention of Royal Burghs, was from c.1507 at Veere, an outport of Antwerp.[1]

Until the 1540s foreign merchants handled nearly half of England's cloth exports. Hanse merchants normally took the larger share, helped by preferential tariffs. In 1552, the government, needing the Adventurers' help in paying off its Antwerp debt, withdrew the Hanse's privileges on the ground that it had misused them. Mary I's government briefly restored them, but in 1555 drastically restricted Hanse trade between England and the Netherlands, and in 1558, when it wanted the Adventurers' co-operation in implementing new customs rates, required the Hansards to pay the same duty on cloth exports as other foreigners. It also imposed new restrictions on Italian and Ragusan merchants. Thereafter the share of English trade carried by foreign merchants fell sharply.

The Adventurers' trade in Antwerp was interrupted by two embargoes in 1563–4 and 1568–73, and in 1582 they finally moved their Netherlands staple to Middelburg, a port in Dutch Zeeland. Meanwhile they also tried a variety of German bases: Emden in 1564, Hamburg in 1567–78, Emden again from 1579 until 1586, and from 1587, the little town of Stade, just outside Hamburg. The advantages of trading in or near Hamburg were the city's well-established links with the great south German fairs and its rapidly developing cloth-finishing industry.[2]

England's Baltic trade gradually increased. She needed more ship's stores for her expanded navy and more grain during the later sixteenth century's poor harvests, and exported some cloth to the Baltic. This growth led to the foundation of the Eastland Company in 1579. Its staple was the little port of Elbing, favoured by the Polish crown. Scotland depended even more heavily on Baltic and Norwegian supplies of timber, iron and grain. Scottish colonies existed in several Baltic ports, and several Scottish traders settled in Poland.[3]

The English expedition to find a north-eastern route to the Far East in 1553 resulted instead in contact with Russia and the Muscovy Company's establishment in 1555. England imported ships' cables, hemp, flax, furs, hides, tallow and wax; Muscovy took cloth and some metals. Relations were far from uniformly smooth. Englishmen nevertheless became the best-informed western observers of Russia. Giles Fletcher, special ambassador in 1588–9, published an eloquently negative account *Of the Rus Commonwealth* (1591).[4]

France remained an important trading partner for both England and Scotland. Bordeaux and La Rochelle were the foremost sources of Britain's and Ireland's wine imports. England imported woad from the area round Toulouse. Vast quantities of sea salt came from the Bay of Bourgneuf. Northern France supplied linen, canvas and paper, especially through Rouen. Dieppe, where there was a Scottish colony, traded with Leith and other Scottish ports. England exported tin, lead and some cloth to France, Scotland fish, hides, coarse cloth and wool, but the balance of trade was in France's favour in both cases. The Scots were exempted from the payment of customs in Normandy in 1510, and throughout France in 1558.[5]

From Spain, England imported wool, dyestuffs, whale oil, iron, wine, olive oil, raisins, silks, salt and fresh fruit. Portugal provided pepper, sugar and salt. To Spain, English merchants took lead, tin, hides, cloth, and later, re-exports from northern Europe. The balance developed in England's favour. The trade, almost entirely conducted by English merchants, was doubly valuable. By ordering the seizure of English ships in 1585, Philip II temporarily silenced the strongest English opponents of war with Spain, and turned many of them into predators upon Spanish commerce. West Country merchants and fishermen largely ousted Iberian rivals from the Newfoundland fisheries and later sold fish to Spain and Portugal themselves.[6]

The interruption of trade with Antwerp and Spain (1568–73) and war between Venice and Turkey (1570–3) encouraged the revival of England's direct trade with the Mediterranean. Italians in London gave important initial help. In 1573 an English ship reached the recently founded Tuscan port of Leghorn. The foremost Mediterranean power was Turkey. In 1580 Sultan Murad III gave English merchants trading privileges. Elizabeth exchanged gifts with Murad, declared that she rejected idolatry (implying that Protestants resembled Muslims in this respect) and requested Turkish help against feared Spanish attack. English merchants were soon exporting cloth to the Levant, and importing Levantine dried fruits, silks, carpets, wine and oil, and eastern spices and indigo. Rivalry developed with the temporarily weakened French, previously Turkey's closest western partners. English interest in things Turkish was reflected in Richard Knolles's *Generall Historie of the Turkes* (1603), and the staging of 'Turkish' plays. Companies founded for trade with Turkey and Venice in 1581 and 1583 were merged as the Levant Company in 1592. Englishmen encroached on Venice's Levantine trade and even preyed on Venetian commerce with their strongly armed ships.[7]

Tudor governments welcomed skilled foreign craftsmen and intermittently (but especially after 1560) tried to encourage the establishment or development of certain industries so as to reduce England's dependence on foreign suppliers. The importance of the immigrants' contribution varied from one industry to another. Walloon and Flemish-speaking refugees arriving in large numbers from the 1560s onwards settled in Norwich, Sandwich, Colchester and elsewhere. They helped to revive and diversify English light cloth manufacture with new or improved techniques and varieties that included mixed fabrics made with linen, silk and cotton. Immigrants also helped to establish or expand starch making, dyeing, silk weaving, stocking knitting and lace making. Frenchmen contributed essential skills to the expansion of iron smelting and gun casting in the Weald between the 1490s and the 1540s. Germans mined copper near Keswick, made iron wire at Tintern, brass near London, steel in Sussex and paper in Kent. Craftsmen from Flanders, Lorraine and France rapidly expanded window-glass manufacture from the 1560s onwards. Netherlanders contributed to a huge growth of brewing in and around London.[8]

Rediscoveries of antiquity

For several centuries before 1500 European scholars had studied elements of the literature and philosophy of the ancient Graeco-Roman world, above all in surviving manuscripts, many of them imperfect copies of ancient originals. Various works by the Greek philosopher Aristotle (384–22 BC) had been re-discovered during the twelfth century, largely through Arab texts. Thinkers later dubbed 'scholastic' had subsequently tried to reconcile partially recovered ancient knowledge with Christian doctrine and used Aristotelian logic to systematize Christian theology.

From the fourteenth century onwards increasing numbers of scholars engaged in critical study of ancient texts. Their interests focused especially on the 'humanities' – grammar, rhetoric, poetry, ethics and history. These 'humanists' aspired to write a more correct and elegant Latin, following the example of ancient authors such as Cicero (106–43 BC). Architects and sculptors also imitated ancient styles. Humanist scholarship inspired what was much later to be called the 'Renaissance', though this 'rebirth' encompassed a range of literary, artistic and scientific activities that sooner or later transcended ancient examples or sources of inspiration. The 'Renaissance' radiated from Italy through most of Europe.

Several Greek texts hitherto unknown, or known only in Latin versions, were discovered. For the first time the serious study of Greek, the language of the foremost ancient sages, spread through western Europe. There was renewed interest in Aristotle's master Plato (c.427–c.347 BC), who had envisaged eternal and immutable forms beyond the mutable visible world, and imagined an ideal state ruled by wisdom. Greek texts of the New Testament could now be studied. From c.1455, printing with moveable type greatly accelerated the circulation of more accurate editions of ancient texts, which in turn eventually helped to stimulate new research in almost every branch of the sciences and humanities.

The first notable cluster of English humanist scholars consisted of four Oxford men who visited Italy: William Grocyn, Thomas Linacre, William Lily and John Colet. The first three learnt Greek, and Grocyn taught it publicly. Colet re-founded St Paul's School to provide an education informed by Christian humanist ideals; Lily served as its high master. The erudition of this Oxford group impressed the most celebrated humanist in Europe, the Dutchman Desiderius Erasmus, during his first visit to England (1499). Erasmus taught theology and Greek at Cambridge from 1511 to 1514, thanks to John Fisher, the university's saintly chancellor. The most famous of Erasmus's English friends was Thomas More, whose *Utopia* (1516), conceived during an embassy to the Netherlands, describes an imaginary non-Christian land, whose society and polity seem in many ways to reflect a Christian spirit more truly than those of nominally Christian Europe, tainted by selfishness, rapacity, idleness and injustice. *Utopia* powerfully combines satire and fantasy to broach fundamental questions with a brilliant lightness of touch. It attracted a substantial European readership. Erasmus and More both hoped for a regeneration of Christian society, but became early opponents of Luther's Reformation.[9]

Several Scottish scholars were in Paris when Erasmus studied there during the 1490s. The most distinguished of them, John Mair, a 'scholastic' in his predominant concerns, and unimpeachably conservative in the theology that he taught for much of his career, nevertheless learnt Greek in Paris and sharply criticized the clergy's shortcomings. He was also a historian, more critical and dispassionate than his near contemporary in Paris and fellow theologian and logician Hector Boece, despite the humanist ambitions evident in Boece's work. Both men taught in Scottish universities; Mair also in Paris, where he gained his international reputation.

Universities and printing presses

Several royal and princely courts, monasteries and noble households contributed to the diffusion of learning. The role of the great universities was nonetheless crucial. Many scholars attended more than one. Several continental universities attracted British students to study for the higher degrees: theology, law and medicine. 'Law' in this context meant the civil and canon laws based on Roman law, not England's unique common law, with its idiosyncratic procedures and esoteric technical language. Expertise in canon or civil law was valued as a qualification not only for legal practice, but also for careers in diplomacy and government. Padua was the pre-eminent centre of civilian and medical studies for English students.[10] Its ruler, Venice, protected Protestant students from interference. Bologna, under papal rule, became less attractive after the Reformation. Many Scots students went to French universities, especially Paris, eminent in theology, but also to Angers, Bordeaux, Bourges, Orleans, Poitiers and Toulouse. Montpellier's outstanding reputation in medicine attracted both Scots and English students. In the southern Netherlands both Louvain and the new foundation of Douai became prime centres for the education of English Catholics. In Protestant Holland, Leiden (founded 1575) soon became famous for medicine. Universities that attracted British Protestants also included Basel and Heidelberg, a stronghold of Reformed theology.

The printing press rapidly became a key instrument for the dissemination of texts among scholars, though the biggest concentrations of printing workshops were to be found in great centres of commerce, not all of which possessed universities. Johann Gutenberg began printing in Mainz c.1455. William Caxton set up the first English press at Westminster in 1476, Walter Chepman and Andrew Myllar the first Scottish one at Edinburgh in 1507–8. However, foreign printers produced about two-thirds of all books printed in England between 1500 and 1530. Many of the books sold in Britain, especially ones in Latin, came from abroad throughout the century. Major centres of printing for English markets included Paris, Louvain, Basel, Rouen and Antwerp. Various foreign presses established an enduring lead in Latin publishing well before 1500. The celebrated Venetian publisher Aldo Manuzio, a friend of Linacre's, was an expert in the publication of Greek texts. Several British authors, including More, Linacre, Mair and Boece, sent work to foreign presses. Some books could not be safely printed in England. English translations of the Bible were proscribed before the mid-1530s. During Mary I's reign, the famous printer-publishers Froben and Oporinus of Basel published work by English Protestants whom they employed or sheltered. Both Protestant and Catholic exiles published polemical works abroad.

The papacy and Britain before the break with Rome

Early in the sixteenth century, the headship of distant popes was neither inspiring nor burdensome for the British churches. The papacy always provided to bishoprics in accordance with royal nominations in England, usually in Scotland. Rome taxed the clergy lightly, received appeals from church court decisions (few from England, more from Scotland, yet not many overall) and issued a steady flow of dispensations. Cardinal-protectors supposedly looked after England's interests at Rome. Four Italian bishops of Worcester also acted as royal agents or advisers. Leo X delegated considerable authority to Henry VIII's minister Thomas Wolsey as legate *a latere*. The relationship between the English crown and the papacy was, until Henry VIII sought annulment of his marriage, broadly satisfactory for both sides. James IV incurred papal excommunication by attacking England in 1513, but this did not have lasting consequences. After 1533 the papacy was anxious to prevent Scotland's following England into schism. James V was favoured. David Beaton became in 1538 the first Scotsman appointed cardinal since 1383. During England's brief reconciliation with Rome, Reginald Pole, member in exile of a group of Italian Catholic reformers, led the Church as cardinal legate and archbishop of Canterbury, but Paul IV's suspicions of Pole's unorthodoxy blighted Mary's reunion even before her death. In 1559–60 the British kingdoms' membership of an organized international Church ceased for good.

Protestants

Evangelical Protestantism was at first dependent on continental sources of inspiration and support. William Tyndale's New Testament was printed at Worms in 1526. Subsequent sanctuary until 1535 in the English House in Antwerp enabled him to publish there his translation of the Pentateuch and other works. Miles Coverdale and John Rogers, chaplain to the Merchants Adventurers, both used Tyndale's version for the complete English Bibles they printed in Antwerp in 1535 and 1537. Tyndale's associate John Frith published there his attack on the doctrine of purgatory (1531).

Thomas Cranmer, a Lutheran in key respects between c.1532 and 1547, married the niece of Nuremberg's chief pastor in 1532. Luther's strongest supporter in England was, however, Robert Barnes, formerly Erasmus's student at Louvain, who assisted the clandestine distribution of Tyndale's New Testament before fleeing in 1528 to Antwerp and then to Wittenberg. With Thomas Cromwell's favour, he later undertook ultimately abortive negotiations with German Protestants. He was burnt for heresy after his patron's fall. Scotland's first Protestant martyr, Patrick Hamilton, burnt at St Andrews in 1528, had visited the Lutheran university of Marburg. After fleeing Scotland for Wittenberg in 1532 Alexander Alesius published an appeal to James V to annul a recent episcopal prohibition of the circulation of the New Testament. John Gaw translated from Danish the first Lutheran tract published in Scots (1533).

After Edward VI's accession in 1547 England became a refuge for distinguished churchmen whose influence helped to ensure that England would be aligned in doctrine with the Reformed rather than the Lutheran Churches. Martin Bucer, Calvin's mentor, and the Florentine Pietro Martire Vermigli became professors of divinity at Cambridge and Oxford respectively. Bucer strongly influenced the revision of the 1549 Prayer Book. Other distinguished exiles at Cambridge were Paul Fagius and Joannes Immanuel Tremellius, a converted Italian Jew (readers in Hebrew), and Francis Dryander, translator of the New Testament into Spanish (reader in Greek). The Sienese Bernardino Ochino preached to Italians in London. In 1550, the Polish nobleman Jan Łaski, previously pastor of Emden, became superintendent of the London Strangers' Church, comprising Dutch and French congregations. The order devised for them later became an influential model for other churches, including that of the English refugees in Geneva and the Scottish Kirk. Calvin's friend Valérand Poullain became superintendent of a short-lived Somerset colony of Walloon weavers. For a time Protestant Europe's hopes focused on England.[11]

After Mary I's accession English exiles established communities in several German or Swiss towns. Emden became the exiles' chief polemical literature production centre. At Strassburg John Ponet wrote his *Short Treatise* justifying tyrannicide. Zurich was home to a harmonious group. At Frankfurt the Scottish reformer John Knox, who in England had already criticized the 1552 Prayer Book for requiring recipients to kneel at Communion, resumed his campaign for its further reform. When Frankfurt defenders of the Prayer Book proved too strong, he and some fellow critics went to Geneva. The congregation there produced a new *Form of Prayers*. Some Geneva exiles worked on a new translation of the Bible (1560), the most widely used in Britain during the next fifty years. The exiled ministers Christopher Goodman and John Knox also published tracts declaring the Christian duty of resistance to ungodly rulers. John Knox was to be the chief architect of the Scottish Kirk that emerged from the revolution of 1559–60. But his ill-timed 1558 attack on female rule infuriated Elizabeth and ensured her hostility towards Geneva.

Many Elizabethan churchmen admired the more fully reformed Churches they had witnessed in exile. The Zurich ministers Heinrich Bullinger and Rudolf Gwalther, anxious not to exacerbate dissent in England, were generally cautious and moderate in their advice to English puritans. Theodore Beza, Calvin's successor at Geneva, was more critical of the English Church's shortcomings. The leading British Presbyterians, Thomas Cartwright, Walter Travers and Andrew Melville, were all at Geneva during the early 1570s. Cartwright later spent some time in the militantly Protestant centre of Heidelberg. He and Travers also served as pastors to the English congregation in Antwerp. More extreme puritans who felt impelled to separate from the Church of England established congregations in Middelburg and Amsterdam.[12]

The foreign churches in London were re-established under Elizabeth. Nicolas des Gallars (1560–3) aligned the French Church with Geneva. Several Englishmen attended or even belonged to the London Strangers' churches. Many puritans saw them as models for further reform of the Church of England. Religious persecution in the Netherlands resulted in a larger inflow of immigrants to London and elsewhere during the 1560s. The biggest provincial community, including both Walloons and 'Dutch', was established in Norwich in 1565. Others were founded at Sandwich (the first, 1561), Canterbury, Colchester,

Maidstone, Southampton, Stamford and Yarmouth. The exiles' numbers probably peaked at about 20,000 before declining after 1590, when many migrated to the liberated northern provinces. Radical heresy among the foreign refugees was a recurrent source of anxiety for the English authorities and some of the foreign church leaders. Three Dutch heretics went to the stake in 1551 and 1575. Portuguese Jews began to arrive in London around 1540. Some of them practised outward conformity and secret Judaism. The small London colony included the physicians Hector Nunes, who served William Cecil as intelligence agent, and Rodrigo Lopes, executed in 1594 on a charge of plotting to poison the queen.[13]

Roman Catholics

Some English Catholics became exiles after Henry VIII's break with Rome. Reginald Pole, Henry's second cousin, condemned Henry's schism in his *Pro Unitatis Ecclesiasticae Defensione*. He was appointed cardinal and legate in 1536. During Edward's reign, a group of English Catholics, including Thomas More's nephew William Rastell, editor of his works, and Nicholas Harpsfield, went to live in Louvain. After 1559 many more exiles gathered there, including a large number of Oxford men. During the years 1564 to 1568 they vigorously defended Catholic doctrine in more than forty publications and engaged in controversy with defenders of the Church of England, especially John Jewel. Copies were smuggled into England in large quantities. In 1568 William Allen founded at the new university of Douai a college to train men to serve as priests in England. Philip II and the papacy supported it financially. The first priests went to England in 1574. The college later moved temporarily to Rheims, in a safely Catholic area of France (1578–93). It was there that the first Roman Catholic New Testament in English was published in 1582. The English Catholic laity abroad included noblemen, gentry, merchants and numerous soldiers. Mary I's ex-councillor Sir Francis Englefield became a valued adviser to Philip II. English booksellers and printers helped see Catholic works through the press in Paris, Antwerp and Rouen.

Pope Gregory XIII ordered the conversion of the English hospice in Rome into a seminary, the English College, and in 1579 placed it under Jesuit direction. Jesuit missionaries, including Robert Persons and Edmund Campion, were sent to England in 1580, inaugurating a continuous Jesuit presence there. Never more than a minority of the Catholic priests in England, they included the most famous martyrs (Edmund Campion, Robert Southwell and Henry Garnet) as well as the authors of the most vivid accounts of missionary work (John Gerard and William Weston). Persons's *Book of Resolution* (Rouen, 1582) was soon adapted for Protestant use. Persons later founded a school at St Omer in Artois, and seminaries at Valladolid (1589) and Seville (1592).

The Jesuits' prominence in the mission and their pro-Spanish sympathies angered some secular priests. Enmity towards the Jesuits reached new heights after the 1598 appointment as archpriest in England of George Blackwell, a man seen by his critics as a tool of the Jesuits. Secular priests critical of what they saw as Blackwell's misgovernment appealed to Rome in 1598 and 1600. The pope eventually limited the archpriest's powers and forbade him to consult the Jesuits. In 1601 the English government secretly facilitated the second appeal in the hope of exacerbating the divisions among the Catholic priests in England. The government encouraged priests opposed to the Jesuits to make a declaration of loyalty to the queen, but offered them very little in return, and a mere thirteen priests made a qualified declaration.[14]

Welsh missionaries included Robert Gwyn, a Douai student, who became a famous preacher and religious writer in Wales, and William Davies (executed in 1593). Morys Clynnog, a *protégé* of Pole's, and subsequently warden of the English hospice, published a Welsh catechism in Milan in 1568. His close friend Gruffydd Robert became confessor to Carlo Borromeo, Milan's reforming archbishop. Owen Lewis served as Borromeo's vicar-general (1580–4).

Several Jesuits were active in Scotland, especially from the mid-1580s onwards. James VI invited James Gordon to court in 1588 and debated doctrine with him. William Crichton undertook a mission from James to the pope in 1599. Robert Abercromby had taught in Poland in the 1560s and ministered to Scots and Englishmen there. He allegedly received Anne of Denmark into the Church in 1599. The leading Scots secular clergy abroad were connected with Mary Stewart. James Beaton, archbishop of Glasgow, served as her ambassador in Paris. Both Beaton and John Lesley, Bishop of Ross, plotted on her behalf. Lesley's friend Ninian Winzet was Knox's most active controversial opponent in Scotland and Antwerp before briefly serving as Mary's confessor in 1571. Mary and Beaton founded a Scots college in Paris that ended up in Douai after several moves. A Scots college was established in Rome in 1600.

The Scots Catholic legists Adam Blackwood, working at Poitiers, and William Barclay, professor of civil law at Pont à Mousson in Lorraine, vigorously defended royal authority. Blackwood attacked Calvinist resistance theory in *Pro regibus apologia* (1581), and published a famous vindication of Mary after her execution. Barclay condemned both Huguenot and Catholic League resistance theories in his *De regno* (1600).[15] Several Scots Catholic noblemen visited the continent, often during short spells of banishment or flight. Both the sixth earl of Huntly and the eighth Lord Maxwell sought Philip II's intervention in Scotland.

Service in foreign wars

Rebellions and civil wars in France and the Netherlands attracted many British volunteers whose motives included religious commitment, desire for honour or useful experience and hope of financial gain. Between 1568 and 1572 ships manned by French, Netherlands and English volunteers and freebooters preyed on Catholic shipping with the connivance of the English government. After St Bartholomew, a force largely consisting of English ships and troops re-supplied Huguenot La Rochelle. From 1572 onwards the Strangers' churches in England raised men and money to help the Netherlands' resistance. Dutch and English merchants despatched money, munitions and materials. In 1572 Thomas Morgan led 300 volunteers to the Netherlands, including the equally redoubtable Welshman Roger Williams. Over 3,000 English and Welsh troops were serving the states-general by 1578, along with 4,000 Scots. (Scottish mercenaries also fought for Muscovy, Denmark and Sweden and the western Highlands exported the notorious 'redshanks' to Ireland.) Three English companies were in Spanish pay in the Netherlands by 1582. The Englishman Sir William Stanley and the Scotsman Sir William Sempill both entered Spanish service, Stanley after changing sides. Service against the Turks attracted several Englishmen. Some fought in the Mediterranean, others in Hungary, including John Smith, later pioneer settler of Virginia.[16]

Royal courts and their connections

In the great game of international politics, rulers' households played a crucial part in radiating royal power. Emulative kings and princes borrowed desirable features from rival courts. Burgundian or French examples influenced almost every aspect of British court culture: organization, etiquette, ceremonial, entertainments, architecture and artistic media. The Burgundian court was at first the more influential, but Francis I made the French court incomparably the most magnificent in northern Europe. With some exceptions, such as music, Spanish courts never had as great a cultural influence in England, despite the fact that the Tudors' most important foreign marriages were with Spanish consorts. Rulers' personal gifts to each other and their representatives intimated the magnificence of their courts and the distinction of their patronage.

Henry VIII was exceptional in meeting his fellow rulers Francis I and Charles V on five occasions, most famously Francis I in the fabulously extravagant setting of the Field of Cloth of Gold near Calais in June 1520. James V and VI of Scotland went abroad to fetch home foreign brides in person (1536 and 1589). Such royal visits were enormously expensive. Rulers had long sent to each other's courts envoys to negotiate matters ranging from trade agreements to royal marriages or military alliances. The maintenance of resident agents, introduced in fifteenth-century Italy, subsequently spread throughout western Europe. Ideally it enabled rulers to keep a finger on the pulses of each other's courts, as well as a closer watch on the development of opinion in the host country.

England's most sustained diplomatic relations were with Rome (while papal supremacy was recognized), France, the Emperor or Spain (until ambassadors were expelled from Madrid in 1568 and London in 1584), the Netherlands and Venice (until 1557). From 1578 onwards agents or ambassadors were maintained at Constantinople. Embassies were occasionally sent to most other European countries. Scotland's more limited means and more restricted range of partners required a smaller and less developed diplomatic service. British diplomatic activity intensified during royal courtships, Henry VIII's 'Great Matter', in response to exceptional instability and political uncertainty in neighbouring countries, and in preparation for offensive or defensive war. James VI's most ambitious diplomatic campaign sought support for his succession to the English throne.[17]

Diplomatic relations were often far from smooth. Some envoys had misgivings about their own monarch's policy. Others, by tactlessly expressing Protestant views, antagonized Catholic monarchs or governments: Charles V (1551), France (early 1560s) and Philip II (1568). Various foreign ambassadors became involved in conspiracies against English governments: both Frenchmen (1553–6) and Spaniards (1571, 1583). Governments relied on many agents besides their accredited representatives. Unstable and unpredictable late-sixteenth-century international politics served as a hothouse for the growth of secret intelligence, facilitated by codes, ciphers, invisible ink, disguises and double identities. Francis Walsingham, Elizabeth I's 'spymaster', was one of several Elizabethan secretaries of state who had earlier served as a diplomat.

Civilians and humanists in royal service

There were various pathways to the higher levels of English royal service, including military experience, expertise in the common or civil law and a humanist education. Several individuals combined at least two of these qualifications. The roles of civilian and humanist were the ones most likely to be combined, and to have involved foreign experience and the development of an international outlook. Both a civilian and a humanist training assisted incisive political analysis, effective exposition of problems and articulate advocacy of solutions. Civilians (usually churchmen until the Reformation) were appropriate choices for diplomatic missions involving knotty legal issues. Humanist cultivation of rhetoric was useful for propaganda, persuasion, congratulation and the verbal projection of monarchical power in addressing both domestic and foreign audiences. Both civilians and humanists, but particularly humanists, used their pens to attract rulers' attention.

The break with Rome divided the ranks of English humanists. Thomas More succeeded Wolsey as lord chancellor, only to resign in 1532 and go to the block for his refusal to accept the royal supremacy. His friend Sir Thomas Elyot set out in his *Boke Named the Gouernour* (1531) a curriculum of humane studies to equip the upper classes for the tasks of government, and above all for that of advising the ruler, eloquently praising the works of Plato and Cicero. Although he later took care to distance himself from More, he disapproved of the king's divorce, and a fruitless mission to Charles V in 1531 was the only major assignment with which Henry entrusted him.[18] In 1534 Thomas Cromwell enlisted Thomas Starkey, who had studied at Padua and served as Reginald Pole's secretary, to handle intelligence from Italy and write propaganda for the Henrician regime. Starkey wrote *An Exhortation ... to Unity and Obedience* (1536), but his association with Pole cost him Thomas Cromwell's trust after Pole had bitterly attacked Henry in writing. Richard Morison, who had studied civil law at Padua (1532–6), but was evangelical in religious outlook, became the regime's most effective propagandist in his defences of the royal supremacy and attacks on sedition. Morison drew on Niccolo Machiavelli's works to underline rebellion's futility and coined the word 'Machiavellist' to denote a penetrating political observer. Machiavelli, Italy's most influential political thinker, had neglected conventional concerns such as justice, political obligation and the relationship between spiritual and temporal power, in favour of the best ways of promoting the vigour and stability of states. His most notorious work *The Prince*, written in 1513, told rulers how to control their subjects. As unofficial tutor to Edward VI, William Thomas, traveller in Italy and author of the first history of Italy in English, submitted for the king's consideration questions inspired by Machiavelli's works.[19]

Under Edward the most influential humanist was John Cheke, regius professor of Greek at Cambridge and the king's official tutor (1544–9). As a propagandist against rebellion, he wrote *The Hurte of Sedicion* (1549). Cheke's close friend Sir Thomas Smith, who had visited various continental universities, including Padua, became regius professor of civil law at Cambridge, and secretary of state in 1548–9 and 1572–6. In his *Discourse of the Commonweal* (written in 1549, published in 1581) he was the first English writer to attribute inflation to the debasement of the coinage, and to advocate economic incentives rather than moral reform as solutions of social problems. His *De Republica Anglorum* (1583), written while he was ambassador in France (1562–5), drew on his experience abroad in order to highlight distinctive features of the English constitution. William Cecil, secretary of state (1550–3, 1558–72), and Elizabeth's principal adviser, had been Cheke's pupil at St John's College. Thomas Wilson, secretary of state (1577–81), and writer of treatises on logic, rhetoric and usury, was another member of Cheke's Cambridge circle. He studied civil law at Padua as an exile in Mary's reign and later suffered torture at Rome. In the preface to his translation of the *Orations* of Demosthenes (1570), Wilson compared the danger to Greek liberty posed by Philip of Macedon in the fourth century BC with the contemporary threat from Philip II. Thomas Hoby, another pupil of Cheke's, published his translation of Baldassare Castiglione's *Book of the Courtier* (1528), one of the most admired books of the Italian Renaissance, in 1561. It unfolds the qualities of the perfect courtier and concludes with that courtier's true goal: to influence his master towards virtue and his people's good. Hoby's promising career was cut short when he died while ambassador to France in 1566.

Scotland's leading humanist, Europe's foremost Latin poet in his generation, George Buchanan studied under John Mair at St Andrew's and Paris, and taught in Bordeaux during the 1540s, where he composed Latin classical dramas based on biblical stories. He served Mary I in Scotland, but worked with Mary's opponents after her fall and justified resistance to her. The brothers William Maitland of Lethington and John Maitland of Thirlestane, secretaries to Mary I and James VI respectively, both completed their education in France.

Tolerant in his religious outlook, William combined wide-ranging knowledge of Protestant doctrine with a thorough grounding in classical studies, acquaintance with humanist scholarship and respect for the civil law. His unavoidably complicated political manoeuvres earned him a reputation as a disciple of Machiavelli.

Literary Renaissances

Ancient and modern European poetry and drama helped to invigorate Britain's flourishing vernacular literatures during the sixteenth century. The incorporation of new words from classical and modern languages enriched both English and Scots. Translation made available hundreds of classical and modern works for the first time. The survival of Welsh was partly due to the translation of Protestant religious texts. Yet two of the most creative Welsh linguists were humanists Catholic in sympathy or allegiance. Gruffydd Robert published the first part of his ground-breaking Welsh grammar in Milan (1567). The brilliant Siôn Dafydd Rhys, author of a pioneering account of Italian pronunciation (Padua, 1569), produced after his return home a Welsh grammar (1592) and a treatise of advice for writers (1597).

The foremost Tudor poets were courtiers or linked with the court by ties of friendship and patronage. Thomas Wyatt, member of Henry VIII's privy chamber, was the first Englishman to write sonnets, imitating Petrarch, foremost poet of the early Italian Renaissance. He also drew on the work of modern Italian poets such as Serafino, Alamanni and Aretino and the Roman poets Horace and Seneca. He wrote of unrequited love, satirized the court and paraphrased the penitential psalms. Henry Howard, earl of Surrey, celebrated Wyatt in elegies, and also wrote Petrarchan sonnets. His greatest innovation was English blank verse, in which he wrote his partial translations of Virgil's *Aeneid*. Edmund Spenser's *Shepheardes Calender* (1579) consists of eclogues, used by Virgil to celebrate the Arcadian realm of bucolic felicity, and developed by modern poets such as the Italian Mantovano and the French Protestant Marot. Spenser married fantasy with criticism in allegorical form. His *Faerie Queene* (1590 and 1596), an extended allegory of the struggles of an embattled Protestant England, was inspired by the examples of Homer, Virgil and the modern Italian poets Ariosto and Tasso, writers of romantic epics. Philip Sidney's *Arcadia* (completed by 1581, and partially revised in 1583-4) implicitly criticized Elizabeth's indecisiveness in confronting Catholic powers. Its principal source was the *Arcadia* (1504) of the Neapolitan Jacopo Sannazzaro. Sidney used pastoral romance to convey a message of Protestant activism.[20]

In the theatre, France preceded England in exploiting classical models and themes for both comedy and tragedy. Much English drama was situated in European countries, above all Italy. Italian *novelle* provided plots for English plays; French comic dialogue offered examples to English playwrights. The achievement of the foremost English playwrights, Thomas Kyd, Christopher Marlowe, Ben Jonson and William Shakespeare, was nevertheless unique.

English drama mixed genres, rejected the constraints of the classical unities of action, time and space, escaped the tyranny of rhyme and achieved extraordinary contrasts and changes of mood and expression.

Middle Scots poetry reached its peak in the decades around 1500 in the work of Robert Henryson, William Dunbar and Gavin Douglas, the first British translator of Virgil's *Aeneid*. Sir David Lyndsay, the finest poet of James V's court, belonged to their tradition. James VI was exceptional in combining the roles of poet and patron. His *Essayes of a Prentise in the Divine Art of Poesie* (1584) included rules for the writing of Scottish poetry. His *Poeticall Exercises* followed in 1591. The Catholic Alexander Montgomerie, a writer of great range and versatility, was the most accomplished of James's court poets. James's 'band' particularly favoured the sonnet. James especially admired the Huguenot poet Guillaume Salluste du Bartas, who visited Scotland in 1587 and translated James's poem on the Battle of Lepanto into French.[21]

Architecture and the visual arts

The architectural Renaissance reached Britain by way of France and the Netherlands. Builders combined elements of classical decoration with native styles and design features borrowed from northern Europe. Royal palaces, including Wolsey's Hampton Court and Whitehall residences, greatly extended by the king, were Henry VIII's largest building projects. Classical decorative elements were executed in terracotta (especially at Hampton Court, by Giovanni da Maiano), or in stucco (Nonsuch Palace, by Nicholas Bellin of Modena, earlier employed by Francis I). Many of the craftsmen who worked on Henry's palaces were Flemish, Dutch, German, French and Italian.

The nobility and gentry, rather than the financially straitened crown, were the big builders after 1547. The Protector's Somerset House in the Strand was the first English mansion to combine such Renaissance features as pedimented windows, classical pilasters, a balustrade and an entrance modelled on a triumphal arch. William Cecil's house at Burghley (1555–87) also includes French Renaissance elements such as colonnades, a Roman staircase and a giant hall fireplace. Robert Smythson, the best-known Elizabethan architect, designed and constructed the great houses of Longleat (1568–80), where he collaborated with a Frenchman, Alan Maynard, and Wollaton Hall (1580–8), most flamboyant of all Elizabethan mansions. He married elements of native 'Gothic' design with ones borrowed from the Italian Sebastian Serlio, author of the immensely influential *Sette Libri dell'architettura*, and his admirer the Dutchman Jan Vredeman de Vries. The outstanding non-residential Renaissance building in England was the Royal Exchange (1566–7). Its central colonnaded piazza was modelled on the Antwerp and Venice bourses.[22]

The work commissioned by James V at Falkland Palace (1537–41), with its attached Corinthian columns and pairs of stone medallions, was the first British architectural project to manifest strong French Renaissance influence. The more exuberant and eclectic Stirling Palace, begun c.1540, includes elements reminiscent of earlier French palaces. Tower houses, the predominant form of domestic building undertaken by Scottish nobles and lairds, sometimes boast overhanging turrets and conical spires reminiscent of fifteenth-century French castles. The earl of Bothwell's Crichton Castle courtyard, built in the 1580s, with its loggia and Italianate diamond-faceted rustication, is altogether more original. James VI's new chapel royal at Stirling Castle (1594) has a central entrance portal in the form of a triumphal arch. A Huguenot model possibly inspired the great square church of Burntisland.[23]

The strong hostility of Reformed Protestants to religious imagery almost extinguished sacred art. Commemorative monuments provided most of the remaining opportunities for sculptors, and portraits for painters. Before the Reformation, the Florentine Pietro Torrigiani, who probably arrived from France around 1506, designed the Westminster Abbey tombs of Henry VII and his wife Queen Elizabeth with seated angels, naked putti, grotesques and garlands. The wider adoption of Renaissance styles in English monuments was a slow and uneven process. Various classical details, including balusters, pilasters, candelabra, vases and garlands, were incorporated in some monuments of the 1520s and 1530s. From the 1550s an increasing number of monuments included classical arches and columns. Effigies began to appear in new reclining or kneeling postures imported from the continent. Framed portrait busts also gained favour. The immigrant craftsmen who worked on funeral monuments included some Frenchmen, but most came from the Netherlands. They and their English imitators provided exuberant decorative elaboration, including coffering, strapwork, ribbonwork, obelisks and allegorical figures. In Scotland the Kirk discouraged the erection of monuments in churches, and far fewer survive.[24]

Nearly all the notable painters who worked in the early Tudor courts were foreigners. The Flemings Lucas and Susanna Horenbout, recruited to Henry VIII's service in 1525, painted exquisite miniature portraits. The greatest artist of Henry's court, Hans Holbein the Younger of Augsburg, arrived for his first stay of 1526–8 with a letter of introduction from Erasmus to Thomas More, whose family he portrayed in a group painting of striking originality. After returning to England c.1532, he worked for the Hanse merchants and drew or painted portraits of most of the leading courtiers and, magnificently, Henry himself. A succession of painters from the Netherlands followed Holbein, including Guillim Scrots, Hans Eworth, Marcus Gheeraerts the Elder and the Younger and Quentin Metsys the Younger. Nicholas Hilliard, the one distinguished English artist, renowned above all for his jewel-like portrait miniatures, wrote the first English treatise on painting. He taught Isaac Oliver, member of a French refugee family from Rouen, but Oliver developed his own distinctive style. Flemish artists painted vividly revealing portraits of James III and IV of Scotland. Two Dutchmen worked in succession as James VI's painter: Arnold Bronckorst and Adrian Vanson. Lord Seton, Mary Stewart's loyal supporter, employed excellent foreign artists, including Frans Pourbus the Elder of Antwerp, to paint himself and his family.[25]

Music

Elizabeth's conservative Reformation allowed church music a place that it lost in Scotland. The distinguished Scottish composer Robert Carver, who worked in Stirling Castle's collegiate church, had no post-Reformation successor. Westminster Abbey, the Chapel Royal, the cathedrals and some university college chapels still employed musicians. Thomas Tallis, gentleman of the Chapel Royal from 1543, and William Byrd, joint Chapel Royal organist with Tallis from 1572, were Catholics at heart but sufficiently adaptable to compose music for both Protestant and Catholic services. Continental composers, especially Roland de Lassus and Giovanni da Palestrina, influenced both Tallis and Byrd. The English and Scottish royal courts were the main centres of secular music. Both employed Italian, French and Flemish musicians. Byrd's friend Alfonso Ferrabosco promoted the madrigal, adopted by Thomas Morley, Thomas Weelkes and John Wilbye. Morley also experimented with the canzonetta (carefree song), Morley and Weelkes with the balletto, an Italian dance soon naturalized along with the stately pavan and the brisker galliard. The lute and the virginals were particularly important in Elizabethan music. The leading English lutenist, the Catholic John Dowland, enjoyed a high European reputation. William Byrd and John Bull (gentleman of the Chapel Royal and first reader in music at Gresham College) were England's foremost composers for virginals, especially of dance music.[26]

Science

Mid-century wars and quests for new trade routes stimulated applied science and mathematics in England. In the 1540s and 1550s the Welshman Robert Recorde, inventor of the '=' sign, expounded mathematics in works of practical instruction, using works by Euclid and modern German mathematicians. Leonard Digges was the first major English writer on applied mathematics. Thomas Gemini, a Flemish instrument maker, published Digges's *Tectonicon* (1556) about land surveying and constructional measurement, using it to advertise his own wares.

During his later years Henry VIII employed Italian engineers who drew fortress plans, the first Englishmen to make scaled maps, and Jean Rotz, a Dieppois map maker of Scots descent who drew a chart of the English Channel. John Dee, a London-born polymath of Welsh extraction, met two leading cartographers, Gerard Mercator and Gemma Frisius, in the Netherlands, studied at Louvain (1548–50) and returned with instruments unavailable in England. He advised both Stephen and William Borough, early Muscovy voyagers, and taught William the use of circumpolar charts. William Borough and other Englishmen soon began to produce improved charts of northern waters. In the 1560s Lawrence Nowell mapped Britain, in the 1570s Humphrey Llwyd Wales, and Christopher Saxton the English counties. Maps became important in estate management and in the drive to control Ireland. In the 1590s Edward Wright produced the first English world map based on

Mercator's projection. In 1561 the Muscovy Company paid Richard Eden to translate Martin Cortes's *Arte de Navigar* (1551), which William Bourne later revised and expanded (1574). The compass maker Robert Norman published *The Newe Attractive* (1581), in which he discussed magnetic dip. In his famous work *De Magnete* (1600), William Gilbert argued that measurements of magnetic dip and compass variation could be used in determining latitude and longitude.

In his great work on the revolutions of the planets (1543) the Polish scholar Copernicus challenged the earth-centred cosmology dominant since late antiquity, arguing that a heliocentric hypothesis was more plausible. Robert Recorde mentioned Copernicus with approval in his *Castle of Knowledge* (1556). Thomas Digges, too, endorsed Copernicus's cosmology in his *Perfit Description of the Caelestiall Orbes* (1576), which also presented an infinite universe. William Gilbert, another Copernican, saw the earth as a giant magnet, and argued that the orientation of its daily rotation was also caused magnetically. The moon was a magnetic satellite of the earth whose attraction of water caused the earth's tides. Gilbert was influenced by some similarly innovative Italian natural philosophers such as Giordano Bruno. Continental astronomers such as Kepler and Galileo read Gilbert's conclusions with enthusiastic interest.

Englishmen also contributed to medicine and natural history. The foremost centres of study, especially Padua, were all on the continent. The two best-known presidents of the Royal College of Physicians, the first, Thomas Linacre (1518–24), and John Caius (1555–60, 1562–3, 1571), gained their medical doctorates at Padua. Both of them studied intensively the works of the celebrated Greek physician Galen. Linacre made internationally admired Latin translations of some of those works, while Caius defended Galen from criticisms, including those of the great anatomist Andreas Vesalius. Caius's detailed account of the sweating sickness was widely read in Europe. William Turner, naturalist and medical graduate of Bologna, but (unlike Caius) a militant Protestant, produced a *Herball* (1551–68) that included a great range of plants from all over Europe. Both Caius and Turner contributed essays to the *Historia Animalium* (1558) of Conrad Gesner of Zurich, the foremost European naturalist. The puritan minister Thomas Penny, an assiduous collector of European plants and insects, also visited Gesner in Zurich in 1565. Penny's friend Thomas Moffet studied medicine at Basel. There he became an admirer of the methods of Paracelsus, renowned advocate of chemical remedies, which Moffet defended (1584). His study of silkworms during a 1580 visit to Italy led to his interest in entomology. He incorporated much of Penny's material in his *Insectorum Theatrum* (1634).

London was the forum where courtiers, gentlemen adventurers, merchants, academics, craftsmen and mariners met, the pot where ideas and practical expertise were blended. The court, naval administration, the great merchant companies, most of the nation's presses, her largest immigrant communities and her biggest concentration of diverse industrial and artisan skills were combined in one place. Thomas Gresham promoted the process of putting theoretical learning to practical uses by endowing free lectures at Gresham College in geometry, medicine and astronomy. Several participants in this London scene were impressively versatile. Thomas Hariot, one of the most brilliant, a man of European reputation, combined expertise in astronomical navigation with interest in pre-European American culture and language, the refraction of light, optics, mathematics, algebra and cartography.

Several foreign refugees or visitors joined London's 'scientific community'. Mathias de L'Obel of Lille worked as a physician as well as superintendent of Lord Zouche's garden. He and his collaborator John Gerard, keeper of Lord Burghley's gardens, both published herbals. Both De l'Obel and James Cool, another botanist, were London neighbours of Thomas Penny and Thomas Moffet. Giordano Bruno, a former friar from Naples, published some of his most radical ideas, including his concept of an infinite universe of solar systems, during a stay in England (1583–5).[27]

Travel

From the 1540s onwards increasing numbers of young Englishmen travelled in Europe in order to observe foreign countries and manners, learn languages and acquire other gentlemenly or professional accomplishments. Some travellers, like Thomas Hoby, who explored Italy in 1548–50, began to record their experiences in diaries. For Hoby, and for Henry Unton and Thomas Bodley later on, travel was a useful preparation for subsequent diplomatic assignments. Philip Sidney, the most celebrated young traveller of the 1570s, made a long tour to equip himself for a major role on the European stage that he was never to fulfil before his death in the 1586 Netherlands campaign. During the 1590s both Lord Burghley and the earl of Essex helped to fund young travellers so that they might supply useful intelligence. The most-visited countries were France, Germany and northern Italy. A few went to Bohemia and even Poland. Some observers mistrusted Italy's powerful allure. Most shunned Rome and Naples during Elizabeth's reign; few appear to have visited Spain.

Dictionaries, grammars and conversation books for the use of learners of foreign languages trickled into print from 1497 onwards. Some of the earliest published English accounts of European travel resulted from pilgrimages to Rome, Santiago de Compostela and Jerusalem. A slightly later pilgrim, Andrew Boorde, undertook much wider-ranging travels (1528–c.1547). His *Introduction of Knowledge* comprises short descriptions of most European countries combining shrewd observations with humorous characterizations. Fynes Moryson was exceptional among Englishmen in the range of his European travels. He visited on two journeys between 1591 and 1597 the Baltic and the Levant as well as all the countries that figured in more familiar variants of the 'grand tour' followed by Elizabethan gentlemen travellers. His subsequent account is outstanding in its vividly recorded detail and its well-informed portrayal of cultural, social and economic differences.

Conclusion

There were numerous links between sixteenth-century Britain and her nearest European neighbours. Scotland's commercial and intellectual connections with France were particularly strong. France and the Netherlands were Britain's main sources of expertise and example in the visual arts. Of all humanists the Dutchman Erasmus had the greatest influence in England. However, study (especially at Padua), sightseeing, diplomacy and (before the Reformation) business at the papal curia took a steady stream of visitors from Britain to Italy. Several of them helped to propagate the influence of Italian ideas and culture in their homelands. England's exceptionally vigorous literary Renaissance owed much to Italy, as did her music.

The Reformation divided Europe. In Britain early Lutheran influence soon gave way to that of Reformed Protestantism. British Protestants fleeing persecution found shelter, support and inspiration in Switzerland and some German cities. Catholics gathered after 1559 especially in the southern Netherlands, France and Italy. Continental seminaries trained priests for missionary work in Britain. Protestant religious exiles from the Netherlands and France contributed to England's economic, scientific and artistic development.

Trade and warfare took men overseas in large numbers. England was more successful than Scotland in extending her trading network between 1550 and 1600 and establishing her commercial presence in southern Europe. But though both countries sent help to beleaguered co-religionists in Europe from the 1560s onwards, a far higher proportion of Scotland's population served in European armies.

8

IDEAS OF BRITAIN AND THE COMING
OF REGAL UNION

Ideas of Britain

The Romans already called the island of Britain 'Britannia' in the first century BC. They subsequently conquered most of the island, but only briefly penetrated Scotland beyond the Forth-Clyde line. Anglo-Saxon invaders eventually conquered approximately the whole area of present-day England and south-east Scotland, mastering Cornwall only in the ninth century. Wales resisted subjugation until after England's own conquest by the Normans.

   The name and idea of Britain were legacies appropriated for their own purposes by the Welsh and the English. The Welsh were widely seen as Britons, descended from the people conquered by the Romans. The Britons who had lived in the parts of Britain occupied by the Anglo-Saxons had been slain, enslaved or driven into flight to the west or overseas to Brittany, little Britain. However, the Welsh, later prophecies declared, would one day recover their lost land of Lloegr (England). Some Anglo-Saxon kings had exacted tribute or oaths of loyalty from Celtic rulers in the areas of what are now Wales and Scotland. The most powerful of them styled themselves 'kings of Britain'.

   Around 1138, the monk Geoffrey of Monmouth completed a mainly fictional narrative *History of the Kings of Britain* that powerfully shaped subsequent ideas of Britain. It tells the island's story between its settlement by Brutus, great-grandson of Aeneas of Troy, and the late seventh century AD. Geoffrey included in his narrative a prophecy that British rule would one day be restored in Britain. Yet he dedicated his work to members of the Anglo-Norman nobility. The Welsh used Geoffrey's *History* to reinforce their sense of their own identity, Anglo-Norman writers to underline the dominant position of 'Engleterre' in Britain. Subsequent accounts expanded and embroidered Geoffrey's narrative and credited Brutus himself with naming England Britain (Brutagne), and giving his younger sons Wales and Scotland, thus appropriating the name 'Britain' for England. This was associated with the idea that

Scotland owed homage to the kings of England. After the Norman conquest several kings of England received such homage. Edward I made the most vigorous efforts to enforce this claimed overlordship.[1]

Against this claim the Scots nobility asserted their own foundation myth in the declaration of Arbroath that they addressed to the pope in 1320. The Scots had 'journeyed from Greater Scythia by way of the Tyrrhenian Sea and the Pillars of Hercules, and dwelt for a long course of time in Spain among the most savage tribes', always unsubdued. Finally they had arrived in 'their home in the west' where they still lived. They had driven out the Britons, utterly destroyed the Picts who had once lived in Scotland and lived free of bondage ever since.

In the fifteenth century some Scotsmen began to use the terms 'Great Britain' or 'Greater Britain' to describe an island within which there were two kingdoms of equal status. John Mair in his *Historia Maioris Britanniae* (Paris, 1521) observed that all those born in Britain were Britons, even though the island was divided into two kingdoms. Mair thoroughly approved of Scottish resistance to Edward I. He nevertheless believed that the Welsh, who were weaker than the Scots, had ultimately benefited from conquest. Union with England would have advantages for Scotland: the English crown had curbed the power of the nobility more effectively than Scottish kings had done. Mair perceived a bigger difference between the 'wild' Highlanders and the Lowland Scots than between the latter and the English. Any union would, however, have to be one of equals. Some elements of the Scottish foundation myth seemed incredible to Mair, but he rejected outright the story of Brutus the Trojan invented by Monmouth. He ridiculed notions of the English crown's rightful overlordship, ultimately based on Monmouth's narrative.[2]

Henry VII encouraged the Italian humanist and papal tax collector Polydore Vergil to write a history of England. The result was a work of a sort new to that country, unprecedented in its scope, the range of sources on which it drew and the author's critical assessment of his texts. Its first three editions were published in Basel (1534–55); the first two covered the years down to 1509, while the third continued until 1537. Britain, according to Vergil, was also named England and Scotland, and was divided into four parts: England, Scotland, Wales and Cornwall. He pointed out that Monmouth's account was in many respects either unsupported by or in conflict with more reliable sources.[3]

Neither Mair nor Vergil successfully banished cherished national foundation myths or heroic narratives. Hector Boece satisfied the expectations of Scottish readers with his credulous and robustly patriotic *Historia Gentis Scotorum* (1527), soon translated into French and Scots, while Mair's great work remained untranslated and largely ignored. The fate of Vergil's *Historia* was different: several English and Welsh writers reviled it as the work of a papal agent who had deliberately concealed or played down the achievements of the peoples of England and Wales, but all serious historians had to take account of it. John Bale, militant Protestant polemicist and historian, attacked Vergil's supposed distortion of early British history yet praised his learning. Bale's own studies, like Mair's, encompassed the whole of 'greater Britain': he published *Illustrium maioris Britanniae scriptorum, hoc est, Angliae, Cambriae, ac Scotiae summarium* (1548), later greatly expanded.

The Tudor period saw the fuller integration of Wales into the English state. The accession of a Welsh dynasty (albeit one whose Welshness had been much diluted by marriage) contributed to this process. Wales provided much of Henry VII's initial support. At the Battle of Bosworth one of Henry's banners depicted a red dragon, symbol of Welsh victory over the Saxons, which thereafter found a secure place in Tudor royal heraldry. Henry traced his descent from ancient British kings, named his first-born son Arthur, observed the day of St David, Wales's patron saint, and employed several Welsh servants in his court. Distinguished Welsh poets enthusiastically celebrated Henry and his British ancestry. Towards the end of his reign he issued charters of privilege that allowed the inhabitants of much of North Wales to hold land and office in England and the English boroughs in Wales.[4]

David Powel, encouraged by Sir Henry Sidney, president of the council in the marches of Wales, published *The Historie of Cambria*, the first history of Wales to appear in print (1584). Powel's chief source for the period down to the late thirteenth century was a manuscript account of the Welsh princes, continuing Geoffrey of Monmouth's *History*, which Humphrey Llwyd had already translated and augmented (1559). The *Historie* documented at length the manifold injustices and oppressions suffered by the Welsh during the conquest, and the 'unreasonable and unconscionable' laws subsequently passed against them. Henry VII had, however, begun to reform their 'thraldom and injuries'. Henry VIII's acts had made Welshmen equal to English subjects in all respects. Powel thought that nothing had been as beneficial to the common people of Wales as their country's uniting to the kingdom of England, which had resulted in uniformity of government. Wales was now as quiet and obedient as any country in Europe. He proudly showed that several recent presidents of the council had had Welsh ancestors. The Pembrokeshire antiquary George Owen of Henllys, who regarded the first two Tudors as 'deliverers' of Wales, observed late in Elizabeth's reign the growth in the numbers and wealth of the Welsh gentry. Since they had been made free to trade and traffic through England, gentlemen and people in Wales had greatly increased in learning and civility. Some had proved to be 'learned men and good members in the Commonwealth of England and Wales'.[5]

The number of Welsh students attending the universities and the Inns of Court grew rapidly. Jesus College, Oxford, founded in 1571 as a result of the efforts of Hugh Price, received the largest number of Welsh undergraduates. Welshmen successful in England or abroad included a number of eminent civil and common lawyers, merchants and soldiers. William Cecil, founder of the foremost political dynasty of later Tudor England, proudly claimed descent from Welsh princes. Humbler migrants spread widely through England.

In his description of Britain, later published as *The Breviary of Britayne* (1573), Humphrey Llwyd accepted the story of Brutus but ridiculed Hector

Boece's claim that the Scots had established a civilized kingdom in Scotland long before the birth of Christ. He cited several classical authorities whose testimony seemed to prove that the Scots had been savage predators who had not become established in Britain before the fifth century AD. Furthermore, the southerners within Scotland were 'not true Scots, but borne and begotten rather of Englishmen'. In his history of Scotland (1582) Scotland's foremost humanist George Buchanan in turn savaged the Brutus myth, but also clung to his belief in a line of Scottish kings traceable to Fergus I, *c.* 330 BC. He also did his best to salvage the notion of the essential cultural unity of the Scottish nation, and the deep roots of the identity that distinguished it from England. His principal concern, however, was to show that Scottish kings had always been accountable to their people. In 1586 William Camden, historian and antiquary, published *Britannia*, a massive, learned and detailed account of the ancient peoples and present constitution and social order of Britain and Ireland, together with a county-by-county description of notable antiquities and distinguished families. Camden claimed that his work had been inspired by love of his country, and the glory of the British name. He travelled widely through England, but did not visit Scotland or Ireland. He in effect demolished the myths of both Brutus and Fergus, and (politely and genially) re-emphasized the deep differences between the 'old' Scots and Scottish Saxons, between Highlanders and Lowlanders, 'descended from the very same Germane originall that we English men are'.[6]

Politics and propaganda before the regal union

The marriage of Margaret Tudor and James IV in 1503 created the possibility of a Scottish succession to the English crown. In 1524 Henry VIII briefly considered James V's marriage to his daughter Mary, but James never figured in any subsequent Henrician plan to settle the succession. Henry was disappointed in his hopes that James would prove a grateful and compliant nephew. In 1542, he pointed out that the kings of England had been superior lords of Scotland ever since the days of Brutus, but asserted that his war with Scotland was due to a series of provocations by James rather than to any desire to exact homage from him. The claim to superiority was later re-asserted by both Henry and Somerset in the course of their efforts to enforce the fulfilment of the 1543 treaty for the marriage of Prince Edward and Mary Stewart.

The most eloquent early advocates of Scotland's union with England were two fervently Protestant Scotsmen, John Elder (in a tract for Henry VIII, *c.*1544) and the Edinburgh merchant James Henrysoun, who published *An Exhortacion to the Scottes to Conforme Them Selfes to the Honorable, Expedient and Godly Union betwene the Twoo Realmes of Englande & Scotlande* (1547). Henrysoun argued that the same people had originally inhabited the whole island of Britain. The blood of various invaders had subsequently been mixed with that of the original stock, but 'the great part of both realms is come of the old Britayns (Britons)'. Henrysoun accepted that the supreme power in the island had rightfully remained with the successors of Brutus's eldest son in England. In any case, Britain (he wrongly believed) had subsequently been re-united under the Emperor Constantine, of British royal descent on his mother's side. Eighteen homages and acknowledgements of subjection by kings of Scotland amply proved their acceptance of the superiority of kings of England. The whole Scottish parliament had assented to the marriage of Mary and Edward, and the treaty had been broken only at the instigation of the devil, the pope, the clergy and the French, who had previously drawn the Scots into ruinous wars. Re-united by marriage, the island empire would be at peace with itself, more prosperous at home, and more formidable abroad. Scots would be near and dear to Englishmen, the more so 'when those hateful terms of Scots and Englishmen, shall be abolished and blotted out for ever, and that we shall all agree in the only title and name of Britons ...'. True knowledge of God's word would be the best means of securing the new concord in men's hearts.[7]

Somerset issued a proclamation on the eve of his invasion of Scotland in 1547 and *An Epistle or Exhortacion, to Unite and Peace* in February 1548, both addressed to a Scottish readership. They employed arguments strongly reminiscent of Henrysoun's, and added some new ones. *An Epistle* pointed out that Scotland was the only other nation to speak the same language as England. God's providence had made possible a union through marriage. Despite England's victory, the Scots were being offered peace, trade, intermarriage, the abolition of hostile laws and English acceptance of 'the indifferent old name of Britaynes again'. There was no intention of depriving any man of his leases or offices, or of changing Scots laws or customs. Any foreign power that came to help Scotland would bring subjection and oppression. Ten years later this warning might have seemed prophetic; at the time it cut little ice. An emphatic riposte to Somerset's propaganda campaign appeared in *The Complaynt of Scotland* (c.1548). This claimed that English rulers, long Scotland's oppressors, were descended from usurpers of the crown of their own country, and had no authority in Scotland.[8]

In 1559 the Lords of the Congregation sought Elizabeth I's help against French intervention. By then, Scots Protestants, though still a minority in their country, were stronger and more numerous than in 1549. The dynastic context had been transformed. Mary Stewart was securely married to the dauphin, soon to be King Francis II. Henry II supported Mary's claim to the English throne. William Cecil saw it as essential to make common cause with Scots Protestants, both on religious grounds and for the sake of England's security. When advocating English intervention in Scotland, Cecil was quite clear that any claim of the superiority of the English crown would only hamper co-operation with the Congregation. In 1560 Scottish commissioners proposed a marriage between Elizabeth and the young third earl of Arran, son of the heir presumptive to the Scottish throne, supporting the proposal with eloquent unionist arguments. Elizabeth turned it down: Arran was dangerously erratic. The marriage would have risked provoking both Mary Stewart and France.

The Treaty of Berwick (February, 1560) provided both that English military aid would be sent to Scotland, and that the earl of Argyll, Highland chief, foremost Protestant magnate in western Scotland, and a Lord of the Congregation, would help to maintain Elizabeth's authority in Ireland. The activities of Scottish mercenaries in Ireland, and MacDonald settlement in north-eastern Ulster, had long concerned governments in Dublin and London. The idea that the head of the clan Campbell, now an ally of the English crown, should help to police Ireland was a strikingly novel one. However, Argyll turned against Elizabeth when she failed to support the rebellion against Mary by Argyll and his allies on her decision to marry Darnley in 1565.[9]

After Francis II's death (December 1560), Scotland once more had an unmarried queen, resident in her native land from August 1561: a queen who had still not repudiated her own claim to the crown of England. Mary might have been prepared to sacrifice that claim in return for recognition as Elizabeth's successor. But Elizabeth regarded such recognition as far too dangerous to the stability of her rule. Mary turned down Elizabeth's 1564 suggestion that she marry Robert Dudley, newly promoted earl of Leicester, probably intended to make her succession more acceptable in England. Meanwhile, Henry VIII's will, which favoured the claim of Catherine Grey and remained eloquently silent about the Stewart line, had not been superseded. Supporters of the Protestant Grey claim and conservative advocates of Mary's who cast doubt on the validity of Henry's will engaged in a pamphlet controversy during the 1560s. William Cecil viewed the Catholic Mary with profound suspicion as a potential tool of the Guises and source of encouragement for English Catholics, and did what he could to prevent her succession. However, even after Mary's flight into England, and involvement in the Ridolfi Plot, Elizabeth refused to consent to her statutory exclusion from the English succession.

Mary's execution in 1587 and the Protestantism of her son James made a Stewart succession seem more acceptable. Apart from assuring James that no right or title he possessed would be prejudiced by his mother's personal guilt, Elizabeth refused to give him positive recognition or encouragement. Equally, however, she failed to promote or support the claims of any of the possible successors who might claim by virtue of her father's will. Looking back from the 1720s, Sir John Clerk of Penicuik judged that '[Elizabeth] so managed [James] with the prospect of succeeding to her throne that the present union of the British crowns can be called her achievement'. Both Mary I and James VI pursued the aim of dynastic union with England. This contributed to making Scotland 'a satellite state', even though both monarchs took care to demonstrate their independence in various ways.[10]

In his pseudonymously published *Conference about the Next Succession to the Crown of England* (1594), the Jesuit Robert Persons marshalled all possible arguments against James's succession, including illegitimacy in his ancestry, the mutual antipathy of the English and Scots, and the incompatibility of the English and Scottish churches. One of the possible successors by virtue of Henry's will would be better, though Persons clearly preferred the claim

112

of Philip II's daughter Isabella, descended from John of Gaunt. Persons succeeded in sowing mistrust and suspicion in some English minds, especially that of the increasingly paranoid Essex. In one respect, however, his efforts were counter-productive: they served to strengthen the conviction of staunch Protestants that James now represented the best prospect of excluding a Catholic successor.

The outspoken parliamentarian Peter Wentworth, imprisoned after indiscreetly revealing his plan to demand a settlement of the succession in the parliament of 1593, wrote a powerful *Discourse* defending James's right that was posthumously published in Edinburgh in 1598. Wentworth sought to counter the potentially powerful objection of 'the natural aversion of the two nations', pointing to what seemed like evidence of God's purpose to unite them, including 'unity of true Religion ... unity of language, likeness of discipline and manners, the long peace and concord of the Princes and countries, the often and next descent of the Scottish king from the blood royal of England, his rare wisdom and love of Religion, with sound knowledge and judgement in matters of the same'. The strongest potential English competitors had been removed. Many feared the favour that James was likely to show Scotsmen. Yet (Wentworth continued) James had already shown notable partiality towards Englishmen. He would be so 'won to us, and englished with us' that Scotland would have more cause to fear their subjection to some English deputy than England to fear subjection to the Scots. Wasn't this the way for the English to subordinate by policy a people whom they had not been able to conquer in centuries? Henry VII, in marrying his daughter to James IV, had rightly been convinced that 'the worthier kingdom would annexe and draw to it the lesser and weaker'. The English would no less keep their pre-eminence above the Scots after submitting to their king than they had kept it over the Welshmen after submitting to Henry VII. James's accession would not only bring increase of subjects, but also make England less dependent on foreign alliances. Ireland, facing England and Scotland combined, would be easier to keep in loyal obedience.[11]

Much of Wentworth's forecast of the long-term benefits that would accrue to England from the regal union proved remarkably prescient. It is impossible to say how far the privy councillors who ensured James's peaceful succession might have accepted Wentworth's analysis. The lack of opposition in England does, however, suggest that Wentworth was right in believing that the 'natural aversion' of Englishmen for Scots had indeed been much diminished.

The cases of Wales and Scotland were very different. For all their pride in their identity and ancient culture, the Welsh were a previously subject people who gained a great deal from Tudor rule, particularly their full integration into the Tudor state. As Wentworth saw only too clearly, previously independent Scotland was likely to find herself the subordinate partner as the result of a regal union. It is all the more striking that Scotland had produced in James Henrysoun the most ardent advocate of union, as she also produced in John Mair the first true historian of Britain. Mair combined patriotism with an appreciation of the benefits of union and of what was necessary for its success that was far ahead of his time. His ideas failed to find a popular audience, and his history found no translator in early modern times.

Unions in mainland Europe

There were no exact continental parallels with British developments. Duchess Anne of Brittany married Charles VIII of France in 1491, but it was not until 1532 that the estates of Brittany were prompted to request full union with France, together with confirmation of Breton privileges. The union became complete in 1536. As a duchy long under one ruler, with its own estates and *parlement*, Brittany had far stronger independent institutions than Wales. Wales gained more from Tudor governmental reforms and the grant of parliamentary representation than Brittany did from the settlement of 1532, while also preserving an ethnic identity at least as strong as Brittany's. The French language had already made substantial advances in eastern Brittany. Although the first printed Breton appeared in 1499 in a trilingual dictionary nearly fifty years before the first book in Welsh, thirty books had been printed in Welsh by 1600, compared with five containing Breton. Brittany's rich tradition of religious art had no counterpart in post-Reformation Wales, but the Welsh Bible and Prayer Book contributed crucially to the survival of the language. Secular poetry and bardic culture may also have been stronger in Wales than in Brittany.[12]

All over Europe, kingdoms entered unions of varying degrees of permanence. In 1526 Hungary, Croatia, Bohemia and the Austrian lands came together in the largest such combination, basis of the later Austrian Empire. Poland and Lithuania, in personal union since 1386, became one commonwealth in 1569. The union of Castile and Aragon, neighbouring kingdoms with related languages in a peninsula separated from the rest of Europe by a formidable mountain range, also bore some resemblance to subsequent British developments. There were, however, significant differences. Despite occasional past conflicts between the two kingdoms, there was no history of enmity stemming from the aggression of the larger kingdom such as existed in Britain. They shared a long experience of wars with the Moors. Some historians thought of the whole peninsula as 'Spain'. It was known to have been under one ruler for long periods before the Moorish invasions.[13] When Philip II forcibly asserted his claim to the Portuguese throne in 1580, the Portuguese *Cortes* soon accepted it.

Geographical contiguity and linguistic and ethnic similarities were not enough to guarantee the success of a union of kingdoms. The troubles of the Union of Kalmar, accepted by Denmark, Norway and Sweden in 1397, were largely due to the misjudged centralizing ambitions and neglect of Swedish interests by kings based in Denmark. Christian II finally wrecked the Union by massacring his Swedish opponents in 1520.

In both Germany and Italy, humanists invoked a national spirit in face of insuperable barriers created by political divisions. The idea of the resistance of hardy, virtuous Germans to a corrupt Rome possibly made some contribution to the spread of the Lutheran Reformation, even though that movement ultimately served to fragment Germany even more severely. In Italy, Niccolo Machiavelli ended *The Prince*, ostensibly a hard-headed work of political advice, with a sudden passionate plea to the Medici to lead an attempt to free the Italian fatherland from the barbarians. His entreaty fell on deaf ears. Machiavelli's patriotic vision was totally unrealistic; instead, Spain became the dominant power in Italy.

PART II

1603–1707

9

THE FAILURE OF STUART KINGSHIP AND THE BRITISH REVOLUTIONS, 1603-60

James VI and I

James VI's unchallenged succession to the English throne was greeted with joy and relief. Peace with Spain was his most important objective abroad. Defeat in Ireland had ended Spanish prospects of dealing England a decisive blow. War weariness was widespread on both sides. The rulers of the Spanish Netherlands strongly desired peace and friendly relations with James.[1] In the Treaty of London (1604), Spain gained no promise of toleration for English Catholics, England no concession of access to America. But the English crown withdrew from the war in the Netherlands, and the treaty inaugurated a period of friendlier relations and a boom for English trade. Within three years of the peace England founded Virginia, her first permanent settlement in America.

James's most cherished domestic policies, closer union between England and Scotland, and religious harmony, will be discussed more fully in subsequent chapters. He swiftly and realistically abandoned over-ambitious hopes of union in face of clear signs of alarm on both sides of the border. He was nevertheless badly bruised by the obstructive and sometimes belligerent opposition that a much narrower set of proposals encountered in the House of Commons in 1606–7. James used prerogative powers to gain some of his ends. He unilaterally assumed the title of King of Great Britain. He also appointed some Scots to his privy council, and many more to his household, though many Englishmen resented these uses of his patronage.

The personal union of 1603 inevitably affected Scotland more than England. She lost her king and his court, but the king was better able to reward service, and the Scots no longer had to meet the costs of the court. Rivalry for favour now focused on Whitehall. The transformation of the borders into the 'middle shires' removed a major source of intermittent turbulence. Scotland enjoyed unusual peace, governed by a firm and experienced privy council in constant touch with the king.

Ireland became an important new field for Anglo-Scottish or British enterprise after James's accession. In 1607, the defeated earls of Tyrconnel and Tyrone, fearing and resenting the Irish government's efforts to weaken their authority over lesser lords, suddenly went abroad, ultimately to Rome. The earls' lordships were confiscated, opening up large parts of Ulster for 'plantation' by British incomers. James welcomed the lord deputy's suggestion that Scots should be involved in the settlement. Both Scots and Englishmen were granted substantial estates. They were supposed to bring in British tenants; some Scots had already been settled in the north-eastern counties before 1607. In practice many Irish tenants remained (besides those Irishmen who were granted some 20 per cent of the land). London companies were required to finance the development of the ports of Derry and Coleraine. By 1622 there were about 12,000 British settlers on the confiscated lands, of whom 54 per cent were Scots.[2]

James made it clear that he disliked religious persecution, but also that he expected outward obedience. He would not tolerate puritan agitation for alteration of church government, or the maintenance of the pope's power over temporal sovereigns. He declared his unswerving loyalty to his Protestant faith. High hopes of changes in policy after his accession on the part of both puritans and Catholics were not fulfilled. Catholic disappointment provoked the Bye Plot of June 1603 and the Gunpowder Plot of 1605. However, the deprivation of some puritan ministers and new legislation against Roman Catholics were followed by relative quietness and no major persecution.

Robert Cecil (earl of Salisbury from 1605) held an unprecedented combination of offices as principal secretary of state, master of the court of wards and (from 1608) lord treasurer. He successfully increased the king's revenues, particularly by means of new impositions on trade following a judgement in their favour in 1606, but failed to curb James's extravagance or to achieve in 1610 the 'Great Contract' by which James would have sacrificed some unpopular prerogative revenues in exchange for a permanent parliamentary income. The young Scotsman Robert Carr became James's intimate favourite after 1607. James made him his personal secretary after Salisbury's death in 1612, and earl of Somerset in 1613. Carr's subsequent insensitive neglect of James, and his involvement in lurid scandal along with his wife Frances Howard, led to his downfall in 1616. The leading Protestant 'patriot' privy councillors had already found James a handsome new favourite, George Villiers, whom James made earl (1617) and duke (1623) of Buckingham and lord admiral (1619).

James intended to maintain friendship with all Britain's neighbours and to promote international peace. His choices of marriage partners for his children were designed to establish links with both Protestant and Catholic Europe. Spain and the United Provinces concluded a twelve years truce in 1609. Within the Empire, however, rival religious alliances were formed: the Protestant Union, led by the Calvinist Elector Palatine (1608), and the Catholic League (1609). A succession dispute concerning the strategically important duchy of Cleves-Jülich on the Dutch border almost led to French military intervention.

A Catholic zealot assassinated Henry IV in 1610 on the verge of hostilities. James helped to achieve a settlement in November 1614. In March 1612 James signed a treaty with the Protestant Union, aiming both to give the Union defensive support and to influence it in favour of peace. Frederick V, the Elector Palatine, married James's daughter Elizabeth in 1613. James had intended a Catholic match for his son Henry (despite Henry's ambition to be a leader of the Protestant cause), but Henry unexpectedly died in November 1612.

Frederick dealt the fatal blow to James's vision of peace when he accepted election to the Bohemian throne in 1619. The estates of Bohemia, a largely Protestant kingdom within the Empire, had already accepted a Habsburg candidate, the Archduke Ferdinand, but found him too zealously Catholic, and renounced their allegiance. Ferdinand's election as Emperor Ferdinand II soon followed. In November 1620 imperial and Catholic League troops defeated Frederick outside Prague, in the first major engagement of what was to become the notoriously destructive 'Thirty Years War' in the Empire. In 1620 Spanish troops began to occupy Frederick's Lower Palatinate, partly in order to secure supply lines to the Netherlands, where the truce of 1609 was due to expire in 1621. James found himself in a nightmarish predicament. Frederick's action had infuriated him, but he could not accept the conquest of the Palatinate without dishonour. He allowed English volunteers to occupy strongholds there. Any serious attempt to help Frederick would require parliamentary subsidies. James's first parliament had ended acrimoniously in 1610. He had swiftly dissolved the 'Addled' parliament of 1614 after complaints about impositions on trade. When his third parliament met in 1621, James undertook to make war to recover the Palatinate if necessary. The Commons made a grant of taxation intended to be generous, but quite insufficient to pay for a continental campaign. Some members were bent on the redress of grievances, particularly monopoly patents. The ancient procedure of impeachment was revived to deal with grantees and the man held ultimately responsible for the grants, the lord chancellor, Francis Bacon.

James had opened negotiations for a marriage between his second son, Prince Charles, and the Spanish infanta Maria in 1614. He hoped this match would seal Anglo-Spanish friendship, provide a dowry large enough to reduce his financial dependence on parliament and lead to the restoration of the Palatinate. But the idea of a Catholic marriage was widely disliked in England. In December 1621, the Commons decided to petition James for war against Spain if she did not withdraw from Frederick's hereditary lands, and for Charles's marriage to a Protestant, which offended the Prince. James angrily rebuked the Commons for interfering in matters beyond their competence. They responded with a protestation defending their freedom of speech in dealing with 'arduous and urgent' matters of state. James then dissolved parliament and ripped the protestation from the Commons Journal. Yet another of James's parliaments had ended in acrimony.[3]

Early in 1623, Buckingham and Charles undertook a highly unconventional courtship journey to Madrid. After an initial welcome, Philip IV (who had become king in 1621) ultimately refused to allow Maria to leave Spain until England's anti-Catholic penal laws had been repealed. Charles and Buckingham returned home furious with what they thought humiliating treatment, and pressed for a war that James still intended to avoid. When his fourth parliament met in 1624, supporters of Charles and Buckingham tried to win the Commons' confidence by proposing that any taxation granted should be specifically appropriated to the war. The Commons offered help towards a war fought on sea and land in close alliance with the Dutch, a project repugnant to James. The lord treasurer, Lionel Cranfield, earl of Middlesex, saw that war would wreck crown finances. Buckingham, his former patron, would not tolerate his opposition. He was impeached on charges of corruption.

A French marriage was then sought as an alternative to the failed Spanish match. Louis XIII, Henry IV's son and successor, accepted a marriage between his sister Henrietta Maria and Prince Charles in December 1624. He promised to help support a predominantly English expedition to the Palatinate under the command of the German Count Mansfeld. Delayed by Anglo-French disagreements about its route, Mansfeld's army set off for the Netherlands, where much of it succumbed to starvation or disease.

James died in March 1625. His failed foreign policy underlined some of his most serious weaknesses as a ruler. He had proved unable to control the actions of Frederick, Charles or Buckingham. He had repeatedly underestimated the difficulties facing him and optimistically misread other men's intentions. In his tenacious pursuit of peace, he had sometimes seemed duplicitous. The collapse of his foreign ambitions wrecked attempts to solve his financial problems and exacerbated England's religious divisions.

Charles I

Charles and Buckingham believed that their plan to help Frederick by fighting Spain would be popular. They had promoted a marriage alliance with France, traditionally Spain's chief opponent. France was, however, not yet ready for war and faced her own internal problems. In order to obtain the marriage treaty, James had promised not to enforce the laws against Catholics, a condition bound to be unpopular in England.

Charles's first parliament met in June 1625, soon after his marriage to the French princess Henrietta Maria. Already there was deep disquiet about royal policy in the Commons. The House infuriated Charles by granting him tonnage and poundage for one year only, instead of for life, as had been customary since 1484. This was due to concern about the use of the crown's prerogative to introduce new impositions. Parliament's grant of subsidies was insufficient for the war. An Anglo-Dutch naval expedition to Cadiz, the year's great enterprise, failed totally because of a late start, inadequate funding and poor discipline. After Charles's second parliament met in February 1626, the Commons tried to impeach Buckingham, the lord admiral. The long list of charges included waste, corruption and incompetence. Charles angrily dissolved parliament without waiting for the completion of a subsidy grant. His hopes for 1626 centred on an anti-Habsburg alliance of England, the United Provinces and Denmark, but a series of setbacks culminated in the defeat of Charles's uncle Christian IV of Denmark at Lutter in August. Charles had been unable to give Christian the financial help he had promised. In September he authorized the raising of a forced loan which, though highly controversial, was remarkably successful.

The marriage treaty had created fresh problems for Charles by binding him to help Louis XIII against his own Protestant rebels. Early in 1626 France nevertheless made a new treaty with Spain. Buckingham held Cardinal Richelieu, Louis XIII's chief minister, personally responsible for what he regarded as shameful duplicity, and plotted Richelieu's overthrow. He planned an English expedition to provoke a rebellion by a coalition of Richelieu's domestic opponents. In 1627 Buckingham led an expedition that attempted to break the siege of Huguenot La Rochelle, but the English army eventually had to withdraw with heavy losses.

England was now at war with both the European great powers, though Charles lacked the resources to fight either effectively. The now inevitable new parliament met in March 1628. MPs' fear and anger focused above all on the unprecedented use of prerogative powers by an unfortunate and incompetent government. Charles had continued to levy tonnage and poundage without a grant. He had raised the forced loan despite the judges' collective refusal to declare it legal and then imprisoned about seventy non-lenders, five of whom had challenged the legality of their imprisonment in vain. The Commons prepared a Petition of Right, seeking to outlaw taxation without parliamentary consent, imprisonment without cause shown, the compulsory billeting of troops on civilians and the enforcement of martial law instead of due legal process. All these grievances stemmed directly from Charles's efforts to wage war. After a non-committal first answer, he finally assented and received a generous subsidy grant.

A Commons remonstrance blaming Buckingham as the cause of the ills afflicting the realm influenced a soldier who assassinated the favourite as he was preparing another expedition to La Rochelle. National rejoicing aggravated Charles's grief. La Rochelle surrendered to Louis XIII's army in October. Parliament met for its second session in January 1629. Charles spoilt his chance of regularizing the collection of tonnage and poundage by trying to avoid publishing his consent to the Petition of Right. A minority of MPs forestalled an inevitable dissolution by passing three resolutions while forcibly holding the speaker in his chair. The resolutions denounced those who introduced religious innovations or untrue religious ideas, those who advised the king to collect tonnage and poundage without Parliament's consent and those who willingly paid it. Charles condemned this action and declared that he would be readier to meet parliament again when his people better understood his intentions and actions. He made peace with France in April 1629 and Spain in November 1630.

Ferdinand II now seemed the decisive victor of the war in Germany, where militant Protestantism had been crushed. Meanwhile, however, the Dutch had held their own, achieving in 1628 the old Anglo-Dutch ambition of capturing the Spanish treasure fleet. In 1630, when the Protestant cause in the Empire seemed at its lowest ebb, help came from a new source. King Gustavus Adolphus of Lutheran Sweden, convinced of the need to check the growth of Habsburg power, led an army to Germany. He decisively defeated Catholic League and imperial forces at Breitenfeld in September 1631. Swedish forces occupied Munich, capital of Ferdinand's principal ally, Maximilian of Bavaria, in 1632. In 1630 Charles I had allowed the marquis of Hamilton to raise 6,000 men to fight under Gustavus, and in 1631-2 he investigated the possibility of an Anglo-Swedish alliance. However, Gustavus died in battle in November 1632. Renewed imperial successes enabled Ferdinand to make the favourable Treaty of Prague (May 1635).

Peace in Germany was already doomed by France's declaration of war on Spain a few days beforehand. The two great powers had long been moving gradually closer to an open confrontation. In 1629-31 Louis XIII had intervened on behalf of a French claimant to the duchy of Mantua in northern Italy, where Spain was the dominant power. Richelieu undermined Ferdinand II by means of generous subsidies to Sweden. He also offered French protection to several German states. Spain could not tolerate this threat to its overland route to the Netherlands, and in March 1635 expelled French troops from Trier.

Unable to make war, Charles favoured James's policy of trying to regain the Palatinate for Frederick or, after Frederick's death in 1632, his son Charles Louis, with Spanish help. Some councillors with strong Catholic leanings, including Richard Weston, earl of Portland, lord treasurer, favoured this course. After 1630, Spanish silver was able to pass through England on its way to Flanders. A secret Anglo-Spanish agreement of 1631, never ratified, even envisaged a joint attack on the United Provinces. Charles's more vigorously Protestant advisers strongly favoured a Dutch alliance. But Anglo-Dutch rivalry in trade and fishing made it seem sensible to contain the United Provinces' growing power. Richelieu wanted to draw Charles into an anti-Habsburg alliance. Henrietta Maria and some councillors and courtiers associated with her backed it energetically. They advised Charles to summon a parliament, but he was not ready for this step. Thousands of British, and especially Scottish, volunteers joined the great continental struggle, but Britain's king took no part in it.[4]

Charles was determined to re-assert his authority, threatened (in his view) by religious discord and financial weakness. Charles and William Laud, archbishop of Canterbury from 1633 onwards, aimed to strengthen the Church, enforce liturgical uniformity and prevent doctrinal disputes. Unfortunately, the numerous critics of these policies associated them with the sorts of undesirable religious innovation condemned in the Commons' Protestation of 1629. By the 1630s, most of the royal revenues were based on the king's claimed prerogatives. A wide variety of sources, many of them unpopular, were tapped. Taxes on foreign trade were, however, the increasingly important mainstay of the royal finances. It was imperative to build up naval strength, not only to protect trade from the depredations of pirates, especially North African corsairs, but also to assert control over eastern coastal fisheries, and to maximize England's ability to facilitate or hamper the passage of foreign ships through the Channel, her most important strategic asset. In 1634, Charles's government levied ship money for the building of the fleet from English coastal counties, and from 1635 onwards extended the levy to all inland counties. Both the peacetime levy of ship money and its imposition on inland counties were unprecedented. In 1638, in John Hampden's case, the judges nevertheless upheld the king's action, albeit by the narrow majority of seven to five. The fleet was expanded, a squadron of royal ships cruised the Channel every year between 1635 and 1641, and an expedition was sent against Moroccan pirates in 1637.

His disastrous mishandling of Scotland ended Charles's attempt to gain greater freedom and authority for the monarchy throughout Britain. Charles did not share his father's enthusiasm for closer union. He believed that Scotland would be easier to govern as a separate country, but showed indifference to Scottish feelings. He began his Scottish reign with an act revoking grants of crown and church property made since 1540. He never envisaged a general resumption of the lands in question, but intended to increase crown revenues and provision for the parish clergy, and to loosen the dependence of lesser landholders on feudal overlords.[5] The whole process caused much resentment and uncertainty. The original scheme was never implemented in full. Charles first visited Scotland in 1633. His elaborate coronation shocked Scottish religious sensibilities. He did his best to stifle debate about taxes in his first Scottish parliament.

Collapse of royal authority in three kingdoms

Charles's imposition of a new Scottish Prayer Book in 1637 provoked riots and a flood of petitions. Charles faced with outraged incomprehension a subsequent general petition, a national supplication organized by several noblemen, the supplicants' establishment of a representative body of the four estates, and the adoption in February 1638 of a new National Covenant, soon distributed for nationwide signature. In November the first general assembly convened for twenty years condemned all innovations in the Kirk since 1617 and abolished episcopacy. The revolution of 1637, like the Scottish Reformation itself, rested on a covenant and was introduced without royal authority.[6]

Charles first moved to suppress the Covenanters in 1639. They easily defeated his supporters in conservative north-eastern Scotland. Charles sent an unwilling and inexperienced English force to the border, but then made a truce. Charles agreed to convene a general assembly and parliament. He could not control the parliament. It protested about Charles's attempt to prorogue it without its consent, and established a committee of estates to await his reply. Charles's setbacks in Scotland undermined his authority in England.

Rather than give up the attempt to subdue the Scots, Charles turned to an English parliament (April 1640). He hoped that a letter from the Covenanters to Louis XIII would outrage members. But they were more concerned with their own grievances: the treatment of the previous parliament, the growth of Catholic influence and breaches of subjects' rights. Facing the Commons' reluctance to grant sufficient taxation without concessions he found unacceptable, and fearing that some members were co-operating with the Scots, Charles swiftly dissolved the 'Short Parliament'.

Might Spain help Charles? He had allowed Spanish troops to march through England on their way to the Netherlands, thus reducing their exposure to Dutch attack at sea. In September 1639 a Spanish armada sailed towards Flanders with reinforcements. Charles's fleet had orders to prevent a Dutch attack on the fleet, but Admiral Tromp largely destroyed it off the English coast. Charles was humiliated. In 1640 hope of Spanish assistance vanished as rebellions exploded in Catalonia and Portugal.

In June 1640 the Scottish parliament re-convened at the date earlier set by Charles, excluded bishops from its ranks and passed an act ensuring that it met at least once every three years in future, in both cases setting examples followed by the English parliament in 1641–2. It formally empowered the committee of estates to govern the kingdom. Encouraged by Thomas Wentworth, earl of Strafford, lord deputy of Ireland, his most resolute adviser, Charles decided on what he hoped would be a swift and decisive campaign against the Scots. He had difficulty in raising an army. Knowing Charles's intentions, and well aware of his weakness, the Scots struck first in August and, brushing resistance aside, seized Newcastle. This unprecedented defeat was possible only because Charles had so little active English support. He agreed in October to pay the Scottish army occupying Northumberland and County Durham until a settlement was reached, and to summon an English parliament to meet in November. Charles had finally been forced into unwilling partnership with Lords and Commons.

Several of the king's closest advisers were impeached. The earl of Strafford, thought to present the greatest continuing danger, was condemned by act of attainder in May 1641. The king sacrificed his ablest servant because he feared for his family's safety in face of London mob pressure. He also accepted major limitations on his prerogatives, to be described in Chapter 11. The Commons condemned religious innovations, but remained deeply divided over further measures of Church reform. In August Charles ratified the treaty providing for the withdrawal of the Scottish army, and visited Scotland in the vain hope of building up support there.

A disastrous new setback for Charles was a formidable rebellion that began in Ireland in October. Strafford had been a firm lord deputy, resolute in following policies that alienated every major Irish group. His efforts to strengthen the Church of Ireland and align it more closely with the Church of England alarmed Irish Protestants. Scots settlers resented the imposition of a 'black oath' to abjure the Covenant. His determination to make Irish administration pay for itself by increasing income from taxation and feudal dues affected all property owners. He alienated both Old English and Old Irish Catholics. In 1628, a delegation of landowners had agreed to support a generous grant of taxation in return for relaxation of the anti-Catholic penal legislation and confirmation of titles to land held for over sixty years. When the next parliament met in 1634 Wentworth got the taxation he wanted, but refused to confirm all the 'Graces'. In 1640, the Irish parliament sent to England a remonstrance against his government.

The Covenanters' triumph and the anti-Catholicism sweeping Britain frightened Irish Catholics. Several Catholic nobles and gentry planned a rising, presenting themselves as loyal subjects forestalling action by subversive puritans. In October 1641 they failed to seize Dublin Castle, but Sir Phelim O'Neill's followers rapidly took over much of Ulster. The rebellion got out of hand. Many settlers were killed or dispossessed. Reports reaching Britain enormously magnified the numbers involved. The rebels' claim that Charles had authorized their measures raised alarm at Westminster to fever pitch.

John Pym, leading manager of the year's reforming legislation, seized this opportunity to present the 'Grand Remonstrance' to the Commons, a long catalogue of the disasters of Charles's reign, parliament's achievements and additional measures judged necessary. A vigorous debate ended in a very close vote in favour of the Remonstrance. Its opponents deplored its provocative tone, its authors' failure to consult the Lords and especially its publication in an apparent appeal to the country. The king increasingly appeared to be defending rather than threatening the constitution. The cause of 'constitutional royalism' at Westminster was nevertheless badly damaged by Charles's subsequent mistakes, culminating in his personal attempt on 4 January 1642 to arrest on charges of high treason the five leaders of the Commons 'junto', John Pym and four other MPs who, forewarned, had already fled. Meanwhile, in London, a broad-based popular movement, deeply hostile to Catholicism and episcopacy, had staged huge demonstrations in Westminster in support of Charles's parliamentary opponents, and taken control of the London Common Council from the City oligarchy after municipal elections in December. The 'Five Members', followed by the rest of the Commons, now took refuge in the Guildhall, seat of London's municipal government. The London Common Council refused to surrender the 'Five Members' on 5 January 1642. Five days later the king left London.

The leaders of the parliamentary majority would not trust Charles with control over any armed forces sent to Ireland, fearing that he might use them against parliament. In March 1642, when he refused assent to the Militia bill, which put the English counties' military resources under parliamentary control, parliament passed it as an ordinance with statutory force. The Lords and Commons made one more attempt to bind Charles to them by presenting Nineteen Propositions (1 June). These requested among other things the future appointment of privy councillors, ministers of state and other officers of trust with the approval of parliament or (between parliaments) of the majority of the privy council; the Church's reformation with Parliament's advice; and a closer alliance with the United Provinces and other states to defend the Protestant religion. (In 1641 Charles had already married his eldest daughter Mary to William of Orange, son of Frederick Henry, stadholder of most of the United Provinces.) Charles's eloquent answer, drafted by former critics of his government who were now 'constitutional royalists', argued that the Propositions threatened the balance of the constitution.

Civil wars

It was not long before parliament voted to raise an army of 10,000 volunteers in June 1642, and Charles raised his standard at Nottingham in August. Parliament controlled much of the machinery of central government, the fleet and the resources of London and of most of south-eastern England. Although the king's only march on London (November 1642) after the indecisive Battle of Edgehill encountered such determined resistance that he did not risk an attack, he held the upper hand for most of 1643. Parliament created new institutions to wage war, and raised new taxes. The king set up his own administration in Oxford, held a rival parliament there and matched or followed Parliament's administrative and fiscal innovations, though on the whole less effectively.

Parliament looked to the Scots for help. The Covenanters, influenced by their army's setbacks in Ireland and fears of a royalist rising in Scotland coupled with an English royalist invasion, were keen on a closer alliance.[7] English parliamentary commissioners sent to Edinburgh agreed in August 1643 on a Solemn League and Covenant with the Scots, ratified by the English parliament in September after an acrimonious debate. A large Scottish army entered England in January 1644, and joined with parliamentary forces to defeat royalists under Charles's nephew Prince Rupert on Marston Moor near York in July. The royalists lost control of the north of England, but Charles won a major victory soon afterwards at Lostwithiel (Cornwall) in September.

Meanwhile 1,600 men recruited in Ireland by Randall MacDonnell, earl of Antrim, landed in western Scotland in July 1644, led by Alasdair MacDonald ('MacColla'). With their help, the marquis of Montrose, the king's lieutenant in Scotland, won several spectacular victories over larger forces. He trounced the earl of Argyll, head of Clan Campbell, the MacDonalds' inveterate foes. Only in September 1645 did David Leslie, with troops returned from England, overcome his army at Philiphaugh.

In England, many members of parliament including Oliver Cromwell, a major contributor to the victory at Marston Moor, were increasingly critical of some parliamentary generals' cautious conduct and resentful of the price of the Scots alliance – a Presbyterian system of church government that they thought intolerably restrictive. The 'Presbyterians' remained a majority, but faced an increasingly restive 'Independent' group. Early in 1645 parliament passed two momentous measures: one provided for the creation of a 'New

Model' Army. The other, the 'Self-denying Ordinance', barred members of both houses from military or civil appointments made by parliament during the war. Modified to allow re-appointments before the Lords accepted it, the Ordinance nevertheless facilitated the promotion of more energetic and resolute senior officers. The New Model Army under Sir Thomas Fairfax broke Charles's main force at Naseby in June, and destroyed his western army at Langport in July. Charles surrendered himself into Scottish custody in May 1646.

The king had been decisively defeated, but all parties still firmly intended to include him in any settlement. Charles considered himself indispensable. He hoped to play his enemies off against each other, and span out negotiations. In July, still in Scots hands, he received in Newcastle the 'Newcastle Propositions', parliament's terms for a settlement. They included Charles's acceptance of the Solemn League and Covenant, parliamentary control of the armed forces for twenty years and parliamentary nomination of all major officers of state and judges. Charles could not accept them. In January 1647 the Scots delivered him to the English parliament.

Parliament now wanted to disband the armed forces as far as possible, and send some of the New Model to deal with the Irish rebellion. The spring of 1647 saw steadily mounting disquiet and anger in the ranks of the army. A petition presented to Fairfax in March expressed their concerns, above all about substantial arrears of pay. A junior officer seized the king in June. Fairfax and his senior commanders approved a *Declaration* demanding the purging of unfit members from parliament and parliamentary reform. After a bitter rift between Presbyterians and Independents in parliament, a London 'counter-revolution' against the Independents and the army and the flight of leading Independent members to seek the army's protection, the army occupied London in August. These events strengthened Charles's conviction that he was indispensable. In July the army had presented him with 'The Heads of the Proposals' for a settlement, agreed by a new General Council of the Army and the leading parliamentary Independents. More generous to the king, these proposals allowed religious freedom for all Protestants, and called for parliament's own reform. Charles indicated that he preferred them to the 'Newcastle Propositions', but did not formally accept them.

The Levellers, radicals outside and inside the army, impatient of slow progress towards a settlement and suspicious of the negotiations with Charles, advocated more thoroughgoing political reforms. *An Agreement of the People*, the fullest statement of their programme so far, was debated at Putney in late October and early November after consideration by the Army's General Council. Senior officers were increasingly concerned about the army's divisions, and in November crushed a Leveller mutiny. Meanwhile Charles escaped to the Isle of Wight, where in December he clinched the 'Engagement' with a Scots party led by the duke of Hamilton. This included a three-year trial period for Presbyterianism in England. Agreement with the Scots 'Engagers' seemed to offer him the prospect of more freedom of action than the possible alternatives. Royalist risings erupted during the spring of 1648 in south-eastern England. Most had been suppressed before the Engagers' army entered England in July. Cromwell and John Lambert routed it south of Preston in August. The defeat precipitated a rising by the Engagers' opponents in Scotland. The English army's programme was unacceptable to the Covenanters. But many Scots did not trust Charles. A majority of the Kirk's general assembly, and a minority of nobles led by Argyll, bitterly opposed the Engagement. Cromwell reached Edinburgh and made an agreement with them in October.

The army's decisive victory in this 'second civil war' strengthened parliament's urgent desire to reach a settlement with Charles. However, the Council of Officers finally decided that negotiations must be ended and the king brought to trial. Parliament rejected their demands in December. The army then purged parliament, excluding many MPs, especially those who had just voted to continue the negotiations with Charles. Many stayed away. The purged Commons agreed to establish a court to try the king. The Lords resisted; the Commons resolved that they themselves had supreme power as the people's representatives. Charles's trial began in Westminster Hall on 20 January. The principal charges were that he had sought to gain unlimited and tyrannical power (instead of the limited power entrusted to him to govern by the laws of the land and for the people's good). He had levied war against parliament and the people it represented, and had renewed that war. After repeatedly refusing to plead, and eloquently challenging the court's legality, he was condemned, and executed on 30 January. Charles's condemnation was the most revolutionary act of a decade of rebellions. It shocked international opinion. The charge's characterization of his rule was unjust, though he had certainly stretched and twisted the law. His repeated misjudgements, dogged insistence on his own authority, denial of concessions until they were unavoidable, efforts to exploit the victors' divisions and refusal to grasp any chance of accommodation had finally sealed his fate. Charles's martyrdom had not been inevitable. His judges had adopted a revolutionary theory of popular sovereignty in order to justify his trial, but they were divided. His co-operation might have saved his life and prevented the abolition of the monarchy.[8]

Interregnum

The 'Rump' parliament now assumed sovereign authority. It appointed a council of state to exercise executive powers, and in March 1649 abolished the monarchy and the House of Lords and promised to dissolve itself as soon as it safely might. In May it declared England a Commonwealth. The Rump was regarded from the start as a provisional government. The army had only reluctantly agreed to a purge rather than dissolution. Levellers in the army, disappointed by senior officers' co-operation with the Rump, instigated mutinies in the spring. They were vigorously suppressed.

The Commonwealth government's first priority was to subdue Ireland. In 1642, at Kilkenny, the leading Irish Catholic clergy and laity had resolved to establish an elected assembly and supreme council. They devised an oath to be taken by Ireland's confederated Catholics, combining allegiance to the king with maintenance of Ireland's fundamental laws and the free exercise of the Roman Catholic religion. The assembly met annually from 1642 until 1648. The Confederation of Kilkenny governed much of Ireland. In September 1643, Charles's commander in Ireland, the marquis of Ormonde, made a truce with the Confederates. This 'Cessation' enabled him to send some troops to England to help Charles. Colonel Robert Monro, commanding Covenanter and parliamentarian forces in Ulster, fought on against the Confederates. A damaging defeat at Benburb in 1646 crippled his army.

After Charles I's execution, the Confederates accepted Ormonde as the new King Charles II's lord lieutenant in order to meet the threat from England. The parliamentarian commander Michael Jones defeated Ormonde at Rathmines near Dublin in August 1649. Cromwell then arrived with a new English force supplied with siege guns, and rapidly took Drogheda and Wexford. Their garrisons (largely English in Drogheda's case) were massacred along with priests. Many towns on or near the coast then surrendered. Cromwell took several more towns and fortresses before leaving Ireland in May 1650. The reconquest was completed in 1652. The Rump's August 1652 Act for the Settling of Ireland penalized all Irish landowners save the English parliament's consistent supporters. Confiscated land was to be transferred to those who had helped suppress the rebellion: English soldiers and 'Adventurers' who had contributed money in accordance with an act of 1642. Government was entrusted to parliamentary commissioners, largely Independent in religion and out of sympathy with other Protestants, let alone the Catholic majority.

The Scots were deeply affronted by the unilateral English execution of Charles I. His eldest son Charles was proclaimed king of Great Britain and Ireland at Edinburgh in February 1649. After signing the Covenants he was received in Scotland in June 1650. The English government decided to strike first. Cromwell invaded Scotland in July. On 3 September he routed a much larger Scottish force at Dunbar. Defeat further divided Scotland. In October, a Remonstrance that drew its main support from the south-west blamed the defeat on those who had trusted the unrepentant Charles II. Argyll and the Committee of Estates condemned the Remonstrance. They also concluded that in order to defeat the invaders former royalists must be recruited as well as solid Covenanters. The commission of the general assembly adopted resolutions to this effect, splitting the Kirk between Resolutioners and Protestors. In January 1651, Argyll set the Scottish crown on Charles's head at Scone. After the English army resumed its Scottish campaign in the summer, Charles invaded England. Cromwell routed his outnumbered force at Worcester on 3 September. Charles eventually escaped to France and a nine-year exile.

Meanwhile the conquest of Scotland continued. A fresh royalist rebellion broke out in the Highlands in 1653. George Monck, the new commander-in-chief there, finally suppressed it in 1655. At least 10,000 English troops were in Scotland throughout the 1650s. Most of the members of the governing council were Englishmen. Even so, efforts to conciliate the Resolutioner majority were fairly successful, and many erstwhile Protestors preferred English to royal rule. In 1651 the Rump decided to seek Scottish consent to Scotland's incorporation into the Commonwealth. In April 1654 Cromwell, by then Lord Protector, issued an ordinance that created a Commonwealth of England, Scotland and Ireland. Irish consent had not been sought.

The military achievements of English parliamentary governments in the island kingdoms between 1642 and 1652 were unprecedented. For the first time they had succeeded in harnessing English resources by regular and efficient taxation, had raised the country's first modern professional army, overthrown the monarchy and subjugated both Ireland and Scotland. The international context of these achievements had been crucial. Locked in exhausting struggle, the European great powers had been unable to intervene in the British wars. After 1636, France and Sweden inflicted several defeats on the Habsburg allies without achieving outright victory. The 1648 Treaties of Westphalia at last ended the 'Thirty Years War' in Germany. Sweden made substantial territorial gains. The 1555 concession of princely religious choice was extended to include Calvinism. Charles Louis recovered the lower, but not the upper, Palatinate. The independence of Switzerland and the Dutch Republic was finally recognized. But intermittent civil wars in France from 1648 to 1653 helped to prolong her war with Spain, which lasted until 1659.

Spain, facing revolts in Catalonia, Portugal and Naples, was unable to help the Irish during the 1640s. The papacy sent a nuncio, the uncompromising Giovanni Battista Rinuccini, whose divisive influence helped to undermine the Irish cause. Henrietta Maria sought, mostly in vain, help from France and Lorraine. In 1645–6 a French envoy worked fruitlessly for an alliance between Charles I and the Scots, and in 1648 Ormonde brought to Ireland weapons that France had paid for. France supported royalist sea captains in 1650. She could not afford war with England, however, and recognized the Commonwealth in 1652. Spain had already done so in 1650.

William II of Orange, stadholder of Holland, Mary Stuart's husband, welcomed royalist exiles in the United Provinces. Charles II set out for Scotland from the Netherlands. William's death in November 1650 seemed to the Rump a golden opportunity to achieve a closer alliance between England and the Provinces. Ambassadors sent in March 1651 found the Dutch deeply divided, with the Orangist party stronger than expected. There was widespread sympathy with Scotland. The Dutch Reformed clergy shared Scottish disapproval of the Rump's toleration of religious radicals. The English mission failed. The Navigation Act of October 1651, largely directed against the Dutch carrying trade, was followed by seizures of Dutch ships. War broke out in May 1652, when the Orangist admiral Martin Tromp refused to strike his topsail in English waters. The English fleet, rapidly expanded since 1649 to counter the depredations of royalist captains and their continental supporters, inflicted severe damage on the less heavily armed Dutch fleet, run down since 1648, and on Dutch commerce. English aggression was fuelled by accumulated resentment at past wrongs received at Dutch hands and English religious militants' belief that the Dutch must be punished for lukewarmness and straying from the path of righteousness.[9] However, although England won the battles close to home, the Dutch struck back at her trade further away, making the struggle seem increasingly futile. The Dutch made few concessions in the peace treaty of Westminster (April 1654).

The Rump, always envisaged as a provisional government, tried the army's patience by failing to undertake thoroughgoing reform or to arrange for a new parliamentary election. It deliberated at length on a bill 'for a new representative'. This did not, however, ensure that men whom the army could trust would be elected. In April 1653 the Lord General Cromwell angrily dissolved it and expelled the members. There followed a short experiment with the Nominated Assembly of 140 chosen by the Council of Officers, including representatives of Scotland and Ireland. The naive radicalism of many of its members soon exasperated Cromwell. Its more moderate members surrendered their powers to him on 12 December.

A large gathering of officers now adopted a new 'Instrument of Government', designed by Major-General John Lambert. Cromwell, solemnly admitted to the office of Lord Protector on 16 December, was to govern with the advice of a council, which was empowered to make war and peace and choose his successor. Parliaments were to be unicameral, each elected within three years of the dissolution of the previous one. England was assigned 400 members, Scotland and Ireland thirty each. Various categories of men judged untrustworthy were either temporarily or permanently barred from standing.

Its course in foreign policy was the most important decision facing the new government. Cromwell favoured profitable use of England's navy. French adventurers were preying on English shipping. But Spain seemed to the council a more convenient enemy than France. The Spanish silver fleet and American colonies retained their old allure. France seemed better placed to threaten England, and might be persuaded to expel the Stuarts. Spain's financial condition was parlous and she had little to offer.

An English fleet sailed in December 1654 to seize Hispaniola, Spain's second largest Caribbean island colony. This poorly organized 'Western Design' failed in its principal objective but in May 1655 took the much smaller island of Jamaica instead. The same month, however, incensed by a massacre of Protestants in Savoy, a French client state, Cromwell demanded a fresh guarantee of freedom of worship. After this had been achieved, an Anglo-French treaty was signed in October which provided for freedom of trade and the expulsion of the Stuarts from France. England then declared war on Spain. In September 1656, English ships captured or sank most of a returning treasure fleet. Robert Blake blockaded Cadiz the following winter. In April 1657 he sank another treasure fleet, preventing the silver it had landed on Tenerife from reaching Spain. In March 1657 England and France at last concluded an offensive alliance, and in June 1658 defeated Spain at the Battle of the Dunes. England gained Dunkirk, previously a base for pirates preying on English shipping.

Cromwell's foreign policy had mixed success. His war with Spain achieved some gains, but necessitated an unsustainable burden of taxation, and severely disrupted English trade. By throwing England's weight against the weaker protagonist in the continental struggle, he assisted the rise of the stronger one, France. The newly strengthened fleet did, however, demonstrate England's naval power in the Mediterranean and Iberian waters, and helped to secure a favourable commercial treaty with Portugal in 1654. The Baltic was an increasingly important area of British trade. During the recent Anglo-Dutch war, the Dutch had been able to close the Sound to the English, thanks to their alliance with the Danes. Cromwell succeeded in obtaining from Denmark the favourable rates of Sound dues she had granted to the Dutch in 1649. However, his hope of bringing Denmark and Sweden together in a Protestant alliance proved to be completely unrealistic.

At home, Britain needed 'healing and settling' after the upheavals it had undergone. The Protectorate's first parliament, meeting in September 1654, would not ratify the Instrument of Government as it stood. The disappointed Protector dissolved it as soon as possible. The vigilant government snuffed out plans for royalist rebellion. A small rising in Wiltshire in 1655 rapidly collapsed. To curb royalist conspiracy, promote moral reformation and reduce the heavy cost of the regular army, Cromwell undertook later in 1655 a deeply unpopular administrative experiment. England was divided into ten districts under major-generals charged with the suppression of conspiracy, disorder and vice, and financed by a 'Decimation Tax' on former royalists.

Military expenditure made it necessary to convene a second parliament in September 1656. It voted against the Decimation Tax and Cromwell abandoned the hated experiment with major-generals. His civilian supporters presented a 'Humble Petition and Advice' in parliament in February 1657, seeking to enhance the authority of the 'single person' and parliament and lessen the army's influence. Cromwell was to become king, and name his own successor, and, subject to approval, the members of his council. There were to be two houses of parliament. The project alarmed and angered senior army officers, but Cromwell accepted it after refusing the title of king.

Cromwell died on 3 September 1658. He had kept Britain quiet, though the acquiescence of most of the population did not betoken positive loyalty. His numerous enemies were too divided to mount a successful attack. He bequeathed an unpopular war and severe financial problems. Once his visionary and compelling personality was removed, nobody else could keep together the key elements of his regime. The inexperienced Richard Cromwell succeeded his father as Protector. His only parliament, which met in January 1659, wished to restrict the army's political role. Senior officers made him dissolve it in April and recall the Rump. Richard's subsequent resignation ended the Protectorate (and its provision for the representation of Scotland and Ireland). The country was deeply unsettled by mounting financial problems, political uncertainty and the revived hopes of various radical groups. Even so John Lambert swiftly crushed in August a royalist rising in Lancashire and Cheshire. When the Rump attempted to cashier Lambert and other senior officers, Lambert expelled it in October. George Monck, commanding the army in Scotland, was determined to prevent a further slide into anarchy. He demanded the re-admission of the Rump. The army's Committee of Safety rapidly lost control of the fleet and much of the army and faced unrest in London. Monck arrived there in February 1660, and soon reinstated all the members purged in 1648 whom he could find. The restored Long Parliament voted for new elections and dissolved itself in March.

There was now an immensely strong current of opinion in favour of monarchy as the best guarantor of order and stability. In retrospect, Charles I's 'tyranny' paled compared with the colossal taxes, army interventions, and political and religious upheavals of recent years. The opponents of monarchy were still vocal, but disorganized. On 4 April, the exiled Charles II issued a skilfully conciliatory declaration at Breda in the Netherlands. On 1 May the newly elected Convention Parliament declared that the government ought to be by king, Lords and Commons.

Conclusion

Between 1619 and 1630 the Stuart kings found themselves trapped by the folly of the Elector Frederick V and their own foreign policy misjudgements in a series of challenging situations that posed irreconcilable demands and exacerbated their otherwise not unmanageable problems. Charles I emerged from his failed wars with Spain and France bruised and humiliated. Avoiding both parliaments and European entanglements, he successfully increased his income. However, he did so by controversial and unpopular use of the royal prerogative. This made peace absolutely necessary.[10] At the same time his religious policy caused widespread unease and offence in England. His attempt to impose deeply unpopular religious innovations on Scotland at this juncture was an extraordinary blunder. His persistence in trying to subdue Scotland plunged his three kingdoms into crisis. Rebellion in Scotland precipitated upheavals in Ireland and England. In both England and Scotland, parliamentary regimes that by-passed the king's authority achieved hitherto unthinkable administrative, military and fiscal innovations. In a final stage of revolution, goaded by the king's obduracy and duplicity, the English army purged parliament and brought about Charles's execution. The Republic established in 1649 then remained at war throughout its existence: in Ireland and Scotland, and with the United Provinces and Spain. It achieved unprecedented displays of English military and naval power, and a short-lived union of the island kingdoms in one state, never repeated before 1801. However, the Republic never devised a constitutional settlement that gave it full legitimacy or reconciled the interests of military men with those of the rest of the political nation. Even during its short life it moved back towards monarchical forms, and the restoration of Charles Stuart seemed the best way out of its worst crisis.

10

FROM RESTORATION TO UNION, 1660–1707

Restoration

Charles II returned from the Netherlands in May 1660 amid general rejoicing. His principal adviser and lord chancellor, Sir Edward Hyde (earl of Clarendon from 1661), was the foremost survivor of the 'constitutional royalists' of 1641. Charles had been restored unconditionally. The legislation that his father had accepted in 1641–2 remained in force unless repealed, but subsequent parliamentary ordinances were void. In April, Charles had promised at Breda to refer to parliament exceptions from a prospective general pardon, 'indulgence' of differences of religious opinion that did not disturb the peace, the settlement of land titles and soldiers' arrears of pay. The first distinctive element of the Restoration settlements was the Convention's decision to grant Charles an annual income of £1,200,000 for life. It recognized that inadequate revenue had pushed the pre-war monarchy into increased reliance on prerogative. But the settlement was not outstandingly generous. Cromwell had been offered £1,300,000 in 1657.[1] For many years after 1660 the income fell short of the sum envisaged. Lands confiscated during the revolutions (including those of the crown) were to be restored to their owners, but not those sold under pressure, to pay fines, for example, which angered many royalist families.

Continuing hostility towards religious and political radicalism resulted in the election of the fiercely royalist 'Cavalier Parliament' that met in May 1661. In its first session the parliament passed the Corporation Act, demanding demonstrations of loyalty to crown and Church from all those involved in governing corporate towns. The 1662 Act of Uniformity drove many puritan ministers into separation from the Church. All individuals coming within the scope of these acts were required to repudiate the Solemn League and Covenant. Acts of 1661, 1664 and 1665 hampered nonconformist worship and ministry. Continuing fear of religious extremists inspired these measures.

In Scotland, the Act Rescissory (March 1661) revoked all legislation since 1633, the date of Charles I's Scottish coronation. Parliament imposed on all office-holders an oath recognizing the king as the only supreme governor of the kingdom and repudiating the Covenants, but Charles I's hated Prayer Book was not re-imposed. Parliament granted the king an annual revenue for life, and empowered him to raise an army of 22,000 men. Some leaders of the Scottish Revolution, notably Argyll, were executed. After 1663, only three more Scottish parliaments were convened before 1689, each for relatively short periods, in 1669–72, 1681 and 1685–6. They were by no means docile, but posed no serious threat to the crown. Charles's minister Lauderdale could tell him complacently, 'Never was king so absolute as you in poor old Scotland'. In Ireland, government by the king's representative (usually from now on a lord lieutenant) was restored. 'Innocent papists' were given a statutory right to recover their lands, but they got back only a fraction of the land confiscated during the interregnum. Catholics, who had owned a share of Ireland's profitable land variously estimated at 59 or 66 per cent in 1641, had at most 29 per cent by the late 1660s.[2]

The English parliament met far more frequently under Charles II than in any previous reign since 1461, largely because the crown now accepted that extra taxation could not be raised without its consent. But revolutionary upheavals had created widespread support for a strong monarchy. The long term growth of royal income, the control of armed forces larger than those existing before the wars, new ways of exploiting remaining royal prerogatives and the crown's improved control of Scotland and Ireland would in time reveal their potential to enhance the restored monarchy's power.

The Treaty of the Pyrenees (1659) ended twenty-four years of war between France and Spain and confirmed France's European ascendancy. France gained territory from Spain. The young king Louis XIV married his cousin the Infanta Maria Teresa in 1660. Charles II proclaimed peace with Spain. The Spanish government had sheltered and supported him in Flanders and Brabant from 1656 to 1660 and hoped for an alliance. Instead, encouraged by his cousin Louis XIV, he made an advantageous match with the Portuguese princess Catherine of Braganza in 1662. She brought with her a substantial dowry and the Portuguese possessions of Tangier and Bombay. Tangier, a potentially useful base, proved too costly to defend, and was abandoned in 1684. Bombay soon became a flourishing commercial centre. British troops helped to thwart Spain's attempted reconquest of Portugal, and English mediation helped secure final recognition of Portugal's independence in 1668. In 1662 Charles sold Dunkirk, newly acquired but costly to garrison, to France.[3]

Anglo-Dutch relations deteriorated between 1660 and 1664 because of continuing commercial rivalries and the fact that many English courtiers and naval officers believed that the Republic could easily be defeated. Charles's brother James, duke of York, lord admiral, who disliked the Dutch for ideological reasons, also hoped to overthrow their commercial dominance by means of naval aggression. In 1664 he ordered attacks on Dutch forts in West Africa and the seizure of the Dutch colony of New Amsterdam (New York). The second Anglo-Dutch war started with enthusiastic parliamentary support in February 1665. The English fleet was better armed, but outside the nearby battle area Dutch ships inflicted terrible damage on English commerce. In 1666, bound by a 1662 treaty, Louis XIV somewhat reluctantly joined the Dutch. Meanwhile, London was devastated first by plague (1665) and then by fire (1666). Cash flow dwindled to a trickle. Charles started peace talks in May 1667. Much of the fleet was laid up. The Dutch penetrated the Medway in June, destroying or capturing several ships. In the peace (July 1667), New York and its dependencies were England's only gain.[4]

Clarendon, Charles's most upright and consistent minister, was unjustly blamed for the war's failure. He was dismissed, then unsuccessfully impeached, and finally banished by parliament. English and Dutch suspicion and fear of the rising power of France soon grew rapidly. In 1667 Louis XIV invaded the Spanish Netherlands, claiming several provinces in lieu of his wife's unpaid dowry. Charles sought from Louis a share of the spoils and an anti-Dutch alliance.[5] Rebuffed, in 1668 he instead offered the Dutch an alliance, which Sweden joined. The treaty, demonstrating that England was a power to be reckoned with, was very popular. Louis bitterly resented what he saw as Dutch impudence and ingratitude. He set about detaching Charles from the alliance.

Their negotiations culminated in the secret Treaty of Dover of May 1670. Charles and Louis agreed to attack the Dutch and partition the United Provinces between themselves and William of Orange, Charles's nephew. Louis promised to subsidize Charles during the war. Charles was to declare himself a Roman Catholic 'as soon as his country's affairs permit' and receive a further payment to help him fulfil this undertaking. Besides Charles, only his brother James, Lord Arlington, senior secretary of state, a crypto-Catholic, and Sir Thomas Clifford, Arlington's client, knew about the treaty. Several other ministers signed in December 1670 a 'pretended treaty' omitting the 'Catholicity' clause. Charles issued a Declaration of Indulgence in favour of Catholics and Protestant dissenters in March 1672, and declared war on the Dutch.

The treaty ensured that France would be on England's side in a future attack on the Dutch. The prospect of subsidies was attractive, but unless the war was exceptionally successful they would certainly not pay for it. The most baffling provision is Charles's undertaking to embrace Catholicism, included on his own insistence. Some of his closest relatives were Catholic, including his recently converted brother James. There is, however, no other good evidence that in 1670 Charles seriously contemplated declaring himself a Catholic. That step would precipitate a seismic political crisis. Whatever the reasons for Charles's commitment, it was extraordinarily reckless. It hung over his head like a sword of Damocles during the following years. There were various possible reasons for Indulgence. It could be presented as a first step towards fulfilment of Charles's undertaking to Louis. There were independent arguments for assuaging the discontent of Protestant nonconformists, and Indulgence for Catholics alone was far too dangerous.[6]

The third Dutch war (1672–4) was disastrous for Charles. A brilliant Dutch naval defence forced the allies to abandon their seaborne attack. Dutch venturers inflicted more damage on English trade than ever before. On land opening of the dykes saved the province of Holland from French invasion. A popular revolution swept William III of Orange to power in Zeeland and Holland in July 1672. In February 1673, the Commons attacked the Declaration of Indulgence. Charles withdrew it and accepted a Test Act designed to prevent Roman Catholics from holding office. James and Clifford resigned. James's Catholicism became public, and a major political issue: as Charles's marriage had remained childless, his brother was heir to the throne. In 1674 the Commons considered bills designed to limit the power of a future Catholic king. In February Charles made peace with the Dutch.

The crisis caused the resignation or removal of the councillors responsible for the failed policies of 1670–2. Sir Thomas Osborne, earl of Danby, lord treasurer from 1673, was financially competent and staunchly loyal to the Church of England. He understood the conservative outlook of the majority of MPs. Yet Charles's policies and the prospect of James's succession had created an insuperable mistrust. Danby's attempts to manage parliament increased suspicion. The Commons proved more restive and unresponsive than they had been in the 1660s, and began to demand stronger action to curb Louis XIV. The Habsburg powers had entered the war against him, but its main result was that France made substantial gains on her eastern borders, chiefly at Spain's expense. In October 1677 Charles agreed to the marriage of James's daughter Mary to William of Orange and went through the motions of preparing for war with France before hostilities ended in 1678. There were fears that Charles might use the army against parliament.

Evidence of a 'Popish Plot' by the Jesuits to assassinate Charles, fabricated by Titus Oates, emerged in the summer of 1678. The mysterious death of the first magistrate to examine witnesses about the Plot, and the discovery of letters to Jesuits, including Louis XIV's confessor, among James's former secretary's papers, gave the Plot added plausibility. Parliament began to investigate it. Panic gripped the political nation. Charles accepted parliament's demand for a new Test Act excluding Catholics from parliament (November 1678). In December, Ralph Montagu, recently ambassador in Paris, produced in the Commons letters written by Danby early that year concerning financial help from Louis XIV. The Commons resolved to impeach Danby. Charles, fearing that earlier dealings with Louis might come to light, first prorogued and then dissolved parliament.

The next parliament (March to May 1679) proved far less manageable and more hostile to the court than its predecessor. A Commons majority welcomed a bill for James's exclusion from the throne. Charles failed to gain support for his alternative – limitations on a Catholic successor – and soon dissolved this parliament. Financial need drove him to summon another for October 1679, which he prorogued seven times until October 1680. Charles's personal presence in the Lords ensured the defeat of another Exclusion Bill in November.

In March 1681, when the next parliament met at Oxford, the Commons were determined to proceed with Exclusion, and Charles immediately dissolved it.

By 1681 the terms 'Whig' and 'Tory' were being applied to the adherents of rival groups or parties that had emerged in opposition to the court and in support of it during the intense political activity of the 'Exclusion Crisis'. Exclusion, the key issue that divided them, though far from the only one, failed for several reasons. Its support was divided between two possible successors: Mary, James's daughter, but a Protestant, married to William of Orange, and the duke of Monmouth, Charles's illegitimate son. The court exploited fears of the return of political instability or even civil war aroused by the Whigs' campaigning tactics. Charles controlled Scotland, Ireland and the London trained bands. Finally, he ceased to be financially dependent on parliament. He got further help from Louis XIV, but even more importantly a commercial boom and improved fiscal administration at last lifted the crown's income out of the shallows where it had been trapped for much of the reign.

Some Whig leaders later plotted risings. The earl of Shaftesbury, against whom a treason charge had earlier failed, fled to Holland in 1682. William Lord Russell and Algernon Sidney, an eloquent republican theorist, were executed in 1683 after the discovery of the 'Rye House Plot' to assassinate the king. Opinion moved against the Whigs. Between 1681 and May 1685, the crown, largely in response to Tory requests, made nearly 100 parliamentary boroughs surrender their charters so that new ones could be issued giving the king more control over their government and (directly or indirectly) their parliamentary franchise. The Exclusionists' efforts to build Protestant solidarity had curbed Charles's desire for toleration. He allowed the persecution of Protestant dissenters.

In Scotland, resentment at the betrayal of the Covenants, aggravated by more immediate grievances, especially the quartering of troops, had caused two main risings, both based in the south-west, where support for the Covenants was strongest. The 'Pentland' rising in 1666 was only defeated after the rebels had nearly reached Edinburgh. News of the Popish Plot sharply increased tension. In May 1679 militant Covenanters assassinated Archbishop Sharp of St Andrews. Another more formidable south-western rebellion was eventually defeated at Bothwell Brig near Glasgow by an Anglo-Scots force headed by the duke of Monmouth. In June 1680 some extremist Covenanters led by Richard Cameron declared that Charles was a tyrant who had forfeited his throne. Cameron was killed, other leaders were later executed and a savage campaign was undertaken against obdurate Covenanters. The rebellions did not seriously threaten Charles's hold over Scotland because they were too localized and lacked support from the nobility.

Charles II died, a deathbed Catholic convert, on 6 February 1685. A parliament was nearly a year overdue.[7] The crown was stronger than at any time since 1603. The yield of Charles's lifetime grant of parliamentary taxation had at last surpassed initial expectations. The majority of the ruling classes, though firm members of the Church of England, had come to prefer a Catholic successor to the prospect of renewed revolution. Charles's devious religious and foreign policies, and his brother's Catholicism, had seriously endangered their support. Yet one of the most flexible of English kings had consistently supported legitimate hereditary succession during the Exclusion Crisis. In the end, with Tory support, he had won.

Downfall of James VII and II

Seldom in British history has a ruler dissipated considerable inherited advantages as swiftly or completely as James VII and II. The once almost unimaginable accession of a Roman Catholic took place amid widespread good will, reinforced by James's pledge to maintain the present government in Church and state. Parliament once again made a lifetime grant of taxation. This, together with sundry later additional grants, gave James exceptional financial security. In Scotland too he had support, successfully built up by judicious use of patronage when he had been Charles's commissioner there in 1679–82. Soon after his accession, the speedily defeated rebellions of his nephew Monmouth in the West Country and the earl of Argyll in Kintyre further strengthened support for the king.

James was determined to gain equal status for his co-religionists with the least possible delay. In October 1685 Louis XIV revoked Henry IV's 1598 Edict of Nantes in favour of France's Huguenots. The step shocked Protestant Europe. Huguenot refugees soon flooded into England. Parliament reconvened in November in the shadow of the Revocation. James's announcement that he had used his dispensing power to commission nearly ninety Catholic army officers alarmed both houses. He quickly prorogued parliament. In July 1686, after dismissing six judges, he secured a judgement in favour of his power to dispense individuals from the Test Acts in the case of Godden vs Hales.

The Tories who had formed the bedrock of Charles II's support would not help James implement toleration. He dismissed leading Tories from the privy council: the marquis of Halifax in 1685, and the earls of Clarendon and Rochester in the winter of 1686–7. Nearly all James's new councillors were Catholics. The earl of Sunderland, Rochester's rival, converted in 1688. In April 1687 James issued a Declaration of Indulgence suspending legislation that denied Catholics and Protestant dissenters key civil and religious rights. Its scope far exceeded that of Charles II's 1672 measure. James declared his wish that all his subjects were Catholics, but undertook to protect the free exercise of the established religion. James hoped the Declaration would win him the support of Protestant nonconformists. Many took advantage of it, but few trusted him.

James intended to have the Test Acts and penal laws repealed by a new parliament. In autumn 1687 lords lieutenant were instructed to ask JPs and deputy lieutenants about their readiness to promote repeal and their support for the Declaration of Indulgence. Three-quarters of the replies were either negative or evasive. A huge purge then took place. In April 1688 James's agents reported optimistically on the prospects of securing a co-operative parliament. James issued an expanded Declaration of Indulgence, and in May ordered it to be read in all English churches. Archbishop Sancroft and six bishops petitioned him to withdraw his directive, pointing out that the dispensing power had often been declared illegal in parliament. James had them prosecuted for seditious libel. The 'seven bishops' were acquitted, to popular jubilation.

On 10 June, however, James received signal reassurance of divine favour. After fifteen years of marriage, his second wife Mary of Modena bore a son. By this time, James had demoralized the crown's natural supporters and alarmed many of his Protestant subjects. Yet his position seemed impregnable. With an ample income, a considerable army and the prerogative of dismissing judges who disagreed with him, it was difficult to see how his rule might be challenged. During the Exclusion Crisis Tories had insisted on the duty of non-resistance to royal authority. This certainly did not mean co-operation in the implementation of the king's policies. The Tories' fundamental principles nevertheless seemed to rule out rebellion.

In Scotland, too, James undermined the crown's support. He dissolved parliament in June 1686 after it had become clear that his offer of free trade with England in return for full religious and civil rights for Scotland's tiny Catholic minority was unacceptable. In 1687 he unilaterally granted freedom of worship to Catholics, Presbyterian 'conventiclers' and Quakers. In Ireland, Richard Talbot, earl of Tyrconnell, lieutenant general of the army, set about turning it into a Catholic force. Lord Deputy from January 1687, he worked to ensure the return of a Catholic parliament. Catholic judges and privy councillors were appointed.

The regime's overthrow could only be initiated from outside Britain. William of Orange, James's nephew and son-in-law, was acutely concerned about developments in England. His great aim since 1672 had been to check the growth of Louis XIV's power. After the peace of 1678 Louis made a series of piecemeal annexations, including Strassburg, one of the great free cities of Germany (1681). Then the king of Poland's march to raise Vienna's last siege by the Turks in 1683 persuaded Louis to make the twenty-year truce of Regensburg in 1684. For protection from further French aggression the Emperor Leopold joined Spain, Sweden, Bavaria and other German princes in signing the League of Augsburg in July 1686. There was no prospect of James II's England assisting this process of containment.

William would have to intervene directly if he was to make England an ally against France. The envoys he sent to England in 1687–8 reported widespread disaffection. The strong preference for peace in the Netherlands, especially in the wealthy province of Holland, remained a major obstacle to intervention. But Louis's insensitive re-imposition in 1687 of a range of heavy tariffs on imported goods transformed Dutch attitudes. James aroused unfounded suspicions of his collusion with Louis XIV when, early in 1688, he unsuccessfully ordered the return of British troops in Dutch service.

William decided to intervene in England. While there to congratulate James on the birth of his son, the Dutch emissary Willem Zuylestein solicited a letter of invitation which was signed by seven Englishmen, five Whigs and two Tories. The seizure of Dutch vessels in French ports in September finally won William Holland's full support. With breath-taking speed and efficiency the Dutch assembled under William's leadership a formidable army and fleet for the invasion of England. Louis XIV inadvertently assisted this perilous venture. At the crucial juncture he invaded the Rhineland in a brutal attempt to intimidate the western German states. He knew of William's plans, but reckoned that embroilment with James would prevent the Dutch from taking an active part in the continental war.[8]

He failed to predict the speed of William's success. Borne by favourable east winds that kept the English fleet in the Thames, the mighty Dutch armada sailed to Torbay, where William landed on 5 November. His declared intention was the earliest possible assembly of a free and lawful parliament. He condemned James's counsellors' illegal policies. James, who had hastily reversed his campaign to pack parliament and some other unpopular measures on the eve of the invasion, panicked in face of William's march, demoralizing his own army. He fled London for France on 11 December 1688, was captured, but was then allowed to make a final escape on 22 December.

Parliamentary monarchy established

James's flight, widespread fears of the possible consequences of his return and William's resolute exploitation of his dominant position now pushed the political nation inexorably but untidily in the direction of James's removal. A deeply divided Convention parliament with a substantial Whig majority met in January 1689. On 28 January the Commons resolved that James had tried to subvert the constitution by breaking the contract between king and people, violated the fundamental laws, withdrawn from the kingdom and abdicated the government, leaving the throne vacant. The fiction of abdication left many Tories unhappy, and the Lords accepted the Commons' resolution only on 6 February. Both houses had meanwhile agreed on 29 January that the government of a popish prince was inconsistent with the safety and welfare of the Protestant religion. Tories reconciled themselves to the exclusion of James's son by means of a convenient fiction: James was not his father. He had been smuggled into the Queen's bed. James's daughter Mary was next in line, but her husband William, himself a grandson of Charles I, was determined to acquire full royal authority. Crucially, his wife and her sister Anne supported him. On 13 February 1689 Parliament therefore offered the crown to William and Mary. William alone was to exercise regal power. After Mary's death from smallpox in December 1694 William was sole ruler until his own death.

Immediately after the offer of the crown a Declaration of Rights was read to William and Mary. In its final form the Declaration mentioned only what were claimed to be existing rights and laws. It declared illegal the power of suspending laws without parliamentary consent and that of dispensing with them as recently exercised, as well as the peacetime maintenance of a standing army within the kingdom without parliamentary consent. In some respects the Declaration was rather vague: it said that the election of MPs ought to be free, for example, and that parliaments ought to be held frequently. The Declaration was incorporated in the Bill of Rights enacted in December 1689, which also excluded Catholics and their spouses from succession to the crown. At their coronation in April, William and Mary had sworn a new oath binding them to rule according to statutes agreed in parliament and maintain the Protestant religion. The most effective curb on William's own power was, however, that unlike his two immediate predecessors he was granted no revenues for life until 1690, and then ones far smaller than those voted to Charles and James. In 1698, after William's war with Louis XIV was over, he was granted a life revenue of £700, 000 to cover civil expenses. Taxes to maintain essential peacetime armed forces had henceforth to be sought from parliament.

Several politicians wanted to lessen the Protestant divisions that James had tried to exploit. But William's call for all Protestants to be admitted to public life went too far for most members of the established Church. The limited Toleration Act of 1689 granted only freedom of worship, not political rights. There could be no statutory toleration of Roman Catholicism, but William did his best to prevent persecution. He dissolved the Convention in February 1690.

In Scotland, James's numerous supporters in the Convention that met in March 1689 were wrong-footed by his peremptory demand for obedience, quite different from William's diplomatic message. John Graham of Claverhouse, Viscount Dundee, one of those most loyal to James, withdrew and raised James's standard. With support from the Highlands, where James's rule had been popular, the Jacobites won the Battle of Killiecrankie in July, but Dundee was slain. Jacobite resistance was finally overcome in May 1690. In August 1691 Highland chiefs were required to swear an oath of allegiance to William by 1 January 1692 in order to qualify for an indemnity. The infamous massacre of MacDonald of Glencoe and nearly 40 members of his clan after he had taken the oath five days late caused widespread outrage and lasting resentment.

Jacobite secession left the Convention dominated by James's opponents. In April 1689 it adopted a Claim of Right which declared that James had forfeited the crown, and denounced episcopal church government. William disliked parts of the Claim and of the associated Articles of Grievances. He and Mary nevertheless accepted the offer of the Scottish crown on 11 May. William's unavoidable reliance on Whig support forced him to accept some unpalatable demands. In July 1689 episcopacy was statutorily abolished. In 1690, Presbyterian government was established, and the committee of articles through which Stuart kings had managed Scots parliaments was abolished. The Scottish religious settlement was more partisan than the English. It made no provision for toleration. The episcopalians were denied freedom of worship.[9]

William faced the most serious resistance in Ireland. James was joyfully welcomed when he arrived there with a small French force in March 1689. A parliament with an overwhelming Catholic majority reversed the Restoration land settlement as far as possible. A Williamite army landed in August, but did not press the attack before William arrived in June 1690. He defeated James's forces at the Battle of the Boyne on 1 July. Despite comparatively small Jacobite losses, the outcome frightened James into leaving Ireland. The bloody Battle of Aughrim in July 1691 broke Jacobite resistance. The Treaty of Limerick, under whose terms 15,000 Jacobite troops left for the continent, ended the war in October. The Irish parliament (now dominated by Protestants) ostensibly ratified the treaty in 1697, but omitted its limited pledge of religious freedom for Catholics. Confiscations reduced the proportion of Irish land owned by Catholics to about 14 per cent by 1703, and acts of 1697 and 1704 prohibited their acquisition of any more land.[10]

The help Louis XIV sent with James to Ireland gave William as king of England his pretext to declare war on France in May 1689. A great European coalition at last contained Louis's aggressive expansionism, but at a terrible cost. At sea, after the French victory at Beachy Head in June 1690, the English and Dutch decisively defeated the French fleet at La Hogue in May 1692. The French then turned, however, to devastating attacks on allied trade. The land war centred on the Spanish Netherlands, in a series of bloody but mainly indecisive battles and sieges of strongholds such as Namur, taken by the French in June 1692 but re-captured by William in 1695. By the Treaty of Ryswick (September 1697) Louis gave up much of the territory he had occupied since 1678 and recognized William as king of Great Britain and Ireland. The Dutch were to garrison several fortresses in the Spanish Netherlands as a 'barrier' between them and the French.

William wished to choose advisers from both parties. He did not want to be bound to one party, or to sacrifice any more of the crown's powers, as he had to do in Scotland. In 1693-4, advised by the adaptable earl of Sunderland, James II's former minister, William decisively altered his government's balance in favour of the Whig politicians most fully committed to the war. In 1694 he also accepted, unwillingly, a triennial act limiting the life of a parliament to three years. By guaranteeing frequent elections, this measure helped keep English politics on the boil for over twenty years. An English financial revolution also began in 1693-4. The Tontine Loan Act (January 1693) and the Tonnage Act (April 1694) inaugurated the long-term servicing of increasingly huge government debts by means of specially appropriated parliamentary taxes. The subscribers to the loan of £1,200,000 authorized by the Tonnage Act were incorporated as the Bank of England. A key figure in these initiatives was the Whig Charles Montagu, chancellor of the exchequer.

The election of 1695 strengthened the Whigs in the Commons. The Whig 'Junto' of Somers, Montagu, Wharton and Russell had continued success in mobilizing loans and Montagu's reform of the coinage. Various English politicians had kept in touch with James's exiled court. Most wanted to ensure

James's favour in case of his restoration rather than help him to return, but their contacts nevertheless contributed to an atmosphere of mistrust. The discovery of a Jacobite plot to kill the king in February 1696 created an unusual surge of loyalty. The Commons voted to associate MPs in an oath to William as rightful and lawful king, splitting the Tories.

After the Peace of Ryswick the Commons demanded that the army should be drastically reduced. In February 1699 William very reluctantly assented to the Disbanding Bill. Hostility to continental involvement was linked with resentment of the Dutch connection and William's generosity towards Dutch favourites and advisers. In 1699–1700 the Junto broke up as its leading members resigned or were dismissed.

William's war badly harmed Scotland's trade. Britain as a whole experienced 'seven ill years' of poor harvests in 1692–8. Scotland suffered two devastating harvest failures in 1696 and 1698. The Scottish economy was less well able to cope with such shocks than its more developed English counterpart. The Scottish government nevertheless supported ambitious commercial initiatives. A 1693 act encouraged foreign trade; another, of 1695, established the Company of Scotland trading to Africa and the Indies. In 1698–9 expeditions sailed to Darien on the Isthmus of Panama, intended as a base for developing both Atlantic and Pacific trade. But Spanish supremacy over the Isthmus was long-established. William, given the extreme delicacy of his relations with Spain, could not possibly support interlopers there, and forbade all English colonies to help the colonists. The venture was abandoned in face of tropical disease and Spanish counter-measures. The catastrophe caused great bitterness towards England and William. (A leading promoter of the scheme was William Paterson, a Scotsman allegedly bred in England, who was also one of the chief planners of the Bank of England.)

William and Mary had no children. In July 1700 Princess Anne's last surviving child died. Settlement of the succession became urgent. William brought prominent Tories into government so as to gain parliamentary support for a statutory solution. The 1701 Act of Settlement provided that if William and Anne both died childless, the next successors were to be Sophia, electress of Hanover, James I's granddaughter, and her heirs. Any successor had to be in communion with the Church of England. Several limitations were placed on the successor's powers. Some of these were soon repealed, but a clause providing that judges should not be removed from office save by addresses of both houses of parliament became operative in 1714.

During 1701 the political nation came to accept the inevitability of a new war despite the immense relief with which it had recently greeted peace. At issue was the control of the Spanish Empire. Charles II, king of Spain since 1665, was a childless invalid. Louis XIV himself was a potential claimant as the grandson of Philip III, and had a son by King Charles of Spain's half-sister. The union of France and Spain was completely unacceptable to England, the Dutch or Austria. William III nevertheless recognized that France must be allowed a share of Spanish territory in order to secure European peace. He concluded two Partition Treaties with Louis in October 1698 and March 1700. This was an extraordinary achievement on the part of two old enemies. The idea of maintaining a balance of power in the service of peace was to exercise a lasting influence over international diplomacy. The sickly Charles II was, however, determined to pass on his inheritance intact, and shortly before he died in the autumn of 1700 signed a will making Louis XIV's younger grandson Philip his successor.[11]

Louis accepted the will. Early in 1701, he declared that Philip could not be excluded from the French succession and occupied strongholds in the Spanish Netherlands, thus blasting the prospects of peace. In August William as king of Britain made a new alliance with the United Provinces and the Emperor whose objectives included re-instatement of the barrier separating the Dutch from France, and freedom to trade with Spanish territories for Britain and the Dutch Republic. When James II died in September, Louis capped his other provocative actions by recognizing James's son as James VIII and III, and (along with Spain) placed an embargo on British trade in a mistaken attempt at intimidation.

William died unexpectedly in March 1702 after a riding accident. He had ensured that England played a fuller and more consistent role in Europe than at any time since 1603. His resolute and single-minded pursuit of his main goals had necessitated an unprecedentedly close partnership with Lords and Commons. That partnership had frequently been a frustrating one for William. The unreliability of so many English politicians, their poisonous rivalries and the querulous parochialism of many MPs had been profoundly depressing. Yet William's initiatives and necessary concessions had accomplished a revolution whose results would endure. Thanks above all to fiscal and financial develop ments of the 1690s, no year would elapse thereafter without a meeting of parliament. The parliamentary monarchy's ability to mobilize resources would make it vastly more powerful abroad than the monarchy had been before 1689. A reserved, lonely monarch never loved by his subjects, William nevertheless influenced England's future course more profoundly than any other modern king. William never visited Scotland. He did, however, advocate the closer union of England and Scotland but without success.

Widespread rejoicing greeted the accession of Anne, committed like William to the Protestant succession, but both English and unswervingly loyal to the Church of England. In May 1702 the allies declared war on France. Thus began the War of the Spanish Succession. John Churchill, duke of Marlborough from 1702, was English captain-general and allied commander in the Netherlands. His brilliance offset England's comparatively small contribution of men to the allied armies. In 1704 he marched 400 miles from the Netherlands to join up with the imperial general Prince Eugen and completely defeat the Franco-Bavarian army at Blenheim. Marlborough then led allied armies to two great victories in the Spanish Netherlands, at Ramillies (May 1706) and Oudenarde (June 1708). In 1702 an Anglo-Dutch fleet destroyed or captured several French and Spanish ships off Vigo. This helped persuade Portugal to join the grand alliance in May 1703, providing a first springboard for an attempt to place the Archduke Charles of Austria on the Spanish throne. An allied fleet sailed from Lisbon in 1704 to attack the French and seized Gibraltar on the way. Catalonia accepted Charles in 1705, and Madrid briefly fell to the allies in 1706.

At home, the moderate Tory Godolphin, lord treasurer, whose only son had married Marlborough's daughter, was the captain-general's indispensable partner. Marlborough's wife Sarah was the queen's principal favourite. Robert Harley, speaker of the Commons, provided essential support and became a secretary of state in 1704. The general election of 1702 resulted in a considerable Tory majority in the Commons. The Tory ranks included the members who had the strongest reservations about the continental war and believed that England should further her own commercial interests by concentrating on a maritime strategy. Military successes nevertheless made the war less unpopular than William's. The Tories' main domestic concern was the threat to the Church of England from what they believed to be the dramatic growth of Protestant religious nonconformity. The strongest support for the war came from the Whigs, a minority in the Commons, but a majority in the Lords. The general election of 1705 brought Whig gains, that of 1708 the only clear Whig majority of Anne's reign.

From a British perspective, the most momentous measure of Anne's reign was the Act of Union between England and Scotland. The making of the Union is separately and more fully discussed in Chapter 15, but some salient elements of its background and passage should be established here. The Revolution of 1688–90 had accentuated the religious differences between England and Scotland and weakened the crown's control over the Scottish parliament. Events of the 1690s, followed by the English Act of Settlement, had alienated many Scots. There was a possibility that Scotland might decide a different settlement of the succession. The outbreak of another French war, unwelcome to many Scots, made this prospect seem more substantial and more dangerous.

A Union was the answer adopted by Anne and her leading English and Scottish ministers. In 1703 negotiations failed, and the Scottish parliament passed a variety of measures designed to protect Scottish sovereignty, religion and trade. The queen's ministers drove Union through by a combination of bullying, concessions and material inducements. They were greatly helped by the fact that Scottish majority opinion, though united in resentment of English behaviour, was divided on most other issues. English and Scottish commissions to negotiate a union were appointed in 1706 and made rapid progress towards agreement. The eventual Treaty of Union created a United Kingdom of Great Britain. The Scottish parliament ratified the treaty in January 1707 despite widespread opposition. The two British kingdoms were united, not through any knitting together of affections, but by the determination of comparatively small groups of politicians.

11

FROM 'FREE' MONARCHY TO PARLIAMENTARY MONARCHY

Constitutional change

International and domestic conflicts

Many European monarchies faced major rebellions or civil wars during the seventeenth century, especially during the 1640s. Their main causes were religious tensions, fiscal pressures and royal encroachments on the privileges of particular social groups, provinces or kingdoms. The Bohemian rebellion began the 'Thirty Years War' (1618–48), with its main theatre in the Empire. Spain, England, the Dutch Republic, Denmark, Sweden and France all became involved. Hostilities continued between France and Spain until 1659, a war of attrition in which France ultimately emerged the victor. War subjected all the participant powers to enormous strain.

In no two states was the pattern of upheaval exactly alike. The Bohemian rising, first in the series, was provoked by the Austrian Habsburg monarchy's efforts to re-impose Catholicism. Catholic Bavaria and Spain helped Ferdinand II to defeat Frederick V. This was the turning point in the long consolidation of the Habsburg dynasty's hold over its various inherited territories. However, Swedish and French intervention in the Thirty Years War thwarted efforts to enhance the Emperor's authority within the Empire as a whole.

The Spanish crown's fiscal and military demands, the erosion of local privileges and, in Portugal's case, Spain's inability to protect Portuguese colonies provoked revolts in the 1640s. Catalonia rebelled in 1640, eventually placed herself under the French crown, and submitted only in 1652. Portugal seceded in 1640 and eventually secured independence in 1668. In 1647, brief but violent anti-tax revolts broke out first in Palermo, then in Naples. Castile, core of the monarchy, held firm.

In France, the crown successfully crushed the last Huguenot rebellions (1621–8). Between 1635 and 1660, however, there were many popular uprisings in the provinces, above all against taxation. During the 1640s new fiscal demands and other grievances caused mounting discontent that culminated during 1648 in protests by the *parlement* and other sovereign courts of Paris and unwilling government concessions. In 1649 a government blockade of Paris was followed by a truce. There ensued a period of complicated political manoeuvres by members of the higher nobility, resistance by provincial *parlements* and intermittent fighting. Only in 1653 was the government's authority fully restored. The ultimate failure of resistance to the crown in these confused civil wars of the Fronde was due to the lack of an agreed leadership or programme, and above all of a single institution like the English parliament capable of focusing and uniting the forces of opposition.

War with France and Spain was the prime cause of the Stuarts' domestic problems during the 1620s. The poisonous legacy of that decade influenced both Charles I's government during the 1630s and the attitudes of the parliaments he faced in 1640. The British monarchy was exceptional in facing resistance in all its three kingdoms, inspired in each case by a different mixture of fears and grievances. The parliamentary governments of England and Scotland were unique in Europe in successfully mobilizing resources for a king's defeat. England was the first European monarchy to become a republic. The experiment was short-lived. Tension between the army, midwife of the Commonwealth, and different parliaments was the republic's fundamental weakness. The monarchy was restored, but gratuitously provoked a second revolution, launched this time by the king's nephew and son-in-law. William III's paramount goal – containment of Louis XIV – necessitated the forging of a new, unique and, in the event, enduring partnership with Lords and Commons.

Parliaments and the limitation of royal independence

It seemed possible, especially during the 1630s and the 1680s, that the British monarchy might become more independent of parliament. Given patience and skill, the Stuart kings might have extended and consolidated royal power. It was above all their religious policies that wrecked their prospects of doing so.

Impositions on trade provided James I and Charles I with their fastest growing revenues from 1608 onwards, despite protests in the Commons. Charles continued to collect tonnage and poundage, ignoring the Commons' limitation of the customary grant to one year in 1625. Ship money became an important new source of revenue in the 1630s. When at last, thanks to the Scots, Charles I had to co-operate with parliament, acts of 1641 completely prohibited both ship money and the levy of taxes on trade without parliament's consent. His reign saw the longest interval ever to occur between parliaments (1629–40). The 1641 triennial act provided that writs for a new parliament should be issued automatically during the third year after the end of the previous session. A new triennial act of 1664 left the issue of writs to the king. Parliaments nevertheless sat nearly every year in Charles II's reign until 1681, above all because he needed additional supplies. When in the 1680s he had an adequate income, he ignored the 1664 act.

After 1688, parliaments never again made the monarch a lifetime grant sufficient to meet all expenses of peacetime government. The crown's dependence on renewed grants ensured frequent sessions. Fears that a parliament tuned by royal management and patronage might be prolonged indefinitely resulted in the 1694 triennial act limiting each parliament to a maximum length of three years. From 1693 onwards various acts also excluded many government employees from the Commons.

The most controversial of the crown's claimed prerogatives during the later seventeenth century were those of dispensing from statutes and suspending them altogether. Charles II's 1672 Declaration of Indulgence provoked a Commons' resolution 'that penal statutes in matters ecclesiastical cannot be suspended but by act of Parliament'. James II's use of the dispensing power worried even his exceptionally loyal parliament. His Declaration of Indulgence was widely regarded as unlawful. The Bill of Rights of 1689 finally established the illegality of the suspending power and also of the dispensing power as it had been used 'of late'.

One of the most important of all royal prerogatives was the appointment of judges and officers of state. One of the Nineteen Propositions of 1642 made its exercise dependent on parliamentary consent, but Charles rejected them. Impeachment, revived in 1621 after nearly 170 years of disuse, became the principal means of getting rid of ministers, including several of the crown's ablest advisers, who no longer commanded parliament's confidence. A clause in the 1701 Act of Settlement provided that judges should remain in office during good behaviour.

Scotland took strong measures to curb the independent exercise of royal power both in 1640–1 and in 1689–90. Parliament passed in 1640 a triennial act that would operate automatically, and reformed the committee of the lords of the articles that managed the parliamentary agenda. In 1641, Charles I reluctantly agreed to appoint officers of state, privy councillors and lords of session with the advice and consent of the estates. All these measures were rescinded after the Restoration. The Scottish Claim of Right (1689) condemned more forcefully than its English counterpart James VII's alteration of the fundamental constitution from a 'legal limited monarchy to an arbitrary despotic power' and declared that he had forfeited the crown. Parliament abolished the lords of the articles in 1690.

Representative institutions declined or disappeared in some European countries. The French estates-general met in 1614 for the last time before 1789. Another meeting planned in 1651 was cancelled. (Demands drawn up in preparation, strikingly similar to English ones, included an end to taxation without consent, the regulation of billeting, the abolition of many offices and regular sessions of the estates-general themselves.) Spanish monarchs convened representative assemblies in their various territories much less often than in the past, or ceased doing so altogether. French and Spanish governments negotiated tax grants with local assemblies, corporations and notables where necessary, but the estates of various French provinces ceased to meet.

The Danish estates met for the last time in 1660. The Swedish *Riksdag* proved more resilient, but nevertheless suffered a temporary eclipse during the later seventeenth century. Previously elective monarchies were declared hereditary both in the Bohemian lands (1627–8) and in Denmark (1660). The nobility of the elective kingdom of Poland in and out of the *Sejm* resisted attempts to strengthen royal authority, but failed to counter threats from hostile neighbours. Royal power and national strength ultimately declined together.

Notions of fundamental law and ancient liberties were potential obstacles to the exercise of arbitrary royal power in many countries. The English judge Sir Edward Coke eloquently expounded the idea that kings should be subject to law. The common law was for Coke the supreme form of law, of immemorial antiquity, protecting king and subject alike. Judges (guardians and interpreters of the law), nevertheless, sanctioned major extensions of royal power in Stuart England. Save for James II, kings seldom had to move or replace judges in order to obtain favourable judgements. The Court of Exchequer's judgement in the crown's favour in Bate's case (1606) made possible a substantial increase in the crown's income from impositions on trade. The judges refused to give an opinion about the legality of the forced loan in 1626, but the court of King's Bench denied bail to those imprisoned for non-payment, on the ground that they had been detained by special command of the king. (Parliament passed acts curbing arbitrary imprisonment in 1640 and 1679.) When some merchants refused to pay tonnage and poundage in 1628, the Court of Exchequer ratified the council's confiscation of their goods. In 1638, albeit by only seven to five, the judges in Hampden's case found that the demand for ship money had been legal. The dispensing power was upheld in Godden vs Hales (1686). Only in the disastrous trial of the Seven Bishops, when two of the judges spoke out against the suspending power, did the crown's proceedings go badly wrong. In practice it was parliaments that limited English monarchs' prerogatives, and then only when operating in unusually favourable political contexts.[1]

French *parlements* sometimes tried to check what they saw as monarchs' unconstitutional exercise of power. Their members were more secure in their positions than English judges. The *parlements* strenuously opposed registration of Henry IV's 1598 Edict of Nantes. The Paris *parlement* won a modification before registering it in 1599; the *parlements* of Toulouse and Rouen held out till 1600 and 1609 respectively. (Louis XIV's widely welcomed revocation of the Edict was registered with alacrity.) The Paris *parlement* protested against unpopular fiscal measures in both 1645 and 1648, and in 1648 the members of the four sovereign courts of Paris met to draw up wide-ranging reform proposals. The government reluctantly accepted them, but rescinded its concessions once it had gained the upper hand in 1652. In 1673 Louis XIV insisted that the *parlements* register edicts before presenting remonstrances against them. In 1675, when heavy new taxes provoked a great wave of revolts, he punished the suspected connivance of the *parlements* of Rennes and Bordeaux with summary exile. Despite protests by *parlements*, the power to order imprisonment remained part of the French crown's prerogative of 'retained' justice.[2]

Political thought

Political upheaval and religious divisions stimulated thought about the location of ultimate authority in the state. The defenders of 'free' or 'absolute' monarchy, from James VI to Bishop Bossuet in Louis XIV's France, argued that the king's power came from God, to whom alone he was answerable for his actions. Justifications of resistance to royal authority usually included claims that kings or their officers had infringed God's commandments or broken established human laws.

Thomas Hobbes, greatest of all English political philosophers, royalist in sympathy, developed his political theory in exile in Paris. In *Leviathan* (1651) he set out his bleak vision of a state of nature in which individual desires were always in potential conflict. All, however, shared one paramount desire: to avoid death. Hence people had entered a covenant with each other to surrender their hitherto untrammelled rights to a sovereign. (Thus Hobbes avoided in his reconstruction of the origins of sovereignty a contract between sovereign and subject.) After the covenant, all laws derived their authority from the sovereign's will. Hobbes insisted that 'the *ghostly* must be subordinate to the *temporal*'. The civil sovereign could legitimately demand complete outward conformity in religion, even though he could not control internal belief.[3]

Hobbes tried to deal with every possible ground for disobedience. He observed, however, that once the state had suffered a final defeat in war, and could no longer protect its members, their obligation to the sovereign was extinguished. In 1651 he returned to England and lived under the Commonwealth. No other English political thinker of the century provoked stronger reactions or more vigorous debate at home and abroad. His critics, especially among the clergy, hated an analysis that so completely divorced earthly sovereignty from scriptural or divine authority.[4] The Tories' preferred political theorist during the Exclusion Crisis was not Hobbes, but Sir Robert Filmer. His *Patriarcha*, published in 1680, but written much earlier, argued that all political authority was ultimately patriarchal.

The breakdown of co-operation between the king and the Lords and Commons in 1641–2 had resulted before long in the assertion of popular sovereignty. Henry Parker, pamphleteering apologist for parliament, tried to show in his *Jus Populi* (1644) that 'Princes were created by the people, for the people's sake' and argued that both kings and laws had been 'first formed and created' by bodies of men similar to English parliaments. The eventual charge of treason against Charles I in 1649 took this position as its starting point.

In Scotland, the Covenanters refurbished a long tradition of resistance to misused royal authority. Samuel Rutherford's *Lex Rex* (1644) justified armed resistance to Charles I. This leading covenanting theorist had read the work of Johann Althaus, a German political thinker and apologist for the Dutch revolt against the absent Philip II, an example very relevant to Scotland's situation. According to Althaus, the 'Ephors', i.e. 'the elders, the estates or the nobility', constituted the supreme magistrate and protected the Covenant between the supreme magistrate and the people. In doing so they had to act in accordance with the fundamental law.[5]

Between 1649 and 1653 England as a republic enjoyed an unprecedented military success that invited comparisons with the Roman republic. English republicans 'found their principal guide to antiquity in Machiavelli', who had written at length about the reasons for that republic's long survival and eventual fall. The leading republican theorist of the 1650s, James Harrington, inspired by the example of the enduring stability of Venice, advocated a complicated balanced constitution. To others, Venice already seemed a stagnant, declining power. (The Dutch confederation never seemed a suitable model for the much more highly centralized English state.)[6]

The Exclusion Crisis generated two further notable justifications of resistance to tyrannical governments that were published some years later. Algernon Sidney asserted in his *Discourses Concerning Government* (1698) that 'All just Magistratical Power is from the People'. In the second of his *Two Treatises of Government* (1690), John Locke envisaged that political societies had been created by the express consent of individuals for the protection of their lives, liberty and property. If those entrusted with power threatened liberty or property, they dissolved the government, absolving the people from obedience. Locke's ideas, popularized and propagated during the following decades, were to be enormously influential in eighteenth-century England.

Political parties

During the 1670s, the labels 'Court' and 'Country' described fluid political alignments in the House of Commons: the government's supporters, and those members who opposed political corruption, popery and arbitrary government. True political parties first emerged during the Exclusion Crisis. The Whigs advocated exclusion of James, duke of York, from the succession for political as well as religious reasons: a Roman Catholic king presented the threat of arbitrary rule. They wanted to unite all Protestants against this threat, and favoured toleration of dissenters, who gave them strong support. Sidney and Locke were their leading theorists.

In contrast the Tories emphasized the divine origins of royal power, the descent of the crown by hereditary right and subjects' duties of obedience and non-resistance. They denied the existence of an original contract. They cherished the ideal of a Church that embraced all members of the nation and inculcated right belief and obedience. James II wrong-footed the Tories by challenging the privileges of the Church and seeking to enlist both Catholics and Protestant religious dissenters in support of his policy of Indulgence. The Tories in the 1689 Convention, where the Whigs dominated the Commons, only reluctantly accepted the vacancy of the throne, the exclusion of Catholics from the succession and the toleration of Protestant dissenters' worship.

The war with France in defence of the Protestant succession that began in 1689 soon became colossally expensive and widely unpopular. It was Whig supporters of William who most wholeheartedly accepted the war and its consequences: close involvement with European allies, together with huge increases in the armed forces, taxation and borrowing. 'Country' MPs of both parties saw these things as necessary evils at best. They wanted to curb financial mismanagement, exclude placemen from parliament and reduce the standing army as far as possible after 1697. Many country gentlemen, especially in south-eastern England, feeling that they were paying an unfair share of taxation, stuffing money into the pockets of financiers and investors in government debt, voted Tory, perceiving a fundamental division between their 'landed interest' and the Whig 'monied interest'.[7]

In the absence of regularly convened representative assemblies, enduring parties did not take shape in any other European kingdom. In the United Provinces, the 'States party' stood for republican liberty, and in practice for the dominance of Holland, by far the richest province within the Union. The Orangists supported the authority of stadholders drawn from the princely house of Orange, especially in face of threats to the safety of the Union. But the English parliament was a very different body from the small gathering of provincial delegates in the states-general, and English parties came to play a more sustained and central part in English politics than those of the States party and the Orangists in Dutch politics.

Seventeenth-century political conflicts involved many of the 'middle sort' of people – traders, craftsmen, manufacturers and professional men. Such people were always divided in their allegiances. Vociferous and determined opposition movements such as the London allies of Charles I's parliamentary critics in 1641, the Levellers a little later and the emergent Whig party drew much of their support from this social stratum. But a vigorous urban Toryism soon emerged. During the 1690s, London's lesser middling sort, with some exceptions such as the weavers, many of whom were nonconformists, increasingly turned Tory, opposing a largely Whig ruling oligarchy.[8]

Party struggles in continental cities were generally far more intermittent and localized than in England. In various Dutch towns, however, citizens or citizen militias took the lead in sweeping William of Orange to power in 1672. In Paris, artisans and shopkeepers largely supported the *parlement* during the Fronde. The Bordeaux *Ormée*, a radical movement of lesser office-holders, emerged in 1651, opposing their own *parlement* and oligarchy.

The vigorous public politics that emerged in England during the seventeenth century fed on information and generated debate. The output of English printing presses hugely increased following the lapses of pre-publication censorship in 1641 and 1679 and its end in 1695. Satire, polemic and newspapers flourished in the hothouse of intensified political activity. In France, there was during the Fronde a flood of pamphlets hostile to Cardinal Mazarin, the chief minister of the Queen Mother, regent for her young son Louis XIV. Regular newspapers first appeared in large numbers during the early seventeenth century in decentralized Germany and the United Provinces. The leading Catholic powers started publishing official gazettes from 1631 onwards, and tried to control other news media by censorship. In England, printed 'corantos' of foreign news published in series first appeared during the 1620s but were prohibited for most of the 1630s. Newspapers containing home news appeared during the civil wars. The official *London Gazette* started in 1666. After 1695 the numbers of British newspapers (including Scottish and English provincial ones) increased rapidly.[9]

Government
Royal courts

The role of the British royal court gradually changed. Charles II, forced at first to subsist on an inadequate income, drastically reduced the household's size and the number of people entitled to feed at his expense, the most extravagant aspect of pre-war court life. James II made further cuts, well aware that good husbandry was part of the price of royal independence. Charles and James lived with less ceremonial, staged fewer costly spectacles and disposed of less patronage, than earlier kings. The divergence in splendour between the English and French courts became more marked. However, William III revived old ceremonies and etiquette in order to underline his royal status and legitimacy, and gave Mary II a colossally expensive, sombrely magnificent funeral in 1695. William and Mary made their court exemplary for its sobriety and sermon-centred piety. The court remained for most of this period the foremost arena of British cultural and artistic activity and innovation. English monarchs built no great palaces to match Philip IV's Buen Retiro or Louis XIV's Versailles, but the Whitehall Banqueting House and the Queen's House at Greenwich were the most innovative English buildings of James I's reign. Despite the financial stringencies of the 1690s, William and Mary undertook at Kensington and Hampton Court England's most extensive royal building programme of the century.[10]

The court remained the realm of favourites and intimate politics. The favourites Somerset and Buckingham gained and consolidated their influence in James I's Bedchamber. Charles II conducted his relationship with Louis XIV from his private apartments, unknown to many of his councillors. Two Dutchmen, Hans Willem Bentinck, earl of Portland, and Arnold Joost van Keppel, earl of Albemarle, helped William III keep hold of the threads of diplomacy and government in four countries. Bentinck, groom of the stool and keeper of the privy purse, was the intermediary between Scottish politicians and the king.

Ministers and councils

Robert Cecil was unique in becoming lord treasurer (1608–12), while also principal secretary. No subsequent minister combined these important offices. Their occupants were usually among the crown's close advisers, but between 1612 and 1628 the favourites Somerset and Buckingham dominated its inner counsels. Charles I had no single leading minister between 1628 and 1640. Clarendon initially performed that role for Charles II, the only lord chancellor after 1555 to do so. Two secretaries of state were responsible for domestic security and foreign and domestic intelligence. In 1640 Charles I gave each secretary responsibility for relations with a distinct group of European countries. A similar arrangement was formalized in 1689 as a division between 'northern' and 'southern' departments. Among the outstandingly able secretaries were Sir Francis Windebank (1632–40), Sir Henry Bennet, Lord Arlington (1662–74),[11] the earl of Sunderland (1679–81, 1683–8), the earl of Nottingham (1689–93) and Robert Harley (1704–8).

Among the more successful of Robert Cecil's successors as lord treasurer before the civil wars were Lionel Cranfield, earl of Middlesex (1621–4), and Sir Richard Weston, first earl of Portland (1628–35). Facing a severe financial situation in 1667, Charles II appointed a treasury commission with unprecedented powers to control revenue and expenditure, which worked hard to make economies and improve procedures. Thomas Osborne, earl of Danby, lord treasurer from 1673 to 1679, was also Charles's principal minister. The treasury was in commission more often than not from 1679 onwards. The drive for greater efficiency and professionalism was maintained. Between then and 1710 Sidney Godolphin, one of the ablest and least corrupt of later Stuart politicians, was the first lord of the treasury (1684–5, 1690–7, 1700–1), lord treasurer (1702–10) and, along with Marlborough, the captain-general, one of Anne's two foremost advisers.

The privy council grew from twelve men in 1598 to forty by 1625 and remained large thereafter. Given the size of the council, kings not surprisingly made their most important decisions in consultation with much smaller groups. Specialized council committees also developed. Privy councils included men of widely different opinions, both protagonists of the 'Protestant cause' and advocates of friendship with Spain under James I and Charles I, 'moderates' determined to win parliamentary co-operation and those of a more authoritarian bent under Charles I, ex-parliamentarians as well as royalists under Charles II. Between 1660 and 1681 and after 1689 skill in parliamentary management became an increasingly important qualification for ministerial leadership. 'Ministries' began to emerge from the privy council. The Whig 'Junto' of the 1690s was a ministry united by shared political outlook and goals.

In Scotland, James VI left behind in 1603 a privy council armed with wide financial and administrative powers, but in constant touch with the king. George Home, earl of Dunbar, lord treasurer of Scotland (1601–11) and chancellor of the exchequer in England (1603–6), uniquely attuned to James's priorities, travelled tirelessly to ensure the enforcement of royal policies in Scotland. After Dunbar's death the able but cautious and conservative Alexander Seton, earl of Dunfermline (chancellor from 1604–22), was James's foremost councillor in Scotland. Charles I marginalized his father's surviving advisers and by-passed the full council. William Graham, earl of Menteith, temporarily saved Charles from the worst consequences of his mistakes until his dismissal in 1633. Thereafter, Charles's appointment of docile and obedient councillors kept him increasingly insulated from Scottish opinion.[12]

After the Restoration, the earl of Lauderdale, secretary (1660–1680), outmanoeuvred his rival Middleton, then stayed in control until the 1679 Covenanters' rebellion by using his long periods of residence in England to keep closely in touch with the king and by skilfully choosing a succession of allies on the Scottish council. James, duke of York, largely governed Scotland himself in 1679–82 and after his accession through his henchmen, the earls of Perth and Melfort, both Catholic converts. William II's unfamiliarity with Scotland and reliance on a small group of advisers allowed his government to be destabilized by individual and family rivalries and Country parliamentary opposition. Parliamentary outrage after the disastrous massacre of the MacDonalds of Glencoe forced the resignation in 1695 of the Master of Stair, secretary. Government efforts to cope with the furious reaction to the Darien affair owed much of their limited success to the divisions of the opposition.[13]

In France and Spain early seventeenth-century rulers entrusted overall direction of government to exceptionally powerful and long-serving ministers: in Spain the duke of Lerma (1599–1619) and the count-duke of Olivares (1622–43), in France Cardinals Richelieu (1624–42) and Mazarin (1642–61). From 1661 the adult Louis XIV, a king of outstanding vigour and ability, governed France personally. He set his distinctive stamp on the hierarchy of councils that he inherited. Some, the more important, advised on policy; others were administrative and judicial. The very highest, primarily concerned with foreign policy, Louis's chief interest, consisted of a few handpicked men with the personal title of minister of state. The other 'policy' councils were devoted to internal affairs and finances. The controller general of finances (Jean-Baptiste Colbert from 1665 to 1683) was a key figure who sat on both of them. There were four secretaries of state (war, navy, foreign affairs and the royal household). The major difference between English and French central government was that French ministers did not need to fear parliamentary criticism or engage in parliamentary management. Louis kept his ministers far longer than the later Stuarts were able to retain theirs, and selected nearly half of them from two families.[14]

In France, the king's *conseil privé* acted as a supreme court of justice. No English conciliar court had had this function. Star Chamber, where councillors sat as a court along with judges, had helped to enforce some of Charles I's unpopular policies. Parliament abolished it in 1641, declaring that the reasons for the court's original establishment no longer existed, and that its decrees were an intolerable burden. It also abolished the Court of Requests and the councils in the North and in the marches of Wales (though the latter, restored in 1660, survived until 1689).

Local government

Justices of the peace remained the key officials of English local government. Their numbers continued to increase. Successive governments used their powers of appointment and dismissal to tune the commission of the peace. Charles I's government sacked some uncooperative men, but the biggest purges took place during the civil wars and interregnum, and under James II. The justices of assize were the most important long-term link between central and local governments. There were some notable episodes of government interference. During the early 1630s the privy council made a commendable effort in the wake of dearth to ensure that the justices were properly enforcing relevant laws, but this campaign could not be sustained. A stable or slightly falling population eased social pressures after the 1650s. The civil wars brought much more serious upheavals. The commissions of the peace faced formidable rivals in the shape of county committees composed of zealous supporters of parliament, some of them of humbler origins than the justices, and a few years after the committees' abolition, the rule of the hated major-generals.

The 1558 legislation that specifically authorized the arming and mustering of county forces lapsed in 1604. Governments nevertheless tried to strengthen the county lieutenancy and militia, especially in coastal areas and during the 1620s, with mixed results. The 1661 Militia Act placed the county forces under royal control and gave them a secure statutory basis and extensive policing powers. Lords lieutenant became more important as the crown's local representatives, exercising political leadership with the help of patronage, and giving advice on the membership of the commission of the peace. Harmony between court and county depended on the maintenance of a delicate balance. The gentry were ready to fund the militia because they saw it as *theirs*, a guarantee of local order, and also an effective substitute for a large peacetime standing army. The lords lieutenant were expected to act as their counties' spokesmen at court. Loyal lieutenants exercised a steadying influence during the Exclusion Crisis. But James II fatally alienated his natural supporters when he replaced some lords lieutenant and purged the commissions of the peace.[15]

After 1603 the Scottish privy council continued to promote peace and more effective local government. Feuding was further discouraged. An Anglo-Scots commission set up in 1605 acted vigorously to pacify the borders. The Highlands continued to be viewed as a quasi-colonial area to be tamed and exploited. The inhabitants fiercely resisted an attempt to colonize the island of Lewis in 1605. Lord Ochiltree's 1608 expedition to the Western Isles, facilitated by the use of English ships, resulted in the capture of a number of chiefs, though the 1609 'Statutes of Iona', requiring them to control violence among their followers, support the Kirk and send their eldest sons to school, were not effectively enforced. The obstreperous earl of Orkney was hanged in 1615 after a local rebellion. James VI, empowered by an act of 1609, introduced commissioners or justices of the peace, similar to the English justices of the peace, though less powerful. James and Charles also considerably increased the total of sheriffs subject to royal nomination.[16]

After the interval of war and English conquest, Restoration Scotland underwent some further institutional change. The Court of Justiciary, the central criminal court, was established in its enduring form in 1672. Commissioners of supply, chosen from among local landowners, collected the 'cess' or land tax from 1665. In the Highlands, the disgrace, rebellion and death of the earl of

Argyll (1681–5) enabled James VII to draw on the support of the Campbells' many enemies.[17]

Armed forces

Neglect and corruption weakened the English navy after the peace with Spain in 1604. However, Buckingham was a politically powerful and energetic admiral, and Charles I was anxious to build up an effective navy during the 1630s. New ships were built, dockyards developed and naval administration and discipline improved. But Charles I did not have the resources to build the balanced fleet of different types of vessel needed to meet the potential threat from the growing navies of rival powers and curb North African pirates. His reign witnessed a dangerous loss of support for the navy amid the wider maritime community whose co-operation was essential in time of war. The victorious parliamentarian and republican regimes created a navy some three times larger than that of 1640. This had a better combination of different sorts of ship and closer links with the merchant community.

After the Restoration, England made great advances in ship design, the application of science to navigation, effective record-keeping, efficient organization of the Navy Board and Ordnance Office, improved professional training for naval officers and adequate victualling. Both Charles II and his brother James, a keen lord admiral, took a close interest in naval matters. The navy failed to realize its potential during the second and third Anglo-Dutch wars partly because of Charles II's cash flow problems. During William's and Anne's wars with France, England's navy benefited from more secure parliamentary funding and from the fact that the two leading maritime powers were allies.

England's naval strength fell behind that of her main rival, the United Provinces, between 1603 and 1642. By 1650 the English navy was the stronger; it may have slipped behind by the 1670s, but between then and 1700 the balance tilted sharply in England's favour. France, beginning the century with a negligible navy, outbuilt England during the ministries of Richelieu and Colbert. Between the 1640s and the 1660s, however, and again after 1695, concentration of France's resources on gruelling land wars seriously reduced her naval strength.[18]

Britain was not engaged in military operations on land between 1603 and 1640 except in the brief expeditions of the 1620s. Professional soldiers had to seek experience in foreign armies. In 1639–40, the Covenanting leadership followed the unique Swedish model of national conscription. Committees determined the local quotas; burgh councils and kirk sessions selected the men to serve. Nearly half of each regiment's officers were to be veterans. Arms, especially muskets, came in large quantities from the Netherlands. The ill-trained and unwilling English forces assembled by Charles I were no match for the Scots.[19]

Civil war led to the creation of the first modern English army. At first both sides relied heavily on volunteers, especially on officers with continental experience. Loyal noblemen and gentlemen raised substantial forces for the king, often drawing on their own tenants and financial resources. The London trained bands played a vital part in parliament's early survival. Further parliamentary armies, notably that of the Eastern Association, were raised from the combined resources of several counties. Both sides introduced conscription in 1643. The New Model Army, initially of 22,000 men, two-thirds infantry, one-third cavalry or mounted infantry, formed in 1645, was better organized, equipped and supplied than any previous English force. At first it was also better paid. England kept a large army for several years after the civil wars. It amounted to some 40,000 men in 1660.

Charles II retained some 3,500 men in England in 1661 as well as forces in Scotland and Ireland. Several British regiments later served in foreign armies or at Tangier. Renewed temporary increases to counter Dutch or French threats stirred intense fears of armed and arbitrary royal power. In 1685, Charles kept just under 9,000 men in England, nearly as many in Ireland and 2,000 in Scotland. Monmouth's rebellion gave James II a pretext to enlarge his forces. In 1688 he had (on paper) over 34,000 men ready to meet William of Orange's invasion. During William's war the initially small British contribution to his continental operations grew steadily until there were 56,000 troops in the Netherlands in 1697. Parliament then insisted on reducing the home army to 7,000, while, however, allowing other forces to be maintained overseas. By 1709, parliament was voting enough money to maintain 150,000 British and foreign troops in Europe.

The army acquired a permanent bureaucracy: the secretary-at-war, the War Office and the paymaster general. After 1689 it came under sustained parliamentary scrutiny. Britain had by 1707 a professional standing army, but one in which discipline left much room for improvement. It depended on impressment in wartime, paid its private soldiers a pittance and allowed them to moonlight to make ends meet. Officers bought their commissions, and expected to profit from them. 'Effectively, the army was rented to its officers who undertook to recruit, clothe, train, and pay their men on behalf of the State.'[20]

Problems of definition make it difficult to estimate the overall size of different states' armies. Many armies included foreign troops. All states expanded their armies in wartime. Certain broad long-term trends nevertheless seem clear. The forces of the Spanish monarchy may have reached 300,000 during the 1630s before a rapid decline. France fielded 70,000–80,000 troops between 1635 and 1642, but possibly as many as 280,000 in 1678, and between 330,000 and 360,000 during the wars of 1689–97 and 1702–14. The United Provinces paid 50,000–70,000 troops during the 1630s, and around 100,000 during the war of the Spanish Succession. With the help of French subsidies, Sweden possibly maintained 120,000 men, including many foreigners, during the early 1630s. Denmark, Prussia and Austria also raised large armies during the seventeenth century. While still relying on voluntary recruitment and contracts with mercenary captains, seventeenth-century governments increasingly resorted to various forms of compulsion, including impressment, the drafting of men in time of war from militias ostensibly raised for defensive purposes and outright conscription. France, during Louis XIV's later wars, drew the largest numbers of men from militias, while Sweden introduced the first national conscription system. The overall proportion of the Scottish population in military service at one time may have equalled Sweden's, but many of her men were fighting in foreign armies.[21]

Taxation

Given the controversial nature of their most important fiscal initiatives, James I and Charles I were surprisingly successful in raising income. They did so above all by taxing foreign trade more effectively. Ship money also proved an effective new peacetime impost in the short term. The crown's feudal revenues, especially those from wardship, also grew. There were other miscellaneous prerogative sources, including burdensome monopolies. Crown lands produced 40 per cent of royal revenue under Elizabeth, 15 per cent in 1635. Charles I's peacetime income grew from just over £618,000 to nearly £900,000 between 1635 and 1640. The Caroline fiscal achievement was precarious, however, and depended on the avoidance of war.[22]

The Long Parliament abolished ship money and monopolies, but could not do without enhanced impositions on trade. In 1643, it imposed new burdens: assessments (direct taxes on a county quota principle); the sequestration of royalists' estates; compulsory loans; and finally the excise, a tax on a wide range of goods produced in England and abroad. The royalists copied the excise. Each side's determination to win the war meant that a significant proportion of the political nation accepted levels of taxation inconceivable before 1640. The parliamentary government also confiscated the lands of the crown, bishops, cathedrals and several prominent royalists, and sold a substantial portion of them. The main sources of parliamentary revenue produced £29,619,877 between 1643 and 1659. Of that sum, assessments produced 41 per cent, customs and excise 35 per cent (in almost equal shares) and sequestrated and confiscated lands 24 per cent.[23]

In 1660 the Convention confirmed the abolition of feudal revenues (1646) and purveyance (1657), and granted Charles II a projected life income of £1,200,000. Customs and excises were to be the main elements. A hearth tax was added in 1662. Charles II's parliaments also voted him substantial direct taxation to pay for wars and emergencies. After an initial serious shortfall, customs revenues surged in 1674–5 and again after 1681. The ordinary revenue touched £1,370,000 by 1684–5. James II's parliament renewed Charles's revenues and granted additional ones for specific purposes. The total amount reached £2,000,000 for much of his reign. Fiscal management was greatly improved. Tax 'farming' was replaced by direct collection of the customs (in 1671) and of the excise (in 1683), accompanied by a drive for greater efficiency.[24]

In 1690 William III was granted the excise for life, and customs for four years (a grant later renewed). During the war with France, parliaments greatly increased the range of excisable and dutiable items, and voted various other taxes. The land tax raised 42 per cent of all wartime tax receipts. The statutory commission of public accounts scrutinized expenditure with a new thoroughness from 1691 to 1697. Many grants were strictly appropriated to specified purposes. A clearer view of what the crown needed for civil government and the royal household resulted in the lifetime grant of the 'civil list' of £700,000 in 1698. Peacetime military expenditure would henceforth require parliamentary votes.[25]

All seventeenth-century governments had to borrow on a large scale, especially to meet the costs of war. London's corporation, gathering money in turn from companies and individuals, was one of the biggest lenders, advancing just over £1,000,000 between 1660 and 1680, and over £592,500 in 1689–93. Other lenders included monopolists (before 1641), farmers of the revenue and officials of spending departments. All of these stood to lose from the withdrawal of government favour. Loans were also raised from goldsmith bankers. When the crown postponed repayment of much of its debt in 1672, it ruined several financiers. William III's government spent over £49,000,000 between 1689 and 1697. Taxes raised not far short of £33,000,000, a stupendous amount by previous standards, but far short of expenditure. The debt, £16,700,000 in 1697, dwarfed all previous government deficits. Parliament underwrote an increasing proportion of it. The million pound loan of 1693 was funded by specific taxes. In 1694 parliament authorized the foundation of the Bank of England. Subscribers were to raise £1,200,000 to lend to the government. Interest payable at 8 per cent was to be funded by fresh duties and excises. The Bank was empowered to raise further loans secured by taxation. By 1714 most of the national debt (then £40,400,000) was funded.[26]

The raising of vastly increased revenues resulted in the creation or re-organization of several offices. 'Full-time employees in the fiscal bureaucracy' increased in number from 2,524 to 4,780 between 1690 and 1708. The great majority was employed in the Customs and Excise offices. The new Excise service was notable for efficiency and probity.[27]

The Scottish crown's income, largely derived from customs, was a tiny fraction of that raised in England around 1600. James VI and Charles I demanded substantial grants from their parliaments. The Covenanters seized bishops' and royalists' lands, and in 1643–4 introduced a land tax and excise on English lines. Taxation under the English occupation was far heavier than it had been in the 1630s. By 1659, the Scottish state's estimated income had reached a high point equivalent to 9.5 per cent of the English state's revenues. Taxes were sharply reduced after the Restoration. They were raised once again during the 1690s. A range of other fiscal expedients followed a big increase in land tax. But England's fiscal burden rose far faster. Scotland's tax yield was less than 3 per cent that of England's in 1707.[28]

The Dutch fiscal achievement was widely admired in England. Holland, the wealthiest province, always raised the lion's share of the revenue. Excises and customs provided nearly 71 per cent of her contribution in 1640. Most of the remainder came from land and house taxes. Despite the fiscal autonomy of each province in the Union, a process of 'continuous bargaining and coalition-making at all levels' resulted in impressively effective collective achievements in face of external threats. Towns had raised loans and sold annuities before 1500; provincial governments had introduced them during the sixteenth century. The Dutch had pioneered assignable debts based on taxes, but 'due to the fragmented character of (their) political structure, never issued a truly national debt backed by a national taxing authority' as England did after adopting 'Dutch finance' in the 1690s. They nevertheless carried a growing burden of public debt without undue strain until Louis XIV's wars nearly quadrupled it between 1670 and 1715.[29]

The French crown relied heavily on direct taxation, above all the *taille*, throughout the seventeenth century. Around 16,000,000 *livres* in 1609–10, the *taille* supposedly reached 57,000,000 in 1648 (62 per cent of total revenue), though in practice arrears of payment mounted steadily. The taille fell disproportionately on poorer peasants, but attempts to adjust the burden by imposing indirect taxes encountered strong local resistance. Expenditure reached new heights during the wars of 1689–97 and 1702–14. Louis XIV's ministers had to introduce new taxes to finance his wars, notably the 1695 *capitation*, which ended noble exemption from direct taxes. Most governments resorted to the creation of offices on a large scale. In a fateful step, Henry IV in 1604 allowed all office-holders to bequeath their offices if they paid an annual tax of a sixtieth of their value. This temporary measure was later repeatedly renewed, entrenching the independence of an army of largely superfluous office-holders, the majority of whom were exempt from various taxes. This system of concealed borrowing 'incarcerated the French monarchs in a fiscal prison of their own making'. In England both crown and office-holders sold some offices, but the crown never did so systematically. The law limited the scope for creating new offices for sale. The French crown also borrowed at relatively high rates of interest due to its poor credit history.[30]

The complexity of France's local fiscal patchwork, together with widespread corruption and inefficiency among existing officials, compelled the crown to create a new administrative layer, sending increasing numbers of special commissioners or *intendants* into the localities during the 1630s. Their foremost responsibility was to ensure that taxes were levied efficiently, but others were later added, including the raising of militia regiments and a wide range of economic tasks. Armed cavalry and a growing number of local subdelegates helped them. Spanish governments, too, sent out commissioners and superintendents in order to improve Castilian tax collection, and, later, to promote economic well-being, but overall they achieved little, partly because of the resentment of existing local authorities.[31]

The Spanish monarchy entered the seventeenth century facing dire financial problems. By 1598 all the ordinary revenues of the crown except its share of American treasure (already falling by 1601) were committed to servicing the long-term debt. With deficits increasing, the crown nevertheless had to seek fresh loans, which reached a peak early in the 1620s. It persuaded the *Cortes* to grant new taxes, made economies in the royal household, reduced official salaries, taxed the interest due to crown creditors, issued base currency, sold town privileges, raised forced loans and rescheduled debts. Royal borrowing became more difficult. Olivares wanted all the kingdoms of the monarchy to contribute to its defence so as to relieve overburdened Castile. In Catalonia his measures to counter a French attack caused full-scale rebellion in 1640. A weakened monarchy ultimately accepted the loss of the northern Netherlands and Portugal. The hopelessly inefficient collection of taxes by the *Cortes* led the crown from the 1660s to negotiate directly with the cities instead.[32]

New taxes, and efforts to improve the yield of existing ones, provoked widespread resistance: hundreds of local risings in France from the 1630s to the 1670s, protests across Castile's northern coastal provinces against a new salt tax of 1631, revolts in southern Italian cities during the 1640s and disturbances in Castilian cities during the later seventeenth century. English riots against excises in the 1640s and 1660s and the hearth tax in the 1660s were less violent and smaller in scale.

Conclusion

The seventeenth century saw the possibility of what James VI and I called a 'free monarchy' disappear in Britain. Adequate revenue was the indispensable basis of such a monarchy. Each time kings made progress towards its achievement their efforts were de-railed by a crisis caused partly or wholly by their own policies: in 1624, 1640 and 1688. Parliaments exacted the sacrifice of royal prerogatives in 1641 and 1689. After 1689, William III's overriding determination to contain the power of Louis XIV at last broke the cycle. Henceforth the English monarchy could not govern without the co-operation of Lords and Commons. Parliamentary consent gave the crown resources far beyond the reach of English monarchs before 1689.

English government grew more efficient in the seventeenth century. Its major achievements were fiscal and administrative reform, naval growth and the creation of a standing army, together resulting in what some historians call a 'fiscal-military state'. The royal household lost some of its importance as the prime focus of political activity to parliaments and to ministries that could manage them. The most important changes were initiated either in the 1640s and 1650s (the introduction of the excise, the creation of England's first modern army and an exceptionally ambitious programme of naval expansion) or in the 1690s (the inception of the national debt). Restoration governments achieved important fiscal and administrative reforms of their own, but not a financial revolution. Meanwhile, the pattern of local self-government in accordance with decisions made in parliaments was confirmed. Central government interference without local support repeatedly proved counterproductive.

Scotland remained a separate kingdom after 1603, but one governed by the ministers of absentee kings. The benefits of the century of regal union included long periods of peace, and the strengthening of local government. But between

1603 and 1702, every one of Scotland's London-based kings, deriving a tiny fraction of their income from Scotland, pursued policies that were against Scottish sentiment or interests. Nevertheless, only in 1637–40 was the combination of grievances sufficiently powerful to generate a national revolution. That revolution's achievements were in various respects even more impressive than those of England's revolution, but they did not save Scotland from English conquest. The Orange Revolution of 1688–9 resulted in more independent Scottish parliaments, and, after the disasters of the 1690s, a determination to safeguard Scotland's interests.

12

THE CONTESTED INHERITANCE
OF REFORMATION

James VI and I

James declared both before and after 1603 that he kept the faith in which he had been brought up but that he rejected the Presbyterians' 'democratic' form of church government. His statements about liturgical practice had been less consistent. In 1604 he convened the Hampton Court Conference of selected higher clergy, privy councillors and five 'godly spokesmen', including some puritans. James shared with puritans a desire for more preaching ministers and a new Bible translation, which he had already proposed to the Scottish clergy. However, he made no concessions to the puritans concerning worship or church government. His insistence that all clergy subscribe their acceptance of the royal supremacy, the Prayer Book and the Thirty-nine Articles resulted in the deprivation of about seventy-five beneficed clergy. After this, however, the Jacobean Church overlooked non-observance of some aspects of the Prayer Book by otherwise quiet and obedient puritan ministers. 'Moderate' puritans saw James as a king sound in his religious belief. He chose George Abbot, *protégé* of the earl of Dunbar, as archbishop of Canterbury in 1611. Abbot was a strict or 'high' Calvinist and uncompromising foe of the papacy, but he had been a useful advocate of episcopacy during a visit to Scotland.[1]

The king disavowed in 1604 any intention of uniting the English and Scottish Churches, but his programme for the Kirk looked like an attempt to bring it closer to the English model. James appointed bishops to every diocese in Scotland, restored their revenues, entrusted them with supervision of synods and presbyteries, and established a court of High Commission to strengthen their authority. In 1606 James summoned Andrew Melville and seven other leading Presbyterians to London to hear English bishops preach on the virtues of episcopacy. Melville, unconvinced, was imprisoned and ultimately exiled. Visiting Scotland in 1617, James caused scandal by having Communion celebrated in the English fashion. He published five articles concerning religious practice. The most contentious ordered that Communion be received kneeling and restored the observance of five church festivals. The 1617 general assembly did not accept the articles, but they were pushed through the next assembly at Perth in 1618, the last to be summoned for twenty years, and through parliament in 1621. James had refused to heed Scots opinion, and divided the Kirk.[2]

James had sought the support of the papacy and other Catholic powers for his succession to the English throne. In 1604, in strikingly conciliatory new language, James publicly acknowledged the present pope's kindness to him, and told parliament that he regarded the Roman Church, 'although defiled with some infirmities and corruptions', as 'our Mother Church'.[3] There was, however, one insurmountable obstacle to friendlier relations: the pope's claimed authority to depose kings. James responded to the 1605 Gunpowder Plot by requiring Catholics to swear an oath repudiating this claim. When Paul V forbade them to take it, James defended it in print, initiating a long controversy with papal champions. Henry IV's assassination by a Catholic fanatic in 1610 renewed James's concern. He nevertheless remained opposed to the severe punishment of loyal lay Catholics. Queen Anne was a discreet Catholic. James's councillors and courtiers included some Catholics or crypto-Catholics. Hopes of a Catholic marriage for Prince Charles resulted in some relaxation of the anti-Catholic penal laws later in the reign.

James allegedly much admired Richard Hooker's partially published treatise *Of the Lawes of Ecclesiastical Politie*, the most comprehensive defence of the Church of England yet written. According to Hooker, biblical texts describing church government were not clear, as the Presbyterians insisted, but had to be interpreted in the light of human reason. Worship, especially celebration of the Lord's Supper, was of paramount importance. Inherited ceremonies had positive value. Hooker died in 1600, but Lancelot Andrewes, one of James's favourite preachers, shared some of Hooker's concerns. He deprecated the seeming arrogance of many puritans in challenging ancient ceremonies and questioning church government. Preaching properly concentrated on Christ as 'object of faith, adoration and emulation'. The faithful offered themselves to God in the sacrament of the Lord's Supper, which also conveyed the enabling grace essential to living the Christian life. Andrewes and some others of similar outlook promoted by James formed a counter-weight to Calvinist churchmen. The Calvinists were more suspicious of anything that to them smacked of idolatry, less attached to ceremonies, implacably hostile to the papacy and more inclined to give preaching a central role in religious practice. James relished the role of arbiter, and prevented theological differences from getting out of hand. But unforeseen pressures would soon threaten his policy of balance.[4]

James worked to preserve the unity of the Dutch Reformed Church by countering what he saw as the divisive influence of the theologian Jacobus Arminius (d. 1609). By questioning the Calvinist doctrines of strict predestination and the irresistibility of God's grace Arminius had caused bitter controversy. The synod of Dordt was convened in 1618 to settle the dispute between Arminius's followers, the Remonstrants, and orthodox Calvinists. The synod, to which James sent a British delegation, condemned the Remonstrants. In England, the influence of Arminius nevertheless mingled with that of existing non- or anti-Calvinist ideas, attracting some prominent English churchmen. Arminius had seen the alternative dangers of false assurance and unnecessary despair stemming from a belief in rigid predestination. Andrewes and his associates deprecated the Calvinists' perceived presumption in their handling of predestination, thought it inappropriate to expound this complicated doctrine in preaching to the unlearned and feared that this might encourage false assurance.

James's Spanish marriage project dismayed his more militantly Protestant subjects, including Archbishop Abbot. While promoting it, James increasingly favoured churchmen who supported his work for peace. He reacted angrily to criticisms of his foreign policy. The crisis that wrecked his diplomacy had been caused by Calvinist political activism. After James's death, Richard Montagu claimed that the king had approved his *Appello Caesarem* (1625) in which Montagu called Calvinists 'puritans', thus damning what had hitherto been orthodoxy by labelling it subversive. It followed that the Church of England was not one of the international sisterhood of Calvinist or Reformed churches. Montagu also characterized the Roman Church as a true Church, albeit an unsound one, and questioned the commonly accepted Protestant identification of the pope as Antichrist. He and like-minded divines moved towards a new conception of the English Church's special 'middle way' between rival confessions.[5]

Charles I

Charles I, probably influenced by a change in James's stance, strongly favoured anti-Calvinist churchmen from the beginning of his reign.[6] He protected Montagu against proceedings by the Commons in 1626, made him a bishop in 1628 and forbade the discussion of potentially controversial doctrines. The first of the Commons' Three Resolutions of 1629 powerfully expressed growing concern about religious innovations. The triumph of the 'Arminian' party, men largely inspired by Andrewes, culminated in William Laud's appointment as archbishop of Canterbury in 1633.

The international context made England's weakness shameful for staunch Protestants during the 1620s. Ferdinand II gave Protestants in Bohemia a stark choice between conversion and expulsion. After the Catholic conquest of the Palatinate, bastion of the Reformed cause in central Europe, Duke Maximilian of Bavaria purged the renowned Calvinist university of Heidelberg and sent its library to Rome. The 1629 Edict of Restitution reversed all secularizations of church lands in the Empire since 1552. The same year the Huguenots were deprived of all the strongholds granted them in 1598, though they kept their civil rights and could still practise their religion.

At the heart of Charles's and Laud's religious policy during the 1630s was decent and reverent worship, especially in the celebration of Holy Communion.

Laud sought stricter enforcement of liturgical conformity. Puritans objected to the altarwise placing of the communion table at the east end of the church, with its overtones of Catholic worship, and to the practice of receiving communion at an enclosing rail. Charles agreed with his father that once services were over, his hard working subjects 'of the meaner sort' deserved recreation to refresh their spirits. In 1633 he re-issued a declaration in favour of Sunday sports originally authorized by his father in 1618. Unfortunately puritans saw this as an attack on strict Sabbath observance.

Charles and Laud, here again developing Jacobean initiatives, tried to prevent any further alienation of church property and encouraged the recovery of what had already been lost. Charles also employed the clergy more extensively in both local and national governments than any previous monarch since the Reformation; here again he was extending his father's practice. He encouraged high esteem for the sacred offices of the priest, who alone could minister the sacraments, and the bishop, whose office he believed to be divinely prescribed for church government.

Henrietta Maria and her chapels, creating a visible Catholic presence at court; the Catholic sympathies or convictions of some of Charles's courtiers and councillors; the reception of two papal envoys in 1634 and 1636, the first in England since 1558; above all Charles's weak foreign policy during the 1630s: all these deeply disturbed staunch Protestants. Laud put pressure on foreign Protestants in England, from 1635 allowing only new immigrants their own liturgy, and insisting that 'strangers' born in England attend their parish churches. Meanwhile Catholics were largely free from persecution, though Charles's government, seeking any possible source of revenue, squeezed greatly increased fines from them.

The formation of new puritan voluntary congregations continued under James and Charles. Some of these were 'semi-separatist' groups whose members sometimes participated in church services. Others went to the Netherlands in order to preserve their separate identity. One group settled in Massachusetts in 1620. Between 1629 and 1640 20,000 people or more left for 'New England', many of them because of more stringent prosecution of nonconforming puritans. Three anti-episcopal pamphleteers Burton, Bastwick and Prynne became the leading 'martyrs' of the persecution when their ears were cropped in 1637. The punishment made the government look ridiculous and led to mass demonstrations of popular sympathy.

Charles's religious policy in Scotland posed a much more fundamental challenge to the nature of the existing Church. His 1633 coronation at Holyrood, with a table set altarwise bearing a crucifix, bishops in vestments and an English communion service, was a deep affront to Scottish traditions and sensibilities. In 1636 he unilaterally imposed new canons on the Kirk. Charles wanted what he saw as decency, uniformity and order in worship rather than spontaneity, variety or improvisation. His introduction of a new Prayer Book in 1637, largely based on the English Book of 1549, provoked a revolution.[7]

Revolution and further Reformation

The Scottish National Covenant of February 1638 rehearsed a 'Negative Confession' (a thorough abjuration of Roman Catholicism first signed by James VI in 1581 in order to win the confidence of kirkmen), and sundry subsequent reforming measures. The Covenant then bound its signatories to defend the true religion thus established, without accepting innovations in worship, or 'corruptions' of church government. The general assembly convened at Glasgow in the autumn condemned the Prayer Book, abolished episcopacy and annulled the 1636 canons and the Five Articles.

The Scots hoped that England would follow their path to Reformation. In 1641, however, parliament could not agree on the abolition of episcopacy. It suppressed the courts of High Commission, which had enforced unpopular ecclesiastical policies. In September the Commons ordered the reversal of Laudian innovations in worship and church furnishings. The November Grand Remonstrance blamed all that had gone wrong since 1625 on 'Jesuited papists', bishops, corrupt clergy, and those councillors and courtiers who worked for foreign powers. The nearly even vote on the Remonstrance revealed a deepening division of opinion, not a reforming unanimity. However, many supporters of episcopacy withdrew from Westminster to join the king. Charles's last unwilling concession was to consent to a bill excluding bishops from the Lords (February 1642). When civil war broke out, puritans were parliament's staunchest supporters.

The need for Scottish aid in 1643 pushed parliament further. In June it established the advisory Westminster Assembly of 121 clergy with some peers and MPs. The Assembly and the two Houses subscribed the Solemn League and Covenant with the Scots. It committed its signatories to 'the reformation of religion in the kingdoms of England and Ireland in doctrine, worship, discipline and government, according to the Word of God and the example of the best reformed churches' and to bringing the three kingdoms' churches 'to the nearest conjunction and uniformity'. Eight Scots commissioners joined the Assembly. Parliament authorized in 1645 a *Directory of Worship* drafted by the Assembly, and approved the Westminster Confession in 1648. It ordered in 1646 the establishment of a framework of Presbyterian church government, which never covered the whole country, and abolished episcopacy. Parliament was determined to retain ultimate control over the Church, and many MPs had no wish to see Presbyterianism on the Scottish model installed in England.

Presbyterian ministers pointed to an incipient breakdown of religion and argued for strong church government to guard against it. However, soldiers such as Oliver Cromwell knew that some men in the army whom Presbyterians viewed as dangerous radicals were among the staunchest fighters for the parliamentary cause. The Army's *Heads of the Proposals* of July 1647 demanded an end to penalties for not attending religious worship. In 1650 the Rump's ordinance 'for the relief of religious and peaceable people' ended compulsory church attendance. In 1653 the Instrument of Government guaranteed toleration of all

Christians provided they did not disturb the liberties of others or the public peace. Adherents of 'popery or prelacy' and those advocating or practising licentiousness were excepted. Sympathetic gentry supported many ejected royalist clergy, and some deprived bishops continued to ordain new clergy. Despite widespread fears of Catholic plotting just before the civil wars, and Charles's opponents' inflammatory anti-Catholic rhetoric, relatively few Catholics suffered death for their religion in 1641–6. Enforcement of anti-Catholic legislation was uneven. Cromwell tried to avoid persecution, and many Catholics enjoyed some freedom of worship under his rule.[8]

The lapse of censorship in 1641, followed by the religious ferment of the revolutionary years, gave birth or new freedom to a number and variety of voluntary religious congregations and sects barely equalled even during the heady early days of Reformation in Germany or the Netherlands. The Independent or Congregational churches, embodied by Covenant, chose their own ministers and carefully assessed would-be members. They retained infant baptism, while the Baptists' fundamental principle was believers' baptism, which required a degree of maturity. The Arminian General Baptists and the Calvinist Particular Baptists could both trace their origins to the period before 1640.

Fastest growing of the many sects that sprang up were the Quakers or 'Friends of the Truth'.[9] The Friends accorded primary authority to the Holy Spirit, which guided the reading of Scripture. They discarded liturgy, ministry and sacraments. In a spirit of universal brotherhood they embraced pacifism, insisted on familiar forms of address and refused conventional expressions of respect such as the removal of hats before social superiors. They also refused oaths and the payment of tithes to the organized Church. The Quaker message appealed to many people whom the Reformation had hitherto largely failed to engage, especially the less literate and inhabitants of remoter regions. The close reading of Scripture and the reconciliation of seemingly conflicting texts practised by many puritans became largely redundant for Quaker evangelists. The subversive potential of their religious and social ideas was widely feared. More shadowy than the Quakers, and certainly far less successful, were the Ranters, who allegedly claimed that all acts done 'in light and love' were right, no matter how sinful in conventional estimation. Less socially disruptive, but theologically threatening, were the few English anti-trinitarians.

Religion was a driving force in popular political activism. The Levellers, who later developed a far-reaching programme of political, economic and legal reforms, came together in 1645 above all in shared concern for religious toleration. One of their leaders, Richard Overton, questioned the separate existence of the soul. Another, William Walwyn, believed that the apostles preached community of goods. In 1649 Gerrard Winstanley the 'Digger' or 'True Leveller' launched in Surrey his experiment in communal cultivation of land following what he believed to be Christian teaching.

Millenarian beliefs were a notable spur to puritan political action. Passages from two of the Bible's prophetic books, Daniel and Revelation, were the basis of predictions that four great earthly monarchies would be succeeded by the thousand-year rule of Christ on earth before the end of the world. The exceptional international turbulence of the 1640s and Charles I's execution strengthened the expectation that the Fifth Monarchy would begin soon. The Fifth Monarchists, whose most vocal spokesmen were army officers and Independent ministers, advocated more rigorous punishment of some breaches of the Ten Commandments. The Rump passed in 1650 new ordinances dealing with sexual offences and violations of the Sabbath. It set up two Commissions for the Propagation of the Gospel in northern England and Wales. A Fifth Monarchist, Colonel Thomas Harrison, headed the Welsh commission, and two other millenarians, Vavasor Powell and Morgan Llwyd, were especially active members. They ejected several clergy, aggravating a shortage of ministers only partly offset by the appointment of itinerant preachers. Harrison was also the principal architect of the Nominated Assembly, which included some Fifth Monarchists. He ardently supported war with the Dutch, believing them to have lapsed from godliness into gross materialism. The Fifth Monarchists bitterly resented what they saw as Cromwell's subsequent betrayal of the cause. Fears that they might seize power in 1659–60 strengthened support for the Restoration.

The abolition of episcopacy had removed the main agency supervising the parish clergy. In 1654 were established a commission of 'triers' to assess the fitness of ministers presented to parish livings, and local commissions of 'ejectors' to expel the unfit. Some ministers joined together during the 1650s in voluntary local associations in order to achieve a more effective preaching and catechizing ministry. But in the absence of an English equivalent of the Scottish kirk session, it was difficult to enforce puritan moral discipline.

Many Scots proudly believed that the Kirk was already the best-reformed Church in Europe. They viewed the growth of English separatism with horror. As has been shown, conflicting responses to the Stuart cause and consequent hostilities with England split the Kirk into supporters and opponents of the Engagement in 1648, and Resolutioners and Protesters in 1650. When the Engagers' catastrophic defeat enabled their opponents to seize power, parliament abolished lay patronage in the Kirk. The division between Resolutioners and Protestors persisted after the English conquest. Despite the imposition of toleration on English lines there was very little Scottish support for any of the sects, though the Quakers gained some converts.

The interregnum saw the only intensive campaign to convert the Irish majority. Funds were set aside to pay clergy and schoolmasters, and the government tried to compel the population to participate in Protestant worship. But the serious shortage of suitable ministers could not be made good in the brief time available.

Restoration

The religious divisions that had developed in England since 1641 prevented united opposition to the restoration of the old church order in 1660. The Convention parliament did not attempt a religious settlement. The Presbyterians, the biggest puritan group, welcomed Charles II's return, but though the king declared his support for a compromise over church government, the Presbyterians were unable to reach agreement with the bishops in 1661. In January 1661 an abortive Fifth Monarchist rising in London aroused fresh fears of religious 'fanatics'. Later that year the Cavalier parliament restored the bishops to the House of Lords and passed the Corporation Act, requiring all officers in borough corporations to take oaths of allegiance and supremacy, abjure the taking of arms against the king together with the Solemn League and Covenant, and receive Holy Communion in Church. The 1662 Uniformity Act required the oaths and abjurations from all clergymen, and imposed an only slightly revised Prayer Book. Most Presbyterians, let alone Independents, could not comply. In all, 1880 English and Welsh parish clergy left their livings before or after the Act, though some later conformed.[10] The 1662 Quaker Act specified severe penalties for Friends' meetings. After conspiracies in the north in 1663, the 1664 Conventicle Act prohibited religious gatherings of five or more people who did not belong to the same household unless they used the Prayer Book. An act of 1665 forbade nonconformist ministers to come within five miles of any corporate town or parish where they had previously been in post unless they took an oath of non-resistance.

The triumphant Church of England received fervent and widespread support from those who had suffered under puritan rule, especially royalist nobility and gentry. Conviction, sentiment and self-interest impelled most of the gentry to support the Church. Separatism had threatened the rights of lay patrons. Uniformity of public worship, the alliance of squire and parson, and hierarchy both in Church and society seemed natural means of securing social stability and control over the lower orders.

The boundary between conformity and dissent was somewhat blurred in practice. In many places the Prayer Book was used selectively and attendance at Communion was poor. Occasional conformity – occasional attendance at church and reception of communion by nonconformists – was widespread. The enforcement of the laws against dissenters depended on the co-operation of lay authorities. This was often hard to obtain, especially in towns where nonconformity was strong, or from gentry of puritan sympathies. Nonconformists still occupied local offices and some parliamentary seats.

Charles II's bishops included both former Laudians and an ex-Presbyterian. Although many men who had entered or continued in the parish ministry between 1645 and 1660 had left the Church, far more survived within it. Some of them favoured the conciliation of moderate dissenters and their 'comprehension' within the Church. Such men were sometimes labelled 'Latitudinarians' for their supposed lack of strong opinions about doctrine, organization and liturgy, though this was a hostile caricature. For surviving Laudians, and some 'enthusiastic converts' among interregnum ministers, the apostolic succession of the episcopate, the saving grace conveyed by the sacraments and the Church's 'incomparable liturgy' were fundamentally important. They revered the memory of the martyred Charles I and strongly upheld doctrines of divine hereditary right and the duty of obedience to royal authority.

Charles II may have valued the authority he enjoyed as supreme governor of the Church, but he lacked his father's emotional attachment to it. Just before his return to England he had declared 'a liberty to tender consciences': no man would be troubled for religious opinions that did not disturb the peace. He probably thought it unwise to provoke Protestant nonconformists through persecution. Catholics had saved him in 1651, and most of his closest surviving relatives were or would become Catholics. In December 1662 Charles declared that he would seek parliament's help in easing the lot of deserving Protestant nonconformists and Roman Catholics. A furious reaction forced his retreat. Charles's Declaration of Indulgence of 1672 allowed Protestant dissenters to worship in licensed chapels and Roman Catholics in their own houses. Parliamentary condemnation of the Declaration compelled its revocation in 1673. The 1673 Test Act required all those holding office under the crown to take the oaths of allegiance and supremacy, make a declaration against transubstantiation and receive Communion in the Church of England. (A second act, in 1678, extended the first and second of these requirements to members of both houses of parliament.)

Fears of Roman Catholicism, never dormant, had been temporarily eclipsed during the early 1660s by what had seemed the more immediate threat posed by 'fanatics'. During the 1670s Catholicism seemed to pose the greatest danger. The Commons passed in 1673 a bill for the ease of Protestant dissenters later mangled by the Lords. Fear of the resurgent power of Catholic France abroad was combined after 1673 with the prospect of a Catholic successor to the throne at home. Over-assertive clericalism at home was also liable to be seen as 'popish'. An intense fear of Catholic machinations powered the Popish Plot scare and the subsequent drive for Exclusion. However, the Exclusionists' efforts to mobilize mass popular support for their cause and their readiness to appeal to Protestant dissenters once again made the danger of civil strife seem to many loyal supporters of the crown more immediate than the popish threat. Tories also held the dissenters responsible for dividing Protestant ranks, and thus doing the pope's work. Charles's response to the crisis of 1673 and to Exclusion was to turn to the men who combined loyalty to Church and king. On both occasions, but particularly from 1681 on, this meant persecution of the dissenters and the abandonment of hopes of relief for either Catholic or Protestant nonconformists. After 1681 the strategy was helped by the reaction against Exclusionist excess. The Quakers, seen as the most dangerous of all nonconformists, suffered worst: about 400 died in prison between 1681 and 1685.[11]

Roman Catholics underwent brief but savage persecution in 1678–80, when twenty-four were executed, and nearly as many died in gaol. James II's accession brought them a new dawn after recent nightmares: eagerly seized opportunities to build chapels and defend the faith in print, the establishment of new religious missions and the triumphal 1687 tour of a newly appointed vicar apostolic (to whom three more were added in 1688).[12]

The unexpected challenge of James II's determined pursuit of general religious toleration was particularly difficult for the Church of England. The bishops were the monarchy's strongest supporters. Many of them were fervent exponents of the doctrine of non-resistance to kings whom they regarded as the Lord's Anointed, representatives of God on earth. James strained their loyalty to the utmost by insisting that they execute commands which seemed to them illegal and ungodly. In 1686 Bishop Compton of London refused to suspend John Sharp for contravening the king's *Directions* forbidding anti-Catholic preaching. The Court of Ecclesiastical Commission that James had established suspended Compton himself. He was to be the one churchman to join in the invitation to William of Orange. The 'seven bishops' carefully explained that their refusal to order the Declaration of Indulgence of April 1688 to be read from the pulpits was due to its illegality, not their want of 'due tenderness to Dissenters'.[13]

James found his strongest dissenting supporters among the Quakers, who had suffered the harshest persecution. More moderate dissenters, especially the Presbyterians, were less enthusiastic. They were perhaps influenced by two arguments eloquently expressed by the Marquis of Halifax in his *Letter to a Dissenter* (1687): James's actions were illegal, and in the long term he was not to be trusted because the Roman Catholic Church could not allow liberty. Many dissenters shared in the general rejoicing at the seven bishops' acquittal. James had achieved the extraordinary feat of making Protestant heroes out of the leaders of a persecuting Church.

The makers of the Restoration in Scotland faced a different situation from the one in England: a deeply divided Kirk, but no proliferation of sects outside it. The Kirk was restored to its state of 1633: with bishops, but without Charles I's deeply loathed innovations. Most of the nobles, sick of upheavals that had finally resulted in loss of their church patronage as well as their heritable jurisdictions, were happy enough by this stage to see bishops restored to a Kirk that remained Presbyterian in its lower reaches and Reformed in worship. A minority of the population, however, including many ministers of the Kirk, was never reconciled to the restoration of episcopal government, the requirement of episcopal collation to parishes or the enforced repudiation of the Covenants. About a quarter of Scotland's ministers had been expelled by 1663. Many of them took sizeable numbers of their congregations with them into illegal conventicles that spread through the Lowlands. Armed risings invoking the Covenants broke out in 1666 and 1679. A few militant Covenanters called for war on Charles II in 1680. Lauderdale favoured 'indulgence' of the more moderate dissenters (after limited submission). The Act of Supremacy of 1669 recognized the king's absolute control over the Kirk. Indulgences were issued on royal authority in 1669 and 1672 in partially successful attempts to bring ministers back into the fold, but a core of determined and militant 'conventiclers' remained. A 1681 Test Act heralded a brutal campaign of repression. James VII's 1687 grant of toleration earned him little support: Catholics and Quakers were few, and Covenanters were unimpressed. But he seriously weakened the authority of the bishops, loyal henchmen of the crown.[14]

Toleration and intolerance

Charles II and James II were the first English rulers openly to present the case for toleration in their Declarations of Indulgence. Religious unity, they pointed out, had proved impossible to achieve. The anticipated advantages of toleration were 'ease and quiet ... the increase of trade and encouragement of strangers'. James's 1687 Declaration was the more eloquent. He admitted that he wished that all his subjects were Catholics. Constraint of conscience had always been directly contrary to his inclination, however, and (he thought) to the interests of government. James's Declaration might be illegal, his long-term intentions widely mistrusted. The toleration he offered was nonetheless more generous and comprehensive than anything granted by statute before the nineteenth century or existing in contemporary Europe.[15]

The United Provinces were unique in their religious diversity, but this was largely due to an 'ambivalent semi-tolerance' rather than whole-hearted toleration. The public Reformed Church comprised over half the population by 1650, perhaps two-thirds by 1700. Catholics were the largest minority, and actually increased in some cities. Anabaptists and Lutherans also formed substantial minorities, though the Anabaptists declined in the long run. There were small but growing Jewish communities and various fringe sects. The oligarchies of some of the wealthy cities favoured toleration. Some provincial authorities nevertheless strongly discouraged or tried to prevent the meetings of various minority groups. The Dutch debate about toleration, part of wider European exchanges, reached its peak between 1680 and 1710. Even at that stage, the Republic experienced 'a partial toleration seething with tension, theological and political'.

During the 1650s a new split within the public Church developed between orthodox Calvinists and more liberal theologians, especially Johannes Cocceius of Leiden, an expert philologist who warned against a uniformly literal interpretation of Scripture. Orthodox anxieties were deepened by new scientific discoveries and speculations that seemed to reinforce these warnings. A Sabbath observance controversy broke out between the 'precisians' and their liberal opponents.[16]

Brandenburg-Prussia followed a different path to ambivalent tolerance from that of the Dutch. The Elector John Sigismund had converted to Calvinism in 1613 hoping that his subjects would follow him, but instead faced strong opposition from people and estates. His 'court reformation' instead resulted in a 'bi-confessional' state. His grandson Frederick William issued an 'edict of tolerance' in 1664 forbidding polemical warfare between the two confessions. In some of his territories, old treaties protected the rights of Catholics. He allowed Protestant sectarian refugees from Poland to settle in Prussia, and some Jews to came to Brandenburg. Frederick William's policy of tolerance was probably inspired in part by economic considerations as well as by personal dislike of the 'violent hatreds' resulting from religious conflict. Largely in order to counter continuing Lutheran hostility towards Calvinism, the Elector Frederick III enlisted Philipp Jakob Spener, a reforming pastor with a strong aversion to arid and acrimonious theological controversy. He supported Spener and several of his associates in the movement dubbed 'Pietist' by its critics in an effort to promote religious harmony and 'cultural integration' in his territories. Halle, where Frederick founded a new university in 1691, became the main centre of Pietist educational and charitable activity.[17]

In western Europe the Huguenots were the only dissident minority of the population of a whole kingdom to enjoy both religious and civil rights, granted by Henry IV's Edict of Nantes. Louis XIV increased the pressure on the Huguenots to convert to Catholicism, gradually from 1661, more insistently from 1681, destroying their churches, curtailing their civil rights, closing their academies, forcibly removing children from their homes and billeting soldiers on households. The final revocation of the Edict of Nantes in 1685 was followed by sporadic atrocities. The reasons for the persecution of the Huguenots varied from time to time, but by 1685 Louis was particularly concerned to demonstrate his orthodoxy as a Catholic monarch at a time when he was involved in a quarrel with the papacy over royal rights in the Gallican Church. He underestimated the extent of Huguenot survival in 1685. Between 140,000 and 160,000 people fled abroad during the persecution, the largest numbers to the Dutch Republic, England, Brandenburg and Switzerland. Even after that, the Protestants of the Cévennes tied down an army when Louis XIV tried to crush them between 1702 and 1704. The revocation and the consequent acceleration of the flight to England were acutely embarrassing for James II. He feared the potentially subversive influence of the Huguenots in England, and their fate undermined English trust in his good intentions.

In no other European country was the end of previous toleration as dramatic as in France, but elsewhere Protestants faced a variety of pressures. Emperor Leopold I closed Protestant churches in Silesia, and tried to curb both noble privileges and religious freedom in Hungary, provoking opposition from both Catholics and Protestants: repression alternated with reluctant concessions between 1670 and 1711. In Poland, the crown discriminated against Protestants in its use of patronage. The Catholic majority among the nobility increasingly blamed Protestantism, the religion of the great enemy Sweden, for national disasters. The *Sejm* forbade conversion from Catholicism (1668) and barred non-Catholics from admission to the nobility (1673).[18]

Roman Catholicism's international power, its recent advances, the cruel persecution in France, the association of popery and arbitrary government, and the danger to Britain from the continent's most powerful Catholic monarch made it impossible to advocate the toleration of Roman Catholicism in 1689. John Locke, foremost of Whig political philosophers, clearly distinguished in his *Letter Concerning Toleration* the responsibilities of civil governments from those of Churches. The former were concerned with the protection of life, liberty and possessions; the latter with the care of souls. The magistrate had no business to try to compel anybody to belong to a particular Church, which was properly a voluntary society. The Roman Church, however, was not to be tolerated. It threatened the basis of civil society itself, by teaching that

Catholics were not obliged to keep faith with heretics, and asserting the Church's right to depose rulers.[19]

William III was anxious to protect Catholics from persecution because of his dependence on Catholic allies. He could do little to curb the anti-Catholic zeal of the Irish parliament, which passed severe penal laws. Legislation of William's and Anne's reigns included measures to confiscate horses and weapons in the hands of Catholics, and prevent them from having their children educated overseas (1695), to banish bishops and members of religious orders (1697), prevent Catholics' acquisition of land and divide their existing estates (1697, 1704). A sacramental test for office holding was introduced in 1704. This adversely affected the Ulster Presbyterians, largest and best organized of Protestant groups, reinforced by further immigration during the 1690s.

After 1688 it seemed very unwise to withdraw toleration from Protestant dissenters in England completely. Experience of James II's reign underlined for many the necessity of preventing Catholic exploitation of Protestant divisions. One way of doing this was to revive the project of comprehension, facilitating the conformity of 'moderate dissenters', while also granting limited toleration to the expected small number who would still find it impossible to conform. This scheme foundered in 1689 on the hostility of defenders of the Church. Finally a rather limited Toleration Act was passed. It gave freedom of worship to Protestant dissenters ready to swear or declare their allegiance and their acceptance of certain fundamental Christian doctrines. Their meeting houses had to be licensed. The Test and Corporation Acts were not repealed, so that dissenters remained in principle barred from public office.

Scotland's religious settlement was far more partisan and intolerant than England's. Against William's wishes, parliament abolished episcopacy in 1689, then royal supremacy over the Kirk in 1690. Presbyterian government was restored, and private church patronage abolished. The general assembly met for the first time since 1653. Over 660 ministers were ousted or left their congregations between 1689 and 1702, many more than after 1660. Several of them were nonjurors who refused to accept William and Mary. Others were punished for their past support for episcopacy. The purge was least effective in the north-east and the Highlands, where support for the episcopalian Church was strongest.[20]

In England, eight prelates, including Archbishop Sancroft and four of the other bishops prosecuted in 1688, and nearly 400 other clergy, felt unable to swear allegiance to William and Mary. These nonjurors lost their places. Many other clergy secretly admired their courage.

Church and dissent after 1689

The term 'High Churchmen' was applied from the later 1680s to those clergymen who were determined to protect the Church and if possible reverse the dissenters' gains. Over 3,900 dissenters' meeting-houses were licensed between 1689 and 1710. However, the dissenters were far less of a threat than they seemed to High Churchmen's fevered imaginations. In all the main dissenting groups, but especially among the Quakers, the development of organizational structures went hand in hand with a loss of missionary fervour. The sects' internal splits over matters of doctrine became more open after 1689. Early efforts at co-operation between Presbyterians and Independents soon broke down.[21]

However, toleration made church attendance more difficult to enforce. The circulation of unorthodox ideas became harder to police when the statute enforcing regulation of print by means of licensing lapsed in 1695. Many High Churchmen felt that the leadership of the Church in face of these challenges was weak or unsound. Some of William's bishops, including John Tillotson, archbishop of Canterbury, were renowned for their moderation towards dissenters and support for comprehension. Tillotson as a young puritan had been a happy conformist during the interregnum. Gilbert Burnet had been a minister in the Church of Scotland. 'Moderate High Church' bishops were reluctant to stir up controversy, so lower-ranking clergy blew the trumpet against the threats to the Church. Anne, unlike William, was a loyal daughter of the Church. She regularly summoned Convocation, which had not met between 1689 and 1701. Clergy there and Tories in the Commons attacked what they saw as the insidious menace of occasional conformity, which enabled many nonconformists to evade the penalties of the legislation excluding dissenters from public life.

Toleration had diminished the Church's ability to exercise social control, especially through the church courts. The general reformation of lives and manners advocated by William himself and others was, however, a cause in which churchmen and dissenters could co-operate. The Societies for the Reformation of Manners, originating within the Church in 1691, soon included dissenters. They prosecuted vice and disorder. More positively, the Society for Promoting Christian Knowledge (founded in 1698) aimed to check the perceived 'decay of Religion' and guard against Catholicism by means of primary religious education. The Society helped to encourage the foundation of large numbers of charity schools. Missionary work among non-Christians, an activity hitherto neglected by the Church of England, was one aim of the Society for the Propagation of the Gospel in Foreign Parts, founded in 1701.

Conclusion

The widespread desire for further reformation and continuing theological disagreements in Protestant Europe threatened to exacerbate the religious divisions created by the Reformation. The island kingdoms formed one of those combinations of territories in which religious differences were particularly marked. England and Scotland each had a different form of Protestant church that commanded the allegiance of the great majority of the population. Most of the Irish people, however, remained Roman Catholics. James VI and I and Charles I wanted their Protestant churches to be 'congruent' or even 'convergent' in their hierarchical government, decent reverence in worship and avoidance of potentially divisive religious controversies. The international crisis of the 1620s and militant Protestant criticism of royal foreign policy resulted in an increasing royal suspicion of the subversive potential of Calvinist Reformed Protestantism at home and abroad. The balance of domestic policy shifted towards stricter uniformity, the promotion of enthusiastic liturgical conformists and an attempt to curb the discussion of key Calvinist doctrines. In Scotland, where James VI's innovations had already split the Kirk, Charles's measures resulted in national resistance. The ensuing civil wars finally doomed hopes that the English might follow the Scottish path to reformation, and allowed an unprecedented variety of religious beliefs and practices to emerge in England.

After 1660 it was hard to envisage the complete eradication of Protestant religious dissent in England, and impossible to imagine the comprehension of all its varieties within the Church. In Scotland, where there was little support for radical sects, the Kirk was split by disagreements about co-operation with the Stuarts between 1648 and 1652, and by the re-imposition of episcopacy and repudiation of the Covenants after 1660. In each kingdom, governments experimented with both persecution and indulgence as possible solutions. It was the unilateral imposition of an unprecedented toleration by the Catholic James VII and II that finally made it impossible to withhold religious freedom from England's Protestant dissenters. The Revolution settlements gave them a more limited but also more secure freedom than James had granted them and in Scotland established a Presbyterian Kirk with a large and unrecognized, though regionally concentrated, episcopalian minority outside it.

Toleration was not extended to Roman Catholics. Since 1603 fear and hatred of Catholicism in England had been fuelled by the successes of Catholic powers in Europe, by major persecutions (above all in the 1620s and 1680s) and by a series of real or imagined Catholic plots (especially in 1605, 1641 and 1678). Catholic designs had assumed their most insidious form when successive kings had appeared to further them, either as the unwitting tools of Catholic schemers or in sinister collaboration with them. Finally, tyranny and popery had come together under the dangerously deceptive guise of a plain-speaking sailor king. James's flight, the exclusion of Catholics from the throne and William's moderation helped to prevent a Protestant backlash in England. But in Ireland, where the great majority of the population remained Catholic, there took place after 1689 another instalment of the dispossession of the old ruling class whose only possible parallel in Europe was to be found in Habsburg Bohemia.

13

COMMERCIAL COMPETITION, INDUSTRIAL DIVERSIFICATION AND AGRICULTURAL SUCCESS

Populations and wars

After 1600 European demographic growth slowed sharply. England's population possibly increased from 4,162,000 to 5,391,000 between 1601 and 1656 — by 30 per cent. Thereafter, with a brief interruption during the 1670s, it fell to 5,036,000 in 1686 before rising to an estimated 5,211,000 in 1701. Both lower fertility and higher mortality checked growth. Reduced economic opportunities discouraged marriage. Real wages fell to their lowest level of this period on the eve of the civil wars, and their subsequent recovery was gradual at first. The first marriage rate reached its nadir just after the Restoration before rising rapidly until the 1680s. Increasing numbers migrated to London and major provincial towns, entering a much more unhealthy environment that drove up overall mortality. London's last great outbreak of plague occurred in 1665, but several other contagious diseases, including smallpox and typhus, combined to keep background mortality at a high level. War deaths and emigration also helped to curb population growth.[1]

Scotland's and Ireland's demographic histories are more obscure than England's. Scotland's population possibly rose to a high point of 1,230,000 before a savage check during the 1690s. Ireland's may have grown from 1,000,000 to 1,970,000 by 1687. Wars ravaged both countries during the 1640s and early 1650s. In the 1690s Scotland suffered from famine, Ireland from war. For several decades, however, both countries were at peace. Irish agricultural production rose. High Irish fertility and immigration levels more than compensated for the emigration of dispossessed Catholics. Emigration from Scotland continued at a high level.[2]

Most European populations grew more slowly than Britain's or Ireland's. The Dutch pattern closely resembled the English: an increase of some 27 per cent between 1600 and 1650, when it stood at 1,900,000, followed by stagnation. In 1700, France still had the largest population in western Europe, between 19,000,000 and 22,000,000, but it had grown very little since 1600. Germany possibly lost a quarter or even a third of its people between 1600 and 1650, and may not have made good the loss by 1700. Mediterranean populations fell sharply between 1600 and 1650, then rose by 1700 to around 13,000,000 in Italy and 9,000,000–10,000,000 in the Iberian Peninsula, levels little different from those of 1600. Plague and famine afflicted several countries far more severely than England. In 1627–31 they caused especially heavy mortality in France and northern Italy.[3]

The seventeenth century saw intense and sustained warfare and exceptionally frequent rebellions. Wars killed both directly, in battles and massacres, and indirectly, when armies spread disease or destroyed or commandeered food supplies. Military operations and increased taxation often disrupted economic activity severely. Britain and Ireland experienced the most intensive civil strife of their modern history. According to the latest estimate, England suffered 180,000 war-related deaths between 1640 and 1652, as well as material damage and exactions of over £46,000,000. The armies brought plague and typhus with them, exacted free quarter, plundered civilian populations and sacked some towns. Trade was severely disrupted. The wars did, however, result in a huge growth in the manufacture of munitions, clothing and leather goods. Surprisingly, the population of England and Wales is believed to have increased, albeit gradually, during the civil wars. Scotland's death toll and tax burden were proportionately far higher than England's. Hostilities caused widespread damage without compensating economic advantages. The consequences of the wars were harshest of all for Ireland, culling 15–20 per cent of the population. Subsequent demographic recovery was nevertheless quite rapid.[4] The British wars were shorter than those suffered by some continental countries. England suffered very brief and partial foreign invasions, in contrast with Germany, Italy, Poland-Lithuania, parts of Scandinavia and Catalonia. The worst affected areas of Germany were repeatedly plundered and contested, while their trade and food supplies were disrupted. The Rhineland suffered renewed devastation later in the century.

Towns and cities

The urban population grew faster in England than anywhere else in Europe. England achieved 30 per cent of the growth in the population living in towns of 10,000 people or more. The Dutch Republic remained the most heavily urbanized country. In 1700, an estimated 39 per cent of its people lived in towns of at least 5,000 inhabitants, compared with 17 per cent in England. Urbanization was, however, accelerating in England, slowing down in the Republic. The comparable French urban population also grew, but as a proportion of the total (10.9 per cent) was far smaller than England's in 1700. In Spain and Italy the urban population had shrunk.[5]

London contained an estimated 200,000 people in 1600, and 575,000 in 1700, by which time it was the largest city in western Europe. Growth was concentrated in the suburbs, especially to the east, where industrial expansion was especially vigorous, and in the West End, in which increasing numbers of gentry and nobility resided for part of the year. Industrial growth also occurred north of the City and in Southwark. Westminster remained the seat of government, but the administration of England's growing fiscal and naval apparatus was largely located near the Tower. Close by were the great dockyards of Deptford, principal centre for naval stores, and Woolwich. Around 1700 some three-quarters of English trade by value went through London. All the great merchant companies were based there. London's myriad consumers, copious supplies of water-borne raw materials and an unrivalled concentration of different skills supported an exceptional range of manufactures. Foremost were textiles, including woollens, mixed fabrics, silks and lace, materials for an army of tailors, milliners and seamstresses. Others were tanning and the making of gloves and footwear; hat making; the finishing of metal goods including handguns, clocks and watches; woodworking (including furniture making and coach-building); baking; shipbuilding and ship repairs; brewing and distilling; glass manufacture; soap making; candle making; printing, and sugar and tobacco processing.

Specialist bankers began to operate before the civil wars. Their numbers increased rapidly after 1660. A market in the hugely increased range of government and private company stocks took shape during the 1690s. The first company specializing in fire insurance was founded in 1680 and the first marine insurance company soon afterwards. The most successful early insurance companies and the first stock exchange developed in coffee houses. By 1663, eighty-two of these fashionable establishments existed in the City alone. Conservatives viewed them with suspicion as channels for the dissemination of unsettling news and rumours and centres of potentially subversive political as well as intellectual and commercial speculation. London's unequalled combination of political and economic functions and its inhabitants' exposure to a great range of printed media helped to create what was probably one of the most literate populations in Europe. London women's literacy seems to have improved especially rapidly during the later seventeenth century.[6]

The capital's speedy recovery from the calamities of the plague and the Great Fire of 1665–6 demonstrated its invincible vitality. Immigration soon reversed the losses to the plague, larger in absolute terms than in any other London outbreak. The Fire, the greatest early modern urban conflagration, destroyed most of the City and huge stocks of merchandise. A colossal construction boom followed. Plans to create a magnificent new city centre came to nothing, but scores of fine new churches and public buildings were built, along with thousands of houses.

London's growth affected the rest of the country in several different ways. Most obviously, its demands for food, fuel, raw materials and other goods stimulated agriculture, extractive industries and the manufacture of a great range of wares such as metal goods that could not so readily be produced in the capital. Those demands helped to develop a national market, and promoted regional specialization. Relatively high wages in the metropolis attracted immigrants. Because London experienced a natural surplus of deaths over births, it relied on constant immigration to maintain, let alone increase its population. It absorbed half of the natural increase of England's whole population. In doing so, it helped to check national demographic growth after the 1650s, and thus maintain the living standards of a substantial proportion of the survivors. New styles and patterns of consumption were established in this great city that were subsequently adopted in the provinces.[7]

Edinburgh's population was about 34,000 by 1691, reflecting its growing importance as a centre of law, government and education, and Leith's continuing role as a major port. A fine Parliament House was finished in 1639. Charles II authorized a major remodelling of Holyrood. His brother James encouraged various initiatives, including the foundation of the Royal College of Physicians (1681) and the Advocates' Library (opened in 1689). The Bank of Scotland was founded in 1695. However, Dublin rapidly overtook Edinburgh after 1650 to reach a population of approximately 60,000 in 1700, becoming the second largest city of the three kingdoms. It was now a commercial, industrial, educational and social as well as administrative centre.[8]

By 1700 London had outgrown the two continental cities, Paris and Naples, that had exceeded it in size in 1600. The growth of Paris had been driven above all by the expansion of royal administration. It was always under far tighter royal control, and largely dominated by wealthy office-holders, tax farmers, clergy and greater noblemen. Several new religious houses were founded. Rigorous royal maintenance of the authority of guilds as instruments of social and quality control restricted commercial and industrial enterprise. The manufacturing sector was more narrowly based than London's. Paris attracted large numbers of poor, but was less successful in employing them than London. An inland city, it was less well placed than London to import supplies from a greater distance than normal when harvests fell short. Naples, parasitic capital of a subject realm, was dominated by feudal landowners who transferred resources from the countryside to support them during their long stays in the capital and pay for goods and services provided by the city or imported from abroad. Popular revolt in 1647, provoked by a new fruit tax, was followed in 1656 by a devastating outbreak of plague. The city contained many fewer people in 1700 than it had in 1600. Amsterdam, with 200,000 people in 1700, contained a proportion of the Dutch Republic's population similar to that of England's in London. It built on its thriving Baltic trade and a Europe-wide network of contacts inherited from Antwerp to become the most successful commercial centre in Europe, with an Exchange Bank (1609), and Stock Exchange (1611), weekly publication of commodity prices and early newspapers. It also became a major industrial centre. However, it never possessed the judicial or administrative functions of a national capital.[9]

England differed from most of the continent in the extent to which its urban population was concentrated in one capital city. In France, for example, there were in 1700 six provincial cities with well over 30,000 inhabitants, some of which, such as Lyons, Nantes and Marseilles, had grown rapidly since 1600. In England only Norwich could boast as many as 30,000 inhabitants in 1700. English provincial towns nevertheless grew more vigorously as a group during the seventeenth century, and especially after 1670, than they had done between 1500 and 1600. By 1700 five, including all the major ports and provincial capitals, had more than 10,000 inhabitants, and a further twenty-six had 5,000–10,000. The appearance of Birmingham, Manchester, Leeds and Liverpool in this group for the first time reflected the quickening pace of economic activity in the North and Midlands. The share of Scotland's population in large and medium-sized provincial towns probably fell after the disruption of the civil wars. Glasgow grew fastest, and began to trade with America, becoming the second largest Scottish city by 1691, with 15,000 people. All Ireland's major provincial cities, especially Cork, grew rapidly after the civil wars.[10]

Trade

Imports were the most dynamic and rapidly changing element in England's seventeenth-century trade. Her industries became increasingly dependent on imported raw materials. From Scandinavia and the Baltic came huge quantities of timber as well as pitch, tar, potash and hemp. Swedish bar iron imports increased ninefold between the 1620s and the 1680s. From southern Europe came not only rapidly growing imports of wines, oil, fresh and dried fruit, but also fine Spanish wool, and raw and thrown silk.

The East India Company enjoyed an extremely profitable minority share in the eastern spice trade, and found other attractive goods in India: indigo, calicoes, sugar, saltpetre and raw silk. English re-exports of pepper and calicoes to Europe grew rapidly after 1660. Between 1622 and 1700 the value of London's tobacco imports rose from £55,000 to £161,000, and that of its sugar imports from £82,000 to £526,000. Two-thirds of England's tobacco imports were re-exported to Europe in 1700, a third of her sugar imports. Tobacco's rapidly falling price made it an item of mass consumption. Virginia was its main source. Several islands on the eastern rim of the Caribbean were settled in the 1620s and 1630s. At first they too grew tobacco, but went over to sugar from the 1640s onwards, as did Jamaica after its conquest in 1655, replacing Portugal as the source of England's supplies. The switch to sugar cultivation in the Caribbean led to the adoption of slave labour, following Portuguese example. After 1660 English merchants became major participants in the infamous slave trade, hitherto dominated by the Dutch. In the best known of all the multilateral networks that made up the English commercial empire, English metal goods and cloth helped pay for slaves shipped to the Caribbean and Virginia. Those colonies' products came to England or through her to European markets. The New England colonies, established by religious separatists from 1620 onwards, did not at first supply England with any major commodity, but imported goods from England and traded with the Caribbean and southern mainland colonies.[11]

The pattern of English domestic exports changed less than those of imports or re-exports. Woollen cloth still accounted for over two-thirds of all exports in 1699–1701. However, in face of a shrinking north-west European market for broadcloths, merchants exported new types of cloth to southern Europe and broadcloths to the Levant. Other English manufactures accounted for only 12 per cent of exports by value.[12]

Direct trade between England and Scotland gradually became more important. However, the regal union also had some negative consequences for Scotland, including disruptive wars with France and the United Provinces. The Dutch were the Scots' major trading associates for much of the seventeenth century. Scots played an active part in Dutch enterprises in South America, the Caribbean, the New Netherlands and even in the East Indies. In principle the Navigation Acts excluded Scots from trade with English colonies. In practice the later Stuarts issued licences to individual Scots entrepreneurs. James VII when duke of York encouraged Scottish activity in New York and Delaware, and a Scottish colony was established in East New Jersey in 1685. But early attempts to establish a Scottish colony in Nova Scotia came to little and the Darien scheme ended in brutal disappointment.[13]

Britain shared in a larger shift in the control of Europe's trade from Italy and Iberia to the north-western European powers, who between them took much of Venice's trade with the Levant, ended Portuguese dominance of far eastern trade and settled Caribbean islands on the doorstep of Spain's American empire. England's foremost commercial rivals during the seventeenth century were the Dutch. Their network of small colonies and trading posts stretched from the East Indies to North America. The Dutch traded in all the major colonial commodities, including spices, sugar, tobacco and dyestuffs. Dealing in more commodities than any other trading nation, they took the lead in developing detailed commodity price lists, trading in stocks and shares, brokerage services, new means of speculative trading, insurance techniques, and instruments of credit and exchange. They established low rates of interest and freight charges. Their reputation for probity, reliability and efficiency was unequalled in Europe.[14]

The Dutch Republic was, however, a small nation with envious neighbours. The long-term costs of defence were heavy. Dutch companies made some strategic mistakes overseas. The West India Company's attack on Brazil in the 1620s was ultimately an expensive failure. The West and East India Companies subordinated their colonies in New Netherlands and at the Cape of Good Hope to their own perceived interests. Failure to strengthen the New Netherlands colony made it vulnerable to eventual English attack. Their far smaller population put the Dutch at a disadvantage compared with the English in developing colonies of settlement.

James I issued the first proclamations designed to protect particular English trades from Dutch competition. The execution of some English representatives on the Indonesian island of Amboina by Dutch officials in 1623 caused huge resentment in England. The Dutch took over much of the trade with England's American colonies during the 1640s, and, once at peace after 1648, drastically reduced the English share of the Baltic trade. England retaliated. The Rump's 1651 Navigation Act provided that imports to England were to be brought only from the country of origin or first shipment, and in ships of England or the country of origin. It reserved imports from most of the non-European world to English ships. A revised act of 1660 limited the general provisions of 1651 to certain listed commodities so far as Europe and the Mediterranean were concerned, and also required that English ships must have an English master and a three-quarters English crew. The chief exports of English colonies had to be shipped to England even if ultimately destined for another country. The 1663 Staple Act required that most European exports to the colonies go via English ports. English commercial shipping tonnage grew rapidly after these acts, probably from 200,000 in 1660 to 340,000 by 1686. The construction of bulk carriers for coal and Baltic goods and armed merchantmen for the risky trades in valuable Mediterranean and colonial goods made major contributions to the total. English merchants took a growing share of Baltic trade. The seizure of New Amsterdam (New York) in 1664 enabled England to plug a crucial gap in her chain of North American colonies, improving her chances of enforcing the Navigation regulations. (It also opened up a new supply of furs, but the Hudson's Bay Company, founded in 1670, soon supplied a far greater quantity.) Dutch captures of English vessels during the second and third Anglo-Dutch wars outweighed English captures of Dutch ones. However, England's commerce benefited greatly from her neutrality when France and the Dutch were still at war between 1674 and 1678.[15]

France began to pose a serious threat to Dutch and English commerce only after 1660. The absence of a single dominant port, the distance between most of the ports and the inland capital, internal geographical obstacles to the emergence of a national market, internal tolls, heavy royal reliance on regressive direct taxes and the sale of offices, and prolonged land wars all militated against the consistent and coherent promotion of overseas trade. Foreign ships carried a substantial proportion of France's exports. In 1627 Richelieu established a company to promote trade and colonization in Canada. Its relative lack of interest in colonization, the difficulty of attracting settlers to a harsh environment and the attempt to reproduce in Canada a Catholic and seigneurial society prevented New France from developing as vigorously as the English North American colonies. The French also settled a handful of West Indian islands and established toeholds in Senegal, soon a source of slaves, and Madagascar.

Colbert brought new energy and purposefulness, seeking to promote commerce by means of protective tariffs, overseas colonies, trading companies and where necessary the use of France's newly enlarged navy. The French Caribbean islands successfully adopted sugar planting. Trade with India was established. French linen was the most highly prized foreign textile in Spain. French fine cloth exports to Turkey rose rapidly during the 1680s. France disrupted English and Dutch trade with the Levant during the 1690s, and by the early eighteenth century she was the dominant commercial power there. First the Dutch (from 1671) then the English (from 1678) met French protectionism with retaliatory tariffs. The Dutch were the prime target of Louis XIV's vindictive enmity and Colbert's policies. Wars with France, especially after 1689, imposed a colossal fiscal burden on the Republic and drove up insurance costs.[16]

The Nine Years' War severely damaged English trade too. Yet after 1702 England experienced a wartime trade boom. The Methuen Treaty of 1703 strengthened her trade with Portugal. Discovery of gold in Brazil helped Portugal to pay for substantial increased imports of woollen textiles and grain from England. Meanwhile, the French made major inroads into the already badly disrupted Dutch trade with Spain and her empire. After 1688 the alliance with England inhibited Dutch interference with English commerce. English merchants strengthened their position in India, where the Dutch concentrated their efforts against the French. England also benefited from rising European demand for the products of India, where her East India Company had bases at Surat, Bombay, Madras and Calcutta. Indian re-exports contributed substantially to an improvement in England's balance of trade after 1700. England was also able to export greatly increased quantities of cloth and grain, largely because military operations severely disrupted Baltic corn exports and reduced cloth production in Germany and the Netherlands.[17]

Industries

England's manufacturing and extractive industries absorbed a rapidly growing workforce. Much of her industrial activity took place in the countryside. In her chief industry, cloth manufacture, various 'new' draperies largely replaced the heavier old cloths, a development that caused severe hardship for many people. 'Old drapery' exports fell by nearly 30 per cent between 1614 and 1640. New and miscellaneous types of fabric made up 47 per cent of London's cloth exports by 1640, and 58 per cent of England's by 1699–1701. The entire English cloth industry was by then far larger, more varied and more competitive internationally than at the height of its mid-Tudor success, and probably exported nearly half of its total production by value, mostly dyed and finished. The manufacture of several other fabrics was introduced or rapidly expanded: lace (widely established by the 1630s), silk (especially from the 1680s), linens, canvas and knitted stockings. Other fast-growing English manufactures included glass, paper, tobacco and sugar processing, metal goods (especially in Sheffield and the West Midlands), ceramics, leather goods and hats. The success of these industries resulted in diminished reliance on imports. Naval shipbuilding and maintenance employed a growing army of workers.[18]

Of all the extractive industries coal was the most strikingly successful. Its cheapness compared with wood, especially in London, encouraged its use in a growing range of manufactures, stimulating technological invention. Imports to London (most of them from the north-east, which produced over 50 per cent of England's coal) more than tripled between 1605–6 and 1699–1700, under-pinning the capital's industrial growth. Coal and coke were adopted as fuels in lime, brick, glass, salt, soap, starch, and alum production, brewing, dyeing, and sugar refining. London's demand encouraged investment in deeper mines and the technology needed to pump and ventilate them and transport coal to the quayside. Lead production rose impressively during the century. The growth of iron, copper and tin production was more uneven. England imported increasing amounts of iron and copper from Sweden, but there was a major revival of the English mining of all three of these metals before 1700. Salt, alum, copperas and saltpetre production also increased.[19]

Scotland's industrial base remained relatively narrow. Her biggest successes were in coal and lead mining, salt-making and linen manufacture. Coal pro-duction grew fifteen-fold between 1560 and 1700, compared with a thirteen-fold growth in England. Linen exports to London increased thirty-six-fold between 1600 and 1700.[20]

In Europe, the United Provinces developed during the seventeenth century a diverse, adaptable and outstandingly successful industrial sector. Textiles, ship-building, brewing, tobacco pipe, soap, paper, glass manufacturing, ceramics, distilling, processing of whale oil, salt, sugar and tobacco employed large num-bers of people. Several of these industries involved the application of highly specialized techniques. Leiden, the pre-eminent centre of textile manufacture, produced from the 1630s rapidly increasing quantities of fine cloths alongside cheaper new draperies made in greater numbers but for a smaller return. The adoption of labour-saving machinery, innovative designs and standardization helped to create the largest and most successful merchant navy in Europe. The famous *fluit*, a cheap bulk carrier, first appeared in the 1590s. Relatively small groups of highly skilled workers drew on the techniques of Antwerp and Venice in making maps and precision instruments and cutting diamonds. The largest cluster of publishers of fine scholarly and scientific books for an international readership was also to be found in Holland. The Dutch became the foremost importers of Swedish copper from 1613 onwards, manufacturing products rang-ing from pots and kettles to Europe's finest weapons as well as promoting Sweden's own armaments manufacture. Effectively used wind and water and substantial peat deposits gave the Dutch abundant energy supplies.[21]

France's successful industries included woollen, linen and canvas textiles and fine paper. Perhaps her most notable achievement was the development of the silk industry established in the sixteenth century until it surpassed Italy's in dyeing, printing and innovative design. The crown (with mixed success) encouraged and protected several projects for the production of other luxury goods, for instance luring Venetian glassmakers to France. It also sought to control or profit from certain key industries, including salt and gunpowder manufacture and mining. Iron forges and furnaces were widely scattered through the kingdom. Small enterprises predominated, and the industry was hampered by relatively poor communications. France's underdeveloped and conservative arms manufacture left her dangerously short of cannon when embarking on war with Spain. Colbert made the most ambitious efforts to develop French industry. While largely relying on small artisan units of production, he helped to establish some big enterprises, such as sugar refineries, the Royal Plate Glass Company, factories for the production of fine cloth by specially recruited Dutch workers and the dockyards necessary to build a formidable navy. However, a prohibition on sailcloth exports in order to hamper Dutch and English shipping backfired, resulting in the development of a flourishing Dutch sailcloth industry. The revocation of the Edict of Nantes two years after Colbert's death resulted in the flight of Huguenot craftsmen who took valuable skills with them to Protestant countries.[22]

Some previously leading European industrial areas suffered severe setbacks. The Thirty Years War disrupted German trade and badly damaged some of the most highly developed German industrial centres. Italy, Europe's main centre of fine manufactures, suffered a series of damaging blows: wars, plagues, disruption of silver imports, the issue of base currency and rising taxes. Northern manufactures such as English and Dutch woollen cloth, English and French glass, and French silks encroached on or took over former Italian markets, and sometimes penetrated Italy itself. Meanwhile Italian guilds resisted attempts to cut costs. Industry increasingly retreated to the countryside and produced basic goods for the home market. In Castile, severe population losses around 1600 hit industries already suffering from foreign competition. Taxation imposed ruinous burdens on urban manufactures. Northern competition challenged the iron industry and shipbuilding (which depended on increasingly expensive imported cordage, sails and naval stores). Difficulties in their markets affected Catalan exports of cloth and iron to Italy and Valencian sales of silk to Castile.

Agriculture

According to one set of estimates, England's agricultural output may have risen by 45 per cent, and output per worker in agriculture by about 60 per cent between 1600 and 1700, despite a probable fall in the percentage of the population engaged in agriculture from 70 to 55. After 1670 the numbers so engaged fell in absolute terms. England's food producers met most of the needs of a non-agricultural population that continued to grow when total population fell after 1660, and by 1707 exported substantial amounts of grain.[23]

How were these successes achieved? Over 4,000,000 acres were probably reclaimed or improved between 1500 and 1700 through the conversion of moorland, forest, marshes, fens, parks, chases, downs and heaths. More and better-fed animals enriched the soil with their dung. The spread of convertible husbandry, in which fodder crops alternated with arable, improved both animal nutrition and the fertility of the soil. The adoption of turnips provided a new source of winter feed. Increasing numbers of farmers flooded water meadows in order to obtain better hay. Seed quality improved as farmers chose seed from the best plants and larger inter-regional markets developed. These markets, and London's insatiable demands, encouraged regional specialization: the 'mainly arable complexion' of the eastern and south-eastern counties and the predominance of livestock or pastoral farming elsewhere. Grain prices fell between 1650 and 1680. The rise in real earnings allowed more people to eat a varied diet, including more meat and dairy products, while the fall in prices pushed farmers and landlords to improve productivity. It has also been argued that farmers' knowledge of superior metropolitan living standards, and desire for consumer goods first widely available in the capital, acted as an additional spur in that direction.[24]

Many landowners tried to increase their incomes not only by promoting new husbandry practices and undertaking schemes of improvement, but also by raising rents, consolidating farms and converting customary tenures to shorter leaseholds. However, yeoman farmers who enjoyed relatively advantageous tenures accomplished much of this period's increase in productivity. For much of the century, they continued to prosper, while smaller farmers found it difficult to hold their own except where farming could be combined with rural industries, or where intensive small plot cultivation was lucrative, as in market gardening, especially around London. According to one widely cited estimate, a quarter of England's agricultural land was 'enclosed' or came to be 'held in severalty, falling completely under the power of one owner to do with as he pleased' between 1600 and 1700, more than in any other century after 1500. However, the flexibility of the open field system and its ability to accommodate innovative husbandry practices must not be underestimated.[25]

Agricultural change was more limited in Scotland than in England, though many landowners were interested in improvement. English demand for meat and wool helped to encourage more commercial cattle and sheep rearing. Holdings were gradually consolidated, and the commutation of rents in kind into money payments encouraged farmers to engage more actively with the market. Liming allowed some extension of the cultivated area, and improved crop rotations were introduced in some Lowland districts. In good years, grain was exported to the continent, though severe famines in 1623 and 1695–9 interrupted a gradual improvement in the reliability of home-produced food supplies.[26]

The conditions that favoured English agriculture, including the proximity of a large and growing non-agricultural population, good river and coastal communications, the absence of internal tolls and only briefly interrupted internal peace, hardly existed elsewhere in combination outside the United Provinces. Obstacles to agricultural progress were widespread. The deleterious effects of warfare and heavy taxation have already been emphasized. Sharp falls in populations, particularly urban populations (especially marked in Spain and Italy), were followed by very slow recovery. Some continental nobilities pursued short-sighted policies with negative consequences: the usurpation of wastelands and commons in much of Castile, for example, or the exploitation of inefficient labour services in Poland, which resulted in a steady decline in grain yields. Seventeenth-century French and Spanish noble landowners relied more heavily than their British counterparts on such sources of income as military service, investment in crown debt, the purchase of offices, jurisdictions and the right to collect taxes. British landowners had stronger incentives to take an interest in their rural estates than did these members of continental nobilities, even though such interest might not be consistently benign or productive.

In France, the Paris market encouraged the consolidation of farms and the adoption of innovative practices in the surrounding area. But inter-regional markets emerged more slowly than in England, hampered both by natural obstacles and by internal tolls. The subsistence farming of tiny holdings remained much more widespread. The relatively small scale of livestock farming, and consequently inadequate supplies of fertilizing dung, necessitated greater reliance on fallow as a means of maintaining soil quality.

Rural developments that threatened the livelihoods of poorer farmers and smallholders not surprisingly caused intermittent popular unrest. The biggest wave of riots against enclosure spread across the Midlands from Northamptonshire in 1607. Threatened loss of shared resources through disafforestation led to a series of protests that reached its peak in 1631. Forcible opposition to fen drainage was most widespread in 1640. Resistance was partially successful in slowing down disafforestation and drainage. Food riots were the other main form of popular direct action, concentrated in years of poor harvest and economic recession, especially 1629–31, 1647–9 and 1693–5.[27]

Numerous rural rebellions took place on the continent, but royal fiscal demands were the main grievance, especially in France. Tenants sometimes turned against landlords, or resisted seigneurial demands (as for labour services in Bohemia in 1680). Only in England, however, were attempts to prevent 'improvement' widespread. Food riots were a major form of popular action in all countries. In the Mediterranean world rural poor swarming into the big cities helped to trigger mid-century rebellions in a way not seen in England.

Political economy

The French writer Montchrétien coined the term 'political economy' to denote study of the management of national resources (1615). Thomas Mun, East India Company director, wrote tracts about English trade a little later, though his *England's Treasure by Forraign Trade* was published only in 1664. Samuel Fortrey, a businessman of Flemish descent, urged in *England's Interest and Improvement* (1663) that England reduce its luxury imports so as to correct its trade deficit with France. Josiah Child identified in *Brief Observations Concerning Trade and the Interest of Money* (1668) fifteen crucial ingredients of Dutch success, most importantly low interest rates.

Concern during the 1660s trade slump about England's ability to compete with her neighbours stimulated her precocious development of political arithmetick, designed to give political economy quantitative muscle. Its pioneer, William Petty, had studied in France and the Netherlands and surveyed Irish lands under the Protectorate. His *Political Arithmetick* (written in 1672–6, but not published until 1690) tried to demonstrate that England had little to fear from French or Dutch competition if she exploited her advantages effectively.

Petty's friend John Graunt, a London shopkeeper, demonstrated in his *Natural and Political Observations* (1662) that London had grown substantially despite its apparent surplus of deaths over births, and calculated the scale of immigration necessary to maintain that growth. He included a London life table. (In 1693, when the government was considering the sale of annuities to raise revenue, Edmond Halley published a more sophisticated table based on data from Breslau in order to 'ascertain the Price of Annuities upon Lives'.) In his famous 'Natural and Political Observations upon the State and Condition of England, 1696', Gregory King, herald and bureaucrat, drew on fiscal records in order to estimate the country's wealth and population. He drew up a comparative account of *per capita* consumption, public expenditure and revenue in England, France and the Netherlands. His figure for England's total population in 1688, 5,500,520, was well under 10 per cent larger than the most recent modern estimate, though he seriously underestimated France's population. The French writers Pierre de Boisguilbert and Marshal Vauban, a distinguished soldier, were notably more pessimistic about France's condition than the English political arithmeticians were about England's. Boisguilbert believed that France's national income had fallen sharply between 1660 and 1695. Vauban made the first serious attempt to calculate France's national income and population, and in 1707 produced estimates more credible than King's.

Social structure

King was unique among European political economists in attempting a detailed analysis of England's social structure. He thought that 38 per cent of household heads could maintain themselves and their dependants (amounting in all to 49 per cent of the population). Household heads were divided into various groups or categories: 1.2 per cent were nobility and gentry, 24.3 per cent freeholders or tenant farmers, 4 per cent members of professions, 3.7 per cent merchants, shopkeepers and tradesmen, and 4.4 per cent artisans. Some of King's categories are not very helpful: they do not distinguish such important groups as substantial manufacturers, merchant-industrialists or bankers, for example. He probably underestimated the size of the nobility and gentry, which had grown faster than the national population. The development of the mortgage enabled landowners to carry a burden of debt for a much longer period than hitherto, and the end of crown wardship (1646, confirmed in 1660) facilitated long-term family strategies. Substantial landowners were the ones best placed to adapt to and benefit from changing market opportunities. Smaller ones found the relatively low prices common in the later seventeenth century and the burden of the land tax in the 1690s harder to cope with. King's estimates of the sizes of different groups may have been unreliable, but he nevertheless noticed some undeniably important social changes. He believed that 'merchants and traders by sea' (fewer than 0.75 per cent of all family heads) were accumulating *per capita* wealth through their surplus of income over expenditure faster than any other social group except the nobility. He attributed larger incomes to greater merchants than any other group below the upper gentry. He concluded that the growing numbers of officials, naval and military officers and 'Persons in sciences and liberal arts' (which would have included groups as diverse as schoolmasters and medical practitioners) exceeded those of the older professions of the law and clergy by a wide margin.[28]

Poverty

King came to the chilling conclusion that 51 per cent of the total population were 'decreasing the wealth of the kingdom', because their necessary expenditure exceeded their income. 'Labouring people and outservants', 'Cottagers and paupers', and common sailors and soldiers were all in this category, as well as vagrants. Private alms and charitable endowments remained important sources of English poor relief, but statutory parish rates became steadily more important during the seventeenth century. Probably only a small minority of parishes levied them in 1600, but by 1700 nearly all did so. They had become the backbone of relief. The Board of Trade calculated that £400,000 was spent on poor relief in 1696, or nearly two-thirds of the £622,000 by which, King estimated, the poor 'decreased the wealth of the kingdom' in 1688. However, much relief was only supplementary or temporary, it was never generous, and provision varied hugely from parish to parish. The various means of punishing the idle and setting the poor to work included houses of correction, the apprenticing of children (especially in the 1630s), manufacturing schemes and 'corporations of the poor' to provide urban relief, work and training.[29]

No other European country had specified as clearly as England the responsibilities of all parishes, rural as well as urban, for the relief of their poor. (Scottish contributions to relief remained largely voluntary during the seventeenth century.) In other countries, provision was concentrated in the cities, whether controlled by municipalities (the prevalent pattern in Protestant Europe) or Catholic institutions. Some cities may have provided for the poor of their immediate hinterlands.

Conclusion

England greatly increased the quantity and variety of its industrial and agricultural output and the range and volume of its commerce during the seventeenth century. Agricultural output possibly rose faster than during any other century of this period. England made for herself a growing variety of goods she had previously imported, and turned coal, an abundant and reliable source of energy, to a growing range of industrial uses. Between 1640 and 1700, imports probably more than doubled, domestic exports almost doubled and re-exports grew nearly fourfold. Around 1700, re-exports amounted to 31 per cent of all England's exports. Tobacco, calicoes and sugar headed the list. Northwestern Europe remained England's most important market, taking 42 per cent of her domestic exports, and 59 per cent of her re-exports. (The corresponding figures for southern Europe were 34 and 11 per cent.)

London was by 1700 western Europe's largest city, and its demands helped drive the rest of the English and Welsh economy, including all the developments outlined above. It led the way in the adoption of new patterns of consumption. The concentration of state institutions and commerce in one centre, government's dependence on revenues from trade and interactions between city, court and country interests helped to maintain a high level of awareness of the importance of overseas trade among policy makers and the political nation in general.

In Scotland there was vigorous growth in some industries such as linen and coalmining, and a stirring of interest in agricultural improvement. By 1700 linen and cattle were the most valuable Scottish exports overall and in her growing trade with England. Unwelcome wars disrupted Scottish commerce with continental partners, especially the Dutch. The Navigation Acts discriminated against Scotland, but did not prevent Glasgow from beginning to trade with America.

By 1700 England and France had made deep inroads into the Dutch dominance of world trade. France's commercial ambitions, backed between the 1660s and the 1690s by a powerful navy, menaced both England and the Dutch Republic, but the latter more directly. France was commercially and industrially much less advanced than the Republic, but possessed far larger territorial, demographic and military resources. England and the Republic combined in 1689 and 1702 to contain threats from France that were not only economic but also territorial and (in England's case) dynastic.

14

CONTACTS AND CONNECTIONS, 1603-1707

Royal marriages and kindred

The Stuarts' marriages, unlike the Tudors', created numerous connections with other European royal families. James VI married Anne of Denmark, sister of Christian IV, Europe's foremost Lutheran ruler. Commercially useful, the connection failed to result in adequate reciprocal assistance in time of need, either from Charles I to his uncle Christian in the 1620s, or from Christian to Charles in 1642.

As has been seen, the actions of the Elector Palatine Frederick V following his 1613 marriage to James's daughter Elizabeth had catastrophic consequences for Stuart foreign and domestic policies. The couple's sons Rupert and Maurice at least fought for Charles I in the civil war, but their elder brother Charles Louis chose to live in London between 1644 and 1649, to Charles I's disgust. Their daughter Sophia bore George, elector of Hanover, eventual successor to the British throne. Prince Charles's personally fruitful marriage to Henrietta Maria (1625) did not result in an Anglo-French alliance or (despite her efforts) effective French help for the Stuarts during the civil wars except for an intermittent asylum for her sons. Charles II's hopes of assistance from his cousin Louis XIV contributed to the weakness and confusion of English foreign policy during his reign.

Charles I chose William II of Orange as his daughter Mary's husband in 1641. He hoped for Dutch financial help and knew that the match would be popular. In 1643 Henrietta Maria brought him money and arms purchased in Holland. William supplied the ships that took Charles II to Scotland in 1650. After 1650 the now widowed Mary gave Charles what help she could, though the states-general disliked the Orange–Stuart connection. Charles II renewed it by supporting the marriage between his brother James's daughter Mary and his sister Mary's son William III. Originally mooted in 1671, it took place in

1677. Charles hoped that it might allay the fears caused by his friendship with Louis XIV and by James's Catholicism.

Charles II's 1661 marriage to Catherine of Braganza usefully strengthened England's Portuguese connection and brought a substantial dowry, but was childless. His brother James married twice: first, in 1660, Clarendon's daughter Anne Hyde, the mother of his Protestant daughters Mary and Anne; secondly, in 1673, Mary of Modena, an Italian client state of Louis XIV's. The birth of James's son by this second marriage in 1688 precipitated William of Orange's intervention in England. Louis XIV provoked two wars with Britain by supporting James II in 1689 and recognizing his son as James III in 1701. Mary II had no children. Her younger sister Anne's many children by her consort Prince George of Denmark predeceased her, the last in 1700. In 1701 parliament settled the succession on the nearest Protestant candidate, Sophia, Electress of Hanover, and her descendants.

Diplomats

The most important foci of British diplomatic activity were the United Provinces, the Spanish Netherlands, France and Spain. Trading interests were an important reason for sending ambassadors and agents to Constantinople, the Hanse towns, Tuscany and Portugal. Some powers became more important as British diplomatic partners, including Sweden (from the 1620s) and the Emperor (from the 1680s). The frequency of missions to such states as Savoy, Venice, Poland and Russia fluctuated markedly. The numbers of British diplomatic representatives increased during the century.

Especially delicate and important missions demanded the appointment of a nobleman or trusted courtier. Most diplomats belonged to the gentry, but some had a commercial background. In some states, such as Spain and the Ottoman Empire, consuls were kept in several different ports. It was essential for a would-be diplomat to gain a patron, sometimes as a tutor to a nobleman's son on his travels. Foreign travel, military service or commerce, acquisition of foreign languages and study of civil law were all potentially useful qualifications. Service as an ambassador's secretary was often the first step in a diplomatic career. One short-term consequence of the regal union was the employment of several Scotsmen, especially in the Baltic area. Some diplomats, like Sir William Temple, who served in the United Provinces (1667–70, 1674–9), were eloquent friends of the countries to which they were accredited. Temple's *Observations upon the United Provinces* (1673) remains one of the best-known accounts of a foreign country by an English diplomat.

The European powers diplomatically most active in England were France, Spain, the United Provinces and (from Charles II's reign) the Emperor. Critics exaggerated the malign or disruptive influence of some diplomats, such as Count Gondomar, Spanish ambassador at James I's court, and Paul Barrillon, Louis XIV's ambassador (1677–88). But the irregular contacts of William III's two emissaries van Dijkvelt and Zuylestein with the opposition to James II really did pave the way for his successful invasion in 1688.

Centres of trade

The Merchants Adventurers maintained staples in one of a succession of Dutch towns and in Hamburg. Their privileges were finally removed in 1689, but they survived as a fellowship. Rotterdam, the Adventurers' staple from 1635 to 1655, became the main centre of the growing Anglo-Dutch trade. The Scots, with their staple at Veere, kept a special connection with Zeeland. The Eastland Company, which included both Englishmen and Scots, was seated in Elbing until 1628, and later in Danzig (though several British merchants remained in Elbing). A 1673 statute greatly curtailed its privileged position. In 1620, 30,000 Scots were believed to be resident in Poland. In Denmark–Norway Scots enjoyed special privileges after James VI's marriage. Scots settled in several parts of Norway, above all in Bergen, and exported Norwegian timber to Scotland. They also settled in Sweden, often after military service. Scotsmen led the way in importing Swedish bar iron to Britain after 1600, though Englishmen later took the predominant share of this trade.[1]

The Dutch rapidly surpassed their English competitors in Russia after the 1590s. After Charles I's execution Tsar Alexis removed English merchants' privileges and restricted them to Archangel. During the later seventeenth century, with Swedish encouragement, English merchants returned to the eastern Baltic port of Narva, then in Swedish hands, as a new gateway to Russia. In 1697, Tsar Peter I travelled to western Europe, hoping to acquire technical and scientific expertise. He visited English and Dutch arsenals, factories and dockyards, and met William III. Peter's drive to put his army into uniform from 1700 onwards contributed to a boom in English cloth exports to Russia.[2]

Britain traded with France through a few major centres, above all Bordeaux, Rouen, Nantes and La Rochelle, and a host of smaller ones. The trade was damaged in the later seventeenth century by hostile tariffs and a temporary ban on French imports in 1689, though its geographical diffusion made it particularly hard to police. Trade with Spain quickly recovered after 1604. A commercial treaty of 1667 established a 'judge conservator' to provide cheap and speedy justice. Treaties of 1654 and 1661 with newly independent Portugal gave English merchants privileges, including tax exemptions. The Methuen treaty of 1703 gave Portuguese wine a preferential rate of duty in return for English cloth's free access to Portugal.

Leghorn in Tuscany, which enjoyed the status of a free port with low duties and free movement of merchandise, was the chief centre of English commerce in the Mediterranean, the hinge between Italian and Levantine trades. English merchants also participated in the trade between northern and southern Italy.[3] The Levant Company paid the English ambassador at Constantinople, and maintained merchant stations there and at Smyrna and Aleppo.

Soldiers

The Dutch army offered the most continuous employment to British soldiers. In 1623 four English and three Scots regiments, totalling 13,420 men, constituted 22 per cent of the States' army. In 1632, 47 per cent of the Dutch field army consisted of British regiments. After the Anglo-Dutch wars there were three English and three Scottish regiments and an Irish one. Many Englishmen served in the Spanish army of Flanders, in Portugal (1662–8) and with the French after 1670. The numbers of Scotsmen serving in foreign armies were highest during the Thirty Years War: possibly 5,000 of 8,000 British troops assisting Frederick V until 1622, 13,400 in Danish service (c.1627–9) and 30,000 in Swedish forces (1629–48). Three Scots regiments were raised for French service between 1632 and 1635, and more men were recruited between 1641 and 1648. In 1655–6, 4,000 Scots troops went to Sweden. Many Catholic Irish joined the Spanish and French armies, including thousands of men banished in the 1650s, and some 12,000 'wild geese' who left for France in 1691. Men from the three kingdoms also served in the Imperial, Venetian, Polish and Russian armies.[4]

Students and travellers

British attendance at foreign universities was by 1700 increasingly concentrated in the Dutch Republic, above all at Leiden, where one-third of the students were reportedly British in 1700, with smaller numbers at Utrecht. Medicine drew an increasing proportion of the students who went overseas. Leiden gradually replaced Padua as the most favoured university for the discipline, though Montpellier and some other schools remained attractive. A growing proportion of British theological students also gravitated towards Dutch universities. Increasing numbers of Scottish students reading law there offset a broader decline in overseas study of civil law. Several Scottish students attended various Scandinavian and German Baltic universities.[5]

Increasing numbers of young Scots and English noblemen and gentlemen undertook European travel as part of their education, especially in France and Italy. The traveller was expected to learn some French and Italian, acquire socially useful accomplishments, see antiquities, buildings and works of art, and gain some understanding of foreign governments and politics. A growing minority took an interest in economic and technological development. Many kept a travel diary or wrote letters. The Stuarts' usual preference for peace with Spain, and their more conciliatory religious stance, resulted in safer access to central and southern Italy. Spain itself attracted relatively few British tourists. Germany, never a prime destination, became much less safe during the Thirty Years War. Some travellers nevertheless ranged far beyond the usual itinerary.[6]

France took the lead in developing aristocratic social skills and etiquette, culinary and sartorial fashions and luxury industries. Paris was considered the most elegant city in northern Europe. France's Reformed Protestant minority, tolerated for most of the seventeenth century, possessed its own academies and was strongly concentrated in certain towns where sound tutors could be found and good sermons heard. Italy gradually ceased to provoke the extreme reactions of intense admiration and horrified fascination that had been common before 1600. The rediscovery of classical antiquity had been assimilated into British culture. Venice remained a considerable power, respected for its independence, and still vigorous in commerce and industry. Venice and Rome were the outstanding architectural, artistic and musical centres.

The Netherlands, especially the United Provinces, were probably more familiar to British people than any other part of the continent. The spectacle of a state that enjoyed harmony despite religious diversity and the absence of monarchical government, together with wealth and success out of all proportion to its extent, population or resources fascinated a succession of English observers.

Confessional links

James I cherished a vision of European religious reconciliation, but the papacy refused to encourage his hopes of an ecumenical council. When Venice and the papacy quarrelled in 1605-6, the friar Paolo Sarpi advocated a Venetian appeal to a general council. James invited him to England. Instead, the apostate former archbishop of Split, Marco Antonio de Dominis, arrived in 1616 with a copy of Sarpi's account of papal manipulation of the Council of Trent, which was printed in London in 1619. Welcomed by James, De Dominis published in England his own attack on papal primacy. Eventually, however, he was reconciled to Rome in 1622.

James's hopes of Christian re-union attracted various foreign Protestants, including the Frenchman Isaac Casaubon, the German Georg Calisen and the Dutchman Hugo Grotius. Calisen and Grotius sought a basis for religious unity in a minimal statement of agreed doctrine. James strongly recommended Pierre du Moulin's ambitious plan for progress towards Christian re-union to the synod of the French Reformed Church in 1614. The Reformed Churches could not, however, function as a base for such a scheme if they themselves were split. James saw the bitter dispute within the Dutch Church over Arminius's doctrines as a scandalous source of division. He had personally liked Hugo Grotius when they met, but could not approve of Grotius's sympathy with the Remonstrants. Grotius later presented to Laud the idea of a union with the Lutheran Church of Sweden. The Scotsman John Durie, previously minister to the Eastland Company at Elbing, supported by the English diplomat Sir Thomas Roe, was working for a union of all the Protestant churches. However, neither Laud nor Charles I was interested in such schemes.[7]

Religious exiles

The United Provinces provided a refuge for a succession of English and Scottish religious nonconformists. One, Thomas Helwys, returned from exile and established the first Baptist congregation in England around 1612. William Brewster, ruling elder of a separatist congregation set up in Leiden in 1609, took a leading part in the settlement of Plymouth (Massachusetts) in 1620.

Many British residents became members of congregations affiliated to the Dutch Reformed Church. English or Scottish ministers were to be found at Amsterdam, Middelburg, Leiden and Delft. The ministers in the Netherlands were, as a group, prolific authors of controversial and theological works. Tracts criticizing the Five Articles of Perth reached Scotland from the Netherlands, as did arms later shipped to the Covenanters.[8]

Many Scotsmen worked as ministers of the Reformed Church in France or professors in Protestant academies there, especially between 1598 and 1629. They included some critics of James VI's church policies. Saumur on the Loire, and French-speaking Sedan, just within the Empire, attracted the largest numbers. Andrew Melville spent his exile in Sedan. The many professorial chairs and academy headships held by Scotsmen testified to their French colleagues' high regard.

Far fewer foreign religious exiles came to England during the early seventeenth century than between 1550 and 1590. They included some high profile individuals like Isaac Casaubon and James I's physician Theodore Turquet de Mayerne. The foreign churches' freedom between 1642 and 1660 turned out to be a mixed blessing for them. They had co-operated in face of Laud's efforts to restrict their worship. Issues of discipline and politics now divided them. English parishes and separatist congregations offered their members alternative spiritual homes.[9]

Increasing pressure on French Protestants after 1661, then the revocation of the Edict of Nantes in 1685, resulted in a new wave of Huguenot immigration that peaked after James II's 1687 Declaration of Indulgence. During the 1630s *all* the foreign congregations in England may have totalled 10,000. An estimated 40,000–50,000 new immigrants fled to England from Louis XIV's persecution. Foreign Protestants in England were now overwhelmingly French rather than Dutch speaking. London was by far the largest centre of Huguenot settlement, with major clusters in the western suburbs, City and eastern suburbs, especially Spitalfields. Outside London, Kent, Devon and East Anglia all received many new immigrants.

Huguenots contributed substantially to England's economic development. Their expertise benefited silk manufacture, especially in Spitalfields, calico printing and the production of carpets, fine paper and linen, and the best felt hats. Huguenots were outstanding manufacturers of superior firearms, clocks and watches; transformed English cabinet making, and produced the finest gold and silver ware. The Huguenots' share in the struggle against Louis XIV was out of all proportion to their numbers. Possibly 2,500 Huguenot officers served in the British armed forces. French-speaking families long established in London assisted the integration of new immigrants. Shared membership of the Threadneedle Street French Church strengthened the bond between them. Seven of the twenty-four initial directors of the Bank of England were of Huguenot or Walloon descent, though only one was a new arrival. However, new refugees probably contributed at least 10 per cent of the investment in government funds started in the 1690s.[10]

Oliver Cromwell convened in 1655 a conference to consider the formal re-admission of the Jews to England. Supporters hoped for their conversion once exposed to the light of Gospel teaching. Opponents feared they would undermine both trade and religion. Opposition was too strong, but Cromwell protected the small, hitherto clandestine London Jewish community, allowed in a few recommended individuals, and permitted Jewish worship. These concessions survived the Restoration. At first Sephardi members, originally from Portugal, dominated the community. The Ashkenazim, from central and eastern Europe, established their independence around 1690. In 1697 Jews were allowed to practise as brokers on the Royal Exchange. Sephardi Jews bought large amounts of Bank of England stock.[11]

Roman Catholics

By 1603 the overwhelming majority of Roman Catholic priests in Britain had been trained on the continent. There were about 300 in England in 1603, possibly 750 in 1640 (including rather fewer than 500 seculars) and between 650 and 700 in 1700. Before 1685 there were normally from twelve to twenty priests in Scotland, operating under the direction of the Sacred College of Propaganda in Rome. Prestigious colleges such as those at Douai and St Omer (both in parts of Flanders seized by Louis XIV) educated boys for the priesthood and lay careers. Several new British monasteries or convents were founded on the continent. The ten English institutions of 1600 increased to nearly 100 by the 1660s, when there were some forty Irish ones and twelve Scottish. Half the English houses were concentrated in the Spanish Netherlands; there were nearly forty in France, largely clustered in and around Paris. The English houses included forty convents of nuns, in whose foundation redoubtable Catholic ladies played an important part. The most remarkable initiative was Mary Ward's 1609 foundation of the Institute of the Blessed Virgin Mary, largely devoted to women's Christian education. The 'English Ladies' met widespread opposition. Urban VIII formally suppressed them in 1631, but later allowed Ward to found a school in Rome.[12]

Rivalries between the Catholic continental powers had repercussions among British Catholics. The papacy favoured France's influence in England in Charles I's reign, but opposed it in James II's. Catholic activity in Henrietta Maria's household led to several conversions after 1625. In 1623, Pope Urban VIII had decided to appoint a vicar apostolic in England. The second man he chose for this position, Richard Smith, was a *protégé* of Richelieu's who was forced to leave England in 1631 to avoid arrest. Conflict between secular clergy and Jesuits connected with rivalry between Henrietta Maria's circle and the 'pro-Spanish' group in Charles's court. Urban VIII sent three envoys to Henrietta Maria, including a Scots Franciscan, the genial George Conn (1636–9). James II approved of Louis XIV's assertion of royal authority over the Church and his revocation of the Edict of Nantes. The papal nuncio and the Spanish ambassador worked together to counter French and Jesuit influence at his court. Pope Innocent XI himself thought James's religious measures precipitate and resented James's attempt to reconcile him with Louis.[13]

Royalist exiles

Hundreds of royalists, many of whom were former army officers, spent some time abroad between 1640 and 1660. The main clusters of exiles formed round Charles II and his mother Henrietta Maria, smaller groups in the Netherlands households of Mary of Orange and Elizabeth Stuart. Charles spent much of his exile in France until 1654 and the Spanish Netherlands from 1656, but also travelled widely in response to possible opportunities. Several royalists served in foreign armies. Others travelled or settled into quiet retirement. Personal quarrels and questions of policy divided the exiles. The 'old royalists', Edward Hyde and his associates, remained Charles's most trusted advisers, though Hyde strongly opposed involvement in Scotland and consequent concessions to the Covenanters. Otherwise, Charles remained consistently loyal to the Church of England, even though Henrietta Maria's Paris household was the natural home of Catholic exiles. Services performed overseas earned some exiles rich rewards. Their experience influenced English culture and fashion. It inclined Charles towards a moderate and inclusive Restoration settlement, but had little direct influence on the details of the settlement or on his subsequent policy.[14]

Political and religious exiles, 1660-85

After 1660, British exiles found their main refuge in the United Provinces, even though three regicides were seized there and later executed. Others went to Germany or Switzerland, where five of them, including Edmund Ludlow, former commander of the Irish army, settled at Vevey. In 1665–6 Algernon Sidney tried unsuccessfully to prompt a Dutch invasion of England and get help for a rising from Louis XIV. Several participants in the Pentland Rising fled to Holland, where two early critics of the Scottish church settlement, Robert McWard and John Brown, had already settled. In 1672–3 William of Orange employed Pierre du Moulin to gather intelligence and try to influence English opinion. One of du Moulin's agents, William Carstares, son of a minister involved in the Pentland Rising, later became William's chaplain and adviser on Scottish affairs.

The earl of Shaftesbury fled to Amsterdam in 1682, followed by several more Whigs, including John Locke, after the 'Rye House Plot' of 1683. Argyll and Monmouth both sailed from Holland on their doomed expeditions in 1685. William did nothing effective to prevent either of them. Polemical tracts attacking the English government flowed from Dutch presses. Gilbert Burnet, an outspokenly anti-Catholic Scottish minister, arrived in Holland in 1686, became William's chaplain in 1688 and translated the *Declaration* of the aims of his intervention in England. It was in vain that James II tried to have exiles extradited, and the British regiments in Dutch pay returned. Several veteran plotters accompanied William to England in 1688.[15]

Jacobites

Louis XIV established James II in the palace of St Germain with generous financial support. Even after the Jacobite defeats in Scotland and Ireland, threats to the new regime in England seemed to remain serious. The bulk of his potential supporters were Protestants, including English nonjurors and Scottish episcopalians, rather than the tiny Catholic minority. Under pressure from Louis, James issued in 1693 a conciliatory declaration guaranteeing the position of the Church of England and promising an amnesty for supporters of the revolution. The Jacobite cause attracted some radical Whigs disappointed by the revolution's outcome. Various Jacobites travelled between England and France, including, in 1695, James's illegitimate son, the duke of Berwick. Conspiracies took shape in 1691–2 and 1695, but adverse winds and naval defeats in 1692, and lack of co-ordination in 1695, aborted plans to provide essential French military support. After 1696, there was a lull in serious conspiratorial activity until 1708.[16]

Literature

Shared indebtedness to antiquity and the early Renaissance ensured innumerable resemblances and connections between British and continental literatures. English writers also borrowed plots from Spanish and Italian novels and plays. English domestication of European genres continued. These included tragicomedy, the pastoral play, the essay, mock encomia and letters combining entertainment and instruction. Sometimes borrowing was direct, but more often the relationship between continental and English works was a complex one. Francis Bacon's *Essays*, for example, are distinctively different from the widely admired works of Michel de Montaigne.

John Milton, the century's foremost English poet, loved the Italian language, had an Italian Protestant friend and in 1638–9 travelled widely in Italy itself. Italian epic poems, sonnets and histories were among his sources of inspiration. But he mostly drew on past achievements rather than the contemporary literature of an Italy dominated by Spain, the papacy and their satellites.[17] The sensuous and ornate poetry of the Neapolitan Giambattista Marino (1569–1625) was widely admired in Britain. John Donne, England's leading 'metaphysical' poet, resembled Marino in his use of 'startling metaphors and brilliant paradoxes', but Donne used them more seriously, and explored their implications more thoroughly and profoundly.[18] Richard Crashaw, influenced by Marino and Spanish mystic writers, converted to Catholicism, and expressed the ecstasy of martyrdom in some of his most characteristic poems. In the 1630s Francis Quarles adapted Jesuit originals to produce the best-known English examples of the immensely fashionable emblem book combining symbolic pictures with maxims and verses. Two outstanding devotional poets, both clergymen from the Welsh Marches and distantly related, George Herbert and Henry Vaughan, used familiar emblems to explore major religious themes. Vaughan, the foremost Welsh poet writing in English, translated many Latin poems, including ones by a Polish Jesuit, Casimir Sarbiewski.

French literary influence, already apparent in the work of the 'Cavalier' poets of the 1630s, was particularly strong after 1660. Several Restoration dramatists owed plot, character or dialogue to Molière or other French playwrights. Some of Corneille's and Racine's plays were staged in translation, and Corneille's classical tragedies influenced English dramatists, notably John Dryden. Several French romances were also translated, including the first epistolary novel published in English (1678). Aphra Behn, prolific female novelist and playwright, swiftly adopted this vehicle. French writers of literary analysis and criticism such as Corneille, Dacier and Boileau strongly influenced English ideas through translations of their work by Dryden and other authors.[19]

Among the poets who stayed in Scotland rather than following James VI to England, the outstanding example, William Drummond of Hawthornden, drew on Petrarch as well as more recent English and continental authors, including Marino. He wrote in both English and Latin. Some Scottish authors were best known to a European audience through their Latin compositions, including John Barclay, writer of Latin romances, who spent the years 1616–21 in Rome; Thomas Dempster, professor at Bologna, author of poems, tragedies and the first biographical dictionary of Scottish writers; and Arthur Johnston, the foremost Scottish Latin poet of his age, editor of the first anthology of Scottish Latin poetry. Three men, all royalist in sympathy, wrote notable works in English. Thomas Urquhart published a classic translation of Rabelais (1653, 1693). Thomas Sydserf's play *Tarugo's Wiles* (1667), based on a Spanish original, includes a caricature of coffee house conversations among scientific virtuosi. Sir George Mackenzie was the first Scotsman to write a pastoral novel in English: *Aretina* (1660), containing a disguised narrative of recent Scottish history.[20]

Architecture

Renaissance architectural ideas reached Britain mainly through French and Flemish channels until Inigo Jones, one of the greatest English architects, surveyor of the king's works from 1615 to 1643, drew on their source through two long visits to Italy. Vincenzo Scamozzi, who worked in Venice and Vicenza and completed various buildings by Andrea Palladio, strongly influenced him. Jones's finest design, the Banqueting House in Whitehall (1619–22), is notable for its grandeur, regularity and coherence, and the uncluttered spaciousness of its interior. The Queen's House at Greenwich (1616–37) has an austere refinement, the Queen's Chapel in St James's Palace (1623–7), a restrained elegance. Jones also designed Covent Garden, London's first classical piazza.[21]

The Netherlands provided the chief source of inspiration, transmitted either through immigrant craftsmen or pattern books, for the largely unknown architects or builders who employed an eclectic mixture of elements of classical and modern styles, incorporating such features as ornate gables and broken pediments. Among known architects, John Webb, Inigo Jones's nephew and pupil, designed some innovative grand houses with splendid staircases, entrance halls and interconnected private rooms. In 1655 he built the first classical portico attached to an English country house. Sir Roger Pratt travelled to France, Italy and the Low Countries during the 1640s, closely analysing different architectural styles. Such features as monumental chimneys, dormer windows set in steep hipped roofs and balustraded roof top platforms distinguished his house designs between 1658 and 1672. Hugh May drew on Dutch classical architecture, especially as represented by the Mauritshuis in the Hague (1640), in his houses of the 1660s. William Talman's design for the south front of Chatsworth House, begun in 1686, echoes French baroque.[22]

Sir Christopher Wren, greatest and most versatile of English architects, swiftly produced a plan for London's rebuilding after the Fire. Appointed surveyor of the king's works in 1669, he designed some fifty new London churches (1670–90), St Paul's Cathedral (1675–1708), the Monument (1671–6), the Royal Observatory (1675–6), Chelsea Hospital (completed in 1693), new ranges at Hampton Court (1689–94), Kensington Palace (1689–96) and the Royal Naval Hospital (from 1696). Wren surpassed all other British architects in his supremely inventive combinations of different classical elements and the range of continental models on which he drew (Italian, French, Flemish and Dutch), especially in his 'Anglo-Dutch' London churches. St Paul's Cathedral is the supreme achievement of English baroque.[23]

In Scotland some courtiers incorporated classical elements into their houses, as at Culross Abbey (from 1608), Winton (1620–7) and Caerlaverock (from 1633). George Heriot's Hospital, Edinburgh (from 1628) shares its symmetry and projecting corner blocks with Culross, but its towers, little turrets and tall chimneystacks have something of the air of a Danish royal palace. The first Scottish architects of international distinction were at work after 1660. Sir William Bruce handled classical elements with assurance and independence in innovative combinations from c.1670 onwards. He was the first British architect to use curved screens to link flanking pavilions to a central block. Louis XIV's château de Marly inspired his design for Hopetoun House (from 1698). Bruce's younger associate James Smith studied in Rome. Smith's compact and elegant houses at Newhailes and Strathleven betray a strong Palladian influence. His Hamilton Palace (1691–1701) radiated a French spirit; Dalkeith Palace (1701–9) echoes William III's Het Loo. He gave both houses Italianate grand porticos. His Canongate Kirk (1688–91) shows an unusual Dutch classical influence.[24]

Sculpture

Most of the best sculptors active in England during the century were immigrants, or Englishmen with continental experience. Maximilian Colt, a native of Arras, master carver to James I, created funeral monuments for Elizabeth I, James's two youngest daughters and the earl of Salisbury. The Huguenot Hubert Le Sueur, who came to England with Henrietta Maria, produced an equestrian statue of Charles I, bronze figures for royal gardens in London and several tombs. Notable English sculptors included Epiphanius Evesham, who became a member of the Paris guild of painters and sculptors, and Nicholas Stone, who probably worked for about six years with Hendrick de Keyser of Amsterdam. Evesham designed the poignantly expressive monument to Lord Teynham (d. 1622) at Lynsted. Stone famously represented John Donne rising from his funeral urn at the moment of resurrection. He also designed garden statuary and architectural sculpture.

Two of the leading Restoration sculptors, the Dane Caius Gabriel Cibber and the Londoner John Bushnell, both travelled to Italy, and Bushnell worked there. Bushnell created some dramatic baroque statues and tombs. Cibber was perhaps the most versatile sculptor active in England during the century. His work included a statue and bust of Charles II, statues for the gates of Bethlem hospital for the insane, bas-reliefs on the Monument commemorating the Great Fire and several good funeral monuments. Grinling Gibbons, master sculptor to William III, of English parentage, but brought up in the Netherlands, brought back skills that enabled him to become the foremost decorative wood carver in England, presenting fruit, flowers and foliage with unprecedented realism. He worked in many country houses, royal residences and the choir of St Paul's Cathedral, inspiring several English imitators. His workshop also produced some fine statues, including one of Charles II on horseback, and became the most successful funeral monument business in England. The Dutch sculptor Arnold Quellin collaborated with Gibbons, and the Fleming John Nost worked as Quellin's foreman.[25]

London-based sculptors executed some of the finest commemorative effigies in Scotland, such as Maximilian Colt's monument to the earl of Dunbar (d. 1611) and John Nost's at Durisdeer to the duchess of Queensberry (d. 1709). However, native artists probably created the canopied tomb and elaborate painted ceiling (1638–9) in the Skelmorlie Aisle at Largs, seventeenth-century Scotland's most distinctive and ambitious commemorative ensemble.

Painting

Most of the leading painters of the Stuart courts were of Netherlands birth or descent, though several leading Jacobean courtiers, the earls of Arundel, Salisbury and Somerset, and the duke of Buckingham, as well as Princes Henry and Charles, became connoisseurs of Italian, and especially Venetian painting. With some notable exceptions, portraiture dominated painting in Britain. James I inherited the Flemish-born brothers-in-law John de Critz and Marcus Gheeraerts II. Paul van Somer arrived c.1616, Daniel Mytens by 1618. Philip IV sent northern Europe's foremost artist Peter Paul Rubens to London as a peace envoy in 1629. Charles I commissioned him to paint ceiling canvases celebrating his father's reign for the Banqueting House in Whitehall, the grandest composition so far executed in England. In 1632 Charles appointed as his principal painter Anthony Van Dyck, who had worked in Rubens's studio, and also spent several years in Italy. Van Dyck achieved a fluidity and dignified grandeur new in English portraiture. Peter Lely, trained in Haarlem, arrived in England in the 1640s, painted the captive royal family, became the most admired artist of the 1650s, and then Charles II's prolific principal painter, best known for the 'sleepy voluptuousness' of his portraits of court beauties. The most inventive and fluent painter in England between 1680 and 1723 was Gottfried Kneller of Lübeck, principal painter from 1689, who had studied under Rembrandt and in Italy. Artists employed in wall and ceiling decoration after Rubens included Thomas de Critz, the Neapolitan Antonio Verrio and the Frenchman Louis Laguerre.[26]

William Dobson, pupil to a German, Franz Klein, was perhaps the best English painter: he immortalized royalist officers in vigorously rugged portraits during the civil war. A versatile amateur and visitor to the Netherlands, Sir Nathaniel Bacon, painted exuberant still life compositions as well as accomplished portraits. Two other portraitists arguably surpassed Lely in certain respects: John Michael Wright, a Catholic convert resident in Rome for over a decade from c.1642, and the miniaturist Samuel Cooper. The portraitist Mary Beale, encouraged by Lely, was the first successful English female artist. The first notable Scottish painter, George Jamesone, who worked in Aberdeen and Edinburgh between c.1620 and 1644, taught Wright. Two somewhat hazier figures, the portraitists John and David Scougall, worked in Edinburgh later in the century. In the 1690s, a Flemish painter of Spanish parentage, John Baptiste de Medina, became Edinburgh's principal portraitist after moving there from London.[27]

Music

English music remained both vigorous and open to new continental influences. Several musicians in royal service belonged to families of Italian or French origin already established in England. Angelo Notari published examples of new Italian styles (1613). Nicholas Lanier, of Huguenot descent, visited Venice, where he probably met Monteverdi, and became the first master of the king's music c.1626. Italian influences can also be discerned in madrigals and fantasia-suites by John Coprario, an Englishman who kept the form of his name given him in Italy, and in the chamber music of Coprario's apprentice William Lawes, the foremost composer of Charles I's reign. Lawes's brother Henry contributed to the first English experiments in opera in the 1650s.[28]

After the Restoration most of England's leading musicians once again benefited from royal patronage exercised through the Chapel Royal or the court. Charles II established a band of violins in the Chapel Royal, following the example of Louis XIV's chapel orchestra. Among Charles II's foreign musicians were Louis Grabu, master of the king's music and leader of the violins, and Giovanni Battista Draghi, his master of Italian music. Englishmen with continental experience included John Banister, royal violinist, composer of theatrical music and pioneer of public concerts; Grabu's successor Nicholas Staggins; Pelham Humfrey, master of the children of the Chapel Royal; and the notably versatile court musician Matthew Locke. John Blow, an organist of the Chapel Royal and outstanding composer of sacred music, used his knowledge of the French composer Lully's work in his opera *Venus and Adonis* (1681). England's greatest composer, Henry Purcell, had studied with John Blow and possibly Matthew Locke. He drew on sources of inspiration ranging from older English polyphony to contemporary Italian vocal and instrumental works. He wrote magnificent verse anthems with orchestral preludes enriched by the influence of Lully and Charpentier. He composed magnificently sombre and poignant music for Mary II's funeral, wrote an opera, *Dido and Aeneas* (1689), much music for the theatre and many grand celebratory odes.[29]

Music in Scotland suffered both from the court's absence and from the Kirk's hostility. However, copious extant collections in print and manuscript indicate the survival of a rich native tradition of anonymous 'airs' and the circulation of both English and continental tunes. Sir John Clerk of Penicuik was exceptional in studying with Arcangelo Corelli in Rome and composing Italianate cantatas.

Science

The seventeenth-century 'scientific revolution' overthrew previously accepted cosmology and opened up a boundless rather than physically limited universe; one whose parts were mechanically interrelated and subject to uniform natural laws rather than different celestial and terrestrial ones. No longer was the earth the universe's centre, but, along with other planets, orbited the sun, one of countless stars. The idea that all things were constructed of different combinations of basic particles and that all living organisms functioned as machines gradually gained widespread acceptance. The three most influential natural philosophers were the Italian Galileo Galilei, through his astronomical discoveries and his study of dynamics; the Frenchman René Descartes, eloquent advocate of a mechanistic universe; and the Englishman Isaac Newton, formulator of the law of universal gravitation. This brief account is a distant view of developments that from a nearer vantage point appear altogether more complicated. Different theories and schools of thought, some of them rooted in classical antiquity, interacted and competed in an intricate process of exchange and debate.

Exceptional individuals made crucial new discoveries and formulated innovative hypotheses, but favourable intellectual, social, economic and organizational contexts were essential for their acceptance. It has been claimed that science benefited in England from the national Church's 'doctrinal minimalism'. Certainly the Catholic Church made far more ambitious claims to police scientific investigation. Free debate and exchange of ideas; intercourse between scholars, gentlemen amateurs, businessmen and craftsmen; aristocratic or royal patronage; the demands of navigation, commerce and industry; and the establishment of learned societies: all these promoted scientific advances. An environment favourable to science already existed in Elizabethan England, especially in London. New scientific clusters and networks developed in the following century.[30]

During the early 1620s Francis Bacon advocated large-scale collaborative endeavour to advance science for the benefit of mankind. Careful observations and experiments leading to systematic accounts of natural phenomena would be necessary in order to ascertain nature's laws. One of those interested in

Bacon's ideas was the German Samuel Hartlib, son of an Eastland Company factor in Elbing. He settled in England. After the civil war, with an official pension, he published a great range of practical scientific tracts, drawing on the ideas of his friends and a network of correspondents. Meanwhile, a group of natural philosophers devoted to 'Experimental Philosophy' began to meet at Gresham College and elsewhere in London in 1645. Hartlib's friend Theodore Haak belonged to this group. Some of its members later joined a new cluster that formed round John Wilkins when he became warden of Wadham College in Oxford. Members of both groups joined in founding in 1660 at Gresham College a society to promote 'physico-mathematical experimental learning' which was to be formally incorporated as the Royal Society in 1662.[31]

The Royal Society was notable for the wide range of its members' interests. Thomas Sprat's *History* (1667) emphasized both its scientific productivity and its immediate practical usefulness. In 1665 it began to publish *Philosophical Transactions*, which reached an international readership. The Society included men of diverse social backgrounds. Two of its founder members were Scotsmen, and eminent overseas investigators were soon elected to the Society. Its indefatigable secretary, Henry Oldenburg, from Bremen, maintained a European correspondence network.

Before 1660, short-lived academies concerned with science had already been founded in Rome, Naples and Florence. The French Académie des Sciences was founded in 1666. The Dutch polymath Christiaan Huygens was a member of both the Royal Society and the Académie. He made several important astronomical observations, invented the pendulum clock and pocket watch, and shared various interests with Isaac Newton, including the nature of light.

The Royal Society became England's pre-eminent forum for the communication and dissemination of scientific ideas, but much activity and discussion took place elsewhere both before and after its foundation. During the century, British practitioners made important contributions to mathematics, the essential basis of scientific measurement and calculation. John Napier of Merchiston published in 1614 his invention of logarithms, swiftly adopted in Europe. Henry Briggs calculated the first base ten logarithms. His friend Edmund Gunter devised several useful navigational and mathematical instruments. Both men were professors at Gresham College. William Oughtred, who knew Briggs and Gunter, developed the slide rule, and introduced the '×' symbol for multiplication. After 1650, John Wallis, deviser of the symbol for infinity, the Scotsman James Gregory and Isaac Barrow all contributed to the development of differential calculus, in which Isaac Newton and Gottfried Leibniz played the decisive part.

The most renowned of English physicians, William Harvey, who had learnt at Padua about Girolamo Fabrizi's work on the venous 'valves', published his discovery of the circulation of the blood and the function of the heart in 1628. Francis Glisson published a pioneering account of rickets (1650) and a description of the liver (1654). Thomas Sydenham, an advocate of close clinical observation and of specific remedies that would help nature to attack the 'morbific matter' causing disease, published *Observationes Medicae* (1676), swiftly printed in three continental editions. He had been influenced by Jan Baptista van Helmont, a critical admirer of Paracelsus.

The discovery of capillaries in a frog's lungs by the Italian microscopist Marcello Malpighi (1661) amplified Harvey's account of blood's circulation. Malpighi also studied skin structure and embryos. He published his discoveries in the *Philosophical Transactions* and was elected Fellow of the Royal Society (FRS). Robert Hooke's *Micrographia* (1665), published by the Royal Society, included hugely magnified illustrations of insects, parts of plants and fabric textures. Hooke coined the word 'cell' for the smallest unit of a living organism. His work inspired the Dutch microscopist Antonie van Leeuwenhoek (FRS 1680), who saw bacteria and human spermatazoa for the first time, and became an especially assiduous Royal Society correspondent.

Hooke and his employer Robert Boyle investigated the pressure and weight of air, as well as its elasticity and compressibility, using the barometer invented by Evangelista Torricelli (c.1643), and a much improved version of the air pump invented by Otto von Guericke (1650), which enabled them to demonstrate that only part of the air was necessary for respiration and combustion. With Hooke's help, Boyle also demonstrated his 'law': that at constant temperature, the volume of gas varies inversely with its pressure. The idea of exploiting pressure led to experiments with diving bells, the Huguenot Denis Papin's invention of the pressure cooker (1679, soon followed by his election as FRS), and his and Thomas Savery's efforts to design steam pumps to drain mines.

The microscope and telescope were both invented in the Dutch Republic in about 1595 and 1608. Galileo's telescopic observations, including the phases of Venus, and the existence of Jupiter's satellites, powerfully reinforced the heliocentric model. Johannes Kepler, his vigorous German supporter, presented elliptical, rather than circular, movement, as one of the three basic laws of planetary motion. Jeremiah Horrocks observed the transit of Venus (1639); he and William Gascoigne confirmed the moon's elliptical motion. In 1675 Charles II founded the Royal Observatory and appointed John Flamsteed Astronomical Observator with the responsibility of mapping the heavens in order to measure longitude more accurately for navigational purposes. Edmond Halley helped by making southern hemisphere observations from St Helena (1676). He also predicted when Halley's Comet would return.

Halley's interest in the subject helped to encourage Newton to complete the work that resulted in his formulation of the law of universal gravitation, presented in his *Principia Mathematica* (1687). Newton's work promoted a new idea of the universe as a self-regulating machine. But Newton, unlike some of his popularizers, regarded God as the omnipresent governor of the universe.[32]

Conclusion

The seventeenth century was the 'Dutch century'. Despite Anglo-Dutch rivalry, connections between the Republic and Britain were close and numerous. Dutch example influenced Britain in countless ways. English landowners employed Dutch drainage engineers, English economists urged the adoption of Dutch commercial practices and English governments followed Dutch example in adopting the excise and funding the crown's debts. British soldiers found training and employment in the Dutch army. The largest numbers of foreign craftsmen, artists and architects working in Britain came from the northern or southern Netherlands. Dutch example influenced English domestic architecture and garden design. Scientific connections between Britain and the Republic were close. British students attended Dutch universities in growing numbers. Many British authors had their works published in Holland, where Europe's foremost presses were concentrated. Dutch writers such as Arminius and Grotius influenced English thought. The Republic provided a refuge and a source of support for English and Scottish religious and political exiles, including Separatists, Covenanters, Whigs and members of the royal family.[33]

France's acknowledged supremacy in matters of taste, in etiquette, fashions and fine craftsmanship was established during this century. French models strongly influenced British literature, architecture and music. The court of Louis XIV enjoyed an unmatched renown. French natural philosophers made major contributions to the advancement of science. France was the country most visited by young British gentlemen travellers, one where until Louis XIV's reign Protestants could enjoy the company of their Huguenot co-religionists.

A profound change nevertheless took place in British perceptions of France and her European role. From being the natural opponent of Habsburg 'universal monarchy' she became the pattern of 'absolute monarchy', an aggressive state threatening her neighbours' territories and economics. No action was better calculated to turn British opinion against Louis XIV than the revocation of the Edict of Nantes. Huguenot refugee merchants and craftsmen brought with them their skills, their international connections and an intense hatred of the government of their native country. The measure reinforced some political economists' belief that the French economy was less formidable and efficient than had previously been thought. Louis's religious persecution and long wars seemed to weaken rather than strengthen the state.

Italy remained throughout the century a powerful source of cultural inspiration. In music and the visual arts, the stimulus came from ongoing activity as well as past examples; in literature, however, the most influential models of Italian excellence were sixteenth-century ones. Italy continued to produce fine natural philosophers and physicians, some of whom were elected to the Royal Society. By 1700, however, north-western Europe had become the preeminent centre of scientific activity. British tourists and connoisseurs visited Italy in increasing numbers, but attendance at Italian universities gradually declined. Discussion of the much-admired Venetian constitution in the 1650s drew attention to its shortcomings as well as its strengths.

Neither Prince Charles's courtship of the Infanta in 1623, the outstanding Anglo-Spanish cultural encounter of the century, nor Charles II's sojourn in the Spanish Netherlands bore fruit in a marriage alliance, or close *entente* between Britain and Spain. Anglo-Spanish trade links remained close and valuable; Spanish plays and novels were a continuing source of inspiration for British authors. However, Spain was not a country that British travellers much wanted to visit, a source of inspiration in the visual arts or the sciences, or an example of successful political or economic policies.

The Baltic and Scandinavia remained an outstandingly important area of Scottish activity. Danish and Swedish service provided Scots with invaluable military experience. Swedish conscription provided a model for the Covenanters. In Germany, England maintained a vigorous commercial presence in Hamburg. A trickle of able and energetic Germans participated fruitfully in English scientific activity. The Palatine marriage was a source of blasted hopes for its keenest supporters and disaster for the House of Stuart. However, the accession of a grandson of that marriage to the British throne in 1714 would bring closer links between Britain and Germany.

15

MAKING THE UNITED KINGDOM

The Jacobean union project

James VI and I set his heart on a closer union between England and Scotland. He defined his goals succinctly in a message to parliament in 1604: 'one worship to God: one kingdom, entirely governed: one uniformity in laws'. His first step would be to change his royal style to 'King of Great Britain'. English MPs disliked this proposal. Some argued that it would invalidate existing English laws. Various MPs expressed a fear recurrent in subsequent debates: that union would encourage hordes of impoverished and greedy Scotsmen to migrate to England. The Scottish parliament resented English hostility, and passed acts that protected Scotland's Kirk and fundamental laws.[1]

The two parliaments nevertheless chose commissioners to consider practical steps towards closer union. The commission's proposals (November 1604) included the repeal of statutes of either country that were hostile to the other, the abolition of border laws, measures to promote Anglo-Scots trade and the naturalization of James's subjects of either kingdom in the other. Even these limited proposals, particularly naturalization, aroused intense opposition in the English parliament in 1606–7. Crudely expressed anti-Scottish sentiments infuriated James. Opponents of the government's programme proposed what they called a 'perfect' union, i.e. the incorporation of Scotland into England in a process similar to the incorporation of Wales. The Scots could not accept such a union. The English parliament accepted (with modifications) only the proposals concerning hostile and border laws.[2]

James's original hopes had been disappointed, but he took various steps by virtue of his own prerogative. He proclaimed in 1604 his adoption of the style 'King of Great Britain', to be used on coins and in proclamations and treaties and in 1606 ordered ships of both nations to carry a new union flag, though Charles I discontinued its use. In Calvin's case (1608) the judges decided that those Scots born after James's English accession were natural born subjects of the king of England. A conference of lawyers met late in 1607 to explore the possibilities of reconciling the two countries' public laws, but without success. Some contemporary observers thought that James's ecclesiastical policies in Scotland were part of a larger project to assimilate the Kirk to the Church of England.

Supporters and opponents of union wrote at least twenty-seven tracts (including nine Scottish and eighteen English ones) of which eleven were printed. Several of them mentioned or reviewed previously established unions. An anonymous Scottish author distinguished four main types: by election, marriage or descent, conquest or bequest, and incorporation. There had been several transient unions by election in eastern Europe. Relevant examples of unions by marriage or descent included Castile and Aragon, Portugal with the rest of Spain, and the Netherlands with the house of Austria. These had often been unstable. Unions by conquest (amongst which he included Henry II's annexation of Ireland to the crown of England) were subject to frequent rebellions. Only incorporation could guarantee that a union would endure. This author therefore called for the adoption of a common name and the common sharing of all freedoms of foreign trade and benefits by treaties. Yet he envisaged the retention of separate parliaments, laws and liberties.[3]

Sir Henry Spelman placed both Wales and Scotland in the same category as Normandy and Brittany, whose princes had always been understood to be vassals of French kings. In the same way, English kings had always understood Wales and Scotland 'to be of the fee and homage of their crowne of England' – a notion that no Scotsman could accept. No other union seemed to correspond exactly with what James hoped to achieve in Britain. However, one of several tracts that mentioned Poland–Lithuania pointed out that the united Commonwealth had not only one elected king, but also one assembly and one currency, though each nation kept its own laws and privileges.[4]

James tried to offset the effects of his departure from Scotland by giving Scotsmen a generous share of patronage in England. He appointed several to the English privy council, and, in an attempt to create a truly British court, 149 to the royal households, especially to his Bedchamber, an almost exclusively Scottish domain until the rise of Buckingham. Many Scots received lavish royal gifts. Unfortunately, English resentment of this largesse strengthened opposition to a fuller union. James also encouraged marriages between English and Scottish noble families. Nearly a quarter of all marriages of Scots peers or their heirs in the years 1603–42 were to English women, but many of these English wives were second or third spouses. A few Scots courtiers put down roots in England, and others had economic interests in both countries. Many more, however, remained firmly centred in Scotland. James VI and I made little progress towards creating a British nobility. Charles I appointed Scotsmen to the English privy council at various times in his reign, and Englishmen to the Scottish council from 1633. But it was the Bedchamber Scots whom he consulted when deciding on his disastrous response to Scottish developments after 1637.[5]

The British revolutions and the disappointment of Scottish hopes

The Scottish revolution ignited by the imposition of the Prayer Book in 1637 was not a separatist movement. The Covenanters presented themselves as zealous defenders of both king and true religion. Close links between Scottish and English Presbyterians had been established during Elizabeth's reign. Some Presbyterians had seen James VI's accession to the English throne as a sign that God intended to bring about a more perfect reformation in England. In a tract composed in 1605, David Hume of Godscroft advocated a union of councils and parliaments. For him, however, the crucial element would be the creation of a British Presbyterian Church, a step towards a fuller European reformation.[6]

Charles's efforts to subdue the Scots collapsed in 1640. They demanded that he summon an English parliament, in which there was considerable initial sympathy with the Scots. Charles had to accept the religious and constitutional changes in Scotland. The Scots also made a wide-ranging series of demands designed to strengthen the union. Most significant for the future were uniformity in church government, closer liaison between the two parliaments, free trade and full native rights for Scots and English in each other's countries, but without English parliamentary support these proved unattainable.[7]

The House of Commons was deeply divided over further measures of church reform by the time Charles ratified the treaty with the Scots in August 1641. Thereafter, different threats from Ireland first precipitated the outbreak of civil war in England, and then, in 1643, the signing of the Solemn League and Covenant between the English parliament and the covenanting regime. Four Scottish commissioners joined the Committee of Both Kingdoms, established in 1644 to ensure the more effective prosecution of the war. For some time it achieved close co-operation as 'the first real institutional tie between the two nations'.[8] As the Westminster Assembly produced a common confession of faith and directory of worship, it seemed that the long cherished Scottish dream of a fully reformed English sister Church was at last coming true. Meanwhile, however, the moment of English dependence on Scottish help soon passed. There was limited support for a Presbyterian church settlement in England. On the one hand there was a widespread attachment to the old Prayer Book, on the other a spread of congregational independency and heterodox opinions that Scots observers found even more alarming. The rift that opened in England in 1647 between parliament, slowly implementing a Presbyterian settlement, and the army, opposed to any such settlement, and ready to offer Charles alternative terms, prompted the moderate Covenanters to come to a new agreement with the king.

By the Engagement of December 1647, Charles committed himself to statutory confirmation of the Solemn League and Covenant and (for three years, pending a final settlement) the establishment of Presbyterianism in England. Charles promised to 'endeavour a complete union of the kingdoms' according to his father's intention, and pending the union's achievement, common sharing of all economic privileges. Charles's execution after the rout of the Engagers' army deeply shocked and angered Scotland, which had not been consulted about her king's fate. Defiantly, the Covenanters proclaimed Charles II king of Great Britain and Ireland. Scots support for him provoked the first English conquest of Scotland. From this unprecedented humiliation a devastated Scottish nation emerged into the bleak light of a new world.[9]

Union by conquest

The Rump declared in October 1651 that Scotland was to be 'incorporated' with England into a single Commonwealth. The Declaration implied that all non-episcopalian Protestants would be tolerated. The Rump then proclaimed in February 1652 a 'Tender of Incorporation', ultimately subscribed by nearly all the Scottish shires and nearly three-quarters of the royal burghs. Parliamentary commissioners appointed three Scotsmen and four Englishmen as commissioners for the administration of justice. An overlapping set of commissioners was to regulate the universities and the Kirk. Two sheriffs-principal were appointed for each county, an English army officer being paired with a Scotsman. Cromwell issued in April 1654 the Ordinance for Uniting Scotland into one Commonwealth with England. This was confirmed by parliament in 1657: it gave Scotland thirty seats in parliament, the same as Ireland; established free trade within Britain; and gave Scots commercial access to England's dominions. All taxes were to be levied proportionally from the whole united Commonwealth, and all servile tenures in Scotland were to be abolished, along with personal homage and a wide range of private and hereditary jurisdictions.[10]

Scotland's government between 1651 and 1660 had positive aspects, not least the administration of impartial if rigorous justice, and (after royalist rebellion in 1653–5) the imposition of an unprecedented degree of order. A ruined country was, however, unable to take full advantage of freedom of trade or pay the expected tax quota fixed in 1652, which soon had to be reduced. The divided Kirk, its general assembly forcibly dissolved in 1653, hated the toleration of Protestant separatists, while the nobility deeply resented the drastic reduction in their local power. Scotland remained a country under military occupation, many of its former leaders excluded from political life. Its MPs at Westminster always included some Englishmen under the Protectorate. Only two of the ten members of the council of Scotland appointed in 1655 were Scotsmen.[11]

Scottish discontents

The restoration of two separate kingdoms in 1660 was widely welcomed. Gone were the visionary ambitions that had drawn the Covenanters into repeated interventions in England. For his part, Charles II was happy to keep Scotland separate from England, and dependent on himself. Scotland was now excluded from the benefits of the English Navigation Acts. Complaints began almost immediately. The Scottish parliament passed a retaliatory Navigation Act in 1661. The deeply unpopular second Anglo-Dutch war made matters worse. Might the Dutch exploit Scottish economic grievances against England to foment unrest? Charles II instigated in 1667 discussions between commissioners appointed by the two parliaments. Some English interests, notably the woollen industry, favoured concessions to the Scots, but north-eastern coal and salt producers, keen to restrict Scottish competition, were better organized. The talks failed. In 1669 Charles ostensibly promoted a closer political union as a way out of the impasse. His motives remain obscure, but were probably tactical. He had no obvious interest in ending Scotland's separate status. Commissioners discussed a proposal including one parliament, commercial union, and separate churches and legal systems – one that largely anticipated the settlement of 1707. (Sir James Dalrymple and Sir George Mackenzie both published accounts of *The Institutions of the Law of Scotland*, in 1681 and 1684 respectively, which underlined the distinctive character of the Scottish legal system and its increasing divergence from English common law, notably through the influence of European civil law.) Lauderdale, prob ably acting on Charles's orders, adopted tactics that wrecked the scheme in November 1670. The secret treaty with Louis XIV may have made Scottish problems seem much less urgent.[12]

In January 1689, William III's Scottish supporters, attending him in London, suggested a union, which he recommended to the Scottish Convention of Estates. It nominated commissioners, but nothing was achieved. William's war with France badly damaged Scotland's trade. The 1696 Navigation Act, designed to strengthen enforcement of previous acts, was in part a response to Scottish commercial penetration of England's American colonies. In face of the East India Company's strong opposition William withdrew his support for the Company of Scotland Trading to Africa and the Indies, a venture promoted by London Scots who mobilized English investment in the Company. William's energetic efforts to frustrate the settlement of Darien in order to avoid offend-ing Spain caused the greatest bitterness.[13]

Scottish anger, consequent difficulties in managing the Scottish parliament and an increasingly uncertain international situation convinced William that a parliamentary union was the only way to ensure control of Scotland. The English parliament proved unresponsive in 1700 and showed complete indif-ference to Scottish opinion when it settled the succession on the Hanoverian line in 1701. William again urged union in his last message to the Commons in 1702. Queen Anne inherited his determination to achieve parliamentary union. However, many of the dominant Tories were hostile to a union with Presbyterian Scotland. English and Scottish commissioners appointed to discuss terms could not agree compensation for the Company of Scotland or for the fiscal burdens of union. In 1703, a new Scottish parliament, angered by the English Act of Settlement, passed bills asserting Scottish independence. The Act Anent Peace and War stipulated that peace and war should be made only with parlia-mentary approval after Anne's death. Anne reluctantly assented to this bill, but refused until its second passage in 1704 to accept the Act of Security. This provided that her successor in Scotland should not be the same person as in

England unless the honour and sovereignty of the crown and kingdom of Scotland, the freedom, frequency and power of parliaments, and the nation's religion, liberty and trade were first secured 'from English or any foreign influence'.[14] Hostility towards England rose to a new pitch after the English East India Company instigated the seizure of a Company of Scotland ship in 1704. An English merchant ship was seized in retaliation and the captain and two crew members tried and wrongfully condemned to death for the murder of the crew of another Company of Scotland vessel.

The union of 1707

The English parliament responded to the hostile Scottish measures of 1703–4 with the 1705 Alien Act. English estates of non-resident Scots would be treated as alien property, and Scotland's most important exports to England and her colonies would be strictly prohibited, unless by Christmas 1705 Scotland had entered into negotiations for union or accepted the Hanoverian succession. The act was the result of co-operation between Godolphin, commanding the court interest, and the Whigs, who were to be strengthened by the 1705 election. Godolphin and his parliamentary supporters realized that union must be achieved in order to ensure the succession of the same dynasty in both countries. The struggle with Louis XIV made Scotland's close partnership essential to England's security. Her military manpower was a crucial resource. Concessions to the Scots would be necessary in order to achieve political union and the channelling of potentially disruptive Scottish commercial ambitions into an integrated British trading network.[15] That summer, the Scottish parliament agreed to the nomination of commissioners, who settled to work in 1706. After the Scots had abandoned their initial demand for a federal union, negotiation focused on matters of detail. The treaty, complete by July 1706, was passed by both parliaments early in 1707, and came into force in July.

Before it confirmed the Treaty of Union the Scottish parliament passed an act securing Presbyterian church government which was rehearsed in the separate Scottish and English acts of parliament ratifying the treaty. The main provisions of the treaty were as follows. There was to be one kingdom, named Great Britain, with one flag, one great seal, a standard coinage and weights and measures, and one parliament. Sixteen Scottish peers were to be elected by their fellows to sit in the House of Lords. Scotland was assigned forty-five MPs, about one-twelfth of the total, much smaller than her share of the population, much larger than her share of taxable wealth. The Hanoverian succession was secured. (Catholics and their spouses were excluded from the throne forever.) All British subjects were to be free to trade throughout the kingdom and its possessions, subject to the same regulations and tariffs. Scotland was to pay a share of the land tax equivalent to about 2.4 per cent of England's, and was exempted from various current English taxes. The English parliament would pay an 'Equivalent' of nearly £400,000 to offset future Scottish liability to the national debt, much of it to be used to compensate Company of

Scotland investors. Scotland kept her own courts and all her heritable offices and jurisdictions. Her existing laws were to remain in force, and her private law was not to be altered except for the 'evident utility' of Scottish subjects. The privileges of the royal burghs were preserved.

The passage of the Union Treaty resulted above all from a transformation in the attitudes of leading English politicians between 1703 and 1705. The English parliament's outrageously cavalier behaviour had provoked the hostile Scottish measures of 1703–4. By 1705, Anne's advisers saw that real concessions were necessary to win over Scottish opinion. The Scottish political nation was deeply divided, a fact reflected in the number of political groupings in parliament: the Court, the Country, the Jacobite Cavaliers and, from 1703, a 'New Party' or 'flying squadron', offshoot of the Country Party. The parliamentary majority of 1703–4 was united only in its opposition to government. There could be no solid alliance between Jacobites and obdurate Presbyterians. The eloquent 'patriot' Alexander Fletcher of Saltoun argued that tight restriction of royal prerogatives would best guarantee Scottish independence. Those who wanted to win material advantages by negotiation found his stance increasingly irrelevant. Leadership was crucial. The queen's commissioner, the young duke of Argyll, showed firmness and adroitness. The duke of Queensberry employed complementary political cunning and attention to tactical detail. The vacillations and possible treachery of the Country Party's duke of Hamilton seriously weakened the opposition.

Robert Harley's cynical opinion was that the English parliament had bought the Scots by paying the Equivalent. Individual Scots were paid considerable sums on various pretexts, and several politicians received peerages. But the major inducement for larger numbers of Scots to accept union was free trade. Safeguards for the Presbyterian establishment, for Scots law and for noble and burgh privileges allayed fears that national institutions would disappear in the new union. The 1707 merger was not popular. A vigorous pamphlet war pitted the claims of sentiment and a proud history against a Unionist vision of increased prosperity and security, presented with particular eloquence by the English Presbyterian Daniel Defoe. There was a widespread preference for a federal union, but that was not on offer, and there was probably less support for a complete break with England than for the incorporating union. There was no reliable alternative ally. French agents encouraged opposition, but the Auld Alliance, associated with Jacobitism and Catholicism, raised spectres of internal quarrels and English military intervention. A federation with the Dutch was never a practical proposition.[16]

All the major European composite monarchies suffered serious strains during the seventeenth century. Each faced its own combination of challenges. The Austrian Habsburgs confronted in Bohemia and Hungary a stubborn defence of religious freedom and the constitutional liberties of historically elective kingdoms. The Spanish Habsburg monarchy's efforts to spread the increasingly intolerable burdens of its external wars to its non-Castilian realms provoked formidable rebellions. The most serious crisis within the Commonwealth of

Poland–Lithuania resulted from religious and other grievances of the Ukraine, transferred from Lithuania to the Polish crown in 1569.

The Stuart monarchy was exceptional in facing two diametrically opposed forms of religious resistance to its authority in its two outlying kingdoms of Ireland and Scotland. During the crisis of the 1640s, as has been shown, the Scots sought to impose their own Reformation on England rather than dissolve the regal union. As their economic grievances became more important, the best solution remained some sort of union with an England whose home market and commercial empire were already very important to the Scottish economy. The warily concluded bargain of 1707 created a unique unitary state governed by one sovereign crown and parliament, comprising the largest free trade area in western Europe, but containing two different established churches, each with its own distinct structure and relationship to the crown, and two separate legal systems.

The Irish and the Welsh

The third Stuart kingdom, Ireland, was temporarily merged in the Commonwealth of England, Scotland and Ireland in the 1650s, but unlike the Scots, the Irish were not consulted. Ireland's subjugation after 1649 differed from Scotland's in being followed by the wholesale expropriation of Catholic landowners. By 1700, although the vast majority of the Irish nation remained Catholic, Protestants owned most of the land and dominated politics. Since 1495 the Irish parliament's legislation had been subject to advance approval by the English crown and council. It could not retaliate against English legislation of 1663 and 1701 limiting the benefits of the 1660 Navigation Act for Ireland, of 1663 and 1666 restricting or banning imports of Irish farm animals, prohibiting importation of colonial goods into Ireland (1671), or forbidding the export of Irish woollens (1699). Ireland's quasi-colonial economic status suited English producers very well. Many Irish Protestants resented that status. One, Sir William Molyneux, insisted in a tract of 1698 on the independence of the Irish parliament. That parliament was sometimes turbulent and difficult to manage, but a vigorous campaign for Irish legislative independence was as yet unthinkable. The Irish parliament supported three resolutions in favour of union with England in 1703–4, 1707 and in 1709, but probably for tactical reasons. Unlike its Scottish counterpart, it lacked means of leverage, and the English parliament had no incentive to change Ireland's status. The partnership of the three kingdoms was re-configured in 1707. Ireland now became subject to the British crown. But the ascendant Protestant magnates maintained their *English* identity and scornfully rejected 'any notion of being "British" since that would have implied a community of interest with the despised Ulster Scots'.[17]

Meanwhile, the Welsh had successfully preserved their own language and sense of shared identity despite their lack of separate political institutions. James VI and I saw the successful union of England and Wales as an argument for the rather different Anglo-Scottish union he envisaged. He showed his awareness of Welsh loyalty. The investitures of two princes of Wales (Henry and Charles) in 1610 and 1616 included Welsh elements. James defended the Council in the Marches as an institution that helped to bind the two nations together. Most of the Welsh gave the dynasty loyal support, along with the established Church. It was in Wales that Charles I had most success in raising forces in 1642. Later in the century, as the nobility and upper gentry ceased to patronize the bards, Welsh poetry survived and flourished with the support of smaller gentry, clergy and farmers. Crucial to the survival of the Welsh language was the printing press. Songs, poems and devotional literature were published in some quantity during the later seventeenth century. Thomas Jones established in Shrewsbury the first provincial press producing Welsh books soon after the lapse of licensing in 1695, and helped to revive *eisteddfodau* (assemblies of Welsh bards) around 1700. The equally vigorous bardic and poetic traditions of Gaelic Scotland and Ireland, with their powerful currents of celebration, lament and criticism, lacked this important medium. Antiquarian studies also flourished widely. Edward Lhuyd, keeper of Oxford's Ashmolean Museum, stood unequalled among scholars in this field. It was a curiously fitting coincidence that his *Archaeologica Britannica*, a comparative account of the 'Languages, Histories and Customs of the Original Inhabitants of Great Britain', should have appeared in the year that witnessed Britain's political union.[18]

PART III

1707–80

16

THE UNITED KINGDOM TESTED

Party conflict and peace-making

War with France was the forge of Britain's union. It made Queen Anne and her ministers determined to ensure that Scotland stood alongside England in an enduring partnership. The exceptional conjunction of circumstances in 1705–7 was not to last. The Union soon underwent early tests. Its widespread unpopularity in Scotland encouraged a French attempt to land James Francis Edward Stuart (James VIII and III) in Scotland with troops in order to precipitate a planned national rising in March 1708. The Pretender caught measles, the delay denied him the necessary element of surprise and the attempt failed.

This episode helped the Whigs in the short run. In May they won a decisive election victory. However, public opinion began to swing against the war. Castile resisted the allied invasion of Spain with unexpected vigour, the Dutch were blamed for failing to support the allied cause strongly enough and the conflict in the Netherlands turned into a bloody war of attrition. Louis XIV was ready to come to terms in 1709, but the allies' unreasonably harsh conditions prolonged the war. When the Habsburg Archduke Charles, their candidate for the Spanish throne, became emperor in 1711, there was a new prospect of the creation of a Habsburg Empire rivalling that of Charles V. This was not what England had gone to war to achieve.

Early in 1710 the trial for seditious libel of the fiery young High-Church controversialist Henry Sacheverell after his intemperate condemnations of toleration and occasional conformity provoked demonstrations that revealed the ministry's deep unpopularity. Anne herself was tiring of the war and determined to assert her independence of Marlborough and his wife. She dismissed Godolphin. The October 1710 election resulted in a Tory landslide. The 1713 election strengthened this dominance still further. Robert Harley was appointed lord treasurer (1711–14), and made earl of Oxford, his rival Henry St John became secretary of state (1710–14), and was created Viscount Bolingbroke (1712).

The ministry opened negotiations with France in 1711 and soon reached substantial agreement. Britain's allies had little choice but to follow suit. Moderate Tory peers combined with Whigs to oppose the ministry's preliminary peace terms in December 1711. Anne created extra Tory peers in order to force them through, and dismissed Marlborough as captain-general. The Utrecht treaties of 1713 left Louis XIV's grandson Philip of Anjou on the Spanish throne, though with a French assurance that France and Spain would not be united. Britain kept Gibraltar, and Minorca, captured in 1708. France ceded claims to Newfoundland, Nova Scotia and Rupert's Land. Britain also obtained the rest of the Caribbean island of St Kitts, recognition of the Protestant succession and a thirty-year contract for the supply of African slaves to the Spanish American empire (Asiento). The Dutch got a 'barrier' of fortresses in the southern Netherlands, but fewer than had been agreed with Britain in 1709. The Emperor Charles, denied the prize of Spain, accepted in 1714 the Spanish Netherlands, Milan, Sardinia and Naples. Britain had emerged as one of the foremost European powers. Her treatment of her allies was deeply resented.

The government passed legislation designed to curb English Protestant dissenters, but introduced toleration for loyal Scottish episcopalians in 1712. The 1709 Treasons Act, which interfered with Scottish judicial procedure, and the attempted imposition of a malt tax on Scotland in 1713 were both contrary to the Treaty of Union, and encountered strong Scottish opposition. In June 1713 an attempt to introduce a bill to repeal the Act of Union failed in the Lords by only four votes.

Hanoverian succession, Jacobite rebellion and Anglo-French co-operation

By the time of Anne's death on 1 August 1714 the Tories were disastrously divided over the succession. Hanoverians outnumbered Jacobites, but the undecided were the largest group. The elector George of Hanover succeeded peacefully to the British crown. James III remained resolutely Roman Catholic and gave his sympathizers no effective lead. George was outraged by the behaviour of the Tory leaders' treatment of Britain's allies and suspicious of their earlier covert dealings with James's court. As a Lutheran with broad-church instincts, he was out of sympathy with High-Church political aims. It was to the Whigs that he gave his confidence, enabling them to establish their enduring political supremacy. A hard-fought general election early in 1715 resulted in a substantial Whig parliamentary majority. Bolingbroke and Ormonde (Marlborough's successor as captain-general) fled to France after impeachment proceedings were started against them. By promptly entering James's service they helped the government's efforts to tar the Tories with Jacobitism.

Hostility to George's regime precipitated Jacobite rebellion in 1715. There was widespread potential popular sympathy in England, but no strong leader and much ineffectual gathering and dithering. John Erskine, earl of Mar, previously secretary of state for Scotland, supporter of Union and Harley's *protégé*, turned active Jacobite after George dismissed him. He raised James's standard at Braemar in September. A mixture of Jacobite loyalties, anti-union feeling, hostility to the Campbells and episcopalian dissatisfaction, especially in the Highlands and north-east, helped him field a substantial force. He nevertheless failed to press his initial advantage against Argyll's outnumbered men at Sheriffmuir in November. In England, only Scottish help enabled a small northern rising to get off the ground. It fizzled out at Preston in November. James made a late, brief appearance in Scotland (December 1715– February 1716). The Jacobites needed foreign help, but the French did not want to provoke a new war. The rebellion's swift defeat strengthened the regime, which further secured its position in 1716 with an act extending the maximum length of parliaments to seven years.

The king pursued ambitions as a German prince, especially during the early years of his reign. George's inability to speak English fluently, his German advisers and German mistress, and his frequent absences in Hanover were the subjects of disrespectful comment. The alleged subordination of British to Hanoverian interests was to be a recurrent theme of opposition criticism until the 1750s. George's Hanoverian ambitions split his first ministry, in which the secretaries of state were Charles Townshend and James Stanhope, hero of the recent war in Spain. Robert Walpole, Townshend's brother-in-law, who already had extensive ministerial experience, became first lord of the treasury in 1715. At this time Sweden lost her hitherto dominant position in the Baltic region through her king Charles XII's defeats in the long and gruelling Great Northern War with Russia and her allies (1700–21). Her neighbours hovered over her empire like vultures. George hoped to acquire the Swedish territories of Bremen and Verden both to give Hanover access to the North Sea and to prevent their falling under Danish control. After he became king of Britain he ensured that the British navy was used in such a way as to facilitate allied hostilities against Sweden, and in October 1715 declared war on her, though only as elector of Hanover. In response, the Swedish ambassador in London plotted with Jacobites for a Swedish invasion of England. Russian occupation of Mecklenburg, bordering on Hanover, underlined the danger posed by Russia's replacement of Sweden as the dominant Baltic power.

Stanhope, supported by his colleague Charles Spencer, earl of Sunderland, worked hard to achieve George's diplomatic objectives. Townshend, however, was deeply concerned about the dangers of British involvement in the Baltic. George moved him from his secretaryship of state. Walpole resigned early in 1717. Opposition Whigs joined with Tories in criticizing the subordination of British policy to Hanoverian interests. To make matters worse, the king's son George, Prince of Wales, quarrelled with his father and allied with the opposition Whigs. However, Charles XII's death in 1718 made it easier to end the Baltic hostilities. Sweden ceded Bremen-Verden to George in 1719. The king now switched to supporting Sweden against Russia, but the British navy was of limited use in shallow Baltic coastal waters and against overwhelming

Russian strength. In 1721 Sweden had to surrender to Russia her extensive territories to the south-east of the Baltic.[1]

The king's desire for help in dealing with these complex northern problems promoted the most dramatic diplomatic development of his reign, the conclusion of an alliance with France in September 1716, joined by the Dutch in December. Louis XIV, who had died in August 1715, had been succeeded by his great-grandson Louis XV. Britain and France had a shared interest in European peace after the recent long and exhausting wars, and for the first time worked together to maintain it. The British government wanted above all to ensure that James Edward never again received French support. Philip V of Spain resented the territorial losses imposed on Spain by the recent treaties, and his exclusion from the French succession even if his young nephew Louis XV died without sons. His ambitions posed the chief threat to the post-war international order. Spain invaded Sardinia in 1717 and Sicily in 1718. Britain and France, hoping to impose a settlement, drew the Empire into their alliance. An English fleet defeated the Spanish off Cape Passaro in August 1718. In December Britain and France declared war on Spain. Spain retaliated by landing a small force in Scotland to stir up Jacobite rebellion, but it was rapidly overcome, and she accepted the alliance's peace terms in 1720.

Soon after the king and the Prince of Wales were reconciled in the spring of 1720, Walpole and Townshend were restored to the government. Their return coincided with the speculative frenzy of the South Sea Bubble. A dizzying rise in the price of South Sea Company stock was followed by a slow fall and then an abrupt collapse in September. The price had been deliberately driven up in order to help the Company raise further share capital after it had rashly taken over a substantial portion of the National Debt, offering company stock in return for government securities. Stanhope died of a stroke in February 1721, and Sunderland, first lord of the treasury since 1718, resigned, but because Walpole and Townshend had been out of office when the scheme had been launched they were not damaged. The crisis, his own financial and political skill in dealing with it, and the unforeseen elimination of his former rivals gave Robert Walpole an unchallenged position of leadership within his party. He again became first lord of the treasury in April 1721, and the Whigs won the unusually hard-fought election of March 1722. George's achievement of his own main aims and the absence of major new challenges to British interests left Walpole exceptionally free to pursue a peaceful foreign policy. Peace made lower taxes possible and encouraged trade. Disgruntled Tories had fewer grievances to chew on. At the same time Walpole sought to manage parliaments and discredit Toryism. An abortive Jacobite plot by Francis Atterbury, bishop of Rochester and a small group of peers in 1722 served this purpose very well. Without posing a serious threat, it underlined for the public the continuing menace of Jacobitism and its links with Toryism.

Walpole controlled Scotland through the Campbell brothers, John, duke of Argyll (d. 1743) and his brother and successor, Archibald, earl of Islay (d. 1761), who acted as political manager. Their Whig rivals, the 'Squadrone', were aligned with Sunderland and Stanhope during the Whig split, thus helping to bring the Campbells into alliance with Walpole. In 1725, the duke of Roxburghe, Squadrone member and third secretary of state since 1716, was dismissed after encouraging opposition to the malt tax in Scotland, thus sealing Campbell dominance. He was not replaced. Islay managed Scottish patronage and also became first governor of the Royal Bank of Scotland, established in 1727, a rival to the Bank of Scotland. English politicians tended to treat Scotland almost like a colony. The dominance of a Scottish political manager and the survival of distinctive national institutions (the law courts and the Kirk) nevertheless helped to ensure the continuance of a separate Scottish political sphere.[2]

Walpole's and Townshend's first major diplomatic challenge came in 1725. Spain and Austria, so recently enemies, concluded an alliance. The Emperor Charles VI, the first Habsburg since the family's rise to prominence to have neither brother nor son to succeed him, wanted to ensure that all the Habsburg lands went to his daughter Maria Theresa. He issued a solemn declaration called a 'pragmatic sanction' to this effect. Philip V, disappointed in his hopes of a French marriage alliance, accepted Charles's regulation of the Habsburg succession and conceded trading rights to the Ostend Company based in the Austrian Netherlands. Britain and France responded with a fresh alliance. In 1726 both Russia and Prussia joined Austria and Spain in accepting the pragmatic sanction. Britain and the Dutch Republic viewed the Ostend Company as a threat to their own eastern trade. Britain started a blockade to prevent Spain's importing silver from America. Spain responded with an unsuccessful siege of Gibraltar in 1727. Lack of effective Austrian support persuaded her to make peace in 1728, and sign a treaty of friendship with Britain and France in 1729.

George I died in June 1727. His son George II had earlier revealed his dislike of Walpole, and was widely expected to discard him. Walpole nevertheless survived the new monarch's accession. George II's wife Queen Caroline was his friend. The king's confidant Spencer Compton shrank from stepping into Walpole's shoes. The crucial importance of Walpole's financial and managerial mastery was demonstrated by his success in gaining a generous civil list grant of £800,000 for the new king. Townshend reportedly resented being eclipsed by his brother-in-law, and his resignation in May 1730 further enhanced Walpole's dominance of the ministry. Walpole's key partner in government was now Thomas Pelham-Holles, duke of Newcastle, secretary of state since 1724. Townshend had been ready to co-operate with France to maintain European equilibrium. But English suspicions of France, never far below the surface, were revived in 1730 by news that France was rebuilding the Dunkirk fortifications.

The end of peace and Walpole's departure

In March 1731 Walpole made the Treaty of Vienna with Charles VI, who abandoned the Ostend Company. In return Britain and the Dutch Republic accepted the pragmatic sanction. This seemed a thoroughly satisfactory outcome, but it was achieved independently of France. Cardinal Fleury, Louis XV's former tutor and principal adviser since 1726, had seen the alliance with England as the best means of maintaining European peace. Anglo-French relations remained peaceful after 1731, but the partnership of the previous fifteen years was over. The interlude of Franco-British co-operation, though short, had been remarkable. Coincidence of interests between the governments of the foremost west European powers, former enemies, had enabled them to act in concert to maintain the peace in a continent whose familiar alignments had disappeared. France was now to draw closer to Spain.

The Treaty of Vienna committed England to assist Austria against an aggressor. In October 1733, France declared war against Austria because Austria and Russia had interfered in the Polish succession. Their troops supported Augustus III of Saxony, chosen by a minority of the Polish electors, against Louis XV's father-in-law, Stanislas Leszczynski, who had been elected by the majority. France and Spain rapidly drove the Austrians out of all their possessions in Italy. Emperor Charles VI felt that Britain should help him, especially by using her naval power in the Mediterranean. But Austria was arguably the aggressor, and Walpole was determined to stay out of the war. By October 1735 Charles was ready to conclude a peace, though only after another three years was it finally ratified. Augustus retained the Polish throne; France guaranteed the Austrian succession; Naples and Sicily went to Philip V's son Don Carlos, thus setting up a third Bourbon dynasty; Stanislas Leszczynski received Lorraine in compensation: it was to go to France after his death. Walpole had kept England out of war, a significant achievement in domestic political terms. He had, however, failed to prevent a substantial enhancement of France's position in western Europe, achieved in partnership with Spain.

Resentment of Walpole's political dominance was growing during the 1730s. His 'Robinocracy' had already attracted criticism and satire during the 1720s. Walpole's first major setback in domestic politics came in 1733. His scheme to improve the yield of tobacco taxes by converting them from customs duties to excises aroused a storm of popular opposition. He was forced to withdraw it. George II supported him and dismissed his leading aristocratic opponents from court. Hatred of the excise nevertheless contributed to an unusually large number of contests in the 1734 election, the only one between 1713 and 1761 in which the Tories increased their seats. The excise scheme was the most important, but by no means the only, cause of unrest during the 1730s. The Gin Act of 1736 also provoked protests and riots. The parliamentary opposition, a loose coalition of different interests, now included disaffected Whigs as well as Tories. Bolingbroke, pardoned in 1723 but still barred from parliament, tried to give it a unifying philosophy. The court Whigs, he argued, had betrayed the principles of the Glorious Revolution. Old party divisions had become meaningless. A new body of 'Patriots' must be forged to fight ministerial corruption and encroachments on English liberty. These arguments failed to create a new party, but they did help to inspire and justify opposition. The quarrel between George II and his son Frederick, Prince of Wales, and opposition efforts to woo Frederick added to Walpole's difficulties.

Walpole's hold over Scotland was weakened by the Porteous affair of 1736. Porteous, captain of the Edinburgh town guard, had ordered his men to fire on an unruly crowd at a smuggler's execution, killing eight people. Condemned, then reprieved, Porteous had finally been lynched by a mob. A bill to fine Edinburgh was opposed by most of the Scottish MPs and by Argyll himself, who joined Walpole's critics.

Tension between Britain and Spain persisted during the 1730s. Spain especially resented British possession of Gibraltar and Minorca. Her other grievances included alleged fraud by the South Sea Company, authorized in 1713 to trade with Spanish America; extensive interloping by unauthorized British merchants; illegal British logwood cutting in Honduras; and encroachment on Spanish Florida by the recently founded British colony of Georgia. The paramount British grievance was Spanish abuse of the right to search suspected smuggling ships. Free of war with Austria after 1735, Spain tried to tighten trade regulation. Merchant grievances, sometimes several years old (the most notorious of which was Captain Jenkins's loss of an ear when his ship was pillaged in 1731), were raised in parliament. Spain agreed to pay some compensation for agreed damages, but many British merchants vociferously opposed what they saw as an inadequate provisional settlement reached in January 1739. Those who demanded punitive action against Spain overestimated Spanish weakness, underestimated the difficulties of fighting a war in the Caribbean and ignored the potential damage to Britain's European diplomacy. Walpole was pushed into a war with Spain that he did not want. In November 1739, Britain's forces captured Puerto Bello on the Isthmus of Panama, but thereafter she achieved no further major objectives, and wound down the maritime war after 1742.[3]

The 1741 election increased the numbers of disaffected Whigs among the members of parliament. The number of Scots MPs at Walpole's command fell sharply. In January 1742 Walpole defeated by only three votes a motion to appoint a committee of enquiry into the conduct of the war. Actual defeat a week later in a relatively unimportant vote, and his friends' strong advice, finally persuaded Walpole to retire. He had been the leading figure in government for a longer period than any other statesman in British history save Lord Burghley, and the first 'prime minister'. His mastery had depended both on keeping the confidence of two successive kings (no mean achievement in itself) and on his ability to lead the Commons, where he had also stayed longer than any previous leading politician. Nobody else since James I (in very different circumstances) had so consistently tried to avoid war. Stanhope and Townshend had worked actively in concert with France to maintain European equilibrium, especially by means of naval power. Walpole had withdrawn from that role. His critics blamed Walpole for passivity in the face of French success during the 1730s. But they were also very much at fault for whipping up the bellicosity that forced him into a mistaken war with Spain.

Return to war with France

The Emperor Charles VI died in October 1740. Frederick II (1740–86) of Prussia was the first to take advantage of the vulnerability of Charles's daughter Maria Theresa, his successor in the Austrian Habsburg lands, by invading the valuable Habsburg province of Lower Silesia in December 1740. Brandenburg-Prussia had become an increasingly powerful state under Frederick William the 'Great' Elector (1640–88), Frederick III (1688–1713) and Frederick William (1713–40). In 1701 Frederick III had been crowned king in Prussia, a former Polish fief lying outside the Holy Roman Empire, as Frederick I. Thenceforth his successors were both king and elector. The rulers of Brandenburg had ancient claims to various parts of Silesia. Frederick now rapidly seized most of the province, thus launching the war of the Austrian Succession (1740–8). In May 1741 France and Spain reneged on their commitment to the pragmatic sanction and agreed to support the Bavarian elector Charles Albert's claim to much of the Austrian Habsburg inheritance, as well as his election as emperor.

How should Britain, involved in her own unsuccessful war with Spain, react to these attacks on Austria? Among the various predators, France and long resentful Spain posed the most serious threat to Britain, especially if those powers, strengthened by continental gains, were to combine in attacking her overseas trade and possessions. Frederick II's dramatic success infuriated his uncle George II, who had long feared Prussia's expansionist ambitions but had hoped for Frederick's co-operation against France. His initially bellicose reaction soon gave way to fear that vastly superior Prussian or French forces might overwhelm Hanover. In September 1741 George, as elector of Hanover, undertook to take no hostile action against France's allies and to support Charles Albert's election as emperor in return for a French undertaking not to attack Hanover. His action horrified his English ministers.

On Walpole's retirement his virulent critic Lord Carteret joined in a ministry with Walpole's leading partners Newcastle and his younger brother Henry Pelham, with Spencer Compton somewhat ineffectually presiding at the treasury. Carteret, a German speaker, was as secretary of state chiefly responsible for foreign policy. His great goal was an anti-French coalition. In order to achieve this he helped persuade Maria Theresa to give up Lower Silesia – she hoped only temporarily. Frederick II withdrew from the war against her. George II ended his agreement with France. Heading the 'Pragmatic Army' of Austrian, British, Hanoverian and Dutch troops, he defeated the French at Dettingen in June 1743.

Carteret's success in constructing an effective anti-French coalition cut no ice with dyspeptic 'patriots' at Westminster. The cry went up that British interests were being sacrificed to Hanover. In an exceptionally vigorous parliamentary and pamphlet debate on British foreign policy there were various strands: some critics strongly supported Britain's continental involvement, but argued that its proper goals had been distorted by Hanoverian interests; others argued for 'navalist' or isolationist policies.[4] In November 1744 the 'old corps' Whig brothers Newcastle and Pelham (first lord of the treasury since

August 1743) demanded Carteret's dismissal, and after his resignation, tried to broaden the government. George, feeling coerced, only partially and grudgingly accepted their recommendations. In February 1746, the ministry strengthened its hold on power by a collective resignation that demonstrated George's inability to assemble an alternative team led by Carteret. Pelham or his brother Newcastle headed every government between 1743 and 1762 with one brief break in 1756–7.

In 1744 war between France and Britain began officially, and in August Frederick II, alarmed by Maria Theresa's successes, invaded Bohemia. Substantial Austrian forces had to be withdrawn from the war against France. Under these fateful circumstances the Whigs' worst nightmare was at last realized. The French government planned an invasion of England in 1744, and invited Prince Charles Edward, son of the 'Old Pretender', James VIII and III, from Rome to join it. Violent storms thwarted the plan. In July 1745 the Prince landed in Scotland, though without French official countenance. Only one ship got through. The prospects of success were poor. Charles Edward received support from only a minority of the Highland clans, and even those chiefs who rallied to him did so despite initial reluctance. A swift and resolute advance and the defeat of a small and ill-led government force at Prestonpans gave the Prince temporary control of Lowland Scotland and access to a larger body of episcopalian supporters in the north-east. Against the advice of his best general, Lord George Murray, Charles Edward invaded England in the hope of precipitating a major rebellion and encouraging French intervention. His English sympathizers nevertheless failed to stir, and British ships trapped a belatedly assembled French invasion force in Boulogne. Threatened by two hostile armies, the Jacobites retreated from England and were finally defeated at Culloden by the duke of Cumberland, the king's son, in April 1746. Their early success had been brilliant but precarious, and the whole enterprise had been doomed by the timidity of English Jacobites and the unwillingness of the French government to undertake a risky intervention in Britain. There ensued savage reprisals, thoroughgoing forfeiture of Jacobites' estates (unlike in 1716) and repressive legislation.[5]

Meanwhile the French had gradually conquered most of the Austrian Netherlands after winning the Battle of Fontenoy in April 1745. In North America and at sea, however, Britain achieved some notable successes at France's expense. In June 1745 New England militiamen, with British naval support, captured the massive fortress of Louisbourg on Cape Breton Island, base for immensely profitable French fisheries. In 1746, the British navy successfully adopted the 'Western Squadron' strategy, designed to blockade western France; and in 1747 it won considerable victories over French fleets off Finisterre and Belle-Île.[6] British attacks also ruined the inter-island trade of the French Caribbean. Only in India were the French successful, capturing Madras in 1746. Peace negotiations, begun in 1746, were completed at Aachen in 1748. Britain and France restored their conquests; most notably, Louis XV gave up the Austrian Netherlands. The issues originally at stake had been largely settled in 1745, when Maria Theresa's husband Francis Stephen had been elected emperor after the death of Charles VII of Bavaria, and she had confirmed the cession of Silesia. So far as Britain was concerned, a war that had begun in central Europe with none of her interests immediately involved had developed in its later stages into a direct confrontation with France. After a peaceful interlude of thirty years the two old adversaries had once again found themselves at war. In another respect the conflict closed a chapter: the last and most dramatic attempt at a Stuart restoration had failed. The Jacobite spectre that had troubled British politics since 1689 had not quite disappeared, but glowed ever more fitfully and feebly.

There was a widespread expectation that peace with France would provide only a breathing space. Tension soon rose between France and Britain in North America. Along the eastern coast, settlers from Britain had created a chain of thirteen colonies containing more people of European descent than any comparable area of America. Economically and socially diverse, and growing rapidly, these vigorous plantations were spreading inland from the seaboard. To the north and west, however, France had laid claim to a vast arc of territory stretching from the St Lawrence and the Great Lakes down the Mississippi to the Gulf of Mexico. Far more thinly settled than the British colonies on the east coast, the arc for much of its length consisted of little more than a chain of recently established and widely spaced forts and trading posts. But the French were busy strengthening their position and in 1754–5 they defeated two attacks in the Ohio valley, leading west to the Mississippi. The French increasingly recognized the importance of overseas commercial and colonial resources to the maintenance of their strength in Europe, just as wise British politicians had long perceived that European alliances were essential to the secure pursuit of overseas commercial and imperial aims.[7]

In March 1754, Henry Pelham died and his elder brother Newcastle succeeded him at the head of the ministry. An attempt to intercept French reinforcements going to Canada failed in 1755. A more general attack on French maritime commerce got under way. Newcastle was anxious not to get involved in full-scale war with France before completing arrangements to contain her in Europe, and above all to make Hanover safe. Maria Theresa, obsessed by hopes of recovering Silesia, understandably regarded Frederick II as her chief enemy. Newcastle, in a dramatic new initiative, turned instead to Russia. Hostile to Prussia, she promised in September 1755 powerful assistance in case of an attack on Britain or Hanover. This in turn persuaded Frederick II of Prussia to accept the Convention of Westminster in January 1756. Britain and Prussia guaranteed each other's dominions against attack and undertook to resist the entry of foreign troops into Germany. This removed the threat to Hanover from an aggressive Prussia, but as a direct result Maria Theresa made a defensive alliance with France in May 1756, and a new agreement with Russia in January 1757. Thus the 'Diplomatic Revolution' was accomplished. Britain declared war on France in May 1756, launching the Seven Years War (1756–63). A French expedition landed on Minorca, which it captured in June. Fresh losses in America and India followed.

Newcastle needed a strong leader in the Commons. He chose Henry Fox, previously secretary at war, who became secretary of state in November 1755. Fox's rival William Pitt, a ruthlessly ambitious politician and former 'patriot' critic of Walpole, but also since 1746 an exceptionally honest and able pay-master-general of the forces, was dismissed the same month after his attacks on leading ministers. Then the disasters of 1756 resulted in the resignations of both Newcastle and Fox. The king's reluctant choice of the duke of Devonshire in partnership with Pitt as secretary of state proved a failure. The ministry was too narrowly based and Pitt's health broke down. In June and July 1757 a more inclusive and enduring ministry was constructed, headed by Newcastle, in which Pitt again served as secretary of state and the chief director of strategy. His stance as a unifying 'patriot' was designed to appeal to a broad spectrum of public opinion, spanning both Whigs and Tories.

In July 1757 the French defeated a largely Hanoverian army under Cumberland at Hastenbeck. Cumberland capitulated in September and Hanover became neutral. After this long-feared humiliation, Frederick II saved Britain's inter-ests in Germany with an astonishing series of brilliant victories over French, Austrian and Russian forces in 1757–8. Frederick, supported by hefty British subsidies, nevertheless found it hard to hold out against relentless Austrian and Russian pressure. Ferdinand of Brunswick, commanding an allied army that included a substantial British contingent, won a signal victory over the French at Minden in August 1759.

Britain's most dramatic successes were achieved outside Europe. In an unprec-edented run of successful operations she stripped France of nearly all her over-seas empire: Canada (1758–60), several French West Indian islands (1759–62) and Gorée on the west African coast (1758). The French and their allies, defeated in Bengal (1757) and south-eastern India (1760), lost Pondicherry, their main base in India, in 1761. French commerce was severely disrupted. In August and November 1759 French fleets from the main bases of Toulon and Brest were defeated off Lagos in Portugal and Quiberon respectively. In 1761 the island of Belle-Île off the coast of France itself was taken. After the achieve-ment of a satisfactory Anglo-Spanish trade treaty in 1750, Spain had remained neutral during the war. But now she viewed British successes with growing anxiety, resented British interference with neutral trade and declared war in December 1761. In 1762 Britain captured both Havana and Manila.

Isolation in Europe, domestic disarray and the loss of the thirteen colonies

George II died in October 1760. His grandson George III immediately made clear his desire for peace. Pitt resigned in 1761 after failing to gain his col-leagues' agreement to a pre-emptive attack on the Spanish treasure fleet. Pitt's powerfully persuasive parliamentary oratory and unswerving purpose had made a crucial contribution to victory that complemented Newcastle's role as financial organizer. Newcastle followed, resigning in May 1762 after arguing in vain for the continuation of Frederick II's subsidy. Back in January 1762 the succession of Frederick's ardent admirer Tsar Peter II had prepared the way for peace between Prussia and Russia. Frederick was able to keep Silesia in his own subsequent peace with Austria, but resented what he regarded as a British betrayal.

Peace with France was the main issue of 1762. An attempt to retain all Britain's recent gains would have prolonged the war. By the Peace of Paris (February 1763) France got back her most prized sugar islands and, for exclusively commercial use, her bases in parts of India that Britain now controlled. Britain gained Canada and Louisiana east of the Mississippi, as well as Florida from Spain and recovered Minorca. The 'Seven Years War' had given many in the two kingdoms a strong sense of shared involvement, not least through the raising of several Scottish regiments to serve in the British army.[8] It had been by far the most spectacularly successful war presided over by any British monarch, but also the most expensive. The peace was generally welcome.

George III gloried 'in the name of Briton'. He married a German, Charlotte of Mecklenburg-Strelitz, but unlike his two predecessors never visited Hanover. He cherished an image of himself as 'patriot king'. He would be above party, an enemy of corruption. Politics under his benign rule would be inclusive not divisive: he would be a king for Tories as well as Whigs, Scots as well as Englishmen. His earliest adviser was his tutor, John Stuart, earl of Bute, son of the sister of the Campbell dukes of Argyll, who replaced Newcastle as prime minister in 1762. Tory gentlemen were glad to be brought in from the cold. George's vision nevertheless failed to generate enthusiasm in the political nation. Bute, the first Scots prime minister, predictably attracted scurrilous Scottophobia on top of bitter criticism from those who claimed that the peace had betrayed British interests. Although he enjoyed a strong position in the Commons, Bute, ill and dismayed, resigned in April 1763.

Four more short-lived ministries ensued before the re-establishment of a lasting administration in 1770. The reliance of the first two Georges on 'old corps' Whigs had resulted in a continuity of government unique in post-Elizabethan English history. By 1762, Walpole and the Pelhams had headed, or been leading partners in, governments for forty years, with only two brief interruptions. But the final disappearance of the dynastic threat, George III's distinctive preferences and the way a successful but stupendously costly war had ended all contributed to factionalism in the 1760s. Pitt and Newcastle, surviving embodiment of old Whiggery, had been affronted by the peace. Bute and the 'king's friends' remained lasting sources of suspicion.

George Grenville, Pitt's brother-in-law, had held office under both Newcastle and Bute, whom he succeeded as prime minister in 1763. Sound, thrifty and effective in the Commons, Grenville had a poor relationship with the king, partly because of his suspicions that Bute was continuing to exercise a malign influence. In 1765, with the help of his uncle Cumberland, George picked the marquess of Rockingham to replace Grenville, heading a largely inexperienced ministry whose only substantial member was Newcastle. Rockingham too became obsessed with Bute's influence, and the behaviour of 'king's friends' who had opposed or failed to support his repeal of Grenville's Stamp Act. George turned in July 1766 to William Pitt, who became earl of Chatham. His deteriorating health made Chatham ineffective. He resigned in October 1768. The duke of Grafton, already acting prime minister, succeeded him. But once Chatham had recovered, he attacked the ministry's measures, thus provoking the resignation of 'Chathamites' within it, and as a result of theirs, that of Grafton himself. The short lives of ministries during the 1760s were not primarily due to the challenges they faced in Britain and overseas, nor to problems in managing parliament, or to electoral reverses, but to difficulties with the king and lack of internal cohesion or leadership. The appointment in January 1770 of the experienced, competent, well-liked and widely trusted Lord North[9] at last inaugurated a new period of ministerial stability.

Chatham's criticism of the Grafton ministry in 1769 had included its handling of three issues: the resurgence of French power, the Middlesex election of 1768 and the grievances of Britain's American colonies. Genoa, faced with a formidable rebellion in Corsica, allowed France to take over the island in 1768–9. Britain's problems in America precluded her doing anything to prevent this, but the rebel leader Pasquale Paoli became a popular hero in London.

In the general election of 1768, Middlesex returned John Wilkes at the top of the poll. Son of a rich London distiller, previously member for Aylesbury, satirist and rake, Wilkes first became notorious for his scurrilous attacks on Bute in his paper *The North Briton*. Wilkes characterized Scots as poor, rapacious and conceited parasites, a nation of tyrants and slaves. He tried to defend the English identity from being submerged in the British one adopted by the king.[10] Shortly after Bute's 1763 resignation, in Number 45 of the paper, he attacked the 'ministerial effrontery' responsible for the king's speech defending the recent peace. A general warrant was issued for the arrest of all involved in the paper's production. (This raised a separate issue: such general warrants were subsequently judged illegal.) Wilkes pleaded parliamentary privilege, but the Commons decided that it did not cover seditious libel. Facing another prosecution, for his obscene 'Essay on Woman', Wilkes fled to France, was outlawed and expelled from the Commons. He returned from impoverished exile in 1768. His libertarian rhetoric appealed to Middlesex's exceptionally large suburban electorate, helping to ensure his election. He surrendered himself into custody, but this caused riots and demonstrations, at one of which Scots grenadiers killed about a dozen participants. Wilkes made a libellous attack on Lord Weymouth for authorizing the use of troops. The Commons thereupon resolved to expel him again. The electors confirmed their choice three times, but the Commons ultimately resolved that his election was invalid. Their resolutions raised the fundamental issue of electors' rights and provoked a spate of petitions from across the country. The affair greatly stimulated public interest in parliamentary debates, and led, in 1771, to a last, ill-advised, attempt to prevent their being reported. Wilkes himself eventually emerged from prison. In 1774 he took his seat as MP for Middlesex after the election, and went on to become lord mayor of London.

Vastly more serious was the discontent of the American colonies, rumbling ominously in the background from 1763 onwards. The grievances of the colonists and the Middlesex electors both, though in very different ways, called in question aspects of the exercise of parliamentary sovereignty. Wilkes became hugely popular in America. Americans in London tried in 1769 to link their cause with his. There had been previous attempts to strengthen the authority and control of central governments over the American colonies, most controversially by James II. The recent war had involved an unprecedented commitment of British military resources to North America. To ministers it seemed only fair that the thirteen colonies should shoulder a larger share of the cost of their defence. (It was unfortunate that this argument was being made at precisely the moment when the cession of neighbouring French territories had given them a new security.) Many colonists objected to the fiscal measures chosen for this purpose: Grenville's Sugar Act and his Stamp Act, demanding stamps on legal documents and newspapers (1764–5). These acts did not place heavy burdens on the colonists. Enforcement of the Stamp Act nevertheless led to widespread riots. Rockingham had it repealed, in face of the king's misgivings, but this concession was followed by the Declaratory Act (1766), declaring that the king had the authority, with Parliament's consent, to make laws binding the colonies, and the imposition of duties on a variety of imported goods (1767), which were expected to prove more acceptable than internal taxes. During the war, efforts had been made to co-ordinate action by the colonies against the French. Now each fresh London initiative led to measures concerted between them. The representatives of nine colonies meeting in the Stamp Act Congress in New York in 1765 adopted a Declaration of Rights and Liberties. In 1769 colonial merchants responded to the new duties by agreeing not to import British goods. In 1770, all the duties were repealed save for those on tea. A pattern was established in which the government modified or withdrew measures when they provoked opposition, and sought some new expedient, all the time continuing to insist on the underlying principle of parliamentary taxation of the colonies. A grievance second only to the fiscal exactions was the billeting of British troops in public houses authorized by the Quartering Act of 1765. The American resistance to taxation without representation and to billeting of troops echoed the English Petition of Right of 1628.

The colony of Massachusetts took a leading role in organizing resistance, and its main town, Boston, saw the most dramatic incidents in the growing conflict – the 'Massacre' of some inhabitants in a brawl with soldiers in 1770, and the destruction of tea in the 'Tea Party' of 1773. North's administration determined to punish Massachusetts by tightening control over its government and closing the port of Boston. Measures aimed at one colony provoked nearly all the others into meeting in the First Continental Congress at Philadelphia in September 1774. In April 1775 the first clashes between British and colonial troops occurred near Boston. The Continental Congress of thirteen colonies declared the independence of the United States in July 1776.

British troops had to evacuate Boston in March 1776. Later that year, however, General Howe took New York, and the aim for 1777 was to cut off New England by taking control of the river Hudson. The surrender at Saratoga of General Burgoyne, marching from Canada to meet Howe, was a relatively small defeat in terms of the numbers involved, but crucial in that it encouraged France to enter the war on the side of the United States in February 1778. Spain followed her in June 1779. The war would now be vastly more expensive both in weight of taxes and in the disruption of British commerce. At first, however, British forces made considerable progress in gaining control of the southern colonies between 1778 and 1780. Not until the autumn of 1781 did General George Washington, with crucial French military and naval support, manage to seal off Lord Cornwallis's army at Yorktown in Virginia and bring about what turned out to be the decisive British surrender of the war. A motion to end the war was carried in the Commons in February 1782, followed less than a month later by North's resignation.

During the previous century Britain had never fought France without European allies. This time she found herself isolated. The seeming instability of British politics during the 1760s, and the lack of consistency and firmness in foreign policy, had created a bad impression in Europe. But the basic problem was that no power had a strong incentive to enter a close alliance with Britain.[11] On the other hand, France, intent on re-assertion of her position as a global commercial and imperial power, had ceased to pose an immediate threat to her mainland European neighbours. A French alliance seemed more useful to Austria than a British one. A Russian alliance (1764) guaranteed Frederick II's security far more effectively than a connection with Britain. An alliance between Britain and Russia herself had attractions for both sides, but proved elusive. Britain was particularly reluctant to become involved in the Russo-Turkish war of 1768–74, though she made it possible for Russia to send warships through the Channel to the eastern Mediterranean in 1769–70. Spain, like France, had lost territory to Britain. The two countries reached the brink of war in 1770 in a dispute over the Falkland Islands that was provisionally settled without being properly resolved. In the early 1770s both France and Britain considered the possibility of a rapprochement, especially when Prussia, Austria and Russia joined in the unscrupulous First Partition of Poland in 1772. However, a French backed *coup d'état* by Gustav III of Sweden the same year complicated the situation. Britain's difficulties in America soon created temptations too strong for France to resist.

Early in 1780 Russia declared armed neutrality, in order to prevent Britain from seizing neutral cargoes destined for her enemies. Nearly all the other non-belligerent coastal powers eventually joined her. Britain particularly resented Dutch refusal of assistance, adoption of armed neutrality and dealings with the Americans. At the end of 1780 she declared war on the Dutch Republic. Britain now faced simultaneously a formidable rebellion by her most populous colonies, an alliance of her foremost ancient enemies and a hostile Europe. Yet an attempt to invade England in 1779 failed, as did the 1779–83 siege of Gibraltar. Despite some setbacks, Britain held her own in India and the Caribbean, where Admiral Rodney convincingly overcame the French in the Battle of the Saints in April 1782. Britain also inflicted crushing defeat on the Dutch.

This great struggle was not the outcome of measures lightly taken by a ministry out of touch with opinion in its own country. On the contrary: North's government enjoyed a solid majority in parliament. American affairs were barely an issue in the election of 1774. North gained an adequate majority in 1780. The Association movement, started in Yorkshire in 1779, presented North with his biggest extra-parliamentary challenge. Yet its concerns were waste and inefficiency, and the need for domestic reform, not the government's policy towards America. To some, North seemed almost to have leant over backwards in his efforts to conciliate the colonies. Alternative policies proposed by Chatham and Edmund Burke in the 1770s seemed vague or impractical. The outbreak of war revealed that opinion in Britain was divided. There were addresses in support of the war and petitions against it. The latter did not, however, express clear support for the colonists' constitutional case. France's entry into the war made it even more difficult to reconcile pro-American opinions with patriotism. Loyalist sentiments were loudly and vigorously expressed in Scotland.[12]

Ireland's reaction to the war was different. Irish Protestant 'patriots' seized the opportunity presented by Britain's difficulties to press for the removal of limitations on Irish trade and then the restoration of the Irish parliament's right to initiate legislation. They succeeded in these aims in 1780 and 1782. Meanwhile, both the Irish and British parliaments passed in 1778 different acts improving the status of Roman Catholics. This comparatively limited legislation provoked the darkest forces in the British psyche. Riots took place in Scotland in 1779, followed by five terrifying days of pillage and destruction in London during the Gordon Riots of June 1780.

Britain made peace at Paris in 1783. She still had a substantial army in America and the support of a considerable minority of loyalists, and was holding her own against France and Spain. The terms agreed with the United States were generous, some felt unnecessarily so. Relatively small concessions were made to America's allies. All those who envied Britain's previous wealth and success or resented her maritime dominance and overbearing diplomacy nevertheless rejoiced at what they saw as her humiliation.

Could the loss of America have been avoided? How big a setback was it for Britain? It is clear in retrospect that British government interference in the thirteen colonies after 1760 started the movement towards formal independence. Americans were already used to a large measure of self-government. In order to become a nation they needed a larger sense of shared identity. In response to the imperial government's demands, Americans developed a new framework for common action, and aspirations that became well nigh impossible for Britain to satisfy save by means of some looser form of association between mother country and colonies. British statesmen never worked this out as a practical proposition. It is hard to believe that a British victory over the colonies once war had been joined could have formed the basis of a lasting settlement. The old relationship had gone forever.

As early as 1765 the French minister Choiseul had rightly foreseen a 'revolution' in America, though he had not expected it so soon. Choiseul also believed that the loss of America would make England so weak that Europe would have no more need to fear her.[13] In that he was wide of the mark. Britain was to benefit hugely from her established commercial links with the expanding United States, remaining their principal supplier of manufactured goods until well into the nineteenth century. During the 1780s, despite her recent humiliating defeat and a stupendous national debt, Britain's economic expansion accelerated. Scotland shared in an exhilarating boom. France, on the other hand, did not gain much from the new nation's commercial independence. Her government tottered under the burden of a debt far smaller than Britain's. Six years after the Treaty of Paris came the cataclysm of the French Revolution.

17

'THIS MIXTURE OF MONARCHICAL, ARISTOCRATICAL AND DEMOCRATICAL POWER'[1]

Monarchy, parliament and parties

All subsequent British monarchs owed their succession to the rejection of James II and his son in 1689. In 1702 James's daughter Anne took the throne that but for the revolution would have been her young half-brother's as James III. A larger number of Catholic descendants of James VI and I had to be set aside to enable George I to succeed. George nevertheless insisted that he succeeded by hereditary right. He firmly rejected the view that parliament had given him the kingdom.[2] Although for the most part he was content to work within the constitutional limitations established since 1688, he pushed against them in pursuing his Hanoverian ambitions during the early years of his reign.[3] George was personally fair, committed to justice, equity and religious toleration. His son George II was a shrewd ruler, interested in government, though he was rather less intelligent than his father, and more irascible, and sometimes chafed under the constitutional limitations on his authority. William Pitt, whose relationship with him was often difficult, nonetheless claimed that 'among many other royal and manly virtues, he possessed justice, truth, and sincerity, in an eminent degree'. George III, idealistic but inexperienced in 1760, was a benevolent king who would become the most popular of the Hanoverians. Between 1714 and 1780, Britain was fortunate in having three conscientious and usually prudent monarchs who were assiduous in government and respected the constitution. Royal Hanoverian concerns were a source of recurrent and sometimes acrimonious debates and disagreements. However, despite the wilful exaggerations of opposition rhetoric, those concerns never threatened British religion and liberties in the way that Stuart policies had so often seemed to do.[4]

The royal household, though greatly reduced in size, remained politically important for much of this period. Various court offices, above all those of lord chamberlain, groom of the stole and gentleman of the bedchamber, still gave privileged access to the monarch. Courtiers were an important group in both houses of parliament, though several other considerations besides political advantage influenced their appointments. The court had lost much of its previous magnificence. Anne maintained royal ceremony and etiquette, but Prince George's death in 1708 and her increasing physical infirmity blighted her court. George I hated formality and had no interest in the trappings of majesty. Frequent receptions – assemblies, levees and drawing rooms – allowed courtiers, loyal politicians and the upper classes access to the Hanoverian monarchs. However, George III 'was the first British monarch to make a distinction between his court and his home, between his public and his private life'. He used St James's Palace for business and public social functions, but shared his family life with a comparatively restricted group of courtiers and guests in his other residences.[5]

The privy council had lost its advisory functions to a much smaller 'cabinet council' or 'cabinet'. The 'cabinet' gradually became identified with the more important ministers. Fewer still had frequent access to the king in his private 'closet'. The most regular visitors early in George III's reign were the first lord of the treasury, the secretaries of state, the leader of the Commons and the secretary at war. The monarch guarded the right to see ministers separately as well as together. The leading ministers also met apart from the monarch. By the late 1730s this 'effective' cabinet met once a week. The chief British royal advisers were with few exceptions men who had served in parliament. George I brought some Hanoverian ministers with him to England, especially Baron Bernstorff, who advised him both on Baltic policy and, unconstitutionally, on British patronage. However, after 1719, when George's main Hanoverian aims had been achieved, the role of his German advisers in Britain was much less important. The third earl of Bute was the other royal adviser who owed his political influence to an extra-parliamentary role: that of tutor, mentor and courtier to George III as Prince of Wales. Despite his undeniable gifts and good intentions Bute's influence certainly contributed to the instability of governments during the 1760s.

All monarchs insisted on the fundamental principle that they were free to choose their ministers. They had to compromise, often under protest. They had to include men they would have preferred to omit, or exclude men they would have liked to include. Anne struggled against an overweening Whig Junto, George I faced the resignation of Walpole when he dismissed Townshend, George II was forced to part with Carteret and found he could not do without Pitt and it took George III ten years to find a satisfactory and congenial prime minister. Patronage was a perennial source of disagreement between monarchs and ministers.

After 1689 it was never again possible to conduct government without annual meetings of parliament. The House of Lords included the English peers

(190 in 1720, 189 in 1780), twenty-six prelates and sixteen Scottish representative peers. After the Union there were 558 seats in the Commons, 122 for counties, 436 for cities, boroughs, Scottish burghs and universities. Many boroughs contained few voters and were controlled by a single landowner or the crown. No town was granted parliamentary representation between Charles II's reign and 1832. In 1715 there were between 330,000 and 340,000 English and Welsh voters and 2,600 Scottish ones. The king's ministers had to be able to command majorities in the House of Commons. Around 1750 there were rather fewer than forty ministers, junior ministers and civil servants. However, there were also some fifty court and household officials, forty-five holders of sinecures, ten crown pensioners and sixty officers in the armed services. The support of this larger group of over 160 placemen was important to government, but could not be taken for granted. They needed careful management. A large number of MPs were dependants or relatives of peers.[6]

The emergence of the first lord of the treasury as 'prime minister' was due above all to his being allowed control of the lion's share of crown patronage, particularly revenue department posts which, though not tenable by members of parliament themselves, could be given to their relatives and friends. The longest serving and most effective prime ministers sat in the Commons, where they gave strong and visible leadership. But all administrations largely consisted of peers who were expected to strengthen the government by wielding their influence on its behalf.

The 1716 Septennial Act deplored the election expenses and 'violent and lasting heats and animosities among the subjects of this realm' that the limitation of parliaments to three years in 1694 had caused. There were only eleven general elections in the sixty-five years 1715–80, the same number as during the twenty-five years 1689–1714. Elections hardly ever led directly to a government's downfall, though in 1741 losses at the polls combined with the defection of previous allies in parliament made Walpole's position untenable. Ministries were far more stable and enduring than before 1716.

The existence of two political parties rested on contrasting ideologies. The Whigs were committed to the Hanoverian succession. They upheld 'revolution principles' to varying degrees. The most important of these were that the monarchy was limited by law and existed for the benefit of its subjects. The principle of hereditary succession was 'just but not inviolable'. All men enjoyed certain natural rights, as John Locke had argued: life, liberty and property. All men had the right to resist manifest tyranny. However, these principles did not imply a belief in political equality. Men were naturally unequal in intelligence and strength. This had inevitably resulted in an unequal distribution of property, whose possession was the essential qualification for active citizenship. Its pre-eminent form was land, but Whigs were prepared to allow moneyed men some role in the political arena. Whigs differed in the extent to which they endorsed Locke's theory of an original contract. Many never accepted it, and only a radical minority claimed that such a contract had ever been made by universal consent. Whigs subscribed to the ideal of a mixed government. Monarchy, aristocracy and democracy were combined and balanced in Britain's sovereign legislature. So long as parliament represented property adequately, most Whigs were not much concerned about the shortcomings of the distribution of seats. The legislature must, however, be free of undue popular pressure. To their critics, who often included resentful 'Country' members of their own party, the Whig oligarchs seemed to have abandoned their principles through their exploitation of patronage, the practice of 'corruption' and the use of court influence to swing elections.[7]

The Tories' greatest weakness after 1714 was the perception that they were Jacobites at heart, or at the very least ambivalent in their attitude to the reigning dynasty. The behaviour of some leading Tories in 1715 had confirmed suspicions about their loyalty, and a small minority were active Jacobites in the 1740s. However, many Tories were firm for Hanover both before and after 1714. Others, who may have hankered after Stuart rule, had no intention of doing anything to bring it about. The Stuarts' Catholicism was a major obstacle to Tory support for them. History showed the danger of trusting a Catholic monarch's promises to protect the Church. Loyalty to the Church was the core principle of eighteenth-century Toryism. During Anne's reign 'the Church in danger' became an increasingly potent rallying cry for Tories obsessed with the threats from religious nonconformity and heterodoxy. George I and George II might be preferable to James III, but the Church seemed to be in danger of emasculation by their Whig ministers. The Whigs also removed or modified some of the handicaps from which Protestant dissenters suffered. Systematic exclusion of Tories from a wide range of offices after 1714 may have led some to change their political loyalties. Yet it also enhanced the solidarity of the excluded and their sense of identity. Its reversal by George III in his attempt to escape the old political framework helped to disperse the Tory party.[8]

Party discipline was relatively weak. Splits, first among the Tories, then the Whigs, occurred even during the years between 1708 and 1720 when partisan feeling was strongest. Most oppositions drew on the support of Whigs, including men who hoped to gain a place in government. All the Country issues that had inspired opposition to ministries before 1707 arose at various times thereafter: placemen, standing armies, ministerial corruption and rising taxes, together with foreign policies involving costly European commitments rather than reliance on naval power to promote Britain's overseas interests. Several of these issues brought Tories and opposition Whigs into temporary co-operation, but fundamental differences of principle precluded a longer-term alliance.

After 1714, the Tories formed a dwindling minority of the bishops and temporal peers in the Lords. For a long time, however, they remained a cohesive force in the Commons. Supported by a substantial proportion of the electorate (a majority in 1722, 1734 and 1741), they did relatively well in the largest constituencies, but held a far smaller share of seats because of the deployment of government influence and the large number of 'pocket' borough seats. They had substantial support among the gentry, the county freeholders, the lower clergy, and urban traders and craftsmen.[9]

The end of the Jacobite threat, George III's inclusive attitude to the Tories and his determination to diminish the crown's reliance on 'old corps' Whigs resulted in political re-alignment and new strands of opposition. The marquess of Rockingham, prime minister in 1765–6, thereafter led the largest Whig opposition group. It opposed the alleged 'secret influence' of the 'king's friends', and advocated more conciliatory treatment of the American colonies, together with 'economical reform' to end wasteful expenditure, redundant offices and the use of government patronage to control the Commons. In the Irishman Edmund Burke it had a powerful parliamentary spokesman, particularly on America, but it comprised only a small minority of peers and MPs.

More radical was the Bill of Rights Society, including a few MPs, formed in 1769 to support John Wilkes. Its aims included shorter parliaments, fairer parliamentary representation and measures against bribery. The onset of the American War diminished support for radicalism, but setbacks helped revive calls for reform. Christopher Wyvill launched in December 1779 a petition for economical reform to curb waste and corruption supported by Yorkshire country gentlemen, a move soon copied in other counties. In March 1780 a London meeting of county and borough deputies, instigated by Wyvill, agreed to form an association to promote the addition of 100 county MPs and annual parliaments. (The association later chose triennial parliaments.) Rockingham's second ministry achieved some economical reforms in 1782, but a limited parliamentary reform bill failed in 1785.[10]

Whig dominance, infrequent elections and the relatively few electoral contests diminished parliament's role as an arena for battles between rival ideologies. However, it passed an unprecedented quantity of legislation. Besides general measures such as those relating to law reform, punishment of crime, relief of religious minorities, economic regulation and colonial government there were vast numbers of local and private acts. Parliament remained, as it had been since before 1500, the forum for the resolution of conflicts of interest between manufacturing and commercial pressure groups, now more numerous than ever before.

Revenues, debts, defence and government

Parliament's most important function so far as the strength of the state was concerned was to vote the taxes necessary to service existing debt and meet the growing burden of expenditure. Britain's revenue possibly more than doubled between 1712 and 1782, from £5,830,000 to £12,900,000. But the estimated national income rose from £60,770,000 to £118,290,000 between 1712 and 1782, so that the total revenue as a proportion of national income rose only slightly, from nearly 10 to nearly 11 per cent. (Between 1685 and 1707, however, England's revenue had quadrupled, and risen from around 3 per cent of national income to 11 per cent.) The growth of the national income helps to explain why there was not more opposition to the growth in taxes, which provided well over 90 per cent of the revenue throughout. The eighteenth century saw a shift from direct taxes, above all the land tax, to indirect taxes, especially excises. As a proportion of all taxes, direct taxes fell from around 50 per cent in the 1690s to about 20 per cent in the 1730s. They briefly rose again to 30 per cent in the 1740s. Commissions appointed by county MPs supervised the collection of the land tax. No searching assessment of individual wealth by government was involved. Various other taxes either increased, or newly introduced, between 1740 and 1783, were designed to fall on people of some wealth, but not just on landowners. They included house and window duties, taxes on coaches, servants and glassware, licence and stamp duties. In the 1720s revenue collection occupied the majority of the estimated total of 12,000 government employees. The Excise employed more men than all the other revenue departments put together. It was noted for its outstanding probity and efficiency, which was a major argument for raising new taxes in the form of excises. After 1720, excises nearly always raised more than 40 per cent of the revenue, and sometimes more than 50 per cent; customs duties never more than 30 per cent.[11]

During wars, revenue always fell far short of government expenditure. In 1714 the British public debt stood at just over £40,000,000. Thereafter it rose to some £160,000,000 by 1780. The proportion of the revenue devoted to debt repayment fluctuated between a third and a half for most of the period 1707–83, reaching peaks of nearly 60 per cent in 1716 and 66 per cent in 1783. As Queen Anne's treasurers, Godolphin and Harley increased the portion of the overall debt that was funded from about 30 per cent to about 75 per cent. It seldom fell below 90 per cent after 1720. Each war brought a rapid increase in the amount of short-term debt, which governments subsequently set about converting into long-term obligations. The development of the market in government securities was crucial to the success of the state's long-term borrowing. Creditors' ability to sell their claims hugely reduced the potential demand for early repayment. After 1713, governments, hitherto dependent on fixed-term and therefore inflexible forms of debt, increasingly resorted to loans without a set repayment date. (In 1722 many fixed-term annuitants were induced to take rising South Sea Company stock in exchange for their securities. The stock's subsequent collapse was to administer a severe short-term shock to the financial system, but the aim of reducing the fixed-term debt had been achieved.) Walpole had some success in temporarily reducing the principal of the debt during the 1720s and 1730s. Henry Pelham skilfully achieved between 1749 and 1757 a reduction in the rate of interest payable on much of the debt. But the overall debt continued to rise.[12]

The number of investors in public debt grew from 10,000 in 1709 to 60,000 in 1756, not counting the many individuals who invested indirectly through banks, companies and other bodies. The state's creditors formed a substantial body of stakeholders in the existing regime's continued stability. Their interest, well represented in parliament, helped somewhat to offset possible opposition to rising taxes. Government funds came to be regarded as a secure form of investment, a sort of insurance that encouraged individuals with the necessary resources to complement their stake in the public debt with riskier investments elsewhere.[13]

Revenue growth was required above all to pay for Britain's armed forces and their operations. The navy was seen to be essential to the defence of Britain and the protection of her commerce, and Britain's prime means of inflicting damage on her foes. Unlike a standing army, it was not perceived as a means of imposing domestic tyranny. Britain had 182 ships of 300 tons displacement and above in 1715, 171 in 1745 and 228 in 1780. Over 40,000 seamen were mustered annually in most wartime years before 1750. The numbers rose to some 82,000 by 1762 and 95,000 by 1782. The navy was the most costly element of Britain's defence apparatus because of the combination of skills and materials needed not only to build and equip the fleet but also to maintain it. Britain retained much more of her fleet in peacetime than did her continental rivals. By developing and expanding her six great dockyards, Britain enhanced her ability to prolong the life of her existing ships. A network of overseas bases enabled British ships to be deployed and supported far from home.[14]

The Admiralty was the crucial link between the government and the navy. Its head, the first lord, was usually a capable naval man as well as a member of the government. Promotion into and within the naval officer corps depended upon experience and proven competence as well as patronage. Naval recruitment was primarily voluntary, but impressment was also necessary, drawing on landsmen as well as some of the experienced seamen essential to fishing and commerce. The administrative continuity and long institutional memory of the Navy Board, responsible for shipbuilding and maintenance, made it somewhat resistant to admiralty interference. Britain's many civilian shipbuilders could, however, be used to supplement the efforts of royal dockyards when the navy needed to be expanded rapidly. The Victualling Board greatly improved its purchasing, processing and storing operations, providing much larger and more reliable supplies more cheaply, and reducing waste. The Ordnance Office supplied cannon to both navy and army. Its Board administered the specialist corps of Artillery and Engineers. The Royal Military Academy at Woolwich trained artillery officers from 1741 onwards.

Wartime armies under British command always included many foreign soldiers as well as 'subject troops' from Britain and Ireland. The average annual number of wartime 'army personnel' for which parliament voted ranged from 62,373 in 1739–48 to 108,484 in 1775–84, not including troops paid for by Ireland (24,000 in 1762). In addition, Britain also subsidized various allies. Numbers were sharply reduced in peacetime. Parliaments, regarding the army with greater suspicion than the navy, never supplied it adequately. However, the Hanoverian kings, advised by the Board of General Officers, took a close, well-informed and generally beneficial interest in their land forces. They regulated the sale of commissions and various aspects of pay and financial management, and enforced standard weapons drill. The British army gained renown for the speed and efficiency of its musket volleys.[15]

From 1713 annual Mutiny Acts authorized the maintenance of an army of given size as well as the administration of military discipline. By the later eighteenth century, a high proportion of British soldiers, both officers and men, came from Ireland or Scotland, particularly the Highlands. (Englishmen continued to dominate the upper ranks of the navy to a greater extent.) Recruitment of private soldiers was primarily voluntary. A series of wartime statutes empowered justices of the peace to conscript unemployed able-bodied men, but this was unpopular.

The militia's efficiency had gradually declined. Renewed fear of foreign invasion in the 1740s, and the militia's ineffectiveness during the Jacobite advance into England in 1745, led to calls for its revival for home defence. Britain was the only major European state without 'a fully organized citizen reserve' for the army. The necessary legislation, passed only in 1757, envisaged a force of 32,000 men, raised by parish ballot, who would serve a three-year term and train for twenty days a year. Further legislation tackled various popular grievances, and militias had been established in most English counties by 1762. Militia units guarded prisoners of war, watched the coast, combated smuggling and suppressed disorder.[16]

The internal directive role of central government had declined, but remained important. Issues that demanded action included the threat of plague in 1721, outbreaks of cattle disease, the prospect of dearth and vagrancy following the discharge of military personnel. The cabinet decided which London death sentences should be commuted, and kept metropolitan crime trends under review. Privy council and parliament undertook enquiries into various social and economic problems. The treasury made grants towards the transportation of criminals to America, measures to deal with London crime, the rebuilding of London debtors' prisons and (for a time) to the London Foundling Hospital. Pensions were paid to increasing numbers of aged and disabled soldiers and sailors.[17]

The framework of English and Welsh local government changed little between 1707 and 1780. The justices of the peace, parish vestries and the urban corporations remained the key elements of the structure, the justices of assize the vital links between centre and localities. The incidence of crime was probably far lower in the early eighteenth century than it had been a hundred years earlier, but it began to rise again after 1760, basically as a result of growing population pressure. Counties built bridges, court houses and gaols; prosecuted, guarded and fed prisoners; and dealt with vagrants. In 1750 the English counties may have spent about £58,000 on these services, by 1780 £148,000. The militia added to the burden on the counties, but the total amount of county taxation was a fraction of that raised by parishes, which were the prime agents of poor relief. In principle they were also responsible for road maintenance within their bounds.[18]

Various agencies were established after Union to assist the government of Scotland: a Court of Exchequer, the Boards of Excise, Customs and Police (all by 1714) and the Board of Trustees (1727), intended to promote economic development, set up in response to Scottish anger over the malt tax. These bodies provided a reservoir of patronage for the men who served as virtual viceroys of Scotland. The abolition of military tenures (1746) and heritable jurisdictions (1747) after the 1745 rebellion ended two distinctive features of Scotland's administrative system. Sheriff deputes appointed by the crown took charge of the sheriffs' courts. Their own deputies ('substitutes') were the main agents of local criminal law enforcement. Justices of the peace were concerned with the maintenance of highways and prisons, wages, vagrancy, and the appointment and supervision of customs and excise officers. County commissioners of supply chosen from among the justices increasingly exercised their more important powers, as well as raising the land tax. Kirk sessions remained responsible for poor relief, and began to raise funds by assessment.[19]

Urban government had developed in a haphazard way. About 156 English towns had both a municipal corporation and parliamentary representation; about twenty-four had a corporation but were not represented in parliament, and there were forty-seven parliamentary boroughs, many of them not true urban settlements at all, that had no corporation. Several towns, including such populous places as Birmingham, had neither corporation nor representation, and were governed by parish vestries and/or manorial courts. However, there was no great demand for the creation of new corporations. Corporate government was widely thought to result in restrictive regulation, maladministration and the enrichment of a small oligarchy.

Improvements, pressure groups and wider political participation

Eighteenth-century men of property, who consented to unprecedented levels of taxation for external defence, looked askance at any measure that threatened a new general tax for internal purposes. Hence the importance of local initiatives and the principle that those who benefited from improvements should pay for them. Groups of parishes combined to establish workhouses for the poor, authorized either by local acts or by a general statute of 1723. By 1770, 500 statutory trusts empowered to levy tolls administered 15,000 miles of turnpike road. The first turnpike act had been passed in 1663, but the great majority of the necessary acts were passed between 1750 and 1770. Harbours were constructed, improved and maintained. The first statutes authorizing the construction of canals were passed in 1755 and 1759, and interest reached rapidly grew thereafter. Numerous acts, especially after 1760, empowered improvement commissioners to levy rates for urban street paving and lighting. Subscription was regarded as the ideal means of raising money for charitable initiatives such as hospitals and schools for the poor, and was much more typical of the eighteenth century than foundation by individual benefactors. Participation by subscribers in organization and government was viewed as the best guarantee that money would not be embezzled or wasted. Five new medical hospitals were founded in London between 1720 and 1745, and twenty-two elsewhere in England by 1780. The Edinburgh Royal Infirmary was founded in 1729. Subscriptions helped to support various specialist institutions, of which the most famous was the Foundling Hospital, begun in 1739.[20]

Rather less than a fifth of the adult male population of early-eighteenth-century England could participate in elections. A far smaller fraction of the population had sufficient property to be eligible to stand for parliament. Vigorous extra-parliamentary activity that was in the broadest sense political was, however, frequent. Much of it was designed to achieve a parliamentary outcome. Freedom of speech and information were limited, yet unevenly, and could sometimes be exercised in striking fashion.

Various interest groups – religious, mercantile, industrial, Irish and colonial – lobbied MPs to secure the passage or repeal of legislation, using committees, agents and printed statements of their cases for action, increasingly in conjunction with propaganda addressed to a larger public. Constituents instructed their members of parliament, especially against the 1733 excise bill. Many petitions and addresses were presented to parliament. Major occasions included the campaigns of 1739–42 against Walpole's conduct of government, against the Jewish Naturalization Act of 1753 and of 1756 for an enquiry into the loss of Minorca. Huge numbers were involved in petitioning for Wilkes's restoration to the Commons in 1769, economical reform in 1780 and repeal of the Roman Catholic Relief Act in 1780. Opponents of turnpike projects petitioned against them. English weavers mounted a concerted campaign of petitions against the importation of foreign calicoes in 1721. Marches and petitions to king and parliament accompanied a massive sailors' strike in 1768.

Riots often accompanied or resulted from petitions and other forms of campaigning. Alternatively, such disturbances might be the only means of protest open to the politically defeated or excluded. In widespread disturbances during 1715–16 crowds voiced their hostility to George I. Individuals in authority sometimes approved of rioting for what they regarded as a good cause. There were frequent riotous protests against legislation planned or passed, including the 1733 excise scheme, the Gin Act (1736), the Militia Act (1757) and the Catholic Relief Act (1778). Some measures were modified or abandoned as a result of popular anger. Food riots in response to poor harvests, high prices and exports from the localities concerned occurred in 1709, 1740, 1756–7, 1766 and 1771–3. There were numerous riots against turnpikes. The Galloway 'levellers' made in 1724 the most concentrated attacks on enclosures that occurred in eighteenth-century Britain. There were scattered protests elsewhere. Textile workers attacked manufacturing machinery in several places between 1776 and 1779. The extension of the malt tax to Scotland provoked riots there in 1725. A smuggler's execution in Edinburgh in 1736 eventually led to the Porteous riots.[21]

The press facilitated and enhanced political participation in various ways. Increasing numbers of newspapers and journals supplied information. Reporting of parliamentary debates was forbidden in principle; however, between 1711 and 1737 reports were published during recesses so as to circumvent the prohibition, and thereafter in summarized or thinly disguised form. The Wilkes affair aroused such keen interest that several newspapers took the risk of carrying current reports. In 1771 an embarrassing conflict between the Commons and the London authorities caused by the attempted enforcement of the ban all but ended efforts to uphold it.

Journals and newspapers also provided opinions. Rival newspapers and journals either offered critical commentary on government policy or supported the ministry for much of Walpole's period in power. A further burgeoning of political commentary and a rapid increase in letters to the press accompanied the growth in the numbers of newspapers during the 1760s. The press also published campaigns by petition or instruction to MPs and served as a means of co-ordinating them.

Continental states: government, revenues and armed forces

For most of the eighteenth century the leading European states achieved considerable internal political stability. Religious differences, previously major sources of internal conflict and disruption, no longer posed a serious threat after the suppression of the last major Hungarian rebellion, partly motivated by Protestant grievances, in 1711.

The other leading monarchies of Europe differed from Britain's in being much less subject to constitutional limitations. None of them had to rule in co-operation with a powerful national assembly. The personality, ambitions and abilities of the monarch remained more important than in Britain. The most vigorous and capable monarchs were all rulers of states that had grown in power and importance since 1648: Peter I (1682–1725), Elizabeth (1741–62) and Catherine II (1762–96) of Russia, Frederick William I (1713–40) and Frederick II (1740–86) of Prussia, and Maria Theresa (1740–80) of Austria. All these rulers aimed to strengthen the institutions of their states, and some of them achieved significant territorial expansion.

Effective central co-ordination of the organs of government was a key aim of several eighteenth-century rulers. Government was partly remodelled on French lines in Philip V's newly centralized Spanish state. In other countries, administrative departments were largely brought under the control of a central Senate (Russia), or Directory (Prussia). In Austria a new State Chancery, Council of State and Supreme Judiciary were established under Maria Theresa. Lacking the close and longstanding links between centre and localities that England possessed in parliament and the assize circuits, continental monarchies established new institutions to oversee local administration. In Spain, Philip V's government copied French practice when it appointed intendants as the crown's local representatives. Prussian rulers appointed boards of councillors in the provinces, charged above all with tax collection, each one under the eye of a supervisory official who reported on its performance. Russian local administration was to develop on similar lines from the 1770s onwards. In Austria and Bohemia, Maria Theresa placed the numerous officials appointed by provincial assemblies under the supervision of crown deputations in 1748.

Estimates of the fiscal revenues of some European states produced in 1763 by French investigators, supplemented by fiscal historians' recent calculations, suggest that two great powers were pre-eminent. France still had the largest annual revenue of any European state, 321,000,000 livres, while Britain with 224,000,000 was some way behind. Next came Spain (131,800,000) followed by Austria (92,000,000), the United Provinces (possibly as low as 85,000,000) and Prussia (49,000,000, but growing rapidly).[22]

France's revenue was larger than Britain's. However, whereas France's population in 1750 was nearly three times greater than Britain's, the French state's revenue was much less than this. Whereas the estimated percentage of Britain's commodity output taken in taxation rose from 17 to 21 between 1715 and 1780, the French percentage thus taken was 11 per cent in 1715, reached a high point of 17 per cent in 1735 and fell back to 12 per cent by 1780. Saddled with a ramshackle fiscal machine, the French monarchy lacked the resolve to carry out necessary reforms. Its fiscal system was perceived as more unfair and oppressive than the British because of the various exemptions enjoyed by different groups and provinces, even though the actual tax burden on individuals was lighter than it was in Britain. Venal offices remained a drain on the budget and an obstacle to effective revenue maximization, though fewer were being sold after 1715. The French crown relied far more heavily on direct taxes than did the British. Collection of indirect imposts was leased to tax farmers in the 'general farm'. French indirect taxes were 'exceptionally heterogeneous and regionally varied', and some 40 per cent of them were levied at internal customs posts, which did not exist in Britain. The system was less transparent and accountable than its British counterpart. Government reliance on the tax farmers for loans was an additional obstacle to reform.[23]

The French government borrowed far less than the British. In effect, Britain's borrowing enabled her to narrow the natural resource gap between her and France. French governments had more difficulty in servicing their debt. They had to pay higher rates of interest than their British counterparts for various reasons, including their six defaults between 1715 and 1771, and their preference for fixed-term borrowing over perpetual securities. Debt service costs absorbed a higher proportion of tax revenues. France was also unable to match England in raising tax revenues for the purpose of servicing loans, partly because its fiscal system seemed less equitable.[24]

Various states achieved important fiscal successes during the eighteenth century. In Austria, the crown responded vigorously to the shock delivered by the loss of Silesia and persuaded most of the Austrian and Bohemian estates to make greatly enhanced contributions towards the support of the army, for longer periods. Brandenburg-Prussia succeeded in building up a substantial reserve before 1740 by staying at peace and improving the collection of income from established sources, including direct and indirect taxes and the royal domain, whose contribution to the crown's finances was much more important than in most other states. Then Frederick II got away with the seizure of Silesia, which already yielded 25 per cent of Austria's revenue, an amount soon to be increased by new efficiency. Overall Prussian revenue rose nearly sevenfold between 1710–14 and 1760–4. Both Austria and Prussia also needed British or French subsidies to fight the two mid-eighteenth-century wars; Prussia also wrung revenue from occupied Saxony. Spain increased tax income from her eastern provinces, and also benefited from longer periods of peace, though without achieving fundamental reforms. One state was no longer a major power after 1710. The United Provinces, the most heavily taxed state in Europe, with the largest public debt in proportion to income, experienced relative economic and demographic stagnation thereafter. Under these circumstances there was little scope for further tax increases.[25]

The eighteenth century saw major changes in the relative and absolute sizes of the armed forces of European states. Between 1720 and 1770, Britain had more ships of the line than the next two strongest naval powers combined. By 1775 France and Spain together possessed slightly more, but Britain outbuilt them during the American War. The French navy shrank between 1705 and 1720, but grew substantially between then and 1780. Administration remained weak. Britain was better at keeping its ships in service. In 1739 Britain had sixteen dry-docks in six dockyards, France three in three, with none in the West Indies before 1780. The French navy was slow to adopt important superior features of British shipbuilding and design. It was difficult for its scattered iron industry to provide the guns the navy needed, and its fleet also suffered from shortages of timber and masts. France had greater difficulty in manning its ships. Spain's was the most impressive naval revival of the eighteenth century. From an almost negligible force in 1715, her navy became the third largest in Europe by 1775, almost as large as France's. A succession of far-sighted navy ministers planned the expansion to protect Spain's empire and trade, and deter would-be aggressors. They developed dockyards and supporting industries, and established a naval college. English ship design was studied, and English and Irish shipwrights were enticed to Spain. Possible naval co-operation between the two Bourbon powers constituted the most serious threat to British maritime supremacy between 1730 and 1780. The Dutch navy shrank pretty steadily between 1710 and 1750. Both Denmark and Russia built up fairly sizeable fleets, though smaller than those of the three leading western powers. They posed no active threat to Britain.[26]

France's army, possibly 330,000 strong in 1756, was larger than any other apart from Russia's for most of this period. Notably successful in conquering the Austrian Netherlands in 1744–7, it nevertheless also suffered humiliating defeats, especially at the hands of Prussia. Subsequent reforms in discipline and organization, and improved artillery design, would bear fruit from the 1790s onwards. The fastest growing armies were those of Prussia and Austria. The Prussian forces possibly increased from 39,000 in 1710 to 80,000 by 1740 and 260,000 in 1760, an astonishing achievement given the disparity between French and Prussian resources. The key elements of Prussian military organization included selective conscription; regimental recruitment from assigned local areas; availability of recruits after basic training as reservists who served two or three months a year until retiring age; selection of cadets for the officer corps from the young sons of the nobility; their training in Berlin at the Cadet Corps School, and promotion according to merit as well as seniority. The army, more than any other institution, created a shared sense of identity in a state without natural frontiers. Frederick William I introduced standardized drill and equipment. The army achieved renown for its rate of fire, its combination of all arms in speedy and decisive attack, and its adroit performance of complex manoeuvres. Nevertheless, Prussia was mauled by formidable Russian forces in 1758–61, and only saved by Russia's withdrawal from war in 1762. Prussia's aggression forced Austria to re-organize and increase its own army. Possibly 108,000 strong in 1740, it grew to 201,000 by 1756. The artillery was standardized and improved; a corps of engineers was created in 1747; new drill regulations for the whole army were issued in 1749, and a military academy was opened in 1752. The crown increasingly took control of promotions, broadened the social basis of the officer corps and introduced decorations for military service in 1757. Maria Theresa's son Joseph II improved the organization of military units and, by 1772, introduced a cantonal system of recruitment controlled by the army rather than the local estates.[27]

Political dissent and the weakness of the state

For much of the eighteenth century Britain was unique in Europe in combining success in international competition with a balanced constitution that allowed for relatively wide and vigorous political participation. The other main countries with national representative institutions were declining powers. Poland's anarchic nobility had condemned it to military impotence. Russian intervention decided its last two royal elections, and in 1772 Russia, Prussia and Austria joined in the first of three partitions that would culminate in Poland's disappearance as an independent nation in 1795. In Sweden, after a constitutional revolution in 1719–20, the king had to rule with the advice of a council whose membership was largely controlled by the *Riksdag*, which was to meet every three years, legislate and raise taxes. Vigorous party conflict, largely concerned with foreign policy, was accompanied by electioneering and (from 1766) pamphlet warfare. Humiliating defeats abroad and instability at home ensured a wide welcome for Gustav III's seizure of power in 1772.

Most of the United Provinces remained without a stadholder after the death of William III in 1702. Against a background of economic problems, tensions between States party supporters and Orangists continued. A limited French invasion in 1747 precipitated a widespread popular rising reminiscent of 1672. The urban ruling class in general and tax farmers in particular were targets of widespread anger. The Orange stadholderate was restored, but the regime failed to satisfy popular hopes, and in the 1780s a new radical movement was to emerge.

France remained the leading European power, but its monarchy was weak. Louis XIV's last gruelling wars had ended in bloody stalemate, and the old king was widely blamed for the nation's suffering. Louis XV proved a timid ruler whose habitual indecisiveness encouraged rivalries among his ministers. The Seven Years War resulted in humiliating defeat for France. Broad agreement among his advisers that reforms were essential in order to enhance the efficiency of the state resulted in a series of initiatives by a succession of ministers, who were often abruptly replaced, further enhancing the impression of weakness and ineffectiveness.

Uniquely in eighteenth-century Europe, the principal vehicles of opposition to the crown were judicial authorities – the *parlements*. In 1715 the regent Orléans restored their right to remonstrate against laws before registration. In 1718 the *parlement* of Paris pointed out that, in the absence of the estates-general, it was the only channel by which the voice of the people could reach the king. Two main issues were to cause friction between the crown and the *parlements* during the eighteenth century. One was the enforcement of the papal bull *Unigenitus*, requested by Louis XIV and promulgated in 1713 in order to suppress Jansenist opinions in the French Church. This caused major confrontations between the crown and the *parlement* of Paris in 1730–2 and 1753–6. A second issue was the introduction of new direct taxes. In 1756 the provincial *parlements* supported the Paris judges in a show of solidarity. 'Radical remonstrances, judicial strikes, and the exile of judges became commonplace.' The entire Breton *parlement* resigned in 1765 in protest against the imposition of fresh fiscal burdens on its poor province. Louis XV replaced the *parlement* with a new court, but in 1769 the *parlement* was restored. In 1771 the chancellor finally took the drastic step of dividing the jurisdiction of the *parlement* of Paris, and turning the judges into salaried officials. He subsequently remodelled or abolished nearly all the provincial *parlements*. Yet after Louis XV's death in 1774, the old *parlements* were restored.[28]

The *parlements* published their remonstrances, showing awareness of the importance of public opinion. The government in turn published justifications of its measures. A torrent of hostile pamphlets greeted the 1771 attack on the sovereign courts. Meanwhile, a member of the Bordeaux *parlement*, the baron de Montesquieu, had published anonymously in 1748 an admired comparative account of different systems of government in his *L'Esprit des lois*. His definition of 'despotism' as the government of one man according to no law but his own caprice strongly influenced the *parlements'* rhetoric in conflict with the crown, and passed into common currency.

France's newspaper press expanded more slowly than England's. The English press bought 12,600,000 stamps in the year 1775, roughly equivalent to 242,300 newspapers a week, while in France, a much bigger country, weekly sales amounted to 90,000 at most in 1783–4. The vigorous and open debate carried on in the English press was absent in France, and news was far more tightly censored and controlled. News *did*, however, circulate, especially in Paris, through a variety of media: gossip, songs, poems, letters, manuscript newssheets, posters, satirical prints, pamphlets and books. Much of the information conveyed was coded or presented in allegorical form. Court scandal was prominent. The open debate and organization of political activity characteristic of the British press by the 1770s were impossible in France, but the revelations of the clandestine media contributed to a pervasive decline in respect for the monarchy.[29]

The most striking characteristic of Britain's political life in the eighteenth century compared with the seventeenth was its stability. This stability had several causes, including the readiness of her kings to work within the limitations of the constitution; their usual reliance on ministers skilful in parliamentary management; the length of parliaments and ministerial tenures; a broad continuity of policy; the confidence of a growing army of government creditors; the efficiency of her fiscal system; economic growth; and Britain's usual success in her foreign wars before 1776. It might seem that the monarchy's alliance with a Whig landowning oligarchy was rather a narrow basis for gaining the acquiescence of most British people. The Tory party was excluded from power and patronage under George I and George II even though it long retained the support of a substantial proportion of the electorate. However, despite the concentration of power in relatively few hands, the number of participants in some form of politics was far larger. There was enormous scope for a range of local initiatives. The existence of a vigorous public sphere depended on relative freedom of information, debate and agitation. Governments made repeated concessions to forcefully and publicly expressed opinions on issues that were important but not fundamental. Britain was unique in Europe in combining strong and effective government with public debate, vigorous popular politics and a sense of freedom.

18

RELIGION IN THE AGE OF REASON AND REVIVAL

The Church of England: problems of an established Church

The Act of Union created a state in which two distinct Churches were established as the 'official' Church in different parts of the kingdom. Britain's ruler, supreme governor of the Church of England, had no such position in Scotland's Presbyterian Kirk. This arrangement had no precise counterpart elsewhere in Europe.[1] However, though not in a unitary monarchy, some territories that had come together under one ruler were far more different from each other in religion than were England and Scotland. Frederick Augustus I of Saxony, who converted to Catholicism in 1697 in order to be elected to the Polish throne, remained elector of Lutheran Saxony, where he refrained from challenging the religious *status quo*. As we shall see, such English interference as there was in Scotland's religious affairs came not from the monarch, but from parliament. Rulers differed considerably in the degree of their personal commitment to national Churches. In England, Queen Anne was especially concerned for the Church's good. She set aside money from her ecclesiastical revenues to improve the incomes of the poorer clergy. The Lutheran George I, by contrast, felt no particular devotion to either of the British Churches. Lacking strong religious feelings of his own, he tried cautiously to promote toleration and to discourage partisan religious strife.

Anxiety about the preservation of the Church's authority generated a ferment of controversy in early-eighteenth-century England. The main forum for the expression of 'High-Church' fears was the Lower House of Convocation. The High Churchmen saw in Anne's reign a chance to curb religious dissent. The paramount concerns of moderate 'Low-Church' prelates were the Protestant succession, international Protestant unity in face of a continuing Catholic threat and avoidance of acrimonious controversy.

Protestant nonconformist sects formed a small but highly visible minority, disproportionately concentrated in towns, especially London. The High

Churchmen's principal target was 'Occasional Conformity' whereby dissenters, especially Presbyterians, might qualify for municipal office by receiving Communion in their parish church once in the year before election. Three bills to tackle the practice had failed in 1702–4. The Lords rejected in 1705 a motion that the Church was in danger. In 1709 the aggressive High Churchman Henry Sacheverell delivered before the London Corporation a sermon ferociously attacking toleration, occasional conformity, heresy and the Whigs. The government's decision to impeach him resulted in riotous attacks on dissenting meeting-houses. Jubilant crowds greeted Sacheverell on triumphal progress after his very mild punishment. Tory victory in the 1710 and 1713 elections resulted in an Occasional Conformity Act (1711) and a Schism Act (1714) designed to force dissenters' schools to close down.

George I's early ecclesiastical appointments tipped the balance against the High-Church party. In 1714 he promised to repeal the recent Tory measures. In Whig eyes the loyalty of High Churchmen was suspect, and their 'popish' desire for the independence of the Church posed a danger to the state. The radical Whig John Toland had identified the chief sources of mischief in the Church as *The Jacobitism, Perjury, and Popery of High-Church Priests* (1710).

Benjamin Hoadly, whom George I made bishop of Bangor (1716), shared Toland's apprehensions about Jacobite leanings among High Churchmen. He too detected 'popery' in the Church, especially in its claim to an infallible authority and denial of an individual right to interpret the Scriptures. In a 1717 sermon before the king Hoadly seemed to deny the scriptural basis for a visible Church authority as distinct from that of the state. The true Church was an invisible society whose membership was 'defined by sincerity alone, not by adherence to any particular doctrine or communion'. George I ordered that the sermon be printed. It stirred a vigorous polemical conflict, the 'Bangorian controversy', between 1717 and 1720.[2] In order to prevent Hoadly's condemnation by Convocation, George prorogued the assembly in 1717. Before 1780 it met only once more, in 1741, for a brief business meeting. The Schism and Occasional Conformity Acts were repealed in 1719. In 1722, Francis Atterbury, bishop of Rochester, a leading High-Church spokesman, was implicated in a Jacobite plot. His involvement, albeit brief, seemed to corroborate suspicions of High Churchmen's disloyalty. His exile by parliament in 1723 was a dramatic coda to twenty years of ecclesiastical conflict.

By 1720, several moderate prelates had been alarmed by what they saw as threats to authority and right belief. Even a staunch supporter of the Whig ministry, Edmund Gibson, bishop of London from 1723, carefully distanced himself from Hoadly's ideas. Despite his Whig political principles, Gibson was also a defender of the Church's rights. He worked to gain episcopal support for the Whig government. In return he wanted the government to ensure the appointment of bishops who were not only Whigs, but also orthodox and learned. Walpole aimed to ease the position of dissenters unobtrusively without rousing fears that the Church was 'in danger'. However, Gibson, alarmed by what he perceived as a current of Whig hostility to the Church's authority, jurisdiction and endowments, ended his partnership with Walpole in 1736.

Eighteenth-century governments wanted a quiet Church and archbishops of Canterbury who would provide political support and avoid rocking the boat. All the primates had good qualities, some of them showed genuine pastoral concern, and most proved on occasion less pliant than prime ministers hoped. However, between 1715 and 1780 only Thomas Secker (1758–68), originally nonconformist, combined breadth of vision with capacity for pastoral and administrative leadership. Secker felt his freedom of action limited by lay suspicions of the clergy. He strongly supported the appointment of a bishop for the American colonies, only for a clergyman, Francis Blackburne, archdeacon of Cleveland, to criticize the plan as evidence of 'popery' in the Church.

Blackburne was a leading participant in a controversy of the 1760s and 1770s over subscription to the Thirty-nine Articles. Opponents of subscription (including Blackburne), believed that it promoted hypocrisy or casuistical interpretation. Belief in the Trinity (Article 1) had been a fundamental Christian doctrine since the fourth century. Samuel Clarke, chaplain in ordinary to Queen Anne, had, however, shown in a carefully worded treatise of 1712 that it lacked clear scriptural foundation. In 1772 some 200 men signed a petition drawn up at the Feathers Tavern in London in support of Blackburne's proposal that a private statement of faith be allowed instead of subscription to the Articles. After its decisive rejection by the Commons, some of those involved seceded from the Church of England to found a Unitarian congregation.

Dissenters in England

Around 1715, according to one estimate, just over 338,000 people belonged to one of the main Protestant dissenting denominations in England, 6.5 per cent of the total population. Over half of them were Presbyterians. Thereafter, the numbers of dissenters dwindled for several decades before revival began in the later eighteenth century. The membership of congregations had become increasingly restricted to the sober and industrious middling ranks of urban society. However, several Presbyterian and Independent academies flourished during the early eighteenth century, and taught children from conformist as well as dissenting families.[3]

Anti-Trinitarian ideas developed among the Presbyterians and General Baptists. A meeting of London dissenting ministers in 1719 failed to agree that subscription to the doctrine of the Trinity was essential. Despite their divisions, however, the leading dissenting ministers retained a distinctive political voice. From the 1760s dissenters were the most consistent critics of the government's American policies.

The small Jewish community in England numbered some 6,000 in the 1730s. Its most famous member, the financier Samson Gideon, gave successive ministries valuable help. In 1753 the government passed an act authorizing the naturalization of individual Jews, but widespread hostility to the measure forced its repeal the following year.

Religious loyalties in Scotland

In Scotland no toleration act had been passed. The substantial episcopalian minority (around 40 per cent of the population in 1690, according to one estimate, largely concentrated north of the Tay) had no official countenance. In England, nonjuring clergy (those who refused to take oaths of loyalty to James II's successors) were a small and dwindling group, but most of the Scottish episcopal clergy were nonjurors. Episcopalians supplied the backbone of support for the Scottish Jacobite cause.

In 1710, Edinburgh magistrates imprisoned one of the episcopalian ministers who had begun to use the English Prayer Book. The incident provoked the Tory-dominated British parliament into passing in 1712 an act to prevent the disturbance of prayer book worship conducted by episcopalian ministers who were ready to take the oath of allegiance. An act of 1719 penalized failure to pray for the reigning sovereign with six months imprisonment of clergy and six months closure of chapels. This statute was not enforced continuously, but a much harsher act was passed in 1746. Only clergy ordained by English or Irish bishops were to be allowed to officiate. Severe penalties were provided both for unqualified officiants and for laity attending their services. Cumberland's soldiers destroyed several chapels, and the act was rigorously enforced for ten years. Enforcement was relaxed from the later 1750s onwards, but episcopalians were still subjected to intermittent harassment. Not until after Charles Stuart's death in 1788 could serious negotiations for the removal of their disabilities begin. When penal legislation was rescinded in 1792, the episcopalian minority possibly made up only 1 per cent of the population.[4]

Another act of 1712 restored to Scottish lay patrons the right of nomination of ministers in the Kirk taken from them in 1690. Both 1712 measures were widely seen as breaching the guarantee for Presbyterianism in the Union Treaty. At first, most patrons did not exercise their right, but many began to do so from the 1730s onwards, albeit in the face of widespread protests. The patronage issue led Ebenezer Erskine and four other ministers to form in 1733 the 'Associate Presbytery', soon known as the Secession Church. The Seceders themselves split in 1747 over the issue of state oaths of loyalty. Thomas Gillespie, another minister uncompromisingly opposed to patronage, formed in 1761 the Relief Church, less inflexibly Calvinist and more liberal in doctrine than the previous Seceders. The other small sects outside the Kirk included Baptists, Congregationalists, the Cameronians and the Glasites (founded c.1730).

Two broad currents of opinion were discernible within the Kirk itself. The Moderates, ascendant from the 1760s onwards, insisted on the need to accept patronage as required by law. They emphasized practical morality at the expense of theological rigour, played down the doctrine of predestination without ever repudiating it and presented a more urbane and liberal face to

Scottish society, one more acceptable to Scotland's political managers. By contrast, the Evangelical or Popular party within the Church promoted fervent preaching, emphasized salvation by grace alone and strongly opposed patronage. Missionary and educational effort in the Gaelic-speaking Highlands, most effectively carried out by itinerant preachers and lay catechists, was strongly Evangelical in character.[5]

Roman Catholicism

'Popery' had become an absurdly over-used term in the internal controversies of the Church of England. But Roman Catholicism itself remained, for Protestants in Britain and elsewhere, all too dangerous. Persecution flared up intermittently in various countries. The Elector Palatine's expulsion of Protestants from the main church in Heidelberg in 1719 resulted in Anglo-Hanoverian and Prussian efforts to get the decision reversed. Formerly tolerant Poland became increasingly hostile towards non-Catholics. After destructive clashes between Lutheran townsmen and Jesuit students in the town of Toruń in 1724 the mayor and several other citizens were sentenced to death. This 'bloodbath' caused outrage in Prussia and Britain. They briefly combined in an alliance whose aims included support for Polish Protestantism. In 1731 the archbishop of Salzburg expelled all Protestants over twelve at eight days' notice. Several Protestant powers, but especially Prussia, took in refugees, though rapprochement with Emperor Charles VI prevented George II's supporting the Salzburgers vigorously. Meanwhile Charles whittled away Protestant privileges in Hungary and pushed forward the endowment of Catholic schools and parishes.[6]

In Catholic Europe the eighteenth century saw the building of many magnificent churches. In Italy, new missionary orders were founded: the Redemptorists, with a particular concern for the poor, and the Passionists. The cults of saints, especially the Virgin, confraternities and the practice of pilgrimage, remained widely popular in the Catholic world. However, the vast wealth of many bishops and monasteries, the huge numbers of monks and nuns, and the laxity of some prelates and older monasteries provided grounds for serious criticism. In France, the crown, without consulting the pope, established a commission that between 1768 and 1784 shut down 426 small religious houses. Several states, beginning with Portugal in 1758, attacked the Jesuits. A unique element in the French situation was the bitter internecine conflict between some senior prelates, supported by the crown, and the Jansenists, who were fierce opponents of the Jesuits. Jansenists in the Paris *parlement* played a key part in the anti-Jesuit campaign, backed by the king's minister Choiseul. Once the spearhead of the counter-Reformation, the order had made many enemies, and came to be seen as an actual or potential obstacle to royal policies. Pope Clement XIII made unavailing protests. When he quarrelled with the duke of Parma in 1768, several Catholic rulers shamelessly combined to intimidate him. His successor Clement XIV suppressed the Jesuits in 1773.[7]

Besides the welcome suppression of the Jesuits, two other events were important in improving relations between Britain and the papacy: Clement XIII's refusal to recognize Charles Edward as king in 1766, and the explicit statutory confirmation in 1774 of the privileged position of the Catholic Church in recently conquered Canada.

The English and Welsh Catholics may have increased from 60,000–70,000 in 1700 to about 100,000 in 1800: even if this were so their *percentage* of the total population shrank from approximately 1.3 to 1.1. Several English Catholic peers and gentry conformed to the established Church, though such families as the Howards continued to provide leadership. In various areas (in much of Wales, for example), Catholic numbers probably declined. In certain old strongholds, however, notably Lancashire and Monmouthshire, they held up well. Urban Catholicism grew markedly, especially in London, where there were 20,000 Catholics in 1730. Many English Catholics could practise their religion regularly but unobtrusively. Except on gentry estates, chapels were usually simple and modest. Richard Challoner, vicar apostolic of the London district (1758–81), was an outstanding bishop: a notable administrator, pastor and devotional writer in plain English. There were possibly fewer than 20,000 Catholics in Scotland around 1760. Most were concentrated in the north-east and the western Highlands and Islands. A succession of devoted members of religious orders ministered to the Highland Catholics, enduring a life of hardship. James Gordon, vicar apostolic, opened a seminary at Scalan (Banffshire) in 1717. A second Scottish vicariate apostolic, of the Highland district, was created in 1727. The first effective appointment was made in 1731.[8]

Anti-popery remained a key element of national identity. The triggers of intermittent anti-Catholic hostility included the Jacobite rebellion and local growth in Catholic numbers. For most of the time, however, peaceable Catholics were left undisturbed. The House of Commons readily passed the 1778 Catholic Relief Act, removing certain seldom imposed penalties on Catholic priests and Catholics educated abroad, and making it possible for Catholics to buy land. A petition against it organized by Lord George Gordon led to ferocious London riots that revealed the depth and strength of continuing popular anti-Catholic prejudice.[9]

Ireland's Catholics remained quiescent between 1715 and 1780. By 1720 pressure on Catholic religious institutions had relaxed, only to be tightened once more in 1744–5 (when, however, there was no Irish rising). After 1766 Clement XIII ceased to accept Stuart nominations to Irish Catholic sees. By the 1730s, only 20–25 per cent of the Irish population was Protestant. The dispossession of the old ruling class was without parallel in Europe. So too was the government failure to achieve conversions among a subject majority. Catholic landowners, the major target of the penal laws, did convert in some numbers, but they possessed only 14 per cent of the land by 1703. Many Protestant landowners reportedly preferred their tenants to be Catholic because that supposedly made them more subservient. Protestant missionary activity had been feeble compared with Roman Catholic efforts on the continent. A well-manned and visible Catholic Church existed, with parish priests, schools, religious orders and hierarchy.[10]

Reasonable religion and irreligion

In Christian history, reason had been the handmaiden of revelation. Reason had had an important role in scriptural exegesis, but certain fundamental doctrines were beyond its reach. The Reformation and the advances of science had profoundly disturbed this relationship. By the eighteenth century, the handmaiden threatened to become the mistress. Philosophers and speculative writers were subjecting the most ancient religious dogmas and even Scripture itself to unprecedented critical scrutiny.

A philosopher more radical than any of the participants in eighteenth-century British debates was the Dutch Jew Baruch Spinoza (1632–77). For Spinoza, God was the 'creative power or potential of Nature, the rules governing the working of the universe'. Miracles, he believed, are impossible. Those phenomena so described are either imaginary or natural events beyond human understanding. The resurrection had to be understood allegorically. The Bible was a collection of texts written at several different times and in different contexts, without any special divine inspiration or internal coherence. Spinoza's work provoked scandal and horror, and in Britain, attacked by a wide variety of churchmen, he largely displaced Hobbes as 'the chief intellectual bogeyman and symbolic head of philosophical deism and atheism'.[11]

In his *Essay Concerning Human Understanding* (1690) and *The Reasonableness of Christianity* (1695), John Locke argued that reason must judge claims to the status of divine revelation, and that reason leads to the inescapable conclusion that God existed, the Creator, 'one eternal first cogitative being'. Jesus had come as the bearer of good news, above all restoring a true knowledge of God hitherto obscured by superstition. He had given clear and reasonable moral guidance, and the Christian's duty was to follow that guidance without anxiety about doctrinal subtleties. John Toland claimed in his *Christianity Not Mysterious* (1696) that 'there is nothing in the GOSPEL Contrary to REASON Nor ABOVE it: And that no Christian Doctrine can be properly call'd A MYSTERY'. The Gospels were usually clear, though occasionally particular statements were so obviously impossible that they had to be interpreted figuratively. Mysteries had crept into the originally plain and open Christian religion as priests and philosophers had gradually contaminated it. In 1724, Anthony Collins, a friend of Locke's, claimed that Christ's coming did not fulfil Old Testament prophecies, which had envisaged an altogether different Messiah. Thomas Woolston, in *Six Discourses* (1727–30), argued that much of the Bible, including accounts of miracles and the resurrection, could not be literally true. Scripture had to be read allegorically.

Several authors invoked evidence from nature in support of religion. In *The Folly and Unreasonableness of Atheism* (1693) Richard Bentley, after admitting that scriptural arguments would not convince atheists, turned to 'the mighty

Volumes of visible Nature; and the everlasting Tables of Right Reason', drawing on Newton's *Principia* for evidence of God's providential design of the universe. Subsequent writers, William Wollaston in 1722 and Matthew Tindal in 1731, argued that the 'Religion of Nature' made human duties clear through reason. Wollaston's claim that his argument was 'so far from undermining true *revealed religion*, that it rather paves its way for its reception' seems somewhat disingenuous. Tindal pointed to inconsistencies and absurdities in the Bible, and rejected the idea that salvation was only to be found through the Gospels.[12]

Writing in the later 1740s and 1750s, the Scottish philosopher David Hume expressed a thoroughgoing scepticism about the grounds for religious belief and practice, 'natural' or otherwise. No religion actually practised on earth approximated to 'natural' religion. The earliest religions, inspired by fear of unexplained phenomena, had been polytheistic. Hume conceded that 'the whole frame of nature bespeaks an intelligent author', but he concluded that the hypothesis was still uncertain because 'entirely beyond the reach of human experience'. It provided no basis for principles of conduct and behaviour. Several writers had seen miracles as authenticating evidence of the truths of revelation. Hume found them utterly improbable.[13]

Fears of rival threats from puritan fanaticism and popish tyranny and superstition had divided both Church and nation between 1660 and 1714. They had been major ingredients in party politics. The ideal of moderation, of the resolute avoidance of extremes, was immensely powerful in early Hanoverian England, even though 'moderate' never became a party label as in Scotland. In this climate the notions of 'reasonable' and 'natural' religion had considerable appeal. What was 'reasonable' was, however, open to considerable disagreement. The argument of the reasonableness of religion could be used against atheism, but it was a double-edged sword. It became increasingly clear that 'natural' religion was a slippery slope rather than a firm ground for faith. By the 1780s, 'The tide was turning against what was increasingly regarded as an overemphasis on natural religion at the expense of revealed'.[14]

Evangelical awakening

Faith and feeling, not reason, had to be the sources of religious renewal. Rational or natural religion did not inspire evangelical effort. Most of the Church of England clergy were quite conscientious pastors. The parish church remained a vital focus of community life. Some churches were enlarged, others newly built to the needs of growing centres of population, though admittedly not enough of them. A huge volume of religious guidance was published for home use. And yet the Church largely lacked a missionary impulse.[15]

The last great early modern flowering of British Protestant evangelical activity was connected with continental revival movements.[16] Philipp Jakob Spener, founder of Pietism, had in 1675 set agenda which included intensified Bible study, fuller lay involvement in religious life, emphasis on practical

Christianity and more effective preaching. He focused 'upon the saving work of God in Christ for man, his salvation and renewal', in which the experience of New Birth was crucial. Spener's admirer August Hermann Francke made the new university of Halle the powerhouse of Pietism, founding there a cluster of widely admired charitable, medical and educational institutions.

Pietist influence spread far and wide through the Empire and Switzerland. A dramatic revival occurred in the Habsburg territory of Silesia, where under Swedish pressure the Emperor Joseph I had agreed to return several churches to the Protestants and allow the building of six new ones. In southern Silesia, Francke helped to establish a 'miniature Halle' round one of the new churches at Teschen, close to both Moravia and Hungary. Teschen became a multilingual evangelical centre, drawing huge crowds to prayer meetings and hymn-singing. From there missionary preachers and Pietist literature reached beleaguered Czech Protestants over the border, assisting local religious revivals.

Count Nikolaus Ludwig von Zinzendorf, who had attended Francke's school in Halle, gave a small group of 'Bohemian Brethren' from Moravia refuge on his estate in Saxony in 1722. After a powerful religious revival in 1727, missionaries of the Moravian Church set out from their settlement of Herrnhut, especially to various parts of America. Moravians soon visited England and the recently established British colony of Georgia. After joining in the foundation of the Fetter Lane religious society in London in 1738, Moravians began to establish English congregations of their own. Their Church was recognized by an act of parliament in 1749, and Zinzendorf himself spent the next few years in England.[17]

A forerunner of revival in Britain was Griffith Jones, rector of Llandowror (Carmarthenshire). Jones became a powerful open-air preacher outside his own parish. After teaching for the Society for Promoting Christian Knowledge (SPCK), he launched between 1731 and 1761 in nearly 1600 different places 'circulating schools' where part-time teachers catechized pupils and taught them to read the Bible in Welsh. Two other preachers, Daniel Rowland from Cardiganshire and Howell Harris from Brecknockshire, experienced conversion in 1735, Rowland possibly as a result of a sermon by Jones. They met in 1737 and subsequently became leaders of the Methodist revival in Wales.

John Wesley, the most famous leader of British religious revival, was the grandson of two dissenting ministers, and son of a Tory clergyman. As a young Fellow of Lincoln College, Oxford, he became in 1729 the leading member of a 'Holy Club' of young scholars, devoted among other things to Bible reading, frequent Communion and practical charitable works. Already by 1733 the name 'Methodist' had been coined for Wesley and his associates: he defined it as 'one that lives according to the method laid down in the Bible'. During an unsuccessful missionary visit to the new colony of Georgia (1735–7), Wesley encountered Moravians and refugees from Salzburg, and read widely in German devotional literature. His conversion experience in 1738 followed conversations with his Moravian friend Peter Böhler. He then visited Herrnhut.

A younger associate of the Wesleys, George Whitefield, who took over the leadership of the 'Holy Club', preached publicly of the New Birth after his own experience of conversion in 1735. He helped to found an orphanage in Georgia, modelled on the one at Halle. Possibly inspired by Howell Harris's example, in 1739 he began open-air preaching to coalminers at Kingswood near Bristol, where he raised money for a school, and soon attracted huge crowds. Wesley followed Whitefield's example when he commenced itinerant ministry and outdoor preaching. He sought out those whom the Church had neglected or barely reached: the inhabitants of remoter parts of the north and west, workers in newly expanding industrial areas, the poor, criminals and the dying. He induced in many of his hearers highly emotional, ecstatic, even to some minds hysterical experiences. Christ had died for all: nobody was predestined to damnation, and anybody who refused God's forgiveness offered through Christ did so of his own free will. Wesley's Arminianism led to a serious rift with Calvinist evangelicals, especially George Whitefield. Jones and Harris were also staunch Calvinists and admirers of Whitefield. Whitefield also helped to stimulate religious revival in Scotland, though he achieved his greatest successes in America, where he died in 1770. Selina, Countess of Huntingdon, who made Whitefield her chaplain, hoped to achieve religious renewal among the aristocracy. She founded chapels, and in 1768, with Howell Harris's help, Trevecca College in Brecknockshire for the training of Methodist ministers.

Whitefield was the most powerful preacher of the Methodist revival, but also overbearing, inconsistent, quarrelsome and disruptive. It was Wesley who became the foremost figure in the Methodist movement because he combined with evangelical power absolute confidence, enormous stamina, inflexible determination and considerable organizing ability. Religious Societies were founded, at first under Whitefield's leadership and then under Wesley's, and soon divided into classes that met weekly for prayer and Bible study. The societies were later grouped in circuits. Wesley recruited a growing team of lay preachers who from 1744 met together with his clerical supporters in a conference that became annual. Wesley nevertheless remained a loyal member of the Church of England and resisted several calls to separate from it. By the time of his death in 1791 there were 72,476 registered Methodists in Britain and Ireland, but possibly three times as many more 'sympathetic attenders' at Methodist services.[18] Skilled craftsmen were especially well represented in Methodist ranks. The Congregationalists and the Baptists, influenced by the Methodist example, also started to make new converts among lower middling groups and manual workers.

Some evangelical preachers addressed more affluent and influential audiences and acted as precursors of a revival within the Church that would help to shape the outlook and behaviour of the upper and middle classes after 1780. George III was, if not Pietist, regular in religious observance, and an example of marital chastity.

Conclusion

The religious history of the eighteenth century shows that the tenacity of long-established fears and prejudices must not be underestimated. The fear of Catholicism in particular persisted throughout the century, as the Gordon riots demonstrated. The furious reaction to the 'Jew Bill' revealed widespread anti-Jewish sentiment. Many churchmen continued to see nonconformity as a threat and remained extremely reluctant to countenance any further concessions to religious dissenters. For most of the time, however, English religious minorities enjoyed considerable tolerance in practice. Foreign observers remarked upon England's religious freedom and the multiplicity of her sects. In Scotland, by contrast, the Jacobite loyalties of nonjuring episcopalians, a sizeable minority, precluded their being granted toleration. Two developments were particularly characteristic of the eighteenth century. First, after an era of religious conflict, ideals of moderation and reasonableness gained considerable appeal. These ideals were in themselves compatible with orthodoxy, but several writers of the century's early decades who claimed to show that religion had a rational or natural basis actually questioned fundamental Christian doctrines. Secondly, Britain experienced a powerful tide of religious renewal. 'Natural' religion could never satisfy the deep and widespread need of spiritual sustenance. The age of reason soon became an age of religious revival, the age of Zinzendorf, Whitefield and Wesley.

19

COMMERCIAL ASCENDANCY AND INDUSTRIAL GROWTH

Populations and societies

During the eighteenth century the population of Europe may have grown by about a half. Between 1701 and 1801, the date of the first national census, the population of England grew by two-thirds, more than the European average, to reach over 8,671,000. Scotland's possibly increased between 1700 and 1801 from 1,100,000 to 1,608,000 (46 per cent). Ireland's population grew faster than any other in Europe, possibly from approximately 2,000,000 to approximately 5,000,000, only briefly checked by famine in 1728–9 and 1740–1. France's population, the largest in western Europe, possibly grew from 21,471,000 to 29,200,000 (36 per cent). Growth elsewhere may have ranged from around 70 per cent in Austria and Bohemia to 10.5 per cent in the United Provinces, with the southern Netherlands, Italy and the Iberian Peninsula in between.[1]

In every country the population is thought to have grown much faster in the second half of the century than the first. Until the 1750s, demographic growth in England was slow and uneven. Population actually fell between 1727 and 1731, when a combination of smallpox and other diseases caused England's most severe mortality crisis since the 1550s, and more briefly in 1741–3. Sustained growth began in the 1750s. The increase was primarily due to rising fertility, which was caused by a steady fall in the female age at marriage, a falling incidence of stillbirths and a rise in births outside marriage. The death rate fell, but less sharply than fertility rose. In mainland Europe, in contrast with England, declining mortality was probably the predominant cause of demographic growth. There were longer periods of relative peace, and during wars, better-organized armies caused less disruption.

The eighteenth century also saw major changes in the distribution of the English population. The proportion living in towns of 5,000 or above increased from 17 to 27.5 per cent, making England second in this respect only to the Dutch Republic, where the proportion fell from 39 to 33 per cent. Thirty per cent of Europe's urban growth took place in England. Scotland's urban sector, though proportionally smaller, grew far faster than England's. The 'rural non-agricultural' inhabitants of England's smaller towns and villages rose from 28 to 36.25 per cent, forming a larger proportion of the population than in most other European countries. Many of them were cottage workers in rapidly expanding rural industries.[2]

The nobility and more substantial gentry remained at the head of society. Great landlords are estimated to have owned 20–25 per cent of England in 1790, and other gentry landlords about 50 per cent. Great landlords occupied an even more powerful position in Scotland. During the eighteenth century, however, men whose fortunes came from sources other than land gained greater social acceptance. Wealthy London merchants and financiers and their sons and daughters were regarded as suitable marriage partners for landowning gentry families. Several Londoners bought country estates, but relatively few tried to establish themselves as great landowners. In 1760, the political economist Joseph Massie believed that wealthy merchants, traders and manufacturers outnumbered gentry among the 2.8 per cent of English and Welsh families with incomes of about £200 a year or more. The notion of a middle social category or class became increasingly current during the eighteenth century. Contemporary observers thought that it was growing in affluence and confidence. Massie's figures are notoriously difficult to interpret, but suggest that this middle class of farmers, innkeepers, members of professions, master manufacturers and 'tradesmen' included between a fifth and two-fifths of all families.[3]

Massie believed that 49 per cent of families had annual incomes below £25. The economic viability of many or most families in this category will have been precarious. During the century many small master craftsmen lost their independence to capitalists who organized domestic production or in some cases concentrated groups of workers in one place. The consolidation and enlargement of farms drew a sharper line between those farmers who belonged to the middle sort and growing numbers of smallholder craftsmen and labourers. Expenditure on poor relief rose from 0.8 per cent of national income in 1696 to 1 per cent in 1748–50 and 1.6 per cent in 1776, sufficient to keep 3.6 per cent of the population fed in 1696, 7.9 per cent in 1748–50 and 9.8 per cent in 1776. Many poor people will have been given only partial support, so that the proportion of the population actually receiving relief will have been far larger than these figures suggest, especially in years of high food prices. In the 1780s, it has been claimed, per capita poor relief expenditure in England was seven times as high as in France, and far more uniformly distributed. The rudimentary safety net provided by the English poor laws supported growing numbers of poor, and, it has been argued, 'underpinned the growth of an economically mobile wage labour force' by encouraging impoverished small landholders to seek paid work instead of hanging on to their holdings. According to an alternative view, poor relief administration was too harsh and unpredictable to influence people's calculations in this way.[4]

The comparatively large urban middle class was perhaps the most distinctive element in Britain's, and particularly England's, social structure. In France, too, the urban population grew during the eighteenth century. By 1750, however, it formed a proportion of the whole that was only about half as large as in England. Successful French merchants enjoyed growing respect, but despite their vigour and prosperity, they were widely regarded as having a status lower than that of urban *rentiers*, men who lived off their investments without working for their living. France's rural population was proportionally as well as absolutely far larger than England's. England's rural industries also absorbed a larger proportion of her population.[5]

Towns and cities

Towns and cities were the main centres of enrichment, consumption and economic growth. Britain's rapidly growing urban sector signalled its economic vigour. London grew from an estimated 575,000 people in 1700 to 958,000 in 1801. However, it stopped growing faster than England's population as a whole during this century. The capital's share of England's overseas trade fell from about three-quarters to under two-thirds between 1700 and 1790, even though it had more than doubled in value. London remained the leading shipbuilding centre, although its share of this activity also declined, and by far the most versatile and productive British industrial hub, although access to particular combinations of raw materials as well as labour encouraged the rapid growth of more specialized provincial centres for the production of clothing and metal wares. London was the pre-eminent centre for the manufacture of such things as fine silver ware, elegant furniture, watches, and surgical and navigational instruments. She surpassed Amsterdam to become Europe's leading financial centre, and benefited from Dutch investment: perhaps a quarter of those holding £500 or more of Bank of England stock in 1723–4 were Dutch. The number of London private banks rose from about twenty-four in 1725 to fifty-two in 1786. The business of insurance underwriting and broking grew steadily. The conurbation expanded in all directions, but especially to the West, where several great landlords developed residential estates. New bridges at Westminster (1750) and Blackfriars (1769) encouraged development south of the Thames. An act of 1711 financed the building of twelve fine new churches. Various government departments were handsomely re-housed. A series of lighting and paving acts authorized a gradual process of rate-financed improvement in the City, Westminster and the suburban parishes. The 551 coffee houses of 1739 served the social, cultural, political and business worlds. Theatres, concert rooms and pleasure gardens provided entertainments and opportunities of seeing and being seen.[6]

The population in other English towns of 5,000 inhabitants and more, less than half London's in 1700, far exceeded it by 1801. In 1750, Bristol, Norwich and Newcastle, all long-established provincial capitals, were still next on the list after London. But the new Midland and northern centres, Birmingham,

Liverpool, Manchester and Leeds, were gaining on them rapidly. Bristol and Liverpool took large shares of the Atlantic slave trade after the Royal Africa Company lost its monopoly in 1698. The industries of these great ports included shipbuilding, tobacco and sugar processing, glass-making and brewing. Birmingham was the foremost centre of metalworking, Manchester of textile manufacture. Several smaller ports, inland industrial centres and resorts (above all Bath, England's leading spa) grew fast during the century. In many towns, brick and stone largely replaced earlier half-timbered structures. Town halls, assembly rooms, exchanges, theatres, churches and chapels were built. Squares and gardens were laid out. Local gentry and the upper ranks of town society attended assemblies, balls, concerts, plays, dinners and race meetings. About 15,750 clubs were established in British towns during the eighteenth century.[7]

Edinburgh's population reached 81,600 by 1801. As Scotland's legal, educational and ecclesiastical capital and foremost centre of fashion it contained a large number of professional people, skilled craftsmen and workers in services, as well as printers and brewers. It remained an important port. After the foundation of the medical school (1728), it became a leading centre of medical science. The New Town, planned in 1766, would become Edinburgh's more elegantly coherent equivalent of London's West End. Glasgow, little more than a third of Edinburgh's size in 1700, was, with 77,000 inhabitants in 1801, nearly as large as Edinburgh. Its prosperity was founded on its combined roles as a port for colonial goods and exports from its industrial hinterland. Glasgow, and Scotland's next largest but far smaller towns, Paisley, Aberdeen and Dundee, were all early centres of the successful linen industry. The second city of the island kingdoms, Dublin, had 182,000 inhabitants by 1800. Its grandeur matched its size and its dignity as a capital, the focus of the social and political life of Ireland's ruling class, adorned with fine new public edifices. Dublin was also a centre of sugar refining, silk and wool textile production, luxury craftsmanship and Ireland's major port. Cork was Ireland's second city, and there were four other rapidly growing towns.[8]

In Europe as a whole the proportion of the population living in towns grew relatively little during the century. In the Netherlands the urban population actually shrank. Capital cities, with their courts, burgeoning bureaucracies and carefully fostered luxury industries, present the most spectacular examples of growth. St Petersburg, founded in 1703 in an empty swamp, had some 192,000 inhabitants by 1784. Berlin's population nearly trebled during the century, while Vienna's doubled, as did those of Naples, Turin and Prague. Paris, Madrid, Copenhagen, Stockholm, Dresden, Königsberg and Munich all grew substantially. Flourishing ports included Hamburg, Bremen, Bordeaux, Nantes, Leghorn and Cadiz. Leipzig was Germany's chief inland trading centre. Textile production led to the notably rapid growth of Nimes in France and Barcelona in Spain.[9]

Domestic and foreign trade

Buoyant home demand was essential to economic expansion. Exports absorbed only 8 per cent of British national output in 1700, 17 per cent in 1800. Very modest population growth during the early eighteenth century, low food prices and rising real wages enhanced disposable income, facilitating patterns of consumption that powerfully influenced economic development. Imports of sugar, coffee, rice and above all tea grew dramatically. Tea, at first a luxury, spread to the middling ranks, then to the labouring classes by c.1750. An increasing proportion of the prosperous middling sort possessed such artefacts as clocks, curtains, pictures, mirrors, chests of drawers, china, knives and forks. English craftsmen successfully imitated and adapted many high quality foreign products and made them available to a larger domestic market. The most famous examples are cottons and ceramics inspired by Asian calicoes and porcelain. Such products also included lead crystal glass, Sheffield plate, mahogany and veneered furniture, carpets and ornamental metal wares. Even the poor, perhaps especially household servants, spent a sizeable amount on clothes. Many owned such items as watches and rings. A huge number of shops – at least one for every forty-three individuals in England and Wales in 1759 – could supply every conceivable want.[10]

Her insular position and numerous rivers, and the proximity of much of her population to crucial coastal routes, all promoted the development of Britain's internal market. After growing relatively slowly between 1709 and 1760, the tonnage of English and Welsh coastal shipping increased by nearly 60 per cent between 1760 and 1780. By 1780 England probably had the densest web of improved roads in Europe, and the construction of a network of canals linking major inland industrial centres to the coast was well under way. They drove down the cost of carrying heavy freight, especially coal. Various other European governments, including those of France and Austria, saw the importance of better internal transport networks. From the 1730s French governments undertook a sustained drive to improve roads and bridges that ultimately resulted in the creation of a fine highway network. River navigation was improved and some new canals were dug. England nevertheless remained the leader in improving internal communications.

The promotion of trade was one of the foremost aims of British foreign policy. Overseas colonies were seen as sources of valuable commodities for import and re-export, and, increasingly, as important markets for British goods. The Navigation Acts had been designed to keep the lion's share of the trade of England and her colonies for English ships. Between 1699–1701 and 1772–4 English exports and re-exports grew by 144 per cent in value, imports by 118 per cent. The growth in the volume of some imported commodities whose price had tumbled as they became items of mass consumption was, however, far greater. Patterns of trade changed in important respects. The development of European textile industries, and measures to protect them, reduced English cloth exports to Europe, including even Spain and Portugal from the 1750s onwards. Imports of continental manufactures also fell. Ireland and Scotland provided increasing quantities of linen. Imports of European raw materials, however, continued to increase, including northern iron, timber, flax and yarn and Mediterranean dyestuffs. Rapidly growing colonies in North America and the Caribbean provided, together with Ireland, the most buoyant markets for exported manufactures of all sorts, including both cloth and a vast range of metal goods, which also helped to pay for the slaves shipped from West Africa to America. The value of English exports of manufactures to America increased more than eightfold between 1699–1701 and 1772–4. The high standard of living of the rapidly growing North American population enabled it to purchase substantial quantities of products of good quality.[11]

In the early 1770s Europe took 63 per cent of English re-exports. Tobacco, coffee and rice re-exports to north-western Europe grew especially strongly. Glasgow became the leading British tobacco port, largely because its merchants' resident agents in the colonies enhanced their effectiveness in combining the shipping of tobacco with the supply of colonists' needs. England met new and stiff French competition in the sugar trade, and the re-export of Indian calicoes slowed down in face of protectionist measures by European governments.

France emerged as Britain's most formidable trading competitor. Between 1715 and 1780, she was at war for about a third of the time, compared with nearly two-thirds in Louis XIV's reign. Between 1716–20 and 1784–8, French foreign trade grew fivefold – faster than British, but from a much lower starting point. All France's European neighbours were substantial commercial partners of hers. Her trade with Germany and northern Europe grew especially strongly. Exports of Languedoc cloths from Marseilles to the Levant increased markedly. The West Indies were the mainstay of France's transoceanic trade. St Domingue (Haiti) became, together with Martinique and Guadeloupe, an immensely rich source of sugar, indigo, tobacco and coffee. By 1740, St Domingue produced as much sugar as all the British West Indian islands combined. France re-exported much of the produce of its West Indian possessions. In North America, the French carried on a successful fur trade. They also enjoyed a lucrative share of the north-west Atlantic fisheries. From a much lower starting point than its British counterpart, the French Company of the Indies became a formidable rival by the early 1740s. Mauritius and Réunion yielded increasing quantities of coffee and sugar.[12]

During the Seven Years War Britain exploited its naval superiority to disrupt France's communications with its overseas possessions and seize many of them. In 1763, France kept what had been the most lucrative elements of her commercial empire, but lost the potentially considerable assets of Canada and Louisiana. In India, the British East India Company's now dominant position enabled it to buy Indian goods more cheaply than its competitors, and use local revenues to pay for its purchases. Britain's trade with Asia leapt ahead, while France's failed to expand significantly. Britain built up a growing and commanding lead over France in exports to the trans-oceanic world, and held a lead in trans-oceanic imports that France threatened only very briefly and intermittently. The prosperity of France's colonial trade depended by the 1780s above all on her West Indian possessions, a rather precarious base. She had no equivalent of the North American colonies that played such a crucial part in Britain's industrial advance as suppliers of raw materials and consumers of

British goods. Britain's commercial success rested on three main pillars: her establishment of an exceptionally well-balanced maritime empire, whose different parts played complementary roles; her naval dominance; and the capacity of her industries to satisfy colonial demands.[13]

The Navigation Acts had succeeded in ousting the Dutch from their position as suppliers of Baltic and northern goods to Britain. Between 1689 and the 1760s statutory bounties encouraged British producers to export substantial grain surpluses, largely replacing the Baltic supplies formerly carried by the Dutch. The Dutch themselves bought British malt and cereals. As their domestic peat extraction became increasingly expensive during the eighteenth century, the Dutch imported more British coal on which they paid tariffs. From the 1690s at latest, much Dutch investment flowed into various branches of British trade with Europe and North America. By 1752–4, England's share of colonial imports was far larger than that of the Dutch Republic. In sugar and tobacco, English dominance was overwhelming. In trade with Asia, the Dutch retained their supremacy in spices and coffee, though the English had taken a huge lead in calico and silk imports, largely because the looser organization of their East India Company allowed more initiative to local buyers. Early in the century, English and other competitors broke into the Dutch-dominated tea trade, sailing directly to Guangzhou. The English were also more successful in financing Asian purchases from the profits of regional trade, especially sales of Indian textiles to China.[14]

Manufacturing industry

British industrial output may have doubled between 1700 and 1780.[15] By 1780, the process later dubbed 'the industrial revolution' was only just beginning; but the changes that made it possible were already well under way. Textiles retained their paramount position among British manufactures. In woollens and worsteds the West Riding of Yorkshire was on the way to primacy. Raw silk imports doubled in value between 1700 and the 1770s, supporting a growing industry in London, the Midlands and Lancashire. Linen production increased rapidly in Scotland and Ireland. The Scottish Board of Trustees gave it financial support, helped set up spinning schools, brought in foreign weavers and bleachers, offered premiums for technological innovations, and subsidized the large-scale growing of flax and the establishment of bleachfields. English linen production grew fourfold between 1720 and 1775, while the quantity of Scottish linen stamped for sale grew nearly eightfold between 1728 and 1783. Indian cotton goods had become very popular by 1700. Pressure from the woollen industry led in 1701 to a statute prohibiting the importation of dyed or printed calicoes, and in 1721 to one prohibiting the purchase, sale or use of all cotton textiles in Britain. However, Lancashire, where the climate favours cotton spinning, had already begun to make a mixed cotton and linen fabric. In 1735 the manufacturers obtained an act making it clear that such fabrics were exempted from the ban. The ban on pure cotton fabrics was finally repealed in 1774.[16]

Coal was by 1700 used both as a domestic fuel and in a wide range of industries. British output nearly tripled between 1700 and 1775. The north-east of England still produced over a third of the 1775 total. Other fields distinguished by remarkable output growth were the West Midlands, Lancashire, Yorkshire and South Wales. Lead, copper and tin were all smelted with coal by 1700, and during the eighteenth century the problems involved in using coke for iron production would be successfully overcome. Copper and lead production rose sharply. Britain continued to import increasing amounts of bar iron from Sweden and Russia until 1790. Meanwhile, however, domestic pig iron output had risen by 172 per cent between 1720 and 1788. Shropshire was responsible for 37 per cent of the 1788 output, South Wales for 18 per cent and Scotland for 10 per cent.[17]

The iron works at Dowlais (Merthyr Tydfil) and on the Carron near Falkirk were both founded in 1759. Both became famous for their production of artillery. By 1750, Birmingham was 'already the greatest centre of hardware manufacture in the world'. Its craftsmen employed all the chief metals to make metal goods ranging from buckles and cutlery to toys, guns, candlesticks and coffeepots. In its Black Country hinterland were to be found locksmiths, spurriers, scythe and chainmakers, and a huge multitude of nailers. Sheffield town likewise specialized in fine knives, razors, edged tools and surgical instruments while forks and cheaper tools were made in the nearby countryside. South-west Lancashire made tools, watch parts, locks and hinges. The north-east took a growing share of English shipbuilding. Other rapidly expanding industries included paper-making, glass-making (especially in the West Midlands and the north-east) and pottery (especially in Staffordshire).[18]

With some notable exceptions, technological advances had generally come to Britain from the continent in previous centuries. Now, in two fields, the use of coal and the mechanization of textile production, England took the lead. Britain was exceptionally well endowed with large coal reserves. The cheapness of coal compared with wood, the proximity of the Tyneside coalfield to the sea and the rapid expansion of London demand had all encouraged the use of coal in a vast range of industrial processes, including soap-making, salt extraction, sugar boiling, dyeing, bleaching and glass-making. Maltsters converted coal into coke. In 1709, Abraham Darby followed their example when he first used coke instead of charcoal to produce pig iron at Coalbrookdale. However, coke pig iron was more expensive than charcoal pig iron and the bar iron made from it was inferior in quality to bar iron made from charcoal pig. By dint of experiment and gradual improvement, the Darby firm eventually succeeded by 1755 in producing cheaper pig iron of greatly improved quality, which soon replaced charcoal pig. Charcoal still had to be used in the re-forging of pig to make bar iron, but Henry Cort ended this dependence on charcoal with his invention of the puddling furnace and rolling mill, patented in 1784. In 1712 the first successful coal-fired steam engine, invented by Thomas Newcomen, was used to drain a coalmine at Dudley. A hundred of these engines were in operation in England by 1733. James Watt improved the engine's fuel efficiency with a separate condenser in 1765 and achieved major advances in the use of steam to drive machinery in the 1780s.[19]

William Lee's invention of the stocking frame (c.1589), the first major English contribution to the mechanization of textile production, had been successfully developed, after initial setbacks, by Huguenot silk-weavers in Spitalfields; it was later used to make woollen and cotton hose in provincial centres. Thomas Lombe set up altogether more complex engines in his water-powered silk-throwing factory at Derby in 1717–18 after his brother had pirated their design from an Italian factory. Other silk factories followed Lombe's, and the design of his premises provided the prototype for later-established cotton factories. English inventors took a decisive lead in the mechanization of cotton fabric manufacture during the eighteenth century. Cotton's tensile strength made it exceptionally suitable for mechanized spinning. John Kay's flying shuttle (1733) greatly accelerated weaving speed. Jedediah Strutt's ribbing machine (1759) facilitated large-scale production of ribbed cotton stockings. By the 1760s there was a demand for much larger quantities of cotton yarn. The resulting cluster of inventions, unprecedented in Britain, was the outcome of sustained effort, exchange of ideas and the swift copying of innovations. The important advances included John Hargreaves's spinning jenny (1764) and Richard Arkwright's water frame (1769). In the early 1770s, together with his partners, Arkwright developed the first successful water-powered cotton mill at Cromford. In 1775 he patented his carding machine. Arkwright also helped to establish cotton manufacture in Scotland. In 1779, Samuel Crompton's 'mule' combined the principles of the spinning jenny and the water frame.[20]

By 1780, there were several large enterprises in Britain, including mills, iron works, naval dockyards, deep mines and a factory making metal wares at Soho (Birmingham) established in 1765. There were many other industries in which workshops smaller than factories but larger than households were the normal units of production. However, the commonest form of industrial organization remained the 'putting out' of materials to a host of cottage weavers, knitters, nailers, cutlers and other craftsmen.

France was England's closest industrial competitor between 1700 and the 1780s. France had flourishing woollen industries and retained its superior position in silk production. In the 1780s the French cotton industry, though certainly far smaller than the English, was growing fast. France's pig iron production was larger than Britain's for most of the century. However, Britain showed more technical inventiveness than France, and this gave Britain an advantage that would prove decisive during the decades after 1780. Britain's more abundant and accessible supplies of coal and her relatively high wages were both stimuli to inventiveness, and the dense clustering of industrial activity in certain regions in England facilitated 'co-operation and cross-stimulus' between the skilled artisans and merchant manufacturers who achieved the major technological advances. Industry was far more dispersed in France than in England. There were also closer contacts between scientists and manufacturers in Britain.[21]

For the Dutch Republic, with her small population and home market, the health of manufacturing was closely bound up with that of overseas trade. The Republic lacked protected colonial markets such as Britain enjoyed. The decline of the Baltic bulk-carrying trade had disastrous consequences for shipbuilding and ancillary industries. Scandinavian competition hurt the Dutch North Sea fisheries. Neighbouring countries' measures to promote and protect their own industries hit Dutch manufacturing and processing enterprises hard. The Austrian Netherlands offer the best examples of such policies. Government policies included protective tariffs, Ostend harbour improvement and industrial investment. Linen, fine cloth and iron manufacture, coalmining, and salt, sugar and tobacco processing grew rapidly from the 1750s. The Dutch, as has been seen, had to rely on foreign coal supplies.[22]

Germany remained industrially backward. There were some flourishing rural industrial areas, but they were unevenly scattered. Germany's rivers were under-exploited, her extensive coal deposits all but untapped. She was politically fragmented, and 'traditional institutions – manorial systems with powerful landlords, village communities, privileged towns, guilds, and merchant companies' remained much stronger than elsewhere in western Europe, regulating, and at the same time restraining, industrial development. Some state efforts to stimulate industry proved inefficient, or benefited only a narrow sector. Brandenburg-Prussia successfully promoted the production of military uniforms and armaments, yet as a whole remained one of the least industrialized states in Germany. The Austrian hereditary lands, by contrast, benefited from more consistent and on the whole effective efforts by the monarchy to promote industrial development, even though they suffered from some of the same disadvantages as Germany. Tariffs were used to assist industry, and in 1775 most internal tolls were removed when a Customs Union was created. Internal communications were improved, and the port of Trieste was developed. Guild privileges were whittled away. The textile, glass and iron industries were nurtured with the help of foreign entrepreneurs who were attracted by means of a variety of incentives. Bohemia's domestic textile industry grew vigorously. Several thriving mills and factories were also established there and in Lower Austria.[23]

Italy fell further behind northern Europe, 'exporting foodstuffs and semi-finished raw materials, and importing manufactured goods'. Italian rulers tried to promote industry, but with less success than elsewhere. Around 1770, two-thirds of Europe's silk was made with Italian raw silk or thread, but France dominated the upper end of the market, and other centres of production were growing fast. It was a similar story with wool, though the flying shuttle was introduced in a new factory near Vicenza in 1738. Skilled urban manufactures such as arms in Milan and glass in Venice declined. Rural industries developed, but their products were cheap and basic.

Spanish industry remained largely backward. Basque iron and Valencian silk production expanded vigorously, but remained conservative in organization and technology. Catalonia was different. Agricultural prosperity raised demand for low- to medium-quality cloth made in mountainous areas. Better quality material made in the coastal cities benefited from a developing national market. In Barcelona, bans on calico imports and grants of special privileges to Catalan producers of substitute fabrics encouraged investment in the cotton industry. During the 1780s, Barcelona contained the largest concentration of cotton factories in mainland Europe.[24]

Agriculture

The concept of a British 'agricultural revolution' is one that many economic historians no longer find useful. The changes once thought to merit that title did undoubtedly take place, but they were spread over a long period. Slow and uneven population growth until the 1750s tended to depress prices, but relatively high real wages, enhanced consumer purchasing power and the needs of burgeoning industry promoted diversification and experiments, while statutory bounties encouraged corn exports to the continent. In 1752–4 agriculture supplied 17 per cent of all exports. Corn imports to make up for domestic shortages became necessary from the 1760s onwards as population grew. Improvements in agricultural methods, some of them already well under way before 1700, included careful selection of seed; heavier manuring; new rotations, with crops that raised soil fertility and provided additional animal fodder; selective breeding; the marling, liming and draining of soils; and the development of agricultural machinery. Some improvements spread slowly. Livestock improvement by selective breeding developed very gradually until after 1780. Jethro Tull's seed-drill and horse-hoe system, of which he published a description in 1733, was not widely adopted. Effective seed-drills were not manufactured in quantity before 1800.[25]

Major changes in organization and tenure continued. More commons and wastes were taken into cultivation. At least 13 per cent of English open field, common pasture and 'waste' was enclosed between 1700 and 1800. Some areas, such as the south-east Midlands, were heavily affected. Most of the enclosure was authorized by private acts of parliament and accomplished after 1750. The average farm continued to grow in size. Many smallholders survived, but they usually relied on wages from agriculture or manufacturing for part of their income. Arthur Young, a famous commentator on eighteenth-century agriculture, believed that enclosure enabled farmers to adopt innovative and more productive methods and emphasized that large farms were necessary in order to generate agricultural surpluses. Historians of agriculture have recently suggested that neither enclosure of existing farmland nor consolidation of farms did much to increase overall production, though both reduced rural employment. Some historians have questioned the hitherto widespread belief that many great landlords were agricultural improvers. They suggest that the prime concern of such landlords was the maximization of income for spending in other fields of activity. That was the paramount aim of the agricultural re-organization undertaken by their agents. The rising prices of the later eighteenth century facilitated rent increases and a transfer of income from workers in agriculture to the big landowner. When great landowners *did* take a genuine interest in agriculture, the results were sometimes disappointing. The real promoters of improvement, in this view, were 'resident owner-occupiers, and substantial tenant farmers'.[26]

Most estimates of agricultural output growth during the century have ranged from just under two-thirds to just over a fifth. Some historians have seen an acceleration of growth after 1750, others a slackening of momentum following a period of impressive progress until 1740 or 1750. The latter view has gained ground recently. Optimistic assessments of the performance of English agriculture underline the 'remarkable achievement' of an agricultural sector that comprised a diminishing proportion of the total population in simultaneously supplying most of the food consumed by a growing non-agricultural population and increasing quantities of industrial raw materials. A more pessimistic assessment emphasizes output's failure to match population growth after 1750 and a resulting fall in living standards.[27]

Early eighteenth-century Scotland fed herself and sometimes exported grain. Cattle exports to England rose considerably after the Union. Landlords increasingly let farms as single tenancies and demanded rents in money instead of kind. Between 1760 and the 1790s, 'changes in farm organisation, cultivation methods, land enclosure and new rotations' were rapidly introduced into the Lowlands, compressing into a few decades changes that had taken generations to accomplish in England. Big landowners, even more dominant in the Scottish countryside than their counterparts were in England, are assigned a major role in the process.[28]

The Irish economy grew rapidly from the 1740s. Exports of Ulster linen, allowed free entry to England from 1696, increased thirteenfold between 1710 and 1770. Linen-weaving was largely concentrated in East Ulster, but spinning of linen yarn for use both within and outside Ireland spread over a far larger area. The south-western Irish counties supplied increasing amounts of beef, pork and butter to provision ships and the American tobacco and sugar colonies. From the 1750s, arable farming expanded, and before long began to supply the English market. Extensive areas of the eighteenth-century Irish countryside contained a rapidly increasing mass of labourers and smallholders, largely subsisting on potato cultivation in varying combinations with agricultural employment and/or flax spinning, or in rotation with flax and oats.[29]

England's agricultural workforce rivalled the productivity of its Dutch counterpart by the 1750s, according to the most recent calculations. Output per worker in agriculture was nearly twice as high in England as in France or Spain, and well over twice as high as in Italy. The eighteenth century nevertheless witnessed some agricultural progress on the continent outside the already advanced farming areas of the Netherlands, especially perhaps in France. Various crops and methods were either adopted for the first time or spread much further than before. The foremost examples were maize and the potato, but many others were involved. The cultivation of 'artificial meadows' of sainfoin, clover and lucerne was extended. Animals were better fed. Fallow was reduced. An improved French road network encouraged greater regional specialization. The huge Parisian market continued to stimulate production in its catchment area. Market gardening developed around several European cities. Clearing, irrigation, draining and endykement, especially in Valencia, Catalonia, Lombardy, the Veneto, Friesland and Brandenburg-Prussia, extended the cultivated area. Over 2 per cent was added to existing farmland in France. The French 'Physiocrats' and the 'Cameralists' of the German-speaking world tried to promote agricultural reforms by publishing treatises, inspiring the foundation of agricultural societies and influencing governments.[30]

Obstacles to improvement were much more formidable in most of continental Europe than they were in Britain. They included the natural aridity of many parts of the Mediterranean world; rocky, mountainous terrain; soils degraded by previous overgrazing and deforestation; and Italy's extensive malarial marshes. Poor internal communications were another obstruction, tackled in France with some success, less effectively in Spain. Some areas, especially parts of northern coastal Spain, southern France and Italy, had become overcrowded through a process of subdivision that had often resulted in holdings too small to support their occupants. It is important, however, to distinguish between holdings like these, and more viable small farms whose tenants made a significant contribution to increasing production, for example in France, where such small tenants predominated. They were far more suited to the cultivation of certain labour intensive crops. In many provinces such farmers initiated or shared in significant improvements during the century.[31]

The survival of seigneurial privileges was much more widespread on the continent than in Britain. So was that of peasant communities, often fiercely defensive of common resources, and strongly attached to inherited methods and rotations. The incidence of seigneurial dues varied enormously not only from one country to another, but within individual countries. Attempts to exploit them met growing hostility in France during the century. However, annoying though they often were, the overall burden of rents and dues in France may have been somewhat lower than that of rents in England. More oppressive were the labour services on the lord's demesne that survived over much of eastern Europe. Abuses, including exaction of excessive services, encroachment on peasant holdings and shifting royal tax payments on to peasants, were widespread in the Habsburg lands. Peasant revolts occurred in these areas, especially Hungary, when they had died out over most of the rest of Europe. Over much of Castile, notoriously rapacious landlords exacted the highest possible rents from impoverished tenants.[32]

Governments attempted various reforms in order to assist agriculture: removal of restrictions on the grain trade, opening up additional lands to cultivators and, in parts of central and eastern Europe, the curbing of oppressive seigneurial practices. The grain trade was freed in France (especially in 1763–4), Spain (1765) and Tuscany (1767). Coinciding with population growth, these measures helped raise prices. They benefited larger farmers or landlords, but smaller ones suffered. Wages fell far behind prices and rents. Food riots in France were over three-and-a-half times as common in 1760–89 as they had been in 1690–1720. French ministers promoted the division of common land, albeit with limited results. Much 'under-exploited' Spanish municipal land was divided between farmers (1766–70), as also was land confiscated from the Church in Sicily, where larger producers were the main beneficiaries. The rulers of Prussia and Hanover tried to improve the lot of serfs on their domains. Maria Theresa's government intensified previous attempts to limit labour services, began to get rid of them on royal estates and gave many peasants the right of independent sale of their produce.[33]

The output of French agriculture probably rose by 25 to 40 per cent between 1709 and 1789. The country suffered its last widespread famine in 1709–10, though poor harvests caused widespread distress during the later 1760s. Italy suffered a devastating famine and disease in 1763–4. In Spain, severe drought caused famine in 1753, harvests deteriorated between 1764 and 1773 and severe crises recurred in the 1780s. In these last two countries the efforts of would-be reformers had limited results.[34]

Conclusion

By 1700 England's economy benefited from a unique combination of advantages. These included fertile soils suitable for complementary arable and pastoral husbandry, tilled by a highly productive workforce; abundant and accessible reserves of coal and several other minerals; good transport links by water; a diverse manufacturing sector; a broad-based domestic market; and extensive colonies that served the home economy in different ways.

During the eighteenth century, Britain became Europe's leading commercial power. Her shipping tonnage probably surpassed that of the Dutch Republic by about 1720. In the early 1770s, Europe (including Ireland) still took just over half of England's domestic exports, and most of her re-exports. The century's dramatic development, however, was the growth of the American market, which by the 1770s already absorbed more of England's manufactured exports than did Europe, where sales declined between 1752–4 and 1772–4. The momentum of British industrial expansion and technological innovation quickened after 1760. Intense competition, vigorous experimentation, technological cross-fertilization between different industries and a broad base of education and technical experience all played their part. Innovation proceeded on a wide front, even though especially dramatic increases in production were to result from inventions in textile machinery, iron smelting and steam power.

After about 1750, Scotland reaped substantial benefits from belonging to what had been in principle an English commercial empire before 1707. By 1758 Glasgow imported more tobacco than all English ports combined. England herself was an increasingly important market for Scottish goods. English example and expertise promoted Scotland's agricultural and industrial development, though her own scientists and inventors also made a crucial contribution.

The decline of the Dutch Republic left Britain with one paramount rival in Europe. France had a population nearly three times as large as Britain's. But her economy was less well-integrated, her urban sector proportionally smaller and less dynamic. France's ports and industrial centres were more scattered. She lacked Britain's rapidly expanding market of colonial consumers. Confrontations with Britain's superior naval power underlined the vulnerability of France's overseas trade. Britain never lost the commanding lead in coal-based technology with which she began the century. The French economy nevertheless developed vigorously until the 1780s. Between 1789 and 1815 it was to suffer grievous setbacks.

20

CONTACTS AND CONNECTIONS, 1707–80

Dynasties: possessors and the dispossessed

The personal union of Britain and Hanover brought together two very different states whose interests were sometimes difficult to reconcile. It was a source of recurrent friction in British politics. George I's Baltic policy split his British ministry in 1716, but his French alliance was useful to both Britain and Hanover. Problems in Hanover's relations with the Emperor and Prussia absorbed much British diplomatic energy during the 1720s. When George II sent Hanoverian troops to support the Emperor in 1734, France avoided giving neutral Britain any pretext for intervention. However, during the phase of renewed conflict with France after 1740, the need to protect a vulnerable Hanover complicated attempts to contain France and caused much anger in England. A French threat to Hanover in 1741, and French defeat of the Hanoverian army in 1757, led to embarrassing, if speedily repudiated, Hanoverian neutrality conventions. George II's concern for Hanover's safety resulted in the treaty with Prussia in 1756 that helped bring about a Franco-Austrian alliance. Britain's allies Frederick II and Ferdinand of Brunswick worsted France in Germany during the Seven Years War. The American War did not threaten Hanover because France cautiously avoided involvement in another German quagmire. Some critics argued that Hanoverian interests unduly influenced government policy between 1741 and 1760, or even that continental involvement was an expensive distraction from Britain's global conflict with France. Hanover's vulnerability clearly did influence British policy. However, Britain would probably have combined with one of the leading German powers in any event, so as to prevent France's concentrating her attention on the maritime struggle.[1]

As early as February 1716, George I made a will providing for the separation of Britain and Hanover, which he thought would benefit both of them. George II kept his father's will secret, yet considered a separation at moments of stress in Anglo-Hanoverian relations, only to drop the idea in face of practical difficulties. His son Frederick also intended to divide the inheritance, but he died too soon, and the personal union was dissolved by the failure of the male line only in 1837. Meanwhile, the royal family's Hanoverian interests led to new German dynastic links. All the Hanoverian kings and Prince Frederick married German princesses. The chief criteria of choice included Protestantism and usefulness to Hanoverian interests. George II's Caroline of Ansbach and George III's Charlotte of Mecklenburg-Strelitz reinforced German cultural connections. George II was both cousin and brother-in-law of Frederick William I of Prussia, and uncle to Frederick II. Feelings of resentment and mistrust nevertheless developed between the kinsmen, temporarily overcome during the Seven Years War. Both George II's daughter Louisa and George III's sister Caroline Matilda married into the reliably Protestant royal house of Denmark, a potential counterweight to Prussia. Caroline Matilda's marriage ended in lurid scandal in 1772. George II married his daughter Anne to William IV, Prince of Orange, in hopes of strengthening the Anglo-Dutch alliance, but William died young. Anne's sister Mary married Frederick II, Landgrave of Hesse-Cassel. Hessian troops in British pay gave valuable help during both the 1745 rebellion and the American War. In 1764 George III's sister Augusta married Prince Charles of Brunswick-Wolfenbüttel, a potentially valuable ally.[2]

The British diplomatic service remained less professional than its French counterpart. The relatively scarce ambassadorial appointments tended to be reserved for noblemen or political associates of those in power. The overall growth of the network, especially at middling and lower levels, nevertheless created opportunities for men who sought a diplomatic career. Britain was more or less continuously represented at most major European capitals, and at many of the minor ones. Paris, The Hague, Madrid, Vienna and Constantinople were always regarded as important. Posts that gained significance in British diplomacy included St Petersburg, Berlin and Naples, while Stockholm, Brussels and Venice lost some of their previous standing. During Poland's personal union with Saxony before 1763 diplomats accredited to the king-elector's court represented British interests in both states. Savoy's strategic position astride the western approaches to Italy from France gave it a diplomatic significance out of all proportion to its wealth or population.

Scots became much more prominent in the diplomatic service after 1707. The percentage of diplomatic posts they occupied rose from under 6 in Anne's reign to 21 between 1760 and 1789. In 1760 Scotsmen were to be found in all the most important ones, and in 1770 in nearly all the increasingly significant central and eastern European posts. These appointments were in part compensation for the under-representation of Scots in the higher ranks of government at home. The Hanoverian diplomatic service remained separate, providing the king-electors with independent sources of information, though British representatives looked after Hanoverian interests in some areas where Hanover did not maintain its own diplomatic presence.[3]

James Francis Edward Stuart remained for his supporters James VIII and III, rightful king until his death in 1766. From 1719, he was resident in Rome, the guest of successive popes. He married a Catholic, Clementina Sobieska (1719), but quarrelled with her. He retained several Protestant courtiers in a court riven by faction. His son Charles Edward led the 1745 rising with great panache until the retreat from Derby. Thereafter, his volatility and indecisiveness proved grave liabilities in Scotland and in exile. Travelling round Europe, paranoid, quarrelsome and increasingly alcoholic, he canvassed wild schemes. During a clandestine visit to London in 1750 he entered the Church of England. In 1766 Clement XIII refused to acknowledge Charles as king. His belated 1772 marriage to a minor German princess was unhappy and childless.[4]

Generous papal support for the Stuarts hugely helped the British government by underlining the threat they posed to British Protestantism. Other powers would give the Stuart cause essential support only when it was in their interest. Jacobites naturally looked to France, as Britain's long-term rival, for the necessary aid. As has been seen, the French expedition of 1708 failed. Alas for the Jacobites, peace or friendship with Britain served France's interests best throughout the period 1713–41. Subsequent French invasion plans were frustrated by storms in February 1744, by the retreat from Derby in 1745 and by British destruction of two French fleets in 1759. Only briefly did other powers encourage the Jacobite cause. The Swedish negotiations of 1716–17 came to nothing, the attempted Spanish invasion of 1719 failed miserably and Jacobite hopes of help from Russia were disappointed. In 1751–3 Frederick II briefly encouraged a Jacobite plot but without serious commitment.

The Jacobite exiles were geographically scattered and divided in religion. The Protestants among them lacked the benefits Catholics derived from supportive networks of colleges, seminaries and merchants. Prince Charles's 1745 venture was made possible by the support of Jacobite bankers and Antoine Walsh, Franco-Irish shipowner of Nantes. Irish and Scottish soldiers in French service fought for Charles. Some renowned British noblemen served the Jacobite cause as both soldiers and diplomats. Repeated disappointments, together with the Pretenders' personal failings, eroded Jacobite support in the long run. The continuing loyalty of many Jacobites to the Stuarts is nevertheless impressive. It might have lasted even longer if Charles had been more stable and had married sooner and more successfully.

Dynastic and religious allegiance helped draw many soldiers from the island kingdoms into the service of continental states. The Dutch army still included a Scottish brigade, but Irish and Scottish regiments in the armies of Catholic powers attracted a higher proportion of the recruits who served abroad than before 1690. Their numbers fell as Jacobite hopes dwindled and the British army recruited many more Scotsmen and Irishmen. The most famous of all British soldiers in foreign service was the Protestant Jacobite James Keith, who fought in the Spanish, Russian and Prussian armies. The Jacobite Admiral Thomas Gordon helped Peter I create the Russian navy. Other Britons taught at the naval academy Peter founded in 1715. British shipbuilders worked in Russia throughout the century. Some of Catherine II's most distinguished admirals were British. Meanwhile, Britain drew in every war on the services of Hessian,

Hanoverian, Dutch or Swiss auxiliaries. Families of French and Swiss origin established enduring links with the British army, and the Huguenot immigrant Jean-Louis Ligonier was ultimately promoted to field marshal.

Religious links and affinities

Embattled European Protestants saw England as a potential refuge and source of assistance. The few refugees from the bitter struggle in the Cévennes who reached England in 1706, the 'French prophets', were seen as a disruptive influence even by the leaders of the existing Huguenot community, but nevertheless made a few English converts. In 1709, following French military devastation and a bitterly cold winter, over 13,000 German immigrants from the Palatinate and elsewhere in south-west Germany arrived in England. Some remained there or went to Ireland, but many more moved to America. They were far less warmly received than the Huguenots had been in the 1680s. They appeared much more suddenly, as a group they were far poorer and the German host community was smaller than its Huguenot counterpart had been before 1685. The arrival of persecuted Salzburgers in the early 1730s was followed by their even prompter despatch to Georgia.[5]

Prince George of Denmark, Princess Anne's husband, established a German Court Chapel in 1700. (Three other German churches had been founded in London between 1669 and 1697.) George's secretary, Heinrich Wilhelm Ludolf, was in touch with Halle, and through him the frail but determined Pietist Anton Wilhelm Böhme, a *protégé* of Francke's, became George's chaplain. Ludolf was appointed commissioner to the Palatine refugees in 1709. Böhme organized spiritual ministry to them. He persuaded the SPCK to support various missionary initiatives. It also maintained a European correspondence network. Böhme's successor as Lutheran court preacher after 1722, Friedrich Michael Ziegenhagen worked to preserve these links. Several English bishops took a keen interest in the fate of European Protestants. They sympathized with them as co-religionists under persecution. They were in principle ready to help them and welcome them to England, but hoped for their assimilation to the Church of England. Some bishops, especially Archbishop William Wake between 1717 and 1725, responded positively to the ultimately abortive schemes that the Brandenburg court preacher Daniel Ernst Jablonski developed for Protestant religious union. Wake also encouraged intercommunion between the churches of England and Zurich. More splendidly unrealistic were his hopes of intercommunion with an independent Gallican Church.[6]

The rhetoric of the Protestant interest was important in debate about Britain's foreign policy. Britain and Hanover supported persecuted Protestants even though this complicated relations with the Emperor and the German Catholic princes. Until the 1750s, however, friendship with one of the foremost Catholic powers, France or Austria, was a crucial element of British policy. Only during the Seven Years War did Britain briefly find herself part of a Protestant coalition against Catholic enemies, though her ally Frederick II hardly saw himself as a Protestant champion.

British Catholics remained dependent on colleges and convents in France, the Austrian Netherlands and Rome for the education of many layfolk and the training of candidates for the priesthood, whose numbers fell sharply until around 1760. The Jesuits made up over a third of the missionary priests at the time of their official dissolution in 1773. They survived as a distinct group because they managed to retain control of one college, at Liège, and because they were given informal recognition by the vicars-apostolic. British and Irish Catholic merchant colonies in several foreign cities, especially Antwerp, Paris, Nantes, Bordeaux, Oporto, Cadiz, San Lucar, Leghorn and Naples, provided further links with the continent. Despite the prominence of Catholics in Jacobite ranks, and the papacy's support for the Stuart cause, most British Catholics, lay or clerical, were not active Jacobites. They suffered only sporadic persecution as a result of the exiled dynasty's activities.[7]

Trade and economic development

Rapidly growing raw material imports from northern Europe had special strategic importance. Russia became Britain's leading trading partner in this region. Around 1734 Britain took the greater part of Russia's hemp and flax exports and rapidly growing quantities of iron from the Ural foundries. Russian iron exports to Britain overtook Swedish by 1765. Britain had the lion's share of Baltic trade by 1750, but Russia was now the dominant northern power, her friendship necessary to safeguard essential naval supplies. Britain concluded important trade treaties with her in 1734 and 1766. By 1789 the rapidly growing British community in St Petersburg probably numbered nearly 1,000 people.[8]

North-western Europe (Germany, the Netherlands and France) took from Britain substantial but gradually declining quantities of woollens, much less valuable but steadily increasing consignments of coal and metal wares, and (until the 1750s) large amounts of grain. British re-exports of coffee, tobacco, calicoes, rice and silk rose sharply in value between 1699–1701 and 1772–4. Linen imports, more valuable than those of all other manufactures put together, fell sharply as Irish and Scottish production increased. So did recorded wine imports, reflecting the effect of anti-French tariffs. The area accounted for a small proportion of Britain's continental raw material imports, including textile yarns and dyes, and (after 1760) grain. During the 1750s, Hamburg, 'the continent's most English city' became the foremost centre of the English re-export trade in north-western Europe. Trade with Holland remained important, but the percentage of English exports going there fell from 24.2 to 12.1 between 1698–1701 and 1756–63.[9]

Southern Europe both bought from Britain and supplied her with a wide range of goods, including raw materials. Portugal, and through her Brazil, formed a buoyant market for lighter English woollens and worsteds, largely paid for with Brazilian gold. Portugal was an especially valuable commercial partner until 1760, i.e. before the most dramatic phase of expansion of trade with the North American colonies. British control of large amounts of Brazilian bullion, together with Portuguese merchants' use of English ships, credit and insurance facilities, assisted the consolidation of London's position as the leading European financial centre. British merchants imported rapidly growing quantities of Port wine. Oporto became 'a city with an English heart'. From the 1760s, Brazilian gold production fell. Growing British imports of Brazilian cotton, the end of English grain exports, efforts to stimulate Portugal's own textile industries and higher import duties to finance Lisbon's rebuilding after the terrible earthquake in 1755 sharply reduced Britain's trade surplus. Spanish exports to Britain included fine wool, olive oil, soap, dye-stuffs, iron, wine, nuts and fruit, in addition to invaluable supplies of silver. Britain's sacrifice of the Asiento in 1750 encouraged her merchants to concentrate on trade with 'Old' Spain, also a channel for exports to America. Despite repeated Franco-Spanish alliances, Britain remained Spain's best European customer during the late eighteenth century, and second only to Germany as a source of Spanish imports. Italy supplied Britain with raw silk, olive oil, wine and currants, and was an important export market, especially for textiles. Meanwhile, Britain's share of western trade with the Ottoman Empire shrank to a fifth by 1789, compared with France's three-fifths.[10]

In previous centuries, Britain had been an apprentice in agricultural and industrial techniques. Now other European countries sought to learn from her. The Newcomen engine was employed in France and parts of Belgium from the 1720s onwards, though in relatively small areas endowed with good coal supplies. Coal-fired bottle furnaces spread rapidly after c.1710. French efforts to introduce new British textile-manufacturing technology after 1745 were assisted by two Lancashire men of Jacobite sympathies: John Holker, who helped establish the production of cotton velvets and vitriol and became inspector-general of foreign manufactures, and John Kay, who introduced his 'flying' shuttle and developed an improved carding machine. They brought skilled workers to France. The English technique of 'watering' silk was introduced by 1756, copperplate printing of cloth during the 1760s and the spinning jenny in 1770. French efforts to obtain the water frame, the mule and the Watt engine began soon after their invention. Michael Alcock, a Birmingham metal manufacturer, also had some success in France. A major effort to introduce coke iron smelting was under way by 1780.[11]

English merchant-entrepreneurs helped develop Bohemia's textile industry. Robert Allason, the best known, established linen manufacturing and processing works in Rumburk and the surrounding countryside from 1713 onwards. Isaac Potter was persuaded to go to Austria in 1720 to help build Newcomen engines for draining Upper Hungary's copper mines. Other English experts followed him. Scandinavian industrial espionage in England facilitated the establishment of a cast-steel works near Stockholm and a window-glass factory in Norway. In Russia, Britons were involved in sugar-processing, roperies, cotton printing and finishing, porcelain manufacture, breweries and gun founding. British craftsmen in St Petersburg included saddlers, shoemakers and makers of spectacles, watches and scientific instruments.[12]

The French physiocrats admired England's agriculture. Their picture of it was in some respects misleading, but powerfully influenced subsequent historical analysis. François Quesnay insisted that an agriculture based on big farms was the most dynamic and productive. In his argument 'the wealthy farmer and proprietor ... incarnate economic rationality'. The physiocrats were also strenuous advocates of free trade in grain. Less controversially, they called for a variety of improvements in husbandry.[13]

Britain was now less reliant on industrial espionage, though as has been seen, Thomas Lombe used diagrams of Italian machines in his Derby silk-throwing factory. But immigrant or recently settled businessmen and craftsmen continued to make a valuable contribution to the British economy. Huguenot goldsmiths and silversmiths did their finest work in the 1730s and 1740s; the Huguenot contribution to the English silk industry reached its peak in the 1740s and 1750s. The most skilled London engravers were Huguenots. Germans were the largest group gaining naturalization between 1715 and 1800. A substantial majority were merchants; some were sugar refiners, professional men or craftsmen. Many skilled Germans, such as musicians, watchmakers, instrument makers, masons, bookbinders, tailors, shoemakers and bakers, did not seek naturalization. One estimate puts the German population of London in 1800 at 16,000–20,000, which will have included many Jews.[14]

British tourists in Europe

The British aristocratic 'Grand Tour' (a phrase received into English around 1748) reached its peak during the eighteenth century. Increasing numbers of other visitors went to the continent for holidays and diversion. Among cities, Paris was the most popular goal, followed by Venice, Florence, Rome and Naples. The zenith of British interest in the Dutch Republic had passed, but it remained one of the most visited countries in Europe. The Hanoverian connection and the increasing elegance of Dresden and Vienna drew smaller but growing numbers to the German-speaking lands. Berlin became a tourist destination for the first time. Some travellers reached the Ottoman Empire, including a few intrepid women, but it remained off the tourist track. Few British tourists visited Iberia.

Useful knowledge, experience and social attainments were still thought to be the principal educational benefits of foreign travel. Aristocratic parents no longer greatly feared religious seduction; indeed, the opportunity to compare Protestant and Catholic countries, noting the deleterious effects of popish superstition, was thought to be educationally valuable. Italy was judged foremost in artistic achievement, though many travellers admired the architecture of Paris and other northern cities, and there was growing appreciation of Germany's musical life.[15]

Enlightenment

The word 'Enlightenment' is a shorthand term for certain changes in the eighteenth-century intellectual climate. Adopted in Britain from Germany only after 1800, it initially had pejorative overtones here. For the German philosopher Immanuel Kant, writing in 1784, its essence lay in man's emergence from immaturity through having the courage to use his own understanding, advanced by public discussion. For Kant, the philosopher king was the prime agent of Enlightenment. In central and eastern Europe, rulers were indeed the key promoters of 'enlightened' measures: the advancement of scientific knowledge, religious toleration, the removal of internal restrictions on trade and industry, and legal, educational and administrative reforms. The original progenitors of what came to be known as the 'Enlightenment' had, however, been active in western Europe.

Some of the seventeenth century's most original thinkers had been born, or had found refuge, in the Dutch Republic, above all Descartes, Spinoza and Locke. Descartes's attempt to lay completely new foundations for philosophy and his application of systematic doubt to inherited conceptions give him a claim to be considered the father of the Enlightenment. Newton's picture of the universe soon superseded that of Descartes, but both believed that it was governed by a benevolent God. Spinoza, on the other hand, denied the existence of such a being.

John Locke published two especially influential books in 1690. His *Essay Concerning Human Understanding* located the basis of all human ideas in experience, and emphasized the limited nature of our knowledge, but at the same time asserted man's possession of a God-given faculty of judgement, and the need to judge revelation by reason as well as faith. The second of his *Two Treatises of Government* found the authority and basis of governments, as we have seen, in an original contract. *Some Thoughts Concerning Education* (1693) emphasized the importance of early experience in making the child – born like a blank slate – into an actively rational and virtuous adult. The third earl of Shaftesbury thought that Locke underestimated men's capacity for a disinterested love of virtue, and believed that social interaction and the exchange of ideas would promote truth. The sceptical Bernard de Mandeville, originally from Rotterdam, had a more pessimistic opinion of individuals' capacity for altruistic action. However, the optimistic message of his *Fable of the Bees, or Private Vices, Public Benefits* (1714) was that men's greed and desire for comfort drove economic growth and redounded to the overall benefit of society.

Some leading philosophers of the early French Enlightenment during the long peace after 1713 greatly admired England. Voltaire lived there in 1726–9. In his *Lettres Philosophiques ou Lettres Anglaises* (1733) he presented England as the land of freedom of thought and speech, and emphasized the breadth of English political participation. Bolingbroke, in exile after serving James III, had advised Voltaire which English books to read, though it was only after his return to France that he seriously studied Locke and Newton, and became the most effective popularizer of Newton's ideas on the continent. In Montesquieu's *Lettres Persanes* on western society and government (1721), their ostensible author, a Persian visitor, reported that love and gratitude were the only bonds the English recognized: royal oppression removed the basis of their obedience.

They maintained that no unbounded power could be lawful. Montesquieu visited England in 1729–31, and his comparative study of political constitutions, *L'Esprit des Lois* (1748), described England as a 'commercial republic disguised as a monarchy'. Denis Diderot admired and translated Shaftesbury (1745). Approached by a bookseller with a proposal to translate Ephraim Chambers's *Cyclopaedia* (1728), he turned the original design into the most famous collaborative project of the French Enlightenment, the *Encyclopédie* (1751–77).

During Enlightenment's high summer between 1740 and 1780, Scotland took the lead within Britain in 'the development of the sciences of man and of political economy, the historical investigation of the progress of society, and the critical application of ideas for human betterment to the existing social and political order'. In England these central concerns of the Enlightenment did not preoccupy leading thinkers to the extent that they did in France, Germany, Italy and Scotland, largely because England already enjoyed liberty and 'the benefits of commerce'. The rather mixed short-term economic results of Scotland's union with her much richer and more powerful partner helped to sustain vigorous discussion of how best to promote her well-being. The Moderate Party was ascendant in the Kirk by the 1760s, but the defenders of orthodoxy were still on guard. Several new Scottish university chairs were created during the early eighteenth century, and medical teaching was greatly expanded. Clubs, masonic lodges and proliferating new societies facilitated the informal exchange of ideas.[16]

Human nature was a central concern of the Scottish Enlightenment. The Ulsterman Francis Hutcheson, professor of moral philosophy at Glasgow (1729–46), associated himself with Shaftesbury, and identified a divinely implanted moral sense and a public sense that inspired kind and benevolent acts. The best action procured 'the greatest happiness for the greatest numbers'. David Hume, most celebrated of the Scottish philosophers, emphasized in his *Treatise of Human Nature* (1739–40) the limitations of human reason, the importance of experience, the role of natural instinct, the power of desires and passions, and the part played by sympathy in the formation of moral sentiments. Hume's philosophical scepticism caused disquiet among more conservative thinkers at home and abroad.

Hume's friend Adam Smith, like Hutcheson professor of moral philosophy at Glasgow, argued in his *Wealth of Nations* (1776), the most comprehensive work of political economy yet written, that the pursuit of individual wealth and the enjoyment of its fruits promoted general economic well-being. Expanding markets facilitated the division of labour, greater productivity and higher living standards. Freedom was essential to the efficient operation of the market. Interference designed to raise prices, lower wages, limit the free movement of workers, or to subsidize or protect producers were all economically damaging. Smith criticized excessive reliance on regulated overseas commerce, advocating greater investment in agriculture and internal trade.

Smith discerned four stages of society: the successive ages of hunters, herders, farmers and commerce. Commerce freed men from dependence on great landowners and opened up prospects of enrichment and individual choice. His conception of stages of social development resembled Hume's. Adam Ferguson in his *Essay on the History of Civil Society* (1767) also traced a general development towards commercial society, but expressed concern about the possibly deleterious effects of wealth on people's civic virtue and martial spirit.

Many works by Scottish philosophers were quickly translated into French and German. Hume was feted in France when he served in the British embassy in Paris (1763–5). Smith also visited France in 1764–6, and had fruitful discussions with French economists. It was Hume who offered Jean-Jacques Rousseau help in finding an English haven despite the radical differences in their views. Rousseau's belief that the development of civilization had destroyed 'natural' man's primitive happiness, set out in publications of 1750 and 1755, and underpinning his educational tract *Émile* (1762), ran directly counter to Hume's philosophical grain. Rousseau's *Du Contrat Social* (1762) maintained that only the 'general will' of the majority of the people acting together could confer true legitimacy on government. Hume had already rejected as historically unrealistic Locke's conception of an original contract. Once in England, Rousseau quarrelled violently with Hume.

Science and medicine

John Francis Vigani, a native of Verona, was appointed as the first professor of chemistry in Britain at Cambridge in 1703. Edinburgh made its first appointment in 1713. Two of the Edinburgh professors, William Cullen (1756–66) and his pupil Joseph Black (1766–96), were called upon for advice on a huge range of industrial processes crucially important to the Scottish economy. Central to the 'chemical revolution' was the investigation and isolation of gases and other elements by Black, Henry Cavendish, James Watt, Samuel Rutherford and Joseph Priestley, though the Frenchman Antoine Lavoisier accomplished the most systematic and effective work in this field.[17]

Both Cullen and Black served as professors of medicine as well as chemistry. Medicine attracted more students to the continent than any other discipline, Leiden more than any other university. Scotland was disproportionately well represented at Leiden, and the Edinburgh medical school, which rapidly established itself as the best in Britain, was organized on the Leiden pattern. Paris also offered a wide range of opportunities for study in medicine, anatomy and kindred disciplines. (Some students went to Utrecht and Groningen. Göttingen University, founded by George II, opened in 1737, and attracted about 250 British students by 1800. Several students, but especially Scotsmen, studied law or theology. Medical study was, however, the single most important reason for attending a foreign university.) Several British, and especially Scottish, doctors practised abroad. In Russia they included Catherine II's personal physician, the doctor who inoculated her against smallpox in 1768, and the supervisor of the St Petersburg inoculation hospital.

Herman Boerhaave of Leiden, teacher of generations of Scottish students, and his pupil Albrecht von Haller of Bern were the foremost medical scholars in Europe for much of this period. Von Haller, who had got to know several leading British physicians during a visit to England in 1727–8, was in 1736 invited by George II to fill the chair of medicine at Göttingen. He made a fundamental distinction between the contractile or 'irritable' fibres (muscles) and the 'sensible' fibres (nerves). Robert Whytt, professor of medicine at Edinburgh, concluded that the 'sentient principle', the soul, distributed all over the body, conveyed impressions in the sensory nerves and initiated motion in the muscles, and engaged in controversy with von Haller.

He published a major work on nervous disorders in 1764. His Edinburgh colleague William Cullen, who coined the word 'neurosis', was one of the European physicians who believed that a great range of diseases were nervous in origin. Cullen also thought that climate, class, culture and gender affected individuals' nervous sensitivity. Patients in many different countries sought his advice.[18]

Two points emerge strongly from the history of British anatomy and surgery during the eighteenth century: the extent of fruitful connections with France and the number of distinguished Scotsmen who practised in London. The Scottish surgeon John Douglas was a rival in lithotomy with the Englishman William Cheselden, who adopted the lateral lithotomy technique used in France by Jacques de Beaulieu, gaining European fame. John Douglas's brother James, William Smellie and William Hunter were all Scotsmen who visited France to gain a professional qualification or experience, and worked as anatomists and men-midwives in London. All these men taught and published. The lectures that Hunter started to give in his newly built London anatomy theatre in 1767 were particularly renowned.

The single most notable success in reducing mortality resulted from the dissemination of a Turkish folk remedy. Lady Mary Wortley Montagu, wife of the British ambassador in Constantinople, described inoculation against the scourge of smallpox in 1717, and was instrumental in its introduction to Britain, where it was adopted on a large scale after 1750. It spread from Britain to mainland Europe.

There were close links between medicine and natural history, especially botany. Johann Jakob Dillenius of Giessen moved to England in 1721, became first president of the London Botanical Society, and later professor of botany at Oxford. The foremost eighteenth-century naturalist, the Swede Karl Linnaeus, visited England in 1736, soon after the publication in Holland of his *Systema Naturae*, partly funded by the Scottish doctor Isaac Lawson. While in England Linnaeus met Dillenius and the distinguished Scottish botanist Philip Miller, chief gardener at the Chelsea Physic Garden, and member of the Florence Botanic Academy. Early use by several British botanists helped to promote the rapid general adoption of Linnaeus's system of classification of all known living things, and binomial nomenclature by genus and species.

Linnaeus's star student, Daniel Solander, came to England in 1760, ultimately became keeper of the natural history collections at the British Museum, and advised the wealthy young naturalist Sir Joseph Banks. Solander accompanied Banks in 1768–71 on James Cook's voyage to Tahiti, New Zealand and Australia, and gathered an important collection of plants. After 1773, Banks made Kew Gardens an internationally renowned botanical centre. Reinhold Forster, a native of Prussia who had recently arrived in England, served as the naturalist on Cook's 1772–5 expedition, accompanied by his son Georg. They jointly published an account of the expedition's botanical findings. Georg's *A Voyage round the World* (1777) achieved great success in Germany on its translation there in 1778.

The Comte de Buffon began to publish his hugely ambitious *Histoire Naturelle* in 1749. De Buffon's translation of one of his early sources of inspiration, Stephen Hales's *Vegetable Staticks* (1727), had appeared in 1735. Hales had among other things measured transpiration in plants and the force of the upward sap-current in their stems, and had demonstrated their absorption of what was subsequently identified as carbon dioxide. In 1748, de Buffon collaborated in Paris with John Needham, the first Catholic priest to be elected FRS, a meticulous investigator of micro-organisms. De Buffon's immense labours led him, among other things, to the controversial conclusions that species had evolved, and that the earth must be far older than the Bible indicated. The Scottish scholar Lord Monboddo drew on de Buffon's studies in his own work on the origin and progress of language, where he presented orangutans as primitive human beings.[19]

Along with botanical and zoological investigation, more accurate mapping of the earth and heavens was among the objectives of eighteenth-century voyages of exploration. 'If the French excelled during this period in the exactness of their observations, the English made such observations possible by the skill and ingenuity of their instrument-makers.' George Graham, inventor of the dead beat escapement and the mercurial pendulum, supplied instruments to the Frenchman P. L. M. de Maupertuis, who in 1738 proved that the earth is flattened at the poles. John Harrison's chronometers, tested in 1760 and 1764, made possible the precise determination of longitude at sea. Jesse Ramsden invented the 'equatorial' and transformed the theodolite. William Herschel, who came to England from his native Hanover c.1758, became a successful musician and composer, and then graduated via mathematics to astronomy. His patient construction during the 1770s of a telescope with a hugely improved magnification led to friendship with some of England's leading astronomers and to his observation of Uranus (1781), the first recorded discovery of a planet.[20]

Most of the scientists mentioned here were elected to the Royal Society, which acted as the major British forum for scientific discussion. In 1740, 49 per cent of the fellowship were foreigners.

Literature

Britain enjoyed especially close literary connections with France. A variety of processes were at work: translation (often almost immediate); adaptation, as authors borrowed themes, plots or characters for work more or less their own; and a gradual percolation of concepts and styles into broader literary consciousness. England owed the development of some ideas central to her literary taste, such as wit, decorum and good sense, to seventeenth-century French literary critics. Alexander Pope's *Essay on Criticism* (1711), modelled on Horace's *Ars Poetica*, possibly surpassed the influential French critic Boileau's *Art Poétique* (1674). Pope's mock-heroic poem *The Rape of the Lock* was modelled on Boileau's *Le Lutrin*.

The plays of Molière, Marivaux and other French authors succeeded on the English stage and provided plots and characters for English authors. French fiction fed the English imagination. Cyrano de Bergerac's 'proto-science fiction narratives' helped inspire Jonathan Swift's *Gulliver's Travels*. François Fénelon's *Les Aventures de Télémaque* (1699), presenting a 'model of the ideal gentleman', was often reprinted in England. The Scots novelist Tobias Smollett, a translator of *Télémaque*, also translated Alain-René Lesage's picaresque *Adventures of Gil Blas* (1749), and acknowledged its influence on *The Adventures of Roderick Random* (1748). Rabelais influenced Smollett, Swift and Sterne. French novels of passion and scandal proved especially popular. Jean-Jacques Rousseau's more serious exploration of the themes of passion and virtue in *Julie, ou la Nouvelle Heloïse* (1761) enjoyed huge success.[21]

French interest in English literature was satisfied by increasing numbers of translations, many of them first published in Holland. Milton's *Paradise Lost* was frequently re-printed. Voltaire published adaptations of some of Shakespeare's plays, and helped to stimulate wider continental discussion of his work. Voltaire was also a warm admirer of Pope, whose better known poems soon appeared in French translations. Pope was one of the contributors to Addison's and Steele's journal *The Spectator* (1711–12, 1714). Pierre Marivaux sufficiently admired its combination of morality with wit to found a *Spectateur français* (1722). Jonathan Swift's satires were also frequently translated. Defoe's *Robinson Crusoe* (1719) and Henry Fielding's picaresque *Tom Jones* (1749) were both popular in France. Samuel Richardson's *Pamela* (1740) and *Clarissa* (1748–9), stories of women who resisted seduction, were swiftly translated. Denis Diderot praised Richardson for writing novels of a new sort 'which raise the spirit, touch the heart, [and] are permeated with a love for what is good'. He here expressed a central idea of the emerging 'cult of sensibility' to which Rousseau powerfully contributed. Laurence Sterne's *Sentimental Journey* (1768) was also a hit in the francophone world.[22]

Many British books were translated into German. Some books, including Defoe's *Robinson Crusoe* and *Moll Flanders*, and Richardson's *Pamela*, were available soon after first publication. Germany appreciated Shakespeare earlier and more fully than France. Some of his admirers wanted to use his work to promote a more authentically German drama, free of the 'tyranny' of classicism. James Macpherson's *Fingal* (1762) and *Temora* (1763), purportedly ancient Gaelic epic poems by the bard Ossian, were received enthusiastically both in Scotland and on the continent, but especially warmly in Germany.[23]

Despite the many links between Germany and England during the eighteenth century, there was relatively little translation from German into English. Literary translation from Italian also fell to a low level. The Italian book that had the biggest impact in Britain was probably Cesare Beccaria's treatise on crimes and punishments (1764), which influenced William Eden's *Principles of Penal Law* (1771) and John Howard's campaign for penal reform. The Spanish picaresque novel, and particularly *Don Quixote*, had a lasting influence in England. Both Fielding and Smollett greatly admired Cervantes.

Visual arts

Several grand tourists acquired European paintings for their houses and had their portraits painted by Italian artists, including the Roman Pompeo Batoni, who perfected the 'swagger portrait', and the Venetian Rosalba Carriera, practitioner of an altogether more intimate and sensual portraiture. The eighteenth century also saw an unprecedented succession of truly British painters of high quality. Portraits were always required, but conversation pieces and landscapes gained in popularity, and some British artists experimented with different sorts of narrative picture. Sir James Thornhill, England's finest baroque wall and ceiling painter, executed major commissions at the Royal Naval Hospital, Greenwich (from 1708), and St Paul's (1716–19). William Hogarth, Thornhill's son-in-law, graduated from satirical prints to moralizing, tragicomic narrative series, conversation pieces and portraits. The Scotsman Allan Ramsay and the prolific and inventive Joshua Reynolds were the most popular of a growing cluster of high-society portrait painters of the middle and later years of this period that also included the Aberdonian Jacobite Cosmo Alexander, George Romney (from the 1760s) and Henry Raeburn (active in Edinburgh from the 1770s). Reynolds's contemporary Thomas Gainsborough painted both landscapes and portraits. Samuel Scott and the Welshman Richard Wilson were fine landscape painters. Also active after 1750 were George Stubbs, outstanding painter of horses, and Joseph Wright, renowned for studies of industrial activity and scenes lit by moon or candle.[24]

Some painters were exposed to continental influence without going abroad. Thornhill owed much to the work of Antonio Verrio and Louis Laguerre. He trained Hogarth, staunch defender of the idea of a truly *English* art whose narratives nevertheless had some affinities with Dutch genre painting. Gainsborough, pupil to the Frenchman Hubert Gravelot, drew especially on Netherlands artists such as Rubens, van Dyck and Jacob van Ruysdael whose work he saw in England. Other artists spent time in Italy. Ramsay studied under Italian masters and at the French academy in Rome; Alexander lived in Rome from 1747 to 1751. Reynolds made a particularly extensive and thorough study of Italian artists' work in the course of a long visit in 1750–2. Wilson owed his mature style above all to Claude Lorrain and Gaspard Dughet, seventeenth-century French artists based in Italy.

In 1768, nine of the thirty-six founding members of the Royal Academy of Arts, most of them painters, had come to England from the continent: four from Italy, four from the German-speaking world and one from France. They included Angelica Kauffmann, a history painter, and Johann Zoffany, producer of lively portraits and ambitious conversation pieces. The Venetians Antonio Pellegrini, Sebastiano Ricci and Jacopo Amigoni and the Frenchmen Philippe Mercier and Jean-Baptiste van Loo had also worked in England. The Venetian Giovanni Antonio Canal (Canaletto), renowned for his cityscapes, spent the years 1746-55 in London.

Hogarth's prints found an audience in Germany, and his *Analysis of Beauty* (1753) was swiftly translated into German, French and Italian. Some British artists gained a reputation in Italy. William Kent painted the cupola of S. Giuliano in Rome (1717). The Scotsman Gavin Hamilton, in Italy from 1756 onwards, was a pioneer of grand neo-classical narrative. His younger compatriot David Allan was a successful painter of historical episodes and popular customs.

Sculptors won public acclaim above all by executing grand funeral monuments, especially in the national pantheon of Westminster Abbey, or public statues. Portrait busts (increasingly popular), house and garden sculpture and carved surrounds for fireplaces or memorial inscriptions were all ways of building up an appreciative clientele. For some decades a group of long-lived artists, all of whom arrived between c.1720 and c.1730, were the leading sculptors in England. They included two Flemings, Pieter Scheemakers and John Michael Rysbrack, and the Frenchman Louis François Roubiliac. One of eighteenth-century Europe's greatest sculptors, Roubiliac, produced some especially inventive and dramatic funeral monuments. Henry Cheere, son of a Huguenot immigrant, was the foremost native sculptor of the mid-century. A new generation of native artists emerged after 1750: Joseph Wilton and Joseph Nollekens, both of them successful sculptors of funeral monuments and portrait busts; Thomas Banks, whose favourite medium was relief sculpture illustrating ancient myth or history; and John Bacon, an important early designer for the ceramic and metalwork industries, who later created some grand monuments. Wilton trained in France; he, Nollekens and Banks all worked or studied in Italy, where Wilton gained a reputation. Another sculptor, Francis Harwood, settled there and established an international clientele.[25]

Architecture

John Vanbrugh designed the magnificently baroque Castle Howard (largely built 1700-12) and Blenheim Palace (1705-20), whose rich detail derived in part from the work of French architects. Nicholas Hawksmoor, Wren's pupil and Vanbrugh's collaborator, conceived from 1712 onwards some grandly monumental structures: the Clarendon Building in Oxford and several new churches in London and achieved a unique combination of classical and Gothic elements at All Souls College, Oxford. James Gibbs, an Aberdeenshire Catholic trained by Carlo Fontana in Rome, designed the magnificent churches of

St Mary le Strand (1714–17) and St Martin's in the Fields (1722–6), Cannons, the duke of Chandos's Edgeware mansion (1716–20) and the domed rotunda of the Radcliffe Camera, Oxford (1737–49).[26]

Andrea Palladio, the great architect of Vicenza and Venice, was a major source of inspiration of the 'Palladian' style favoured by the Whig nobility, though by no means the only one. The Scotsman Colen Campbell designed between 1712 and 1725 a series of Palladian houses, including Wanstead, Stourhead, Mereworth and (for Walpole) Houghton. The Venetian Giacomo Leoni, who arrived in England c.1714, also employed Palladio's style. The earl of Burlington chose Campbell to remodel Burlington House in London. Palladio's work, which Burlington studied in Italy, also inspired his elegant Twickenham villa. In Italy he found William Kent, who became his *protégé*. Together with Thomas Coke they designed Coke's house at Holkham (from 1733), with its splendid columned hall. Kent also designed the new treasury buildings in Whitehall (1733–7) and the Horse Guards (1750–9). John Wood, practitioner of urban Palladianism, developed his native Bath and designed civic buildings for Bristol and Liverpool.[27]

James Stuart, son of a Scots mariner living in London, set off on foot for Rome in 1742, studied there until 1750, visited Athens and published with Nicholas Revett *Antiquities of Athens* (1762). 'Athenian' Stuart nevertheless drew much of his inspiration from buildings of the Roman period. Robert Adam, in Rome from 1755 to 1757, also published a famous book about the Emperor Diocletian's palace at Split (1764). Adam, from a Scottish family of architects, was the most inventive and prolific of eighteenth-century members of his profession, drawing on all classical architecture rather than making Palladio a privileged guide. His designs ranged from Kedleston Hall's south front (c.1760) to the Adelphi buildings in London (1768–72), a riverside warehouse arcade surmounted by elegant town houses. Lord Bute commissioned Adam to design his own house at Luton Hoo (1767–74) and ensured his appointment as royal architect (1761), along with William Chambers, who had trained in both Paris and Rome. In his elegantly powerful masterpiece, the new Somerset House (1776–1801), Chambers married Palladian and French styles. His admirer James Wyatt, who returned from six years in Venice and Rome in 1768, was the rising star of the 1770s.[28]

The grounds surrounding country houses were manipulated so as to produce more pleasing vistas, and studded with garden buildings that allowed architects more scope for experiment than the houses themselves, including a variety of temples, towers, grottoes, Gothick ruins and Chinese pavilions. Claude Lorrain's depictions of sublime landscapes containing distant temples may have been a powerful influence. In 1712, Joseph Addison advocated designing gardens in a way that would work with, and sometimes improve, rather than subdue, Nature. The outstanding designer of the eighteenth-century English garden was Lancelot 'Capability' Brown, who started his career working with William Kent at Stowe in the 1740s. 'English gardens' were subsequently designed in many continental countries. The first source of a French reaction against formal gardens was, however, interest in Chinese design, hence the French term '*jardin Anglo-Chinois*'. William Chambers's pagoda in the Royal Gardens at Kew (1761) was then the tallest European building in the Chinese style. The 'Gothick' style, the other non-classical source of inspiration for garden buildings, was also used in residential architecture from the 1760s onwards, partly in a supposed re-assertion of English or British identity against more recently imported classical styles.[29]

Music

Eighteenth-century England enjoyed an immensely vigorous musical life, though the foremost composers working there were Germans or Italians. George Frideric Handel, born in Halle, and already well-known in both Germany and Italy, first visited London in 1710, and in 1713 was given a salary by Queen Anne. His royal commissions included his *Water Music* (1717), *Zadok the Priest*, for George II's coronation in 1727, and *Music for the Royal Fireworks*, to celebrate the peace of 1748, attended by 12,000 people on its first public performance in Green Park. Handel staged many of his forty-two operas at the Theatre Royal, Covent Garden, from 1735 onwards. The most famous of his twenty-nine oratorios, *Messiah*, was first performed at Dublin in 1742. Handel combined royal favour with exceptional commercial success. Many other German musicians worked in England. Johann Christoph Pepusch arrived *c*.1697 after starting his career at the Prussian court. Director of the orchestra at the theatre in Lincoln's Inn Fields (1716–32), the duke of Chandos's musical director at Cannons (1719–23), where Handel was also employed, and co-founder of the Academy of Ancient Music (1726), Pepusch composed the overture for John Gay's immensely popular satirical *Beggar's Opera* (1728). After some years in Italy, Christoph Gluck briefly held an appointment at the King's Theatre in 1745–6, composing two operas. Karl Friedrich Abel came from Dresden in 1759, Johann Christian Bach from Italy in 1762. Both served Queen Charlotte, and in 1764 or 1765 they joined forces in the long-running Bach–Abel subscription concerts at the concert hall in Soho Square.[30]

In 1700, Italy was the most important source of external influences on English musical taste. Arcangelo Corelli, the great violinist-composer, was especially widely admired. Among the Italian composers and musicians who spent several years in England were the violinist Francesco Geminiani, who had been taught by Corelli as well as Alessandro Scarlatti, cellist Giovanni Battista Bononcini, who composed a funeral anthem for the duke of Marlborough, and oboist Giuseppe Sammartini, who joined the household of Frederick, Prince of Wales.

Several gifted English composers benefited from the presence of foreign masters. Thomas Arne, perhaps best known as the composer of *Rule Britannia* (1740), was influenced by Handel, but in important respects developed independently, especially during his later career. Geminiani taught two notable composers, Charles Avison and Michael Festing; Pepusch helped train William

Boyce, one of the four Englishmen who occupied the honourable post of master of the king's music throughout this period. Some English musicians such as Thomas Roseingrave and Thomas Linley Jr went to Italy for training.

Conclusion

The exclusion of the Catholic Stuarts resulted in a Hanoverian personal union that was, in the eyes of many Englishmen, a highly undesirable encumbrance. The exiled dynasty in Rome was an alternative focus of loyalty for Jacobites at home and dispersed across the continent from San Lucar to St Petersburg. Britain was one of the most powerful European countries in the eighteenth century, yet in 1745 it looked, briefly, as though her government might be overthrown by a pretender who had landed with a handful of men. The leading Protestant power, would-be protector of Protestant interests, Britain often needed Catholic allies. Britain's political, economic and literary achievements were widely admired. Foreign observers praised her freedom, European governments were keen to learn about her industries and her leading writers were widely translated. At the same time, her architecture, visual arts and music were powerfully shaped by continental influences. More British painters were active than ever before. Many of them, and some of the most distinguished architects of the kingdom, were Scotsmen. The foremost musicians, and several of the best sculptors, working in Britain were Germans, Italians or Flemings. Many of Britain's leading artists and architects trained in Italy or spent time there. The Hanoverian dynasty strengthened connections with Germany. It was nevertheless with France, despite the renewal of hostilities between the two countries in the 1740s, that Britain enjoyed the closest and most sustained intellectual contacts. Scotland came into her own as a leading participant in the high Enlightenment. Coincidentally, Scotsmen took a growing share in Britain's diplomatic representation, especially in eastern Europe. During the 1770s, the torch of political virtue passed to America; there was widespread European pleasure in Britain's discomfiture. Yet in the very year of the Declaration of Independence appeared Adam Smith's *Wealth of Nations*, swiftly translated into French and German, one of the most immediately influential works of the Enlightenment.

21

TRUE UNION?

Scotland and government

The Union brought little increase in Scottish influence on policy or politics
at Westminster to compensate for the loss of Scotland's parliament and the
abolition of her privy council in 1708. Some Scotsmen were appointed
British privy councillors, but they seldom held one of the higher offices or
belonged to the cabinet. One of the two secretaries of state usually took care
of Scottish business. A third principal secretaryship to which Scotsmen
were appointed existed for most of the period 1709–25, but thereafter only
in 1742–6.

During the years 1725–42 and 1746–61 the key intermediaries in the government's management of North Britain were John Campbell, second duke of
Argyll, and his brother Archibald, earl of Islay, John's successor as duke
(1743–61). Their forebears, long amongst Scotland's greatest magnates, had
been zealous Protestants, Covenanters and Whigs. The family held land in
the Scottish Highlands and Lowlands and in England. Both born in Surrey,
the brothers spent much of their time on their estates just outside London.
John, a formidable soldier and a bold and ruthless politician, had helped to
achieve the Union and subsequently the defeat of the 1715 rebellion. Islay,
justice general of Scotland (1710–61), patronized 'ingenious men' and was
also a skilful manager, deploying crown patronage to ensure support for the
government from Scottish MPs and elected peers. Andrew Fletcher, Lord
Milton, lord justice clerk from 1735, acted as Islay's agent in Scotland. When
Argyll quarrelled with Walpole in 1739, Islay remained loyal and soon rebuilt
his influence after his brother's death. George II's coolness towards him
helped to ensure that he never became secretary of state, but between 1761
and 1763, Bute, his sister's son, briefly became secretary of state, then prime
minister. Bute made his brother his Scottish manager, but after 1765 there
was no one intermediary between London and Scotland for the rest of this
period.[1]

Church, law and Union in Scotland

The most distinctively national Scottish institution preserved in 1707 was the Kirk. As a result 'whereas Scottish Presbyterianism was largely politically unionist and ecclesiastically nationalist, the Episcopal Church was the reverse'.[2] Episcopal clergy and laity often found considerable sympathy in Tory circles in England. There were links between Scottish and English nonjuring clergy. The insistence of a Tory-dominated United Kingdom parliament on limited toleration and the rights of patrons in 1712 was a bitter pill for Presbyterians to swallow. It was contrary to the spirit of the explicit guarantee given in the Treaty of Union. Arguably, however, the Westminster parliament's interference had beneficial results so far as the preservation of the Union was concerned. The proscribed episcopal Church was the prime source of Jacobite support. Many of the local landowners who supported it deeply resented the abolition of church patronage. The restoration of patronage, exercised with increasing confidence from the 1730s onwards, may have been one reason for the evident decline of episcopal adherence even before 1745. It probably assisted both the reconciliation of landowners with the Kirk and the rise of 'Moderation' within it. Toleration functioned as something of a safety valve, conditional though it was on the readiness of the clergy to manifest loyalty to the reigning monarch. This limited toleration will have been unacceptable to firm Jacobites, but it created room for the sorts of accommodation and compromise to which the more flexible members of proscribed minorities have so often resorted, as well as the possibility of a non-Jacobite episcopalianism in Scotland. A few episcopal clergy ordained by English or Irish bishops attracted sizeable congregations in eastern coastal towns, which suggests that the strategy had some success.

The Treaty of Union had provided that the Westminster parliament should not alter Scottish laws that concerned private rights unless for the 'evident utility' of Scottish subjects. All existing heritable and lifelong offices and jurisdictions were to be preserved. The Court of Session was to remain in Scotland, with its existing authority and privileges. Only those who practised in the court were to be eligible for appointment as lords of session. The existence of an independent Scottish legal system and the differences between English and Scots law, particularly the latter's indebtedness to Roman law, and greater openness to continental influences, were not important sources of tension in the Union. English law did, however, begin to influence Scots law. The House of Lords heard a growing number of appeals in civil cases. English influence was probably strongest in the field of commercial law. Jacobite activity provoked the sharpest legislative responses from Westminster. Parliament extended the English law of treason to Scotland in 1709 after the failure of Jacobite plans for a rising in 1708. The change was bitterly opposed by Scottish MPs. Military tenures and heritable jurisdictions were abolished in 1746–7 as a result of the government's determination to curtail the power of the Highland chiefs over their tenants. The duke of Argyll and the Scottish Whigs supported this change. Compensation of £493,000, to be distributed among loyal landowners, made it more acceptable. Meanwhile, between 1707 and 1745, Edinburgh lawyers' attitudes towards Jacobitism had probably changed from being predominantly sympathetic to being 'noticeably hostile'.[3]

The Highlands

Well before 1745 trade in cattle and linen yarn and the building of new roads under the supervision of General Wade between 1725 and 1737 had already furthered the process of integrating the Highlands with the rest of Scotland. But Highland clans supplied the core of Prince Charles's armed following, even though several sympathetic chiefs did not give effective support and others were neutral or Whig in sentiment. Cumberland's officers targeted rebel clans with savage reprisals that included indiscriminate killings and the destruction or confiscation of property. The Disarming Act of 1746 ordered the surrender of all weapons, and forbade any male in Scotland other than the king's soldiers to wear '*Highland Clothes*' or 'Tartan, or party-coloured Plaid or Stuff'. Highlanders were subsequently recruited into the British army in large numbers. A statute of 1752 annexed to the crown forfeited Jacobite estates covering a huge area. The commissioners appointed to manage them in 1755 were supposed to promote agricultural improvement, industrial development, Presbyterianism and loyalty to the crown. Their achievement fell far short of these aims, but they identified various projects for future development. They also hastened the disappearance of traditional townships 'through the creation of single-tenant farms, planned villages and crofting communities'. The resulting relocation of inhabitants served as a model for the subsequent 'clearance' of people from inland glens increasingly grazed by sheep or cattle to coastal strips where a rapidly rising potato-dependent population fished or burned seaweed for industrial purposes. In Argyllshire Campbell influence and the proximity of Glasgow promoted improved farming and the linen industry.[4]

Scottish and Welsh languages and literatures

English was the medium employed by Scottish authors best known outside Scotland, including James Thomson, an early and influential poet of nature, and the novelists Tobias Smollett and Henry Mackenzie. Several poets wrote in both Scots and English for a Scottish audience. Allan Ramsay, early-eighteenth-century Scotland's foremost poet, 'is at his best when he writes in the two languages tangled together'. Some other poets wrote 'in an English shaded with Scots rhymes and locutions'. However, writers of serious prose wanted to write a pure English, purged of Scotticisms, to secure full participation in the polite and learned discourses of the new Britain.[5]

About a quarter of Scots people spoke Gaelic; few could read it. Jacobite defeats gave rise to poignant Gaelic poetical laments. Yet the Gaelic language was not proscribed, and the first printed collection of Gaelic poetry, by Alexander MacDonald, erstwhile participant in the '45, appeared in 1751. MacDonald celebrated love, nature and the Highland way of life. James Macpherson published the first volume of translations from Gaelic in 1760, and then his Ossianic epics, which included translated elements of Gaelic verse. They depicted a heroic but comfortably distant past, and helped associate Gaelic culture closely with romantic melancholy and lament for ancient heroes. Yet Gaelic poetry still lived and developed. Duncan Bàn Macintyre published poems on bagpipes, mountains, deer and the sad changes brought by poor land management (1768).[6]

The preservation of Wales's identity depended above all on her language's stubborn survival. Spoken by most of her people, it was defended by some of her gentry. The brothers Lewis and Richard Morris of Anglesey sought out ancient Welsh poetry and music. In 1751 Richard Morris instigated the foundation of the Cymmrodorion Society, whose aims included the support of living Welsh authors and the recovery of ancient manuscripts. It also campaigned against the appointment of non-Welsh speakers to Welsh parish livings. In the 1760s some leading North Welsh gentry helped finance church court proceedings against one such man. He escaped deprivation, but not the judge's severe criticism.[7]

Printing presses were established in Cardiganshire in 1718 and Carmarthen in 1721. Several more followed before 1780. Ten Welsh books a year appeared during the 1730s, forty in the 1770s. A succession of Welsh grammars and dictionaries were published, culminating in the Rev. John Walters's *Dissertation on the Welsh Language*, and his voluminous dictionary, with newly coined words (1770–94). The press facilitated the survival of Welsh poetry and music, old and new, and the production of many Welsh chapbooks and almanacs. For a small country, eighteenth-century Wales produced an extraordinary number of poets and other authors: farmers, craftsmen and parish clergymen. The 'Morris Circle' encouraged several of these men, including the brilliant but unstable Anglesey poet Goronwy Owen. Lewis Morris, Evan Evans and Rhys Jones published ancient poems by 'British bards'. Welsh Methodism inspired powerful hymns. William Williams 'incomparably the greatest Welsh poet of the eighteenth century' published hymns, epic religious narratives, sermons and pastoral guidance. Among the gentry and along the borders, however, Welsh was under pressure. A sense of embattlement and a determination to hold fast to national identity are recurrent strands in eighteenth-century Welsh poetry.[8]

London played its own part in promoting Welsh culture by facilitating a concentration of patriotic exiles in one place. The pro-Hanoverian Society of Ancient Britons was founded there in 1715. The convivial monthly tavern meetings of the Cymmrodorion brought together men of many different social backgrounds. Members of the Gwyneddigion, founded in 1770 for men from North Wales, had to be able to speak Welsh, and met for serious discussion of Welsh issues as well as jollity.

Britons?

The Welsh had always been British. The 1662 Act of Uniformity called their language the 'British or Welsh tongue'. Scots, or some of them, were readier than the English to adopt a British identity. The Scotsman James Thomson apostrophized 'Happy Britannia!' in *The Seasons* (1727) and wrote the words of *Rule Britannia* (1740). Tobias Smollett named his short-lived pro-government journal *The Briton* (1762–3), and made the eponymous hero of *Roderick Random* (1748) a 'North Briton', an appellation accepted by some Scots in England, and mischievously used by Wilkes as the title of his journal (1762–3). No Englishman called himself a 'South Briton'.

A new spate of satirical prints greeted the growing prominence of Scots after 1760. They were portrayed as poor, servile and rustic, but intensely cunning, greedy and ambitious. It took a Scotsman to draw a subtler, gentler caricature that Englishmen were ready to adopt as a national symbol. John Arbuthnot, a Scottish physician and writer in England, published *The History of John Bull* (1712). John was 'an honest plain-dealing Fellow, Cholerick, Bold, and of a very unconstant Temper'. John, 'ruddy and plump', was crammed with good food, while his 'pale and wan' sister Peg (Scotland) 'had only a little Oatmeal and Water, or a dry Crust without Butter'. Scots living in England were well aware of Bull's inconstant temper: walking in London soon after Culloden together with a fellow Scotsman, Smollett warned him that 'John Bull ... is as haughty and violent to-night as he was abject and cowardly on the Black Wednesday when the Highlanders were at Derby'.[9]

Scots in England

Anti-Scottish sentiment did not discourage Scots from seeking fame and fortune in England. The painter Allan Ramsay and the architects Colen Campbell, James Gibbs and Robert Adam all achieved success there. The London Scots literary network included John Arbuthnot, James Thomson, David Malloch, Tobias Smollett and James Boswell. Samuel Johnson, Boswell's friend, mainly used Scottish amanuenses in compiling his *Dictionary*. Andrew Millar and John McMurray (as John Murray) founded successful London publishing houses in 1728 and 1768 respectively. The Carmarthen press of the Scotsman John Ross (1763) was one of the most efficient and productive in Wales.

The excellence of Scottish medical education, and especially the Edinburgh school, attracted a growing number of English students. Comparatively limited opportunities in North Britain encouraged many Scottish medical men to migrate to England. The practice of surgery in the armed forces was a well-trodden path to a successful English career. A host of Scots made their mark in London, including Sir David Hamilton, physician-in-ordinary to Queen Anne, the famous accoucheurs William Smellie and William Hunter, George Armstrong, specialist in children's diseases, and John Clephane, physician to St George's Hospital. Several practised successfully in provincial England. James Johnstone, who settled in Worcestershire in 1751, became one of the foremost West Midlands physicians.

Relatively few lawyers made the transition from the independent Scottish bar. Bute's favour assisted one who did so, Alexander Wedderburn, ultimately the first Scots lord chancellor of Great Britain. Boswell recalled that his compatriot had been schooled in English pronunciation, 'too late in life for a Caledonian to acquire the genuine English cadence, yet … he got rid of the coarse part of his Scotch accent, retaining only so much of the "native woodnote wild", as to mark his country; which, if any Scotchman should affect to forget, I should heartily despise him'.[10] Another Scot, William Murray, Lord Mansfield, trained for an English legal career and became chief justice of king's bench and 'one of England's greatest judges'. His known commitment to religious toleration led to the destruction of his house during the Gordon riots.

Sixty Scots gained parliamentary seats in South Britain between 1754 and 1790, though the Lords refused until 1782 to admit more Scotsmen to their own ranks than the Act of Union had envisaged. There was a growth of intermarriage between English and Scottish peers that was particularly marked in the case of the daughters of Scottish peers. Scotsmen were increasingly prominent in the diplomatic service, in the army (where about a quarter of all regimental officers in the mid-eighteenth century were Scots) and in imperial trade and administration. The first governor of British Canada was a Scotsman, as were nearly half the men appointed administrators by the East India Company in Bengal during the decade 1775–85, and 60 per cent of the men authorized to operate there as independent merchants.[11]

England was 'far and away the major source' of new technology and expertise adopted by Scotland in her industrial development. Englishmen were involved in lead mining at Leadhills and Strontian, and in the successful Bonawe ironworks in Argyll (1752–3). The chemist John Roebuck, and the merchant Samuel Garbett, began sulphuric acid manufacture at Prestonpans in 1749. They were partners with a Scottish shipowner, William Caddell, in founding the Carron ironworks (1759), which after early teething troubles made its reputation by producing the 'carronade' cannon. James Watt, who had studied instrument making in London before returning to Glasgow, entered into partnership first with Roebuck, and then with another Englishman, Matthew Boulton, to develop and manufacture his greatly improved steam engine. Coke smelting, the coal-fired reverberating furnace, the flying shuttle and new cotton spinning machinery were all introduced from England.[12]

Britain and Ireland

Ireland remained throughout the eighteenth century outside the United Kingdom yet dependent on the British crown. The Catholic majority, among whom Jacobite sentiments were widespread, 'were leaderless, demoralized, and disarmed'. The Scots Irish Presbyterians of Ulster were excluded from political participation along with the Catholics. Forty-five per cent of Ireland's inhabitants born in the years 1771–81 spoke Irish. As in Scotland, there was a vigorous Celtic literary culture, but Irish poetry did not find its way into print. The ascendant Protestant landowning families, a small minority, enjoyed a full and varied social life. They employed many distinguished native and immigrant architects, designers and artists. A growing number of Irish news-papers were published. The Dublin Society encouraged innovation and improvement in farming and manufactures. Yet Ireland made no contribution to the Enlightenment comparable with Scotland's. Trinity College Dublin edu-cated members of the ruling class and future ministers of the Church of Ireland, but no great political economist or natural scientist taught there, and it had no medical school.[13]

The Act of Union provoked the Anglo-Irishman Jonathan Swift into writing *The Story of the Injured Lady*, in which Ireland figures as England's lover, cast off in favour of a sluttish, ill-tempered, Presbyterian Scotland. The Protestant Irish nobility and gentry had close and numerous links with England. (Presbyterian Ulster had its own religious and intellectual links with Scotland.) Some great Anglo-Irish families had estates in both countries. Wealthy Anglo-Irishmen often had their sons educated in England. Would-be Irish barristers had to attend one of the London Inns of Court. Many Irish officers served in the British army.[14] Several successful Irish artists worked in England. Richard Steele, Jonathan Swift, Oliver Goldsmith and Richard Brinsley Sheridan were the most celebrated of many Irish contributors to London's literary life. According to Boswell, Sheridan's father shared in giving Alexander Wedderburn elocution lessons.

Members of the Irish Protestant ruling class felt themselves Englishmen in face of threats of Catholic subversion, but Irishmen when confronted with irksome reminders of their kingdom's inferior status. The Declaratory Act passed by the British parliament in 1720 asserted that the kingdom of Ireland was 'subordinate and dependent upon the imperial crown of Great Britain'. The British House of Lords was the final court of appeal for Ireland; the British parliament had the power to legislate for that kingdom. This caused wide-spread Irish anger. In 1724 Ireland refused to accept a new issue of low denom-ination copper coins struck in England. Jonathan Swift, dean of St Patrick's in Dublin, ridiculed the notion of a 'depending kingdom' in one of the pam-phlets he wrote attacking the coins.[15]

The episode underlined the importance of avoiding offence to Irish Protestant sensibilities. For several years the Irish executive managed parliaments reason-ably successfully with the help of Irish 'undertakers'. But from the 1750s, par-liaments showed an increasingly restive 'patriot' spirit. The Commons rejected money bills in 1753 and 1769. Fears that a union with Britain might be rushed into law caused 3,000 angry people to occupy the Dublin parliament house in 1759. Politicians in England began to express anxiety about Irish desire for independence. The pace of events accelerated during the 1770s. The army in Ireland was withdrawn to fight in America. Fears of French invasion led to a rapid growth of volunteer companies for Ireland's defence in 1779–80, creating a citizen force 60,000 strong. Coincidentally, the adverse economic effects of the American War caused an upsurge of agitation for the removal of restrictions on Irish trade. In 1780 the British parliament granted Ireland free trade with British colonies. The 'patriots', led by Henry Grattan, now determined to remove their most fundamental grievance: Ireland's legislative dependence. Following Britain's defeat in America, the patriots achieved their goal in 1782–3. The British parliament repealed the 1720 Declaratory Act and recognized the Irish parliament's exclusive legislative rights.[16]

The spread of radical political activism in the 1790s and unsuccessful popular uprisings in 1798 eventually convinced the Westminster government that union with Great Britain was essential in order to control Ireland. That union, accomplished in 1801, disappointed the Catholic majority's hopes of emancipation, and never brought Ireland benefits comparable with those eventually accruing to Scotland after her union with England in 1707.

Unions: some European comparisons

The creation of the British state had no exact counterpart in eighteenth-century Europe. The transformation of a multiple monarchy into a centralized state in Spain resulted, not from a treaty between sovereign kingdoms, but from the unilateral incorporation of the hitherto distinct dominions of the crown of Aragon. Bourbon troops occupied them between 1707 and 1714 after they had supported Charles III against Philip V in the war of the Spanish Succession. Philip regarded the inhabitants as rebels who had forfeited their ancient privileges. He resolved to subject them all to the laws of Castile and to a reformed judicial and fiscal system under a 'New Plan'. Local *Cortes* and councils were abolished and traditional officials were replaced by *corregidores*. Castilian became the sole language permitted for legal and official purposes. Within a few decades, however, the Catalan economy, damaged by the war, resumed a vigorous growth, assisted by greater freedom of trade within Spain.[17] The almost contemporaneous British and Spanish unions have both lasted until the present day. Both have, however, devolved extensive powers to national or provincial governments within the kingdom in recent decades. It remains to be seen whether British devolution is only a transitional stage on the road to the dissolution of the union.

It was the rulers of Brandenburg-Prussia who achieved the most remarkable consolidation of a new state, created out of several distinct territories acquired by means ranging from marriage to conquest, complemented by tenacious and energetic diplomacy. This state, unlike Britain and Spain, lacked natural boundaries apart from stretches of the Baltic coast. In the long run it was destined to form the core of a new Germany, with which its identity would merge. Prussia's rival, the Habsburg monarchy, embracing the kingdoms of Bohemia and Hungary, and several archduchies and duchies, with outlying territories in Italy and the Netherlands, ethnically, linguistically and religiously diverse, faced particularly formidable obstacles to centralization and fuller integration that it only partly overcame during this period.

Unions of different kingdoms, duchies and electorates that retained distinct identities under a single ruler remained very common in eighteenth-century Europe. The unions of Great Britain with Hanover, and Poland with Saxony, might be described as 'weak' in that the rules of succession in each partner realm were different. Combinations of different kingdoms sharing the same rules of succession included Denmark with Norway and Naples with Sicily. The regal union of Britain and Ireland stands out as exceptional in two main respects. Nowhere else was one kingdom subordinate not just to the monarch but also to the parliament of another kingdom. Nowhere else did the great majority of the people in a lesser kingdom share a religion different from that of its ruling class and the dominant realm.

Conclusion

The United Kingdom succeeded as an entity because despite widespread Anglo-Scottish suspicions and hostility, and evidence of English condescension, the majority of both 'political nations' had more to gain than to lose through its continuance. Scotland's internal divisions, in various respects more serious than England's, helped to prevent the emergence of a national movement in favour of renewed independence during the critical early decades. Despite Scotland's meagre share in central policy making, she was within a few decades to share to the full in the benefits of British commerce and empire. England herself and the trading and colonial network she had created offered a huge range of opportunities to able and ambitious Scots.

The creation of the British unitary state never eradicated the core identities of its constituent nations. The union of 1707 guaranteed the survival of distinctive Scottish institutions. Within it there eventually developed a secondary, British, level of national consciousness that co-existed with the primary ones.[18] Ireland's separate but dependent status contributed to the development of her sense of a distinct national identity. At the same time her internal divisions and the discrimination suffered by most of her population created a legacy of problems that eventual union would not solve.

22

CONCLUSION

In 1762, a Swedish politician, Count Carl Gustaf Tessin, remarked that England appeared irresistible. The former prey of successive invaders, 'on the outermost edge of Europe', England, after suffering 'so many internal convulsions', now dictated peace terms, imposing its authority on France, Spain, Portugal and Holland.[1] Like many other foreign observers, Tessin used 'England' as though it were synonymous with Britain. The remarkable transformation he described has been a central theme of this book. Religious, economic and constitutional developments all played a part.

Protestantism was initially established in both England and Scotland with minority support. It subsequently put down strong roots in both countries. The religious innovations of Edward VI's reign had by 1553 broadly aligned the English Church with 'Reformed' Protestantism in doctrine, though from a Calvinist perspective its worship remained half reformed, its government unreformed. After the brief Marian Counter-Reformation, Elizabeth I restored a fine-tuned version of Edward's settlement, but to the disappointment of more ardent Protestants refused to go any further. Scotland began her own Calvinist Reformation in 1560. Reformation (albeit in different versions) brought the British kingdoms closer together. England's and Scotland's shared Protestantism encouraged English support for James VI's eventual succession. At the same time it weakened both countries' links with previous continental allies. The serious internal problems of the French monarchy prevented it from intervening in Scotland. Fears and tensions due to new religious differences lay at the root of the rising Anglo-Spanish antagonism of the later sixteenth century. They contributed to the efforts to lessen England's dependence on the Antwerp market from the 1550s onwards, and reinforced the resolve to maintain an effective English navy. Protestant bellicosity encouraged armed English intrusion into Spain's transatlantic imperial sphere. Hostility to a Spain still perceived as the leading Catholic power lasted well into the seventeenth century. Louis XIV eventually became, in Protestant eyes, the chief Catholic tyrant. England received waves of foreign Protestant refugees from persecution in the Netherlands and France. Many of them brought manufacturing skills new to England, most notably in the making of 'new draperies'. Those who settled in London reinforced its character as a Protestant metropolis. A succession of real or imagined Catholic plots in England combined with accounts of persecution to nourish a virulent English anti-Catholicism.

Under exceptional circumstances, Elizabeth I became, reluctantly, the linchpin of the Protestant cause at war in north-western Europe during the 1580s and 1590s. Her Stuart successors had scant desire to assume this role, which would have limited their freedom of manoeuvre in foreign affairs. The Stuart kings' relations with Catholic powers caused suspicion and criticism among their anti-Catholic subjects. In addition, all British monarchs between 1559 and 1688 faced the misgivings or opposition of some subjects who felt either that Protestant reforms at home had not gone far enough, or that Protestantism itself was under threat from royal designs. Charles I provoked revolution by attempting to impose unwelcome liturgical changes on Scotland, and James II by his unconstitutional efforts on behalf of Catholics.

Commerce was the chief motor of Britain's economic transformation. The dominance of Antwerp had channelled a growing proportion of English trade and its profits through London. The merchants of London both promoted and benefited from the opening up of new markets and sources of supply after 1550. The expansion and diversification of London's trade contributed substantially to the extraordinary growth that would make it the biggest city in western Europe by 1700. London's growth stimulated England's agriculture and industry and promoted the development of a national market. Governments took several steps to maximize native merchants' share of England's commerce, culminating in the mid-seventeenth-century Navigation Acts. Scottish negotiators sought free trade with England and her dominions in 1641, and it eventually became a powerful inducement for Scots to accept Union.

The golden eggs of commerce presented a tempting spectacle to cash-strapped English governments. From 1608 onwards, after income from various previous sources had diminished, the crown increasingly relied on impositions on overseas trade raised by virtue of royal prerogative, and therefore independent of parliamentary consent. This caused serious disagreement between Stuart kings and several parliaments from 1610 onwards. The grievances of religious innovation and taxation of trade without consent came together in the three resolutions of 1629. Charles I managed to rule without his English parliament from 1629 to 1640. However, as a result of provoking the Scots into invading England in 1640, he was forced into an unstable partnership with parliament. London's support enabled parliament to resist the king and wage, with Scottish help, an eventually successful war against him. From the crucible of civil wars emerged a state that enjoyed revenues far beyond the reach of the pre-war monarchy, England's first modern army, and a greatly enlarged navy. But despite the striking military and naval successes of the regimes of the interregnum in both the British Isles and overseas, the Republic was eventually brought down by its internal divisions. The Stuart monarchy was restored, and by 1685, having weathered the Exclusion Crisis, and with its income from parliamentary grants powerfully boosted by booming trade, looked formidably strong. James II's misjudged religious policy, and the century's second invasion of England, this time by William of Orange, ended a second move towards a more authoritarian sort of monarchy.

The revolution of 1688–9, the ensuing war with France, the settlement of the succession in 1701 and the Union of 1707 created and secured a Protestant and parliamentary monarchy in the United Kingdom of Great Britain. With parliament's consent, this monarchy maintained the world's most powerful navy, raised revenues far beyond the reach of its predecessors before 1689 and carried a huge and mounting debt. Successive governments were able to fight expensive wars in defence of Britain's interests both overseas and in Europe, where she supported coalitions that opposed her rival, France. Britain's population and geographical area were far smaller than France's, but the greater efficiency of her fiscal system and the greater strength of her government's credit allowed her to mobilize far larger resources per capita. Britain maintained a much more sustained and intensive effort in curbing the power of France after 1689 than had England in her earlier opposition to Spain and the Dutch Republic. Spain's decline had been due primarily to her long and exhausting wars with the Dutch and France. The Navigation Acts and Anglo-Dutch wars had impaired Dutch commercial dominance, but Louis XIV menaced the Republic more directly, helping to bring about William III's expedition to England in 1688.

Each of the continental powers with whom Britain went to war was at other times a friend or ally. During the seventeenth and eighteenth centuries there was also a vigorous traffic in scientific and philosophical ideas between France, England and the Dutch Republic. England learnt from Dutch commercial, fiscal and financial practice. The Republic influenced British architecture and supplied many of the painters who worked at the Stuart courts and elsewhere in Britain. French literature and music were widely admired in later Stuart Britain, and some architects experimented with French styles. The long peace between 1713 and 1741 strengthened Franco-British cultural exchanges, which were now less one-sided. There was a keen French interest in English literature, institutions and political life, as well as science and technology. The dialogue survived the mid-century wars, and the writers of the Scottish Enlightenment enjoyed particular esteem.

Throughout this period large numbers of merchants, students, soldiers, diplomats, travellers and religious or political exiles from Britain visited or lived on the European mainland. There were changes in their numbers and distribution over time. English merchant networks developed and expanded from the later sixteenth century onwards, especially in southern Europe and the Baltic. The new Dutch universities, particularly Leiden, attracted increasing numbers of British students, while the allure of Padua gradually diminished. However, a stay in Italy became an almost standard element of the experience of ambitious British artists and architects during the eighteenth century. The practice of tourism, whether grand or economical, useful or simply pleasurable, hugely increased. The multitude of British soldiers in foreign service reached a peak during the Thirty Years War, declining thereafter.

Scotland's engagement with Europe had distinctive features. The proportion of her population involved was almost certainly far greater than in England's case. Many Scots were driven to seek their fortunes abroad by limited opportunities at home. Scotland's trading network, including settlements in such places as Danzig, Veere and Dieppe, was, especially in earlier years, separate from England's. The mass of Scottish petty traders working in Poland had no English counterpart. Substantial numbers of Scottish students and teachers sojourned in French universities and academies. Above all, Scots soldiers served abroad in far larger numbers than Englishmen. During the later seventeenth century, fewer Scots migrated to mainland Europe, more to Ireland. During the eighteenth, the expanding British Empire absorbed an increasing share of Scottish energy and enterprise. Growing numbers of Scotsmen lived as settlers, planters, factors, merchants, soldiers and administrators in British colonies.

The transformation of Britain described in these pages and her emergence as a great power had adverse consequences for many both within and beyond her shores, and left enduring problematic legacies. The Catholics, a minority in Britain, but a large majority in Ireland, suffered from harsh penalties. Those in Britain who fought and lost during the early modern centuries ranged from Englishmen who defended their inherited religion against Tudor innovations to the clansmen hunted and killed in the wake of Culloden. Agricultural and industrial changes brought great long-term benefits, but also carried considerable human costs. Victims of Britain's global expansion notoriously included over 2,500,000 slaves transported from Africa to wretched toil in America by 1780. The cost to European health of two great staples of Anglo-American trade, tobacco and sugar, is beyond calculation.

Today Britain still faces problems whose roots can be traced to conflicts and challenges considered in this book. The relationship between Britain and Ireland and, specifically, the condition of Northern Ireland cannot be understood without reference to this period. Ambivalences already apparent well before 1780 still complicate British participation in the European Union. The begetter of the most successful colonies in North America still seeks to maintain a 'special relationship' with the United States. Finally, the survival of the Union of Great Britain whose creation has been described in this volume now seems less assured than it did in 1780.

NOTES

Introductory note

1. Edward James, *Britain in the First Millennium* (London and New York, 2001), p. 5.
2. William Reese, *An Historical Atlas of Wales from Early to Modern Times* (London, 1959), pp. 53–4 and plates 28, 55–7.
3. James, *Britain*, p. 2.
4. Glenn Burgess, 'Introduction: The New British History', in Glenn Burgess (ed.), *The New British History. Founding a Modern State, 1603–1715* (London and New York, 1999), pp. 13–14; Jonathan Scott, *England's Troubles: Seventeenth-century English Political Instability in European Context* (Cambridge, 2000), pp. 8–16. For the classic exposition of the 'archipelagic' conception of British history, embracing both Britain and Ireland, see J. G. A. Pocock, 'British History: a Plea for a New Subject', *Journal of Modern History*, 47(1975), pp. 601–28.
5. Anthony Pagden, 'Prologue: Europe and the World Around', in E. Cameron (ed.), *Early Modern Europe: An Oxford History* (Oxford, 1999), pp. 1–28; M. S. Anderson, *Britain's Discovery of Russia 1553–1815* (London, 1958), pp. 4, 28; Franklin Le Van Baumer, 'The Conception of Christendom in Renaissance England', *Journal of the History of Ideas*, 6(2) (1945), pp. 131–56.
6. Margaret Aston, *The Fifteenth Century: The Prospect of Europe* (London, 1968), p. 1.
7. Compare James, *Britain*, p. 2.

Chapter 1   Britain and Europe in 1500

1. Thomas Hearne (ed.), *Joannis Lelandi antiquarii de Rebus Britannicis Collectanea* [Collections of John Leland the Antiquary Concerning British Matters], vol. iv (6 vols, London, 1774), pp. 286–94.
2. C. G. A. Clay, *Economic Expansion and Social Change: England 1500–1700: II. Industry, Trade and Government* (Cambridge, 1984), pp. 103–4.
3. P. Brand, 'The Formation of the English Legal System, 1150–1400', in Antonio Padoa-Schioppa (ed.), *Legislation and Justice* (Oxford, 1997), pp. 105–7.
4. William Reese, *An Historical Atlas of Wales from Early to Modern Times* (London, 1959), pp. 40–2, and Plates 45, 55; Glanmor Williams, *Renewal and Reformation: Wales c.1415–1642* (Oxford, 1993), pp. 31–54, 242–3.
5. David Grummitt, '"One of the Mooste Pryncipall Treasours Belongyng to His Realme of England": Calais and the Crown, c.1450–1558', in D. Grummitt (ed.), *The English Experience in France c.1450–1558: War, Diplomacy, and Cultural Exchange* (Aldershot, 2002), pp. 46–62.
6. S. J. Connolly, *Contested Island: Ireland 1460–1630* (Oxford, 2007), pp. 26–41, 47.
7. Connolly, *Contested Island*, pp. 41–5, 62–6; Steven G. Ellis, *Tudor Ireland. Crown, Community and the Conflict of Cultures, 1470–1603* (London, 1985), pp. 68–83.
8. Connolly, *Contested Island*, pp. 10–14, 49; Ellis, *Tudor Ireland*, pp. 46–7.

9. Michael Lynch (ed.), *The Oxford Companion to Scottish History* (Oxford, 2001), pp. 252, 572; Peter G. B. McNeill and Hector L. MacQueen (eds), *Atlas of Scottish History to 1707* (Edinburgh, 1996), pp. 58–61.

10. McNeill and MacQueen, *Atlas*, pp. 15, 242–3; Ian D. Whyte, *Scotland before the Industrial Revolution. An Economic & Social History c.1050–c.1750* (London, 1995), p. 113.

11. Lynch, *Companion*, pp. 471–2; Julian Goodare, *State and Society in Early Modern Scotland* (Oxford, 1999), pp. 45–8; McNeill and MacQueen, *Atlas*, pp. 207, 211.

12. McNeill and MacQueen, *Atlas*, pp. 426–7, 442–5; Whyte, *Scotland*, pp. 253–9; Norman Macdougall, *James IV* (East Linton, 1997), pp. 100–5, 115–16, 180–9; Michael Lynch, *Scotland. A New History* (London, 1991), pp. 155–6.

13. David Potter, *A History of France 1460–1560. The Emergence of a Nation State* (Basingstoke, 1995), pp. 116, 149–54.

14. John H. Munro, 'Medieval Woollens: The Western European Woollen Industries and their Struggles for International Markets, c.1000–1500', in D. T. Jenkins (ed.), *The Cambridge History of Western Textiles* (Cambridge, 2003), pp. 293–4.

15. Macdougall, *James IV*, pp. 229–32.

16. Lynch, *Companion*, p. 264.

17. Macdougall, *James IV*, p. 200.

18. Charlotte Augusta Sneyd (trans.), *A Relation ... of the Island of England ... about the Year 1500* (Camden Society Old Series, vol. 37, 1847), p. 31.

Chapter 2   Dynastic wars and religious changes, 1500–58

1. John M. Currin, 'England's International Relations 1485–1509: Continuities amidst Change', in Susan Doran and Glenn Richardson (eds), *Tudor England and Its Neighbours* (Basingstoke, 2005), pp. 32–4.

2. David Potter, 'Foreign Policy', in Diarmaid MacCulloch (ed.), *The Reign of Henry VIII: Politics, Policy and Piety* (Basingstoke, 1995), pp. 101–33, esp. 108–9, 114–18, 123–8; Elizabeth Frances Rogers (ed.), *The Correspondence of Sir Thomas More* (Princeton, 1947), p. 518.

3. Norman MacDougall, *James IV* (East Linton, 1997), pp. 206–8, 223–43, 261–4, 272–6.

4. Peter Gwyn, *The King's Cardinal: The Rise and Fall of Thomas Wolsey* (London, 1990), pp. 100–1, 156–8, 359.

5. G. W. Bernard, *War, Taxation and Rebellion in Early Tudor England: Henry VIII, Wolsey and the Amicable Grant of 1525* (Brighton, 1986).

6. Virginia Murphy, 'The Literature and Propaganda of Henry VIII's First Divorce', in Diarmaid MacCulloch (ed.), *The Reign of Henry VIII: Politics, Policy and Piety* (Basingstoke, 1995), pp. 135–58, esp. 135–50.

7. Jamie Cameron, *James V: The Personal Rule* (East Linton, 1998), pp. 9–129.

8. Steven G. Ellis, *Tudor Ireland: Crown, Community and the Conflict of Cultures 1470–1603* (London, 1985), pp. 108–31, 194; S. J. Connolly, *Contested Island: Ireland 1460–1630* (Oxford, 2007), pp. 73–90.

9. Cameron, *James V*, pp. 130–52, 169–81, 245–8, 260–2, 264.

10. Marcus Merriman, *The Rough Wooings: Mary Queen of Scots, 1542–1551* (East Linton, 2000), pp. 58–136.

11. Mary Ann Lyons, *Franco-Irish Relations, 1500–1610: Politics, Migration and Trade* (Woodbridge, 2003), pp. 34–43; Connolly, *Contested Island*, pp. 92–3, 101–14.

12. Barrett L. Beer and Sybil M. Jack, *The Letters of William, Lord Paget of Beaudesert, 1547–1563, Camden Miscellany*, xxv (Camden 4th Series, vol. 13, 1974), pp. 76–8.

13. By her second marriage, to Charles Brandon, duke of Suffolk.

14. David Loades, *Mary Tudor: A Life* (Oxford, 1989), pp. 288–9, 302–4.

Chapter 3 Elizabeth I, Mary Stewart and James VI, 1558–1603

1. Stephen Alford, *The Early Elizabethan Polity: William Cecil and the British Succession Crisis, 1558–1569* (Cambridge, 1998), pp. 142–57.
2. Susan Doran, *Monarchy and Matrimony: The Courtships of Elizabeth I* (London, 1996), pp. 73–98.
3. John Guy, *'My Heart is My Own': The Life of Mary Queen of Scots* (London, 2004), pp. 279–436.
4. Mack P. Holt, *The French Wars of Religion, 1562–1629* (Cambridge, 1995), pp. 83–4.
5. Doran, *Monarchy and Matrimony*, pp. 190–4.
6. Susan Doran, 'Revenge Her Foul and Most Unnatural Murder? The Impact of Mary Stewart's Execution on Anglo-Scottish Relations', *History*, 85 (2000), pp. 489–512.
7. Colin Martin and Geoffrey Parker, *The Spanish Armada* (2nd edn, Manchester, 1999).
8. Paul E. J. Hammer, *Elizabeth's Wars: War, Government and Society in Tudor England, 1544–1604* (Basingstoke, 2003), pp. 216–8, 224 8, 232–3; J. McGurk, *The Elizabethan Conquest of Ireland: The 1590s Crisis* (Manchester, 1997); Hiram Morgan (ed.), *The Battle of Kinsale* (Bray, Co. Wicklow, 2004).
9. Paul E. J. Hammer, *The Polarisation of Elizabethan Politics: The Political Career of Robert Devereux, 2nd Earl of Essex, 1585–1597* (Cambridge, 1999), pp. 257–60, 389–404.
10. Pauline Croft, '"The State of the World Is Marvellously Changed": England, Spain and Europe 1558–1604', in Susan Doran and Glenn Richardson (eds), *Tudor England and Its Neighbours* (Basingstoke, 2005), pp. 185–6, 188–90.
11. Hiram Morgan, '"Never Any Realm Worse Governed": Queen Elizabeth and Ireland', *TRHS* (6th series, vol. xiv, 2004), pp. 295–308.

Chapter 4 Rulers and subjects

1. S. J. Gunn, *Early Tudor Government, 1485–1558* (Basingstoke, 1995), pp. 163–6; Julian Goodare, *State and Society in Early Modern Scotland* (Oxford,1999), pp. 11–12; David Potter, *A History of France, 1460–1560: The Emergence of a Nation State* (Basingstoke, 1995), pp. 32–3, 39–41, 51–6; G. R. Elton, *The Tudor Constitution: Documents and Commentary* (2nd edn, Cambridge, 1982), pp. 17–20; Julian Goodare, *The Government of Scotland 1560–1625* (Oxford, 2004), pp. 89–102.
2. J. H. Burns, *Lordship, Kingship and Empire: The Idea of Monarchy, 1400–1525* (Oxford, 1992), pp. 59–69; Brendan Bradshaw, 'Transalpine Humanism' and J. H. Burns, 'Scholasticism: Survival and Revival', in J. H. Burns (ed.), assisted by Mark Goldie, *The Cambridge History of Political Thought 1450–1700* (Cambridge, 1991), pp. 128–30, 150–1; Dale Hoak, 'The Coronations of Edward VI, Mary I, and Elizabeth I, and the Transformation of the Tudor Monarchy', in C. S. Knighton and Richard Mortimer (eds), *Westminster Abbey Reformed* (Aldershot, 2003), pp. 114–15, 147–50; Potter, *History of France*, pp. 37–8, 40; Glenn Richardson, *Renaissance Monarchy: The Reigns of Henry VIII, Francis I and Charles V* (London, 2002), pp. 20–2; Goodare, *Government of Scotland*, p. 91.
3. Jamie Cameron, *James V: The Personal Rule 1528–1542* (East Linton, 1998), p. 264; cf. Niccolo Machiavelli, *The Prince* (first published in Rome in 1532), Chapter xvii.
4. David Starkey (ed.), *The English Court from the Wars of the Roses to the English Civil War* (Harlow, 1987); John Adamson (ed.), *The Princely Courts of Europe, 1500–1750: Ritual, Politics and Culture under the Ancien Régime 1500–1750* (London, 1999).
5. J. A. Guy, 'The Privy Council: Revolution or Evolution?', in Christopher Coleman and David Starkey (eds), *Revolution Reassessed: Revisions in the History of Tudor Government and Administration* (Oxford, 1986), pp. 59–85; Goodare, *State and Society*, p. 73; Goodare, *Government of Scotland*, pp. 128–52.

6. Natalie Mears, *Queenship and Political Discourse in the Elizabethan Realms* (Cambridge, 2005), pp. 33–103; Patrick Collinson, 'The Monarchical Republic of Elizabeth I', in Patrick Collinson, *Elizabethans* (Hambledon and London, 2003), pp. 51–5; Stephen Alford, *The Early Elizabethan Polity: William Cecil and the British Succession Crisis, 1558–1569* (Cambridge, 1998), pp. 109–15.

7. Stanford E. Lehmberg, *The Reformation Parliament, 1529–1536* (Cambridge, 1970); Stanford E. Lehmberg, *The Later Parliaments of Henry VIII, 1536–1547* (Cambridge, 1977); Jennifer Loach, *Parliament and the Crown in the Reign of Mary Tudor* (Oxford, 1986); Jennifer Loach, *Parliament under the Tudors* (Oxford, 1991), pp. 1–96.

8. From John Aylmer, 'An Harborowe for Faithfvll and Trewe Svbiectes' and Sir Thomas Smith, 'De Republica Anglorum', in G. R. Elton, *The Tudor Constitution: Documents and Commentary* (Cambridge, 1982), pp. 16, 240; G. R. Elton, 'Parliament in the Sixteenth Century: Functions and Fortunes', *Historical Journal*, 22 (1979), pp. 255–78; G. R. Elton, *The Parliament of England, 1559–1581* (Cambridge, 1986), pp. 350–79.

9. Paul E. J. Hammer, *Elizabeth's Wars: War, Government and Society in Tudor England, 1544–1604* (Basingstoke, 2003), p. 240; T. E. Hartley (ed.), *Proceedings in the Parliaments of Elizabeth I, Volume III 1593–1601* (London, 1995), pp. 72–3, 92–6, 289–97, 370–414.

10. Keith M. Brown and Alastair J. Mann, 'Introduction' and Alan R. MacDonald, 'The Parliament of 1592: A Crisis Averted?', in Keith M. Brown and Alastair J. Mann (eds), *Parliament and Politics in Scotland, 1567–1707* (Edinburgh, 2005), pp. 11–26, 57–81; Goodare, *Government of Scotland*, pp. 72–3, 278, 287–8.

11. M. A. R. Graves, *The Parliaments of Early Modern Europe* (Harlow, 2001), Chapters 3–4.

12. J. H. Shennan, *The Parlement of Paris* (London, 1968), pp. 116, 193–6, 206, 209–10, 218; Janine Garrisson, *A History of Sixteenth-century France, 1483–1598: Renaissance, Reformation and Rebellion* (Basingstoke, 1995), pp. 181, 185, 199, 346; Potter, *History of France*, pp. 115–6, 131; Bernard Barbiche, *Les Institutions de la Monarchie Française à l'Époque Moderne* (2nd edn, Paris, 2001), pp. 109–10, 340–7.

13. Goodare, *Government of Scotland*, pp. 173–245; Margo Todd, *The Culture of Protestantism in Early Modern Scotland* (New Haven and London, 2002), pp. 127–314.

14. Antonio Padoa-Schioppa (ed.), *Legislation and Justice* (Oxford, 1997), pp. 123–58, 175–96, 229–68, 291–312; Richardson, *Renaissance Monarchy*, pp. 100–9; Steven Gunn, 'State Development in England and the Burgundian Dominions, c.1460–c.1560', in Jean-Marie Cauchies (ed.), *L'Angleterre et les pays bourguignons: relations et comparaisons XVe–XVIe siècle* (Neuchâtel, 1995), pp. 142–6; Norman Davies, *God's Playground: A History of Poland. Volume I The Origins to 1795* (Oxford, 1981), pp. 141, 212.

15. C. J. Harrison, 'The Petition of Edmund Dudley', *English Historical Review*, 87 (1972), pp. 82–99; Helen Miller, *Henry VIII and the English Nobility* (Oxford, 1986), pp. 44–75; Edward Hall, *Hall's Chronicle: Containing the History of England, during the Reign of Henry the Fourth and the Succeeding Monarchs to the End of the Reign of Henry the Eighth*, ed. Henry Ellis (London, 1809), p. 698.

16. Norman MacDougall, *James IV* (East Linton, 1997), pp. 160–6; Cameron, *James V*, pp. 98–117, 169–81; 274–9; Janine Garrisson, *A History of Sixteenth-century France, 1483–1598: Renaissance, Reformation and Rebellion* (Basingstoke, 1995), pp. 220–7; Henry Kamen, *Philip of Spain* (New Haven and London, 1997), pp. 231–3, 285–92.

17. Jeremy Black, *A Military Revolution? Military Change and European Society 1550–1800* (Basingstoke, 1991), esp. pp. 1–9. Very useful survey and discussion of thesis of 'The Military Revolution, 1560–1660' advanced by Michael Roberts (see *Essays in Swedish History* (London, 1967), pp. 195–225) and criticized by Geoffrey Parker, partly on the ground that crucial changes had begun earlier, most recently in his *The Military Revolution: Military Innovation and the Rise of the West, 1500–1800* (Cambridge, 1996), pp. 6–44.

18. N. A. M. Rodger, *The Safeguard of the Sea: A Naval History of Britain, 660–1649* (London, 1997), pp. 205–37, 267–71, 327–46.

19. Hammer, *Elizabeth's Wars* is the most recent survey.

20. Goodare, *State and Society*, pp. 132–58; MacDougall, *James IV*, pp. 229–32, 267–9; Rodger, *Safeguard*, 167–9, 171–2.

21. Jan Glete, *War and the State in Early Modern Europe: Spain, the Dutch Republic and Sweden as Fiscal-military States, 1500–1660* (London and New York, 2002), esp. 76–83, 87–9; Richardson, *Renaissance Monarchy*, pp. 63–70; Luis Ribot Garcia, 'Types of Armies: Early Modern Spain', in P. Contamine (ed.), *War and Competition between States* (Oxford, 2000), pp. 37–52.

22. Steven Gunn, David Grummitt and Hans Cools, *War, State and Society in England and the Netherlands 1477–1559* (Oxford, 2007), pp. 20–3; Glete, *War and the State*, pp. 155–67.

23. Michael J. Braddick, *The Nerves of State: Taxation and the Financing of the English State, 1558–1714* (Manchester, 1996).

24. Cameron, *James V*, pp. 255–62; Goodare, *State and Society*, pp. 102–23.

25. Richard Bonney, 'France, 1494–1815' and Juan Gelabert, 'Castile, 1504–1808', in Richard Bonney (ed.), *The Rise of the Fiscal State in Europe c.1200–1815* (Oxford, 1999), esp. pp. 138–42, 201–15; Potter, *History of France*, pp. 136–64; J. H. Elliott, *Imperial Spain 1469–1716* (London, 1963), pp. 193–7, 224, 279–81.

26. Wim Blockmans, 'The Low Countries in the Middle Ages' and Marjolein 't Hart, 'The United Provinces, 1579–1806', in Richard Bonney (ed.), *The Rise of the Fiscal State in Europe c.1200–1815* (Oxford, 1999), pp. 284–8, 302–5, 309–23.

27. Potter, *History of France*, pp. 161–3.

28. Steven G. Ellis, *Tudor Ireland: Crown, Community and the Conflict of Cultures 1470–1603* (London, 1985), esp. pp. 175–80, 228.

29. Hiram Morgan, *Tyrone's Rebellion: The Outbreak of the Nine Years War in Tudor Ireland* (Woodbridge, 1993), pp. 219–21.

30. T. F. Mayer, *Reginald Pole: Prince and Prophet* (Cambridge, 2000), pp. 13–41; J. H. M. Salmon, 'Catholic Resistance Theory, Ultramontanism, and the Royalist Response, 1580–1620', in J. H. Burns (ed.), assisted by Mark Goldie, *The Cambridge History of Political Thought, 1450–1700* (Cambridge, 1991), pp. 241–3.

31. Robert M. Kingdon, 'Calvinism and Resistance Theory, 1550–1580', in J. H. Burns (ed.), assisted by Mark Goldie, *The Cambridge History of Political Thought, 1450–1700* (Cambridge, 1991), pp. 193–206, 214–18; Roger A. Mason (ed.), *John Knox: On Rebellion* (Cambridge, 1994).

32. Kingdon, 'Calvinism and Resistance Theory', pp. 206–14; Salmon, 'Catholic Resistance Theory', pp. 221–31.

33. Julian H. Franklin, 'Sovereignty and the Mixed Constitution: Bodin and His Critics', in J. H. Burns (ed.), assisted by Mark Goldie, *The Cambridge History of Political Thought, 1450–1700* (Cambridge, 1991), pp. 298–309.

34. Neil Rhodes, Jennifer Richards and Joseph Marshall (eds), *King James VI and I: Selected Writings* (Aldershot, 2003), pp. 199–279.

Chapter 5   Reformations

1. The more recent of the numerous general histories of the European Reformation include Euan Cameron, *The European Reformation* (Oxford, 1991); Diarmaid MacCulloch, *Reformation: Europe's House Divided, 1490–1700* (London, 2003); and Patrick Collinson, *The Reformation* (London, 2003). A very readable and copiously illustrated older account is A. G. Dickens, *Reformation and Society in Sixteenth-century Europe* (London, 1966).

Alec Ryrie (ed.), *Palgrave Advances in the European Reformations* (Basingstoke, 2006) is a useful recent collection of essays.

2. Eamon Duffy, *The Stripping of the Altars: Traditional Religion in England c.1400–c.1580* (New Haven and London, 1992), pp. 9–376.

3. Diarmaid MacCulloch, *Thomas Cranmer: A Life* (New Haven and London, 1996); Diarmaid MacCulloch, 'Henry VIII and the Reform of the Church', in Diarmaid MacCulloch (ed.), *The Reign of Henry VIII: Politics, Policy and Piety* (Basingstoke, 1995), pp. 159–80, esp. 178; and George Bernard, *The King's Reformation: Henry VIII and the Remaking of the English Church* (New Haven and London, 2005); Alec Ryrie, 'The Strange Death of Lutheran England', *Journal of Ecclesiastical History*, 53(1) (2002), pp. 64–92.

4. D. MacCulloch, *Tudor Church Militant: Edward VI and the Protestant Reformation* (London, 1999); Diarmaid MacCulloch, *The Later Reformation in England, 1547–1603* (2nd edn, Basingstoke, 2001), pp. 57–8, 106.

5. Eamon Duffy, *Fires of Faith: Catholic England under Mary Tudor* (New Haven and London, 2009); Thomas F. Mayer, *Reginald Pole: Prince & Prophet* (Cambridge, 2000); Christopher Haigh, *English Reformations: Religion, Politics and Society under the Tudors* (Oxford, 1993), pp. 203–18.

6. Norman L. Jones, *Faith by Statute: Parliament and the Settlement of Religion, 1559* (London, 1982); MacCulloch, *Tudor Church Militant*, pp. 186–95; H. Horie, 'The Lutheran Influence on the Elizabethan Settlement, 1558–1563', *Historical Journal*, 34 (1991), pp. 519–38.

7. Alec Ryrie, *The Origins of the Scottish Reformation* (Manchester, 2006); Claire Kellar, *Scotland, England and the Reformation* (Oxford, 2004).

8. I. B. Cowan, *The Scottish Reformation: Church and Society in Sixteenth-century Scotland* (London, 1982); Gordon Donaldson, *The Scottish Reformation* (Cambridge, 1960), pp. 53–182; Margo Todd, *The Culture of Protestantism in Early Modern Scotland* (New Haven and London, 2002).

9. Mark Greengrass, *The French Reformation* (Oxford, 1987); R. J. Knecht, *The French Wars of Religion, 1559–1598* (Harlow, 1989); Mack P. Holt, *The French Wars of Religion, 1562–1629* (Cambridge, 1995).

10. Alastair Duke, *Reformation and Revolt in the Low Countries* (Hambledon and London, 2003), pp. 1–59, 71–124, 199–293, esp. 199, 269; Andrew Pettegree, *Emden and the Dutch Revolt: Exile and the Development of Reformed Protestantism* (Oxford, 1992); Wiebe Bergsma, 'The Low Countries', in Robert W. Scribner, Roy Porter and Mikuláš Teich (eds), *The Reformation in National Context* (Cambridge, 1994), pp. 67–79.

11. Patrick Collinson, *The Elizabethan Puritan Movement* (London, 1967), pp. 59–167, 191–207, 243–316, 403–31; Patrick Collinson, *Archbishop Grindal, 1519–1583: The Struggle for a Reformed Church* (London, 1979), pp. 233–78; MacCulloch, *Later Reformation*, pp. 24–51.

12. Collinson, *Puritan Movement*, pp. 432–7; MacCulloch, *Later Reformation*, pp. 69–78; Nicholas Tyacke, *Anti-Calvinists: The Rise of English Arminianism c.1590–1640* (Oxford, 1987), pp. 29–32.

13. Christopher W. Marsh, *The Family of Love in English Society, 1550–1630* (Cambridge, 1994).

14. Conrad Russell, *The Causes of the English Civil War* (Oxford, 1990), pp. 33–8.

15. Alan R. MacDonald, *The Jacobean Kirk, 1567–1625: Sovereignty, Polity and Liturgy* (Ashgate, 1998), pp. 13–18, 21, 25–7, 30–100.

16. Haigh, *English Reformations*, pp. 268–95; Felicity Heal, *Reformation in Britain and Ireland* (Oxford, 2003), pp. 425–57.

17. Glanmor Williams, *Renewal and Reformation: Wales c.1415–1642* (Oxford, 1993), pp. 305–25.

18. Jane Dawson, 'The Protestant Earl and the Godly Gael: The Fifth Earl of Argyll (*c.*1538–1573) and the Scottish Reformation', in D. Wood (ed.), *Life and Thought in the Northern Church c.1100–c.1700: Essays in Honour of Claire Cross* (*Studies in Church History*, Subsidia 12, London, 1999), pp. 337–63.

19. Nicholas P. Canny, 'Why the Reformation Failed in Ireland: une question mal posée', *Journal of Ecclesiastical History*, 30 (1979), pp. 423–50; Steven G. Ellis, *Tudor Ireland: Crown, Community and the Conflict of Cultures 1470–1603* (London, 1985), pp. 183–227; Heal, *Reformation*, pp. 380–6; S. J. Connolly, *Contested Island: Ireland 1460–1630* (Oxford, 2007), pp. 184–200.

20. Geoffrey Parker, 'Success and Failure during the First Century of the Reformation', *Past and Present*, 136 (1992), pp. 43–68, 77–82.

21. M. Mullett, *The Catholic Reformation* (London, 1999); Robert Bireley, *The Re-fashioning of Catholicism, 1450–1700* (Basingstoke, 1999); N. Davidson, *The Counter Reformation* (Oxford, 1987); Parker, 'Success and Failure', pp. 70–6; John O'Malley, 'The Society of Jesus', in R. Po-chia Hsia (ed.), *A Companion to the Reformation World* (Oxford, 2004), pp. 223–36.

22. Henry Kamen, *Inquisition and Society in Spain in the Sixteenth and Seventeenth Centuries* (London, 1985), esp. pp. 62–100, 215–18; Massimo Firpo, 'The Italian Reformation', James R. Palmitessa, 'The Reformation in Bohemia and Poland' and William Monter, 'The Inquisition', in R. Po-chia Hsia (ed.), *A Companion to the Reformation World* (Oxford, 2004), pp. 169–204, 255–71; R. J. W. Evans, *The Making of the Habsburg Monarchy 1550–1700: An Interpretation* (Oxford, 1979), pp. 1–20, 41–62.

23. Michael A. Mullett, *Catholics in Britain and Ireland, 1558–1829* (Basingstoke, 1998), pp. 1–23; Christopher Haigh, 'From Monopoly to Minority: Catholicism in Early Modern England', *Transactions of the Royal Historical Society*, 5th series, 31 (1981), pp. 129–47; Christopher Haigh, 'The Continuity of Catholicism in the English Reformation', in Christopher Haigh (ed.), *The English Reformation Revised* (Cambridge, 1987), pp. 176–208; Michael C. Questier, *Catholicism and Community in Early Modern England: Politics, Aristocratic Patronage and Religion, c.1550–1640* (Cambridge, 2006); Patrick McGrath, *Papists and Puritans under Elizabeth I* (London, 1967), pp. 177, 255–6.

24. Mullett, *Catholics*, pp. 27–32; Williams, *Renewal and Reformation*, pp. 327–31.

25. Mullett, *Catholics*, pp. 33–54; Peter G. B. McNeill and Hector L. MacQueen (eds), *Atlas of Scottish History to 1707* (Edinburgh, 1996), pp. 406–7.

26. Mullett, *Catholics*, pp. 55–63; Ellis, *Tudor Ireland*, pp. 221–3.

27. G. R. Elton, *The Tudor Constitution: Documents and Commentary* (2nd edn, Cambridge, 1982), pp. 365–7.

Chapter 6 Population growth and new horizons

1. E. A. Wrigley and R. S. Schofield, *The Population History of England 1541–1871: A Reconstruction* (London, 1981), p. 566; E. A. Wrigley, R. S. Davies, J. E. Oeppen and R. S. Schofield, *English Population History from Family Reconstitution, 1580–1837* (Cambridge, 1997), pp. 614–15; Bruce M. S. Campbell, 'Benchmarking Medieval Economic Development: England, Wales, Scotland, and Ireland, *c.*1290', *Economic History Review*, 61(4) (2008), pp. 896–945, esp. 925; Glanmor Williams, *Renewal and Reformation: Wales c.1415–1642* (Oxford, 1993), p. 408; Ian D. Whyte, *Scotland before the Industrial Revolution. An Economic & Social History c.1050–c.1750* (London, 1995), p. 113; S. J. Connolly, *Contested Island: Ireland 1460–1630* (Oxford, 2007), p. 405; Jan de Vries, *European Urbanization 1500–1800* (London, 1984), p. 36; R. Mols, 'Population in Europe 1500–1700', in C. Cipolla (ed.), *The Fontana Economic History of Europe: The Sixteenth and Seventeenth Centuries* (London, 1974), p. 38; Massimo Livi-Bacci, *The Population of Europe* (Oxford, 2000), p. 8.

Notes

2. Peter Clark (ed.), *The European Crisis of the 1590s* (London, 1985), pp. 7, 8–9, 116–18, 126–7, 158–60, 199–201, 214, 232–3; Vicente Pérez Moreda, 'The Plague in Castile at the end of the Sixteenth Century and Its Consequences', in I. A. A. Thompson and Bartolomé Yun Casalilla (eds), *The Castilian Crisis of the Seventeenth-century: New Perspectives on the Economic and Social History of Seventeenth-century Spain* (Cambridge, 1994), pp. 32–59.

3. David Hackett Fischer, *The Great Wave: Price Revolutions and the Rhythm of History* (New York and Oxford, 1996), pp. 65–91; J. R. Wordie, 'Deflationary Factors in the Tudor Price Rise', *Past and Present*, 154 (1997), pp. 32–70.

4. E. Anthony Wrigley, 'Urban Growth and Agricultural Change: England and the Continent in the Early Modern Period', *Journal of Interdisciplinary History*, xv(4) (1985), p. 688; Robert C. Allen, 'Economic Structure and Agricultural Productivity in Europe, 1300–1800', *European Review of Economic History*, 4 (2000), pp. 8–9.

5. Francis Sheppard, *London: A History* (Oxford, 1998), p. 363; Stephen Inwood, *A History of London* (London, 1998), pp. 159–60.

6. Inwood, *London*, pp. 89–96, 126–68, 204–15.

7. C. G. A. Clay, *Economic Expansion and Social Change: England 1500–1700: II. Industry, Trade and Government* (Cambridge, 1984), pp. 106–12; G. D. Ramsay, *The City of London in International Politics at the Accession of Elizabeth Tudor* (Manchester, 1975), pp. 22–3, 33–50; Robert Brenner, *Merchants and Revolution: Commercial Change, Political Conflict, and London's Overseas Traders, 1550–1653* (Cambridge, 1993), pp. 11–23; Roger Finlay and Beatrice Shearer, 'Population Growth and Suburban Expansion' and A. L. Beier, 'Engine of Manufacture: The Trades of London', in A. L. Beier and Roger Finlay (eds), *The Making of the Metropolis: London 1500–1700* (Harlow, 1986), pp. 40–6, 141–67; Lien Bich Luu, *Immigrants and the Industries of London, 1500–1700* (Aldershot, 2005), pp. 1–196, 219–43, 259–315; J. U. Nef, *The Rise of the British Coal Industry*, vol. ii (2 vols, London, 1932), pp. 21, 157, 213–15.

8. Inwood, *London*, pp. 162–9, 172–8; Ramsay, *City of London*, pp. 50–60; Ian W. Archer, 'The Government of London, 1500–1650', *London Journal*, 26(1) (2001), pp. 22–3; M. J. Power, 'London and the Control of the "Crisis" of the 1590s', *History*, 70(230) (1985), pp. 371–85.

9. Wrigley, 'Urban Growth and Agricultural Change', p. 686; Peter Clark and Paul Slack, *English Towns in Transition 1500–1700* (Oxford, 1976), p. 9.

10. Michael Lynch, *Scotland: A New History* (2nd edn, London, 1992), pp. 173–7; Whyte, *Scotland before the Industrial Revolution*, pp. 172, 195.

11. Lynch, *Scotland*, pp. 174–5; T. M. Devine and Gordon Jackson, *Glasgow: I. Beginnings to 1830* (Manchester, 1995), pp. 44, 233; Peter G. B. McNeill and Hector L. MacQueen (eds), *Atlas of Scottish History to 1707* (Edinburgh, 1996), p. 233; Whyte, *Scotland before the Industrial Revolution*, pp. 170–1, 179–82, 196–201; Keith M. Brown, Alastair J. Mann and Roland J. Tanner, *The Scottish Parliament: An Historical Introduction*, vol. 5. *The Early Modern Parliament*, at http://www.rps.ac.uk/static/historicalintro5.html [accessed 21 September 2010]

12. Connolly, *Contested Island*, pp. 30–2, 346–7.

13. Beier and Finlay, *Metropolis*, p. 3; De Vries, *Urbanization*, pp. 270–8; Oreste Ranum, *Paris in the Age of Absolutism. An Essay* (2nd edn, University Park, PA, 2004), pp. 1–69; Gregory Hanlon, *Early Modern Italy, 1550–1800: Three Seasons in European History* (Basingstoke, 2000), pp. 69–70; Gigliola Pagano de Divitiis, *English Merchants in Seventeenth-century Italy* (Cambridge, 1990), pp. 17–23.

14. David R. Ringrose, *Madrid and the Spanish Economy, 1560–1850* (Berkeley, 1983); G. V. Scammell, *The World Encompassed: The First European Maritime Empires, c.800–1650* (London, 1981), pp. 276–9, 290–8.

15. D. S. Chambers, *The Imperial Age of Venice, 1380–1580* (London, 1970), pp. 187–94; Scammell, *World Encompassed*, pp. 132–52; Brian Pullan, *Crisis and Change in the Venetian Economy in the Sixteenth and Seventeenth Centuries* (London, 1968), esp. pp. 76, 149–50; Richard Mackenney, *Sixteenth Century Europe: Expansion and Conflict* (Basingstoke, 1993), pp. 91–3; Pagano de Divitiis, *English Merchants*, pp. 19–21.

16. De Vries, *Urbanization*, pp. 270–8; R. Pike, *Enterprise and Adventure: The Genoese in Seville and the Opening of the New World* (Ithaca, 1966); P. Benedict, *Rouen during the Wars of Religion* (Cambridge, 1981); Ramsay, *City of London*, pp. 1–28; Jonathan I. Israel, *The Dutch Republic: Its Rise, Greatness, and Fall, 1477–1806* (Oxford, 1995), pp. 307–27; Scammell, *World Encompassed*, pp. 64–5; Mackenney, *Sixteenth Century Europe*, p. 88.

17. M. L. Bush, *Rich Noble, Poor Noble* (Manchester, 1988), pp. 153–69; Anne Katherine Isaacs and Maarten Prak, 'Cities, Bourgeoisies, and States', in Wolfgang Reinhard (ed.), *Power Elites and State Building* (Oxford, 1996), pp. 208–34; Israel, *Dutch Republic*, pp. 125–8, 341–5; Archer, 'Government of London', pp. 20–1.

18. Clay, *Industry, Trade and Government*, pp. 1–13; Keith Wrightson, *Earthly Necessities: Economic Lives in Early Modern Britain* (New Haven and London, 2000), pp. 87–9; H. Kellenbenz, 'Rural Industries in the West from the End of the Middle Ages to the Eighteenth Century', in P. Earle (ed.), *Essays in European Economic History 1500–1800* (Oxford, 1974), pp. 45–88.

19. Clay, *Industry, Trade and Government*, pp. 46–62; N. A. M. Rodger, *The Safeguard of the Sea: A Naval History of Britain, 660–1649* (London, 1997), p. 214; John Hatcher, *The History of the British Coal Industry: I. Before 1700: Towards the Age of Coal* (Oxford, 1993), pp. 497–501.

20. Clay, *Industry, Trade and Government*, pp. 108–25.

21. Ralph Davis, *English Overseas Trade 1500–1700* (London and Basingstoke, 1973), pp. 11–31; Clay, *Industry, Trade and Government*, pp. 128–9.

22. Fischer, *Great Wave*, pp. 81–3; Mauricio Drelichman, 'The Curse of Moctezuma: American Silver and the Dutch Disease', at http://www.econ.ubc.ca/discpapers/dp0311.pdf [accessed 21 September 2010]

23. Kenneth R. Andrews, *Trade, Plunder and Settlement: Maritime Enterprise and the Genesis of the British Empire, 1480–1630* (Cambridge, 1984), pp. 116–34, 200–22.

24. Ralph Davis, *The Rise of the English Shipping Industry* (London, 1962), pp. 1, 3–8, 15; K. R. Andrews, *Elizabethan Privateering: English Privateering during the Spanish War 1585–1603* (Cambridge, 1964), pp. 222–38, esp. 229–31.

25. Jonathan I. Israel, *Dutch Primacy in World Trade 1585–1740* (Oxford, 1989), pp. 12–68.

26. Martin Rorke, 'English and Scottish Overseas Trade, 1300–1600', *Economic History Review*, 59(2) (2006), pp. 265–88, esp. 275, 278–85; Whyte, *Scotland before the Industrial Revolution*, pp. 272, 278.

27. Allen, 'Economic Structure and Agricultural Productivity', pp. 8, 17.

28. D. M. Palliser, *The Age of Elizabeth: England under the Later Tudors 1547–1603* (London and New York, 1983), pp. 161–72, 178–201.

29. John Walter and Roger Schofield, 'Famine, Disease, and Crisis Mortality in Early Modern Society', in J. Walter and R. Schofield (eds), *Famine, Disease and the Social Order in Early Modern Society* (Cambridge, 1989), pp. 17–35; Wrightson, *Earthly Necessities*, pp. 160–2, 198–9.

30. Allen, 'Economic Structure and Agricultural Productivity', p. 21; Israel, *Dutch Republic*, pp. 111–12, 332–7; Norman Davies, *God's Playground: A History of Poland: I. The Origins to 1795* (Oxford, 1981), p. 257; Douglas F. Dowd, 'The Economic Expansion of Lombardy, 1300–1500: A Study in Political Stimuli to Economic Change', *Journal of Economic History*, 21 (1961), pp. 143–60; S. J. Woolf, 'Venice and the Terraferma: Problems of the Change from Commercial to Landed Activities', in Brian Pullan, *Crisis*

and Change in the Venetian Economy in the Sixteenth and Seventeenth Centuries (London, 1968), pp. 179–81; Hanlon, *Italy*, p. 96; Fernand Braudel, *The Mediterranean and the Mediterranean World in the Age of Philip II* (2 vols, London, 1972–3), vol. i. pp. 71–85.

31. John A. Marino, 'Economic Structures and Transformations', in John A. Marino (ed.), *Early Modern Italy 1550–1796* (Oxford, 2002), pp. 57–9; Hanlon, *Italy*, pp. 97–102; Gonzalo Anes, 'The Agrarian "Depression" in Castile in the Seventeenth Century', in I. A. A. Thompson and Bartolomé Yun Casalilla (eds), *The Castilian Crisis of the Seventeenth Century: New Perspectives on the Economic and Social History of Seventeenth-century Spain* (Cambridge, 1994), pp. 60–70; Philip Benedict, 'Civil War and Natural Disaster in Northern France', M. Greengrass, 'The Later Wars of Religion in the French Midi', Peter Burke, 'Southern Italy in the 1590s: Hard Times or Crisis?' and Timothy B. Davies, 'Village-building in Sicily: An Aristocratic Remedy for the Crisis of the 1590s', in Peter Clark (ed.), *The European Crisis of the 1590s* (London, 1985), pp. 84–134, 177–208.

32. For recent account of developments in British agrarian societies see Wrightson, *Earthly Necessities*, pp. 70–7, 132–41, 144–6, 182–90.

33. Enrique Llopis Agelán, 'Castilian Agriculture in the Seventeenth Century: Depression, or "Readjustment and Adaptation"?' in I. A. A. Thompson and Bartolomé Yun Casalilla (eds), *The Castilian Crisis of the Seventeenth-century: New Perspectives on the Economic and Social History of Seventeenth-century Spain* (Cambridge, 1994), pp. 88–92; Benedict, 'Civil War and Natural Disaster', pp. 97–8; Greengrass, 'Later Wars of Religion', p. 123.

34. Aldo de Maddalena, 'Rural Europe 1500–1750', in C. Cipolla (ed.), *The Fontana Economic History of Europe: The Sixteenth and Seventeenth Centuries* (London, 1974), pp. 308–10; Jerzy Topolski, 'Economic Decline in Poland from the Sixteenth to the Eighteenth Centuries', in P. Earle (ed.), *Essays in European Economic History 1500–1800* (Oxford, 1974), pp. 130–5, 138–41; Israel, *Dutch Republic*, pp. 106–9, 348–53.

35. Tom Scott and Bob Scribner (eds), *The German Peasants' War: A History in Documents* (London, 1991); Anthony Fletcher and Diarmaid MacCulloch (eds), *Tudor Rebellions* (4th edn, London and New York, 1997), pp. 144–6; Benedict, 'Civil War and Natural Disaster', pp. 90–1, 94; Greengrass, 'Later Wars of Religion', pp. 119–22.

36. Felicity Heal and Clive Holmes, *The Gentry in England and Wales 1500–1700* (Basingstoke, 1994).

37. J. Gwynfor Jones, *Early Modern Wales c.1525–1640* (Basingstoke, 1994), pp. 9–25; T. Jones Pierce, 'Landlords in Wales', in Joan Thirsk (ed.), *The Agrarian History of England and Wales: IV 1500–1640* (Cambridge, 1967), pp. 366–81; Keith M. Brown, *Noble Society in Scotland: Wealth, Family and Culture, from Reformation to Revolution* (Edinburgh, 2000), pp. 1–21; Keith M. Brown, *Kingdom or Province? Scotland and the Regal Union, 1603–1715* (Basingstoke, 1992), pp. 33–40, esp. 40; Allan I. Macinnes, *Clanship, Commerce and the House of Stuart, 1603–1788* (East Linton, 1996), pp. 1–24, esp. 24.

38. Bush, *Rich Noble, Poor Noble*, pp. 7–11, 111–12; Israel, *Dutch Republic*, 337–41.

39. M. L. Bush, *Noble Privilege* (Manchester, 1983), pp. 27–34, 80–3, 158–9; M. L. Bush, *The English Aristocracy: A Comparative Synthesis* (Manchester, 1984), p. 17; Davies, *God's Playground*, pp. 352–5; Stuart Carroll, *Blood and Violence in Early Modern France* (Oxford, 2006).

40. Robert Jütte, *Poverty and Deviance in Early Modern Europe* (Cambridge, 1994), pp. 105–25; Janine Garrisson, *A History of Sixteenth-century France, 1483–1598: Renaissance, Reformation and Rebellion* (Basingstoke, 1995), p. 63.

41. Paul Slack, *The English Poor Law 1531–1782* (Basingstoke, 1990), pp. 14–21, 59–61; Steve Hindle, *On the Parish? The Micro-politics of Poor Relief in Rural England c.1550–1750* (Oxford, 2004), pp. 379–405, 451–2; Julian Goodare, *The Government of Scotland 1560–1625* (Oxford, 2004), pp. 120–1, 195; Inwood, *London*, p. 156; Whyte, *Scotland before the Industrial Revolution*, pp. 108–9.

42. Jütte, *Poverty and Deviance*, pp. 125–37.

43. David Cressy, *Literacy and the Social Order: Reading and Writing in Tudor and Stuart England* (Cambridge, 1980), pp. 19–41, 104–64; R. A. Houston, *Literacy in Early Modern Europe: Culture and Education 1500–1800* (London and New York, 1988), pp. 131–2.

44. Rosemary O'Day, *Education and Society 1500–1800: The Social Foundations of Education in Early Modern Britain* (London and New York, 1982), pp. 25–42, 217–30; Houston, *Literacy*, pp. 25–39.

45. Houston, *Literacy*, p. 86.

46. Andrew Pettegree, 'Centre and Periphery in the European Book World', *Transactions of the Royal Historical Society*, 6th series, 18 (2008), pp. 101–28; Cyndia Susan Clegg, *Press Censorship in Elizabethan England* (Cambridge, 1997), pp. 10–12, 19–29, 37–45.

Chapter 7   Contacts and connections: Renaissance and Reformation

1. G. D. Ramsay, *The City of London in International Politics at the Accession of Elizabeth Tudor* (Manchester, 1975), pp.3–4, 22–6; Ian D. Whyte, *Scotland before the Industrial Revolution: An Economic and Social History c.1050 c.1750* (London and New York, 1995), pp. 74, 171.

2. Ramsay, *City of London*, pp. 62–70; T. H. Lloyd, *England and the German Hanse, 1157–1611: A Study of Their Trade and Commercial Diplomacy* (Cambridge, 1991), pp. 293–343.

3. R. W. K. Hinton, *The Eastland Trade and the Common Weal* (Cambridge, 1959), pp. 1–7; Peter G. B. McNeill and Hector L. MacQueen (eds), *Atlas of Scottish History to 1707* (Edinburgh, 1996), pp. 262–3, 265.

4. M. S. Anderson, *Britain's Discovery of Russia 1553–1815* (London, 1958), pp. 1–32.

5. C. G. A. Clay, *Economic Expansion and Social Change: England 1500–1700: II. Industry, Trade and Government* (Cambridge, 1984), pp. 4, 38, 39, 41, 57, 61, 104, 124, 140n; Theodora Keith, *Commercial Relations of England and Scotland, 1603–1707* (Cambridge, 1910), pp. 4–5.

6. Pauline Croft, 'English Commerce with Spain and the Armada war, 1558–1603', in Simon Adams and Mia Rodriguez-Salgado (eds), *England, Spain and the Gran Armada, 1558–1604: Essays from the Anglo-Spanish Conferences, London and Madrid, 1988* (Edinburgh, 1991), pp. 236–63; Clay, *Economic Expansion and Social Change: II*, pp. 132–3.

7. G. D. Ramsay, 'The Undoing of the Italian Mercantile Colony in Sixteenth Century London', in N. B. Harte and K. G. Ponting (eds), *Textile History and Economic History* (Manchester, 1973), pp. 44–9; Kenneth R. Andrews, *Trade, Plunder and Settlement: Maritime Enterprise and the Genesis of the British Empire, 1480–1630* (Cambridge, 1984), pp. 88–93, 97–8; S. A. Skilliter, *William Harborne and the Trade with Turkey, 1578–1582: A Documentary Study of the First Anglo-Ottoman Relations* (Oxford, 1977), esp. pp. 74–5; Nabil Matar, *Islam in Britain, 1558–1685* (Cambridge, 1998), pp. 12, 23, 56, 123–4, 130; Arthur Leon Horniker, 'Anglo-French Rivalry in the Levant from 1583 to 1612', *Journal of Modern History*, 18(4) (1946), pp. 289–308.

8. B. A. Holderness, 'The Reception and Distribution of the New Draperies in England' and Luc Martin, 'The Rise of the New Draperies in Norwich, 1550–1622', in N. B. Harte (ed.), *The New Draperies in the Low Countries and England, 1300–1800* (Oxford, 1997), pp. 217–43, 245–74; Joan Thirsk, *Economic Policy and Projects: The Development of a Consumer Society in Early Modern England* (Oxford, 1978), pp. 24–56; Nigel Goose, 'Immigrants and English Economic Development in the Sixteenth and Early Seventeenth Centuries', in Nigel Goose and Lien Bich Luu (eds), *Immigrants in Tudor and Early Stuart England* (Brighton, 2005), pp. 136–44, 153; Lien Bich Luu, *Immigrants and the Industries of London, 1500–1700* (Aldershot, 2005), pp. 259–315.

9. Jonathan Woolfson (ed.), *Reassessing Tudor Humanism* (Basingstoke, 2002) is a recent collection of useful essays; see esp. 'Introduction', pp. 1–21.

Notes

10. Jonathan Woolfson, *Padua and the Tudors: English Students in Italy, 1485–1603* (Cambridge, 1999).

11. A. G. Dickens, *The English Reformation* (London, 1964), pp. 231–4; Diarmaid MacCulloch, *Tudor Church Militant: Edward VI and the Protestant Reformation* (London, 1999), pp. 27, 68, 79–80, 88, 141, 167–70, 174, 182–4; M. Anne Overell, *Italian Reform and English Reformations c.1535–c.1585* (Aldershot, 2008), pp. 17–60, 81–102.

12. Patrick Collinson, *The Elizabethan Puritan Movement* (London, 1967), pp. 79–82, 107–10, 151–4, 233–4, 295–6; B. R. White, *The English Separatist Tradition from the Marian Martyrs to the Pilgrim Fathers* (Oxford, 1971), pp. 47–50, 96–105.

13. Patrick Collinson, 'Europe in Britain: Protestant Strangers and the English Reformation' and Edgar Samuel, 'London's Portuguese Jewish Community, 1540–1753', in Randolph Vigne and Charles Littleton (eds), *From Strangers to Citizens: The Integration of Immigrant Communities in Britain, Ireland and Colonial America, 1550–1750* (London and Brighton, 2001), pp. 57–67, 239–40; Andrew Pettegree, *Foreign Protestant Communities in Sixteenth-century London* (Oxford, 1986), pp. 20, 44–5, 63, 65–6, 138, 163–81, 272–6, 287–8; Ole Peter Grell, *Calvinist Exiles in Tudor and Stuart England* (Aldershot, 1996), pp. 5, 29, but see alternative estimates in Laura Hunt Yungblut, *Strangers Settled Here Amongst Us: Policies, Perceptions and the Presence of Aliens in Elizabethan England* (London and New York, 1996), pp. 9–35; Patrick Collinson, *Archbishop Grindal 1519–1583; The Struggle for a Reformed Church* (London, 1979), pp. 134–52.

14. Arnold Pritchard, *Catholic Loyalism in Elizabethan England* (London, 1979); Sandra Jusdado, 'The Appellant Priests and the Succession Issue', in Jean-Christophe Mayer (ed.), *The Struggle for the Succession in Late Elizabethan England: Politics, Polemics and Cultural Representations* (Montpellier, 2004), pp. 199–216.

15. J. H. M. Salmon, 'Catholic Resistance Theory, Ultramontanism, and the Royalist Response, 1580–1620', in J. H. Burns (ed.), assisted by Mark Goldie, *The Cambridge History of Political Thought 1450–1700* (Cambridge, 1991), pp. 234–6, 660, 663.

16. David J. B. Trim, 'The "Secret War" of Elizabeth I: England and the Huguenots during the Early Wars of Religion, 1562–77', *Proceedings of the Huguenot Society*, 27 (1999), pp. 189–99; David J. B. Trim, 'Protestant Refugees in Elizabethan England and Confessional Conflict in France and the Netherlands', in Randolph Vigne and Charles Littleton (eds), *From Strangers to Citizens: The Integration of Immigrant Communities in Britain, Ireland and Colonial America, 1550–1750* (London and Brighton, 2001), pp. 68–79; 90, 113; Paul E. J. Hammer, *Elizabeth's Wars: War, Government and Society in Tudor England, 1544–1604* (Basingstoke, 2003), pp. 90, 113; Roger B. Manning, *An Apprenticeship in Arms: The Origins of the British Army 1585–1702* (Oxford, 2006), pp. 28, 81–3, 86, 90; Albert J. Loomie, *The Spanish Elizabethans* (London, 1963), p. 132. I am grateful to David Trim for sharing with me material from his database of British soldiers serving as volunteers in foreign armies.

17. Gary M. Bell, *A Handlist of British Diplomatic Representatives 1509–1688* (London, 1990), esp. pp. 2–4, 10–15, 40–59, 66–103, 170–94, 252–6, 283–4, 288–9; Susan Doran, 'James VI and the English Succession', in Ralph Houlbrooke (ed.), *James VI and I: Ideas, Authority and Government* (Aldershot, 2006), pp. 32–3.

18. Maria Dowling, *Humanism in the Age of Henry VIII* (London, 1986), pp. 37–68; Alastair Fox and John Guy, *Reassessing the Henrician Age: Humanism, Politics and Reform 1500–1550* (Oxford, 1986), esp. Alastair Fox, 'Sir Thomas Elyot and the Humanist Dilemma', pp. 52–73.

19. Sydney Anglo, *Machiavelli: The First Century. Studies in Enthusiasm, Hostility, and Irrelevance* (Oxford, 2005), pp. 98–108.

20. Kenneth Muir, *Life and Letters of Sir Thomas Wyatt* (Liverpool, 1963), pp. 222–60; W. A. Sessions, *Henry Howard, the Poet Earl of Surrey: A Life* (Oxford, 1999), esp. pp. 260–88; David Norbrook, *Poetry and Politics in the English Renaissance*

(revised edn, Oxford, 2002), pp. 53–139; Blair Worden, *The Sound of Virtue: Philip Sidney's* Arcadia *and Elizabethan Politics* (New Haven and London, 1996).

21. Robert Crawford, *Scotland's Books: The Penguin History of Scottish Literature* (London, 2007), pp. 72–9, 86–104, 108–13, 147–54; Neil Rhodes, Jennifer Richards and Joseph Marshall (eds), *King James VI and I: Selected Writings* (Aldershot, 2003), pp. 4–10, 21–120.

22. Simon Thurley, *The Royal Palaces of Tudor England: Architecture and Court Life 1460–1547* (New Haven and London, 1993); John Summerson, *Architecture in Britain, 1530–1830* (9th revised edn, New Haven and London, 1993), pp. 23–74; Mark Girouard, *Robert Smythson and the Elizabethan Country House* (revised edn, New Haven and London, 1983); Alice T. Friedman, *House and Household in Elizabethan England: Wollaton Hall and the Willoughby Family* (Chicago and London, 1989).

23. Andrea Thomas, *Princelie Majestie: The Court of James V of Scotland, 1528–1542* (Edinburgh, 2005), pp. 72–8; Deborah Howard, *Scottish Architecture: From the Reformation to the Restoration, 1560–1660* (Edinburgh, 1995), pp. 16–33; Miles Glendinning, Ranald MacInnes and Aonghus MacKechnie, *A History of Scottish Architecture: From the Renaissance to the Present* (Edinburgh, 1996), pp. 6–50.

24. Brian Kemp, *English Church Monuments* (London, 1980), pp. 58–88; Adam White, 'England *c*.1560–*c*.1660: A Hundred Years of Continental Influence', *Church Monuments*, 7 (1992), pp. 34–9, 44–5.

25. Karen Hearn (ed.), *Dynasties: Painting in Tudor and Jacobean England 1530–1630* (London, 1995), pp. 1–181; Susan Foister, *Holbein in England* (London, 2006); National Galleries of Scotland, at http://www.nationalgalleries.org/collection/scottish_az/ [accessed 21 September 2010]

26. A. L. Rowse, *The Elizabethan Renaissance: The Cultural Achievement* (London, 1974), pp. 95–151; John Caldwell, *The Oxford History of English Music: 1. From the Beginnings to 1715* (Oxford, 1991), pp. 267–502.

27. Rowse, *Elizabethan Renaissance*, pp. 235–320 offers a readable, if also in some respects outdated survey of the developments outlined in this section. See Marie Boas, *The Scientific Renaissance 1450–1630* (London, 1962) for the international context, and Deborah E. Harkness, *The Jewel House: Elizabethan London and the Scientific Revolution* (New Haven and London, 2007) for London networks.

Chapter 8 Ideas of Britain and the coming of regal union

1. Alan MacColl, 'The Meaning of "Britain" in Medieval and Early Modern England', *Journal of British Studies*, 45 (2006), pp. 248–69, esp. 257–9.

2. Arthur H. Williamson, *Scottish National Consciousness in the Age of James VI: The Apocalypse, The Union and the Shaping of Scotland's Public Culture* (Edinburgh, 1979), pp. 97–102; Roger A. Mason, 'The Scottish Reformation and the Origins of Anglo-British Imperialism', in Roger A. Mason (ed.) *Scots and Britons: Scottish Political Thought and the Union of 1603* (Cambridge, 1994), pp. 162–3, 166–9, 184–5.

3. Sir Henry Ellis (ed.), *Polydore Vergil's English History from an Early Translation, ... Vol I. Containing the First Eight Books* (Camden Society Old Series, vol. 36, 1846), pp. 1, 26–33.

4. Glanmor Williams, *Renewal and Reformation: Wales c.1415–1642* (Oxford, 1993), pp. 237–44.

5. David Powell, *The Historie of Cambria, Now Called Wales* (London, 1584), Preface to the Reader, and pp. 387–401; Williams, *Renewal and Reformation*, pp. 459, 462.

6. Humphrey Llwyd, *The Breuiary of Britayne* (London, 1573; STC 16636), pp. 6–9; George Buchanan, *The History of Scotland ... Faithfully Rendered into English* (London, 1690, Wing B5283A), pp. 94–7; William Camden, *Britain, or a Chorographicall Description of*

the Most Flourishing Kingdomes, England, Scotland, and Ireland, trans. Philemon Holland (London, 1610; STC 4509), The author to the reader, and pp. 5–9, 119, 124–6; Williamson, *Scottish National Consciousness*, pp. 122–7.

7. Marcus Merriman, *The Rough Wooings: Mary Queen of Scots, 1542–1551* (East Linton, 2000), pp. 44–5, 269–73; James A. H. Murray (ed.), *The Complaynte of Scotland* (Early English Text Society, extra series, vol. 17, 1872), pp. 207–36.

8. Murray (ed.), *Complaynte*, pp. 1–188, 237–46; Merriman, *Rough Wooings*, pp. 272–7.

9. Jane E. A. Dawson, 'William Cecil and the British Dimension of Early Elizabethan Foreign Policy', *History*, 74(241) (1989), pp. 205–10, 213–16.

10. Julian Goodare, *State and Society in Early Modern Scotland* (Oxford, 1999), pp. 262, 312.

11. Peter Wentworth, *A Pithie Exhortation to Her Maiestie for Establishing Her Successor to the Crowne. Whereunto Is Added a Discourse Containing the Author's Opinion of the True and Lawfull Successor to Her Maiestie* (Edinburgh, 1598; STC 25245), pp. 67–82.

12. David Potter, *A History of France, 1460–1560: The Emergence of a National State* (Basingstoke, 1995), p. 113; Gwenaël Le Duc, 'Breton Literature (I): Beginnings to *c*.1900'; Geraint Evans, 'Printing, Early History in the Celtic Languages', in John T. Koch (ed.), *Celtic Culture: A Historical Encyclopaedia* (Santa Barbara, 2006), pp. 267–72, 1459.

13. Juan de Mariana, *The General History of Spain from the First Peopling of It By Tubal*, trans. J. Stevens (London, 1699, Wing M599), pp. 1, 6–8, 74–98.

Chapter 9 The failure of Stuart kingship and the British revolutions, 1603–60

1. Pauline Croft, '*Rex Pacificus*, Robert Cecil, and the 1604 Peace with Spain', in Glenn Burgess, Rowland Wymer and Jason Lawrence (eds), *The Accession of James I: Historical and Cultural Consequences* (Basingstoke, 2006), pp. 140–54.

2. Nicholas Canny, *Making Ireland British 1580–1650* (Oxford, 2001), pp. 183–226. The proportion of Scots was far higher in Antrim and Down, which had not been confiscated.

3. Conrad Russell, *Parliaments and English Politics, 1621–1629* (Oxford, 1979), pp. 133–4; J. P. Kenyon, *The Stuart Constitution 1603–1688: Documents and Commentary* (Cambridge, 1966), p. 47.

4. Kevin Sharpe, *The Personal Rule of Charles I* (New Haven and London, 1992), pp. 70–97.

5. David Stevenson, *The Scottish Revolution 1637–44: The Triumph of the Covenanters* (Newton Abbot, 1973), p. 36.

6. Edward J. Cowan, 'The Making of the National Covenant', in John Morrill (ed.), *The Scottish National Covenant in Its British Context, 1638–51* (Edinburgh, 1990), pp. 68–89.

7. Ian Gentles, *The English Revolution and the Wars in the Three kingdoms 1638–1652* (Harlow, 2007), pp. 205–6.

8. See Jason Peacey (ed.), *The Regicides and the Execution of Charles I* (Basingstoke, 2001), esp. Sean Kelsey, 'Staging the Trial of Charles I', p. 86 and D. Alan Orr, 'The Juristic Foundation of Regicide', pp. 117–37.

9. Steven C. A. Pincus, *Protestantism and Patriotism: Ideologies and the Making of English Foreign Policy, 1650–1668* (Cambridge, 1996), pp. 25–75.

10. So thought Duke Maximilian of Bavaria: see Ronald G. Asch, *The Thirty Years War: The Holy Roman Empire and Europe 1618–48* (Basingstoke, 1997), p. 113.

Chapter 10 From Restoration to Union, 1660–1707

1. J. P. Kenyon, *The Stuart Constitution, 1603–1688: Documents and Commentary* (Cambridge, 1966), p. 353.

2. Gillian H. MacIntosh, 'Arise King John: Commissioner Lauderdale and Parliament in the Restoration Era' and Alastair J. Mann, '"James VII, King of the Articles": Political Management and Parliamentary Failure', in Keith M. Brown and Alastair J. Mann (eds), *Parliament and*

Politics in Scotland, 1567–1707 (Edinburgh, 2005), pp. 163–83 (esp. 181), 184–207; S. J. Connolly, *Divided Kingdom: Ireland 1630–1800* (Oxford, 2008), p. 137 and n. 27.

3. R. A. Stradling, 'Spanish Conspiracy in England, 1661–1663', *English Historical Review*, 87(343) (1972), pp. 269–86.

4. Gijs Rommelse, *The Second Anglo-Dutch War (1665–1667): Raison d'état, Mercantilism and Maritime Strife* (Hilversum, 2006), esp. pp. 11–13, 195–201; J. R. Jones, *The Anglo-Dutch Wars of the Seventeenth Century* (London, 1996), pp. 30, 56–60, 88–94, 107–78.

5. Ronald Hutton, *Charles II: King of England, Scotland, and Ireland* (Oxford, 1989), p. 255.

6. Extensive discussions of Charles's motives in Ronald Hutton, *Charles II*, pp. 263–73 and John Miller, *Charles II* (London, 1991), pp. 142–82.

7. According to the provisions of the modified version of the 1641 Triennial Act passed in 1664.

8. For the continental context of the Revolution of 1688, see Jonathan I. Israel, 'The Dutch Role in the Glorious Revolution' and Wouter Troust, 'William III, Brandenburg, and the Construction of the anti-French Coalition, 1672–1688', in Jonathan I. Israel (ed.), *The Anglo-Dutch Moment. Essays on the Glorious Revolution and Its World Impact* (Cambridge, 1991), pp. 105 22, 299–333; J. R. Jones, *The Revolution of 1688 in England* (London, 1972), pp. 176–208, 250–55, 267–80.

9. Ian B. Cowan, 'Church and State Reformed? The Revolution of 1688–9 in Scotland', in Jonathan I. Israel (ed.), *Anglo-Dutch Moment: Essays on the Glorious Revolution and Its World Impact* (Cambridge, 1991), pp. 163–83.

10. D. W. Hayton, 'The Williamite Revolution in Ireland, 1688–91', in Jonathan I. Israel (ed.), *The Anglo-Dutch Moment. Essays on the Glorious Revolution and Its World Impact* (Cambridge, 1991), pp. 185–213; Connolly, *Divided Kingdom*, pp. 178–93, 197–203.

11. For two recent discussions, see John C. Rule, 'The Partition Treaties, 1698–1700: A European View', in Esther Mijers and David Onnekink (eds), *Redefining William III: The Impact of the King-Stadholder in International Context* (Aldershot, 2007), pp. 91–105; David Onnekink, 'Anglo-French Negotiations on the Spanish Partition Treaties (1698–1700): A Re-evaluation', in Glenn Richardson (ed.), *'The Contending Kingdoms': France and England 1420–1700* (Aldershot, 2008), pp. 161–77.

Chapter 11 From 'free' monarchy to parliamentary monarchy

1. J. P. Kenyon, *The Stuart Constitution: Documents and Commentary* (Cambridge, 1966), pp. 90–124, 420–47; for a recent re-assertion of the importance of common law thought for constitutional development, see Alan Cromartie, *The Constitutionalist Revolution: An Essay on the History of England, 1450–1642* (Cambridge, 2006).

2. Janine Garrisson, *A History of Sixteenth-century France, 1483–1598: Renaissance, Reformation and Rebellion* (Basingstoke, 1991), p. 397; Yves-Marie Bercé, *The Birth of Absolutism: A History of France, 1598–1661* (Basingstoke, 1996), pp. 162–7, 178; John J. Hurt, *Louis XIV and the Parlements: The Assertion of Royal Authority* (Manchester, 2002), pp. 38–59; Bernard Barbiche, *Les Institutions de la Monarchie Française à l'Époque Moderne* (2nd edn, Paris, 2001), pp. 51–4.

3. Thomas Hobbes, *Leviathan or, the Matter, Forme and Power of a Commonwealth Ecclesiasticall and Civil*, ed. Michael Oakeshott (Oxford, 1960), pp. 112, 215.

4. Mark Goldie, 'The Reception of Hobbes', in J. H. Burns (ed.), with the assistance of Mark Goldie, *The Cambridge History of Political Thought 1450–1700* (Cambridge, 1991), pp. 589–615.

5. Edward J. Cowan, 'The Making of the National Covenant', in John Morrill (ed.), *The Scottish National Covenant in Its British Context, 1638–51* (Edinburgh, 1990), pp. 78–83.

6. Blair Worden, 'English Republicanism', in J. H. Burns (ed.), *The Cambridge History of Political Thought 1450–1700* (Cambridge, 1991), pp. 443–55, 464–70; Jonathan Scott,

Notes

England's Troubles: Seventeenth-century English Political Instability in European Context (Cambridge, 2000), pp. 290–341.

7. On the birth of political parties in England, see Tim Harris, *Politics under the Later Stuarts: Party Conflict in a Divided Society 1660–1715* (London, 1993).

8. Gary S. de Krey, 'Political Radicalism in London after the Glorious Revolution', *Journal of Modern History*, 55 (1983), pp. 585–617.

9. Mark Knights, *Representation and Misrepresentation in Later Stuart Britain: Partisanship and Political Culture* (Oxford, 2005), pp. 220–71; Bob Harris, *Politics and the Rise of the Press: Britain and France, 1620–1800* (London, 1996), pp. 6–10, 53–4; R. A. Houston, *Literacy in Early Modern Europe: Culture and Education 1500–1800* (London, 1988), pp. 177–8.

10. On seventeenth-century royal courts, see Neil Cuddy, 'Reinventing a Monarchy: The Changing Structure and Political Function of the Stuart Court, 1603–88', in Eveline Cruickshanks (ed.), *The Stuart Courts* (Stroud, 2000), pp. 59–76 and Andrew Barclay, 'William's Court as King', in Esther Mijers and David Onnekink (eds), *Redefining William III. The Impact of the King-Stadholder in International Context* (Aldershot, 2007), pp. 243–59.

11. Charles II's most important minister between 1668 and 1672: see Ronald Hutton, *Charles II, King of England, Scotland and Ireland* (Oxford, 1989), pp. 254–86.

12. Keith M. Brown, *Kingdom or Province? Scotland and the Regal Union, 1603–1715* (Basingstoke, 1992), pp. 89–101.

13. Ronald Hutton, 'The Triple-crowned Islands', in Lionel K. J. Glassey (ed.), *The Reigns of Charles II and James VII & II* (Basingstoke, 1997), pp. 75–80; Mark Goldie, 'Divergence and Union: Scotland and England, 1660–1707', in Brendan Bradshaw and John Morrill (eds), *The British Problem c.1534–1707: State Formation in the Atlantic Archipelago* (Basingstoke, 1996), pp. 220–45, esp. 231–6; Allen I. Macinnes, 'William of Orange – "Disaster for Scotland"?', in Esther Mijers and David Onnekink (eds), *Redefining William III: The Impact of the King-Stadholder in International Context* (Aldershot, 2007), pp. 202–23, esp. 210–11, 220–1.

14. Barbiche, *Institutions de la Monarchie Française*, pp. 178, 258–61, 279–300.

15. Anthony Fletcher, *Reform in the Provinces: The Government of Stuart England* (New Haven and London, 1986), pp. 5–11, 24–6, 56–60, 92–4, 282–348.

16. Jenny Wormald, 'The Happier Marriage Partner: The Impact of the Union of the Crowns on Scotland', in Glenn Burgess, Rowland Wymer and Jason Lawrence (eds.), *The Accession of James I: Historical and Cultural Consequences* (Basingstoke, 2006), pp. 69–87; Brown, *Kingdom or Province?*, pp. 91–2, 94, 103–4, 140, 165, 175; Julian Goodare, *The Government of Scotland 1560–1625* (Oxford, 2004), pp. 175–81, 203–7, 220–45.

17. Michael Lynch, *Scotland: A New History* (2nd revised edn, London, 1992), pp. 296–7.

18. N. A. M. Rodger, *The Safeguard of the Sea: A Naval History of Britain, 660–1649* (London, 1997), pp. 347–94; N. A. M. Rodger, *The Command of the Ocean: A Naval History of Britain, 1649–1815* (London, 2004), pp. 1–163, 607–8; Richard Harding, *The Evolution of the Sailing Navy, 1509–1815* (Basingstoke, 1995), pp. 31–104.

19. Edward M. Furgol, 'Scotland Turned Sweden: The Scottish Covenanters and the Military Revolution, 1638–1651' in John Morrill (ed.), *The Scottish National Covenant in Its British Context 1638–51* (Edinburgh, 1990), pp. 134–40.

20. Ian Gentles, *The English Revolution and the Wars in the Three Kingdoms 1638–1652* (Harlow, 2007), p. 251; J. D. Davies, 'International Relations, War and the Armed Forces', in Lionel K. J. Glassey (ed.), *The Reigns of Charles II and James VII & II* (Basingstoke, 1997), pp. 218–20; John Childs, 'The Restoration Army, 1660–1702' and David Chandler, 'The Great Captain-general 1702–1714', in David G. Chandler and Ian Beckett (eds), *The Oxford History of the British Army* (Oxford, 1994), pp. 46–66, 67–91, esp. 47, 52, 57, 62 (quotation), 69, 73, 80.

21. Jeremy Black, *A Military Revolution? Military Change and European Society 1550–1800* (Basingstoke, 1991), pp. 6–7; Ruth Mackay, *The Limits of Royal Authority: Resistance and Obedience in Seventeenth-century Castile* (Cambridge, 1999), pp. 7, 82–8; David Parrott, *Richelieu's Army: War, Government and Society in France, 1624–1642* (Cambridge, 2001), p. 220; Frank Tallett, *War and Society in Early-modern Europe, 1495–1715* (London, 1992), pp. 69–85.

22. Kevin Sharpe, *The Personal Rule of Charles I* (New Haven and London, 1992), pp. 105–30.

23. Ian Gentles, *English Revolution*, pp. 106–10.

24. Geoffrey Holmes, *The Making of a Great Power: Late Stuart and Early Georgian Britain 1660–1722* (Harlow, 1993), pp. 88–92, 432–3; C. D. Chandaman, 'The Financial Settlement in the Parliament of 1685', in H. Hearder and H. R. Loyn (eds), *British Government and Administration: Studies Presented to S. B. Chrimes* (Cardiff, 1974), pp. 144–54, esp. 152; Howard Tomlinson, 'Financial and Administrative Developments in England, 1660–88', in J. R. Jones (ed.), *The Restored Monarchy 1660–1688* (Basingstoke, 1979), pp. 100–2.

25. Holmes, *Making of a Great Power*, pp. 267–8, 337, 432–3; John Brewer, *The Sinews of Power: War, Money and the English State, 1688–1793* (Cambridge, Mass., 1988), p. 95.

26. C. G. A. Clay, *Economic Expansion and Social Change: England 1500–1700: II. Industry, Trade and Government* (Cambridge, 1984), pp. 272–5, 278–9; Brewer, *Sinews*, pp. 30, 40, 118, 121; Holmes, *Making of a Great Power*, pp. 270–1, 432.

27. Brewer, *Sinews*, pp. 66–8.

28. Julian Goodare, *State and Society in Early Modern Scotland* (Oxford, 1999), pp. 318–22.

29. Marjolein 't Hart, 'The United Provinces, 1579–1806', in Richard Bonney, *The Rise of the Fiscal State in Europe c.1200–1815* (Oxford, 1999), pp. 309–25, esp. 311; Larry Neal, 'The Monetary, Financial and Political Architecture of Europe, 1648–1815', in Leandro Prados de la Escosura (ed.), *Exceptionalism and Industrialisation: Britain and Its European Rivals, 1688–1815* (Cambridge, 2004), pp. 176–80, esp. 178.

30. Bercé, *Birth of Absolutism*, pp. 21–3, 136–7; Brewer, *Sinews*, pp. 16–17; Julian Swann, 'The State and Political Culture' and William Doyle, 'Politics: Louis XIV', in William Doyle (ed.), *Old Regime France 1648–1788* (Oxford, 2001), pp. 152–3, 184.

31. Bercé, *Birth of Absolutism*, pp. 137–9; Swann, 'The State', pp. 147–9; Juan Gelabert, 'Castile, 1504–1808', in Richard Bonney (ed.), *The Rise of the Fiscal State in Europe c.1200–1815* (Oxford, 1999), pp. 222, 227–8.

32. Gelabert, 'Castile', pp. 215–26.

Chapter 12 The contested inheritance of Reformation

1. Neil Rhodes, Jennifer Richards and Joseph Marshall (eds), *King James VI and I: Selected Writings* (Aldershot, 2003), pp. 223–4, 299; Alan Cromartie, 'King James and the Hampton Court Conference', in Ralph Houlbrooke (ed.), *James VI and I: Ideas, Authority and Government* (Aldershot, 2006), pp. 61–80, esp. 64–74; Pauline Croft, *King James* (Basingstoke, 2003), pp. 158, 165–6.

2. Alan R. MacDonald, *The Jacobean Kirk, 1567–1625: Sovereignty, Polity and Liturgy* (Aldershot, 1998), pp. 101–86.

3. James F. Larkin and Paul L. Hughes, *Stuart Royal Proclamations. Vol. I Royal Proclamations of King James I 1603–1625* (Oxford, 1973), p. 73; Rhodes *et al.* (eds), *James: Selected Writings*, pp. 299–300.

4. Peter Lake, 'Lancelot Andrewes, John Buckeridge, and Avant-garde Conformity at the Court of James I', in Linda Levy Peck (ed.), *The Mental World of the Jacobean Court* (Cambridge, 1991), pp. 113–33, esp. 124; Kenneth Fincham and Peter Lake, 'The Ecclesiastical Policy of King James I', *Journal of British Studies*, 24(2) (1985), pp. 169–207.

5. Nicholas Tyacke, *Anti-Calvinists: The Rise of English Arminianism c.1590–1640* (Oxford, 1987), pp. 47, 104, 149–51; Anthony Milton, *Catholic and Reformed: The*

Roman and Protestant Churches in English Protestant Thought 1600–1640 (Cambridge, 1995), esp. pp. 112–13, 152–3, 526–8.

6. Richard Cust, *Charles I: A Political Life* (Harlow, 2005), pp. 14–16, 82–103.

7. John Morrill, 'The National Covenant in Its British Context', in John Morrill (ed.) *The Scottish National Covenant in Its British Context, 1638–51* (Edinburgh, 1990), pp. 1–30, esp. 1–11.

8. John Coffey, *Persecution and Toleration in Protestant England 1558–1689* (Harlow, 2000), pp. 90, 142, 158–9; Michael A. Mullett, *Catholics in Britain and Ireland, 1558–1829* (Basingstoke, 1998), pp. 70–5; Austin Woolrych, *Britain in Revolution 1625–1660* (Oxford, 2002), p. 587.

9. Ronald Hutton, *The British Republic 1649–1660* (Basingstoke, 1990), pp. 95–8.

10. John Spurr, *The Post-Reformation: Religion, Politics and Society in Britain 1603–1714* (Harlow, 2006), p. 147.

11. Spurr, *Post-Reformation*, p. 168.

12. Coffey, *Persecution and Toleration*, pp. 90, 186; Mullett, *Catholics*, pp. 77–81.

13. J. P. Kenyon, *The Stuart Constitution: Documents and Commentary* (Cambridge, 1966), p. 442.

14. Julia Buckroyd, *Church and State in Scotland 1660–1681* (Edinburgh, 1980); Peter G. B. McNeill and Hector L. MacQueen (eds), *Atlas of Scottish History to 1707* (Edinburgh, 1996), pp. 145–7, 395–400; Michael Lynch, *Scotland. A New History* (2nd edn, London, 1992), pp. 287–97; Keith M. Brown, *Kingdom or Province? Scotland and the Regal Union, 1603–1715* (Basingstoke, 1992), pp. 149–52, 155–63, 167–8.

15. Kenyon, *Stuart Constitution*, pp. 407–8, 410–13.

16. J. L. Price, *Dutch Society 1588–1713* (Harlow, 2000), pp. 130, 142–3, 198–9, 206; Jonathan I. Israel, *The Dutch Republic: Its Rise, Greatness, and Fall, 1477–1806* (Oxford, 1995), pp. 637–76, esp. 675.

17. Christopher Clark, *Iron Kingdom: The Rise and Downfall of Prussia, 1600–1947* (London, 2006), pp. 115–31.

18. R. J. W. Evans, *The Making of the Habsburg Monarchy 1550–1700: An Interpretation* (Oxford, 1979), pp. 120–3, 237–8; Janusz Tazbir, 'The Fate of Polish Protestantism in the Seventeenth Century', in J. K. Fedorowicz (ed.), *A Republic of Nobles* (Cambridge, 1982), pp. 198–217, esp. 208.

19. John Locke, *A Letter Concerning Toleration*, ed. James H. Tully (Indianapolis, 1983), pp. 26–8, 50.

20. Ian B. Cowan, 'Church and State Reformed? The Revolution of 1688–9 in Scotland', in Jonathan I. Israel, *The Anglo-Dutch Moment: Essays on the Glorious Revolution and Its World Impact* (Cambridge, 1991), pp. 174–81; Brown, *Kingdom or Province*, pp. 176–8; McNeill and MacQueen, *Atlas*, p. 401.

21. Geoffrey Holmes, *The Making of a Great Power: Late Stuart and Early Georgian Britain 1660–1722* (Harlow, 1993), p. 353; B. R. White, 'The Twilight of Puritanism in the Years before and after 1688', in Ole Peter Grell, Jonathan I. Israel and Nicholas Tyacke, *From Persecution to Toleration: The Glorious Revolution and Religion in England* (Oxford, 1991), pp. 315–30.

Chapter 13 Commercial competition, industrial diversification and agricultural success

1. Totals given to nearest 1,000: see E. A. Wrigley, R. S. Davies, J. E. Oeppen and R. S. Schofield, *English Population History from Family Reconstitution, 1580–1837* (Cambridge, 1997), pp. 195, 348, 614; E. A. Wrigley, 'British Population during the "Long" Eighteenth Century, 1680–1840', in Roderick Floud and Paul Johnson (eds), *The Cambridge Economic History of Modern Britain: I. Industrialisation, 1700–1860* (Cambridge, 2004), p. 78.

2. R. A. Houston, *The Population History of Britain and Ireland 1500–1750* (Basingstoke, 1992), p. 29; S. J. Connolly, *Contested Island: Ireland 1460–1630* (Oxford, 2007), p. 405.

3. Jan De Vries, *European Urbanization, 1500–1800* (London, 1984), p. 36; Jean-Pierre Bardet and Jacques Dupâquier (eds), *Histoire des Populations de l'Europe: I. Des origines aux prémices de la révolution démographique* (Paris, 1997), pp. 313, 429, 447–9, 468–9, 492, 519; Yves-Marie Bercé, *The Birth of Absolutism: A History of France, 1598–1661* (Basingstoke, 1996), pp. 111–16.

4. Ian Gentles, *The English Revolution and the Wars in the Three Kingdoms 1638–1652* (Harlow, 2007), pp. 433–56; Wrigley *et al.*, *English Population History*, p. 614; Connolly, *Contested Island*, p. 405.

5. E. Anthony Wrigley, 'Urban Growth and Agricultural Change: England and the Continent in the Early Modern Period', *Journal of Interdisciplinary History*, xv(4) (1985), pp. 688, 709, 714, 718; De Vries, *European Urbanization*, pp. 30, 39.

6. Stephen Inwood, *A History of London* (London, 1998), pp. 310, 317, 341–4, 349–50, 352–3, 986; Peter Earle, *The Making of the English Middle Class: Business, Society and Family Life in London, 1660–1730* (London, 1989), pp. 18–34; David Cressy, *Literacy and the Social Order: Reading and Writing in Tudor and Stuart England* (Cambridge, 1980), pp. 72–5, 132–5, 144, 175–82.

7. E. A. Wrigley, 'A Simple Model of London's Importance in Changing English Society and Economy 1650–1750', *Past and Present*, 37 (1967), pp. 44–70.

8. David Harris Sacks and Michael Lynch, 'Ports 1540–1700', in Peter Clark (ed.), *The Cambridge Urban History of Britain, II 1540–1840* (Cambridge, 2000), pp. 419–20; Helen M. Dingwall, 'Edinburgh: 2. 1650–1750', in Michael Lynch (ed.), *The Oxford Companion to Scottish History* (Oxford, 2001), pp. 219–20; Colm Lennon, 'The Changing Face of Dublin, 1550–1750', in Peter Clark and Raymond Gillespie (eds), *Two Capitals, London and Dublin, 1500–1840* (Oxford, 2001), pp. 39–52; S. J. Connolly, *Divided Kingdom: Ireland 1630–1800* (Oxford, 2008), p. 164.

9. Oreste Ranum, *Paris in the Age of Absolutism. An Essay* (2nd edn, University Park, PA, 2004), pp. 87–378; John Robertson, *The Case for the Enlightenment: Scotland and Naples 1680–1760* (Cambridge, 2005), pp. 71–5, 78–9; Clé Lesger, 'Clusters of Achievement: The Economy of Amsterdam in Its Golden Age', in Patrick O'Brien, Derek Keene, Marjolein 't Hart and Herman van der Wee, *Urban Achievement in Early Modern Europe: Golden Ages in Antwerp, Amsterdam and London* (Cambridge, 2001), pp. 63–80; De Vries, *European Urbanization*, pp. 271, 275, 277.

10. De Vries, *European Urbanization*, pp. 271, 274–5; Wrigley, 'Urban Growth and Agricultural Change', p. 686; Ian D. Whyte, *Scotland before the Industrial Revolution: An Economic and Social History c.1050–c.1750* (London, 1995), pp. 174, 176, 284–5, 288–90; Sacks and Lynch, 'Ports', p. 419.

11. C. G. A. Clay, *Economic Expansion and Social Change: England 1500–1700: II. Industry, Trade and Government* (Cambridge, 1984), pp. 154–82; Ralph Davis, *English Overseas Trade 1500–1700* (London, 1973), pp. 26–36, 55.

12. Clay, *Industry, Trade and Government*, pp. 142–9.

13. Allan I. Macinnes, *Union and Empire. The Making of the United Kingdom in 1707* (Cambridge, 2007), pp. 143–5, 150–1, 157–8, 164–9.

14. Jonathan Israel, *Dutch Primacy in World Trade 1585–1740* (Oxford, 1989), pp. 12–120.

15. Clay, *Industry, Trade and Government*, pp. 184–91; Israel, *Dutch Primacy*, pp. 278, 294, 298–9; J. L. van Zanden and E. Horlings, 'The Rise of the European Economy 1500–1800', in Derek H. Aldcroft and Anthony Sutcliffe (eds), *Europe in the International Economy 1500–2000* (Cheltenham, 1999), p. 36.

16. Pierre H. Boulle and D. Gillian Thompson, 'France Overseas', in William Doyle (ed.), *Old Regime France 1648–1788* (Oxford, 2001), pp. 105–18; Israel, *Dutch Primacy*, 231, 282–91, 307–13.

17. D. W. Jones, 'Sequel to Revolution: The Economics of England's Emergence as a Great Power, 1688–1712' and K. N. Chaudhuri and Jonathan I. Israel, 'The English and Dutch East India Companies and the Glorious Revolution of 1688–9', in Jonathan I. Israel (ed.), *The Anglo-Dutch Moment: Essays on the Glorious Revolution and Its World Impact* (Cambridge, 1991), pp. 389–406, 407–38.

18. Clay, *Industry, Trade and Government*, pp. 21, 36–43, 121, 142–52, 216.

19. Robert C. Allen, *The British Industrial Revolution in Global Perspective* (Cambridge, 2009), pp. 82, 86–8; John Hatcher, *The History of the British Coal Industry. I: Before 1700: Towards the Age of Coal* (Oxford, 1993), pp. 501–2; Clay, *Industry, Trade and Government*, pp. 46–63.

20. Whyte, *Scotland*, pp. 276–8, 286–8; Allen, *British Industrial Revolution*, p. 82.

21. Israel, *Dutch Primacy*, pp. 114–18, 193–6, 259–69, 346–58; Violet Barbour, 'Dutch and English Merchant Shipping in the Seventeenth Century', *The Economic History Review*, 2(2) (1930), pp. 261–90.

22. Joël Félix, 'The Economy', in William Doyle (ed.), *Old Regime France 1648–1788* (Oxford, 2001), pp. 19–25; Pierre Chaunu and Richard Gascon (eds), *Histoire Economique et Sociale de la France*, vol. I 1450–1660 (Paris 1977), pp. 352–3; Ernest Labrousse *et al.*, *Histoire Économique et Sociale de la France*, vol. II 1660–1789 (Paris, 1970), pp. 220–33; John U. Nef, *Industry and Government in France and England 1540–1640* (Ithaca, 1957), pp. 59–88; David Parrott, *Richelieu's Army: War, Government and Society in France, 1624–1642* (Cambridge, 2001), pp. 66–7; Israel, *Dutch Primacy*, p. 349.

23. Wrigley, 'Urban Growth and Agricultural Change', p. 700; Robert C. Allen, 'Economic Structure and Agricultural Productivity in Europe, 1300–1800', *European Review of Economic History*, 4 (2000), pp. 17, 21.

24. C. G. A. Clay, *Economic Expansion and Social Change: England 1500–1700: I. People Land and Towns* (Cambridge, 1984), pp. 102–41; Keith Wrightson, *Earthly Necessities: Economic Lives in Early Modern Britain* (New Haven and London, 2000), pp. 161–2, 230–5; Allen, *British Industrial Revolution*, pp. 59–63, 76–7.

25. Wrightson, *Earthly Necessities*, pp. 162–4, 182–90, 209–12, 277–88; J. R. Wordie, 'The Chronology of English Enclosure, 1500–1914', *Economic History Review*, 36(4) (1983), pp. 483–4, 502; Allen, *British Industrial Revolution*, pp. 63–74.

26. Whyte, *Scotland*, pp. 132–49.

27. A. Charlesworth (ed.), *An Atlas of Rural Protest in Britain, 1548–1900* (London, 1983), pp. 33–43, 74–80.

28. Joan Thirsk and J. P. Cooper (eds), *Seventeenth-century Economic Documents* (Oxford, 1972), pp. 780–1; recent analyses in Geoffrey Holmes, *The Making of a Great Power: Late Stuart and Early Georgian Britain 1660–1722* (Harlow, 1993), pp. 69–81; Wrightson, *Earthly Necessities*, pp. 270–2.

29. Paul Slack, *The English Poor Law 1531–1872* (Basingstoke, 1990), pp. 23–30; Steve Hindle, *On the Parish? The Micro-politics of Poor Relief in Rural England, c.1550–1750* (Oxford, 2004).

Chapter 14   Contacts and connections, 1603–1707

1. Steve Murdoch, 'Kith and Kin: John Durie and the Scottish Community in Scandinavia and the Baltic, 1624–34' and Leos Müller, 'Britain and Sweden: The Changing Pattern of Commodity Exchange 1650–1680', in Patrick Salmon and Tony Barrow (eds), *Britain*

and the Baltic: Studies in Commercial, Political and Cultural Relations 1500–2000 (Sunderland, 2003), pp. 23–7, 61–76.

2. M. S. Anderson, Britain's Discovery of Russia 1553–1815 (London, 1958), pp. 33–4; Enn Küng, 'English Commercial Activity in Narva during the Second Half of the Seventeenth Century', in Patrick Salmon and Tony Barrow (eds), Britain and the Baltic: Studies in Commercial, Political and Cultural Relations 1500–2000 (Sunderland, 2003), pp. 77–108; D. W. Jones, War and Economy in the Age of William III and Marlborough (Oxford, 1988), pp. 182, 184–6.

3. Gigliola Pagano de Divitiis, English Merchants in Seventeenth-century Italy (Cambridge, 1990), pp. 17–23, 59, 70–1, 182–5.

4. Murdoch, 'Kith and Kin', pp. 30–3; Steve Murdoch, 'Mercenaries in Europe', in Michael Lynch (ed.), The Oxford Companion to Scottish History (Oxford, 2001), pp. 418–19; Roger B. Manning, An Apprenticeship in Arms: The Origins of the British Army 1585–1702 (Oxford, 2006), pp. 41–93; John Childs, 'The Restoration Army 1660–1702', in David G. Chandler and Ian Beckett, The Oxford History of the British Army (Oxford, 1994), pp. 51–2.

5. Murdoch, 'Kith and Kin', p. 33 (Åbo, Uppsala, Lund, Copenhagen, Soro, Kiel, Rostock and Königsberg).

6. John Stoye, English Travellers Abroad, 1604–1667: Their Influence in English Society and Politics (revised edn, New Haven and London, 1989).

7. W. B. Patterson, King James VI and I and the Reunion of Christendom (Cambridge, 1997), pp. 35–72, 124–78, 222–92; Anthony Milton, Catholic and Reformed: The Roman and Protestant Churches in English Protestant Thought 1600–1640 (Cambridge, 1995), pp. 347, 444–6; H. R. Trevor-Roper, 'Hugo Grotius and England', in Simon Groenveld and Michael Wintle (eds), The Exchange of Ideas: Religion, Scholarship and Art in Anglo-Dutch Relations in the Seventeenth Century, vol.II (Britain and the Netherlands, 1994), pp. 42–67; Murdoch, 'Kith and Kin', pp. 34–45.

8. Laura Stewart, '"Brothers in Treuth": Propaganda, Public Opinion and the Perth Articles Debate in Scotland', in Ralph Houlbrooke (ed.), James VI and I: Ideas, Authority and Government (Aldershot, 2006), p. 163; Geoffrey Parker, The Military Revolution: Military Innovation and the Rise of the West, 1500–1800 (New York, 1988), pp. 69, 74.

9. Hugh Trevor-Roper, Europe's Physician: The Various Life of Sir Theodore Turquet de Mayerne (New Haven and London, 2006); Ole Peter Grell, Calvinist Exiles in Tudor and Stuart England (Aldershot, 1996), pp. 53–97, 120–46.

10. Robin D. Gwynn, Huguenot Heritage: The History and Contribution of the Huguenots in Britain (London, 1985), pp. 24, 32–3, 35–6, 65–78, 144–59; Robin Gwynn, 'The Huguenots in Britain, the "Protestant International", and the Defeat of Louis XIV', in Randolph Vigne and Charles Littleton (eds), From Strangers to Citizens: The Integration of Immigrant Communities in Britain, Ireland and Colonial America, 1550–1750 (London and Brighton, 2001), pp. 412–24.

11. David S. Katz, The Jews in the History of England, 1485–1850 (Oxford, 1994), pp. 109–41, 180, 185, 187.

12. John Bossy, The English Catholic Community, 1570–1850 (London, 1975), pp. 216–18; J. C. H. Aveling, The Handle and the Axe: The Catholic Recusants in England from Reformation to Emancipation (London, 1976), pp. 87–8, 90, 94–8; Peter G. B. McNeill and Hector L. MacQueen (eds), Atlas of Scottish History to 1707 (Edinburgh, 1996), pp. 408–9.

13. Michael C. Questier (ed.), Newsletters from the Caroline Court, 1631–1638: Catholicism and the Politics of Personal Rule (Camden, 5th series, vol. 26), pp. 1, 4–5, 21–5; Steven C. A. Pincus, 'The European Catholic Context of the Revolution of 1688–89: Gallicanism, Innocent XI, and Catholic Opposition', in Allan I. MacInnes and Arthur H. Williamson (eds), Shaping the Stuart World, 1603–1714: The Atlantic Connection (Leiden, 2005), pp. 79–116.

14. Geoffrey Smith, *The Cavaliers in Exile, 1640–1660* (Basingstoke, 2003), pp. 6, 10, 30, 47, 68–70, 91, 116–20, 125–6, 191–5, 212.

15. See the trilogy by Richard L. Greaves, *Deliver Us from Evil: The Radical Underground in Britain, 1660–1663* (New York, 1986), esp. pp. 92–5, *Enemies under His Feet: Radicals and Nonconformists in Britain, 1664–1677* (Stanford, 1990), esp. pp. 12–15, 23–32, 58–68, 102, 184–9 and *Secrets of the Kingdom: British Radicals from the Popish Plot to the Revolution of 1688–89* (Stanford, 1992), esp. pp. 252–325; also Ginny Gardner, *The Scottish Exile Community in the Netherlands, 1660–1690* (East Linton, 2004) and K. H. D. Haley, *William of Orange and the English Opposition, 1672–4* (Oxford, 1953).

16. Daniel Szechi, *The Jacobites: Britain and Europe 1688–1788* (Manchester, 1994), pp. 30–2, 51–63; Frank McLynn, *The Jacobites* (London, 1985), pp. 21–5.

17. Mario A. di Cesare (ed.), *Milton in Italy: Contexts, Images, Contradictions* (Binghamton, 1991).

18. Frank J. Warnke, 'Marino and the English Metaphysicals', *Studies in the Renaissance*, 2 (1955), pp. 160–75.

19. Paulina Kewes, 'Drama', Jennifer Birkett, 'Prose Fiction: Courtly and Popular Romance' and Philip Smallwood, 'Literary Criticism', in Stuart Gillespie and David Hopkins (eds), *The Oxford History of Literary Translation in English, 3: 1660–1790* (Oxford, 2005), pp. 317–24, 340–3, 374–6; Jeffery Barnouw, 'Britain and European Literature and Thought', in John Richetti (ed.), *The Cambridge History of English Literature, 1660–1780* (Cambridge, 2005), pp. 423–5, 427.

20. Robert Crawford, *Scotland's Books: The Penguin History of Scottish Literature* (London, 2007), pp. 182–200.

21. Giles Worsley, *Inigo Jones and the European Classicist Tradition* (New Haven and London, 2007).

22. John Summerson, *Architecture in Britain, 1530–1830* (9th edn, New Haven and London, 1993), pp. 133–56, 173–9, 242–5.

23. Kerry Downes, *The Architecture of Christopher Wren* (2nd edn, Reading, 1988); Summerson, *Architecture*, pp. 179–238.

24. Miles Glendinning, *A History of Scottish Architecture: From the Renaissance to the Present* (Edinburgh, 1996), pp. 35–7, 40–1, 53–4, 58–9, 65–8, 83–90, 93–102.

25. Margaret Whinney, *Sculpture in Britain, 1530–1830* (Harmondsworth, 1964), pp. 17–62, plates 11–13, 15–22, 24, 26–31, 36–47.

26. Ellis Waterhouse, *Painting in Britain, 1530–1790* (4th edn, Harmondsworth, 1978), pp. 51–62, 70–80, 92–100, 125–31, 138–43; Karen Hearn (ed.), *Dynasties: Painting in Tudor and Jacobean England 1530–1630* (London, 1995), pp. 171–219, 226–7; Oliver Millar, *The Age of Charles I: Painting in England, 1620–1649* (London, 1972); Oliver Millar, *Sir Peter Lely* (London, 1978); J. Douglas Stewart, *Sir Godfrey Kneller and the English Baroque Portrait* (Oxford, 1983).

27. Waterhouse, *Painting*, pp. 65–6, 68–9, 80–5, 91, 106–10, 113–14, 121–3 150–1; Malcolm Rogers, *William Dobson, 1611–46* (London, 1983); Hearn, *Dynasties*, pp. 166, 220–3.

28. John Caldwell, *The Oxford History of English Music: 1. From the Beginnings to 1715* (Oxford, 1991), pp. 447, 479–80, 495, 497, 510–12, 523–7, 539–42, 553–7.

29. Caldwell, *The Oxford History of English Music*, pp. 515–22, 549–54, 561–615; John Caldwell, 'England: 4. From the Restoration to the Accession of Queen Victoria', in Alison Latham (ed.), *The Oxford Companion to Music* (Oxford, 2002), p. 421.

30. L. W. B. Brockliss, 'The Scientific Revolution in France', David Goodman, 'The Scientific Revolution in Spain and Portugal' and John Henry, 'The Scientific Revolution in England', in Roy Porter and Mikuláš Teich (eds), *The Scientific Revolution in National Context* (Cambridge, 1992), pp. 55–89, 158–77, 178–209, esp. 192; Michael Hunter,

Science and the Shape of Orthodoxy: Intellectual Change in Late Seventeenth-century Britain (Woodbridge, 1995), esp. pp. 1–18, 101–34.

31. Charles Webster, *The Great Instauration: Science, Medicine and Reform 1626–1660* (London, 1975). For a brief comment on the role Webster attributed to puritan millenarianism, see Henry, 'Scientific Revolution', pp. 179–80.

32. Richard S. Westfall, *Never at Rest: A Biography of Isaac Newton* (Cambridge, 1980), pp. 302–6, 317–18, 351, 448, 508–10, 647, 653, 748, 777–8.

33. Charles Wilson, *Holland and Britain* (London, 1946).

Chapter 15 Making the United Kingdom

1. Bruce Galloway, *The Union of England and Scotland 1603–1608* (Edinburgh, 1986), pp. 20–5.

2. Galloway, *Union*, pp. 65–76, 93–130.

3. Galloway, *Union*, pp. 56–7, *The Jacobean Union: Six Tracts of 1604*, ed. Bruce Galloway and Brian P. Levack (Scottish Historical Society, 4th series, vol. 21, Edinburgh, 1985), pp. 39–74.

4. Galloway, *Jacobean Union*, pp. 163–8, 221–2.

5. Keith M. Brown, 'The Scottish Aristocracy, Anglicization and the Court, 1603–38', *Historical Journal*, 36(3) (1993), pp. 543–76, esp. 552, 556, 573; Neil Cuddy, 'The Revival of the Entourage: The Bedchamber of James I, 1603–1625', in David Starkey (ed.), *The English Court: From the Wars of the Roses to the Civil War* (Basingstoke, 1987), pp. 173–225.

6. Arthur H. Williamson, 'Radical Britain: David Hume of Godscroft and the Challenge to the Jacobean British Vision', in Glenn Burgess, Rowland Wymer and Jason Lawrence (eds), *The Accession of James I: Historical and Cultural Consequences* (Basingstoke, 2006), pp. 48–68.

7. David Stevenson, *The Scottish Revolution 1637–44: The Triumph of the Covenanters* (Newton Abbot, 1973), pp. 220–3.

8. Brian P. Levack, *The Formation of the British State: England, Scotland, and the Union 1603–1707* (Oxford, 1987), p. 64.

9. S. R. Gardiner (ed.), *The Constitutional Documents of the Puritan Revolution 1625–1660* (3rd edn, Oxford, 1906), pp. 347–53; David Stevenson, *Revolution and Counter-revolution in Scotland, 1644–1651* (London, 1977), pp. 129, 132–3.

10. F. D. Dow, *Cromwellian Scotland 1651–1660* (Edinburgh, 1979), pp. 31–2, 35–42, 55, 49–51, 58–61, 120–1.

11. Dow, *Cromwellian Scotland*, pp. 148–51, 165, 185–7, 237–40.

12. William Ferguson, *Scotland's Relations with England: A Survey to 1707* (Edinburgh, 1977), pp. 153–7.

13. Allan I. Macinnes, *Union and Empire: The Making of the United Kingdom in 1707* (Cambridge, 2007), pp. 172–88.

14. Ferguson, *Scotland's Relations*, p. 209.

15. Macinnes, *Union*, p. 277.

16. Anthony Aufrere (ed.), *The Lockhart Papers*, vol. I (2 vols, London, 1817), p. 327; Michael Lynch, *Scotland: A New History* (revised edn, 1992), pp. 310–17; T. M. Devine, *The Scottish Nation, 1700–2000* (London, 1999), pp. 3–16; Christopher A. Whatley, *Bought and Sold for English Gold? Explaining the Union of 1707* (2nd edn, East Linton, 2001); Stewart Jay Brown and Christopher A. Whatley (eds), *The Union of 1707: New Dimensions* (Edinburgh, 2008); Karin Bowie, *Scottish Public Opinion and the Anglo-Scottish Union, 1699–1707* (Woodbridge, 2007); Macinnes, *Union*.

17. S. J. Connolly, *Divided Kingdom: Ireland 1630–1800* (Oxford, 2008), pp. 170, 208–13; David Hayton, 'Constitutional Experiments and Political Expediency, 1689–1725', in Steven G. Ellis and Sarah Barber (eds), *Conquest and Union: Fashioning a British State, 1485–1725* (London, 1995), p. 304.
18. Glanmor Williams, *Renewal and Reformation: Wales c.1415–1642* (Oxford, 1993), pp. 473–7, 215–16; Geraint H. Jenkins, *The Foundations of Modern Wales, 1642–1780* (Oxford, 1987), pp. 213–44; Philip Jenkins, 'The Anglican Church and the Unity of Britain: The Welsh Experience, 1560–1714', in Steven G. Ellis and Sarah Barber (eds), *Conquest and Union: Fashioning a British State, 1485–1725* (London, 1995), pp. 115–38.

Chapter 16 The United Kingdom tested

1. On the complexities of Baltic policy, see Ragnhild Hatton, *George I Elector and King* (London, 1978), pp. 180–201, 216–22, 235–42; Brendan Simms, *Three Victories and a Defeat: The Rise and Fall of the First British Empire 1714–1783* (London, 2007), pp. 108–34, 142–6, 153–5.
2. John Stuart Shaw, *The Political History of Eighteenth-century Scotland* (Basingstoke, 1999), pp. 24–6, 30, 43–5, 55–6, 59–69, 87, 97, 101–2; Michael Lynch, *Scotland: A New History* (revised edn, London, 1992), pp. 323–5.
3. Basil Williams, *The Whig Supremacy 1714–1760* (2nd edn revised by C. H. Stuart, Oxford, 1962), p. 207 (Spanish grievances); N. A. M. Rodger, *The Command of the Ocean: A Naval History of Britain, 1649–1815* (London, 2004), pp. 234–40.
4. Simms, *Three Victories*, pp. 315–22.
5. Daniel Szechi, *The Jacobites: Britain and Europe 1688–1788* (Manchester, 1994), pp. 95–103; Allan I. Macinnes, *Clanship, Commerce and the House of Stuart, 1603–1788* (East Linton, 1996), p. 246; Murray G. H. Pittock, *Jacobitism* (Basingstoke, 1998), 98–9, 111–12.
6. Rodger, *Command*, pp. 250–4.
7. Simms, *Three Victories*, p. 369.
8. Shaw, *Scotland*, p. 74; Linda Colley, *Britons: Forging the Nation 1707–1837* (New Haven and London, 1992), pp. 53, 103–5; Stephen Conway, *War, State and Society in Mid-eighteenth-century Britain and Ireland* (Oxford, 2006), pp. 193–212.
9. Paul Langford, *A Polite and Commercial People: England 1727–1783* (Oxford, 1989), pp. 388, 521–4.
10. Colley, *Britons*, pp. 105–17.
11. Michael Roberts, *Splendid Isolation 1763–1780* (Reading, 1970); Jeremy Black, *A System of Ambition? British Foreign Policy 1660–1793* (2nd edn, Stroud, 2000), pp. 234–46.
12. Langford, *Polite and Commercial People*, pp. 536–40, 547–9, 553–4; Colley, *Britons*, pp. 139–41.
13. 'Mémoire présenté à Louis XV par le duc de Choiseul', in A. Soulange (ed.), *La Diplomatie de Louis XV et la Pacte de Famille* (Paris, 1894), p. 251.

Chapter 17 'This mixture of monarchical, aristocratical and democratical power'

1. David Armitage (ed.), *Bolingbroke: Political Writings* (Cambridge, 1997), p. 125.
2. Ragnhild Hatton, *George I, Elector and King* (London, 1978), p. 119.
3. Especially in his use of the fleet. He instigated in 1715 the repeal of a clause in the 1701 Act of Settlement that forbade the monarch to leave England without parliamentary consent: Hatton, *George I*, p. 158.
4. Hatton, *George I*, pp. 287–90, 294; Charles Chenevix Trench, *George II* (London, 1973), pp. 176–7, 227, 268–71, 299–300; William Cobbett (ed.), *The Parliamentary History of England, from the Earliest Period to the Year 1803. Vol. 16: A.D. 1765–1771* (London,

1813), column 849; John Brooke, *King George III* (London, 1972), pp. 56–7, 90, 260–2, 307–13, 316–17.

5. R. O. Bucholz, *The Augustan Court: Queen Anne and the Decline of Court Culture* (Stanford, CA, 1993), pp. 209–48; John M. Beattie, *The English Court in the Reign of George I* (Cambridge, 1967), pp. 1–65, 249–78; Brooke, *George III*, pp. 282–9.

6. John Cannon, *Aristocratic Century: The Peerage of Eighteenth-century England* (Cambridge, 1984), p. 15; Chris Cook and John Stevenson, *The Longman Handbook of Modern British History 1714–1995* (3rd edn, London, 1996), pp. 83–4; Geoffrey Holmes, *The Making of a Great Power: Late Stuart and Early Georgian Britain, 1660–1722* (Harlow, 1993), p. 330; Betty Kemp, *King and Commons 1660–1832* (London, 1959), pp. 95–7.

7. H. T. Dickinson, 'Whiggism in the Eighteenth Century', in John Cannon (ed.), *The Whig Ascendancy: Colloquies on Hanoverian England* (London, 1981), pp. 25–42.

8. Linda Colley, *In Defiance of Oligarchy: The Tory Party, 1714–60* (Cambridge, 1982); Frank O'Gorman, *The Long Eighteenth Century: British Political and Social History 1688–1832* (London, 1997), pp. 147–52, 159 n. 12.

9. Colley, *In Defiance of Oligarchy*, pp. 118–45.

10. John Cannon, *Parliamentary Reform 1640–1832* (Cambridge, 1972), pp. 61–7, 76–80, 85–6, 92–4.

11. Patrick K. O'Brien and Philip A. Hunt, 'The Rise of a Fiscal State in England, 1485–1815', *Historical Research*, 66 (1993), pp. 164, 166, 175; Paul Langford, *A Polite and Commercial People: England 1727–1783* (Oxford, 1989), p. 645; John Brewer, *The Sinews of Power: War, Money and the English State, 1688–1783* (Cambridge, Mass., 1988), pp. 65–7, 98.

12. Brewer, *Sinews of Power*, pp. 114–17, 119–26.

13. Brewer, *Sinews of Power*, p. 126; Larry Neal, 'The Monetary, Financial and Political Architecture of Europe, 1648–1815', in Leandro Prados de la Escosura (ed.), *Exceptionalism and Industrialisation: Britain and Its European Rivals, 1688–1815* (Cambridge, 2004), pp. 174–5.

14. N. A. M. Rodger, *The Command of the Ocean: A Naval History of Britain, 1649–1815* (London, 2004), pp. 608, 636–8; Brewer, *Sinews of Power*, pp. 30, 34–7; Daniel A. Baugh, 'Naval Power: What Gave the British Navy Superiority?', in Leandro Prados de la Escosura (ed.), *Exceptionalism and Industrialisation: Britain and Its European Rivals, 1688–1815* (Cambridge, 2004), pp. 238–43, 245–8.

15. Alan J. Guy, 'The Army of the Georges, 1714–1783', in David G. Chandler and Ian Beckett (eds), *The Oxford History of the British Army* (Oxford, 1994), pp. 92–111.

16. Ian F. W. Beckett, *The Amateur Military Tradition 1558–1945* (Manchester, 1991), pp. 63–8.

17. Joanna Innes, 'The Domestic Face of the Military-fiscal State: Government and Society in Eighteenth-century Britain', in Lawrence Stone (ed.), *An Imperial State at War: Britain from 1689 to 1815* (London, 1994), pp. 96–127.

18. Christopher W. Chalklin, *English Counties and Public Building, 1650–1830* (London, 1998), pp. 51–3; J. A. Sharpe, *Crime in Early Modern England 1550–1750* (London, 1984), pp. 57–63; O'Gorman, *Long Eighteenth Century*, p. 293, *Parliamentary Papers*, xli (1839), pp. 11–13 (assuming West Riding county rates to have raised about 5 per cent of the total, as there suggested).

19. Michael Lynch, *Scotland: A New History* (revised edn, London, 1992), pp. 324–5, 339; Rosalind Mitchison, *Lordship to Patronage: Scotland 1603–1745* (London, 1983), pp. 142–5; Bruce P. Lenman, *Integration and Enlightenment: Scotland 1746–1832* (Edinburgh, 1992), p. 25; Johan Findlay, *All Manner of People: The History of the Justices of the Peace in Scotland* (Edinburgh, 2000), pp. 63–74.

20. Paul Slack, *The English Poor Law 1531–1782* (Basingstoke, 1990), pp. 40–3, 50–1, 63; Langford, *Polite and Commercial People*, pp. 134–45, 391–417; Paul Langford, *Public*

Life and the Propertied Englishman 1689–1798 (Oxford, 1991), pp. 163, 182–3, 222–32, 493–500.

21. Langford, *Polite and Commercial People*, pp. 44–7, 264–6, 291–2, 442–5, 550–1, 669, 721; Nicholas Rogers, *Whigs and Cities: Popular Politics in the Age of Walpole and Pitt* (Oxford, 1989); Andrew Charlesworth (ed.), *An Atlas of Rural Protest in Britain 1548– 1900* (London, 1982), pp. 44–50, 81–94; Andrew Charlesworth (ed.), *An Atlas of Industrial Protest in Britain, 1750–1990* (Basingstoke, 1996), pp. 18–31; H. T. Dickinson, 'Popular Politics and Radical Ideas', in H. T. Dickinson (ed.), *A Companion to Eighteenth-century Britain* (Oxford, 2002), pp. 97–111.

22. Richard Bonney, 'The Eighteenth Century II. The Struggle for Great Power Status and the End of the Fiscal Regime', in Richard Bonney (ed.), *Economic Systems and State Finance* (Oxford, 1995), pp. 336–7.

23. Peter Mathias and Patrick O'Brien, 'Taxation in Britain and France, 1715–1810. A Comparison of the Social and Economic Incidence of Taxes Collected for the Central Governments', *Journal of European Economic History*, 5 (1976), pp. 601–50, esp. 608–9, 622; Brewer, *Sinews of Power*, p. 128.

24. Richard Bonney, 'Towards the Comparative Fiscal History of Britain and France during the "Long" Eighteenth Century', in Leandro Prados de la Escosura (ed.), *Exceptionalism and Industrialisation: Britain and Its European Rivals, 1688–1815* (Cambridge, 2004), pp. 191–215; Brewer, *Sinews of Power*, pp. 130, 133.

25. Charles W. Ingrao, *The Habsburg Monarchy 1618–1815* (2nd edn, Cambridge, 2000), pp. 161–4; Richard Bonney, 'Struggle' and 'Revenues', in Richard Bonney (ed.), *Economic Systems and State Finance*, pp. 332–5, 460–3; Juan Gelabert, 'Castile, 1504–1808' and Marjolein 't Hart, 'The United Provinces, 1579–1806', in Richard Bonney (ed.), *The Rise of the Fiscal State in Europe, c.1200–1815* (Oxford, 1999), pp. 229–35, 322–3; D. W. Jones, *War and Economy in the Age of William III and Marlborough* (Oxford, 1988), p. 29.

26. Rodger, *Command of the Ocean*, pp. 211–12, 222, 232–4, 294, 310, 411, 418, 608; Baugh, 'Naval Power', pp. 238–48.

27. Jeremy Black, *A Military Revolution? Military Change and European Society 1550–1800* (Basingstoke, 1991), p. 7; Christopher Clark, *Iron Kingdom: The Rise and Downfall of Prussia, 1600–1947* (London, 2006), pp. 95–101, 157–8, 200–4; Jeremy Black, *European Warfare 1660–1815* (London, 1994), pp. 129–31, 153–4; Ingrao, *Habsburg Monarchy*, p. 183.

28. Julian Swann, 'The State and Political Culture' and 'Politics: Louis XV', in William Doyle (ed.), *Old Regime France 1648–1788* (Oxford, 2001), pp. 157, 196–7, 203–4, 209–12, 215–21.

29. Bob Harris, *Politics and the Rise of the Press: Britain and France, 1620–1800* (London, 1996), pp. 12, 59; Robert Darnton, 'An Early Information Society: News and the Media in Eighteenth-century Paris', *American Historical Review*, 105(1) (2000), pp. 1–36.

Chapter 18 Religion in the age of reason and revival

1. Brian P. Levack, *The Formation of the British State. England, Scotland and the Union, 1603–1707* (Oxford, 1987), pp. 136–7. More than one religion had long been recognized within the Holy Roman Empire, an entity very different from the United Kingdom.

2. Andrew Starkie, *The Church of England and the Bangorian Controversy* (Woodbridge, 2007).

3. Colin Haydon, 'Religious Minorities in England', in H. T. Dickinson (ed.), *A Companion to Eighteenth-century Britain* (Oxford, 2002), pp. 241–51; Michael R. Watts, *The Dissenters: from the Reformation to the French Revolution* (Oxford, 1978), pp. 450–78.

4. F. C. Mather, 'Church, Parliament and Penal Laws: Some Anglo-Scottish Interactions in the Eighteenth Century', *English Historical Review*, 92 (1977), pp. 540–72.

5. Stewart J. Brown, 'Religion in Scotland', in H. T. Dickinson (ed.), *A Companion to Eighteenth-century Britain* (Oxford, 2002), pp. 260–70; Ian D. Whyte, *Scotland before the Industrial Revolution: An Economic and Social History c.1050–c.1750* (London, 1995), pp. 322–7; Michael Lynch, *Scotland: A New History* (revised edn, London, 1992), pp. 363–5; Allan I. Macinnes, *Clanship, Commerce and the House of Stuart, 1603–1788* (East Linton, 1996), pp. 177–80.

6. Andrew Thompson, *Britain, Hanover and the Protestant Interest, 1688–1756* (Woodbridge, 2006), pp. 61–167.

7. W. R. Ward, *Christianity under the* Ancien Régime *1648–1789* (Cambridge, 1999), pp. 34–52, 56–62, 186–90, 228.

8. Haydon, 'Religious Minorities', pp. 241–51; Michael A. Mullett, *Catholics in Britain and Ireland, 1558–1829* (Basingstoke, 1998), 88–101, 104–12, 138–47, 152–76; Bruce P. Lenman, *Integration and Enlightenment: Scotland 1746–1832* (Edinburgh, 1981), p. 12.

9. Colin Haydon, *Anti-Catholicism in Eighteenth-century England c.1714–80: A Political and Social Study* (Manchester, 1994), esp. pp. 204–44.

10. S. J. Connolly, *Divided Kingdom: Ireland 1630–1800* (Oxford, 2008), pp. 249–58, 262–7, 277–9.

11. Jonathan I. Israel, *Radical Enlightenment: Philosophy and the Making of Modernity 1650–1750* (Oxford, 2001), pp. 162, 221–2, 229, 231, 449.

12. William Wollaston, *The Religion of Nature Delineated* (1722), esp. p. 153; Matthew Tindal, *Christianity as Old as the Creation* (1730).

13. David Hume, *Philosophical Essays Concerning Human Understanding* (London, 1748), pp. 198–9, 220; David Hume, 'The Natural History of Religion', in his *Four Dissertations* (London, 1757), esp. pp. 1–15.

14. John Walsh and Stephen Taylor, 'Introduction: The Church and Anglicanism in the "Long" Eighteenth Century', in John Walsh, Colin Haydon and Stephen Taylor (eds), *The Church of England c.1689–c.1833: From Toleration to Tractarianism* (Cambridge, 1993), pp. 40–1, 43, 53–9.

15. Walsh and Taylor, 'Introduction', pp. 8–18, 22–9.

16. W. R. Ward, *The Protestant Evangelical Awakening* (Cambridge, 1992), pp. 54–159.

17. Colin Podmore, *The Moravian Church in England, 1728–1760* (Oxford, 1998).

18. Henry D. Rack, *Reasonable Enthusiast: John Wesley and the Rise of Methodism* (London, 1989), esp. pp. 437–8; G. M. Ditchfield, *The Evangelical Revival* (London, 1998), pp. 39–77.

Chapter 19 Commercial ascendancy and industrial growth

1. Jan de Vries, *European Urbanization 1500–1800* (London, 1984), p. 36; Jean-Pierre Bardet and Jacques Dupâquier (eds), *Histoire des Populations de l'Europe: I. Des origines aux prémices de la révolution démographique* (Paris, 1997), pp. 254–5, 449; E. A. Wrigley, 'British Population during the "Long" Eighteenth Century', in Roderick Floud and Paul Johnson (eds), *The Cambridge Economic History of Modern Britain: I. Industrialisation, 1700–1860* (Cambridge, 2004), p. 64; Michael Anderson, 'Population Patterns', in Michael Lynch (ed.), *The Oxford Companion to Scottish History* (Oxford, 2001), pp. 487–9; S. J. Connolly, *Divided Kingdom: Ireland 1630–1800* (Oxford, 2008), pp. 164, 345, 351; Gilles Pison, 'The Population of France in 2000', *Population et Sociétés*, 366 (2001), p. 2.

2. Wrigley, 'British Population', pp. 57–95, esp. pp. 66–86; E. Anthony Wrigley, 'Urban Growth and Agricultural Change: England and the Continent in the Early Modern Period', *Journal of Interdisciplinary History*, 15(4) (1985), pp. 700, 709, 714; De Vries, *European Urbanization*, p. 39.

3. F. M. L. Thompson, 'The Social Distribution of Landed Property in England since the Sixteenth Century', *Economic History Review*, 2nd series, 19(3) (1966), pp. 510, 514;

Stephen Inwood, *A History of London* (London, 1998), pp. 354–7; Peter Mathias, 'The Social Structure in the Eighteenth Century: A Calculation by Joseph Massie', *Economic History Review*, 2nd series, 10(1) (1957), pp. 30–45; Paul Langford, *A Polite and Commercial People: England 1727–1783* (Oxford, 1989), pp. 62–4; P. J. Corfield, 'Class by Name and Number in Eighteenth-century Britain', *History*, 72(234) (1987), pp. 38–61.

4. Paul Slack, *The English Poor Law 1531–1872* (Basingstoke, 1990), pp. 30–4; Peter M. Solar, 'Poor Relief and English Economic Development before the Industrial Revolution', *Economic History Review*, 2nd series, 48(1) (1995), pp. 1–22; Steve King, 'Poor Relief and English Economic Development Reappraised', *Economic History Review*, 50(2) (1997), pp. 360–8.

5. Wrigley, 'Urban Growth and Agricultural Change', pp. 700, 718; Gail Bossenga, 'Society', in William Doyle (ed.), *Old Regime France 1648–1788* (Oxford, 2001), p. 48.

6. Francis Sheppard, *London: A History* (Oxford, 1998), p. 363; Inwood, *London*, pp. 251–62, 311–20, 335–8, 344–54, 358–60.

7. Wrigley, 'Urban Growth', pp. 686, 688, 690–1; Christopher Chalklin, *The Rise of the English Town 1650–1850* (Cambridge, 2001), pp. 6–8, 12–16; Peter Borsay, 'Urban Life and Culture', in H. T. Dickinson (ed.), *A Companion to Eighteenth-century Britain* (Oxford, 2002), pp. 196–208.

8. Joyce Ellis, 'Regional and County Centres 1700–1840' and Gordon Jackson, 'Ports 1700–1840', in Peter Clark (ed.), *The Cambridge Urban History of Britain: II. 1540–1840* (Cambridge, 2000), esp. pp. 679, 710; Connolly, *Divided Kingdom*, pp. 164, 363–7, 504.

9. De Vries, *European Urbanization*, pp. 30, 39, 270–8; Wrigley, 'Urban Growth', p. 714; Anthony Cross, *By the Banks of the Neva: Chapters from the Lives and Careers of the British in Eighteenth-century Russia* (Cambridge, 1997), p. 16.

10. John Rule, 'Manufacturing and Commerce', in H. T. Dickinson (ed.), *A Companion to Eighteenth-century Britain* (Oxford, 2002), p. 137; John Rule, *The Vital Century: England's Developing Economy 1714–1815* (London, 1992), pp. 251–63; Maxine Berg, 'Consumption in Eighteenth- and Early Nineteenth-century Britain', in Roderick Floud and Paul Johnson (eds), *The Cambridge Economic History of Modern Britain: I. Industrialisation, 1700–1860* (Cambridge, 2004), pp. 357–87; Ralph Davis, 'English Foreign Trade, 1700–1774', in W. E. Minchinton (ed.), *The Growth of English Overseas Trade in the Seventeenth and Eighteenth Centuries* (London, 1969), pp. 119–20.

11. Davis, 'English Trade', pp. 119–20.

12. Pierre Léon, 'Élan industriel et commercial', in Ernest Labrousse *et al.* (eds), *Histoire Économique et Sociale de la France: II. Des derniers temps de l'age seigneurial aux préludes de l'âge industriel (1660–1789)* (Paris, 1970), pp. 503–9; François Crouzet, *Britain Ascendant: Comparative Studies in Franco-British Economic History* (Cambridge, 1990), pp. 12–20, esp. 18; Joël Félix, 'The Economy' and Pierre H. Boulle and D. Gillian Thompson, 'France Overseas', in William Doyle (ed.), *Old Regime France 1648–1788* (Oxford, 2001), pp. 26, 105–38.

13. Javier Cuenca Esteban, 'Comparative Patterns of Colonial Trade: Britain and Its Rivals', in Leandro Prados de La Escosura (ed.), *Exceptionalism and Industrialisation: Britain and Its European Rivals, 1688–1815* (Cambridge, 2004), pp. 35–66, esp. pp. 46–53, 59.

14. David Ormrod, *The Rise of Commercial Empires: England and the Netherlands in the Age of Mercantilism, 1650–1770* (Cambridge, 2003), pp. 334–51; Niels Steensgaard, 'The Growth and Composition of the Long-distance Trade of England and the Dutch Republic before 1750', in James D. Tracy (ed.), *The Rise of Merchant Empires: Long-distance Trade in the Early Modern World, 1350–1750* (Cambridge, 1990), pp. 102–52, esp. 148–50.

15. Geoffrey Holmes and Daniel Szechi, *The Age of Oligarchy. Pre-industrial Britain 1722–1783* (London, 1993), pp. 383, 388.
16. Rule, *Vital Century*, pp. 101–10; Ian D. Whyte, *Scotland before the Industrial Revolution: An Economic and Social History c.1050–c.1750* (London, 1995), pp. 301–3; Holmes and Szechi, *Age of Oligarchy*, p. 391; Paul Mantoux, *The Industrial Revolution in the Eighteenth Century* (revised edn, London, 1961), pp. 198–203.
17. Holmes and Szechi, *Age of Oligarchy*, p. 390.
18. Rule, *Vital Century*, pp. 118–25.
19. Robert C. Allen, *The British Industrial Revolution in Global Perspective* (Cambridge, 2009), pp. 156–63, 217–28; Rule, *Vital Century*, pp. 116–17.
20. Christine Macleod, 'The European Origins of British Technological Predominance' and James Thomson, 'Invention in the Industrial Revolution: The Case of Cotton', in Leandro Prados de La Escosura (ed.), *Exceptionalism and Industrialisation: Britain and Its European Rivals, 1688–1815* (Cambridge, 2004), pp. 111–26, 127–44; Allen, *British Industrial Revolution*, pp. 182–208.
21. Crouzet, *Britain Ascendant*, pp. 21–4, 26–32, 43; Allen, *British Industrial Revolution*, esp. pp. 138–40.
22. Jonathan Israel, *The Dutch Republic: Its Rise, Greatness, and Fall 1477–1806* (Oxford, 1955), pp. 998–1003, 1087–90.
23. Sheilagh C. Ogilvie, 'The Beginnings of Industrialization', in Sheilagh C. Ogilvie (ed.), *Germany: A New Social and Economic History. 2: 1630–1800* (London, 1996), pp. 263–308; Charles W. Ingrao, *The Habsburg Monarchy 1618–1815* (2nd edn, Cambridge, 2000), pp. 138–9, 167–8, 212–13.
24. Gregory Hanlon, *Early Modern Italy, 1550–1800* (Basingstoke, 2000), pp. 333–9, esp. 334; John Lynch, *Bourbon Spain 1700–1808* (Oxford, 1989), pp. 216–23; J. K. J. Thomson, 'Proto-industrialization in Spain', in Sheilagh C. Ogilivie and Markus Cerman, *European Proto-industrialization* (Cambridge, 1996), pp. 92–7.
25. Gordon Mingay, 'Agriculture and Rural Life', in H. T. Dickinson (ed.), *A Companion to Eighteenth-century Britain* (Oxford, 2002), pp. 144–9; Robert C. Allen, 'Agriculture during the Industrial Revolution 1700–1850', in Roderick Floud and Paul Johnson (eds), *The Cambridge Economic History of Modern Britain: I. Industrialisation, 1700–1860* (Cambridge, 2004), pp. 108–10.
26. Mingay, 'Agriculture', pp. 146, 149–51; J. R. Wordie, 'The Chronology of English Enclosure, 1500–1914', *Economic History Review*, 36(4) (1983), p. 502; Patrick K. O'Brien and Daniel Heath, 'English and French Landowners, 1688–1789', in F. M. L. Thompson (ed.), *Landowners, Capitalists and Entrepreneurs: Essays for Sir John Habbakuk* (Oxford, 1994), pp. 29–32, 40–4, 51–2, 61; Allen, 'Agriculture', pp. 110–14.
27. Mingay, 'Agriculture', p. 151; Allen, 'Agriculture', pp. 102, 114–16; Robert C. Allen, 'Tracking the Agricultural Revolution in England', *Economic History Review*, 52(2) (1999), pp. 209–35, esp. 216.
28. T. M. Devine, 'Scotland', in Roderick Floud and Paul Johnson (eds), *The Cambridge Economic History of Modern Britain: I. Industrialisation, 1700–1860* (Cambridge, 2004), pp. 392–4, 404–10.
29. Connolly, *Divided Kingdom*, pp. 349–61.
30. Allen, 'Agriculture', p. 98; Serge Bianchi, Michel Biard and Alan Forrest 'La "révolution agricole" du xviiie siècle, in Serge Bianchi *et al.*, *La terre et les paysans en France et en Grande-Bretagne du début du XVIIe siècle à la fin du XVIIIe siècle* (Paris, 1999), pp. 158–66; Lynch, *Bourbon Spain*, p. 205; Heide Wunder, 'Agriculture and Agrarian Society', in Sheilagh C. Ogilvie (ed.), *Germany: A New Social and Economic History. 2: 1630–1800* (London, 1996), p. 83.

31. Bianchi *et al.*, *La Terre*, pp. 167, 170–1, 173; Philip T. Hoffman, *Growth in a Traditional Society: The French Countryside 1450–1815* (Princeton, 1996), pp. 162–5, 190–1.

32. O'Brien and Heath, 'English and French Landowners', pp. 26–7; Bossenga, 'Society', pp. 62–6; Ingrao, *Habsburg Monarchy*, pp. 135, 171–2, 185–7; Lynch, *Bourbon Spain*, pp. 199–205.

33. Félix, 'The Economy', p. 18; Bianchi *et al.*, *La Terre*, pp. 143–5, 163; Bossenga, 'Society', p. 67; Lynch, *Bourbon Spain*, p. 212; Ogilvie, *Germany*, p. 89; Hanlon, *Italy*, pp. 330–2; Ingrao, *Habsburg Monarchy*, pp. 185–7.

34. Félix, 'The Economy', p. 19; Hanlon, *Italy*, pp. 329–30; Lynch, *Bourbon Spain*, p. 208.

Chapter 20 Contacts and connections, 1707–80

1. Jeremy Black, 'Hanover and British Foreign Policy 1714–1760', *English Historical Review*, 120(486) (2005), pp. 303–39; Brendan Simms, *Three Victories and a Defeat: The Rise and Fall of the First British Empire* (London, 2007). Two articles helpfully survey Britain's relations with Europe during the eighteenth century: J. S. Bromley's brilliant 'Britain and Europe in the Eighteenth Century', *History*, 66(218) (1981), pp. 394–412; and Stephen Conway, 'Continental Connections: Britain and Europe in the Eighteenth Century', *History*, 90(299) (2005), pp. 353–74.

2. Ragnhild Hatton, *George I: Elector and King* (London, 1978), pp. 157–8; Simms, *Three Victories*, pp. 130–2, 440–1, 461–2, 526–7; Clarissa Campbell-Orr, 'Dynastic Perspectives', in Brendan Simms and Torsten Riotte (eds), *The Hanoverian Dimension in British History, 1714–1837* (Cambridge, 2007), pp. 213–51.

3. David B. Horn, *The British Diplomatic Service, 1689–1789* (Oxford, 1961), pp. 115–22, esp. 117–18.

4. Frank McLynn, *The Jacobites* (London, 1985), pp. 158–70, 188–207; Daniel Szechi, *The Jacobites: Britain and Europe 1688–1788* (Manchester, 1994), pp. 113–21.

5. Hillel Schwartz, *The French Prophets: The History of a Millenarian Group in Eighteenth Century England* (Berkeley, 1980); Alison Olson, 'The English Reception of the Huguenots, Palatines and Salzburgers, 1680–1734: A Comparative Analysis', in Randolph Vigne and Charles Littleton (eds), *From Strangers to Citizens: The Integration of Immigrant Communities in Britain, Ireland and Colonial America, 1550–1750* (London and Brighton, 2001), pp. 481–91.

6. W. R. Ward, *The Protestant Evangelical Awakening* (Cambridge, 1992), pp. 256–7, 304–8; Sugiko Nishikawa, 'The SPCK in Defence of Protestant Minorities in Early Eighteenth-century Europe', *Journal of Ecclesiastical History*, 56(4) (2005), pp. 730–48; Sugiko Nishikawa, 'Henry Compton, Bishop of London (1676–1714) and Foreign Protestants', in Randolph Vigne and Charles Littleton (eds), *From Strangers to Citizens: The Integration of Immigrant Communities in Britain, Ireland and Colonial America, 1550–1750* (London and Brighton, 2001), pp. 359–65; Norman Sykes, *William Wake, Archbishop of Canterbury, 1657–1737*, vol. I (2 vols, Cambridge, 1957), pp. 254–314, vol. II, pp. 60–80, 267–9.

7. J. C. H. Aveling, *The Handle and the Axe: The Catholic Recusants in England from Reformation to Emancipation* (London, 1976), pp. 253–4, 307–8, 314.

8. M. S. Anderson, *Britain's Discovery of Russia 1553–1815* (London, 1958), pp. 125–6; Ian Blanchard, 'Russia and International Iron Markets, ca. 1740–1850', p. 3, at http://www.ianblanchard.com/ [accessed 21 September 2010]; Anthony Cross, *By the Banks of the Neva: Chapters from the Lives and Careers of the British in Eighteenth-century Russia* (Cambridge, 1997), pp. 9–43, 46–8.

9. Ralph Davis, 'English Foreign Trade, 1700–1774', in W. E. Minchinton (ed.), *The Growth of English Overseas Trade in the Seventeenth and Eighteenth Centuries* (London, 1969),

pp. 119–20; David Ormrod, *The Rise of Commercial Empires: England and the Netherlands in the Age of Mercantilism, 1650–1770* (Cambridge, 2003), pp. 190, 316, 337.

10. H. E. S. Fisher, 'Anglo-Portuguese Trade 1700–1770', in W. E. Minchinton (ed.), *The Growth of English Overseas Trade in the Seventeenth and Eighteenth Centuries* (London, 1969), pp. 144–64; Jean O. McLachlan, *Trade and Peace with Old Spain, 1667–1750* (Cambridge, 1940), pp. 16–17, 122–40; D. B. Horn, *Great Britain and Europe in the Eighteenth Century* (Oxford, 1967), pp. 345, 357.

11. John R. Harris, *Industrial Espionage and Technology Transfer: Britain and France in the Eighteenth Century* (Aldershot, 1998), pp. 52–127, 173–202, 238–61, 290–313, 327–9, 361–89.

12. A. Klima, 'English Merchant Capital in Bohemia in the Eighteenth Century', *Economic History Review*, 2nd series, 12(1) (1959), pp. 34–48; Harris, *Industrial Espionage*, pp. 290, 507–26; Eric Robinson, 'The Transference of British Technology to Russia, 1760–1820', in Barrie M. Ratcliffe (ed.), *Great Britain and Her World, 1750–1914* (Manchester, 1975), pp. 2–12; Cross, *By the Banks*, pp. 67–70, 225–43.

13. Yves Charbit, 'The Political Failure of an Economic Theory: Physiocracy', *Population*, 57 (2002), pp. 855–84, esp. p. 861.

14. Panikos Panayi, *Germans in Britain since 1500* (London, 1996), pp. 29–48; Graham Jefcoate, 'German Immigrants and the London Book Trade, 1700–70' and Margrit Schulte Beerbühl, 'Naturalization and Economic Integration: The German Merchant Community in 18th-century London', in Randolph Vigne and Charles Littleton (eds), *From Strangers to Citizens: The Integration of Immigrant Communities in Britain, Ireland and Colonial America, 1550–1750* (London and Brighton, 2001), pp. 504, 511–18; Robin D. Gwynn, *Huguenot Heritage: The History and Contribution of the Huguenots in Britain* (London, 1985), pp. 70, 73.

15. Jeremy Black, *The British Abroad: The Grand Tour in the Eighteenth Century* (Stroud, 1992).

16. John Robertson, *The Case for the Enlightenment: Scotland and Naples 1680–1760* (Cambridge, 2005), pp. 42, 45–6; Roger Emerson, 'The Contexts of the Scottish Enlightenment', in Alexander Broadie (ed.), *The Cambridge Companion to the Scottish Enlightenment* (Cambridge, 2003), pp. 9–30.

17. David Daiches, 'The Scottish Enlightenment' and R. G. W. Anderson, 'Joseph Black', in David Daiches, Peter Jones and Jean Jones (eds), *The Scottish Enlightenment 1730–1790: A Hotbed of Genius* (Edinburgh, 1986), pp. 24–34, 93–114.

18. E. Ashworth Underwood, *Boerhaave's Men at Leyden and After* (Edinburgh, 1977); Roy Porter, *The Greatest Benefit to Mankind: A Medical History of Humanity from Antiquity to the Present* (London, 1997), pp. 245–93.

19. Buffon et l'histoire naturelle: l'édition en ligne, at http://www.buffon.cnrs.fr/ [accessed 21 September 2010]; Daiches, 'Scottish Enlightenment', pp. 19–20; Aaron Garrett, 'Anthropology', in Alexander Broadie (ed.), *The Cambridge Companion to the Scottish Enlightenment* (Cambridge, 2003), pp. 81–2.

20. Charles Singer, *A Short History of Scientific Ideas to 1900* (Oxford, 1959), pp. 307–8, 316–21; Dava Sobel, *Longitude* (London, 1996); M. Daumas, *Scientific Instruments of the Seventeenth and Eighteenth Centuries and Their Makers*, ed. and trans. M. Holbrook (London, 1972), pp. 171, 231–2.

21. Paulina Kewes, 'Drama', Stephen Ahern, 'Prose Fiction: Excluding Romance', Jennifer Birkett, 'Prose Fiction: Courtly and Popular Romance' and Peter France, 'Voltaire and Rousseau', in Stuart Gillespie and David Hopkins (eds), *The Oxford History of Literary Translation in English* (Oxford, 2005), pp. 322–5, 329–37, 343–5, 387–9.

22. Jeffery Barnouw, 'Britain and European Literature and Thought', in John Richetti (ed.), *The Cambridge History of English Literature, 1660–1780* (Cambridge, 2005),

pp. 442–3; Harold W. Streeter, *The Eighteenth Century English Novel in French Translation* (New York, 1936); J. Assézat and Maurice Tourneux (eds), *Oeuvres Complètes de Diderot* (20 vols, Paris, 1875–77), vol. 5, pp. 211–17.

23. Lawrence Marsden Price, *Die Aufnahme Englischer Literatur in Deutschland, 1500–1960* (Bern and Munich, 1961), pp. 43–304.

24. Bruce Redford, *Venice and the Grand Tour* (New Haven and London, 1996), pp. 81–104; Elizabeth Einberg (ed.), *Manners and Morals: Hogarth and British Painting 1700–1760* (London, 1987); William Vaughan, *British Painting: The Golden Age from Hogarth to Turner* (London, 1999), pp. 6–97, 103–4, 162–71, 182–5, 204–11; John Brewer, *The Pleasures of the Imagination. English Culture in the Eighteenth Century* (London, 1997), pp. 201–321.

25. Margaret Whinney, *Sculpture in Britain, 1530–1830* (Harmondsworth, 1964), pp. 83–141, 145–70, 175–82, plates pp. 56–99, 107–14, 117–22, 126–9, 136–7.

26. Sir John Summerson, *Architecture in Britain, 1530–1830* (9th edn, New Haven and London, 1993), pp. 251–71, 280–4, 286–7, 290–2, 324–33.

27. Summerson, *Architecture*, pp. 295–323, 359–64.

28. Summerson, *Architecture*, pp. 381–409, 424–6.

29. Marie Luise Gothein, *A History of Garden Art*, ed. Walter P. Wright, vol. II (first published 1928, 2 vols, New York, 1979), pp. 277–307; Tom Turner, *Garden Design in the British Isles: History and Styles since 1650*, at http://www.gardenvisit.com/history_theory/library_online_ebooks/tom_turner_english_garden_design/ [1998 revised web edition of *English Garden Design: History and Styles since 1650* (Woodbridge, 1986) accessed 21 September 2010].

30. John Caldwell, 'England: 4. From the Restoration to the Accession of Queen Victoria', in Alison Latham (ed.), *The Oxford Companion to Music* (Oxford, 2002), pp. 421–2; John Caldwell, *The Oxford History of English Music: II. c.1715 to the Present Day* (Oxford, 1999), pp. 1–85, 96–110, 123–38.

Chapter 21 True union?

1. John Stuart Shaw, *The Political History of Eighteenth-century Scotland* (Basingstoke, 1999), pp. 27–37, 63–81, 93–107; Bruce P. Lenman, *Integration and Enlightenment: Scotland 1746–1832* (Edinburgh, 1992), pp. 41–2; John M. Simpson, 'Who Steered the Gravy Train, 1707–1766?', in N. T. Phillipson and Rosalind Mitchison (eds), *Scotland in the Age of Improvement: Essays in Scottish History in the Eighteenth Century* (Edinburgh, 1970), pp. 47–72.

2. Murray G. H. Pittock, *Inventing and Resisting Britain: Cultural Identities in Britain and Ireland, 1685–1789* (Basingstoke, 1997), pp. 44–5.

3. T. M. Devine, *The Scottish Nation, 1700–2000* (London, 1999), p. 18; Allan I. Macinnes, *Clanship, Commerce and the House of Stuart, 1603–1788* (East Linton, 1996), pp. 215–16; John Clive, 'The Social Background of the Scottish Renaissance', in N. T. Phillipson and Rosalind Mitchison (eds), *Scotland in the Age of Improvement: Essays in Scottish History in the Eighteenth Century* (Edinburgh, 1970), p. 237; Michael Lynch, *Scotland: A New History* (revised edn, London, 1992), pp. 338–9.

4. Macinnes, *Clanship*, pp. 210–26.

5. Robert Crawford, *Scotland's Books: The Penguin History of Scottish Literature* (London, 2007), pp. 243–67, 298–9, 313–17, 321–7.

6. Crawford, *Scotland's Books*, pp. 299–313, 317–20.

7. Geraint H. Jenkins, *The Foundations of Modern Wales* (Oxford, 1987), pp. 228–9, 345–6, 390–1, 401.

8. Philip Jenkins, *A History of Modern Wales, 1536–1990* (London, 1992), pp. 72–3; Jenkins, *Foundations*, pp. 217, 393–422.

9. Linda Colley, *Britons: Forging the Nation 1707–1837* (New Haven and London, 1992), pp. 114, 121; Crawford, *Scotland's Books*, pp. 234–6; Alexander Carlyle, *The Autobiography of Dr Alexander Carlyle of Inveresk* (Boston, 1861), p. 155.
10. James Boswell, *Boswell's Life of Johnson* (new edn, London, 1953), pp. 273–4.
11. Colley, *Britons*, pp. 125–8; John Cannon, *Aristocratic Century: The Peerage of Eighteenth-century England* (Cambridge, 1984), pp. 87–8.
12. Devine, *Scottish Nation*, pp. 62, 116; Ian D. Whyte, *Scotland before the Industrial Revolution: An Economic and Social History c.1050–c.1750* (London, 1995), p. 305; Ian D. Whyte, *Migration and Society in Britain 1550–1830* (Basingstoke, 2000), p. 108; Paul Mantoux, *The Industrial Revolution in the Eighteenth Century* (revised edn, London, 1961), pp. 318–33.
13. S. J. Connolly, *Divided Kingdom: Ireland 1630–1800* (Oxford, 2008), pp. 259–62, 290–5, 327–34, 367–9, 371–4; Toby Barnard, *A New Anatomy of Ireland: The Irish Protestants, 1649–1770* (New Haven and London, 2003), pp. 41–80; 106–12, 115–16, 'Irish Artists: 18th Century' in *Encyclopaedia of Irish and World Art* at http://www.visual-arts-cork.com/irish-artists-eighteenth-century.htm [accessed 21 September 2010].
14. Barnard, *New Anatomy*, pp. 30, 34–5, 37, 116–18, 129, 136, 193 8.
15. Jonathan Swift, *A Letter to the Whole People of Ireland, by M. B. Drapier* (Dublin, 1724), pp. 14–15.
16. Connolly, *Divided Kingdom*, pp. 240–8, 386–411.
17. John Lynch, *Bourbon Spain* (Oxford, 1989), pp. 60–6, 117–18.
18. Brian P. Levack, *The Formation of the British State: England, Scotland, and the Union 1603–1707* (Oxford, 1987), pp. 209–13.

Chapter 22 Conclusion

1. *Tessin och Tesssiniana* (Stockholm, 1819), p. 370, quoted by Michael Roberts, *Splendid Isolation 1763–1780* (Reading, 1970), p. 4.

SHORT BIBLIOGRAPHY

Only books published since 1980 have been included. Priority has been given to broad surveys, and especially to works that make connections or comparisons between the different British nations, or between Britain and Europe. Some surveys of the histories of the different British nations and of the history of Europe have also been included.

Britain and the British Isles

British history and relations between the island kingdoms

Brewer, J., *The Sinews of Power: War, Money and the English State, 1688–1783* (Cambridge, MA, 1988).

Brigden, S., *New Worlds, Lost Worlds: The Rule of the Tudors, 1485–1603* (London, 2000).

Canny, N., *Making Ireland British 1580–1650* (Oxford, 2001).

Collinson, P. (ed.), *The Short Oxford History of the British Isles: The Sixteenth Century* (Oxford, 2002).

Ferguson, W., *Scotland's Relations with England: A Survey to 1707* (Edinburgh, 1977).

Floud, R. and Johnson, P. (eds), *The Cambridge Economic History of Modern Britain. I: Industrialisation, 1700–1860* (Cambridge, 2004).

Galloway, B., *The Union of England and Scotland 1603–1608* (Edinburgh, 1986).

Gentles, I., *The English Revolution and the Wars in the Three Kingdoms 1638–1652* (Harlow, 2007).

Heal, F., *Reformation in Britain and Ireland* (Oxford, 2003).

Holmes, G., *The Making of a Great Power: Late Stuart and Early Georgian Britain 1660–1722* (Harlow, 1993).

Holmes, G. and Szechi, D., *The Age of Oligarchy: Pre-industrial Britain, 1722–1783* (Harlow, 1993).

Houston, R. A., *The Population History of Britain and Ireland 1500–1750* (Basingstoke, 1992).

Hutton, R., *The British Republic 1649–1660* (Basingstoke, 1990).

Kearney, H., *The British Isles: A History of Four Nations* (2nd edn, Cambridge, 2006).

Kellar, C., *Scotland, England and the Reformation, 1534–1561* (Oxford, 2003).

Kishlansky, M., *A Monarchy Transformed: Britain 1603–1714* (London, 1996).

Levack, B. P., *The Formation of the British State: England, Scotland, and the Union 1603–1707* (Oxford, 1987).

Macinnes, A. I., *Union and Empire: The Making of the United Kingdom in 1707* (Cambridge, 2007).

Mason, R. A. (ed.), *Scots and Britons: Scottish Political Thought and the Union of 1603* (Cambridge, 1994).

Merriman, M., *The Rough Wooings: Mary Queen of Scots, 1542–1551* (East Linton, 2000).

Morrill, J. (ed.), *The Scottish National Covenant in Its British Context, 1638–51* (Edinburgh, 1990).

Mullett, M. A., *Catholics in Britain and Ireland, 1558–1829* (Basingstoke, 1998).

Nicholls, M., *A History of the Modern British Isles, 1529–1603: The Two Kingdoms* (Oxford, 1999).

Russell, C., *The Fall of the British Monarchies 1637–1642* (Oxford, 1991).

Ryrie, A., *The Age of Reformation: The Tudor and Stewart Realms 1485–1603* (Harlow, 2009).

Smith, D. L., *A History of the Modern British Isles 1603–1707: The Double Crown* (Oxford, 1998).

Short bibliography

Whatley, C. A., *Bought and Sold for English Gold? Explaining the Union of 1707* (2nd edn, East Linton, 2001).

Woolrych, A., *Britain in Revolution 1625–1660* (Oxford, 2002).

Wormald, J. (ed.), *The Short Oxford History of the British Isles: The Seventeenth Century* (Oxford, 2008).

Wrightson, K., *Earthly Necessities: Economic Lives in Early Modern Britain* (New Haven and London, 2000).

British identity

Colley, L., *Britons: Forging the Nation 1707–1837* (New Haven and London, 1992).

Murdoch, A., *British History 1660–1832: National Identity and Local Culture* (Basingstoke, 1998).

Pittock, M. G. H., *Inventing and Resisting Britain: Cultural Identities in Britain and Ireland, 1685–1789* (Basingstoke, 1997).

Robbins, K., *Great Britain. Identities, Institutions and the Idea of Britishness* (Harlow, 1998).

Some essay collections

Bradshaw, B. and Morrill, J. (eds), *The British Problem c. 1534–1707: State Formation in the Atlantic Archipelago* (Basingstoke, 1996).

Bradshaw, B. and Roberts, P. (eds), *British Consciousness and Identity: The Making of Britain 1533–1707* (Cambridge, 1998).

Burgess, G. (ed.), *The New British History. Founding a Modern State, 1603–1715* (London, 1999).

Ellis, S. G. and Barber, S., *Conquest and Union: Fashioning a British State, 1485–1725* (London, 1995).

Fletcher, A. and Roberts, P. (eds), *Religion, Culture and Society in Early Modern Britain: Essays in Honour of Patrick Collinson* (Cambridge, 1994).

Grant, A. and Stringer, K. J., *Uniting the Kingdom? The Making of British History* (London, 1995).

Macinnes, A. and Ohlmeyer, J., *The Stuart Kingdoms in the Seventeenth Century: Awkward Neighbours* (Dublin, 2002).

Smout, T. C. (ed.), *Anglo-Scottish Relations from 1603 to 1900* (Oxford, 2005).

Stone, L. (ed.), *An Imperial State at War: Britain from 1689 to 1815* (London, 1994).

National histories

Clay, C. G. A., *Economic Expansion and Social Change: England 1500–1700* (2 vols, Cambridge, 1984).

Connolly, S. J., *Contested Island: Ireland 1460–1630* (Oxford, 2007).

Connolly, S. J., *Divided Kingdom: Ireland 1630–1800* (Oxford, 2008).

Coward, B., *The Stuart Age: England 1603–1714* (3rd edn, Harlow, 2003).

Dawson, J. E. A., *Scotland Re-formed, 1488–1587* (Edinburgh, 2007).

Devine, T. M., *The Scottish Nation, 1700–2000* (London, 1999).

Ellis, S. G., *Tudor Ireland. Crown, Community and the Conflict of Cultures, 1470–1603* (London, 1985).

Foster, R. F., *Modern Ireland 1600–1972* (London, 1988).

Hoppit, J., *A Land of Liberty? England 1689–1727* (Oxford, 2000).

Jenkins, G. H., *The Foundations of Modern Wales, 1642–1780* (Oxford, 1987).

Langford, P., *A Polite and Commercial People: England 1727–1783* (Oxford, 1989).

Lenman, B. P., *Integration and Enlightenment: Scotland 1746–1832* (Edinburgh, 1992).

Lynch, M., *Scotland. A New History* (2nd edn, London, 1992).

Mitchison, R., *Lordship to Patronage: Scotland 1603–1745* (London, 1983).

Smith, A. G. R., *The Emergence of a Nation State: The Commonwealth of England 1529–1660* (2nd edn, London, 1997).

Whyte, I. D., *Scotland before the Industrial Revolution. An Economic & Social History c. 1050–c. 1750* (London, 1995).

Williams, G., *Renewal and Reformation: Wales c. 1415–1642* (Oxford, 1993).

Williams, P., *The Later Tudors, 1547–1603* (Oxford, 1995).

Wormald, J., *Court, Kirk, and Community: Scotland 1470–1625* (London, 1981).

Wormald, J. (ed.), *Scotland: A History* (Oxford, 2005).

Continental immigrants in Britain

Gwynn, R. D., *Huguenot Heritage: The History and Contribution of the Huguenots in Britain* (London, 1985).

Pettegree, A., *Foreign Protestant Communities in Sixteenth-century London* (Oxford, 1986).

Vigne, R. and Littleton, C. (eds), *From Strangers to Citizens: The Integration of Immigrant Communities in Britain, Ireland and Colonial America, 1550–1750* (London and Brighton, 2001).

Britain and continental Europe: connections and comparisons

Adamson, J. (ed.), *The Princely Courts of Europe, 1500–1750: Ritual, Politics and Culture under the* Ancien Régime *1500–1750* (London, 1999).

Allen, R. C., *The British Industrial Revolution in Global Perspective* (Cambridge, 2009).

Black, J., *A Military Revolution? Military Change and European Society 1550–1800* (Basingstoke, 1991).

Black, J., *The British Abroad: The Grand Tour in the Eighteenth Century* (Stroud, 1992).

Black, J., *Convergence or Divergence? Britain and the Continent* (Basingstoke, 1994).

Black, J., *A System of Ambition? British Foreign Policy 1660–1793* (2nd edn, Stroud, 2000).

Burns, J. H. (ed.), with the assistance of Mark Goldie, *The Cambridge History of Political Thought 1450–1700* (Cambridge, 1991).

Cameron, E., *The European Reformation* (Oxford, 1991).

Clark, P. (ed.), *The European Crisis of the 1590s* (London, 1985).

Claydon, T., *Europe and the Making of England, 1660–1760* (Cambridge, 2007).

Crouzet, F., *Britain Ascendant: Comparative Studies in Franco-British Economic History* (Cambridge, 1990).

De Vries, J., *European Urbanization, 1500–1800* (London, 1984).

Doran, S., *England and Europe in the Sixteenth Century* (Basingstoke, 1999).

Doran, S. and Richardson, G. (eds), *Tudor England and Its Neighbours* (Basingstoke, 2005).

Graves, M. A. R., *The Parliaments of Early Modern Europe* (Harlow, 2001).

Grummitt, D. (ed.), *The English Experience in France c. 1450–1558: War, Diplomacy, and Cultural Exchange* (Aldershot, 2002).

Gunn, S., Grummitt, D. and Cools, H., *War, State and Society in England and the Netherlands 1477–1559* (Oxford, 2007).

Henshall, N., *The Myth of Absolutism: Change and Continuity in Early Modern European Monarchy* (London, 1992).

Israel, J. I. (ed.), *The Anglo-Dutch Moment. Essays on the Glorious Revolution and Its World Impact* (Cambridge, 1991).

Johnson, D., Crouzet, F. and Bédarida, F. (eds), *Britain and France: Ten Centuries* (Folkestone, 1980).

Jones, J. R., *The Anglo-Dutch Wars of the Seventeenth Century* (London, 1996).

Lloyd, T. H., *England and the German Hanse, 1157–1611: A Study of Their Trade and Commercial Diplomacy* (Cambridge, 1991).

MacCulloch, D., *Reformation: Europe's House Divided, 1490–1700* (London, 2003).

Mijers, E. and Onnekink, D. (eds), *Redefining William III: The Impact of the King-Stadholder in International Context* (Aldershot, 2007).

Ormrod, D., *The Rise of Commercial Empires: England and the Netherlands in the Age of Mercantilism, 1650–1770* (Cambridge, 2003).

Pagano de Divitiis, G., *English Merchants in Seventeenth-century Italy* (Cambridge, 1997).

Porter, R. and Teich, M. (eds), *The Enlightenment in National Context* (Cambridge, 1981).

Porter, R. and Teich, M. (eds), *The Renaissance in National Context* (Cambridge, 1992).

Porter, R. and Teich, M. (eds), *The Scientific Revolution in National Context* (Cambridge, 1992).

Prados de la Escosura, L., *Exceptionalism and Industrialisation: Britain and Its European Rivals, 1688–1815* (Cambridge, 2004).

Richardson, G., *Renaissance Monarchy: The Reigns of Henry VIII, Francis I and Charles V* (London, 2002).

Salmon, P. and Barrow, T. (eds), *Britain and the Baltic: Studies in Commercial, Political and Cultural Relations 1500–2000* (Sunderland, 2003).

Scott, J., *England's Troubles: Seventeenth-century English Political Instability in European Context* (Cambridge, 2000).

Scribner, R. W., Porter, R. and Teich, M., *The Reformation in National Context* (Cambridge, 1994).

Simms, B., *Three Victories and a Defeat: The Rise and Fall of the First British Empire, 1714–1783* (London, 2007).

Simms, B. and Riotte, T. (eds), *The Hanoverian Dimension in British History, 1714–1837* (Cambridge, 2007).

Stoye, J., *English Travellers Abroad, 1604–1667: Their Influence in English Society and Politics* (revised edn, New Haven and London, 1989).

Szechi, D., *The Jacobites: Britain and Europe 1688–1788* (Manchester, 1994).

Thompson, A. C., *Britain, Hanover and the Protestant Interest, 1688–1756* (Woodbridge, 2006).

Ward, W. R., *Christianity under the Ancien Régime 1648–1789* (Cambridge, 1999).

Some surveys of European history

Black, J., *Eighteenth-century Europe* (2nd edn, Basingstoke, 1999).

Blanning, T., *The Pursuit of Glory: Europe 1648–1815* (London, 2007).

Bonney, R., *The European Dynastic States 1494–1660* (Oxford, 1991).

Cameron, E. (ed.), *Early Modern Europe: An Oxford History* (Oxford, 1999).

Doyle, W., *The Old European Order 1660–1800* (2nd edn, Oxford, 1992).

Mackenney, R., *Sixteenth Century Europe: Expansion and Conflict* (Basingstoke, 1993).

Munck, T., *Seventeenth Century Europe: State, Conflict and the Social Order in Europe 1598–1700* (Basingstoke, 1990).

Pettegree, A., *Europe in the Sixteenth Century* (Oxford, 2002).

Sturdy, D. J., *Fractured Europe: 1600–1721* (Oxford, 2002).

INDEX

Index

Index

Index

Index

Index

Index

Index

Prynne, William   170
Puerto Bello   233
Puerto Rico   36
Purcell, Henry   209–10
puritans   65–66, 68, 167–74
Putney   129
Pym, John   127
Pyrenees, Treaty of   137

Quakers   142, 172–73, 175–76, 180
Quarles, Francis   205
Queensberry, James Douglas, 2nd duke
    of   221
Quellin, Arnold   208
Quesnay, François   292
Quiberon, battle of   237

Rabelais, François   206
Racine, Jean   206
Raeburn, Henry   299
Ragusa   89
Ramillies, battle of   147
Ramsay, Allan (painter)   299, 308
Ramsay, Allan (poet)   306
Ramsden, Jesse   297
Ranters   172
Rape of the Lock, The (Pope)   298
Rastell, William   95
Rathmines, battle of   131
Reasonableness of Christianity, The
    (Locke)   266
rebellions   52
    against taxes   52, 53, 83, 149, 152, 165
    agrarian   83, 193
    religious   52, 176, 140
    see also riots
rebellions, national and provincial
    Bohemian   121
    Castilian, of *Comuneros*   54
    Catalan   126, 132, 149, 165
    Irish   17–18, 21, 30, 36–37, 53–54,
        126–27, 130–31
    Jacobite   228–29, 235, 251–52, 287–88,
        304
    Morisco   29
    Naples   149
    Netherlands   29, 31–34, 36, 54, 96–97,
        153
    Pilgrimage of Grace   19, 46
    Portuguese   149
    Scottish   27, 53, 125–26, 140, 170–71

Swedish   54
    see also wars, civil
Recorde, Robert   103–04
Redemptorists   264
Reformation
    English   61–62, 65–66, 68
    French   64–65
    German   58
    Scottish   63–64, 67–69
    Swiss   58–59
Reformed Protestantism   26, 58–59,
    62–63, 65, 93–95
    see also Calvinism
Reichstag see diet
Relief Church   263
religion, reasonable and natural   266–67
Rembrandt Harmenszoon van Rijn   209
Remonstrants   169, 201
Renaissance   91
Restoration   173–76
Réunion   276
revenue: some sources (England and United
        Kingdom)
    assessment   162
    clerical taxation   51, 61
    decimation tax   134
    debasement   50–51
    excise   162–63, 165, 213, 232, 249
    feudal dues   51, 52, 162, 194
    forced loans and benevolences   14, 48,
        51–52, 123, 152
    impositions   120–22, 150, 152, 162, 314
    lands   50, 162
    land tax   163, 194, 220, 249, 252
    malt tax   228, 231, 252, 253
    monopolies   44, 51, 121, 162
    parliamentary subsidies   44, 51, 120, 122
    purveyance   51
    ship money   125, 150, 152, 162
    tonnage and poundage   50, 122–23,
        150, 152
Revett, Nicholas   301
revocation, act of   125
Reynolds, Joshua   299
Rheims   95
Rhine   7
Rhodes   16
Rhys ap Gruffydd, Sir   17
Rhys, Siôn Dafydd   100
Ricci, Sebastiano   300
Richardson, Samuel   298

Index